# GOLF

THE LEGENDS OF THE GAME

# GOLF

## THE LEGENDS OF THE GAME

ALISTAIR TAIT

FIREFLY BOOKS

**Dedication**

This book is dedicated to my three girls, Linda, Aubrey and Olivia, but most of all Linda for putting up with an obsession.

A FIREFLY BOOK

Published by Firefly Books Ltd. 1999

A QUINTET BOOK



First Printing

**Canadian Cataloguing in Publication Data**

Tait, Alistair

Golf: the legends of the game

Includes index.

ISBN 1-55209-435-9

1. Golfers - Biography. 2. Golf - History. I. Title.

GV964.A1T34 1999 796.352'092'2 C99-930962-5

**U.S. Cataloguing in Publication Data**

Tait, Alistair

Golf: the legends of the game/Alistair Tait. - 1st ed.

[352]p. : col. ill.; cm.

Includes index.

Summary: short biographies of the top 300 golfers in the history of the game.

ISBN 1-55209-435-9

1. Golf. 2. Golfers. I. Title.

796.352 c21' 1999 CIP

Published in Canada in 1999 by
Firefly Books Ltd.
3680 Victoria Park Avenue
Willowdale, Ontario
M2H 3K1

Published in the United States in 1999 by
Firefly Books (U.S.) Inc.
P.O. Box 1338, Ellicott Station
Buffalo, New York
14205

This book was designed and produced by
Quintet Publishing Limited
6 Blundell Street, London N7 9BH

Creative Director Richard Dewing
Designer Rod Teasdale
Project Editor Diana Steedman
Editor Nicole Foster

Manufactured in Singapore by United Graphic Pte Ltd
Printed in China by Leefung Asco Printers Ltd

# Contents



## Special Features

# Introduction

Golf has a unique feature over all other sports - it's the only one where you can truly walk in the footsteps of your heroes. Think about it. How much of a chance will you ever get of playing tennis at Wimbledon? Probably zero unless you are extremely well connected. How about ice hockey at Madison Square Garden? Unless you are a professional, then forget it. A few innings at Yankee Stadium? No way. Most fans of other sports will never experience what their heroes do in the great sporting arenas of the world. Golfers can.

The great championship venues help define golf. Augusta, St Andrews, Pinehurst, Pebble Beach, and the many great courses around the world have provided the theaters for some of the greatest moments in golf. Yet many of them are accessible to the public. The average 18-handicapper can play from the same spots that Nicklaus, Hogan, Palmer, Snead, Faldo, Norman, Els and the other greats of the game have played from. There are a few exceptions, of course.

Augusta is a members' only course and doesn't allow casual visitors. But who knows, you may know somebody who knows somebody who knows somebody else, and one day find yourself walking down the steep slope that is the 10th fairway. In most other cases you can get onto the championship courses. The great British links courses all take visitors. You may need to write months in advance and produce a letter verifying your handicap to play the likes of, say, Muirfield and Royal St George's, but you can play. As for St Andrews, the home of golf, that is a *public* course. All you have to do is put your name in the daily ballot and wait to see if it comes up. If it does you could find yourself walking in the footsteps of just about every great player in the history of the game. When you walk through the Valley of Sin that fronts the 18th green, you can take comfort from the fact that your heroes have walked the same path.

Other sports suffer from restrictions that bind the player to the same scenery day in and day out. The tennis circuit may move around the world but when the first ball is served it is played on a court exactly the same dimension as anywhere else in the world. The same is true of basketball, ice hockey, football, soccer, and many other sports. Professional golfers have the beauty of playing on a different course every week. From Pebble Beach to St Andrews, from Royal Melbourne to Wentworth, golf offers a vast array of courses to sample. Yet it all started from one main source—the Old Course at St Andrews.

No one actually designed the Old Course *per se*. The townsfolk simply stuck holes in the ground and played out to the end of the peninsula and back again. Whatever they encountered along the way they simply played around or over. Thankfully no one has tried to copy the Old Course. Designers, both past and present, have let their imaginations run wild. The result has been that golf's major tournaments are held over courses that not only test the greatest players, but that are situated in some of the most scenic spots around the world.

Yes, golfers are truly blessed. Fans of other sports can only watch with envy. We can watch and then go out and try to emulate the accomplishments of the legends in this book.

Who said golf is a good walk spoiled?

MASTERS

# The True Champions

Golf is the last bastion of true sportsmanship. In what other sports do you see players calling penalties on themselves as you do in golf? It certainly doesn't happen in football, or ice hockey, or baseball, or basketball, and when did you ever see a professional tennis player tell the umpire that the call he just made in the player's favor was actually wrong? Never.

There are many examples of golfers calling penalties on themselves for infractions only they could possibly have seen. In an age when other sportsmen actually try to bend the rules, golf is a sport where strictly adhering to the letter of the law is paramount.

In the first round of the 1925 US Open at Worcester, Massachusetts, Bobby Jones's ball moved in the long grass beside the 11th green as Jones addressed it. He told an official to add a stroke to his score. When the official objected, Jones insisted the stroke be added. It was. When praised for his honesty, Jones responded by saying: "There is only one way to play this game."

Jones's way was the honest way. No one else saw him commit the infraction, yet Jones could not have lived with himself had he ignored the misdemeanor. It was costly, too. That extra stroke cost him the championship. Jones tied for the 72-hole lead and lost the subsequent 36-hole playoff for the title.

Nearly 70 years later, Davis Love III was playing in the 1994 Western Open when he called a two stroke on himself. Love had to move a coin marking his ball on one green to let a fellow competitor have a clear putt at the hole. Love replaced his ball, holed his putt, then went to the next tee. It wasn't until later he realized he had not moved the coin back to its proper spot and had putted from the wrong place on the green. The two-stroke penalty meant he missed the cut.

These are not isolated incidents. Golf is littered with such examples throughout its long history. That's what makes the men and women in this book true champions. They haven't got to the top through taking shortcuts, through trying to buck the system. They've earned their way there through guts, determination, talent, and sheer hard work.

This book is full of people who have dedicated their lives to golf, to arguably the hardest of all sports to play. More importantly, they have done so with respect for the traditions of the game and their fellow competitors. Of all sports, golf is the one that stands out not only for its honesty and fair play, but for the way its heroes conduct themselves.

That's evident from some of the greatest so-called battles in golf's rich history. Very few, if any, have been conducted in the hostile atmospheres that prevail in other sports.

Take Tom Watson and Jack Nicklaus's famous Duel in the Sun at Turnberry in 1977. Nicklaus played brilliant golf for four days, golf good enough to have won the title in other years. Yet Watson beat him by one stroke. Nicklaus didn't storm off the course afterward in a fit of petulance. Instead he put his arm around Watson and said "well done." The two men walked off the final green arm in arm, knowing they'd both played golf of the highest standard and the better man had won.

Golf has been like that since time immemorial. Vardon, Jones, Zaharias, Hogan, Berg, Palmer, Nicklaus, Watson, Lopez, Ballesteros, Norman, Davies, Els, Woods—they all play the game with grace, with dignity. They are all in this book because they are truly great champions and have deported themselves in the way a champion should.

But what makes a true champion?

In the case of the players mentioned above, their records can be measured in major championships, and they have stacks of them. But there are others in this book who haven't won major championships. This book is also full of players who got as much out of their game as their talent, their dedication, and hard work would allow them to do. There are players in this book who never won majors, but they are here perhaps because of the way they conducted themselves, or perhaps because of what they gave back to the game.

Chi Chi Rodriguez is a fine example of a player who never won a major, never really came close, but who is in these pages for what he gave to the game, for what he does and has done for charity. The same goes for Peter Jacobsen. This American player has won only a handful of tournaments, but he is one of the game's greatest ambassadors. Or how about Casey Martin? A player who hasn't even made it on to the US Tour yet, but who has overcome a crippling handicap to compete in the US Open. Remember, the mark of a true champion isn't always measured by the number of trophies on the mantelpiece.

The players in these pages come from every part of the spectrum. Their stories are as diverse as the courses the game is played on. However, one thing all of them have in common is that these men and women have mastered this beautiful game in their own unique way. That makes them true champions in anybody's book.

# Tommy Aaron

AARON WAS KNOWN AS A POOR FINISHER EARLY IN HIS CAREER. HOWEVER, IT WAS HIS FINAL ROUND 68 WHICH WON HIM THE 1973 MASTERS.

## Fact File

**BORN** 1937, Gainesville, Georgia, USA

**CAREER HIGHLIGHTS**
1969 Canadian Open
1970 Atlanta Classic
1973 Masters

**INTERNATIONAL HONORS**
Ryder Cup: 1969, 1973
Walker Cup: 1959

Tommy Aaron's name will always be linked with the Masters for two reasons. Aaron won the 1973 Masters, the only major the Georgia native ever won, but five years earlier he was involved in one of the most unfortunate incidents in Masters history.

Bob Goalby won the Masters in 1968 in strange circumstances. That was the year Roberto de Vicenzo inadvertently signed for a four at the 17th hole in the final round when he had actually taken a three. Under the Rules of Golf, Vicenzo's score had to stand. Had he spotted the error he would have tied with Goalby and been involved in a playoff for the prestigious green jacket. Instead he finished second. Aaron was the player marking de Vicenzo's scorecard that day.

Of course no one was more upset than Aaron, but it was a genuine mistake and de Vicenzo was gentleman enough to absolve Aaron of any blame.

Five years later the tall bespectacled Georgian would stand in the winner's circle at Augusta National. There can be no greater honor for a Georgia golfer than to win the Masters, and by doing so Aaron laid to rest an old ghost.

As an amateur, Aaron finished runner-up to Charles Coe in the 1958 US Amateur Championship, and played in the 1959 Walker Cup at Muirfield, where he helped his country to a nine to three victory. He later attended the University of Florida and in 1960 turned professional.

From early in his career, Aaron was known as a good starter in tournaments. He would often open with rounds under 70, only to fade over the weekend. For example, on no less than nine occasions prior to his first PGA Tour victory, Aaron finished second or equal second. Then in 1969 he won the Canadian Open in a playoff with Sam Snead. Aaron shot a final round 64 to tie Snead, before winning the playoff, proving that he could finish tournaments as well as start them. A year later he won the Atlanta Classic. Then in 1972 he traveled to France and won the prestigious Lancôme Trophy.

It was a good finish that won Aaron the Masters green jacket. A final round 68 in 1973 gave him the win he most wanted. That win helped him make the 1973 US Ryder Cup team, the second and last time Aaron played in the match. The other appearance came in 1969 at Royal Birkdale.

Upon reaching 50, Aaron embarked on a successful senior career which saw him win the 1992 Kaanapali Classic held on the beautiful island of Hawaii.

# AMY ALCOTT

ALCOTT HAS WON JUST ABOUT EVERY TOP HONOR IN GOLF. ONLY THE LPGA CHAMPIONSHIP HAS ELUDED HER.

Amy Alcott turned professional after a short amateur career which saw her win the 1973 USGA Junior Girls' Championship at the age of just 17. Two years later she triumphed professionally when she won the 1975 Orange Blossom Classic, her first of many LPGA tournament wins.

It didn't take Alcott long to notch up wins on the LPGA Tour. By 1983 she had won 16 tournaments, including two major championships, the 1979 Du Maurier Classic (then called the Peter Jackson Classic) and the 1980 US Women's Open. Those wins took her career earnings past the $1 million mark, making her the sixth LPGA player in history to surpass the mark. Alcott was not finished, not by a long shot.

In 1983 Alcott gained her third major when she won her first Nabisco Dinah Shore tournament. Alcott obviously feels comfortable on the Mission Hills course at Rancho Mirage, California, venue for the Dinah Shore, because she has made this particular major almost her own property. She has won it three times, more than any other player. She also established the record for the lowest score in the event when in 1991 she shot a four-round total of 273 to win. (Dottie Pepper broke that record in 1999.)

When Alcott won the 1988 Nabisco Dinah Shore, her $80,000 first prize took her past the $2 million mark. By 1994 she had increased her earnings to $3 million, courtesy of another victory in the Dinah Shore, and several other tournaments as well.

The 5-foot, 6-inch professional has only ever had one teacher throughout her career, relying on the expert eye of Walter Kellyer.

Alcott has given much to charity over the course of her career. In the 1980s, she created a $50,000 endowment for the UCLA Children's Hospital and its Neonatal Intensive Care Unit. Her work in charity has won her several honors, including the 1984 LPGA Good Samaritan Award and the 1984 National Multiple Sclerosis Achievement Award.

In the 1990s, Alcott suffered a broken kneecap, which kept her out of competitive action for nearly four months. However, she was soon back trying to win titles on the LPGA Tour.

Alcott's hard work over three decades was finally rewarded when she was admitted into the LPGA Hall of Fame. By that time she had recorded 29 wins on the LPGA Tour.

Alcott only needs to win the LPGA Championship to make it a clean sweep in the majors.

## FACT FILE

**BORN** 1956, Kansas City, Missouri, USA

**CAREER HIGHLIGHTS**
1979 Du Maurier Classic
1980 US Women's Open
1983 Nabisco Dinah Shore
1988 Nabisco Dinah Shore
1991 Nabisco Dinah Shore

# Helen Alfredsson

HELEN ALFREDSSON IS ONE OF THE TOUGHEST COMPETITORS IN WOMEN'S GOLF, A PLAYER WHO TRULY WEARS HER EMOTIONS ON HER SLEEVE.

## Fact File

**BORN** 1965, Göteborg, Sweden

**CAREER HIGHLIGHTS**
1989 WPGET Rookie of the Year
1990 Weetabix Women's British Open
1992 LPGA Rookie of the Year
1993 Nabisco Dinah Shore
1997 McDonald's WPGA Championship of Europe

**INTERNATIONAL HONORS**
Solheim Cup: 1990, 1992, 1994, 1996, 1998

Sweden has produced a number of excellent tournament professionals, both men and women, but Helen Alfredsson has to be one of the best to emerge from Scandinavia.

Alfredsson started playing golf at the age of 11, and it wasn't long before she was playing it to an exceptionally high level. She was the Swedish National champion six times before she turned professional, winning the title successively between 1981 and 1984, then in 1986 and 1988. She also won the 1984 Belgium Junior International Championship.

Alfredsson made the transition to professional golf with ease. She was the 1989 Rookie of the Year on the European Tour. Then in 1990 she finished third on the Order of Merit after winning the Weetabix Women's British Open at Woburn Golf Club, one of the biggest tournaments in European women's golf.

Alfredsson is one of the toughest players in ladies' golf. She never gives up and her emotion shows on just about every shot. She has been a perennial Solheim Cup player for Europe since the event began in 1990. During those matches she has compiled a record of seven wins, nine losses and two halves; excellent, considering Europe won only one of those matches, the 1992 contest at Dalmahoy.

Just as she was a success in Europe almost from the moment she turned professional, Alfredsson also didn't waste any time stamping her mark on the LPGA Tour when she moved to the United States. She won the Rookie of the Year Award in 1992, and in the same season went to Japan and won the Itoki Classic.

Alfredsson's sophomore year was even better. She was a contender in most tournaments she played, especially the majors. The 5-foot, 10-inch Swede lifted her first big trophy, winning the Nabisco Dinah Shore. She also contended strongly in two other majors, tying for second in the US Women's Open and placing third in the LPGA Championship. In all she notched up nine top-ten finishes that season.

The former model crossed the $1 million mark in 1995, and the $2 million barrier in 1998. She continues to earn lots of money with good-quality golf, not only in America, but around the world. To her credit, the Swedish star has never forgotten her European roots. She has been one of the strongest supporters of the women's professional golf tour in Europe over the years, splitting her schedule between the States and Europe to try to play as many events in Europe as possible. Indeed, Alfredsson won the opening event of the 1998 European season and went on to win the Order of Merit.

# FULTON ALLEM

ALLEM HAS TWO MILLION DOLLAR CHALLENGE VICTORIES TO HIS NAME. HIS BEST CAME WHEN HE WON THE 1993 NEC WORLD SERIES OF GOLF.

South Africa has produced a host of great golfers over the years, from the greatest the country has ever seen, Gary Player, to one who may exceed Player's records, Ernie Els. While not quite attaining the honors of these two, Fulton Allem is one of the best players to emerge from the South African Republic.

Allem took golf up at the age of seven after encouragement from his father. As with many South Africans, Gary Player was Allem's idol when he was a boy growing up and learning the game.

Allem turned professional in 1976, but it took him nine years before he made his mark in pro golf. After no less than 18 second-place finishes on the South African Tour, Allem won the 1985 Palaborwa Classic, but that was just an appetizer of what was to come that year. That victory gave him entry into the Million Dollar Challenge at Sun City, South Africa. The man whose interests include riding and breeding horses, made the most of his invitation to play with the game's true thoroughbreds. He took the $1 million first prize, setting himself up financially for life.

Allem won the Million Dollar Challenge again in 1988, by which time he had won eight events in his native South Africa, including back-to-back South African PGA Championships in 1986 and 1987.

The sturdy South African joined the US Tour in 1987 but it took him four years before he triumphed in America. The victory came just in the nick of time.

Allem appeared to be losing his US Tour card in 1991. Heading into the last event of the season, the South African was placed 143rd on the money list. With only the top 125 at the end of the year qualifying for the 1992 season, Allem knew he had to play well. He did. Allem played the last two rounds in 11 under par to win by a stroke over Billy Ray Brown, Mike Hulbert, and Tom Kite.

Allem won twice in 1993, lifting the Southwestern Bell Colonial and the NEC World Series of Golf. He did so respectively over Colonial Country Club in Fort Worth, Texas, and Firestone Country Club in Akron, Ohio, two of the tougher courses on the US Tour. Indeed, on the latter course he fired a final round 62, ten under par, to win the tournament and earn himself a ten-year exemption on the US Tour.

## FACT FILE

**BORN** 1957, Kroonstad, South Africa

**CAREER HIGHLIGHTS**
1985 Million Dollar Challenge
1988 Million Dollar Challenge
1991 Independent Insurance Agent Open
1993 Southwestern Bell Colonial
1993 NEC World Series of Golf

**INTERNATIONAL HONORS**
Presidents Cup: 1994

# PETER ALLISS

REGARDED AS THE BEST IN THE BUSINESS, ALLISS HAS BEEN COMMENTATING ON GOLF FOR RADIO AND TELEVISION FOR OVER THIRTY YEARS.

## FACT FILE

**BORN** 1931, Berlin, Germany

**CAREER HIGHLIGHTS**
1957 PGA Championship
1962 PGA Championship
1964 Vardon Trophy
1966 Vardon Trophy
1966 PGA Championship

**INTERNATIONAL HONORS**
Ryder Cup: 1953, 1957, 1959, 1961, 1963, 1965, 1967, 1969

After retiring from a successful career in full-time competitive golf, Peter Alliss turned his attention to a career that has made him more famous than his exploits on the golf course, a career which has made him a household name.

Alliss is known throughout the world for his work as a television commentator. He has been a regular fixture on the BBC's televised golf coverage for nearly 30 years, and has worked for the ABC network on US golf tournaments. Indeed, such is his stature worldwide that he is generally recognized as the best in the business.

The Berlin-born but thoroughly English-bred Alliss made no fewer than eight appearances in the Ryder Cup. He played on the winning side just once, when Great Britain & Ireland won the biennial match at Lindrick in 1957. He also appeared in the historic match of 1969, when Jack Nicklaus graciously conceded a missable two-and-a-half-foot putt to Tony Jacklin on the final green, ensuring the trophy was shared for the first time.

The son of Percy Alliss, Peter Alliss was always destined to follow in his father's footsteps as a professional golfer. Indeed, he would eventually compile a more successful record than his father.

Born in Berlin when his father was the resident professional at the Wannsee Club in the German city, Alliss turned professional at the tender age of 15. He won his first professional event in 1952, when he won the British Assistants Championship. In 1953 he made his first appearance in the Ryder Cup at Wentworth, but it wasn't an experience he will recall with particular fondness.

Alliss faced Jim Turnesa in the singles and was level with the American coming to the 18th green of the West course at Wentworth. Two putts from the edge of the green would have given Alliss and the Great Britain & Ireland side a valuable point. However, Alliss took four to lose the match. Had he won, the USA would have lost the Cup.

The erudite golfer always admitted that putting was his weakness. While it let him down in his first Ryder Cup, it did not stop him from winning tournaments all around the world. In Britain alone, Alliss won a host of great tournaments. Included among those was the British PGA, which he won on three occasions (1957, 1962, 1966), the prestigious but now defunct Daks tournament (1954, 1963), and many others. He also won the Spanish Open twice (1956, 1958), the Italian Open (1958), and the Portuguese Open (1958).

Besides his television work, Alliss is a popular after-dinner speaker. He has also designed or helped design numerous courses around the world, including The Belfry, scene of many Ryder Cups, which he co-designed with Dave Thomas. The voice of golf has co-written or authored many golfing books over the years.

# Jamie Anderson

**ANDERSON WAS ONE OF THE BEST GOLFERS TO EMERGE FROM ST ANDREWS, THE HOME OF GOLF. HE IS ONE OF ONLY FOUR MEN TO WIN THREE CONSECUTIVE BRITISH OPEN CHAMPIONSHIPS.**

James Anderson, or Jamie as he was better known, played golf at a time when the best players came from the home of golf, St Andrews. Anderson was as good a St Andrews golfer as there has ever been.

He grew up in the Fife town and started playing golf at the age of ten. Of course in his time the town was fortunate to have two of the greatest golfers in the world at the time in the shape of the Morrises, the famous father and son duo who won eight Opens between them. Old Tom Morris won the Open Championship four times between 1861 and 1867. His last victory was followed by his son Young Tom, who won the championship four consecutive times between 1868 and 1872, the only player ever to accomplish that particular feat. Not far behind them came Anderson.

Son of the famous St Andrews caddie David Anderson ("Old Daw" as he was known), Jamie Anderson first announced his intentions of winning the British Open in 1873 when he finished second to Tom Kidd at St Andrews. Four years later, Anderson entered the winner's circle when he won the 1877 British Open at Musselburgh.

Anderson's second victory in the world's oldest golf tournament came a year later at Prestwick. He won it in impressive style. Knowing he had to cover the last four holes in 17 strokes to win, Anderson declared his intention, and then achieved it. An ace at the 17th hole, the first hole in one in championship golf, helped Anderson win the title.

Anderson won his third and final British Open the following year on his beloved St Andrews, to become only the second man, and one of only four, to this day, to win three consecutive titles. He finished runner-up to Robert Ferguson in 1881, but never won the tournament again.

The Fife man was known as a percentage player who believed in keeping the ball in play. He wasn't long off the tee, but he hit the ball straight and was a fine iron player and a good putter. He once played 90 holes at St Andrews and later revealed that he never hit one bad shot or played a stroke other than the way he had intended to play it.

In his later years, he was the professional at Ardeer Golf Club in Ayrshire, Scotland. He was also renowned for being a good clubmaker, a business he set up on his own before taking the post at Ardeer.

## Fact File

**BORN** 1842, St Andrews, Fife, Scotland

**DIED** 1912

**CAREER HIGHLIGHTS**
1877 The Open Championship
1878 The Open Championship
1879 The Open Championship

# Willie Anderson

WILLIE ANDERSON IS THE ONLY PLAYER TO WIN THREE CONSECUTIVE US OPENS, AND ONE OF FOUR TO WIN THE TITLE FOUR TIMES. THERE IS NO TELLING HOW MANY HE WOULD HAVE WON HAD HE NOT DIED AGED 32.

## Fact File

**BORN** 1878, North Berwick, Scotland

**DIED** 1910

**CAREER HIGHLIGHTS**
1901 US Open
1902 Western Open
1903 US Open
1904 US Open
1904 Western Open
1905 US Open
1908 Western Open
1909 Western Open

There's no telling just how many major championships Willie Anderson would have won had his life not been taken from him when he was in his prime golfing years.

Anderson died of arteriosclerosis at just 32 years old in 1910. Until that time he had won four US Opens and four Western Opens—in his day one of the biggest championships in golf, a major championship in the eyes of many.

Born in Scotland in 1878, Anderson was just one of many Scotsmen who emigrated to the United States and gained huge success on the fairways. Tommy Armour was one, Jim Barnes was another.

Anderson was the first player to record four US Open wins, and still the only man to win the title for three consecutive years. (Bobby Jones, Ben Hogan, and Jack Nicklaus subsequently equaled Anderson's record of four titles.)

Anderson emigrated to America at the age of 14 in 1892 on the advice of a member of the Spalding family. He played his first US Open at Chicago Golf Club in 1897 at the age of 19, finishing runner-up by just one stroke to Joe Lloyd. However, it would not take him long to step into the winner's circle.

The Myopia Hunt Club in Hamilton, Massachusetts, was a course Anderson obviously felt comfortable on.

The Scottish-born American won two of his four titles there, both times beating the same man.

Anderson won his first championship at Myopia in 1901, when he defeated Alex Smith in an 18-hole playoff. Smith shot 86 in the fifth and deciding round to Anderson's 85. It must be borne in mind that these scores were shot in the days when rounds in the 80s were commonplace. Four years later, Anderson won for a second time at Myopia, again defeating Smith, this time in regulation play and by two strokes, 314 to 316.

The North Berwick native won his second US Open in a playoff, defeating David Brown by a score of 82 to 84 at Baltusrol in 1903, the first of his three consecutive American national championships. His opening round of 73 set a new championship record. However, his 331 total in the 1901 championship is still a US Open record for the highest score for four rounds, one that is likely to stand forever.

The Western Open was also a favorite tournament of Anderson's, a title he won four times between 1902 and 1909. The 1909 tournament was Anderson's last big win, as the following year he died. He had played three 36-hole matches the week before his death, and appeared in good health. Needless to say, his demise came as a shock to those around him.

# Isao Aoki

AOKI IS LIVING PROOF THAT IT DOES NOT TAKE A TEXTBOOK SWING TO WIN AT THE VERY HIGHEST LEVEL. THE JAPANESE GOLFER HAS WON MANY TITLES WITH HIS UNORTHODOX STYLE OF PLAY.

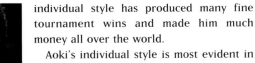

Japanese golfers have never found it easy to make the transition from home soil to tournaments in foreign lands. One who has found much success away from home is Isao Aoki.

Aoki is perhaps the most famous of Japan's great golfers. Indeed, he was one of the pioneers of Japanese golf, founding the way for others, such as Tommy Nakajima, and Jumbo and Joe Ozaki, to follow in his footsteps.

Aoki first came to prominence when he won the 1978 World Match Play Championship at Wentworth. Aoki overcame New Zealand's Simon Owen three and two in the 36-hole final to become the first and only Japanese player to lift the trophy. The following year he lost to American Bill Rogers in the final.

Modern golf is renowned for players who swing the club in a conventional manner. Contemporary teaching has produced players who basically adhere to the same fundamentals. Not Aoki. His game is different because of the way he uses his hands in the swing. Aoki crouches over the ball at address, with his hands very low. The result is a swing that involves a lot of hand action. It's a motion that runs counter to modern thinking which says the body, the legs and torso, should control the golf swing. Yet Aoki's individual style has produced many fine tournament wins and made him much money all over the world.

Aoki's individual style is most evident in his putting stroke. The head of his putter sits well clear of the grass at address, and it looks unorthodox and ungainly. Yet the best part of Aoki's game is his putting.

His manner of play was born out of the way he started to play the game. When he was just a boy, Aoki was given his first set of clubs by an American serviceman. They were far too long for him, but Aoki had nothing else. It was use them or not play golf at all. This is the reason why his hands are low in the address position.

Aoki never won one of the game's four major championships during his prime, but he came close in the 1980 US Open. Aoki finished second to Jack Nicklaus at Baltusrol, as the dominant golfer of the time recorded his fourth, and last, US Open victory. Aoki's score of 274 would have won the title in most other years, but he fell two strokes short of Nicklaus's record score.

Upon turning 50, Aoki embarked on a successful senior career. He has won more titles and made more money on that circuit than he did on the regular US Tour.

## Fact File

**BORN** 1942, Abiko, Chiba, Japan

**CAREER HIGHLIGHTS**
1978 World Match Play Championship
1983 European Open
1983 Hawaiian Open

# AMEN CORNER

Those fortunate enough to get into Augusta National, home of the Masters, usually head straight for Amen Corner, a glorious stretch of turf at the bottom end of the course where many green jackets have been won and lost.

Amen Corner was the phrase given to the 11th, 12th, and 13th holes by Herbert Warren Wind, the doyen of American golf writers. He had seen so many adventures and misadventures over these three holes that he thought they were worthy of a name. He remembered an old Dixieland song called "Shouting at Amen Corner," used it in his 1958 Masters report in *Sports Illustrated*, and the name stuck. Never have three holes been more aptly titled. Amen to those who pass through the corner without meeting disaster.

The first time Masters competitors see water at Augusta is on the par-4 11th hole. A pond eats into the left-hand side of the green, forcing players to aim to the right. The flag is usually situated perilously close to the pond on the final day of the Masters. Ben Hogan always said that if his ball was lying on the 11th green then he had miss hit his approach shot. Hogan always aimed to the right of the green, relying on a chip and putt to make his par.

It was on the 11th that Larry Mize struck one of the most famous shots in Masters' history. In a playoff for the 1987 title with Greg Norman, Mize missed the green by about 30 yards. He then holed a miraculous pitch shot to win the green jacket.

Nick Faldo won his first two Masters titles on the 11th. There he holed a long birdie putt to defeat Scott Hoch in a playoff for the 1989 title. The following year he won with a par on the hole, after playoff opponent Ray Floyd had dumped his second shot into the pond.

The 12th hole looks insignificant on paper. At around 155 yards, it calls for little more than a 6-iron even for the average handicap player. But there's nothing average about the hole. Jack Nicklaus calls it the most demanding par-3 in the world.

To play well on this hole, the tee shot has to be hit over the pond fronting the green to a putting surface that is only about 12 yards wide. Anything hit short will hit the bank fronting the green and roll back down into the pond. Anything long leaves a treacherous chip to the flag, with the water beckoning in the background. Tom Weiskopf once made a 13 here by hitting five balls into the pond before reaching the green. And Fred Couples' ball defied gravity in 1992 when it stopped on the bank inches from the water. Couples was able to chip and putt for his par before saying a quiet Amen and heading for the 13th tee.

The dogleg left, par-5 13th hole only plays about 465 yards, par-4 length really for the professionals. It calls, however, for a perfectly drawn tee shot around the trees, then a dangerous mid to long iron over Rae's Creek to reach the putting surface. Many players have watched their dreams drown on this hole. Curtis Strange hit into the creek in 1985. It meant he had to say farewell to the green jacket. In 1954, Billy Joe Patton took on the creek and lost.

The hole does reward true champions, though. Bernhard Langer made an eagle three at 13 in 1993 after hitting an excellent drive and a glorious 3-iron to the heart of the green. Langer went on, that same year, to win his second Masters.

If you're ever fortunate enough to enter Augusta National, head for Amen Corner. You may never want to leave this little bit of heaven.

ABOVE: THE 11TH HOLE IS THE FIRST TIME PLAYERS ENCOUNTER WATER AT AUGUSTA NATIONAL.

ABOVE RIGHT: JACK NICKLAUS CALLS THE 12TH AT AUGUSTA THE MOST DEMANDING PAR-3 IN THE WORLD.

RIGHT: THE DOGLEG 13TH CALLS FOR A GOOD DRIVE TO HAVE ANY HOPE OF REACHING THE GREEN IN TWO SHOTS.

LEFT: A SMALL STREAM CALLED RAE'S CREEK PROTECTS THE 13TH GREEN. MANY GOLFERS HAVE FOUND THE CREEK AND THROWN AWAY THEIR CHANCE AT THE TITLE.

# George Archer

ARCHER IS ONE OF THE TALLEST GOLFERS IN THE GAME'S HISTORY. HE CAPPED A FINE CAREER BY WINNING THE 1969 MASTERS, OVERTAKING BILLY CASPER IN THE FINAL ROUND.

## Fact File

**BORN** 1939, San Francisco, California, USA

**CAREER HIGHLIGHTS**
1967 Greater Greensboro Open
1969 Bing Crosby National Pro-Am
1969 Masters
1972 Los Angeles Open
1972 Greater Greensboro Open

They say tall people don't make good golfers. The ideal height for a golfer is supposed to be somewhere between 5-feet, 8-inches and 6 feet. George Archer sure proved that theory wrong.

At 6-feet, 6-inches tall, Archer is one of the tallest ever to have played the game. Indeed, he is the tallest major champion in golf history.

Archer's one and only major title came in the 1969 Masters. The Californian entered the final round behind overnight leader Billy Casper, who would win the title the following year. Casper played the front nine holes in 40 strokes to give Archer a three-stroke lead going into the final nine holes. Despite a nervous back nine, Archer emerged victorious to win by one stroke from Casper, Tom Weiskopf, and Canada's George Knudson.

Before Archer turned professional in 1964, he worked on a cattle ranch. Yet he emerged from his tenure as a cattle hand without ever learning to ride or rope a horse. In fact, he had probably never so much as put a saddle on a horse while "working" on the ranch. Archer was the beneficiary of the cattle ranch's owner, a rich Californian who agreed to sponsor him on the US Tour. Rather than roping cattle, Archer spent his days working on his golf swing, hitting hundreds and hundreds of practice shots.

Almost immediately, Archer made an impression on the American professional circuit. He won his first tournament in 1965, the Lucky International. Two years later he won in Greensboro, North Carolina, before winning two events in 1968, the Pensacola and New Orleans Opens.

Archer warmed up for the 1969 Masters by winning the Bing Crosby National Pro-Am in January, a victory that gave him a $25,000 first-place cheque, a huge sum in those days.

Archer was known for being one of the best putters on the American circuit during his prime. During the 1980 Sea Pines Heritage Classic at Harbor Town Golf Links, South Carolina, the tall professional set a new US Tour record (since broken) for the fewest putts over 72 holes. Archer needed only 95 for his four days' work. During his Masters win, he had to hole a slick, 15-foot downhill putt on Augusta's 15th hole during his final round. He duly did so to save par. Had he missed he would have been involved in a four-man playoff.

Strangely enough, despite his success, Archer never played in the Ryder Cup.

# TOMMY ARMOUR

ARMOUR, THIRD FROM LEFT, COMPETES IN THE FORERUNNER TO THE RYDER CUP, IN 1926 AT WENTWORTH. FROM THE LEFT ARE JOE KIRKWOOD, ARCHIE COMPSTON AND AUBREY BOOMER. ARMOUR IS STILL REGARDED AS ONE OF THE FINEST SHOTMAKERS TO PLAY THE GAME.

Tommy Armour received the best start in golf—he was coached by six-time British Open winner Harry Vardon.

The Silver Scot, as Armour was called, was born in Edinburgh and started to play golf at an early age. His enthusiasm for the game came from watching exhibition matches featuring Vardon and James Braid, two members of golf's great triumvirate. He later took lessons from Vardon.

Armour served in World War I, losing an eye in combat. After the war he returned home and resumed playing. He competed in two British Amateur Championships and won the 1920 French Amateur Championship. In 1921 he appeared in the forerunner of the Walker Cup matches. A year later he went with the team to the first official Walker Cup match, played at Long Island, New York. He remained in America after the match and turned professional in 1924.

Armour's first success in America came in the 1927 US Open at Oakmont, one of America's toughest courses. He tied with Harry Cooper over the regulation 72 holes, before defeating Cooper by three shots in the playoff. In 1930, Armour added a second major championship to his list of honors when he beat Gene Sarazen by one hole in the final of the USPGA Championship. Then in 1931 Armour returned home to Carnoustie to win the British Open.

By this time Armour had taken out US citizenship, so although he was born in Scotland, he goes down as an American winner of the oldest championship in golf. Indeed, Armour holds the unique distinction of having represented Great Britain & Ireland as an amateur, in 1921, and America as a professional, in 1926 when a match was held between British and American professionals a year before the Ryder Cup officially started.

Armour possessed a golf swing that wasn't just good enough to win tournaments, but that was graceful and stylish to boot. He had strong hands that allowed him complete control over the golf club. So good was his swing that when Armour hit balls, other professionals would stop to watch.

After his playing career, Armour enjoyed a hugely successful career as a teacher at Boca Raton, Florida, and Winged Foot, near New York. While his services did not come cheap, his lesson book was always full. His book *How to Play Your Best Golf All the Time* is still regarded as one of the best ever written on the game.

## FACT FILE

**BORN** 1895, Edinburgh, Scotland

**DIED** 1968

**CAREER HIGHLIGHTS**
1927 US Open
1927 Canadian Open
1930 Canadian Open
1930 USPGA Championship
1931 The Open Championship
1934 Canadian Open

# Paul Azinger

AZINGER WON THE 1993 USPGA CHAMPIONSHIP IN A PLAYOFF WITH GREG NORMAN. HIS FINEST VICTORY CAME IN 1995 WHEN HE OVERCAME ILLNESS TO RETURN TO COMPETITIVE ACTION.

## Fact File

**BORN** 1960, Holyoke, Massachusetts, USA

**CAREER HIGHLIGHTS**
1987 Phoenix Open
1990 MONY Tournament of Champions
1992 Tour Championship
1992 Memorial Tournament
1993 USPGA Championship

**INTERNATIONAL HONORS**
Ryder Cup: 1989, 1991, 1993
World Cup: 1989
Presidents Cup: 1994 (co-captain)

There are many heart-warming stories in golf. Paul Azinger's is one of the warmest.

Despite a swing that includes an unorthodox, strong left-hand grip, Azinger is one of the most successful professionals on the US Tour. Between turning professional, in 1981, and 1993, Zinger, as he is known, won 11 times in America. Then disaster struck.

Azinger had complained of a pain in his right shoulder for a number of years. It wasn't until the end of the 1993 season that he knew why the shoulder troubled him so. He was diagnosed as having cancer in his right shoulder blade.

He underwent treatment during 1994 that included chemotherapy and radiation to cure the disease. It was successful and Azinger returned to professional golf in 1995. He penned a book called *Zinger*, which deals with his fight against cancer, and in 1995 he received the Ben Hogan Trophy, awarded to individuals active in golf who have overcome physical handicaps to return to competition.

It was always odds-on that Azinger would win his battle against cancer, for they don't come much tougher than the tall Florida State University graduate. Over the years, Zinger has shown that he's one of the most determined of golfers in the pressure of any tournament.

His resilience was shown in his first appearance in the 1989 Ryder Cup at The Belfry. Most rookies would not want to face the formidable Seve Ballesteros in their first Ryder Cup singles match, but Azinger seemed to relish the occasion. One up going to the last hole, he appeared to have thrown the match away when he pulled his tee shot into a water hazard. He dropped another ball then conjured up an amazing shot with a fairway wood to get his ball into a greenside bunker. That may have been the reason why Seve's approach shot also found water. Nevertheless Seve played his fourth shot to 20 feet, while Azinger blasted out of the bunker to within five feet of the cup. When Seve holed his downhill putt it meant Azinger had to hole the five-footer to win his match and give his team a valuable point. The putt never looked like missing and Azinger had proved he could stand the most immense pressure in golf.

His ability to cope well under pressure was also evident in his first major championship win. Azinger had to face the formidable and odds-on favorite Greg Norman in a playoff for the 1993 USPGA Championship. Azinger won at the second extra hole.

# Ian Baker-Finch

**AFTER WINNING THE 1991 BRITISH OPEN AT ROYAL BIRKDALE, THE TALL AUSTRALIAN WENT INTO A SLUMP THAT FORCED HIM OUT OF THE GAME.**

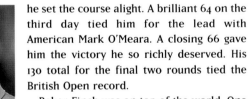

Ian Baker-Finch's story is one of the saddest in golf. The tall, popular Australian had to quit tournament golf after he made just six cuts in 49 tournaments over three years. Yet there was a time when he was unquestionably one of the best players in the world.

When Ian Baker-Finch won the 1991 British Open, he finally got his hands on the trophy that had eluded him twice during his career. The Australian had paid his dues and there was no more worthy winner of the old trophy than he.

Baker-Finch had first threatened to win the game's oldest tournament when he led at St Andrews in 1984 in his first British Open. Not many first timers win the British Open, and so it proved for Baker-Finch. He closed with a 79 to place ninth as Seve Ballesteros won his second championship. Six years later, he featured at St Andrews again, when a brilliant third round 64 put him five shots behind Nick Faldo. However, Faldo was too good that year and the Australian eventually placed sixth. But he wasn't to be denied the following summer.

While it had been a poor finish that denied him his first chance at the title in 1984, in 1991 Baker-Finch made sure he finally got his name on the trophy with a brilliant finale to the championship. After rounds of 71, 71, the Australian was four behind the leaders when he set the course alight. A brilliant 64 on the third day tied him for the lead with American Mark O'Meara. A closing 66 gave him the victory he so richly deserved. His 130 total for the final two rounds tied the British Open record.

Baker-Finch was on top of the world. One of the best putters in the game, there was no telling how many more majors he would win. Throughout his career he had been building to the victory, winning tournaments all over the world. He had served his apprenticeship well, finally won his first major and was ready to conquer the world. Then it went all downhill from there.

Baker-Finch did win the Australian PGA Championship in 1993, but he made only 12 cuts on the US Tour that season, tumbling to 114th on the US Tour money list. The following season he made just six of 20 to place 167th on the money list. Then came complete disaster. In 1995 and 1996, Baker-Finch went 27 tournaments and never made a cut.

In 1997, Baker-Finch hit an all-time low when he tried to play the British Open. In tough conditions in the opening round, he shot 92, 21 over par and then withdrew from the championship.

Now working as a TV commentator, Baker-Finch hasn't ruled out a comeback in the future. All of golf would welcome him back.

## Fact File

**BORN** 1960, Nambour, Queensland, Australia

**CAREER HIGHLIGHTS**
1985 Scandinavian Open
1988 Australian Masters
1989 Colonial National Invitational
1991 The Open Championship
1993 Australian PGA Championship

**INTERNATIONAL HONORS**
World Cup: 1990, 1991
Alfred Dunhill Cup: 1992

# John Ball

NO PLAYER HAS BEEN ABLE TO MATCH BALL'S TALLY OF EIGHT BRITISH AMATEUR CHAMPIONSHIPS. HE WAS ONE OF THE BEST PLAYERS OF HIS DAY, AMATEUR OR PROFESSIONAL, WHICH HE PROVED WHEN HE WON THE 1890 BRITISH OPEN.

## Fact File

**BORN** 1861, Hoylake, England

**DIED** 1940

**CAREER HIGHLIGHTS**
1888 British Amateur
1890 British Amateur
1890 The Open Championship
1892 British Amateur
1894 British Amateur
1899 British Amateur
1907 British Amateur
1910 British Amateur
1912 British Amateur

Without question, John Ball was the best amateur golfer Great Britain has ever produced. He can thank his father for that.

Ball's father was the proprietor of the Royal Hotel in Hoylake. The hotel was situated beside links land that would become the Hoylake golf course, later the Royal Liverpool Golf Club. The course was constructed when Ball was just a boy of eight or nine, and it was on these famous links that the youngster spent much of his youth, indulging a passion for the game that would become his life.

Not surprisingly, Ball quickly developed into a fine player. At just 15 years old he competed in his first British Open Championship, placing sixth. At 17 he won the first of eight British Amateur Championships. Ironically, despite being the game's outstanding amateur player, Ball never successfully defended any of his titles.

Ball proved that he was more than just a great amateur golfer when he captured the British Open in 1890, becoming the first amateur to win the coveted trophy. Ball won his only professional event at Prestwick, Scotland, and it must have galled the Scots to see the first Englishman win the Open in their own backyard. In fact, along with Bobby Jones of the United States, Ball holds the distinction of being the only player to hold the British Amateur and British Open championships in the same year.

Ball was renowned for being a good driver of the ball, a very accurate iron player, an excellent putter, and a player with the coolest of temperaments. In short he had everything needed to play competitive golf at the top level. He has been described as "wiry and active, and immensely strong." His swing was also controlled and very repetitive.

Ball's feat of eight British Amateur titles in 24 years came at a time when the game was full of outstanding amateur players. Also in their primes at the time, were players like Harold Hilton, Freddie Tait, and Horace Hutchison, to name just a few. That he could dominate the game with these players around was proof that Ball was one of the best the game has ever seen, amateur or professional.

It is a testament to his skill that for three years during his outstanding amateur career, Ball played no golf at all. He was away fighting in the Boer War, where he served in the Cheshire Yeomanry. Yet when he returned he had lost none of his talent.

Ball competed in his last British Amateur Championship at the age of 60 on his beloved Hoylake. He got as far as the sixth round.

# BRIAN BARNES

BARNES HOLDS THE UNIQUE DISTINCTION OF BEATING JACK NICKLAUS TWICE IN RYDER CUP SINGLES MATCHES—ON THE SAME DAY.

Brian Barnes holds a unique place in the history of the Ryder Cup: he once faced Jack Nicklaus twice in the same day in singles matches. That would strike terror into the heart of most golfers. Not "Barnesy." He beat Nicklaus both times.

The occasion was the 1975 match at Laurel Valley, Pennsylvania, and Nicklaus, by his own admission, was playing the best golf of his life as he approached the contest. That season alone he had won his fifth Masters, his fourth USPGA Championship, and the World Open at Pinehurst, North Carolina.

Nicklaus had already taken two-and-a-half points out of a possible three prior to the final day singles matches. He was last out in the morning series (they played two sessions of singles on the final day in the matches between 1961 and 1975) and faced Barnes, who had only earned one half point from his three previous matches. It looked a foregone conclusion that Nicklaus would win the contest easily. Barnes had other ideas, however.

The English-born Scotsman won the first encounter with relative ease, defeating Nicklaus by the embarrassing margin of four and two. Nicklaus wasn't happy and made a point of asking American captain Arnold Palmer to play him last so he could have the chance of facing Barnes again. Palmer replied, and as the two stood on the first tee in the afternoon, Nicklaus said to Barnes, "You've beaten me once, but there ain't no way you're going to beat me again." But Barnes wasn't listening.

Despite Nicklaus starting with two straight birdies to take the early lead, Barnes stuck to his task and once again got the better of Nicklaus, this time by the score of two and one. It remains the biggest upset in Ryder Cup history.

Brian Barnes was one of the original Butten Boys. This was a handful of talented British golfers assembled by Ernest Butten, head of a management consultancy, and managed by 1951 British Open champion Max Faulkner with the sole purpose of producing a home-grown British Open winner. If it weren't for a third-round score of 80 in 1968, Barnes might have fulfilled Butten's wish. Barnes finished six strokes behind eventual winner Gary Player.

While his encounter with Nicklaus is his biggest victory on the golf course, Barnes triumphed in his personal life in the early 1990s when he overcame an addiction to alcoholism. Barnes has gone on to become a successful senior golfer.

## FACT FILE

**BORN** 1945, Addington, Surrey, England

**CAREER HIGHLIGHTS**
1964 British Youths' Open Amateur Championship
1975 French Open
1976 Sun Alliance PGA Match Play Championship
1995 Senior British Open
1996 Senior British Open

**INTERNATIONAL HONORS**
Ryder Cup: 1969, 1971, 1973, 1975, 1977, 1979
World Cup: 1974, 1975, 1976, 1977

# Severiano Ballesteros

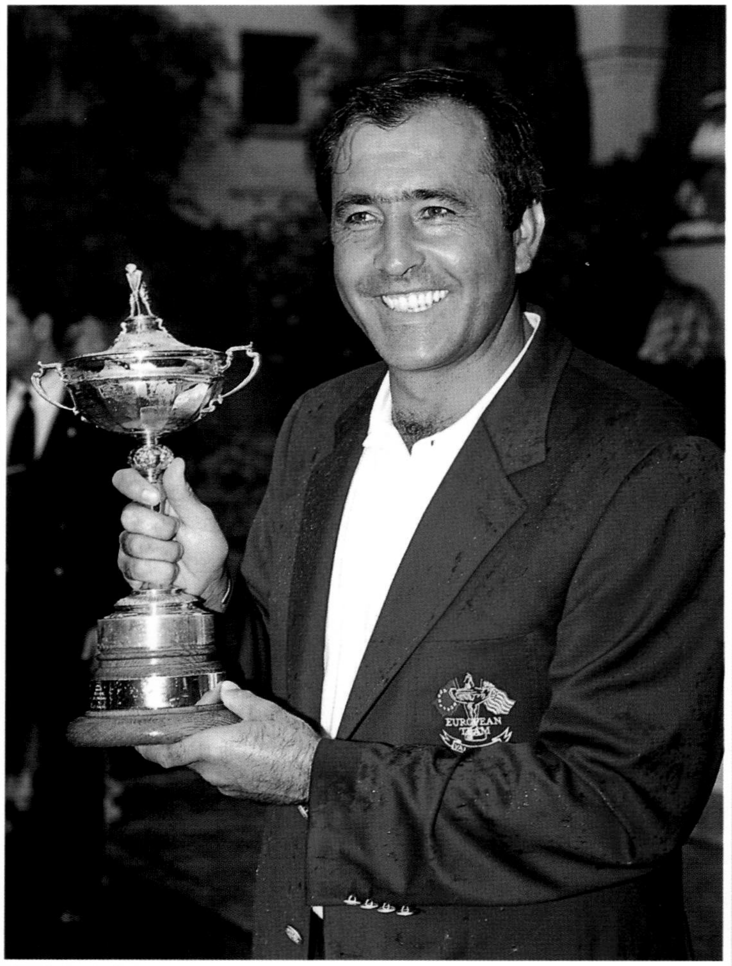

No player has done more for the growth of European golf than Severiano Ballesteros. Just as Arnold Palmer helped promote the game's image in North America in the late 1950s and early 1960s, Seve performed a similar service in Europe in the late 1970s and early 1980s and European golf owes him a lot.

Ballesteros breathed new life into European golf. His swashbuckling style, his go-for-broke attitude, his ability to make birdies or save par from seemingly impossible situations thrilled galleries everywhere. One such occasion occurred on the final day of the 1979 British Open at Royal Lytham & St Annes. Ballesteros drove his ball into a parking lot well to the right of the 17th fairway. It seemed certain he would lose a shot. However, he got a free drop and then went on to make birdie. It was that shot that earned him the dubious nickname "the car park champion," a title that did not bother him.

While people marveled at his skill in finding ways to get the ball into the hole from almost anywhere, to Ballesteros it came naturally. As a boy growing up in Spain, Severiano had started playing golf with an old 3-iron. Alone on the beach at Pedrena, he would practice for hours, hitting hundreds of shots off the smooth sand, using his imagination to get the ball from A to B, no matter where B was.

It was the emergence of Ballesteros as a predominant force that saved the Ryder Cup. Until 1977, the Ryder Cup had been a one-sided affair between the USA and Great Britain & Ireland. Jack Nicklaus realized the future of the match was in jeopardy if the contest didn't become more competitive. In Seve he saw a way to even things up.

After another USA victory in 1977, Nicklaus proposed that future matches be between the USA and Europe. The suggestion was taken on board and Ballesteros and fellow countryman Antonio Garrido played in the 1979 match. Europe lost, but the way was paved for future European stars such as Jose Maria Olazabal and Bernhard Langer to compete in the biennial match. Six years after Ballesteros made his debut in the match, Europe recorded a historic win at The Belfry in 1985, with Ballesteros leading the way. Europe won again in 1987 for the first time on American soil, again with Severiano leading from the front. Suddenly it was game on, and now the Ryder Cup is the biggest event in golf.

Nicklaus was astute enough to realize that Ballesteros was a world-class star. He knew the Spaniard's victory in the 1979 British Open was no fluke. Nicklaus was right. Seve Ballesteros was here to stay.

To his British Open win, Seve added the 1980 Masters, becoming the first European to win the coveted green jacket. At just 23 years old, he was also the youngest golfer to win at Augusta. That record would stand for another 17 years, until Tiger Woods won in 1997.

Seve added another Masters green jacket to his growing list of tournament wins when he triumphed at Augusta in 1983. In 1984, Seve recorded his most emotional victory to date when he won the British Open over the Old Course at St Andrews, the traditional home of golf.

Another British Open was added in 1988, again at Royal Lytham & St Annes. It was in this championship that Ballesteros proved he was the best when his back was to the wall.

The Spaniard entered the final round two shots behind overnight leader Nick Price, who had thrown away the British Open at Troon six years before. Price told his caddie Dave McNeilly that all they had to do that day was shoot 69 and the trophy would be theirs. Price duly shot 69—and lost the Open by two shots. Seve shot 65 to win his third British Open, and his second at Royal Lytham.

It is in the Ryder Cup though that Seve has featured most prominently. Of all the European players since 1979, Seve has been the mainstay. So it was fitting that when the match went to Spain for the first time in 1997, Seve captained the European side. He was as inspirational a captain as he was a player, seemingly involved in every match on the course on all three days. Despite being heavy underdogs, Seve's side won.

Severiano Ballesteros is used to winning. Throughout his career he has won tournaments all over the world, notching up in excess of 85 victories, including the World Match Play Championship five times.

## Fact File

**BORN** 1957, Pedrena, Spain

**CAREER HIGHLIGHTS**
1979 The Open Championship
1980 Masters
1983 Masters
1984 The Open Championship
1988 The Open Championship

**INTERNATIONAL HONORS**
Ryder Cup: 1979, 1983, 1985, 1987, 1989, 1991, 1993, 1995, 1997 (captain)
World Cup: 1975, 1976, 1977, 1991
Alfred Dunhill Cup: 1985, 1986, 1988

ABOVE: FROM 1979 THE RYDER CUP MATCHES PITTED THE USA AGAINST A EUROPEAN TEAM, INCLUDING BALLESTEROS. HERE HE HOLDS THE 1997 CUP WON AT VALDERRAMA IN SPAIN.

RIGHT: BALLESTEROS IN FULL FLOW. THE POPULAR SPANIARD'S ABILITY TO SAVE PAR FROM ALMOST ANYWHERE HAS THRILLED GALLERIES AROUND THE WORLD.

# JIM BARNES

JIM BARNES PLAYS THE 14TH GREEN AT ROYAL LIVERPOOL DURING THE 1924 BRITISH OPEN. HE DID NOT WIN ON THAT OCCASION, BUT THE FOLLOWING YEAR OVERCAME MACDONALD SMITH IN TESTING CONDITIONS AT PRESTWICK IN SCOTLAND.

## FACT FILE

**BORN** 1887, Lelant, Cornwall, England

**DIED** 1966

**CAREER HIGHLIGHTS**
1916 USPGA Championship
1919 USPGA Championship
1921 US Open
1925 The Open Championship

It is too bad the Ryder Cup came along after Jim Barnes's prime, because the English-born American was one of the best head-to-head golfers of his generation.

In Barnes's day the USPGA Championship was a match play event (it became a stroke-play tournament in 1958), and he won the first two tournaments ever played. Barnes also lost in two finals, twice to Walter Hagen, in 1921 and 1924. In nine appearances in the tournament, Barnes won 24 matches and lost just seven. Moreover, he shares the record of the biggest winning margin in the history of the event, recording a 12 and 11 victory in his first two matches in 1923.

Barnes began playing golf in his native Cornwall, becoming an assistant professional at Lelant Golf Club at the age of 15. He emigrated to the United States four years later and finished fourth in the 1913 US Open Championship at The Country Club, Brookline, Massachusetts. He eventually won America's national championship in 1921, when he lifted the trophy at Columbia Country Club in Chevy Chase, Maryland, by nine strokes over Fred McLeod and his match play nemesis, Walter Hagen.

Barnes was a tall golfer who was nicknamed "Long Jim" because of his height. Quiet and self-assured, Barnes was known as a methodical golfer whose game was well respected by his peers.

The naturalized American was always proud of his English heritage, so it was fitting that he should return home in 1925 to win the British Open. Prestwick was the scene of Barnes's only victory in the event, yet it should have been Macdonald Smith who won that year. Barnes was five strokes behind Smith going into the final round and only emerged victorious after Smith's final round collapse. Barnes's steady play in windy conditions no doubt came from spending his youth hitting balls on the Cornish coast.

However, it was in match play that Barnes excelled. For example, in the first USPGA Championship the tall golfer entered the afternoon round one down against Jock Hutchison, after both golfers had scored identical morning rounds of 77. Despite his apparent shyness, Barnes announced his intentions on the first tee after the break. "I always do better after lunch," Barnes told the assembled gallery. He lived up to his promise, defeating Hutchison on the final green to win one up and earn himself $500 and a diamond medal.

Barnes wrote two books in his time. In 1919 he produced a title called *Picture Analysis of Golf Strokes*, and in 1925 he penned *Guide to Good Golf.*

# Andy Bean

BEAN HAS WON THE DORAL EASTERN OPEN THREE TIMES, EACH TIME OVER "BLUE MONSTER," PROVING HE IS ONE OF THE BEST TO PLAY ON THE US TOUR.

For a ten-year period between the mid 1970s and mid 1980s, Andy Bean looked like a genuine contender to Jack Nicklaus's mantle as America's best golfer.

Although he has not won a major, Bean won 11 times on the US Tour between 1977 and 1986. Three of those victories came in the Doral Eastern Open. Doral is known on the US Tour as one of the toughest tournaments to win. The event is played on the famous Blue course, dubbed the "Blue Monster" by American professionals because of its severity. The fact that Bean has won the event three times proves he is worthy of inclusion on any list of great golfers.

Bean was destined to be a golfer from an early age. He grew up on Jekyll Island, Georgia, where his father had an interest in a golf course. When he was 15 years old, Bean moved to Florida when his father bought a golf course at Lakeland. What more could a budding golfer want?

Upon reaching university age, Bean attended the University of Florida where he played on the golf team. Indeed, he won All-American honors and captained the Florida team. He turned professional in 1975 and earned his US Tour card at the 1975 US Tour Qualifying School. It didn't take him long to make his mark in professional golf, winning for the first time at Doral in 1977.

Bean's best year on the US Tour came in the 1978 season, when he triumphed three times, winning the Kemper Open, the Danny Thomas Memphis Classic, and the prestigious Western Open. That was good enough to give him third spot on the US Tour Order of Merit that season, a position he matched in 1984. In fact, between 1977 and 1986, Bean finished in the top-ten on the American money list five times, and inside the top 35 every year.

Bean came closest to winning a major championship when he finished second by two strokes to Tom Watson at Royal Birkdale in the 1983 British Open. He also finished runner-up to Jack Nicklaus at Oak Hill in the 1980 USPGA Championship, when Nicklaus lifted his fifth title by seven strokes.

The 6-foot, 4-inch Floridian appeared in two Ryder Cup matches. He first played in 1977, when he compiled a record of two wins and one loss in the three matches he played. Ten years later he equaled that tally, with one of his wins coming against Ian Woosnam in the final day singles matches.

Tendinitis in the late 1980s caused Bean to cut back on his playing schedule during the 1990s. He should, however, prove a force in senior golf.

## Fact File

**BORN** 1953, Lafayette, Georgia, USA

**CAREER HIGHLIGHTS**
1977 Doral Eastern Open
1978 Western Open
1982 Doral Eastern Open
1984 Greater Greensboro Open
1986 Doral Eastern Open

**INTERNATIONAL HONORS**
Ryder Cup: 1979, 1987

# Patty Berg

BERG IS ONE OF THE GREATEST WOMEN GOLFERS EVER. DESPITE MANY INJURIES, SHE WON 57 TOURNAMENTS, INCLUDING THE 1946 US WOMEN'S OPEN.

## Fact File

**BORN** 1918, Minneapolis, Minnesota, USA

**CAREER HIGHLIGHTS**
1938 US Ladies' Amateur
1946 US Women's Open
1947 Pebble Beach Open
1949 Texas PGA Championship
1958 American Women's Open

**INTERNATIONAL HONORS**
Curtis Cup: 1936, 1938

Patty Berg stands as one of the best women ever to play golf. The red-haired, blue-eyed girl from Minnesota won every top honor in the game in a career that spanned well over four decades.

Berg first attained notoriety as a teenage prodigy winning top amateur events all over the US. Only three years after taking up the game at the age of 13, Berg won the 1934 Minneapolis City Championship. Four years later she won the US Amateur Championship. Between 1934 and 1940, when she turned professional, Berg won no less than 28 amateur tournaments. Included in that stretch were two appearances in the Curtis Cup, in 1936 and 1938.

Her winning ways continued into the professional game. Between 1940 and 1962 she won 57 tournaments. She won six titles before the Women's Professional Golf Association was even formed. During that period she recorded her only victory in the US Women's Open, which she won in 1946. In 1948 she won seven times before becoming a founding member of the LPGA. Indeed, Berg served as its first president.

After helping form the LPGA, Berg won 44 times on the Tour. She was the leading money winner three times, in 1954, 1955, and 1957. She won the Vare Trophy for the lowest scoring average in 1953, 1955, and 1956.

Berg was famous throughout the world for the clinics she gave to help promote the game, including becoming the first woman golfer to do a golf exhibition in Japan. She is an attractive woman which, combined with her outgoing personality, made people warm to her. She did much to further women's golf and gave a lot of time to charity throughout her career. For this work she has received many awards. For example, in 1963 she won the Bob Jones Award for sportsmanship. In 1976 she became the first woman to receive the Humanitarian Sports Award from the United Cerebral Palsy Foundation.

The LPGA established the Patty Berg Award in 1978 which is given annually to a person for outstanding contributions to women's golf.

Unfortunately, Berg has been plagued with injury throughout her career, including sitting out for 18 months after a car crash in 1941, cancer surgery in 1971, hip surgery in 1980, and back surgery in 1989. Like the way she played golf, however, Patricia Jane Berg has met each challenge head on, and triumphed.

# Thomas Bjorn

THOMAS BJORN MADE HISTORY IN 1997 WHEN HE BECAME THE FIRST DANISH PLAYER TO APPEAR IN THE RYDER CUP. DURING THE 1998 SEASON, HE WON THREE EUROPEAN TOUR EVENTS.

Ian Woosnam dubbed Bjorn the "Great Dane" when they teamed together in the 1997 Ryder Cup at Valderrama, Spain. Despite the fact that Bjorn was making his first appearance in the biennial match, the Welshman was impressed with what he saw in the Dane's ability.

Woosnam and Bjorn were paired together in the second day's fourball matches against the strong American pairing of Brad Faxon and Justin Leonard, the British Open champion that year. The European pair triumphed by the score of two and one. As far as Woosnam was concerned, it was Bjorn who carried them to victory.

Bjorn then halved his singles match with British Open Champion, Leonard on the final day. It was a tremendous display, for Bjorn was four down in the match at one point, but clawed his way back to earn a valuable half point in Europe's historic victory.

Bjorn is by far the best golfer Denmark has produced. In fact, he was the first Danish player to appear in the Ryder Cup. Bjorn and his brother Soren started playing golf as youngsters because their parents played at Jutland's Silkeborg Club. However, it was the long-hitting Thomas who excelled at the sport. Bjorn emerged as a true world-class player when he won the inaugural Loch Lomond World Invitational in 1996 over a quality field. He made history on that occasion too, becoming the first Danish player to win a regular European Tour event.

The 6-foot Danish star learned his trade on the European Challenge Tour. After a successful amateur career in his homeland which saw him win back-to-back Danish Amateur Championships in 1990 and 1991, and represent his country in European and World amateur team events, Bjorn turned professional in 1993. In 1995 he concentrated on using the European Challenge Tour as his avenue to the main European Tour. It proved a wise move. Bjorn won four titles en route to topping the 1995 Challenge Tour Order of Merit with over £40,000, a record at the time.

Bjorn placed tenth on the European Tour's final Order of Merit in 1996, the following season he finished in 15th spot and in 1998 he moved up to sixth. The 1998 season was a banner year for the Dane. He rubber-stamped his potential with two tournament victories, capturing the Heineken Classic in Australia, and the Spanish Open.

## Fact File

**BORN** 1971, Silkeborg, Denmark

**CAREER HIGHLIGHTS**
1990 Danish Amateur
1991 Danish Amateur
1996 Loch Lomond Invitational
1998 Heineken Classic
1998 Peugeot Open de Espana

**INTERNATIONAL HONORS**
Ryder Cup: 1997
World Cup: 1996, 1997

# Tommy Bolt

THE "THUNDER BOLT" LAUNCHES INTO A SHOT. HE HAD A REPUTATION FOR THROWING CLUBS, BUT DESPITE HIS TEMPERAMENT, BOLT WON THE 1958 US OPEN AT SOUTHERN HILLS, OKLAHOMA.

## Fact File

**BORN** 1919, Haworth, Oklahoma, USA

**CAREER HIGHLIGHTS**
1952 Los Angeles Open
1953 Tucson Open
1955 Tucson Open
1958 US Open
1958 Colonial National Invitational

**INTERNATIONAL HONORS**
Ryder Cup: 1955, 1957

Of all the golfers of the past 100 years, Tommy Bolt is the one noted for having the worst temper in the game, a reputation that earned him the dubious nickname "Thunder Bolt." The popular image of Bolt is of him having just mishit a shot, and sending the offending club soaring into orbit.

Stories of Bolt and his volcanic temper are part of golf's rich tradition. It has been said that Bolt always advised golfers to throw clubs forward if they were going to indulge in such acts of petulance—that way they would not have to waste time walking back to retrieve them.

Another Bolt story concerns the time he won his only major championship, the 1958 US Open at Southern Hills, Tulsa, Oklahoma. A report in one of the local newspapers stated that Bolt was 49 years old. Bolt was in fact 40 at the time. When he entered the press tent as leader after 36 holes, Bolt pretended to be angry at the Tulsa writer for adding another nine years to his life. When the writer apologized profusely for what he called a typographical error, Bolt's reply cut him down to size.

"Typographical error, hell," said Bolt. "It was a perfect four and a perfect nine."

In truth there were probably two reasons why Tommy Bolt never won more major championships. One was that his early career coincided with those of Ben Hogan and Sam Snead, while his later playing days clashed with the beginning of the Arnold Palmer era. Then there was his putting.

Bolt was never the player on the greens that he was from the tee. He was known for being one of the best shot makers in the game, a great driver of the ball, brilliant fairway wood player and very accurate with his irons. Sadly, his putting didn't quite complement the rest of his game. On more than one occasion after missing a short putt, Bolt would look up at the sky and say, "Why don't You come down here and play me one time?"

Yet despite his temper and his flawed putting stroke, Bolt still managed to win 15 times on the US Tour. And his victory in the US Open in 1958 was an exhibition of near flawless golf. Southern Hills was set up with fairways so narrow the players almost had to walk single file down the middle of them. The rough was so deep that Bolt would have had a tough time finding a club had he had reason to throw one that week. Yet Bolt ran away with the championship, winning by four shots over Gary Player.

# Sir Michael Bonallack

UNTIL HIS RETIREMENT IN 1999, MICHAEL BONALLACK WAS SECRETARY OF THE ROYAL & ANCIENT GOLF CLUB. HIS OFFICE OVERLOOKED THE OLD COURSE AT ST ANDREWS.

It would take more than the space provided here to list all of Sir Michael Bonallack's successes in amateur golf. Besides the highlights listed, Bonallack also won the Berkshire Trophy, the Lytham Trophy, the Hampshire Hog, the St George's Champion Grand Challenge Cup, the Prince of Wales Challenge Cup, and many other important amateur events. He also represented England more times than any other amateur golfer. In short, he is arguably the best amateur Britain has ever produced.

Despite winning the English Open Amateur Stroke Play Championship four times, it was at match play that Bonallack excelled. His five victories in the British Amateur Championships have never been equaled, nor are ever likely to be given the way good amateur players gravitate to professional golf nowadays. That Bonallack never ventured into the professional ranks seems odd. His own answer was that he didn't think he was good enough.

Bonallack's refusal to turn professional was the amateur game's good fortune. It was particularly fortuitous for the Walker Cup.

Bonallack played in every Walker Cup between 1957 and 1973. In fact, he has played more matches in the event than any other British or Irish player, having played 25 times. Only one other player has played more matches in the biennial contest between America and Great Britain & Ireland. That honor goes to the American Jay Sigel, who played 33 times in nine matches.

Such was his stature in the amateur game that Bonallack was player captain of the Great Britain & Ireland Walker side twice. Unfortunately, American dominance of the contest meant Bonallack played on seven losing sides and in one drawn match. In the only match in which he appeared when Great Britain & Ireland won, the 1971 match at St Andrews, Bonallack was fortunate enough to lead his team to victory as captain.

Expert opinion was fairly unanimous that the tall Englishman never possessed the most classic of golf swings. However, it did the one thing that every good swing needs to do—it stood up to the pressure of championship golf. Besides that, Bonallack had a deadly short game. When he defeated Alan Thirlwell in the 1963 English Amateur Championship at Burnham and Berrow, Bonallack got up and down in two strokes from off the green no fewer than 22 times in the 36-hole final.

Bonallack was awarded the Order of the British Empire in 1971 for his services to golf, and was knighted in 1998. In 1983 he assumed the position of secretary to the Royal & Ancient Golf Club of St Andrews, a role he fulfilled until his retirement in the year 2000.

## Fact File

**BORN** 1934, Chigwell, Essex, England

**CAREER HIGHLIGHTS**
1961 British Amateur
1965 British Amateur
1968 British Amateur
1969 British Amateur
1970 British Amateur

**INTERNATIONAL HONORS**
Walker Cup: 1957, 1959, 1961, 1963, 1965, 1967, 1969 (captain), 1971 (captain), 1973

# The Toughest Par-4

A quick straw poll of any group of professionals to determine the toughest par-4 in all of golf will normally throw up one particular hole time and time again—the 17th on the Old Course at St Andrews.

At 461 yards, the Road Hole, as it is called, is a formidable par-4, but what makes the hole, what defines it, what strikes terror into nearly everyone who plays it, is a small pit of sand just before the green. Known simply as the Road Bunker, this little pit of sand has influenced the outcome of many British Opens.

In the old days, the drive at 17 was played over railroad sheds. Nowadays, competitors aim over reconstructed sheds with a sign that reads "Old Course Hotel," named after the hotel to the right of the tee. Caddies have differing views on what letter they want their player to aim over, often depending on what type of flight their employer puts on the ball. Once the drive is safely negotiated, the fun really begins.

It takes a brave golfer to take on the Road Bunker and come away with a three. The decision is whether or not to go for the flag, which on the final day of the British Open is normally placed directly behind the bunker, or to play safe to the right. The latter option calls for a long chip to get the ball close enough to make a putt for par.

When Severiano Ballesteros won the 1984 British Open at St Andrews, he took the safe option, despite being one of the best shotmakers in the world. Ballesteros knew that to take on the pin would be to tempt fate. Seve made his par. Playing behind him, Tom Watson also decided to play safe. However, Watson's second shot ran through the fairway, across the road behind the green and ended up just in front of the wall that defines the out of bounds. Watson could only stab at the ball to get it onto the green and make a bogey five.

The Road Hole can get you in more ways than one. The road is in play. When Italy's Constantino Rocca earned his way into a playoff for the 1995 championship with John Daly, he did so by chipping off the road behind the 17th. Rocca chipped close enough to make par.

But back to the bunker. The Road Bunker became truly notorious in 1978 when Japan's Tommy Nakajima took four shots to get out of the little bunker en route to a nine on the hole. The bunker has been known as the "Sands of Nakajima" ever since. John Daly found the bunker in the final round of the 1995 championship. The American's ball came to rest almost flush against the face of the bunker. Daly lay the face of his sand wedge wide open and somehow got the ball on the green. It cost him a bogey, but he won the title in a playoff with Rocca.

Daly's shot was shown close up on television from a TV camera placed inside the bunker. It recorded a lot of action over the four days.

TOP: THE ROAD BEHIND THE 17TH GREEN THAT GIVES THE HOLE ITS NAME.

ABOVE: THE FLAG IS ALMOST ALWAYS TUCKED BEHIND THE BUNKER IN THE FINAL ROUND OF THE BRITISH OPEN.

BELOW: THE ROAD BUNKER IN PROFILE WITH THE TOWN AND THE ROYAL & ANCIENT CLUBHOUSE BEHIND.

FAR RIGHT: AN AERIAL SHOT REVEALS THE FULL EXTENT OF THE ROAD HOLE. THE DRIVE HAS TO BE PLAYED ALMOST OVER THE EDGE OF THE OLD COURSE HOTEL, AND NEEDS TO FIND THE FAIRWAY.

# Julius Boros

BOROS HAD ONE OF THE BEST SWINGS IN THE GAME OF GOLF. THE CONNECTICUT PRO USED IT TO WIN THREE MAJOR CHAMPIONSHIPS.

## Fact File

**BORN** 1920, Fairfield, Connecticut, USA

**DIED** 1994

**CAREER HIGHLIGHTS**
1952 US Open
1960 Colonial National Invitational
1963 Colonial National Invitational
1963 US Open
1968 USPGA Championship

**INTERNATIONAL HONORS**
Ryder Cup: 1959, 1963, 1965, 1967
World Cup: 1953, 1968

They say life begins at 40. It certainly did for Julius Boros. Anyone looking at Boros's tournament wins will notice that most of them came on the back nine of his life, so to speak. Indeed, Boros was a late starter to golf. He didn't turn professional until 1950, when he was 30 years old. He didn't have to wait long to make his mark in the game, however. Boros won the 1952 US Open at Northwood Country Club, Dallas, taking the title by four shots over Ed "Porky" Oliver.

It was no mean feat to win the US Open in the early 1950s, for in those days Ben Hogan had a near stranglehold on America's national championship. Boros was a good enough golfer in his day to stand up to Hogan, or anyone else who got in his way for that matter. He also tied for second in 1956, and finished third in 1960, before winning it for a second time in 1963, 11 years after his first win.

Boros's second US Open victory came as something of a surprise because he had been in a slump for a few years. Yet he won it again by defeating another great golfer—Arnold Palmer.

Palmer was the man to beat in the early 1960s, and Boros accomplished the feat head to head. After 72 holes of the 1963 US Open at The Country Club, Brookline, Massachusetts, Boros was tied with Palmer and Jack Cupit. Given Palmer's stature at the time, most players would have bowed under the pressure of facing him and his army of fans in a playoff for one of the game's biggest tournaments. Not Boros.

The late bloomer of Hungarian extraction always played well in the big events. He had an easy-going manner and a swing to match. It was a long and free-flowing swing for such a big man, and it made Boros one of the best ever to play the game. His swing was so effective that even well into his late 40s Boros was still racking up tournament wins.

Boros's victory in the 1968 USPGA Championship at Pecan Valley, San Antonio, Texas, came in his 48th year, making him the oldest winner of the tournament. The victory surprised no one, especially Arnold Palmer. Once again Palmer had to play second fiddle to Boros, finishing one stroke behind in second place with Bob Charles.

The double US Open winner also excelled in Ryder Cup action. In 16 appearances in the four Cups he played in, Boros lost only three times. Of the other matches, he won nine and halved four.

# PAT BRADLEY

BRADLEY EARNED THREE MAJORS VICTORIES IN 1986 AND MADE HISTORY AS THE FIRST WOMAN TO WIN THE WOMEN'S GRAND SLAM.

Pat Bradley's mother used to ring a bell on the back porch of her New England home each time her daughter won a tournament, regardless of the time of day. The bell must have got on the neighbors' nerves, because it was rung many times. At last count Bradley had 31 LPGA Tour wins. Fortunately for the neighbors the bell now resides in the World Golf Hall of Fame.

Bradley is one of the greatest competitors on the LPGA Tour. In 1986 she made history when she triumphed in three of the four women's major championships, winning the Du Maurier Classic, the LPGA Championship, and the Nabisco Dinah Shore, becoming the first player to win all four of the women's modern majors. The only major she missed out on that year was the US Women's Open, which she won in 1981. In total that season Bradley won five tournaments, to end the year as leading money winner. She also won the Vare Trophy for the lowest scoring average on Tour.

The New Englander has set many milestones in the women's game. Besides becoming the first person to win all four majors, she was also the first player to surpass the $2, $3, and $4 million dollar marks, feats she accomplished in 1986, 1990, and 1991 respectively. In 1991 alone she won $763,118. More importantly, she also recorded her 30th win that year to gain entry into the LPGA Hall of Fame.

Bradley started playing golf in her native New England, and credits her late father, Richard, for influencing her career. She won the New Hampshire Amateur Championship in 1967 and 1969, then the New England Amateur Championship in 1972 and 1973. She attended Florida International University and won all-American honors in 1970 before turning her attention to professional golf.

In 1988, Bradley was diagnosed as having Graves' disease and had to undergo treatment. She resumed her winning ways when she returned to the Tour in 1989, finishing first in the Ai Star Centinela Hospital Classic. She then won three times in 1990, and four times in 1991. Her comeback from illness earned her the 1991 Golf Writers Association of America's Ben Hogan Award. She has also received many other honors during her career, including the 1989 Jack Nicklaus Family of the Year Award.

Bradley has participated in three Solheim Cups, appearing on the winning side all three times.

## FACT FILE

**BORN** 1951, Westford, Massachusetts, USA

**CAREER HIGHLIGHTS**
1980 Du Maurier Classic
1981 US Women's Open
1985 Du Maurier Classic
1986 Du Maurier Classic
1986 USLPGA Championship
1986 Nabisco Dinah Shore

**INTERNATIONAL HONORS**
Solheim Cup: 1990, 1992, 1996

# Harry Bradshaw

ENTIRELY SELF-TAUGHT, BRADSHAW WAS ONE OF THE BEST GOLFERS OF HIS GENERATION. THE POPULAR IRISHMAN CAME CLOSE TO WINNING THE BRITISH OPEN WHEN HIS BALL CAME TO REST IN A BROKEN BOTTLE.

## Fact File

**BORN** 1913, Delgany, County Wicklow, Ireland

**DIED** 1990

**CAREER HIGHLIGHTS**
1947 Irish Open
1949 Irish Open
1953 Dunlop Masters
1955 Dunlop Masters

**INTERNATIONAL HONORS**
Ryder Cup: 1953, 1955, 1957
World Cup: 1958

Ireland's Harry Bradshaw will always be remembered for one of the most unusual rules-of-golf incidents ever to occur in the British Open, one that caused the rules to be rewritten.

In the second round of the 1949 British Open at Sandwich, Bradshaw's tee shot on the fifth hole came to rest inside a broken bottle. Nowadays players would simply call for a rules official who would come within minutes and adjudicate. There wasn't the abundance of rules officials in 1949, however, as there is now. Unsure of how to proceed and whether or not he was allowed relief, Bradshaw simply closed his eyes and played the shot. Glass flew everywhere but the ball traveled only about 30 yards.

Whether or not the Irishman would have won had he not been presented with this strange situation remains a moot point. However, history reveals that Bradshaw's score of 77 in the second round was incompatible with his three other scores of 68, 68, 70. Clearly, he was unsettled in round two. Despite that he tied with South Africa's Bobby Locke after four rounds. Locke won the ensuing playoff by 12 strokes.

Had an official been on hand on the fifth hole, Bradshaw would not have been granted relief under the rules. However, that incident caused the game's lawmakers to alter the rules to favor any future player in a similar situation.

Like many fine Irish players, Bradshaw was entirely self-taught, a wholly natural player with a swing not many could copy—or would have wanted to! Bradshaw's grip was totally unorthodox, with three fingers of the right hand overlapping the left. His movement at the ball was a deliberate sway. Yet his wonderful rhythm meant he returned the clubhead to the ball solidly every time.

Besides winning many tournaments in Ireland in the 1940s, Bradshaw won some big tournaments on the British professional circuit. He twice won the Dunlop Masters, one of the biggest tournaments in British and European golf.

Bradshaw was also a fine Ryder Cup player. In the three matches in which he played, his record was two wins, two losses and one half. He appeared on the 1957 side that won at Lindrick, contributing a half point from his match against Dick Mayer.

Bradshaw was the epitome of the easy-go-lucky Irishman. His affable personality made him an approachable figure both on and off the golf course.

# JAMES BRAID

ALONG WITH HARRY VARDON AND J. H. TAYLOR, BRAID DOMINATED GOLF AT THE BEGINNING OF THE 1900S. HE MADE HISTORY IN 1910 AS THE FIRST PLAYER TO WIN FIVE BRITISH OPENS.

Enter many clubhouses around the world, and you will often come across a very famous painting of three golfers. The artist who painted the picture was Clement Flower, and in the middle of the painting stands the immortal James Braid, the first man to win five British Open Championships.

The painting, of course, is of the Great Triumvirate, the name given to the three British golfers who dominated the game at the turn of the 20th century. To the right of Braid is John Henry Taylor, to his left is Harry Vardon. Between them they won 16 British Open Championships, and countless other tournaments around the country.

Braid came from farming stock. His father was a plowman in the Fife town of Elie. Braid senior never played golf, which probably explains why he wasn't too supportive when his son took up the game professionally. However, Braid junior had been attracted to the beautiful Elie links from an early age. After leaving school at the age of 13 to become an apprentice carpenter, Braid played amateur golf and won his first tournament at Braid Hills in Edinburgh.

In 1893 Braid turned professional and worked as an apprentice clubmaker at the Army and Navy Stores in London. Braid was afforded one luxury in London that he hadn't been allowed in his native Scotland—he could play golf on Sundays. The Scotsman played his first professional match that year, and entered his first British Open the following season at Sandwich. It was the first time the Open had been held outside Scotland, and Taylor recorded his first win in the game's oldest tournament.

Braid did not win his first British Open until 1901, by which time Taylor and Vardon had won three each. Yet the Scotsman would soon overtake his two English counterparts, winning his fifth within nine years of his first victory. Of course Taylor would soon equal Braid's record, and Vardon would overtake both of them by winning his sixth in 1914.

In Braid's day there wasn't the abundance of professional events that there is in the modern game, so much of Braid's golf was played in challenge matches against Vardon, Taylor, and other great players from that era.

When Walton Heath was built in 1904, Braid was appointed the club's first professional, and his association with the club lasted until his death in 1950.

During his life, Braid designed many courses around the world. A Braid Golf Society exists which plays only on courses that Braid designed. The members never run out of places to play, for Braid designed courses all over the British Isles, including great courses such as Gleneagles, Southport & Ainsdale, and many more.

## FACT FILE

**BORN** 1870, Earlsferry, Fife, Scotland

**DIED** 1950

**CAREER HIGHLIGHTS**
1901 The Open Championship
1905 The Open Championship
1906 The Open Championship
1908 The Open Championship
1910 The Open Championship
1910 French Open

# Gordon Brand Jr

BRAND IS A LONG-SERVING MEMBER OF THE EUROPEAN TOUR. WHEN THE SCOTSMAN IS PLAYING WELL, HE IS A MATCH FOR ANYONE IN THE GAME.

## Fact File

**BORN** 1958, Kirkcaldy, Scotland

**CAREER HIGHLIGHTS**

1979 British Youths' Open Amateur Championship

1984 Panasonic European Open

1987 Scandinavian Enterprise Open

1989 Benson & Hedges International Open

1993 GA European Open

**INTERNATIONAL HONORS**

Ryder Cup: 1987, 1989

World Cup: 1984, 1985, 1988, 1989, 1990, 1992, 1994

Alfred Dunhill Cup: 1985, 1986, 1987, 1988, 1989, 1991, 1992, 1993, 1994, 1997

Walker Cup: 1979

After an outstanding amateur career in which Brand won just about everything, the Scots-born son of the professional at Knowle Golf Club in Bristol turned pro and immediately made his mark in the paid ranks.

Brand gained his European Tour card by winning the 1981 European Tour Qualifying School. He then lifted two trophies in his first year on Tour, winning the Coral Classic and the Bob Hope British Classic. Those two victories earned him the 1982 European Tour Rookie of the Year Award.

The Scot with the English accent is a gritty competitor, who can beat the best on his day. He is known as a good putter and can shoot very low rounds. For example, when he won the 1993 European Open at East Sussex National, Brand opened with a first round score of 65, seven under par. Brand not only established a course record for the East course, but beat the rest of the field by three shots over one of the toughest layouts in England. He went on to win the tournament by seven shots.

The Scotsman has been a perennial fixture for Scotland in the Alfred Dunhill Cup at St Andrews, and the World Cup, in which he has played seven times. Sadly, in his ten appearances for Scotland at St Andrews in the former event, Brand has never been on a winning side.

Brand has been a valuable member of two European Ryder Cup sides, often teaming up with friend and fellow countryman Sam Torrance. Brand was a member of the victorious 1987 European side that made history by becoming the first team to win on US soil, when the Europeans defeated Jack Nicklaus's side 15-13 in the match at Muirfield Village, Ohio. The Scotsman contributed a valuable one-and-a-half-points from a possible four in that match, including a half point from his singles encounter with Hal Sutton on the final day.

When Europe retained the trophy in the tied match at The Belfry in 1989, Brand teamed up with Torrance in the first day fourballs to defeat the strong American pair of Curtis Strange and Paul Azinger. However, it was mainly due to Brand's nerve that the Scots couple won the valuable point.

Leading two up with two to play, the Scotsmen looked to be odds-on favorite to win until Strange took the 17th with a long eagle putt. Brand finally secured the point when he hit a 40 yard bunker shot to eight feet at the last, then bravely sunk the putt. The mark of a true champion.

# Gay Brewer

GAY BREWER CAPTURED HIS ONLY MAJOR CHAMPIONSHIP IN 1967, WHEN HE WON THE MASTERS, AND HE WENT ON TO WIN ON THE US TOUR AND AROUND THE WORLD.

Gay Brewer had his first taste of major championship glory when he tied with Jack Nicklaus in the 1966 Masters. Jack Nicklaus was the defending champion that year, having won his second green jacket in 1965.

Brewer had a chance to win the tournament outright at the 72nd hole. However, he took three putts from the back of the final green and found himself in a playoff with Nicklaus and Tommy Jacobs. Nicklaus won the ensuing playoff to become the first golfer to win the Masters in successive years, but Brewer's experience was to stand him in good stead for the following season.

After his bitter disappointment of the previous year, the Ohio professional arrived at Augusta National in 1967 determined to atone for his defeat at the hands of Nicklaus. He did just that.

While it was Brewer's putting that let him down in 1966, it was his mastery of the greens that won him the tournament in 1967. Brewer played brilliantly all four days, but he never attained the lead until he holed a ten-foot putt on the 11th hole of the final round. Over the last seven holes Brewer's putting was excellent and he never gave challenger Bobby Nichols a chance. Brewer had survived the pressure and went on to win his only major championship.

Brewer's swing wasn't known as a thing of great beauty. It had a distinctive loop at the top, but it repeated under pressure. It was good enough to make him one of the best players during the 1960s. However, his success didn't come only on home soil.

Brewer was a good enough player to master the vagaries of links golf. In 1967 he triumphed over the Old Course at St Andrews in the Alcan Golfer of the Year Championship, defeating fellow American Billy Casper in a playoff to take the £23,000 first prize. A year later Brewer successfully defended his title at Royal Birkdale.

That Brewer was a quality player was underlined when he won the 1967 Pensacola Open. His score for the four rounds was an incredible 26 under par. It was in that same year that Brewer made his Ryder Cup debut. He played five times in the match, winning three and losing two in his side's victory. In 1973 he contributed two-and-a-half points from a possible four, again to help America win the match.

Brewer faced Neil Coles and Bernard Gallacher in singles on the final day of the 1973 Ryder Cup at Muirfield, Scotland. His love of links golf obviously helped, for Brewer lost neither match, halving with Coles and easily defeating Gallacher by the score of six and five.

## Fact File

**BORN** 1932, Middletown, Ohio, USA

**CAREER HIGHLIGHTS**
1967 Masters
1967 Alcan Golfer of the Year Championship
1968 Alcan Golfer of the Year Championship
1972 Pacific Masters
1972 Canadian Open

**INTERNATIONAL HONORS**
Ryder Cup: 1967, 1973

# Mark Brooks

**Brooks is one of the best putters on the US Tour, a factor that helped him win the 1996 USPGA Championship. The Texan birdied the final hole twice on the last day to win the title.**

## Fact File

**BORN** 1961, Fort Worth, Texas, USA

**CAREER HIGHLIGHTS**
1988 Canon Sammy Davis, Jr.—Greater Hartford Open
1991 Greater Milwaukee Open
1994 Kemper Open
1996 Shell Houston Open
1996 USPGA Championship

**INTERNATIONAL HONORS**
Presidents Cup: 1996

Mark Brooks turned professional in 1983 after much success as an amateur. In 1979 alone, he won the Texas State Amateur Championship, the Southern Amateur Championship and the Trans-Mississippi Amateur Championship. He won the Texas State Amateur again in 1981. He was also a three-time All-American player at the University of Texas.

However, Brooks's transition from the unpaid to the paid ranks didn't come as easily as his amateur record suggested it would be. He had to attend the US Tour Qualifying School four times before he finally became a regular Tour player after the 1988 season. He retained his playing card that year courtesy of his first PGA Tour win, the Canon Sammy Davis, Jr.—Greater Hartford Open.

Between 1988 and 1994, Brooks was one of the best players on the US Tour. With the exception of a poor season in 1989 when he tumbled to 115 on the US money list, Brooks finished no worse than 66th during that period. However, in those six years he had never really been a threat in the major championships.

His stature as a major player improved in 1995 when he finished third in the British Open over the Old Course at St Andrews. In fact, had he not driven into

a small pot bunker on the 16th hole in the final round, Brooks may have stolen the championship from eventual winner John Daly. The winds gusted up to 50 miles per hour over the Old Course on that final day, yet Brooks felt right at home. As a youngster growing up in Texas, Brooks knew how to play in strong winds.

Besides an almost instinctive ability to shape shots in windy conditions, Brooks is one of the best putters in the business when he is on form. He proved that in winning the 1996 USPGA Championship at Valhalla Golf Club, Louisville, Kentucky.

The greens at Valhalla in 1996 were very slick, resulting in many three putts over the four days. Brooks had no such problem in that department. The Texan led the field that week in putting, needing only 104 putts for his four rounds. It was his ability to hole out that not only got him into a playoff for the title, but earned him the victory.

Brooks had to hole a five-foot birdie putt in regulation play to tie Kenny Perry, who had already finished. Brooks sank the putt with ease. In the ensuing one-hole playoff, he sank another birdie putt, this time from four feet, on the 18th green to win. Brooks had made two birdies on the 540-yard, par-5 hole inside 20 minutes.

# Ken Brown

NOW A SUCCESSFUL TELEVISION COMMENTATOR, KEN BROWN WAS A STALWART OF THE EUROPEAN TOUR DURING THE 1970S AND '80S. THE TALL SCOTSMAN PLAYED IN FIVE RYDER CUP SIDES, GAINING THE TROPHY TWICE.

Early in the 1990s, Ken Brown decided it was time to make a career move. He packed his clubs away and started a successful career as a television commentator. He is now a permanent fixture on Sky Sports. When he is not tramping the fairways of the European Tour describing the shots facing Europe's leading professionals, he is commentating on golf tournaments from around the world.

Brown knows what he's talking about. For nearly ten years he was one of the stalwarts of the European Tour. Between 1976 and 1985, Brown recorded four victories in Europe. He was also a regular Ryder Cup player during that period, missing the biennial contest only once when he didn't make the 1981 European side.

Brown was a contemporary of Mark James, and the two created a stir at the 1979 Ryder Cup when failure to adhere to the team's dress code and general insubordination cast the pair as the terrible twosome of the side. Both men were fined for their actions. It's ironic then that Brown was very much in favor for the 1985 and 1987 matches.

In 1979, Brown had been a thorn in the side of European Ryder Cup captain John Jacobs. In the matches of 1985 and 1987, Brown made the side as a wild card pick of captain Tony Jacklin. The lanky Scotsman of English birth teamed up with Bernhard Langer in the 1985 match to contribute a valuable point to America's first loss in the match since 1957. Brown and Langer defeated Ray Floyd and Lanny Wadkins three and two in the second-day foursomes matches.

Brown was also a member of the historic 1987 European side that won the cup for the first time in America, when Europe won at Muirfiled Village, Ohio.

The 6-foot, 2-inch golfer was one of the most deliberate players in the game. Indeed, he had a reputation for being one of the slowest players in golf.

Brown spent four years on the US Tour during the mid 1980s before returning to Europe. He found success there, too. In 1987 he captured the Southern Open in Columbus, Georgia. The victory came just one week after Europe had retained the Ryder Cup. Brown was obviously still on a high because he took the Southern Open by seven strokes, recording scores of 65, 64, 69, 68, for his only US Tour win.

On his day Ken Brown could beat the best in the game—and often did.

## Fact File

**BORN** 1957, Harpenden, Hertfordshire, England

**CAREER HIGHLIGHTS**
1974 Carris Trophy
1978 Carrolls Irish Open
1983 KLM Dutch Open
1984 Glasgow Open
1987 Southern Open

**INTERNATIONAL HONORS**
Ryder Cup: 1977, 1979, 1983, 1985, 1987
World Cup: 1977, 1978, 1979, 1983

# Jimmy Bruen

IRELAND'S JIMMY BRUEN HAD ONE OF THE STRANGEST GOLF SWINGS EVER SEEN. NICKNAMED THE "BRUEN LOOP," THE SWING HELPED HIM TO MANY AMATEUR VICTORIES, INCLUDING THE 1946 BRITISH AMATEUR.

## Fact File

**BORN** 1920, Belfast, Northern Ireland

**DIED** 1972

**CAREER HIGHLIGHTS**
1936 British Boys' Amateur
1937 Irish Close Amateur Championship
1938 Irish Close Amateur Championship
1938 Irish Open Amateur Championship
1946 British Amateur

**INTERNATIONAL HONORS**

Ireland's Jimmy Bruen was one of the greatest amateur champions despite having perhaps the strangest swing in the history of golf, known throughout the game as the "Bruen Loop."

A six-footer who resided in Cork, Ireland, Bruen was a big hitter. He was known to hit the ball 300 yards, a distance almost unheard of in the 1930s and '40s when he was at his peak. Bruen would take the club away normally from his address position, but by the time it got to the top of the backswing, the clubhead was almost directly over the ball. Experts marveled at how Bruen was able to return the clubhead to the ball, but he did so with amazing results. His strong hands would whip the club into the impact area and the ball would explode off the clubface.

Bruen came to prominence in Ireland during the 1930s, when he won just about every amateur award going. As an 18-year-old, Jimmy made the 1938 Walker Cup side which played the Americans at St Andrews. It was his first of three matches.

Prior to the match, Bruen played a practice round with the then British Open champion Henry Cotton. Cotton went round the Old Course in 69. Bruen matched him stroke for stroke. Cotton was suitably impressed, particularly because he had played well to compile his score.

Bruen helped Great Britain & Ireland win the match that year, although he did lose his singles match to Charlie Yates.

World War II halted Bruen's playing career. However, in 1946 Bruen took the game's top amateur honor when he triumphed in the British Amateur Championship at Birkdale. The Irishman defeated the 1937 champion Robert Sweeny by the score of four and three.

Unfortunately, Bruen suffered a serious hand injury that curtailed his career. He tore ligaments in his right hand while helping a friend move a piano. Bruen still played amateur championships, and appeared in two further Walker Cups in 1949 and 1951. Never again quite the same player as he was in his youth, the hand injury forced him to retire from the 1951 match. His last appearance in tournament golf was at the 1960 British Amateur Championship at Portrush, not far from his birthplace. The pain in his right hand recurred then, too, and Bruen had to retire from the tournament.

The popular, powerful hitter died of a heart attack in 1972 after a golfing visit to Penina, Portugal, where he and his wife had a home.

# JACK BURKE JR

TEXAN GOLFER JACK BURKE JR WON THREE MAJORS DURING HIS CAREER. HE HELD A NEAR FLAWLESS RYDER CUP RECORD.

Like most Texans, Jack Burke Jr was a great player in inclement weather. Growing up in the strong winds that swept across the Texas Panhandle, Burke learned from an early age to maneuver the ball in any breeze, no matter how strong. It was that ability that nearly won him his first major championship.

Burke finished second in the 1952 Masters, behind Sam Snead. The wind was so bad on the final day, that Burke's 69 was the only score under 70 to be recorded. Had it been a lesser player in the lead, Burke may have snuck in and stole the title. However, Snead scored 72 to finish four strokes clear.

Burke's turn came in 1956. That year also saw the Masters affected by inclement weather, yet it was the collapse of Ken Venturi, then an amateur, that allowed Burke to win on the hallowed turf of Augusta National. Venturi was four strokes ahead of the field after three rounds, but a nervous 80 on the final day meant Burke's one under par 71 was good enough to win him the title.

The Masters victory obviously inspired Burke, for he went on to record his finest ever season on the US Tour that year.

There are not many golfers who can claim to have won two majors in one season, but Burke is one of them. Just two months after his Masters victory, Burke traveled to the Blue Hill Golf and Country Club in Canton, Massachusetts, and won the USPGA Championship. He defeated Ted Kroll three and two in the 36-hole final, later claiming it was his chipping and putting that enabled him to win the title.

The USPGA was contested at match play in those days, and Burke was one of the best at that form of golf. That he enjoyed head-to-head golf was evident from his appearances in the Ryder Cup.

The two-time major winner has a near flawless record in the Ryder Cup. He made the American team five consecutive times from 1951 to 1959, and only lost one match he played in. His record stands at an incredible seven wins and that one solitary loss. Ironically, the loss came in the 1957 match, when as playing captain he went down five and three to Peter Mills, as Great Britain & Ireland won the match for the first time since 1933.

In 1973, Burke was named captain again. This time he led from the sidelines and inspired his team to a 19-13 victory at Muirfield, Scotland.

## FACT FILE

**BORN** 1923, Fort Worth, Texas, USA

**CAREER HIGHLIGHTS**
1952 Texas Open
1952 Houston Open
1956 Masters
1956 USPGA Championship
1963 Texas Open

**INTERNATIONAL HONORS**
Ryder Cup: 1951, 1953, 1955, 1957 (captain) 1959, 1973 (non-playing captain)

# Mark Calcavecchia

CALCAVECCHIA'S VICTORY IN THE 1989 BRITISH OPEN WAS ACHIEVED IN THE FIRST FOUR-HOLE PLAYOFF IN THE TOURNAMENT'S HISTORY. THE NEBRASKAN PROFESSIONAL DEFEATED WAYNE GRADY AND GREG NORMAN TO LIFT THE OLDEST TROPHY IN GOLF.

## Fact File

**BORN** 1960, Laurel, Nebraska, USA

**CAREER HIGHLIGHTS**
1986 Southwest Golf Classic
1987 Honda Classic
1989 The Open Championship
1989 Nissan Los Angeles Open
1995 BellSouth Classic

**INTERNATIONAL HONORS**
Ryder Cup: 1987, 1989, 1991
Alfred Dunhill Cup: 1989, 1990
Presidents Cup: 1998

Mark Calcavecchia was thrilled when his parents decided to move from Nebraska to Florida when he was 13, because it meant he could play golf every day. Calcavecchia didn't waste his days either.

All those hours spent playing and hitting golf balls in the Florida sunshine made the man they call "Calc" one of the best players on the US Tour. It also helped him win a major.

After attending college at the University of Florida where he played on the golf team, Calcavecchia turned professional in 1981. It took him five years to find success on the US Tour, winning the 1986 Southwest Classic. Calc has never looked back since.

He recorded four more victories—the 1987 Honda Classic, the 1988 Bank of Boston Classic, and the Phoenix and Los Angeles Opens in 1989—before he attained his first major.

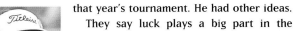

Calcavecchia arrived at Royal Troon in 1989 to play in only his third British Open. In two previous tries he had tied for 11th in 1987 and missed the cut in 1988. His 11th place finish at Muirfield in 1987 and his two early season victories notwithstanding, Calcavecchia wasn't really seen as a major threat in that year's tournament. He had other ideas.

They say luck plays a big part in the winning of any championship; well, Calcavecchia certainly got some in 1989. Playing the 12th hole in the final round, the American found himself in a horrible lie beside the green. He needed a good chip to even get the ball close to have a chance of making par. He didn't get it close, he holed it. It enabled him to go on and tie for the 72-hole lead. Calcavecchia found himself in a playoff with Australians Greg Norman and Wayne Grady.

That year the Royal & Ancient Golf Club of St Andrews decided to try a new four-hole playoff, with the player with the least amount of strokes after the four holes emerging the winner. Norman was the odds-on favorite, but on the fourth extra hole he drove his ball into a fairway bunker 322 yards off the tee and ruined his chances. Calcavecchia then hit a glorious 5-iron to seven feet from 190 yards on the final hole and holed the putt.

That shot alone was the work of a true champion. It enabled Calcavecchia to win the British Open Championship and to take his place among the game's great players.

# Jose Maria Canizares

CANIZARES'S GREATEST MOMENT IN GOLF WAS IN THE 1989 RYDER CUP AT THE BELFRY. THE SPANIARD'S SINGLES TRIUMPH OVER KEN GREEN MEANT EUROPE HELD THE TROPHY.

They say life begins at 40. For Jose Maria Canizares it began at 42.

When Canizares retires to Spain after his playing days are over and looks back on his career, one moment will probably stand out among his great achievements in golf. He'll no doubt sit back and think about one September afternoon in 1989, September 24 to be precise.

Canizares was involved in Ryder Cup action that afternoon. In fact, he was deep in a singles battle with the tough American player Ken Green. The Spaniard had played beautifully over the back nine against Green. Three birdies from Canizares meant they came to the 18th tee all square. Both men hit the fairway. Both hit the green. Canizares was past the flag, Green short of it. The Spaniard hit his first putt to within four feet of the hole, Green's ended five feet away. The American missed his par putt, and the pressure was now on Canizares. And what pressure.

The Ryder Cup was resting on the Spaniard's broad shoulders. About 20 minutes earlier, Christy O'Connor Jr had upset Fred Couples by hitting a glorious 2-iron onto the last green to win his match and give the European side 13 points. With 14 points needed to retain the Ryder Cup, Canizares had to hole his tricky four-footer. He did, and the European side went delirious.

Had Canizares missed the putt, Europe would have lost the Ryder Cup, for the last four Europeans out on the course that day lost their matches.

Of course, Jose Maria Canizares was used to the pressure of a Ryder Cup. The 1989 match was his fourth appearance in the biennial competition. He had appeared in losing contests in 1981 and 1983, then helped Europe win the match for the first time in 28 years at The Belfry in 1985. On that occasion the Spaniard went unbeaten, earning two-and-a-half points out of the three matches he played in. He even defeated the 1984 US Open champion Fuzzy Zoeller two up in the singles.

Canizares is known for his carefree attitude toward the game he plays for a living. His philosophy was summed up when asked what it meant to him to make the 1989 Ryder Cup team. He replied: "For me there are many things more important in my life than just playing golf—like my family. It was fantastic to get back into the Ryder Cup side, but it would not have been the end of the world had I missed out."

## Fact File

**BORN** 1947, Madrid, Spain

**CAREER HIGHLIGHTS**
1972 Lancia D'Oro
1980 Avis-Jersey Open
1980 Bob Hope British Classic
1981 Italian Open
1983 Bob Hope British Classic

**INTERNATIONAL HONORS**
Ryder Cup: 1981, 1983 1985, 1989
World Cup: 1974, 1980, 1982, 1983, 1984, 1985, 1987, 1989
Alfred Dunhill Cup: 1985, 1987, 1989

# DONNA CAPONI

WHEN CAPONI WON THE 1970 US WOMEN'S OPEN, SHE BECAME ONLY THE SECOND PLAYER IN HISTORY TO WIN THE TITLE IN CONSECUTIVE YEARS.

## FACT FILE

**BORN** 1945, Detroit, Michigan, USA

**CAREER HIGHLIGHTS**
1969 US Women's Open
1970 US Women's Open
1975 Colgate European Open
1979 LPGA Championship
1981 LPGA Championship

Donna Caponi is one of a select group of golfers who made the US Open their first win. That puts her in some pretty classy company with 12 other women professionals who have accomplished the same feat. Jack Nicklaus did the same thing in men's golf.

Caponi turned professional immediately after finishing high school. The 5-foot, 5-inch, red-haired, blue-eyed golfer was a good all-round sportswoman in her youth. She learned golf from her father Harry and won the Los Angeles Junior title in 1956 at the age of 11. She joined the LPGA Tour in 1965 as a 20-year-old and it took her just four years to join golf's elite club of major winners.

Caponi won twice in 1969, taking the US Women's Open and the Lincoln-Mercury Open. Those wins were no fluke. A year later she successfully defended her US Women's Open title to become only the second player since Micky Wright in 1958-59 to win the title in consecutive years.

The Detroit native was a prolific winner between 1969 and 1981. She won 24 tournaments during that period, including once in Europe when she lifted the 1975 Colgate European Open trophy. Her best season in the '70s came in 1976 when she won four times—the Peter Jackson Classic, the Portland Classic, the Carlton tournament, and the Mizuno Japan Classic. Those victories propelled her to her first $100,000-plus season as a professional. Her winnings that year totalled $106,553, good enough for second on the LPGA money list.

Caponi won her third major in 1979, when she was victorious in the LPGA Championship. It was a victory that set her up for her most lucrative season as a professional. In 1980 Caponi won five times—the LPGA National Pro-Am, the Colgate Dinah Shore Winner's Circle, the Corning Classic, the United Virginia Bank Classic, and the ERA Real Estate Classic. Her earnings for the year added up to $220,619.

The following season Caponi added another five tournament wins to take her career earnings over the $1 million mark. Included in that tally was a second LPGA Championship, taking her final total in the majors to four. Not bad, considering that for much of her career the Nabisco Dinah Shore and the Du Maurier Classic either weren't in existence or hadn't yet been designated major championship status.

Caponi's last regular LPGA Tour victory came in 1981, when she won the Boston Five Classic. After her competitive days were over, Caponi turned her attention to broadcasting.

# JoAnne Carner

AS JOANNE GUNDERSON, CARNER HAD A BRILLIANT AMATEUR RECORD. SHE DID NOT DISAPPOINT AS A PROFESSIONAL EITHER, WINNING MANY TIMES ON THE LPGA TOUR.

JoAnne Carner is one of the best women ever to play the game of golf. In fact, the great Sam Snead called her the best woman golfer he had ever seen. High praise indeed.

Carner won everything there was to win in women's amateur golf. She was so busy racking up amateur victories that she didn't turn professional until she was 30, and only did so because she had no more mountains to conquer in the amateur game.

As schoolgirl JoAnne Gunderson, she won the US Junior Girls' title one year and the US Women's Amateur Championship the next. That was in 1956 and 1957. She would go on to win the US Women's Amateur Championship a record five times. She played in four Curtis Cups, compiling an excellent record of six wins, three losses and one half.

With nothing left to win in amateur golf, Carner turned her attention to professional golf. She won the 1969 Burdine's Invitational in Miami before turning professional, the last such player to win an LPGA event as an amateur.

It didn't take Carner long to put together a winning record in professional golf to match her amateur record. She won once in 1970, her first year on the LPGA Tour, and was awarded the Rookie of the Year title. In 1971 she won her first US Women's Open to become the only woman in history to win the US Junior Girls' title, the US Women's Amateur, and the US Women's Open.

Carner added a second US Women's Open title in 1976 but never captured the LPGA Championship, although she was twice runner-up, in 1974 and 1982. Throughout her career on the regular LPGA Tour, Carner won 42 titles. She topped the money list three times, won the Player of the Year award three times, and picked up five Vare Trophies for having the lowest scoring average on the LPGA Tour.

In her prime, Carner was an athletic golfer who believed in keeping the game as simple as possible. Her swing wasn't a thing of great beauty. It was very short, with the clubhead pointing straight up into the air at the top of the backswing. However, Carner was very strong and hit the ball a long way.

She was inducted into the LPGA Hall of Fame in 1982 after recording her 35th LPGA victory when she won the Chevrolet World Championship of Women's Golf. In 1994 she captained the US Solheim Cup side to victory over Europe at the Greenbrier, West Virginia.

## Fact File

**BORN** 1939, Kirkland, Washington, USA

**CAREER HIGHLIGHTS**
1971 US Women's Open
1974 Rolex Player of the Year
1976 US Women's Open
1981 Rolex Player of the Year
1982 Rolex Player of the Year

**INTERNATIONAL HONORS**
Solheim Cup: 1994 (captain)
Curtis Cup: 1958, 1960, 1962, 1964

# THE SHOT HEARD AROUND THE WORLD

The inaugural 1934 Masters was missing a few players that would have greatly enhanced the field. Gene Sarazen was one of them. He had to skip the first ever tournament because he had already committed himself to an exhibition. He more than made up for his absence a year later.

By the time the Masters began, Sarazen had already won all three of golf's major championships. He had two US Opens, three USPGA Championships and one British Open, which he won at Princes in 1932. In its infancy, the Masters wasn't known as a major, but because it was Bobby Jones's tournament, it was soon to become one.

In the 1935 tournament, Craig Wood was safely in the clubhouse after compiling a four-round total of 282. He had finished second the year before, one stroke behind Horton Smith. Wood had played the last eight holes of the 1935 Masters in four under par to surge ahead of the field and was being complimented by other professionals. Only a miracle could stop him from winning his first Masters. That's just what happened. Sarazen found out on the 15th hole that Wood had birdied the last hole to jump three shots ahead of him. It meant he needed four birdies over the last four holes to win, and three to tie. A tall order over any course, let alone one as difficult as Augusta National.

The diminutive professional hit a good drive down the 15th fairway. In those days the hole measured 485 yards, and after a drive of 285 yards, Sarazen still had 200 yards to go. It wasn't a straightforward 200 yards, though. A large pond fronts the green at 15, and the professionals have to decide whether to go for the green or lay up short of the water. It's not an easy decision, for even taking the latter option can leave a hellish pitch. Sarazen had no choice, he had to go for it. He selected a 4-wood to play the shot and hit the ball as hard as he could. The ball flew over the pond, landed on the green and rolled into the hole for a two, or a double eagle. It was a miraculous shot, a once in a lifetime stroke of luck. In one fell swoop Sarazen had tied Wood for the lead. Pars at the next three holes put him in an 18-hole playoff the following day, which Sarazen won by five strokes.

The stroke has often been called the "shot heard around the world," and it made headlines around the globe. Already a prestigious tournament, the shot only added to the tournament's image. Only a handful of people actually saw Sarazen make the shot. The galleries in those days weren't anywhere near what they are at today's tournament. One of those watching was Bobby Jones himself, who had wandered down to watch Sarazen finish. It was a stroke the master of Augusta approved of highly.

RIGHT: GENE SARAZEN'S 4-WOOD SHOT AT THE 15TH HOLE IN THE 1935 MASTERS FOUND THE HOLE AND PUT HIM INTO A PLAYOFF FOR THE TITLE, WITH CRAIG WOOD, WHICH SARAZEN WON.

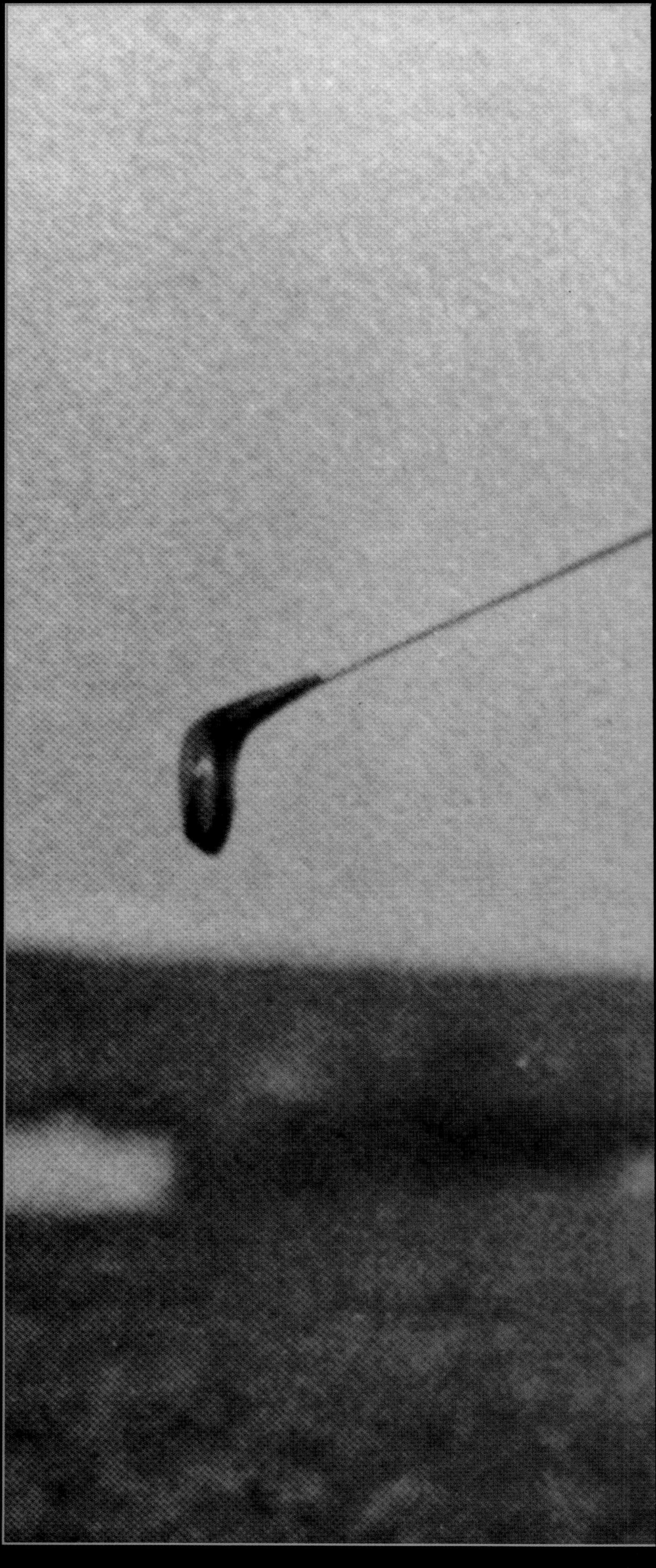

# Joe Carr

Carr's three British Amateur victories made him the pre-eminent amateur golfer during the 1950s, a position he held until the emergence of Michael Bonallack.

## Fact File

**BORN** 1922, Dublin, Ireland

**CAREER HIGHLIGHTS**
1953 British Amateur
1956 Open Championship Silver Medal
1958 Open Championship Silver Medal
1958 British Amateur
1960 British Amateur
1991–92 Captain of the Royal & Ancient Golf Club of St Andrews

**INTERNATIONAL HONORS**
Walker Cup: 1947, 1949, 1951, 1953, 1955, 1957, 1959, 1961, 1963 (captain), 1965 (captain), 1967

Like many of his fellow countrymen, Joe Carr has two qualities you expect to find in Irish golfers. He was largely self taught, and he had an easy-going, happy-go-lucky attitude, factors that made him a winner.

Despite his devil-may-care approach, Carr was one of the finest golfers the amateur game has ever seen. Between the end of World War II and the rise of Sir Michael Bonallack, Carr was the best amateur player in the British Isles. The Dubliner won the British Amateur Championship three times, in 1953, 1958, and 1960. He also took part in every Walker Cup match between 1947 and 1967. His 20 matches in the event is second only to Bonallack among Great Britain & Ireland players.

Carr wasn't a large man. In fact he was quite slim during his prime, but he hit the ball a good distance. His power came from his height and a pair of very strong hands. Carr wasn't the most accurate driver of the ball, but he had a knack for recovering from seemingly impossible situations. His forte was his bunker play, which was better than that of some professionals.

The Irishman's career was long and illustrious. He won the East of Ireland Championship at County Louth in 1941 at the age of 17. It was his first of 12 victories in the event. Indeed, he won every major Irish amateur championship, including the Irish Amateur Close Championship six times, including three years in succession from 1963 to 1965. He captured the West of Ireland Championship at County Sligo 12 times. He triumphed in the South of Ireland Championship at Lahinch three times. In his native national championship, the Irish Amateur Open, Carr won the event four times before it was discontinued in 1960.

Sadly, despite all his Walker Cup appearances, Carr never played on a winning side. The closest he came was when he appeared in the tied match at Baltimore, Maryland, when the two sides matched each other at 11 points apiece.

However, Carr just wasn't the type to sulk in the face of defeat. That was evident when he was awarded the Bobby Jones Award in 1967 for outstanding sportsmanship in golf. It was fitting that Carr should get the award that was named after one of the best American golfers the game has ever seen, for the Irishman was well liked by American galleries. His affable manner and his gritty performances endeared him to Americans who watched him compete in many Walker Cup matches.

In 1991 and 1992, Carr was awarded one of the biggest honors in all of golf when he was made captain of the Royal & Ancient Golf Club.

# BILLY CASPER

CASPER'S FINEST VICTORY CAME IN THE 1966 US OPEN IN CALIFORNIA, WHERE HE DEFEATED FAVORITE ARNOLD PALMER IN A PLAYOFF. THAT WAS HIS SECOND US OPEN TITLE, SEVEN YEARS AFTER HIS FIRST.

Billy Casper turned professional in 1954 while he was still in the navy. Within five years he won his first major championship, the 1959 US Open at Winged Foot.

Although Casper had already won six times on the US Tour, and despite finishing second in the USPGA Championship the previous year, his win in the 1959 US national championship came as a surprise to a lot of people. Many thought the Californian wasn't ready for the rigors of championship golf. They were wrong. Casper was one of the greatest players ever to play professional golf, and one of the best putters the game has ever seen.

It was while winning his first major championship that Casper showed he was a master on the greens. For his four rounds at Winged Foot, Casper needed only 112 putts, an average of just 28 per round.

The victory seemed to give Casper's career a huge boost. He won three more times in 1959, and over the next five seasons he notched another 18 tournaments before his biggest season ever on the US Tour.

Now an established player, Casper started his 1966 campaign with a win in the San Diego Open Invitational, so he was one of the favorites when he showed up at the Olympic Club in San Francisco for the US Open.

The 1966 US Open had Arnold Palmer's name written all over it. Palmer was cruising toward a seven-shot victory over Casper with just nine holes left in the championship; Casper was basically playing for second place. Palmer, however, didn't just want to win, he also knew he had a chance of breaking Ben Hogan's 72-hole record of 276, set in 1948. Palmer went for broke.

The tactic went horribly wrong. Out in 32, Palmer took 39 strokes to come home. Meanwhile Casper quietly covered the back nine in four under par and found himself in an 18-hole playoff the next day. Casper duly won that by four strokes, again coming from behind over the closing nine holes, this time making up a two-stroke deficit.

Casper won twice more before the season ended to top the US Tour money list with over $122,000.

In 1970, Casper won his final major championship when he won the Masters in a playoff with Gene Littler. It wasn't surprising that Casper won at Augusta, given his superb putting touch. What is surprising is that he didn't win more Masters. The only other time he came really close was in 1969, when he finished runner-up to George Archer.

It is a credit to his game that Casper won 51 times on the US Tour, the sixth highest win total ever. He was also a Ryder Cup player for eight consecutive matches between 1961 and 1975, and captained the side in 1979.

## FACT FILE

**BORN** 1931, San Diego, California, USA

**CAREER HIGHLIGHTS**
1959 US Open
1966 US Open
1966 Player of the Year
1970 Masters
1970 Player of the Year

**INTERNATIONAL HONORS**
Ryder Cup: 1961, 1963, 1965, 1967, 1969, 1971, 1973, 1975, 1979 (captain)

# Bob Charles

THROUGH THE 1998 SEASON CHARLES REMAINED THE ONLY LEFT-HANDED GOLFER TO WIN A MAJOR. THE NEW ZEALANDER WON THE 1963 BRITISH OPEN AT ROYAL LYTHAM TO WRITE HIS NAME IN GOLF HISTORY.

## Fact File

**BORN** 1936, Carterton, New Zealand

**CAREER HIGHLIGHTS**
1963 British Open
1968 Canadian Open
1969 Piccadilly World Match Play
1972 Dunlop Masters
1974 Swiss Open

**INTERNATIONAL HONORS**
World Cup: 1962, 1963, 1964, 1965, 1966, 1967, 1968, 1971, 1972
Alfred Dunhill Cup: 1985, 1986

When New Zealander Bob Charles won the 1963 British Open at Royal Lytham & St Annes, he not only became the first Kiwi golfer to win the oldest championship in golf, but the first left-hander as well.

Left-handers don't feature too prominently in this book of true champions of the links. Phil Mickelson is the only other player, in fact. It's not because of any prejudice against left-handed people—it's just that not too many of them have played the game to any great level, especially in the 1950s and '60s. That's what makes Charles so unique in golf history.

In Charles's time, golf was a game for right-handed people. Probably 95 percent of the clubs manufactured were right-handed, and many left-handed people were forced to either play right-handed—many did—or not play at all. Charles was one of the lucky ones who was able to start from scratch with left-handed clubs.

The tall New Zealander is generally regarded as one of the best putters the game has ever seen. Allied to very accurate driving and iron play that very rarely put him in any trouble, it made him a formidable force in any tournament.

The former bank clerk won the British Open by virtue of his play on the Royal Lytham greens. After rounds of 68, 72, 66, Charles came to the 72nd hole at Lytham needing to hole a five-foot putt to shoot 71 and tie American Phil Rodgers for the lead. The silky stroke didn't let him down. Neither did it do so in the 18-hole playoff the next day. More excellent putting helped Charles to an eight-stroke victory and his only major championship.

Charles contended for more majors in the '60s. He was runner-up in two consecutive British Opens at the end of the '60s, losing to Gary Player in 1968 at Carnoustie, and to Tony Jacklin when the British Open returned to Royal Lytham in 1969. He was also third in 1964 and 1970. In the American majors, Charles came closest to winning the USPGA Championship, finishing tied for second with Arnold Palmer when Julius Boros won at Pecan Valley in 1968.

Besides the British Open, the New Zealander won nine tournaments in Europe, including the 1969 World Match Play Championship. Across the Atlantic he wasn't as successful, winning only four times on the US Tour between 1963 and 1974. However, his most successful period came on the US Senior Tour where he won 22 times between 1986 and 1994.

# Howard Clark

ONE OF THE GAME'S GRITTIEST GOLFERS, CLARK HAS PLAYED ON SIX RYDER CUP TEAMS. ON THREE OCCASIONS THE YORKSHIREMAN'S CONTRIBUTION HAS HELPED EUROPE TRIUMPH.

Howard Clark was taught golf by his father, a scratch county player. By the age of 11, young Howard was very serious about the game. So serious that by 16 his handicap was the equal of his father's.

Clark won the 1971 British Boys' Championship at Barassie, Scotland, as a 17-year-old. During his amateur career he played for England at boys', youth, and senior levels. He capped that career with one appearance in the Walker Cup, when he played in the 1973 match at Brookline, Massachusetts. In his three games in the match, Clark won once, lost once, and halved once by a score of 12 to eight. He turned professional shortly afterwards with a handicap of plus two.

Clark has been one of Europe's best professionals since he joined the European Tour in 1974. He has been a stalwart of six Ryder Cup teams, appearing on winning sides three times. The gritty Yorkshireman has defeated some pretty big names along the way.

In 1981 he beat Tom Watson by the comfortable score of four and three in a losing cause at Walton Heath in Surrey, England. At The Belfry in 1985, he downed Mark O'Meara one up in Europe's first victory in the Ryder Cup match for 28 years. He beat Dan Pohl by the same score at Muirfield Village in 1987 when Europe won for the first time on American soil, and won by a similar margin over Peter Jacobsen in Europe's comeback victory at Oak Hill Country Club in 1995.

In his early years in the biennial match, Clark usually partnered Sam Torrance, but in recent years he has teamed up with fellow Yorkshireman Mark James, the 1999 European captain. The two proved formidable in the tied match at The Belfry in 1989. They were unbeaten in the two fourball matches they played, defeating the strong American pairings of Lanny Wadkins and Fred Couples, and Curtis Strange and Payne Stewart.

As he has proved in the Ryder Cup, Clark is a strong player who can beat the best in the world when he is on his game. That was evident when his four-round total of 272 earned him individual honors in the 1985 World Cup of Golf at La Quinta, California.

Clark is one of an elite group to have won more than ten tournaments on the European Tour. His first big win came when he won the 1984 PGA Championship over the West Course at Wentworth.

In typical Yorkshire fashion, Clark does not suffer fools gladly. In fact, he can appear one of the dourest competitors on the European circuit. John Paramor, the European Tour's chief referee, once told a gathering of rules officials at St Andrews that they hadn't experienced a difficult ruling until they had dealt with Howard Clark. Despite that, Clark has a very dry sense of humor off the golf course.

## Fact File

**BORN** 1954, Leeds, England

**CAREER HIGHLIGHTS**
1971 British Boys' Amateur
1978 Portuguese Open
1984 Whyte & Mackay PGA Championship
1985 World Cup of Golf Individual
1988 English Open

**INTERNATIONAL HONORS**
Ryder Cup: 1977, 1981, 1985, 1987, 1989, 1995
World Cup: 1978, 1984, 1985, 1987
Alfred Dunhill Cup: 1985, 1986, 1987, 1989, 1990, 1994, 1995
Walker Cup: 1973

# Darren Clarke

DARREN CLARKE TURNED PROFESSIONAL ON THE ADVICE OF SAM TORRANCE. IT DID NOT TAKE THE NORTHERN IRELAND PROFESSIONAL LONG TO MAKE HIS MARK ON THE EUROPEAN TOUR.

## Fact File

**BORN** 1968, Dungannon, Northern Ireland

**CAREER HIGHLIGHTS**
1990 Irish Close Amateur Championship
1993 Alfred Dunhill Cup
1996 Linde German Masters
1998 Benson & Hedges International Open
1998 Volvo Masters

**INTERNATIONAL HONORS**
Ryder Cup: 1997
World Cup: 1994, 1995, 1996
Alfred Dunhill Cup: 1994, 1995, 1996, 1997, 1998

When Darren Clarke won the 1993 Alfred Dunhill Cup in Belgium, he fulfilled the expectations of a lot of people. Not least of whom was Sam Torrance.

As an amateur in 1990, Clarke was competing in the Irish Open at Portmarnock with Torrance and D.J. Russell. While waiting to play on the 14th tee, Sam asked Clarke what his future plans were. Clarke said he would probably turn pro after the Walker Cup the following year. Almost in unison the two professionals told Clarke not to bother.

The two saw in the 21-year-old a player who could make a huge impact on the European Tour. Torrance in particular knew of the amateur's potential: his father, Bob, was Clarke's coach. The Dungannon man turned pro shortly afterwards.

The Walker Cup aside, Clarke had won many tournaments in amateur golf, particularly in Ireland. In 1990 alone he won the North of Ireland Championship on his favorite course, Royal Portrush, where he is a fully paid-up member. He won the South of Ireland Championship at Lahinch, and the Irish Close Amateur Championship at County Louth. Not since the days of Joe Carr had one player so dominated the Irish amateur game. To no one's surprise, especially Torrance's, Clarke easily won his European Tour card at the end of the season. Yet it would be another two-and-a-half seasons before he made his European Tour breakthrough in Belgium.

Unfortunately Clarke went backward after his maiden victory. It took him another two seasons to win his second tournament, when he won the 1996 Linde German Masters. Since then he has been one of Europe's best players.

Clarke can shoot really low scores when he is playing well. The 6-foot, 2-inch resident of Sunningdale, England, holds or shares no fewer than six course records. One of them was scored in the final round of the 1998 Volvo Masters, Europe's equivalent of the Tour Championship, and nearly pushed him to his first European Tour number one title.

Clarke entered the season-ending Volvo Masters at Montecastillo, Spain, knowing he had to win to have any chance of topping the 1998 European Order of Merit. Colin Montgomerie and Lee Westwood, the two men in front of Clarke on the money list, had to finish worse than ninth and third respectively to allow the Northern Ireland golfer to have any chance. Clarke played his part perfectly, compiling a round of 63 to tie the course record and win the tournament. Unfortunately, Montgomerie finished third to deny Clarke the number one spot, but the Ulsterman's victory was good enough to earn him the European number two spot.

Clarke came closest to winning his first major championship when he finished second at Royal Troon in 1997. Later that year he made his first appearance in the Ryder Cup.

# NEIL COLES

NEIL COLES WON MANY TOURNAMENTS ON THE EUROPEAN TOUR BEFORE BECOMING A SUCCESSFUL SENIOR PLAYER. HIS RECORD IN THE RYDER CUP IS SECOND ONLY TO NICK FALDO.

Until Nick Faldo appeared in the 1995 Ryder Cup at Oak Hill Country Club in Rochester, New York, Neil Coles held a prestigious cup record: he had appeared in more matches than any other player. Between 1961 and 1977, Coles played 40 matches in his eight appearances in the biennial affair. In those eight contests, Coles only ever sat on the sidelines three times and watched his team-mates.

Coles is one of the most consistent golfers ever to play on the European Tour. In a career that spanned more than 30 years on the main European Tour, Coles won 22 times before going on to become a successful competitor on the European Senior Tour. On that circuit he has won such prestigious events as the Senior British Open, in 1987, and the PGA Seniors' Championship three times.

Coles is such a model of consistency that he appeared in the top 12 of the European Order of Merit for 20 straight years. He twice won the official money list, achieving that honor in 1963 and 1970. When he won the 1982 Sanyo Open at San Cugat, Spain, he set a record for the oldest winner on the European Tour. Coles was 48 years and 14 days old when he lifted the trophy.

Not surprisingly, Coles commands a great deal of respect in the game, especially among his peers. For example, he is chairman of the board of directors of the PGA European Tour.

Despite appearing in so many Ryder Cups, Coles sadly never experienced the joy of playing on a winning team. He did play, however, in the famous 1969 match at Royal Birkdale, when the honors were shared for the first time in Ryder Cup history. Coles earned three-and-a-half points from the six matches he played to help secure the tie. In the previous match at the Champions Club in Houston, Texas, Coles recorded a unique double when he twice defeated Doug Sanders by a score of two and one in singles play on the final day.

The closest Coles ever came to winning a major championship was when he tied for second behind Tom Weiskopf at Troon in the 1973 British Open. He also finished third at Royal Birkdale in 1961. The British Open was the only major Coles ever contested. An acute fear of flying meant that he traveled away from England infrequently. Coles never competed in the Masters, the US Open, or the USPGA Championship.

## FACT FILE

**BORN** 1934, London, England

**CAREER HIGHLIGHTS**
1964 British Professional Match Play
1965 British Professional Match Play
1966 Dunlop Masters
1976 PGA Championship
1982 Sanyo Open

**INTERNATIONAL HONORS**
Ryder Cup: 1961, 1963, 1965, 1967, 1969, 1971, 1973, 1977
World Cup: 1963, 1968

# Glenna Collet

COLLET WAS OFTEN REFERRED TO AS THE FEMALE BOBBY JONES, BECAUSE OF HER COMPLETE DOMINANCE OF THE WOMEN'S AMATEUR GAME. COLLET'S SIX US WOMEN'S AMATEUR VICTORIES HAVE YET TO BE MATCHED.

## Fact File

**BORN** 1903, New Haven, Connecticut, USA

**DIED** 1989

**CAREER HIGHLIGHTS**
1922 US Women's Amateur
1925 US Women's Amateur
1928 US Women's Amateur
1929 US Women's Amateur
1930 US Women's Amateur
1935 US Women's Amateur

**INTERNATIONAL HONORS**
Curtis Cup: 1932, 1934 (captain), 1936 (captain), 1938, 1948, 1950 (captain)

Glenna Collet was a natural sportswoman who came from a well-to-do family in New Haven, Connecticut. As a youngster she excelled at tennis and baseball, of all things. It was to discourage her from the latter sport that Collet's mother got her involved in tennis, which eventually led her to golf.

Collet didn't start playing golf until she was 14. She became fascinated by the game and threw herself into it with the same sort of enthusiasm with which she was to later play the game.

Collet quickly established herself as an outstanding player. When she was 19 she won the first of her record six US Women's Amateur Championships. She would win it again in 1925, then for three consecutive years between 1928 and 1930. Her last win came in 1935.

Collet was so much better than the rest of her peers in the ladies' amateur game that she was often called the female Bobby Jones, who was dominating the men's amateur game at the time. During the 1920s, Collet added the Canadian Ladies' Open twice, 1923 and 1924, and the French Ladies' Open in 1925.

With her superiority undisputed in America, Collet traveled to Great Britain to try to win the Ladies' British Open Amateur Championship. Collet had two memorable encounters with Joyce Wethered in the British Ladies'. In 1925 Wethered defeated Collet in the third round by the score of four and three at Troon, despite the fact that Collet was only one over par. Wethered went on to win the third of her four championships. Their next meeting came in the 1929 final at St Andrews. Collet held a five-hole advantage after 11 holes, courtesy of brilliant golf around the Old Course. However, after 18 holes her lead was cut to two and she was four down after 27 holes. Wethered eventually won three and one to earn the last of her four titles.

The talented American appeared in the final at Formby the following year but lost four and three to 19-year-old Diana Fishwick.

In five Curtis Cups as a player, Collet won four matches, lost two and halved once, and never appeared on a losing team. She captained the side three times as a player and was the non-playing captain of the 1950 American team when her side triumphed seven-and-a-half to one-and-a-half points.

Collet later became Mrs Vare upon her marriage. The LPGA Tour honored Collet by naming a trophy after her. The Vare Trophy is awarded annually to the player with the lowest scoring average on Tour.

# ARCHIE COMPSTON



COMPSTON LOVED A WAGER. THE HIGHER THE STAKE THE BETTER. HE RELISHED A CHALLENGE AND ONCE BEAT WALTER HAGEN BY A SCORE OF 18 AND 17 OVER A 72-HOLE MATCH.

Golf club professionals, especially in Great Britain, owe a lot to Archie Compston. He was responsible for helping to break down the barriers that existed in the early days between professionals and the members they served.

The lot of a golf club professional wasn't a happy one in Compston's day. They were treated little better than caddies, usually not even allowed inside the clubhouse to mingle with the members. Compston helped change that.

The tall, 6-foot, 4-inch professional was friendly with the Prince of Wales, who later abdicated the throne to marry Mrs Simpson and became the Duke of Windsor. The Prince was a keen golfer and took lessons from Compston. On one occasion, he took his teacher to a posh London club for a game of golf. When the club secretary pointed out that Compston wouldn't be allowed inside the clubhouse, the Prince announced that if Compston wasn't allowed to go in the clubhouse, then neither would he. The two men dined elsewhere, but it was the start of a breakthrough for club professionals.

Compston won many tournaments in his day, and finished runner-up in the British Open to James Barnes at Prestwick in 1925. He led the 1930 British Open at Hoylake after a record third round score of 68. However, he slumped to an 82 in the fourth round.

His biggest claim to fame was beating Walter Hagen by the landslide score of 18 and 17 at Moor Park Golf Club, Hertfordshire, England in a 72-hole match.

Compston loved to bet, and the more money he could possibly wager the better. He used to bet his members on the first tee at Coombe Hill, where he was the club professional. Compston would stand on the tee and ask the players what they thought they would shoot. When they said, say, 80 or 90, Compston would tell them they had no chance and would offer them £5 a stroke over or under par. Five pounds was a lot in those days, and Compston made quite a bit of money out of it. He would then go out to the eighth hole to see how his bets were doing, and often put more money down with the members. This sideline was so profitable that Compston was questioned by the authorities about it, as betting wasn't taxable in those days.

In later life, Compston retired to Bermuda for health reasons, where he was the resident professional at the Mid-Ocean Club.

## FACT FILE

**BORN** 1893, Wolverhampton, Staffordshire, England

**DIED** 1961

**CAREER HIGHLIGHTS**
1925 British Professional Match Play
1925 Gleneagles Tournament
1927 British Professional Match Play
1928 Eastern Open

**INTERNATIONAL HONORS**
Ryder Cup: 1927, 1929, 1931

# Charles Coody

AS AN AMATEUR, COODY WON 30 TOURNAMENTS IN HIS HOME STATE OF TEXAS. HIS GREAT TRIUMPH WAS WINNING THE 1971 MASTERS, A VICTORY WHICH MIGHT HAVE COME TWO YEARS EARLIER.

## Fact File

**BORN** 1937, Stamford, Texas, USA

**CAREER HIGHLIGHTS**
1964 Dallas Open
1969 Cleveland Open
1971 Masters
1971 World Series of Golf
1973 John Player Classic

**INTERNATIONAL HONORS**
Ryder Cup: 1971

Charles Coody won only three times on the US Tour, but one of those victories came in the Masters, a tournament he should have won at least twice.

Coody was a great amateur player who won 30 tournaments in his home state of Texas, some while he was a lieutenant in the US Air Force. He began golf at the age of 13 after he contracted polio and wasn't allowed to play contact sports. He later attended Texas Christian University and qualified to play in the 1960 and 1961 US Open. In 1962 he made the semi-finals of the US Amateur Championship before turning professional a year later, when he was 26 years old.

Given his excellent record in Texas, it wasn't surprising that Coody's first win came on home soil in the 1964 Dallas Open. Coody didn't win again until 1969 when he triumphed in the Cleveland Open. However, he should have won the Masters that year.

Coody had a chance to win on the final day of the 1969 Masters but dropped shots on the final three holes by playing too conservatively. He finished in fifth place. Coody's game went sour the following year after his clubs were stolen. The loss of his favorite driver played a big part in his loss of form and

confidence. Coody went through some 20 drivers before he found a suitable replacement.

Coody also won in Great Britain during his prime. In 1973 he won twice in Britain, with one of his victories coming at Turnberry in the John Player Classic. The conditions for that tournament were appalling, with high winds and rain. As a Texan, though, Coody was used to playing in the wind, and it was no surprise he emerged victorious.

He made one appearance in the Ryder Cup, playing in the 1971 match.

Coody got another chance at winning the Masters in 1971. He established an early lead which he lost but stayed within sight of the leaders. His main contenders that year were Jack Nicklaus and Johnny Miller. Against those two most golfers would have crumbled under the pressure, but Coody had learned from his disappointment of 1969. The Texan birdied two of the final four holes to win the title he coveted most. It was his last win on the regular US Tour.

Upon turning 50, in 1987, Coody went on to become a successful player on the US Senior Tour. He had more success on that circuit than the regular Tour, winning five times between 1989 and 1996.

# John Cook

JOHN COOK FINISHED SECOND TO NICK FALDO IN THE 1992 BRITISH OPEN AT MUIRFIELD, SCOTLAND. THE TALENTED CALIFORNIAN HAS BEEN ONE OF THE US TOUR'S MOST CONSISTENT PLAYERS DURING THE 1980S AND '90S.

John Cook will remember the 1992 British Open at Muirfield, Scotland, for the rest of his life. Except for one short missed putt and a failure to save par on the 72nd hole, the Californian could have won his first major title on those magnificent links.

Cook had a two-shot lead over Nick Faldo after 16 holes in the final round of the 1992 British Open. When Faldo cut the lead to one with a birdie on the 15th, Cook knew he needed to play the last two holes well to stop the Englishman from winning his third British Open.

Cook got off to a good start when he reached the par-5 17th hole in two shots. When he lagged his first putt up to within three feet of the hole, it looked like he would go down the last with a comfortable two-shot lead. However, the man from California missed the short putt to put undue pressure on himself going down the last. He split the fairway with his drive on 18 but then pushed his 2-iron second shot into the crowd. He received a free drop but could not get the ball up and down in two strokes, taking a bogey five.

When Faldo birdied the 17th, it meant he suddenly had a one-shot lead. A par at the last gave him his third Open win. Cook's play over the last two holes had cost him dearly.

Cook has been close in a number of majors during his excellent career. He also finished second in the USPGA Championship in 1992, finishing in a four-way tie behind Nick Price at Bellerive Country Club, St Louis. In 1993 and 1994 he finished sixth and fourth respectively in the USPGA. He also placed fifth in the 1994 US Open.

Cook was a very good amateur player when he was growing up in California where his family had moved when he was young. Although he was highly sought after by universities in his home state, he was persuaded to attend Ohio State University by Jack Nicklaus and Tom Weiskopf. There he was a three-time All-American between 1977 and 1979, and played on the 1979 NCAA championship team.

Given his love of southern California, it came as no surprise that Cook's first big win on the US Tour came in the 1981 Bing Crosby National Pro-Am at Pebble Beach on the Monterey Peninsula. Cook won the tournament in a five-man playoff. His second victory also came in a playoff, when he won the 1983 Canadian Open after going six extra holes with Johnny Miller.

## Fact File

**BORN** 1957, Toledo, Ohio, USA

**CAREER HIGHLIGHTS**
1978 US Amateur
1981 Bing Crosby National Pro-Am
1983 Canadian Open
1992 Las Vegas Invitational
1996 FedEx St Jude Classic

**INTERNATIONAL HONORS**
Ryder Cup: 1993
World Cup: 1983

# HARRY COOPER

A COURSE RECORD BY TONY MANERO DENIED ENGLISH-BORN COOPER A POSSIBLE VICTORY AT THE 1936 US OPEN AT BALTUSROL, NEW JERSEY.

## FACT FILE

**BORN** 1904, Leatherhead, Surrey, England

**CAREER HIGHLIGHTS**
1926 Los Angeles Open
1932 Canadian Open
1934 Western Open
1937 Los Angeles Open
1937 Canadian Open

Harry Cooper, or the "Lighthorse" as he was known, a nickname given to him by the famed sports writer Damon Runyan, won some 31 times on the US Tour. He should have been a shoe-in for the Ryder Cup, but was considered ineligible as he was born in England.

Cooper won some big tournaments on the US Tour, including two Los Angeles Opens, two Canadian Opens and a Western Open. In the latter tournament, one of the biggest events in Cooper's time, he defeated Ky Lafoon in a playoff to take the title in 1934.

The English-born professional was part of a team sponsored by the Spalding company. The team, led by Lawson Little, traveled around the United States, usually in a luxury train, putting on clinics and exhibitions. Besides Cooper, the team consisted of Horton Smith, Jimmy Thomson, and Little. Thomson was a big hitter and at clinics would demonstrate how to hit the driver, Little hit long irons, Smith gave lessons on the short game, and Cooper was the middle iron genius.

Before the 14-club rule was introduced in 1936, Cooper could often be found with up to 26 clubs in his bag. The new rule did not make him any less effective though, for Cooper came close to winning a few majors during his career.

When Horton Smith won his second Masters in 1936, Cooper was just one stroke behind him. The Lighthorse had actually led Smith by three shots going into the final round, but shot a disappointing 76 to say goodbye to the title. That started a good run for Cooper in the tournament. He finished in the top five in three of the next four years, finishing second again in 1938, two strokes behind Henry Picard.

Throughout the 1930s, Cooper threatened to win the US Open. He was fourth in 1930, third in 1934, second in 1936, fourth in 1937, and third in 1938. Only a course-record 67 by Tony Manero in the final round at Baltusrol in 1936 denied him the championship. Cooper shot a closing 73 and finished two strokes behind Manero's winning total of 282.

Cooper once gave Ben Hogan a lesson, helping the Texan with his grip. Hogan wasn't inclined to take lessons from anybody, so Cooper must have known his stuff. "I saw Hogan at the New Orleans Open in 1937 and he was having a hell of a time fighting that duck hook," Cooper once said about the lesson. "On the range I noticed that Ben was letting go of the club with his left hand at the top of his backswing and then regripping it stronger than he had at address. Ben never made mention of that tip in public, but I think he was grateful. Every time I see him, he comes over and gives me a big hug."

# Sir Henry Cotton

SIR HENRY COTTON IN FULL FLOW AT ROYAL ST GEORGE'S IN SANDWICH, ENGLAND DURING THE 1939 BRITISH OPEN. HE WON THE BRITISH OPEN THREE TIMES DURING HIS CAREER.

Until Nick Faldo came along in the 1980s, Sir Henry Cotton was the best golfer Great Britain had ever produced. Indeed, in many eyes Cotton is still the best golfer to hail from the British Isles.

The Maestro, as he was called, won the British Open three times during a period when no other Briton won it more than once. More importantly, he won it each time in style.

Sandwich was the scene of Cotton's first British Open win, and his triumph remains one of the most impressive in British Open history. Cotton started the tournament by shooting rounds of 67, 65, a record that wasn't equalled for another 56 years and wasn't broken for 58 years. Both Faldo and Greg Norman matched Cotton's opening two-round total of 132 at St Andrews in 1990, with Faldo bettering Cotton's record by two shots in 1992 at Muirfield.

After a third round 72, Cotton stood ten shots ahead of the field in 1934. Stomach cramps caused him to falter in the final round, but he still won his first British Open by five shots to end ten years of American dominance in the tournament.

His next two British Opens were just as impressive. He won the 1937 British Open at Carnoustie over a field that included the entire US Ryder Cup team. He shot a final round 71 in appalling weather conditions to win. It was a magnificent round given the circumstances. He also produced a score of similar magnitude in his third and final victory. Cotton's 66 in the second round at Muirfield in 1948 set a course record and was all the more impressive because it was watched by King George VI of England. Regal stuff indeed.

Cotton was not only the finest golfer of his age, he also did much to improve the lot of British professional golfers. Before Cotton came along, professionals were treated as second-class citizens, often not even allowed to enter the clubhouse of the club which employed them. Cotton raised the status of professional golfers. He was of the opinion that members of his profession were valuable assets to the clubs that employed them and believed they should be treated accordingly.

In later years, Cotton entertained promising young British professionals at his base in Penina, Portugal, where he would pass on the wisdom of his experience. One such player was Faldo, who would eventually equal Cotton's record of three British Open wins. Faldo once related how Cotton would make him play two balls from the tee, then make him play the ball in the worse lie.

Cotton wrote several books on golf in his later years, designed many golf courses, including his beloved Penina, and even performed a golf show at the London Palladium.

He played in three Ryder Cups and was captain twice. Shortly before his death he learned that he was to be knighted in 1987 for his services to the game.

## Fact File

**BORN** 1907, Holmes Chapel, Cheshire, England

**DIED** 1987

**CAREER HIGHLIGHTS**
1934 The Open Championship
1937 The Open Championship
1946 French Open
1947 French Open
1948 The Open Championship

**INTERNATIONAL HONORS**
Ryder Cup: 1929, 1937, 1947 (captain), 1953 (captain)

# Fred Couples

ONE OF THE MOST NATURAL, RELAXED, AND LONG-HITTING, GOLFERS IN THE MODERN GAME, COUPLES LIVED UP TO EXPECTATIONS WHEN HE WON THE 1992 MASTERS.

## Fact File

**BORN** 1959, Seattle, Washington, USA

**CAREER HIGHLIGHTS**
1983 Kemper Open
1984 Players Championship
1992 Masters
1995 Dubai Desert Classic
1996 Players Championship

**INTERNATIONAL HONORS**
Ryder Cup: 1989, 1991, 1993, 1995, 1997
World Cup: 1992, 1993, 1994, 1995,
Alfred Dunhill Cup: 1991, 1992, 1993, 1994
Presidents Cup: 1994, 1996, 1998

A funny thing happened to Fred Couples on the par-3 12th hole at Augusta National in the final round of the 1992 Masters. Couples underhit his tee shot to the treacherous little hole. It landed on the very front edge of the green, spun back, and started down the bank that leads up from the pond fronting the green. Couples waited for the ball to slide into the water, but it stopped—miraculously, inches from the pond.

Call it divine intervention, call it luck, but Couples's ball did not go in the water as it should certainly have done. Couples was able to chip the ball up from the bank and make par. He went on to win his first major championship.

Couples is one of the most natural talents in the game today. His Masters win was merely what people had been expecting of him for years. He had been close in majors before. Until that victory, the easy-going Seattle native had recorded no less than 14 top-ten finishes in the major championships, four of which came in the Masters.

Couples's strength lies in his ability to hit the ball huge distances with a golf swing that looks long and lazy. After a slight but pronounced pause at the top of the backswing, Couples lashes into the ball, sending it enormous distances.

He also has another trait that has helped him become one of the greatest players in the game. Couples is one of the most laid-back professionals in the game. In the heat of intense competition, he often gives the appearance of just being out for a stroll. Underneath that calm outer façade, however, is an intense competitor able to beat the best in the game.

Through the 1980s and '90s Couples has probably been the best American player in the world. The big hitter is a threat in every tournament in which he plays, and has many victories around the world, including stellar Ryder Cup and World Cup records. For example, along with Davis Love III, Couples helped the United States win a record four consecutive World Cups between 1992 and 1995.

Back problems throughout his career have done much to stop Couples attaining even more honors in the game. But even with a bad back, Couples is still one of the favorites in any tournament he enters, majors included.

# BRUCE CRAMPTON

CRAMPTON WAS KNOWN AS THE "IRONMAN" DURING HIS CAREER ON THE US TOUR. HE ONCE PLAYED A SUCCESSION OF 38 TOURNAMENTS WITHOUT TAKING A BREAK.

Bruce Crampton was known as the "Ironman" during his prime on the US Tour. The nickname came after Crampton once went 38 straight tournaments without a break. In fact, he missed only one tournament on the US Tour during the 1964 season, and only because his clubs had been stolen.

Crampton won the Australian Open in 1956 and came to Britain the same year, along with fellow countryman Norman Von Nida, who taught Crampton as a youngster. Like his elder compatriot, Crampton wasn't afraid to speak his mind, a trait that wasn't always well received in many quarters.

The Australian joined the US Tour in 1957, and became one of its leading players. Between 1957 and 1977 Crampton won 14 tournaments in the United States, including such prestigious titles as the Western Open (1971), the Bing Crosby National Pro-Am (1965), the Colonial National Invitational (1965), the Westchester Classic (1970), and many others.

He had his best season in 1973, when he won four times—the Phoenix Open, Dean Martin Tucson Open, Houston Open, and the American Golf Classic. He also finished second five times that season to end the year number two on the money list behind Jack Nicklaus. The 1973 season also saw him become the first foreign player in 36 years to win the Vardon Trophy for the lowest scoring average, an award he again won in 1975.

While the Australian never won a major championship, he did come close. He finished runner-up in majors four times, and each time he placed second to the same man—Jack Nicklaus. He did it twice in 1972, in the Masters and US Open. He also finished behind Jack in two USPGA Championships, at Canterbury Country Club in Cleveland, Ohio, in 1973, and at Firestone Country Club in Akron, Ohio, in 1975. A fine second round 63 in the latter tournament set a USPGA Championship record for the lowest score ever in the tournament. Unfortunately Crampton followed with a 75 in the third round, and his 69 on the last day fell short by Nicklaus's winning margin of two strokes.

The Australian retired from competitive golf in 1977 to go into the oil business, where he made a lucrative living. He returned in 1985 to prepare for the Senior Tour. It was a wise career move, for Crampton won seven tournaments the following season to top the money list with over $450,000. Crampton has since enjoyed even more success on the over-50 circuit, winning over 20 times.

## FACT FILE

**BORN** 1935, Sydney, Australia

**CAREER HIGHLIGHTS**
1956 Australian Open
1965 Bing Crosby National Pro-Am
1965 Colonial National Invitational
1971 Western Open
1975 Houston Open

**INTERNATIONAL HONORS**
World Cup: 1957

# The 'Olden Bear Wins his Sixth

No golfer has been captured on film more than Jack Nicklaus. As winner of 18 majors since 1962, his every triumph has been photographed, but one image stands out above the rest. It shows Nicklaus in a yellow shirt with his putter held aloft. The photo was taken in what was perhaps the most emotional tournament in the history of golf. The picture was taken on the 17th green at Augusta National in the final round of the 1986 Masters. The Golden Bear had just holed his third shot for a birdie three to share the lead with Greg Norman. Nicklaus would go on to par the final hole to cap a memorable afternoon.

Nicklaus started the final round of the 1986 Masters in ninth place, four strokes off the lead. Ahead of him were players like Greg Norman, Tom Kite, Seve Ballesteros, Tom Watson, and defending champion Bernhard Langer, a virtual Who's Who of world golf.

It took a while for the Bear to waken from his slumber. Pars through the first eight holes, the so-called easier part of Augusta National, didn't signal that he was about to mount a serious challenge. All of a sudden Nicklaus started playing like he did when a young man, and the Augusta galleries were whipped into a frenzy.

The charge started at nine, where he made birdie, then he added another at ten then 11, three of the hardest par-4s in the world. A bogey at 12 seemed to have thwarted his chances, but Nicklaus was like a man possessed that final day. Nicklaus's family had pasted a newspaper article on the refrigerator of their rented home that week which said he was finished. Their hope was that it would fire up the head of the family. It did, although somewhere inside Nicklaus wondered if his career was over. "I kept saying to myself, 'Done, washed up, finished.' I was trying to make myself mad, but it didn't really work too well because I thought it might be true."

The bogey at 12 finally did the trick, Nicklaus was angry at himself for making bogey on the par-3 and promptly birdied the 13th. A par at 14 was followed by an eagle at the 15th, then a birdie at 16 and another at the 17th. Nicklaus had covered the last ten holes in seven under par. His 30 on the back nine set a course record. He had shot 65 in the final round.

Best of all, Nicklaus had his son Jack Jr caddying for him that week. After holing out on the 18th, the two walked arm in arm off the green to rapturous applause.

Greg Norman could have forced a playoff with a par at the final hole but pushed his approach shot wide and made bogey. Tom Kite could have tied with Nicklaus as well, but his ten-foot birdie putt at the last just slid past the hole. Nicklaus was not to be denied his sixth Masters victory.

TOP: NICKLAUS SPLASHES OUT OF SAND ON HIS WAY TO VICTORY.

RIGHT: BERNHARD LANGER IS GIVEN THE HONOR OF PLACING A SIXTH GREEN JACKET ON NICKLAUS.

FAR RIGHT: NICKLAUS SEALED THE VICTORY WITH A BRILLIANT BIRDIE PUTT ON THE 17TH HOLE.

# Leonard Crawley

CRAWLEY LEFT AN INDELIBLE MARK ON THE WALKER CUP. IN THE 1932 MATCH THE ENGLISHMAN DENTED THE CUP WHEN HIS APPROACH SHOT BOUNCED OVER THE GREEN AND HIT THE TROPHY DISPLAY.

## Fact File

**BORN** 1903, Nacton, Suffolk, England

**DIED** 1981

**CAREER HIGHLIGHTS**
1931 English Amateur
1934 Gleneagles Silver Tassie
Golf correspondent for the *Daily Telegraph* for 25 years

**INTERNATIONAL HONORS**
Walker Cup: 1932, 1934, 1938, 1947

Leonard Crawley was not only a good golfer, but an excellent cricketer as well. He played at county level for Essex and Worcestershire and traveled with the Middlesex Cricket Club (MCC) on a Tour of the West Indies in 1926.

However, golf was Crawley's first love. He was one of Britain's finest amateur players, with one of the best swings in the game. In his book *Thanks for the Game*, Sir Henry Cotton describes the Crawley swing. "He succeeded in playing his scratch golf or better, with a unique slow backswing action, which was very inspiring to watch," wrote Cotton.

Crawley was a good enough player to have won the 1931 English Amateur Championship at Hunstanton. He came close to winning the title twice more, reaching the finals of 1934 and 1937 only to lose both matches. He played in the Walker Cup four times, comprising a record of three wins and three losses from the six games in which he competed. One of those wins came when he was the only Great Britain & Ireland player to win a match at Brookline, Massachusetts, in the 1932 biennial contest. Crawley defeated George Voight by one hole to earn the only Great Britain & Ireland full point in a comprehensive defeat at the hands of the Americans.

Crawley's appearance in the 1932 match was unique for another reason. An over-strong second shot to the 18th with a 4-iron bounced over the green, landed on a piece of concrete and bounced up and actually hit the Walker Cup, on display on a table behind the green. Crawley was of the belief that the dent he put in the cup should remain there since it happened in the heat of the action, so to speak. To his dismay, however, the Americans had the cup repaired.

While he appeared on three losing teams, Crawley was a member of the 1938 side at St Andrews when Great Britain & Ireland won the Cup for the first time.

Given his outstanding talent, it is strange that Crawley never won more amateur championships. Cotton provides the answer to that enigma in *Thanks for the Game*. "His putting was suspect," wrote Cotton, "which I believe was responsible for him not cleaning up in the amateur game."

Upon retiring from competition, Crawley wrote about golf for the *Daily Telegraph*.

# Ben Crenshaw

CRENSHAW IS ARGUABLY THE BEST PUTTER IN THE MODERN GAME. HIS SUPERB TOUCH HAS ENABLED HIM TO WIN TWO MASTERS TITLES, IN 1984 AND 1994.

Ask most players in the world for the putting stroke they would most like to have, and many will pick the one belonging to Ben Crenshaw. The Texan is one of the best putters the game has ever seen, even when he has to putt with a 1-iron, as he did to great effect while playing against Eamonn Darcy in the 1987 Ryder Cup at Muirfield Village, Ohio, after Crenshaw had broken his putter in anger.

It's because of his smooth stroke that Crenshaw has won two Masters titles, in 1984 and 1994. Only the best putters can conquer Augusta National's slick, sloping greens, and it's perhaps surprising that Crenshaw has won there only twice.

Crenshaw's first victory at Augusta came in 1984, but it could have come much sooner. Three times the Texan finished runner-up in the Georgia Classic in 1976, 1978 and 1983 before his maiden victory. Crenshaw putted brilliantly in 1984, including a monster 60-foot putt on the tenth green, to win by two shots over Tom Watson. There was no more popular winner than Crenshaw.

His second victory was perhaps even more special, as it came after the loss of someone who had a profound influence on Crenshaw's career.

The famous golf coach Harvey Penick taught Crenshaw how to play golf, from when he was a youngster growing up in Austin through his years on the US Tour. In the spring of 1994, Crenshaw visited a frail Penick at his home in Austin, Texas. From his sick bed, Penick gave Crenshaw one final lesson. It was on his putting stroke, and the old coach told Crenshaw not to let the blade get ahead of his hands in the stroke. Not long after the meeting Penick died. During Masters week Crenshaw and Tom Kite, another long-time student of Penick, served as pall bearers at the funeral of the revered coach.

Not many men would have been able to play, but Crenshaw knew it was what Penick would have wanted. He not only played, he won the tournament. It was one of the most emotional victories in Masters history. Upon holing out on the 18th, Crenshaw broke down. He later credited Penick with the victory, saying he felt the coach had been the 15th club in his bag over the four days.

A keen historian of the game, with a large collection of books at his home in Austin, Crenshaw is widely respected throughout golf for his strong adherence to golf's traditions. He has played in four Ryder Cups and was made the captain of the 1999 match at the Country Club, Brookline, Massachusetts.

## Fact File

**BORN** 1952, Austin, Texas, USA

**CAREER HIGHLIGHTS**
1973 San Antonio-Texas Open
1976 Bing Crosby National Pro-Am
1984 Masters
1992 Centel Western Open
1994 Masters

**INTERNATIONAL HONORS**
Ryder Cup: 1981, 1983, 1987, 1995, 1999 (captain)
World Cup: 1987, 1988
Alfred Dunhill Cup: 1995

# Fred Daly

DALY LEARNED TO PLAY GOLF ON THE LINKS OF ROYAL PORTRUSH, NEAR HIS HOME IN NORTHERN IRELAND. HE CAPPED A DISTINGUISHED CAREER BY WINNING THE 1947 BRITISH OPEN AT ROYAL LIVERPOOL.

## Fact File

**BORN** 1911, Portrush, County Antrim, Northern Ireland

**DIED** 1990

**CAREER HIGHLIGHTS**
1946 Irish Open
1947 British Open
1947 British Professional Match Play
1948 British Professional Match Play

**INTERNATIONAL HONORS**
Ryder Cup: 1947, 1949, 1951, 1953

Fred Daly was a small man who hailed from Portrush on the Antrim coast north of Belfast, a town that boasts Royal Portrush, one of the best links courses in the world, and the perfect place on which to learn golf. Daly was a fortunate man to have it in his backyard, so to speak, as he was growing up. Daly not only played on the course, but caddied there as well. It was on these links that he learned to drive the ball long and straight, and how to maneuver the ball in the strong winds that sweep across the course from the Irish Sea.

Prior to World War II, the little man from Portrush collected many championships in Northern Ireland. After the war Daly won the 1946 Irish Open at Portmarnock. He won the Irish Professional Championship twice, in 1946 and 1952, to add to his first win in the event in 1940.

The Ulsterman's biggest victory, however, took place in the British Open, which he won at Hoylake. Daly was fortunate to post a good score in the final round before the wind got up, but he still played well under the pressure to earn his victory.

The little man was known as one of the best putters in the game. In winning the British Open, he holed two

long putts on his march to victory, holing from 60 feet at the 13th and from about 35 feet on the 18th to take the title from Reg Horne and the good American, amateur player Frank Stranahan.

It was this ability to hole putts under pressure that made Daly one of the best players after the War. Yet he never looked comfortable over the ball. He seemed twitchy, waggling the putter countless times, and taking numerous glances at the hole before he actually struck the ball. Yet more often than not the ball would drop in the cup.

Daly played on four Ryder Cup teams, his last appearance coming in the 1953 match over the West Course at Wentworth in Surrey, England. There he contributed two points from the two matches he played in to very nearly give Great Britain & Ireland victory. His side lost the match by six-and-a-half to five-and-a-half points, and Daly teamed up with fellow Irishman Harry Bradshaw to win a foursomes match against Cary Middlecoff and Walter Burkemo, with Daly holing the winning putt. Then in the singles he steamrollered over Ted Kroll, inflicting a nine and seven defeat on the American, one of the biggest singles wins in Ryder Cup history.

# John Daly

JOHN DALY'S TROUBLED PRIVATE LIFE HAS NOT PREVENTED HIM FROM WINNING TWO MAJOR CHAMPIONSHIPS. FANS THROUGHOUT THE WORLD LOVE HIS "GRIP IT AND RIP IT" STYLE OF PLAY.

John Daly literally came out of nowhere to win the 1991 USPGA Championship at Crooked Stick Golf Club, Carmel, Indiana. Daly only got into the field at the 11th hour when Nick Price withdrew to be present at the birth of his child. Daly was the ninth alternate but got in when three players ahead of him declined the invitation. Daly drove through the night to get to Crooked Stick in time to play the open round.

Despite not even playing a practice round, Daly went round the difficult Pete Dye-designed Crooked Stick layout in 69 on day one to be up among the leaders. Further rounds of 67, 69, and 71 gave him the championship by three strokes over Bruce Lietzke. It was one of the most popular wins ever in major championship golf.

The crowds loved the way Daly played the game. Although he was born in California, Daly had grown up in the backwoods of Arkansas. He was a country boy with only one motto—"grip it and rip it." At Crooked Stick, he simply stood on every tee and hit the ball as hard as he could.

Daly won his second major championship when he triumphed at St Andrews in the 1995 British Open. The Old Course seemed made for John Daly that week. The American came to St Andrews with a new driver that hit the ball with a lower trajectory than he was used to. Lee Trevino had predicted a few years earlier that St Andrews was perfect for Daly because there was so much room for him. Daly could hit the ball miles left off every tee and still have a second shot. So it proved.

However, Daly's victory at St Andrews didn't come just from the distances he hit the ball. He had a remarkable touch around the greens that week. He also remained patient throughout the championship. Known as a player to get down on himself when things are going wrong, Daly stuck to his task in 1995. He could have been forgiven for throwing in the towel on the final round when the field had to play in winds that sometimes reached 30 miles an hour. However, a closing 71 put him in a four-hole playoff with Italy's Constantino Rocca, which Daly won to capture his second major and his first British Open.

Daly's private life has often kept him from even more honors in golf. An alcoholic at some stages of his career, Daly gave up the bottle in the late 1990s. He has also gone through two divorces and a few scrapes with the law. Despite that, fans love to watch him grip it and rip it.

## Fact File

**BORN** 1966, Carmichael, California, USA

**CAREER HIGHLIGHTS**
1991 USPGA Championship
1992 BC Open
1994 BellSouth Classic
1995 The Open Championship

**INTERNATIONAL HONORS**
Alfred Dunhill Cup: 1993, 1998

# Beth Daniel

DANIEL DOMINATED THE 1990 LPGA TOUR WITH SEVEN WINS AND 18 TOP-TEN FINISHES. INCLUDED IN THAT PERFORMANCE WAS A VICTORY IN THE 1990 LPGA CHAMPIONSHIP.

## Fact File

**BORN** 1956, Charleston, South Carolina, USA

**CAREER HIGHLIGHTS**
1975 US Ladies' Amateur
1977 US Ladies' Amateur
1979 LPGA Rookie of the Year
1990 Women's Kemper Open
1990 LPGA Championship

**INTERNATIONAL HONORS**
Solheim Cup: 1990, 1992, 1994, 1996
Curtis Cup: 1976, 1978

The 1990 LPGA season saw one player dominate the women's game as no other player had ever done. Beth Daniel not only won the LPGA Order of Merit that year, she set new records in doing so.

Daniel won seven times in 1990, and in total had 18 top-ten finishes. Her performance that year gave her a second Order of Merit title to add to her first, ten years earlier. She became the first player to win over $700,000 in one season, then became the first to win over $800,000, ending the year with over $860,000 in earnings.

Daniel was always destined to be a great professional. She was a two-time winner of the US Ladies' Amateur Championship, and appeared in two Curtis Cups, compiling one of the best records of any player. Daniel played in eight games in her two matches, winning seven and losing only once.

She was the LPGA Rookie of the Year in 1979, earning her maiden victory when she triumphed in the Patty Berg Classic. Daniel went on to win four tournaments the following season, and ended the year leading the Order of Merit. She also won her first Player of the Year award in 1980.

Between joining the Tour in 1979 and the end of the 1985 season, Daniel won 14 times, including a five-season win in 1982. Then her game disappeared—Daniel went nearly four years without a victory. However, she came back with a bang.

Daniel won four tournaments in 1989, but that was just a warm-up for the following season. Her most important victory in her seven wins in the 1990 season came in the LPGA Championship at Bethesda, Maryland.

The 5-foot, 11-inch South Carolina professional has been a perennial Solheim Cup player. Her numbers in that competition are nearly as good as her Curtis Cup record. Through the four matches she had played from 1990 to 1996, Daniel had won seven matches, lost three and halved just two. Needless to say she is a determined character who is almost unbeatable when she is playing her best.

Daniel has had various injuries in recent years, which have hampered her play and prevented her adding more victories to her resume. She suffered from muscle spasms and a shoulder injury in 1997 and only played nine events that season. She returned the following year but went winless. Even though she is now in her 40s, Daniel is still a force to be reckoned with in women's golf.

# LAURA DAVIES

PROBABLY THE LONGEST HITTER IN THE WOMEN'S GAME, DAVIES FINDS THE SAME DISTANCE AS MANY MALE PLAYERS. THE ENGLISHWOMAN HAS WON FOUR MAJOR CHAMPIONSHIPS.

Just as Seve Ballesteros injected new life into men's European professional golf in the 1970s and 1980s, Laura Davies did the same thing for the women's game in the 1980s and 1990s.

Davies is one of the greatest players in women's golf. Wherever she plays in the world, attendances increase at the gate. Fans flock to see her hit the ball as far, sometimes farther, than some men.

Davies is to women's golf what John Daly and Tiger Woods are to the men's game. She hits the ball so far that sometimes she is hitting wedge second shots while some of her opponents are hitting 3-and 4-irons, or even longer clubs.

Like Daly, Davies has a simple approach to golf. She simply hits the ball as hard as she possibly can then finds it and hits it again. She doesn't believe in applying mechanics to her game and has never really had a formal lesson in her life.

When Davies joined the Women's European Tour in 1985, she borrowed money from her mother to get started. She was soon able to pay her back. Davies's first victory came within a month, when she triumphed in the Hennessy Cognac Cup in France. She finished the season atop the European Order of Merit. She won the Rookie of the Year award, too.

In 1986 Davies won the Women's British Open at Royal Birkdale, and again topped the Order of Merit. Her first major victory, however, came the following year.

In 1987 Davies was refused an invitation to a US women's tournament. The LPGA commissioner, John Laupheimer, defended the move by claiming that no British woman had ever proved herself in America. He was soon to be proved wrong. Davies won the US Women's Open after she defeated Japan's Ayako Okamoto and the popular American JoAnne Carner in a playoff. The big-hitting Englishwoman took the lead in the playoff with birdies at the 14th and 15th and went on to win the title, much to the shock of many Americans.

Since then Davies has made her presence felt on the LPGA Tour, winning many tournaments, including the LPGA Championship and the Du Maurier Classic. Indeed, she has twice won the former championship.

Davies splits her time between the United States and Europe, returning from the United States as often as she can to support her home Tour.

Renowned for her penchant for betting, Davies is known to have more than the odd interest in what's happening at the track while she is competing. She is also a keen footballer who even has her own pitch at her home in West Byfleet, England.

## FACT FILE

**BORN** 1963, Coventry, England

**CAREER HIGHLIGHTS**
1986 Weetabix Ladies' British Open Championship
1987 US Women's Open
1993 McDonald's LPGA Championship
1996 McDonald's LPGA Championship
1996 Du Maurier Classic

**INTERNATIONAL HONORS**
Solheim Cup: 1990, 1992, 1994, 1996, 1998
Curtis Cup: 1984

# Rodger Davis

RODGER DAVIS, THE SARTORIALLY ELEGANT AUSTRALIAN PLAYER.

## Fact File

**BORN** 1951, Sydney, New South Wales, Australia

**CAREER HIGHLIGHTS**

1986 Whyte & Mackay PGA Championship
1986 National Panasonic Australian Open
1990 Peugeot Spanish Open
1991 Volvo Masters
1993 Air France Cannes Open

**INTERNATIONAL HONORS**

World Cup: 1985, 1987, 1991, 1993
Alfred Dunhill Cup: 1986, 1987, 1988, 1990, 1992, 1993

Rodger Davis is to the European Tour what Payne Stewart is to the American circuit—he is the only player to dress in plus-fours, or knickers, as they are sometimes called.

Davis is different from Stewart though, he has his names on both socks. One says Rodger, the other says Davis. He isn't one to get lost at any golf tournament.

Davis is one of the longest serving members on the European Tour. The 1998 season was his 22nd European campaign, his 25th as a professional. During that time the nattily dressed Australian has won many tournaments around the world.

A former captain of the Australian junior team, Davis trained to be an accountant before deciding on a career in golf. He was a plus two handicap player when he turned professional in 1974. Within three years, he had won his first professional event. The 1977 season saw him triumph three times in his native Australia, winning the McCallum's South Coast Open, the Rosebud Invitational, and the Nedlands Masters. Those victories allowed him to finish in the top 50 in the Australasian Order of Merit, which in those days meant a ticket to the European Tour.

Davis played only a few events in Europe in the late 1970s, preferring to combine tournaments on the Australasian Tour where he has been highly successful. Through the 1998 season Davis had won 19 times on the Australasian circuit.

His maiden European Tour win was the 1981 State Express Classic. One of his biggest victories came in the 1986 PGA Championship, when he defeated Des Smyth in a playoff at Wentworth to win the prestigious title. Five years later he added another big tournament when he won the 1991 Volvo Masters at Valderrama, one of the toughest courses in Europe. Davis won the tournament from the formidable trio of Nick Faldo, Bernhard Langer, and Seve Ballesteros, who finished second, third, and fourth respectively. Davis earned £100,000 for the victory.

On two occasions Davis has been in contention for the British Open. In 1979 he finished fifth at Royal Lytham and St Annes when Ballesteros won his first British Open. Then in 1987 he placed second at Muirfield behind Nick Faldo. An opening 64 gave him the first round lead. Scores of 73, 74 were followed by a closing 69 to give Davis a chance at the title. That was the year Faldo made 18 straight pars in the final round to win. Davis finished one stroke back.

# JIMMY DEMARET

DEMARET PLAYS A BUNKER SHOT DURING THE 1954 BRITISH OPEN AT ROYAL BIRKDALE. THE TEXAN WON THE MASTERS THREE TIMES, THE FIRST PLAYER TO ACHIEVE THAT RECORD.

Jimmy Demaret was one of the most colorful golfers ever to play the professional game—literally.

In an age when professionals dressed conservatively in blacks and whites and grays, Demaret was a breath of fresh air. The Texan loved bright clothes, and he wore every color imaginable: lavender, pink, gold, red, orange, you name it he wore it. He thought nothing of spending $125 for trousers, $250 for coats, small fortunes in those days. He shipped ladies' pastel fabrics from abroad then had tailors make up clothes from them. He had hundreds of hats of all styles. He had his own shoes made to match his trousers. Talk about dressed to kill.

More importantly, Demaret had the golf game to back up his lavish attire. In 1940 Demaret won six straight tournaments, culminating with his first Masters victory. That was an achievement in itself, but it's all the more impressive when you consider he was working as a nightclub singer at the time. Demaret was just a little bit different from the run-of-the-mill professional who played the US Tour in the 1930s, '40s and '50s.

The Texan was also a journalist's dream. Not only did he look different and, could play the game, but he had a sharp wit about him as well. He was the Lee Trevino of his day. A sports writer would ask Demaret a simple question and the Texan would deliver a line the journalist felt he just had to use. He was the unpaid, unofficial public relations man for professional golf.

Demaret left Houston, Texas, to become a Tour pro in 1935. He had a car, his clubs, and $600 loaned to him by a few rich friends, and unquestionable talent. He soon lost the lot playing pool, but when he eventually got round to playing golf, he won enough to get him started in his first few tournaments and he never really looked back afterward.

Demaret was the first player to win three Masters titles. In 1948 he was runner-up to Ben Hogan in the US Open at Riviera, Los Angeles. The two men were total opposites. Hogan was conservative in his dress, never spoke and never partied, and practiced more than anyone on Tour. Yet they were great friends. They formed a formidable foursomes partnership in the 1947 and 1951 Ryder Cup, winning both matches they played. Indeed, the two share a unique record in the Ryder Cup, they won every match in which they played. Hogan's record reads played three and won three, while Demaret played in six matches in his three Ryder Cups and won all six.

Demaret won 31 times on the US Tour during his long and illustrious career.

## FACT FILE

**BORN** 1910, Houston, Texas, USA

**DIED** 1983

**CAREER HIGHLIGHTS**
1940 Masters
1940 Western Open
1947 Masters
1947 US Tour's leading money winner
1950 Masters

**INTERNATIONAL HONORS**
Ryder Cup: 1947, 1949, 1951

# Bruce Devlin

DEVLIN DIDN'T MAKE AN IMMEDIATE IMPACT ON THE US TOUR AFTER MOVING FROM AUSTRALIA, BUT ONCE HE FOUND HIS FEET HE BECAME ONE OF THE TOUR'S MOST CONSISTENT PERFORMERS.

## Fact File

**BORN** 1937, Armidale, New South Wales, Australia

**CAREER HIGHLIGHTS**
1959 Australian Amateur
1960 Australian Open
1963 French Open
1966 Colonial National Invitational
1969 Byron Nelson Golf Classic

**INTERNATIONAL HONORS**
World Cup: 1963, 1966, 1970

When Bruce Devlin won the 1995 FHP Healthcare Classic, he not only won his first title on the US Senior Tour, but he ended a 22-year winless streak. Devlin defeated Dave Eichelberger in a playoff for the title.

Devlin was expected to win more on the over-50 circuit, because during his regular Tour career he was a consistent player who won eight times in the 1960s and 1970s.

Devlin was a plumber by trade, but was so successful as an amateur golfer that he decided to try to make his living as a professional. The 6-foot, 1-inch Australian finished as joint individual leader in the 1958 World Amateur Team Championship at St Andrews. He won the 1959 Australian Amateur and then followed it up the next year by winning the Australian Open. That was the win that made him realize he could play at the highest level. So he packed away his tool bag and headed for the land of the rich and free: America.

It took Devlin a while to actually start making money on the US Tour. He joined the American professional circuit in 1962, but in that season and the following year he won so little money that he was very nearly forced to give up through lack of funds. Then he won the 1964 St Petersburg Open and he was off and running.

After that maiden victory, Devlin became one of the most consistent players on the US Tour. He won a further seven tournaments, including such prestigious events as the Colonial National Invitational (1966), the Byron Nelson Golf Classic (1969), and the 1972 Houston Open. Devlin's best year came in 1970, when he captured the Bob Hope Desert Classic and the Cleveland Open. Those two victories and a number of top-ten finishes saw him attain his highest ranking on the US Tour when he finished 11th on the US money list.

Devlin made a number of return trips to Australia during his time on the US Tour, visits that brought him victories on his home territory. He won the 1963 New Zealand Open, and was a three-time champion in the Australian PGA Championship, in 1966, 1969, and 1970.

He also made a number of successful trips to Europe. In 1966 Devlin won the Carling World Tournament at Royal Birkdale, England, and the Alcan Golfer of the Year at Portmarnock, Ireland in 1970. The latter victory was particularly impressive as it was accomplished in strong winds. Devlin won the title by seven shots.

# Leo Diegel

LEO DIEGEL HAD A MOST UNUSUAL PUTTING STROKES THE GAME HAS SEEN. IT WAS SO UNUSUAL, THAT THE TERM "DIEGELING" WAS INVENTED TO DESCRIBE IT. THIS PHOTO DEPICTS THE MOVEMENT PERFECTLY. IT WAS AN UNUSUAL STROKE, BUT HIGHLY EFFECTIVE.

Leo Diegel is probably the first golfer to ever have a putting method named after him. Diegel employed one of the most unusual putting strokes ever seen in the history of the game. He contorted his arms into such a position that his forearms were virtually parallel with the ground as he stroked the ball. The word "diegeling" was created to describe the motion.

Although Diegel was one of the best golfers of the 1920s, he should have won more during his career. He would get himself into good positions after the opening two rounds and then ruin all his good work with a poor third or fourth round. Indeed, his poor score on day three became known as a "third round Diegel."

Yet the likable professional won many big events. He became a Canadian Open specialist in the 1920s, becoming the first man to win the title four times, taking his fourth championship in 1929. He won two USPGA Championships in 1928 and 1929, interrupting Walter Hagen's monopoly over the tournament. Indeed, Diegel beat Hagen both times in his march to victory.

Despite those wins, Diegel was susceptible under pressure, and could have won at least three more majors had he been made of sterner stuff. For example, he was one of a group of four players who finished runner-up to Ted Ray in the 1920 US Open. He was third in the 1930 British Open and joint second in 1930. In 1933 he had a chance to win but had an air shot on the final green, when two putts would have put him in a playoff with Craig Wood and Densmore Shute.

Diegel was aware of his frailties and even admitted his nerves kept him from winning more. "They keep trying to give me a championship," he once said, "but I won't take it!"

Diegel played in four Ryder Cups, making his first appearance in the inaugural 1927 match. He inflicted a seven and five defeat on Ted Ray in the singles, to partly avenge Ray's win in the US Open seven years earlier. Diegel also recorded a walkover singles score two years later when he gave Abe Mitchell a nine and eight drubbing. In the six matches he played in four appearances in the biennial competition, Diegel won three and lost three.

## Fact File

**BORN** 1899, Detroit, Michigan, USA

**DIED** 1951

**CAREER HIGHLIGHTS**
1924 Canadian Open
1925 Canadian Open
1928 Canadian Open
1928 USPGA Championship
1929 Canadian Open
1929 USPGA Championship

**INTERNATIONAL HONORS**
Ryder Cup: 1927, 1929, 1931, 1933

# Flory van Donck

FLORY VAN DONCK IS THE BEST PROFESSIONAL EVER TO EMERGE FROM BELGIUM. THE ELEGANT SWINGER WON MANY EUROPEAN TOUR EVENTS DURING THE 1950s, INCLUDING HIS NATIONAL OPEN CHAMPIONSHIP FIVE TIMES.

## Fact File

**BORN** 1912, Brussels, Belgium

**CAREER HIGHLIGHTS**
1953 German Open
1954 French Open
1956 German Open
1957 French Open
1958 French Open

**INTERNATIONAL HONORS**
World Cup: 1954, 1955, 1956, 1957, 1958, 1959, 1960, 1961, 1962, 1963, 1964

It's too bad that continental European golfers were not eligible for the Ryder Cup in the 1950s and 1960s, because Flory van Donck would have played in the match many times.

Van Donck is the best golfer Belgium has ever produced. One look at his record affirms that—he won many titles in the early days of the European Tour.

An elegant swinger of the club who has been one of the most gentlemanly golfers to walk Europe's fairways, van Donck was a threat in most tournaments in which he competed on the main continent of Europe. He won his own Belgium Open five times, including three in a row in 1939, 1946, and 1947 (there were no tournaments held during World War II). He won the Dutch Open five times between 1936 and 1953, the German Open twice, the Italian Open twice, the Swiss Open twice, the French Open three times, the Portuguese Open once, and the Venezuelan and Uruguayan Opens once each.

Van Donck represented Belgium ten times in the World Cup, then named the Canada Cup, and he wasn't there merely as cannon fodder for the bigger international names. Van Donck lost a playoff for the individual title in 1955 in Washington State, when his 279 total equaled British Open specialist Peter Thomson and 1954 US Open champion Ed Furgol. Furgol won the ensuing playoff. Van Donck finished third in the individual title to Ben Hogan at Wentworth in 1956. The tall Belgian professional did win the individual title in 1960 at Portmarnock, Ireland. It was a big accomplishment for van Donck, considering that the field included legendary names like Arnold Palmer, Sam Snead, Gary Player, Thomson, Bobby Locke, and Christy O'Connor.

Van Donck came close to winning the British Open on a number of occasions. He made serious contentions for the championship between 1955 and 1959, finishing no worse than fifth during that period. He was second twice during that run: in 1956 at Hoylake he was three strokes behind Thomson's winning total of 286, then in 1959 he was runner-up to Gary Player at Muirfield. He was actually one stroke behind the leaders going into the final round, and three ahead of Player. However, the South African closed with a 68 to Van Donck's 73 to take the title.

Van Donck had an unusual putting style, one not dissimilar to Japan's Isao Aoki. He held his hands very low so that the toe of the putter was off the ground. However, he used it to good effect. Besides his numerous victories in Europe, he won the European Order of Merit in 1953.

# OLIN DUTRA



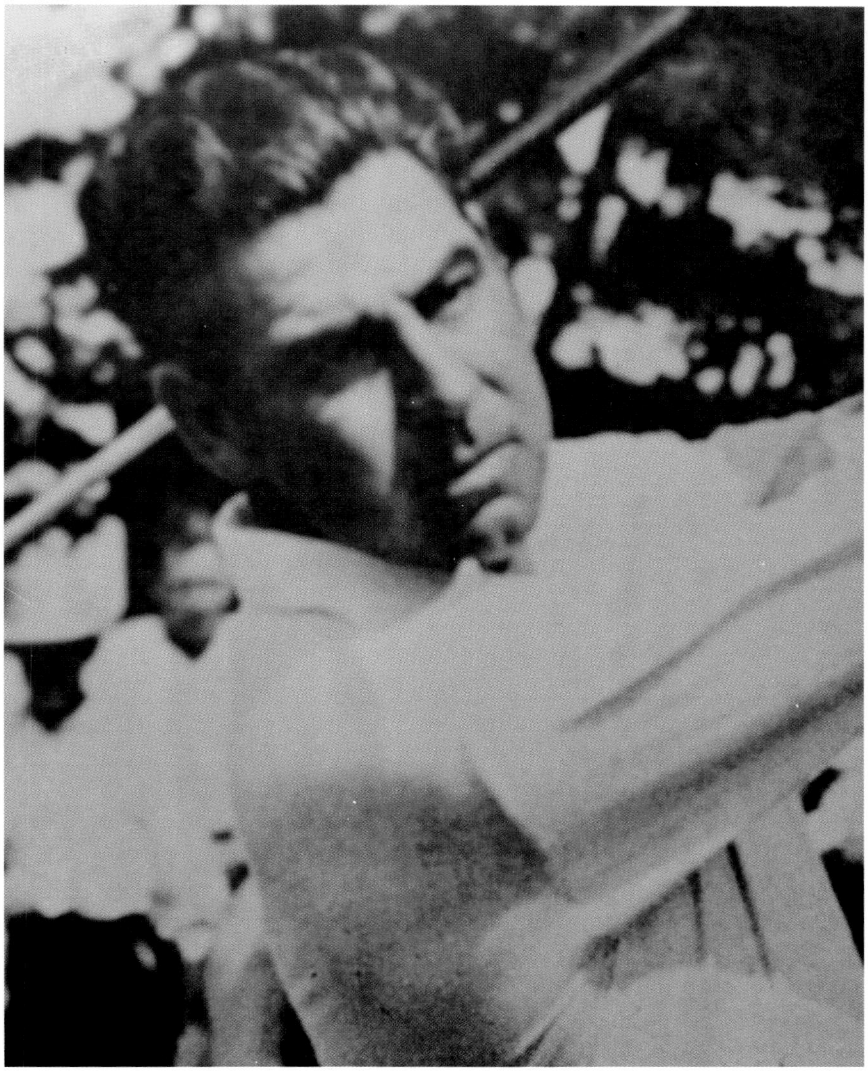

OLIN DUTRA'S PERFORMANCE IN THE 1932 USPGA CHAMPIONSHIP GOES DOWN AS ONE OF THE BEST IN THE TOURNAMENT'S HISTORY. DUTRA WAS 19 UNDER PAR FOR THE 196 HOLES HE PLAYED AT KELLER GOLF CLUB IN ST PAUL, MINNESOTA.

Olin Dutra is one of two brothers who played professional golf in the 1930s. His brother Mortie was also a professional, but Olin was the better of the two, good enough to win two majors during his career.

The California native was known as one of the hardest workers in the game during his days on the North American tournament circuit. That was obvious from his teenage years. He worked in a hardware store before turning professional, and would get up before dawn three times a week to practice. He did this for a number of years, and even continued the habit when he turned pro.

Dutra won the Southern California Professional Championship five times between 1928 and 1933, only missing out on the 1931 event. His first major victory came in the 1932 USPGA Championship at Keller Golf Club in St Paul, Minnesota. Dutra led the 36-hole qualifying round with a score of 140 to signal his intentions in the championship proper.

There was nobody to touch Dutra in the 36-hole match-play stages. He cruised through the opening rounds easily. His first match was a nine and eight whitewash of George Smith. Then he recorded five and four defeats over Reggie Myles and Herman Barron before facing Ed Dudley in the semi-finals. That was his closest match, but Dutra still ran out a three and two winner. He wrapped up the tournament with a four and three victory over Frank Walsh in the final.

Dutra took the golf course to pieces over the five matches he contested. He was 19 under par for the 196 holes he played. It goes down as one of the most dominant victories in the history of the tournament.

Dutra turned in another excellent performance when he won the 1934 US Open at Merion. Trailing Gene Sarazen and feeling ill, Dutra turned in two splendid performances on the final day to win. Rounds of 71, 72 saw him win his only US Open title.

Not surprisingly, Dutra's golf earned him a spot on two US Ryder Cup teams. He played in the 1933 and the 1935 matches at Ridgewood Country Club, New Jersey. Despite his obvious liking for match play, he won only one of the four matches in which he played, a four and two singles win over Alf Padgham in the 1935 contest. It made up for Dutra's first singles encounter in the Ryder Cup, which was a nine and eight thrashing at the hands of Abe Mitchell in 1933, one of the biggest margins of defeat in Ryder Cup history.

## FACT FILE

**BORN** 1901, Monterey, California, USA

**DIED** 1983

**CAREER HIGHLIGHTS**
1931 Southwest Open
1932 USPGA Championship
1934 US Open

**INTERNATIONAL HONORS**
Ryder Cup: 1933, 1935

# David Duval

IT TOOK DUVAL 86 TOURNAMENTS ON THE US TOUR BEFORE HE WON, BUT ONCE HE DID THERE WAS NO STOPPING HIM. AFTER HIS FIRST VICTORY, DUVAL THEN WON NINE OF THE NEXT 29 EVENTS IN WHICH HE PLAYED.

## Fact File

**BORN** 1971, Jacksonville, Florida, USA

**CAREER HIGHLIGHTS**
1997 Tour Championship
1998 NEC World Series of Golf
1998 US Tour leading money winner
1999 Mercedes Championship
1999 Bob Hope Desert Classic

**INTERNATIONAL HONORS**
Presidents Cup: 1996, 1998
Walker Cup: 1991

No player in the history of the US Tour has ever shot 58, a score that would equate to an almost perfect round of golf. David Duval may be the first.

When Duval shot 59 to win the Bob Hope Desert Classic at the PGA West course in La Quinta, California, in January 1999, he became one of only three players in US Tour history to break 60. The previous two were Al Geiberger at the Colonial Country Club, Texas, in 1977, and Chip Beck at Sunrise Golf Club, Las Vegas, in 1991. The experts agree, however, that Duval's was the best of the three.

Duval has been labeled a golfing machine in some quarters of the media. While Tiger Woods collects all the accolades as the most exciting player in golf, Duval quietly wins tournaments and earns money by the truckload. His win in the Bob Hope tournament enabled him to start the year by winning twice and earning $1 million in a month.

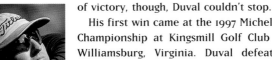

For all his success in the late 1990s, Duval was seen as something of a choker for much of the early part of his career. Great things were expected of him when he graduated from Georgia Tech and joined the Tour in 1993. Although he finished second a number of times, Duval found it hard to win. It took him 86 tournaments on the US Tour to finally triumph. Once he got the taste of victory, though, Duval couldn't stop.

His first win came at the 1997 Michelob Championship at Kingsmill Golf Club in Williamsburg, Virginia. Duval defeated Grant Waite and Duffy Waldorf in a playoff to earn his maiden win. He then won his next two tournaments, winning the Walt Disney World/Oldsmobile Classic, in another playoff, and the season-ending Tour Championship at the Champions Club, Houston, Texas. Duval had earned just under $1,270,000 in four weeks. The streak continued into 1998. Duval won four times to top the US Tour money list. In fact, after taking 86 tournaments to finally win, Duval then won nine in just 29 events.

Part of the Florida native's phenomenal success comes from what appears to be total unflappability on the course. His trademark is wraparound sunglasses, that have earned him the nickname Darth Vader, after the *Star Wars* character. The glasses hide his emotions, but many believe he does not suffer from emotion on the golf course. That certainly seemed true when he compiled his 59. Needing an eagle at the last to break the 60 barrier, Duval calmly hit a 5-iron to six feet and holed the putt.

Duval's father, Bob, is a successful player on the US Seniors Tour.

# STEVE ELKINGTON



ONE OF THE BEST SWINGERS IN THE PROFESSIONAL GAME, ELKINGTON CONFIRMED HIS STATUS IN THE GAME BY WINNING THE 1995 USPGA CHAMPIONSHIP AT RIVIERA COUNTRY CLUB IN LOS ANGELES.

If a poll were to be conducted among professional golfers to try to reveal the player with the best swing in golf, Steve Elkington's name would probably top the list. Quite simply, the Australian is one of the best swingers of a golf club ever to play the game.

Elkington was always destined to play at the top level. He was an extremely talented amateur who won the Australian Amateur Championship and the Doug Sanders World Junior Tournament. From Sydney, Australia, he moved to the University of Houston on a golf scholarship where he was a two-time All-American, and a member of the team that won the 1984 and 1985 NCAA Championships.

Big things were expected of Elkington when he joined the US Tour, and he's lived up to expectations.

The Elk, as he is nicknamed, won his first US Tour event in 1990 when he won the Kmart Greater Greensboro Open. He won again in 1991, when he won The Players Championship, one of the biggest tournaments in golf, and an event sometimes referred to as golf's fifth major championship. He won the title again in 1997.

The 6-foot, 2-inch Australian is one of the most consistent players on the US Tour. For example, he has won at least one tournament in every year of the 1990s with the exception of 1993. Even in his so called "slump" year, Elkington still managed to win just over $675,000 to end the season 17th on the US money list. He finished third in the Masters that year, and also has a fifth place finish at Augusta, in 1995.

Now based mainly in Houston, Texas, Elkington earned his first major championship when he won the 1995 USPGA Championship at Riviera Country Club, Los Angeles. It's a golf course known as "Hogan's Alley" because of the number of times the immortal Ben Hogan won over the layout. And Hogan would have been proud that someone with a text-book swing like Elkington's lifted the trophy.

In what he called "the round of my life," Elkington posted a final round seven under par 64 to set a new championship record of 267, 17 under par. That score was matched later by Scotland's Colin Montgomerie to force a playoff. The Australian won at the first extra hole when he sank a 25-foot birdie putt. It was a victory many had expected from the stylish swinger.

## FACT FILE

**BORN** 1962, Inverell, Australia

**CAREER HIGHLIGHTS**
1990 Kmart Greater Greensboro Open
1991 Players Championship
1992 Infiniti Tournament of Champions
1995 USPGA Championship
1999 Doral Ryder Open

**INTERNATIONAL HONORS**
World Cup: 1994
Alfred Dunhill Cup: 1994, 1995, 1996, 1997, 1998
Presidents Cup: 1994, 1996, 1998

# Woods Cruises to Victory

It's amazing what a good brisk walk can do to a round of golf. It took Tiger Woods the distance of just 50 yards between the ninth green and the tenth tee at Augusta National to turn a disastrous round into a brilliant one. It paved the way for one of the most dramatic victories in the history of golf.

The first day of the 1997 Masters was miserable. The wind was blowing strong and the course was giving the players nightmares. Scores in the high 70s were common. After shooting 40 for the front nine, Woods appeared to be heading that way as well. Then he figured out what he was doing wrong. After a bogey at the ninth, his fourth of the round, he realized his backswing was too long. By the time he got to the tenth tee, he had solved the problem. He shortened his backswing and came home in 30 to shoot a two under par 70. From that moment on the tournament was his for the taking.

Rounds of 66 and 65, saw him enter the final round with a nine-shot lead, the biggest in Masters history. It wasn't a case of if Woods would win the tournament, but by how much. After the third round, Colin Montgomerie came into the press center and practically conceded the tournament to Woods. "There's no way Tiger Woods does not win tomorrow," said the Scotsman. He knew what he was talking about. He had just played alongside Tiger and watched him burn up the course. Jack Nicklaus was ready after two rounds to give Woods the green jacket, saying it was the first time in his life that he'd ever given up on a tournament after a couple of rounds. That was an indication of just how superior Woods was that week.

Tiger Woods did not just win the 1997 Masters, he made the tournament his own. He set or equaled no less than 18 records in winning what many people saw as the first of many green jackets. Indeed, Nicklaus and Arnold Palmer believe Woods will win more than the two of them combined —and they won ten!

Among the records he set in 1997 were: the low 72-hole score of 270, 18 under par, breaking the previous record of 271 shared by Nicklaus and Ray Floyd; he became the youngest champion at 21 years, three months, and 15 days; his 12-shot winning margin set the record for the biggest in Masters' history; and on it went.

He literally reduced Augusta National to a pitch and putt course over the four days. For example, the longest iron Woods hit to any par-4 green during the four rounds was a 7-iron to the tenth, and that was because he hit a 2-iron off the tee.

Nicklaus, the six-time master of Augusta National, thought he had seen everything in his long career, but even he was overawed by Woods's brilliance. "It's a shame Bob Jones isn't here," said Nicklaus. "He could have saved the words he used for me in 1963 for this young man, because he's certainly playing a game with which we're not familiar."

**Right: Woods holes his final putt on the 72nd hole to record a remarkable victory.**

**Far Right, top: Woods's power helped him tame Augusta National as no player had ever done before.**

**Far right, bottom: Emerging from the crowd. Woods was head and shoulders above everyone else at Augusta National in 1997.**

# Ernie Els

ELS'S TWO US OPEN VICTORIES PROVE THAT THE MAN THEY CALL THE "BIG EASY" IS ONE OF THE GREATEST PLAYERS OF THE MODERN GAME. ELS'S LENGTH AND HIS EASYGOING NATURE HAVE MADE HIM ONE OF THE BEST PLAYERS IN THE PRESSURE OF A MAJOR TOURNAMENT.

## Fact File

**BORN** 1969, Johannesburg, South Africa

**CAREER HIGHLIGHTS**
1994 Toyota World Match Play Championship
1994 US Open
1995 Toyota World Match Play Championship
1996 Toyota World Match Play Championship
1997 US Open

**INTERNATIONAL HONORS**
World Cup: 1992, 1993, 1996, 1997,
Alfred Dunhill Cup: 1992, 1993, 1994, 1995, 1996, 1997, 1998
Presidents Cup: 1996, 1998

They call Ernie Els the "Big Easy" because of the way he nonchalantly strolls around a golf course. Even in the biggest tournaments in the game, Els appears completely calm. That was evident when the South African won his second US Open at the Congressional Club, near Washington DC, in 1997.

The mark of a true champion is the ability to hit great shots under the most intense pressure, and in the 1997 US Open Els played one of the best shots ever hit in the cauldron of major championship golf.

The 17th at Congressional is a long par-4 of 480 yards with a green jutting into a pond. On the final day, the pin was treacherously placed on the left hand corner of the green, very close to the water. After a fine drive, Els had 212 yards to the flag. Most players would have aimed for the front right portion of the green, hoping to knock a long putt close and hole out for a safe par. That was what Els's caddie, Ricky Roberts wanted him to do. It's what playing partner Colin Montgomerie did. Playing before Els, the Scotsman hit his approach shot short and right of the green, leaving himself a fairly straightforward chip and putt for par. However, Els is made of stronger stuff.

The South African selected a 5-iron and hit the ball just to the right of the flag with a touch of right to left draw. The ball covered the flag all the way and landed on the back of the green about 15 feet from the flag. It was a truly heroic shot under the circumstances, and earned him his second US Open.

Montgomerie, meanwhile, chipped to five feet and then missed his par putt. Minutes later, Tom Lehman faced a similar shot to the one Els had played, but put his ball in the water to the left of the green. Els then had to hole a par putt of about four feet on the final green to win the championship.

The South African won his first major over Colin Montgomerie as well. The two were involved in a playoff with Loren Roberts in the 1994 US Open at Oakmont, Pennsylvania. Els showed then that he was made of the right stuff by winning the playoff after a disastrous start.

Although Els is proud of his two US Open victories, he has always admitted that he thought his first major triumph would come in either the Masters or the British Open. The Masters because he hits the ball high and draws the ball from right to left, the shape of shot most required at Augusta National. And the British Open because it was the tournament he grew up dreaming about winning when he was a youngster.

Els first played in the British Open as a gangly 6-foot, 3-inch 19-year-old amateur at Royal Troon in 1989, where he missed the cut. His next appearance came in his great 1992 season by which time he had filled out to about 210 pounds, with broad shoulders that signaled only one thing: power.

Els is one of the longest hitters in the game, yet his power seems to come from one of the longest, laziest swings the game has ever seen. Like his demeanor, though, his swing is deceptive, for it is one of the best in the game, especially under pressure.

# Chick Evans

BOBBY JONES WAXED LYRICAL ABOUT EVANS AFTER THE INDIANA NATIVE WON THE 1920 US AMATEUR CHAMPIONSHIP. IT WAS EVANS'S SECOND VICTORY IN THE TOURNAMENT AND THE VICTORY WAS EXTRA SWEET BECAUSE IT CAME OVER FRANCIS OUIMET.

If you read Bobby Jones's excellent autobiography *Down the Fairway,* you will come across the name Chick Evans many times in the text. That's no surprise. Evans was one of the pre-eminent amateur golfers in America in the 1920s.

Evans was older than Jones by some 12 years, so the Indiana native naturally beat Jones to many honors. Most notable were his victories in both the US Amateur Championship and the US Open in 1916, the first man to take the two prestigious titles in the same year. Jones equaled the feat in 1930, and the two remain the only players to win the two tournaments in the same year.

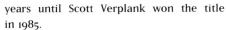

After starting the game as a caddie in his boyhood years, Evans went on to put together an outstanding amateur record by a very early age. For example, he won six Chicago City Amateur Championships, the first in 1907 when he was only 17. Three years later Evans won his first big professional event when he triumphed in the 1910 Western Open, a tournament that at the time rivaled the US Open in stature. It was a feat not even Jones accomplished in his career. For many years Evans's win in the event was the only one recorded by an amateur. That record stood for 75 years until Scott Verplank won the title in 1985.

An outstanding talent in most areas of the game, Evans's Achilles' heel was on the greens. It was for that reason that Evans sometimes carried as many as four or five putters to tournaments. However, he had no such problems in 1916. When he lifted his only US Open trophy, Evans had set a new 72-hole scoring record of 286, a mark that stood for 20 years until Tony Manero bettered it by four strokes at Baltusrol in 1936.

Evans and Jones didn't only become rivals, they also became friends. In *Down the Fairway,* Jones has this to say about Evans's win in the 1920 US Amateur Championship: "Chick Evans was the man of destiny at the Engineers Club and he won the championship, playing against Francis Ouimet in the finals the best golf I have ever seen in our national amateur event." Evans and Jones had many encounters, including one in the semi-finals of the Western Amateur, where Evans got the better of his younger opponent. The victory led Jones to say this about Evans, "Chick is one of the gamest and best competitive golfers the world ever saw."

## Fact File

**BORN** 1890, Indianapolis, Indiana, USA

**DIED** 1979

**CAREER HIGHLIGHTS**
1910 Western Open
1911 French Amateur
1916 US Amateur
1916 US Open
1920 US Amateur

**INTERNATIONAL HONORS**
Walker Cup: 1922, 1924, 1928

# Nick Faldo

NO PLAYER IN THE MODERN AGE HAS WORKED HARDER AT BECOMING A CHAMPION THAN NICK FALDO.

## Fact File

**BORN** 1957, Welwyn Garden City, Hertfordshire, England

**CAREER HIGHLIGHTS**
1987 The Open Championship
1989 Masters
1990 Masters
1990 The Open Championship
1992 The Open Championship
1996 Masters

**INTERNATIONAL HONORS**
Ryder Cup: 1977, 1979, 1981, 1983, 1985, 1987, 1989, 1991, 1993, 1995, 1997
World Cup: 1977, 1991, 1998
Alfred Dunhill Cup: 1985, 1986, 1987, 1988, 1991, 1993

If hard work, perseverance and singleness of mind are the hallmarks of a great champion, then Nick Faldo is one of the greatest the sport has ever seen.

Faldo was a successful European Tour pro between 1976 and 1984, winning ten European tournaments and one US Tour event. In 1983 he won five times in Europe alone, yet he wasn't happy. Faldo was convinced his swing wasn't good enough for the rigors of major championship golf, and majors were what Faldo wanted most. Enter David Leadbetter.

Leadbetter was a failed tournament professional who had turned his attention to teaching. Although English born, Leadbetter had grown up in Zimbabwe alongside future star players like Nick Price, David Frost, and Mark McNulty. In the early 1980s Leadbetter had developed a growing reputation as a coach to these players, and so it was to Leadbetter that Faldo went to revamp his swing. In fact, he asked the coach to throw the book at him. Leadbetter warned his new student that it would be a two-year process, but Faldo was willing to make the sacrifice.

Two years later Faldo got his just rewards, winning the 1987 British Open Championship at Muirfield with a final round that was comprised of 18 straight pars. Faldo's dream of winning golf's greatest championships had become a reality.

In the late 1980s and early 1990s, Faldo was the man to beat going into any major championship. In a three-year period between 1989 and 1992, Faldo won four more majors, two British Open Championships, and two Masters Tournaments. Indeed, he won the Masters two years in succession in 1989 and 1990, becoming only the second man since Jack Nicklaus in 1965 and 1966 to record consecutive victories. That was fitting, for Faldo only took up golf at the age of 14 after watching Nicklaus play in the Masters on television.

The man from Welwyn Garden City, Hertfordshire, England added his third Masters title in 1996. That was the year he defeated Greg Norman in an epic duel which saw him come from six strokes behind the Australian going into the final round. Faldo eventually won by five shots.

The Englishman's demeanor off the course hasn't always endeared him to the press or the galleries. His personal life, which includes two divorces, has been well documented in the tabloids over the years. Many see him as arrogant and aloof, lacking in manners. However, most respect him for the way he plays the game. At his best he is almost unbeatable under pressure. That's one of the reasons for an outstanding record in the Ryder Cup. In 11 consecutive appearances between 1977 and 1997, Faldo has amassed a record of 23 wins, 19 losses, and four halves—proof that he's one of the best when under the gun.

# MAX FAULKNER

FAULKNER IS ONE OF THE MOST COLORFUL CHARACTERS EVER TO PLAY GOLF IN THE BRITISH ISLES. HE FOUND THE GAME SO EASY THAT HE OFTEN RESORTED TO HITTING TRICK SHOTS IN PRACTICE JUST TO EASE THE BOREDOM. FAULKNER'S GREATEST TRIUMPH CAME IN THE 1951 BRITISH OPEN.

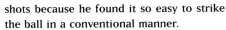

The night before Max Faulkner won the 1951 British Open at Royal Portrush, in Northern Ireland, he was approached by an autograph hunter who asked the Englishman if he would sign his name "Max Faulkner, Open Champion 1951." It wasn't an unreasonable request, given that Faulkner had the lead. However, most professionals wouldn't have wanted to tempt fate with such an audacious act. But then Faulkner wasn't like most professionals.

The English golfer was one of the most colorful people ever to play professional golf. As Jimmy Demaret was to American golf, so Faulkner was to the British game. He had a penchant for colorful clothes and didn't appear to take the game as seriously as most of his peers.

Faulkner was known for outrageous acts. Once when playing against Dai Rees in the British Match Play Championship, Faulkner was five up after eight holes, whereupon he announced to Rees that he was going to play with his head! Faulkner then proceeded to stand on his hands and walked to the next tee on them. It was a crazy thing to do for Faulkner's arms ached for the rest of the round. As it turned out, Rees won the match.

The Sussex-born professional once admitted that he often found golf boring because it came so easily to him. Faulkner said he used to practice hitting trick shots because he found it so easy to strike the ball in a conventional manner.

Despite times when he lacked the concentration needed to push through to victory, Faulkner won many important tournaments. He still remains the only golfer to win the British Open outside mainland Britain. After Faulkner's win, it took 18 years before another British professional lifted the coveted trophy. That honor fell to Tony Jacklin in 1969.

Faulkner also won the Dunlop Masters in 1951, making that season his best ever year as a professional golfer. He won the Spanish Open three times, the British Match Play Championship, and the Portuguese Open, which he won when he was 52 years old.

The outgoing Englishman played in five Ryder Cups, but wasn't too successful in the biennial competition. He played in eight matches in his five appearances and won only once, losing the other seven. At least his only win was a good one. It came in 1953 when he defeated Sam Snead one up in singles play. However, he was a member of the 1957 team that won the trophy at Lindrick when Great Britain & Ireland won the Cup for the first time in 24 years.

In later years, Faulkner did his best to help young British professionals, giving much advice to players like Tommy Horton and Brian Barnes, who eventually became his son-in-law.

## FACT FILE

**BORN** 1916, Bexhill, Sussex, England

**CAREER HIGHLIGHTS**
1951 The Open Championship
1952 Spanish Open
1953 Spanish Open
1953 British Professional Match Play
1957 Spanish Open

**INTERNATIONAL HONORS**
Ryder Cup: 1947, 1949, 1951, 1953, 1957

# BRAD FAXON

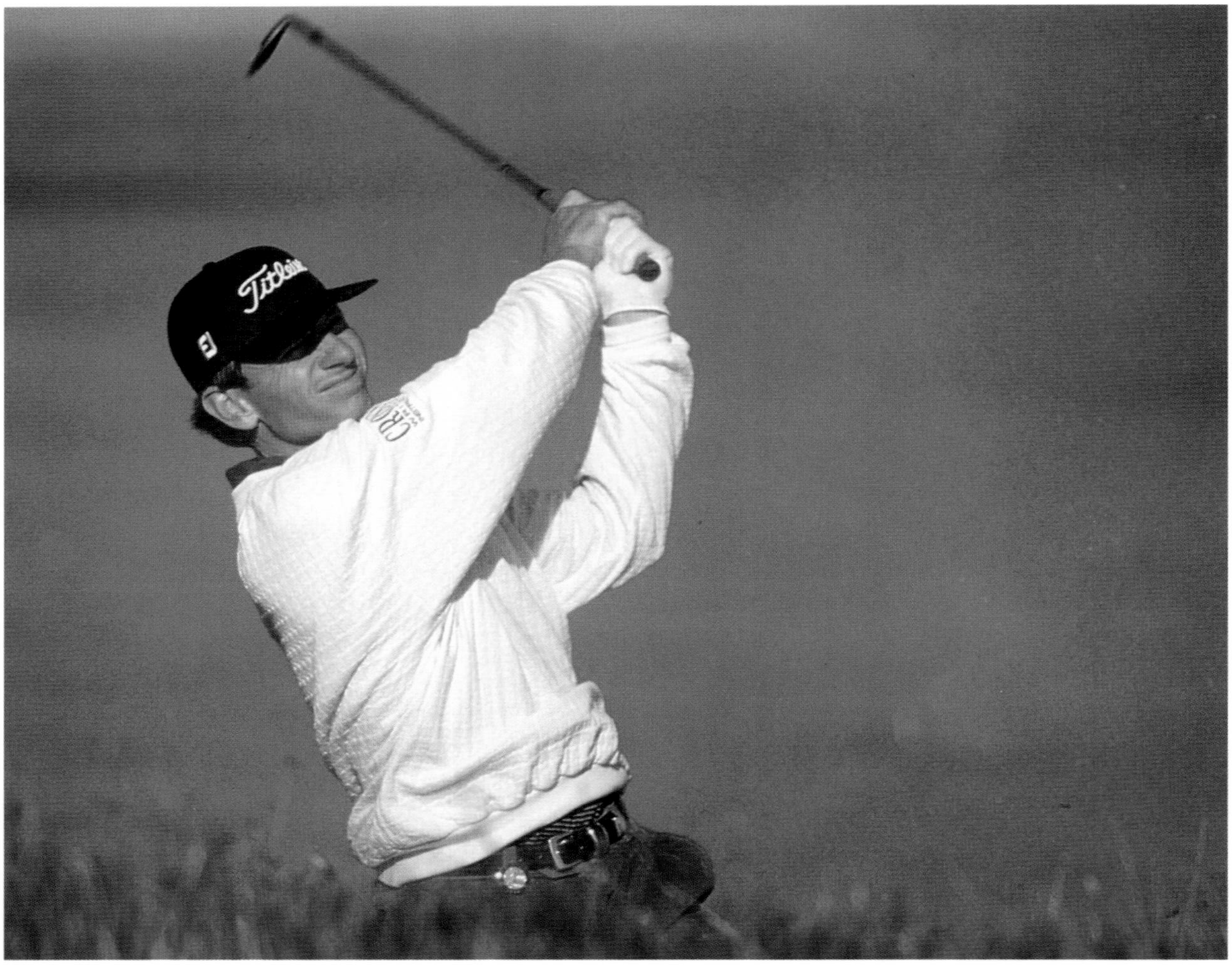

ONE OF THE BEST PUTTERS ON THE US TOUR, FAXON SET A US TOUR RECORD IN 1996 WHEN HE WON $1 MILLION WITHOUT WINNING A TOURNAMENT.

## FACT FILE

**BORN** 1961, Oceanport, New Jersey, USA

**CAREER HIGHLIGHTS**
1986 Provident Classic
1991 Buick Open
1992 New England Classic
1992 The International
1996 Freeport-McDermott Classic

**INTERNATIONAL HONORS**
Ryder Cup: 1995, 1997
Alfred Dunhill Cup: 1997
Walker Cup: 1983

US Tour professionals have a name for when a player hits his tee shot into the trees, pitches it back onto the fairway, knocks his third to 30 feet and then holes the putt. They call it a "Faxon par," after Brad Faxon, who seems to have been doing that his entire career.

Faxon is renowned for his ability to make par even after the most disastrous tee shots. Along with Loren Roberts, Ben Crenshaw, and a few select others, Faxon is one of the best putters on the US Tour.

The 6-foot, 1-inch professional admits he's not the straightest or the longest off the tee, but he knows he's got the short game to rectify any damage he does with his long clubs. Besides, he believes that's the most important part of the game. "No matter how good you hit the ball, you always have to use your short game," Faxon once said.

The New Jersey man attended Furman University, where he graduated in 1983 with an economics degree. That same year he made his one and only appearance in the Walker Cup at Hoylake. He helped the American team to victory by winning three and losing once in the four matches he played. He turned professional the same year and got his card at the US Tour Qualifying School.

It took Faxon a while to settle in on Tour. He barely held onto his card after the 1985 season, finishing 124th of the 125 who retained their cards for the following season. His maiden win came in 1986 when he triumphed in the Provident Classic. That's when the rest of the Tour realized Faxon could putt, for he shot a final round 63 to win.

Sixty-three was the same score Faxon shot in the final round of the 1995 USPGA Championship at Riviera Country Club, Los Angeles. It was important for Faxon, too, because though he didn't win the tournament—that honor went to Steve Elkington—his score did get him into his first Ryder Cup match. The Rhode Island resident knew he needed a good last round to make the side. He got off to the best possible start, shooting a seven under par 28 on the front nine. All of a sudden, a 59 for the first time in a major championship looked to be on the cards. However, the putts didn't drop for him on the inward holes and Faxon came back in 35. His 63 earned him fifth place and a trip to Oak Hill Country Club, Rochester, New York, for the Ryder Cup.

Faxon set a record in 1996 when he became the first player to win more than $1 million ($1,055,050) in a season without recording a victory. He finished second four times and never missed a cut in the 22 tournaments he entered.

# ROBERT FERGUSON

FERGUSON DOMINATED THE BRITISH OPEN IN THE EARLY 1880S, WINNING THREE CONSECUTIVE TOURNAMENTS BETWEEN 1880 AND 1882. HE NEARLY WON THE CHAMPIONSHIP AGAIN IN 1884 BUT WAS DENIED VICTORY IN A PLAYOFF WITH WILLIE FERNIE.

Musselburgh was one of the first venues for the British Open, hosting the championship six times between 1874 and 1889. It was fitting then that one of the town's finest sons should have such a huge impact on the championship's history.

Robert Ferguson was born in Musselburgh, and started caddying on the town's links when he was just eight. Naturally, he learned a lot from the players who employed him, and spent as much of his spare time as possible playing. He soon developed into a fine golfer.

When Ferguson was 18, he borrowed a bag of clubs and entered a tournament at Leith. All the best professionals of the day were entered, but Ferguson came away with the £10 top prize. It helped raise his status to such an extent that Sir Charles Tennant put up the money to sponsor Ferguson in many matches. In 1868 and 1869, Tennant financed Ferguson to play a series of matches against Old Tom Morris, with Ferguson beating the St Andrews man six times.

Musselburgh was one of the hotbeds of Scottish golf during Ferguson's time. The town had already produced British Open champions in the shape of the Park brothers, Willie and Mungo. Willie had won the British Open three times and Mungo once by the time Ferguson got his name on the trophy. Later, Willie Park Jr would also add his name to Musselburgh's roll of honor, winning the championship twice.

Ferguson took over from Jamie Anderson as the dominant player in the British Open. Anderson won the tournament three times in succession between 1877 and 1879, only to be followed by three straight wins by Ferguson from 1880 to 1882. Ferguson's first victory in the championship came on his home course. The local boy won the third British Open to be held at Musselburgh, lifting the trophy within sight of the house where he was born. Wins at Prestwick and St Andrews the following two years completed his hat-trick of victories, making him one of only four men to win the championship three times in succession (the others being Tom Morris Jr, J. Andersen, and Peter Thomson.)

Ferguson finished runner-up to Willie Fernie in 1883. He needed three threes over the trial round's last three holes of the final round to tie Fernie and duly got them to finish on 159. He lost the playoff by one stroke despite being one ahead standing on the last tee. Fernie drove the final green and holed a long putt for a two to deny Ferguson his fourth successive championship.

## FACT FILE

**BORN** 1848, Musselburgh, Lothian, Scotland

**DIED** 1915

**CAREER HIGHLIGHTS**
1880 The Open Championship
1881 The Open Championship
1882 The Open Championship

# Vicente Fernandez

ONE OF THE BEST PLAYERS TO HAIL FROM ARGENTINA, FERNANDEZ WAS A STALWART ON THE EUROPEAN TOUR WHERE HE WAS RENOWNED FOR BEING ONE OF THE BEST TEACHERS IN THE GAME.

## Fact File

**BORN** 1946, Corrientes, Argentina

**CAREER HIGHLIGHTS**
1970 Dutch Open
1979 Colgate PGA Championship
1992 Murphy's English Open
1996 Burnet Senior Classic
1997 Bank One Boston Classic

When Vicente Fernandez played the European Tour between 1971 and 1996, he was known by the nickname "Chino." It was a name used quite often by other European professionals, especially on the practice ground.

Fernandez is widely respected as having one of the best eyes for a golf swing in the game. The approachable Argentinian would often be stopped by other professionals, Seve Ballesteros among them, who would say something like, "Chino, could you just have a quick look at my swing." An hour later, Fernandez would still be there passing on his wealth of experience.

Fernandez had a good start in golf. Early in his career he caddied for Chi Chi Rodriguez at the 1962 World Cup, where he no doubt learned much from the talented Puerto Rican. He was also fortunate that Argentina had a golf superstar in Roberto de Vicenzo, who won the British Open in 1967 at Hoylake. The elder Argentine was a huge influence on Fernandez's career.

Now a successful Senior Tour professional, Fernandez was always one of the stalwarts of the European Tour. He won the 1968 and 1969 Argentine Opens before arriving on the European Tour in 1970. (He has since won his own national championship a further six times, including a streak of four consecutive wins between 1984 and 1987.) That year he won the Dutch Open, the first of five victories on the European Tour.

Fernandez also won in 1975 when he lifted the Benson & Hedges Festival, the forerunner of the current Benson & Hedges International Open. In 1979 he won his biggest European Tour title when he triumphed in the Colgate PGA Championship at St Andrews. Fernandez won the title by beating Gary Player and Italy's Baldo Dassu by one stroke. It would be another 11 years before the little Argentine won his next title, taking the Tenerife Open, held in the Canary Islands.

His last victory in Europe came in dramatic fashion. Fernandez won the 1992 Murphy's English Open at The Belfry when he rattled a monster birdie putt, measured at 87 feet, into the hole on the final green to take the title by one stroke. Chino celebrated by doing a somersault on the green.

Upon turning 50, Fernandez joined the US Senior Tour. It didn't take him long to enter the winner's circle on that circuit. His first victory came in the 1996 Burnet Senior Classic, when he triumphed over Bruce Crampton and J.C. Snead, with Raymond Floyd one shot further behind. He then won the 1997 Bank One Boston Classic the following season.

# Jim Ferrier

AUSTRALIA'S JIM FERRIER WON ONLY ONE MAJOR, THE 1947 USPGA CHAMPIONSHIP, BUT HE CAME CLOSE TO WINNING THE US OPEN AND THE MASTERS DURING HIS CAREER.

Jim Ferrier only ever made a name for himself in one of the four major championships, but he came close to winning all three of the American majors.

Ferrier's one major championship victory came in the 1947 USPGA. The Australian won the championship at the Plum Hollow Country Club in Detroit, Michigan, but not before spending money to draft in a little police assistance.

In the first final since 1937 that didn't include Sam Snead, Ben Hogan, or Byron Nelson, Ferrier faced Michigan native Chick Harbert. The Australian spent the night before the final worrying about fan interference. Ferrier was concerned that the galleries would try to help Harbert by either kicking his ball out of the woods or kicking Ferrier's into them. So Ferrier employed two policemen to patrol each side of the fairway to watch out for over-enthusiastic fans. Ferrier later said, "It was the best $100 that I have ever spent."

The championship was won by Ferrier's magical putting touch. Known as a great short iron player during his career, Ferrier was also very adept on the greens. The Australian needed only 52 putts during the 35-hole match as he won the championship by the score of two and one.

That was the start of a great run for Ferrier. He added Canadian Opens in 1950 and 1951 after finishing runner-up in the tournament to Dutch Harrison in 1949. By the time his career was over, Ferrier won 18 times on the US Tour.

In his native Australia, Ferrier won 25 tournaments as an amateur. Four times he won the Australian Amateur, winning the title back to back in 1935 and 1936, and 1938 and 1939. He also won two Australian Opens while still an amateur. He traveled to America in 1940 where he competed in the US Amateur Championship. Doubts were raised about his amateur status because he had penned a book entitled *How I Play Golf*. Although he played the tournament as an amateur, he turned professional shortly afterward.

Besides his USPGA title, Ferrier came close to winning the Masters when he finished second in 1950. He was just two strokes from forcing a playoff with Jimmy Demaret, who won his third Masters. A closing 75 cost him dearly. He had a number of other good performances in the Masters, finishing third (1952), fourth twice (1946, 1948), and sixth (1947).

Ferrier also came close in a couple of US Opens. In 1947 he finished sixth in St Louis, and closing rounds of 74, 75 at Merion in 1950 saw him miss a playoff by two strokes with Hogan, Lloyd Mangrum and George Fazio, which Hogan won.

Ferrier served as a sargent in the US Army in World War II before continuing his golf career.

## Fact File

**BORN** 1915, Manly, New South Wales, Australia

**DIED** 1986

**CAREER HIGHLIGHTS**
1938 Australian Open
1939 Australian Open
1947 USPGA Championship
1950 Canadian Open
1951 Canadian Open

# Dow Finsterwald

FINSTERWALD LOST IN THE LAST USPGA MATCH PLAY FINAL EVER HELD, TO LIONEL HEBERT IN 1957. THE OHIO NATIVE MADE AMENDS THE FOLLOWING YEAR WHEN HE WON THE FIRST CHAMPIONSHIP CONTEST AT STROKE PLAY.

## Fact File

**BORN** 1929, Athens Ohio, USA

**CAREER HIGHLIGHTS**
1957 Tucson Open
1958 USPGA Championship
1959 Greater Greensboro Open
1960 Los Angeles Open
1960 Greater New Orleans Open Invitational

**INTERNATIONAL HONORS**
Ryder Cup: 1957, 1959, 1961, 1963

During his prime in the 1950s, Dow Finsterwald was known as a player whose main asset was hitting the ball straight and keeping it in play. The strategy was highly effective, because the Ohio professional was one of the best players on the US Tour during that time.

Finsterwald's best two seasons came in 1957 and 1958, when he won 11 times. Included in those wins was his only major championship victory.

Until 1957, the USPGA Championship had been a match play event. In 1958 it was contested by stroke play for the first time. It was entirely fitting that the first stroke play championship in the tournament's history was won by Finsterwald. At Miami Valley Golf Club in Dayton, Ohio, the previous year, Finsterwald had beaten Sam Snead by a score of two and one in the fourth round on his way to the final. He lost to Lionel Hebert in the 36-hole championship match by the score of three and one. A bogey at the 34th hole, after he had hit his ball into a creek fronting the green, ultimately cost him the championship. Finsterwald went two down and Hebert won the match with a par at the next hole.

The disappointment of losing the tournament was erased the following year when Finsterwald lifted the trophy at Colorado Springs. The Ohio professional again had to overcome Snead. Going into the final round, Snead was two shots ahead of Finsterwald, but the losing 1957 finalist bettered Snead's score by six strokes, 67 to 73, to win. Snead eventually finished third with Billy Casper taking second place.

The 1958 USPGA Champion came close to winning the Masters in 1962. He tied with Arnold Palmer and Gary Player after 72 holes but lost the ensuing playoff, scoring 77 against Palmer's 68 and Player's 71.

Finsterwald played on four Ryder Cup sides and put together a very respectable record of nine wins and three losses. In 1957, at Lindrick in Yorkshire, England his rookie year, he lost to Christy O'Connor by the embarrassing score of seven and six. He exacted revenge four years later when he downed O'Connor two and one in the final day's morning singles matches. In 1963, at East Lake Country Club in Atlanta, Georgia, he and Arnold Palmer formed a good partnership when they won both matches they played together.

Finsterwald once shot a round of 60 as an amateur in the 1950 St Louis Open. So it came as no surprise when Finsterwald won the 1957 Vardon Trophy on the US Tour for the lowest scoring average.

# JACK FLECK

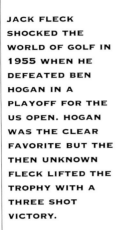

JACK FLECK SHOCKED THE WORLD OF GOLF IN 1955 WHEN HE DEFEATED BEN HOGAN IN A PLAYOFF FOR THE US OPEN. HOGAN WAS THE CLEAR FAVORITE BUT THE THEN UNKNOWN FLECK LIFTED THE TROPHY WITH A THREE SHOT VICTORY.

There have been many giant killers in major championship golf—Scott Simpson beating Tom Watson in the 1987 US Open, Bob Tway winning at the death over Greg Norman in the 1986 USPGA Championship, Larry Mize chipping in at the second playoff hole to deny Norman the 1987 Masters, immediately spring to mind—but none come bigger than Jack Fleck.

When Ben Hogan arrived at the Olympic Club in San Francisco for the 1955 US Open, he had already won the title four times. He was the greatest player of his generation and the heavy favorite to better the record of four US Open titles he shared with Bobby Jones and Willie Anderson.

Everything nearly went as planned for Hogan. He scored rounds of 72, 73, 72, 70 for a four-round total of 287, seven over par on the tough par-70 layout. Thinking he had won, he handed his golf ball to an official when he came off the final green, telling him it was for Golf House, the USGA museum. At the time, Fleck stood on the tenth tee, just one stroke behind Hogan, but no one gave him much of a chance of winning.

What not many people knew was that Fleck had prepared well for the 1955 US Open. He had arrived at the Olympic Club a week early and had played 44 holes each day, practicing shots from out of the deep rough just off the fairways and surrounding the greens. Despite that, he shot an opening 76 to lie nine shots behind Tommy Bolt. Rounds of 69 and 75 put him just three shots behind Hogan entering the last round.

Fleck started well over the final nine holes in his attempt to catch Hogan. He made pars at ten, 11, 12, and 13 to stay within one stroke. A bogey at 14, however, meant he needed to birdie two of the last four holes to force a playoff. He got one at the 15th and then made another at the 18th to tie with Hogan.

Even in the playoff no one expected Fleck to win. Deep down, Fleck probably didn't either. Ben Hogan was his hero.

It was David and Goliath stuff. Hogan had the best swing in golf. Fleck had never had so much as a formal lesson in his entire life. Hogan was already a legend in the game. Fleck was a club pro who was known as a poor putter. Yet the Iowa professional won the playoff. He shot 69 to Hogan's 72 to earn one of the biggest titles in golf, and record one of the greatest upsets in the game's history.

Although Fleck won the 1960 Phoenix Open, he never again came close to attaining the height he reached in 1955.

## FACT FILE

**BORN** 1921, Bettendorf, Iowa, USA

**CAREER HIGHLIGHTS**
1955 US Open
1960 Phoenix Open

# Ray Floyd

THEY DON'T COME MUCH TOUGHER THAN RAY FLOYD. THE NORTH CAROLINA PROFESSIONAL HAS WON EVERY TOP HONOR IN GOLF WITH THE EXCEPTION OF THE BRITISH OPEN CHAMPIONSHIP.

## Fact File

**BORN** 1942, Fort Bragg, North Carolina, USA

**CAREER HIGHLIGHTS**
1969 USPGA Championship
1976 Masters
1982 USPGA Championship
1986 US Open
1992 Senior Tour Championship

**INTERNATIONAL HONORS**
Ryder Cup: 1969, 1975, 1977, 1981, 1983, 1985, 1989 (captain), 1991, 1993
Alfred Dunhill Cup: 1985, 1986

Ray Floyd is one of an elite bunch of players to have won three of the game's four majors. Others in the club include Tom Watson, Lee Trevino, Arnold Palmer, Sam Snead, and Byron Nelson. Pretty classy company.

The only major tournament missing from his *cv* is the British Open. The closest Floyd came in that major was in 1978 at St Andrews, when he finished in a four-way tie behind Jack Nicklaus. He also finished third in 1981 and fourth in 1976, but he never managed to win the oldest trophy in golf.

Pity, for Floyd deserved to win all four majors. During his prime, there was no better player in the heat of a big tournament than the North Carolina native. That was evident when at the age of 51 years and 20 days, Floyd was selected as a wild-card pick by American Ryder Cup captain Tom Watson. Floyd became the oldest player to play in the biennial competition. He didn't let Watson down either. Despite his age, Floyd played four times in the match, winning three times and losing just once. On the last day he beat Jose Maria Olazabal two up to contribute to the American victory.

Ray Floyd turned professional in 1961 and joined the US Tour in 1963. In his early days he was known to indulge in the extra-curricular activities that went with being a professional golfer. He was burning the candle at both ends when he met his future wife, Maria, who basically told him it was time to take the game seriously. Floyd listened.

Floyd had won the 1969 USPGA Championship at the NCR Country Club in Dayton, Ohio, to record his first major. When he met Maria he was in the middle of a six-year winless streak. That changed soon after he got married in 1974.

When Floyd won the Masters in 1976, he led the field from wire to wire. Not only that, he tied Jack Nicklaus's 72-hole record of 271. The two men shared the record until Tiger Woods shot 270 in 1997.

In 1982 Floyd won his third major championship when he added a second USPGA Championship, winning the title by three strokes over Lanny Wadkins at the tough Southern Hills course in Tulsa, Oklahoma. For a few years it seemed that would be Floyd's last major championship, but he had one more left in him.

The tournament Floyd most wanted to win as his regular Tour career wound down was the US Open. He had finished in the top ten twice, but the championship seemed certain to elude him as Floyd got older. Then in 1986, at the age of 43, he won the title at Shinnecock Hills, Long Island. Though he was calm, cool and collected while winning the tournament, afterward Floyd broke down in tears. The ice man had finally cracked.

Floyd is now a successful player on the US Senior Tour, with many victories on that circuit.

# Doug Ford

DOUG FORD WON MANY TOURNAMENTS DURING THE 1950S AND 1960S, INCLUDING TWO MAJOR CHAMPIONSHIPS. FORD WON THE 1955 USPGA CHAMPIONSHIP AND THEN TRIUMPHED IN THE 1957 MASTERS WITH A SUPERB 66 IN THE FINAL ROUND.

Doug Ford doesn't go down as one of the biggest legends of the game. He isn't up there with the Sneads, Hogans, Palmers, Nicklauses, and others, but he's right underneath them. What's more, he toppled at least a couple of them in his day.

Ford was one of the best American professionals in the 1950s. At the end of each season you would always find his name close to the top of the US money list, usually in the top 20, but sometimes in the top ten.

Ford came to prominence when he won the 1955 USPGA Championship at Lake Worth, Florida, defeating Cary Middlecoff four and three in the 36-hole final. It wasn't surprising that Ford won the USPGA Championship when it was contested at match play, for he was a good head-to-head player. During his time he beat a few good names in match-play situations. For example, in 1952 he defeated Sam Snead in a playoff for the Jacksonville Open. He also downed Arnold Palmer in a playoff for the 1961 "500" Festival Open Invitational.

It is no surprise then that Ford has a good record in the Ryder Cup. The Connecticut professional played in the biennial competition four times and came away with a respectable record of four wins, four losses, and one half point. He twice got the upper hand on Harry Weetman in singles play.

Ford won many tournaments, including the Los Angeles Open, the Canadian Open, which he won twice, the Greater Greensboro Open, and the Western Open. The last tournament was a big event during Ford's day, considered by many to rank with the US Open and the Masters. Ford won the 1957 tournament at Plum Hollow in Detroit, Michigan. But 1957 also saw him record the biggest win of his career.

At the Masters that spring, Ford was three strokes behind leader Sam Snead going into the final round and needed to play well to have any chance of putting pressure on the tournament favorite. He did exactly that. Ford shot a final round 66 to win the tournament by three strokes. He set a record for the lowest final round in the tournament's history. It stood for another 11 years until Bert Yancey shot 65 in 1968.

The following year Ford finished tied at second, along with Fred Hawkins and behind Arnold Palmer. Ford's four round total of 285 was one stroke short of Palmer's winning score.

Ford was known as a player who liked to play the game quickly. He would arrive at his ball, assess the situation and play his shot without too much deliberation. He was also one of the best putters during his day, which explains why he was so successful at Augusta National, where only the best putters win the green jacket.

## Fact File

**BORN** 1922. New Haven, Connecticut, USA

**CAREER HIGHLIGHTS**
1955 USPGA Championship
1957 Masters
1957 Los Angeles Open
1959 Canadian Open
1963 Canadian Open

**INTERNATIONAL HONORS**
Ryder Cup: 1955, 1957, 1959, 1961

# David Frost

South African David Frost has one of the best swings in the modern game. It's so good that top coach David Leadbetter used it as the model for his first instructional book.

## Fact File

**BORN** 1959, Cape Town, South Africa

**CAREER HIGHLIGHTS**
1989 Million Dollar Challenge
1989 NEC World Series of Golf
1990 Million Dollar Challenge
1992 Million Dollar Challenge
1997 MasterCard Colonial

**INTERNATIONAL HONORS**
Alfred Dunhill Cup: 1991, 1992, 1993, 1994, 1995, 1997
Presidents Cup: 1994, 1996

Wine is one of David Frost's passions, so much so that the South African has his own vineyards in his homeland. He has a 300-acre estate with 100 acres of vines. If the wine is anything like Frost's golf swing, then it will be vintage stuff.

Frost is known for having one of the best golf swings in the game. It's so good that when the renowned golf instructor David Leadbetter released his first instructional book, he based the illustrations on Frost's swing. Leadbetter and Frost played together as juniors, and later on Leadbetter became Frost's coach, helping him build a swing that would serve him well in the professional ranks.

The swing stood the test of time, for Frost won tournaments throughout his career. He turned professional in 1981, and within three years he had won the Air France Cannes Open on the European Tour. He joined the US Tour in 1985, and won his first tournament when he triumphed at the 1988 Southern Open, defeating Bob Tway in a playoff for the title. He also won again that season, adding the Northern Telecom Tucson Open to his list of honors.

His first really big pay-day, however, came in 1989 when Frost became an instant millionaire by winning the Million Dollar Challenge at Sun City in his native South Africa, the richest tournament in golf. He quickly doubled his earnings in the tournament, returning the next year to successfully defend his title. He also won in 1992.

Frost is just one of a number of players to deny Greg Norman a tournament with a miraculous shot. Frost won the 1990 USF&G Classic by holing out from a bunker on the 72nd hole to win the title from Norman by one stroke.

The South African's first really big win on the US Tour occurred in the 1989 NEC World Series of Golf. He defeated Ben Crenshaw at the second extra hole in a playoff for the title, and also gained a ten-year exemption on the US Tour.

In 1993 Frost won tournaments in successive weeks when he followed a win in the Canadian Open with victory in the Hardee's Golf Classic. In doing so he became the first player since Johnny Miller in 1975 to successfully defend one title the week after winning a tournament.

Besides $3 million in first prizes in his homeland, Frost has also won championships around the world. He is a two-time winner of the Hong Kong Open on the Asian Tour, recording back-to-back victories in 1993 and 1994.

# Ed Furgol

ED FURGOL IS LIVING PROOF THAT THE LEFT ARM DOESN'T HAVE TO BE STRAIGHT IN THE BACKSWING. THE NEW YORK PROFESSIONAL WON THE 1954 US OPEN, EVEN THOUGH HE HAD A DEFORMED LEFT ARM.

One of the myths of golf is that the left arm has to be kept rigidly straight during the swing. Had that been the case then Ed Furgol would never have played the game.

Furgol injured his left arm in a playground accident when he was a small child. The bones weren't set properly and his arm became permanently damaged. The muscles in the arm atrophied and throughout the rest of his life his arm was bent at an angle of 70 degrees. Not the best possible start for someone intent on playing golf, yet Furgol overcame the handicap to go on to win one of the biggest tournaments in the game. Sheer determination and hard work made Furgol a true champion.

The New Yorker developed a swing in which all the left hand did was guide the club to the top of the swing. His backswing was short as a result of his handicap, but he compensated by letting his body and right arm supply the power in his swing. He was powerful enough to compete as an amateur for a number of years before turning professional. During his days as an unpaid player he won the North and South Amateur championship, one of the most prestigious events in the North American amateur game. Furgol turned professional shortly afterward.

The 1954 season was Furgol's biggest as a professional. He won the Phoenix Open after defeating Cary Middlecoff in a playoff for the title. He also put his name in the history books when he won the US Open that year.

Baltusrol in Springfield, New Jersey, was the venue for the 1954 US Open. These were the days of Ben Hogan's dominance in the event, and the great man entered the championship in 1954 as defending champion. He was the heavy favorite, along with other stars such as Sam Snead, Cary Middlecoff, Jack Burke Jr, and a host of others. Furgol was just another player making up the field. Besides, a player with such a handicap wasn't expected to win America's premier golf tournament. But no one bothered to tell Furgol that.

After 71 holes, Furgol came to the last tee with the outright championship lead, but was forced to wait nearly 20 minutes to allow players ahead of him to finish the hole. When he finally played his tee shot, he hooked it into the rough. All he could do was play out to an adjoining fairway but he made a great par to finish the tournament with a four-round total of 284. It was goodenough for a one-stroke victory over Gene Littler, and one of the most remarkable wins in golf history.

## Fact File

**BORN** 1919, New York Mills, New York, USA

**DIED** 1997

**CAREER HIGHLIGHTS**
1945 North and South Amateur
1954 Phoenix Open
1954 US Open

**INTERNATIONAL HONORS**
Ryder Cup: 1957

# Unknown Shocks the World of Golf

The Country Club at Brookline, in Massachusetts, venue for the 1999 Ryder Cup, saw one of the biggest upsets in golf history. An unknown 20-year-old amateur took on two giants of the professional game and beat them comfortably, to send shock waves around the world of golf.

Harry Vardon had won five British Open titles by 1913. Along with James Braid and J. H. Taylor, he was a member of the Great Triumvirate, the three best golfers in the world at the time. When he competed in the 1913 US Open at Brookline, he entered the tournament as one of the heavy favorites. So too did fellow countryman Ted Ray, a huge man who hit the ball a long way, and had proved himself by winning the previous year's British Open at Muirfield.

After two rounds the English pair were first and second respectively, with Vardon leading Ray by two shots, and by four from a young Walter Hagen and an unknown amateur by the name of Francis Ouimet. After three rounds the English pair were tied with Ouimet on 225. No one gave Ouimet much of a chance. Conditions on the final day were poor, and the course was playing long, due to heavy rain. Both Vardon and Ray struggled in with 79s to share the lead on 304. Playing behind them, Ouimet was struggling. He had gone to the turn in 43 and needed to play exceptionally well over the final nine just to finish near the leaders. Two birdies over the closing six holes meant he finished tied for the lead.

Ouimet actually lived across the street from the course. He was a part-time caddie who occasionally got to play the course that lay across the road from his home. His only previous claim to fame had been winning the Massachusetts State Championship and reaching the semi-finals of the US Amateur, where he lost to eventual winner Jerome Travers. He had only entered the US Open because the USGA wanted to increase the size of the field, and so that he could get a closer look at Vardon. Little did he know how close he would get.

No one gave the amateur a chance in the playoff against two such powerful golfers as Vardon and Ray, two of the best players in the world at the time. No amateur had ever won the United States Open before. Ouimet changed all that. The local boy not only won the playoff, he virtually cruised to victory. He shot a one over par-72 to beat Vardon by five strokes, and Ray by six.

The effect on American golf was phenomenal. It took golf from the back to the front pages of nearly every newspaper in the country. It was headline stuff, a complete fairy tale, a David versus Goliath story. Although there were emerging golfers in the United States who would soon conquer the world—Hagen, Jones, Sarazen—Ouimet's win has often been seen as the catalyst that made the nation a golfing superpower.

FAR RIGHT: FRANCIS OUIMET LINES UP HIS PUTT TO THE FINAL HOLE IN HIS HISTORIC PLAYOFF FOR THE 1913 US OPEN, AS HARRY VARDON (CENTER) AND TED RAY (RIGHT) LOOK ON.

FRANCIS OUIMET

TED RAY

HARRY VARDON

# Jim Furyk

JIM FURYK IS ANOTHER PROFESSIONAL WHO HAS REACHED GREAT HEIGHTS IN THE GAME WITH A SWING THAT IS ANYTHING BUT ORTHODOX.

## Fact File

**BORN** 1970, Westchester, Pennsylvannia, USA

**CAREER HIGHLIGHTS**
1993 NIKE Mississippi Gulf Coast Classic
1995 Las Vegas Invitational
1996 United Airlines Hawaiian Open
1997 Argentine Open
1998 Las Vegas Invitational

**INTERNATIONAL HONORS**
Ryder Cup: 1997

You couldn't teach someone to swing a golf club the way Jim Furyk does. The 6-foot, 2-inch professional has one of the least orthodox swings not only on the US Tour, but in the world of professional golf. He takes the club back outside the line to the target and loops it back inside on the way down. It may look ugly, but it works.

Furyk's swing works for one main reason: he's never tried to change it. Many players get to the professional ranks with a golf swing that is less than orthodox. Suddenly they find themselves among players with text-book swings and feel they have to change to be able to reach the top level. Of course, they end up going backwards and some even fail as a result, or after years of trying to change they revert to their original swing.

Furyk has been smart enough to stay with the swing that got him into the professional ranks in the first place. He's only ever had one teacher, his father Mike, who recognized early on that there was no point fixing what wasn't broken.

After graduating from the University of Arizona, where he was a two-time All-American, Furyk turned professional in 1992. In 1993 he played the NIKE Tour and won the Mississippi Gulf Coast Classic.

Unfortunately, he didn't play well enough for the remainder of the season to get his US Tour card. He got his card after tying for 37th spot out of the 40 qualifiers at the 1993 US Tour Qualifying School. In 1994 he established himself by finishing inside the top 80 on the Tour, then won his first tournament in 1995 when he won the Las Vegas Invitational, an event he also won in 1998.

Although Furyk didn't win in 1997, he did play in his first Ryder Cup at Valderrama, Spain. There he proved he was one of the best players in the world.

It initially seemed that Furyk was going to come away from Spain without winning a single point. On the first two days he played two matches and lost them both. He then went head to head with European star Nick Faldo in the singles. After the disappointment of the previous two days, he would have been forgiven for crumbling under the pressure. He didn't. Although Faldo played well over the 18 holes, Furyk played better. Every time it seemed Faldo would win a hole with a great shot, Furyk either matched the shot or rescued the hole by chipping in from off the green.

Even though the Americans lost the match, by beating Europe's top golfer Furyk proved that he was a world-class player.

# BERNARD GALLACHER

IT TOOK SCOTLAND'S BERNARD GALLACHER 11 ATTEMPTS BEFORE HE FINALLY FOUND SUCCESS IN THE RYDER CUP. GALLACHER CAPTAINED THE EUROPEAN TEAM THAT LIFTED THE CUP IN 1995 AT OAK HILL, NEW YORK.

No one rejoiced more than Scotland's Bernard Gallacher when Europe won the 1995 Ryder Cup at Oak Hill Country Club, in Rochester, New York. After years of failure, Gallacher had finally taken part on a winning side.

Gallacher was a Ryder Cup stalwart for first Great Britain & Ireland and then Europe between 1969 and 1983. Yet he never won the coveted trophy as a player. The closest he got was when he made his debut in the tied 1969 match at Royal Birkdale. The Scotsman took a valuable singles point that year, beating Lee Trevino by a score of four and three in the afternoon singles on day three.

Gallacher was something of a terrier in his day. He wasn't a great player from the tee, but he had one of the best short games in European golf. He used to stay snapping at the heels of an opponent until he finally got the better of him. He did that to Jack Nicklaus when he defeated him in singles play in the 1977 Ryder Cup at Royal Lytham & St Annes. He also deployed a strange tactic to help him overcome the game's greatest player.

Gallacher was aware of just how intimidating a player Nicklaus was, and he didn't want to feel as if he was inferior to the American. So he decided before the match that he was going to avoid eye contact with Nicklaus. When the two shook hands on the first tee, Gallacher avoided Jack's eyes, focusing instead on his opponent's chest. So it went throughout the round. Gallacher never looked Nicklaus in the eye. It worked. The Scotsman won the match one up. That's when he finally looked Nicklaus in the eye. When the two shook hands on the 18th, Gallacher looked at Nicklaus long and hard.

In 1991, the Scotsman took over the Ryder Cup captaincy from Tony Jacklin, under whom he had served as a vice-captain. Gallacher lost a heartbreaker at Kiawah Island that year, when Bernhard Langer missed an eight-foot birdie putt on the final green after a brave fight back against Hale Irwin. Gallacher also lost the 1993 match at The Belfry when his side lost 15—13 to the United States.

Gallacher finally got his hands on Sam Ryder's Cup when his underdog side won at Oak Hill Country Club in Rochester, New York. Two points down going into the singles, Gallacher's team rallied to win on the final day. No one jumped higher than Gallacher when Ireland's Philip Walton won his match with Jay Haas on the final green to clinch the victory.

After years of outstanding service to European golf that saw him win 14 tournaments, and serve so valiantly in Ryder Cup action, Gallacher finally got his just rewards. He retired immediately afterwards and is now playing on the European Seniors Tour.

## FACT FILE

**BORN** 1949, Bathgate, Scotland

**CAREER HIGHLIGHTS**
1969 Schweppes PGA Championship
1974 Carrolls International
1974 Dunlop Masters
1975 Dunlop Masters
1979 French Open

**INTERNATIONAL HONORS**
Ryder Cup: 1969, 1971, 1973, 1975, 1977, 1979, 1981, 1983, 1991 (captain), 1993 (captain), 1995 (captain)
World Cup: 1969, 1971, 1974, 1982, 1983

# SERGIO GARCIA

THE LEGEND IN WAITING. GOLF EXPERTS BELIEVE SPAIN'S SERGIO GARCIA WILL WIN MAJOR CHAMPIONSHIPS THROUGHOUT HIS CAREER.

## FACT FILE

**BORN** 1980, Castellon, Spain

**CAREER HIGHLIGHTS**
1995 European Amateur
1997 British Boys' Amateur
1997 French Amateur
1997 Spanish Amateur
1998 British Amateur

His nickname is "El Nino," and it's a name that suits Spain's Sergio Garcia, for the youngster is one of the best young players ever to storm through the amateur game.

Garcia has been compared to Seve Ballesteros and Jose Maria Olazabal as one of Spain's future world-class players. He certainly has the credentials and the background to fulfill those expectations.

Garcia first picked up a golf club at the age of three. He was given good advice from the start: his father is the professional at the Mediterraneo Club de Campo just to the north of the family home town of Castellon, Spain. By the time he was 12, Garcia Jr was the club champion. At age 13 he was playing off scratch.

The precocious youngster played in the European Tour's Mediterranean Open as a 14-year-old and made the cut. At 17 he won his first professional tournament as an amateur when he triumphed in the Catalonian Open with three successive 64s.

Given his pedigree, it's no surprise that Garcia has won over 70 tournaments as an amateur. After winning such prestigious tournaments as the French and Spanish Amateurs, and the European Amateur, which he won at 15 to become the youngest ever winner in the event's history, Garcia added the biggest tournament in amateur golf. The Spanish sensation won the British Amateur at Muirfield to cap off his career in the unpaid ranks.

Garcia groomed himself for professional golf by entering 13 professional tournaments in 1998. He didn't look out of place among the pros. Although he didn't win, he only missed one cut. He twice set a NIKE Tour record for the lowest 72-hole score by an amateur, shooting 280 (eight under par) in the NIKE Monterrey Open, and then bettering the record by returning a 272 (nine under par) in the NIKE Greensboro tournament. He also set the low 72-hole record by an amateur on the European Tour when he shot 277 (11 under par) in the 1998 Spanish Open.

Needless to say, as an amateur Garcia was never intimidated by playing with professionals, no matter their stature in the game. That was evident when he played a practice round with Tom Lehman in the 1998 Standard Life Loch Lomond tournament. Lehman was the defending champion and had won the British Open in 1996, yet it didn't stop Garcia from issuing a challenge to the powerful American golfer. "What are we playing for?" Garcia asked Lehman on the first tee.

Precocious? You can say that again!

# Jane Geddes

NEW YORKER JANE GEDDES TOOK ONLY THREE YEARS AFTER TURNING PROFESSIONAL TO WIN HER FIRST MAJOR CHAMPIONSHIP, THE 1986 US WOMEN'S OPEN. A YEAR LATER SHE ADDED ANOTHER WITH VICTORY IN THE LPGA CHAMPIONSHIP.

Jane Geddes first came to prominence in women's golf when she returned a 64 in the 1985 Du Maurier Classic in Montreal, Canada. It was the lowest round of Geddes's career, and it enabled her to post a second place finish behind eventual winner Pat Bradley.

Insiders knew Geddes was a player for the future. She had starred on the Florida State Women's golf team, helping the university to the 1981 AIAW national championship. Geddes turned professional after leaving university, and joined the LPGA Tour in 1983.

A year after just missing out on her first major championship in Canada, the 5-foot, 5-inch Geddes triumphed in another of the four majors women play: she won the 1986 US Women's Open at the NCR Country Club in Dayton, Ohio. The victory was her first on the LPGA Tour, making her one of 13 players to claim the US Women's Open as her first win as a professional. Her fine play continued the following week when she won the Boston Five Classic, joining Louise Suggs as the only players in the history of the LPGA to win an event the week after victory in the US Women's Open. (Korea's Se Ri Pak joined this pair when she accomplished the feat in 1998.)

Geddes's fine play continued the following season when she won five times. She successfully defended her Boston Five Classic, won the Jamie Farr Toledo Classic, and triumphed in two sudden death playoffs. She was victorious in the Women's Kemper Open when she defeated Cathy Gerring in extra holes, and did the same to Robin Walton to win the GNA/Glendale Federal Classic. However, her biggest win that year came in the Mazda LPGA Championship, the second major championship of her career.

Her fine play in 1987 allowed Geddes to finish third on the LPGA Tour money list with nearly $400,000.

It didn't take Geddes long to reach the $1 million mark in her career. Although she went winless in 1988 and 1989, Geddes crossed into the seven-figure bracket courtesy of 12 top-ten finishes in 1989. She passed $2 million in 1994, and the $3 million mark in 1997 when she finished fourth in the HEALTHSOUTH Inaugural. That year also saw the New York State native post her best-ever career stroke average of 71.34, although she didn't win a tournament that season.

Geddes also won the Ladies' British Open. She was victorious in the 1989 tournament at Ferndown, Dorset, England, setting a record of 274 over 72 holes.

## Fact File

**BORN** 1960, Huntingdon, New York, USA

**CAREER HIGHLIGHTS**
1986 US Women's Open
1987 LPGA Championship
1987 Women's Kemper Open
1989 Ladies' British Open
1994 Chicago Challenge

**INTERNATIONAL HONORS**
Solheim Cup: 1996

# Al Geiberger

AL GEIBERGER MADE HISTORY IN 1977 WHEN HE BECAME THE FIRST PLAYER IN US TOUR HISTORY TO BREAK 60, SHOOTING A 59 IN THE SECOND ROUND OF THE DANNY THOMAS MEMPHIS CLASSIC.

## Fact File

**BORN** 1937, Red Bluff, California, USA

**CAREER HIGHLIGHTS**
1966 USPGA Championship
1976 Western Open
1977 Danny Thomas Memphis Classic
1977 First player to shoot 59 on US Tour
1993 Infiniti Senior Tournament of Champions

**INTERNATIONAL HONORS**
Ryder Cup: 1967, 1975

June 10, 1977, will forever remain etched in Al Geiberger's mind: that was the day he set a record that was to define his career, that was to make him one of golf's immortals.

Playing in the second round of the Danny Thomas Memphis Classic at the Colonial Country Club, Geiberger became the first man to break 60 in a professional tournament. Colonial is not considered one of the easiest courses on the US Tour, but Geiberger took it to pieces.

Heavy rain had made the greens very receptive, and Geiberger was helped because the heavy rain meant the "lift, clean and place" rule was being used. Still, it was the same for everyone, and Geiberger was the only player to break 60 that day.

Rattling in a 40-foot putt for birdie on the opening hole, the California native was off and running. Geiberger carded 10 more birdies and one eagle to score the 59. Included in his round was a 30-yard pitching wedge shot which he holed for an eagle. He came to the last green needing to hole a 10-foot putt for birdie to make history. Known as one of the best putters in the game, Geiberger had no trouble making the putt.

The 6-foot, 3-inch professional won 11 times on the regular US Tour. One of those wins came in the 1966 USPGA Championship, when he won the title by four strokes at Firestone Country Club in Akron, Ohio, one of the toughest courses on the US Tour. Another victory came in the 1976 Western Open, one of the most prestigious events on the US Tour. However, those wins paled in comparison to what Geiberger accomplished in Memphis, Tennessee. It earned him the nickname "Mr 59," and he even had cards made up with that written on them.

Ten years later, a commemorative tournament was held with $1 million on offer to anyone who could shoot the magical score. No one came close. Geiberger himself shot 69.

The record stood for 14 years until Chip Beck shot 59 at Sunrise Golf Club, Las Vegas. David Duval also equaled the score in January 1999.

Geiberger played in two Ryder Cups and holds an excellent record in the competition. He played nine matches and lost only once, with five wins and three halves.

Geiberger is now a respected figure on the US Senior Tour, where he has won many tournaments. In 1996 he was voted the Comeback Player of the Year by his peers, after he had four top-10 finishes and won his first tournament in three years, the Greater Naples IntelliNet Challenge, in three years.

# Bob Goalby

GOALBY'S BIGGEST CAREER WIN CAME IN THE 1968 MASTERS, BUT THE VICTORY WAS TAINTED BECAUSE IT CAME AFTER A SCORE CARD ERROR BY ARGENTINA'S ROBERTO DE VICENZO.

Bob Goalby was involved in one of the saddest incidents in Masters history. Goalby won the 1968 Masters to record the biggest win of his professional career, but the victory was unfortunately tainted by a rules error.

Roberto de Vicenzo played the final round of the 1968 Masters in 65 shots, or so he thought. The Argentinian made a birdie three on the 17th hole after he knocked a pitching wedge approach shot to three feet and holed the putt. However, Tommy Aaron, his playing partner and scorecard marker, mistakenly wrote a four on de Vicenzo's card. The 45-year-old de Vicenzo missed the error and signed the card after the round. Under the rules of golf, the four had to stand, changing the Argentine's score from a 65 to a 66.

The 65 would have put de Vicenzo into a tie with Bob Goalby and a playoff should have taken place. De Vicenzo's error meant Goalby was declared the winner of the green jacket.

It was an unfortunate incident in two ways. One, it denied de Vicenzo the chance to win his only Masters title. Two, it took the sheen off what was a fine performance by Goalby to tie de Vicenzo.

What has usually been overlooked in this affair is that Goalby played superb golf on the final day, golf good enough to have won him the title outright. The Illinois native shot a final round 66 to come from two strokes behind Gary Player after three rounds to tie for the lead. Included in that 66 was a brilliant eagle at the 15th hole, where Goalby hit a 3-iron to 10 feet and made the putt to tie de Vicenzo.

Goalby sympathized with de Vicenzo at the presentation ceremony, and was gracious enough to say he would have preferred to win the title in a playoff. De Vicenzo was equally magnanimous, blaming the error on himself and praising the quality of Goalby's golf.

Although the win surprised many in the game, it shouldn't have. Goalby was a quality player in his day. A natural sportsman who played quarterback for the University of Illinois football team, the six-footer won 11 times on the US Tour. He once scored eight straight birdies in the final round of the 1961 St Petersburg Open to win the tournament. It's a record he set and now shares with Fuzzy Zoeller and Dewey Arnette.

Goalby played in one Ryder Cup, making his only appearance in 1963 at East Lake Country Club in Atlanta, Georgia. Of the five matches he played, Goalby won three, lost one, and halved the other.

He was one of the founders of the US Senior Tour.

## Fact File

**BORN** 1929, Belleville, Illinois, USA

**CAREER HIGHLIGHTS**
1958 Greater Greensboro Open
1961 Los Angeles Open
1968 Masters
1970 Heritage Classic
1971 Bahamas National Open Championship

**INTERNATIONAL HONORS**
Ryder Cup: 1963

# Johnny Goodman

JOHNNY GOODMAN (LEFT), PICTURED HERE WITH BOBBY JONES, WAS THE LAST AMATEUR TO WIN THE US OPEN, IN 1933. DESPITE TURNING PRO LATER, HE NEVER ENJOYED THE SAME SUCCESS AS AN AMATEUR.

## Fact File

**BORN** 1908, Omaha, Nebraska, USA

**DIED** 1970

**CAREER HIGHLIGHTS**
1927 Trans-Mississippi Amateur
1931 Trans-Mississippi Amateur
1933 US Open
1935 Trans-Mississippi Amateur
1937 US Amateur

**INTERNATIONAL HONORS**
Walker Cup: 1934, 1936, 1938

The story of Johnny Goodman is a classic rags to riches tale of a boy who grew up with nothing to become one of the best golfers the amateur game has ever seen.

Born in Omaha, Nebraska, Goodman was the fifth of 10 children and was an orphan when he was still at school. Out of necessity, he had to leave school to earn money to feed his younger brothers. He finished his education by attending night school.

Like many players of that era, Goodman's first experience of golf came as a caddie. He developed a swing that was short and compact, and it was good enough to turn him into a fine amateur player.

He first came to prominence when he won the 1927 Trans-Mississippi Amateur. In 1929 he traveled to Pebble Beach, California, to contest the US Amateur. His mode of transportation was somewhat different from the rest of the field. Goodman rode a cattle car to the tournament on a cattleman's pass given to him by a friend. The journey couldn't have been too arduous, for Goodman upset the form book when he put out Bobby Jones, the tournament favorite, in the first round.

Goodman didn't win the US Amateur that year. He had to wait eight more years before winning that tournament. But he would triumph in the US Open before taking America's premier amateur award, just as Bobby Jones, Francis Ouimet, and Chick Evans had done before him.

The 1933 US Open at North Shore Country Club in Glenview, Illinois, was the scene of Goodman's famous victory. The Nebraska native won the tournament courtesy of a second round 66. That gave him a lead he never surrendered, although he did make things hard for himself. Goodman took a six-shot lead over Ralph Guldahl into the final round and hung on to win by a stroke. His victory in the championship was the last by an amateur.

Goodman played in three Walker Cups between 1934 and 1938, although many felt he should have been in the US team in 1932. During his three matches, Goodman compiled a record of four wins and two losses from the six games he took part in.

Shortly before World War II, Goodman turned professional. However, he never enjoyed the success as a paid player that he did playing just for pride.

# WAYNE GRADY

AUSTRALIAN WAYNE GRADY GREW UP COMPETING AGAINST PLAYERS LIKE IAN BAKER-FINCH AND GREG NORMAN. LIKE THOSE TWO HE FOUND SUCCESS IN THE MAJORS, WINNING THE 1990 USPGA CHAMPIONSHIP.

As a youngster, Wayne Grady grew up dreaming about one day becoming a pilot in the Australian Air Force. Instead, golf got a grip on him and he settled for a career on the sod instead of one in the sky.

Grady actually had two attempts at turning professional. The Brisbane native turned pro at the age of 16, but later regained his amateur status before turning professional for good at the age of 21.

The 5-foot, 9-inch professional grew up competing against such talented Australians as Ian Baker-Finch and Greg Norman, among others. Indeed, Grady was coached for several years by Charley Earp, who also coached Norman. Grady turned professional in 1978 and that same year he won the Westlakes Classic in Australia to justify his change of mind about playing professional golf.

Like many Australians, Norman included, Grady played the European Tour for a number of years before trying his hand in America. He won the 1984 German Open on the European circuit before joining the US Tour.

In 1989 Grady won the Manufacturers Hanover Westchester Classic, to record his maiden victory in America. He defeated Ronnie Black in a playoff to take the title. That proved he had the game to win against the best. However, he nearly took the biggest trophy in golf the same year.

The Australian had never really featured in a major championship until he came to Royal Troon in July 1989 to play in the British Open. After three rounds, Grady held a one-stroke lead over the field. Last out on the final day, he played the final round with Tom Watson, who was chasing his sixth British Open to tie Harry Vardon for most wins in the tournament. Grady returned a final round 71 but found himself in a playoff with Mark Calcavecchia and old sparring partner, Greg Norman.

Royal Troon saw the Royal & Ancient Golf Club of St Andrews adopt a four-hole playoff system for the first time to determine the winner. Sadly for Australia, Grady and Norman couldn't take the title. Calcavecchia won his first major championship.

Grady made up for his near miss the following year when he won the 1990 USPGA Championship at Shoal Creek. This time he took a three-stroke lead into the final round over Fred Couples. With just six holes left, Couples was one shot ahead, but bogeys at the next four holes (while Grady was making pars) cost Couples the title. Grady won his first major by three strokes and was one of only three players to break par over the four days. Couples and third-place finisher Gil Morgan were the others.

## FACT FILE

**BORN** 1957, Brisbane, Australia

**CAREER HIGHLIGHTS**
1984 German Open
1988 Australian PGA Championship
1989 Manufacturers Hanover Westchester Classic
1990 USPGA Championship
1991 Australian PGA Championship

**INTERNATIONAL HONORS**
World Cup: 1978, 1983, 1989
Alfred Dunhill Cup: 1989, 1990, 1991
Presidents Cup: 1998 (vice-captain)

# David Graham

AUSTRALIAN DAVID GRAHAM PRODUCED ONE OF THE GREATEST FINAL ROUNDS EVER PLAYED IN THE US OPEN. GRAHAM HIT ALL 18 GREENS IN REGULATION EN ROUTE TO WINNING THE 1981 US OPEN AT MERION.

## Fact File

**BORN** 1946, Windsor, Australia

**CAREER HIGHLIGHTS**
1972 Cleveland Open
1976 American Golf Classic
1979 USPGA Championship
1980 Memorial Tournament
1981 US Open

**INTERNATIONAL HONORS**
World Cup: 1970
Alfred Dunhill Cup: 1985, 1986, 1988
Presidents Cup: 1994 (captain)

David Graham produced one of the finest rounds ever played in the US Open, when he won the title in 1981 at Merion Golf Club. Graham played near flawless golf in the final round to lift his second major championship.

The US Open is famous for presenting the most penal conditions of any major championship. Deep rough off the fairway and around the greens is the norm. Rock hard putting surfaces is another characteristic, making it hard for the professionals to keep their balls on the greens. It was all the harder that year because Merion is a course with very small putting surfaces. The key to playing it well is to approach the greens from the right angles. In the final round of the 1981 US Open, Graham did that to perfection.

The Australian entered the last day three strokes behind George Burns. Graham then shot a three under par 67, hitting all 18 greens in regulation to win the title by one stroke from Burns and Bill Rogers. Afterwards Rogers had this to say about Graham's feat: "David hit 18 greens in regulation and in the last round of the US Open, that is unbelievable." Graham became the first Australian to win America's national championship.

The 5-foot, 10-inch professional earned eight victories in his regular US Tour career. Besides the US Open, Graham also won the 1979 USPGA Championship at Oakland Hills Country Club, Detroit, Michigan. On that occasion, he again played near flawless golf on the last day to get into contention. Graham shot a final round 65 despite taking a double bogey six on the 18th hole. That slip put him into a tie with Ben Crenshaw. The Australian won the title at the third extra hole.

Graham nearly added a third major championship to his trophy cabinet when the British Open was held at Royal St George's in Sandwich, England, in 1985. Graham had a two-stroke lead after 14 holes of the final round. However, while he made bogeys over the closing holes, Scotland's Sandy Lyle made birdies to win the championship.

Now a successful senior player in America, Graham has also won many tournaments around the world. In 1970 he teamed up with Bruce Devlin to win the World Cup of Golf. He has also won such diverse titles as the Thailand Open (1970), the French Open (1970), Caracas Open (1971), Mexico Cup (1978), New Zealand Open (1979), and the Brazilian Classic (1980). Graham also won the World Match Play Championship in 1976.

# Lou Graham

TENNESSEE PROFESSIONAL LOU GRAHAM WON HALF HIS US TOUR VICTORIES IN PLAYOFFS, INCLUDING THE 1975 US OPEN, THE BIGGEST WIN OF HIS CAREER.

Lou Graham was a bit of a playoff specialist in his prime. Half of his US Tour victories came in extra holes, including the biggest win of his career.

In the 1975 US Open at Medinah Country Club, Chicago, Illinois, Graham came from 11 strokes behind after 36 holes to tie for the championship lead with John Mahaffey. Graham triumphed in the 18-hole playoff the following day, shooting 71 to his opponent's 73. It was only Graham's third US Tour win. His first had come in 1967 when he won the Minnesota Golf Classic. His second occurred in 1972 when he defeated Hale Irwin, David Graham, and Larry Ziegler in a playoff to win the Ligget and Myers Open.

The Tennessee native also came close in the United State's national championship in 1977, when he finished runner-up to Hubert Green at Southern Hills. However, his best season was to come two years later.

Graham won three times in 1979, triumphing in the IVB-Philadelphia Golf Classic, the American Optical Classic and the San Antonio Texas Open. The Philadelphia title was taken when Graham overcame Bobby Wadkins in a playoff. What was particularly remarkable about Graham's three victories was that they happened within a span of just eight weeks.

Graham took up golf as a 10-year-old and later received a scholarship to attend Memphis State University. After three years of university, Graham enrolled in the army and served on the President's Honor Guard. He turned professional in 1964 and joined the US Tour the same year.

The six-footer played on three Ryder Cup teams between 1973 and 1977 where his liking for head-to-head confrontations was put to good use in the biennial competition. In nine matches played he won five, lost three and halved just once. In the 1975 match, held at Laurel Valley in Pennsylvania, he proved a valuable asset in the fourballs and foursomes. He had three different partners during the competition, and successfully teamed up with each one of them. In the first day fourballs he linked up with Tom Weiskopf to defeat Ireland's Eamonn Darcy and Christy O'Connor Jr. On the second day he joined Gene Littler in a fourball match against Bernard Gallacher and Brian Barnes and won five and three. In foursomes on the second day he paired with Al Geiberger to beat Darcy and Guy Hunt three and two.

His ability to dovetail nicely with other professionals was again evident that year when he helped Johnny Miller win the World Cup of Golf in Bangkok.

Graham was inducted into the Tennessee Golf Hall of Fame in 1990.

## Fact File

**BORN** 1938, Nashville, Tennessee, USA

**CAREER HIGHLIGHTS**
1967 Minnesota Golf Classic
1975 US Open
1979 IVB-Philadelphia Golf Classic
1979 American Optical Classic
1979 San Antonio Texas Open

**INTERNATIONAL HONORS**
Ryder Cup: 1973, 1975, 1977
World Cup: 1975

# HUBERT GREEN

DOUBLE MAJOR WINNER HUBERT GREEN WAS ONE OF THE BEST PLAYERS ON THE US TOUR DURING THE 1970s AND 1980s. HE WON 19 TIMES DURING HIS CAREER ON THE REGULAR US TOUR.

## FACT FILE

**BORN** 1946, Birmingham, Alabama, USA

**CAREER HIGHLIGHTS**
1971 Houston Open
1976 Doral-Eastern Open
1977 US Open
1977 Irish Open
1985 USPGA Championship

**INTERNATIONAL HONORS**
Ryder Cup: 1977, 1979, 1985

Hubert Green is one of the best players ever to play the US Tour, but watching the 1977 US Open Champion for any prolonged length of time could drive you crazy.

Green would force other professionals to look away because he would waggle the club and look over the ball at his target so many times. Sometimes he would go through 30 waggles before he would actually strike the ball. Some players would count the number of times the Birmingham, Alabama, professional would waggle the club, then compare the number with other players who had done their own additions in previous pairings with Green.

Green often wasn't aware he was taking so long to hit the ball. It was just that he was so focused on the shot at hand that he had no idea he was taking repeated looks at the hole. Yet, when Green finally did hit the ball, he did so with authority.

As a youngster, Green was encouraged by his father to play all sports. The reason he finally turned to golf was that it was the last one left for him to play. Green eliminated sports as he found out that he either wasn't good enough or wasn't big enough to play to a

reasonable standard. Although his golf swing was very unorthodox, with a lot of hand action, it was good enough to allow him to take up the game professionally.

In a regular Tour career that spanned 26 seasons before he joined the US Senior Tour in 1997, Green won no less than 19 tournaments. Try as he might over the last 11 years of his career, he just couldn't reach that magical figure of 20.

The biggest wins of his career came in the 1977 US Open and the 1985 USPGA Championship.

Southern Hills in Tulsa, Oklahoma, was the venue for the 1977 US Open. A tough course normally, the USGA had made it even more difficult for America's national championship. Green won the title from Lou Graham with a two under par total of 278.

In 1985 he surprised everyone by taking the USPGA Championship from Lee Trevino at Cherry Hills, Denver, Colorado. Although he had been a prolific winner in the 1970s, Green had won only twice in the previous five years. However, he took a three-shot lead into the final round and held on to beat Trevino, the sentimental favorite, by two strokes. It was Green's last regular US Tour win.

# TAMMIE GREEN

PREGNANCY DIDN'T STOP TAMMIE GREEN FROM COMPETING IN THE 1998 SOLHEIM CUP. GREEN HELPED THE UNITED STATES TO VICTORY OVER EUROPE BY WINNING ONE OF HER MATCHES.

Tammie Green did something in the 1998 season that no player has ever done—she became the first pregnant golfer to compete in the Solheim Cup. While she might have had other things on her mind, Green did herself proud by winning one of the three matches she played. Daughter Tina Marie was born in December 1998, three-and-a-half months afterward. Since she's already appeared in one of the biggest golf competitions in the women's game, it may be a safe bet that she'll consider a future career on the fairways.

Green made sure she had a good season before taking time off to give birth. The 1998 season saw her win her seventh career victory when she captured the LPGA Corning Classic. Her 21 events during the season took her over the $3 million barrier, winning just over $338,000 for the year.

Her good play in 1998 was a continuation of an excellent season the year before; 1997 was a big comeback year for the Ohio professional. She had gone three years without a win and, despite a number of top-10 finishes, she just couldn't seem to get to the finish line first no matter what she did.

In 1996 Green had to undergo surgery for a ruptured ovarian cyst, and it took her a while to regain the consistency that saw her win tournaments on the LPGA Tour. Her comeback was marked by a victory over some of the biggest names in women's golf. Green had to fend off Annika Sorenstam, Nancy Lopez, and Karrie Webb to win the Sprint Titleholders Championship. Opening rounds of 66 and 67, gave Green the lead over the field and she hung on to win by two shots over Sorenstam.

Green's victory in the 1989 Du Maurier Classic was her first in a major championship, but she said her victory in the Sprint event felt like she had won her second. She won the tournament, she commented afterward, by believing in herself, "You try to get the negatives away from you and try to think positively. You believe in yourself and have the confidence that you can win and are good enough to play against these players."

The comeback was complete when Green won the Giant Eagle Classic. Again, Green had to overcome one of the best players in women's golf, Laura Davies. Green defeated Davies in a playoff for the title. The former 1987 Rookie of the Year had her best financial year ever in 1997, winning just under $600,000.

## FACT FILE

**BORN** 1959, Somerset, Ohio, USA

**CAREER HIGHLIGHTS**
1989 Du Maurier Classic
1993 Rochester International
1997 Sprint Titleholders Championship
1997 Giant Eagle LPGA Classic
1998 LPGA Corning Classic

**INTERNATIONAL HONORS**
Solheim Cup: 1994, 1998

# Jack the Giant Killer

Much has been written about the 1955 US Open at the Olympic Club in San Francisco, when an unknown golfer by the name of Jack Fleck defeated Ben Hogan, one of the immortals of the game, in a playoff for the title. It was so unbelievable that, even now, it doesn't seem possible.

It certainly didn't seem possible then. Hogan, with 63 career wins, two Masters titles, two USPGA Championships, one British Open, and already four US Opens, was the greatest player of his generation. Fleck was an unknown from Iowa. Yet it happened.

When Hogan sat in the locker room at the Olympic Club after the final round, after posting a score of 287, everyone thought he had won his fifth US Open to break the record of four he shared with Willie Anderson and Bobby Jones. Then he was told Fleck was still in with a chance. "Is Fleck good enough to tie you?" Hogan was asked. "He must be good," replied the Texan. "He uses Hogan clubs." Just a few weeks before the US Open, Fleck had gone to Fort Worth, Texas, to get a new set of clubs from the Hogan factory. The great man himself had let him in the door. Hogan was right. Fleck birdied two of the last four holes to tie for the lead. An 18-hole playoff ensued and no one gave Fleck a chance.

Years later, Fleck spoke about what happened at Olympic Club. For some reason he couldn't explain, he had a great week with his putter, a part of his game that usually gave him trouble. "I did get a funny feeling in my hands, something telling me I could make just about anything I putted. I'd frankly never felt that kind of confidence before," revealed Fleck, over 40 years later. His putting was good enough to help him tie for the lead, but would it stand up to the pressure of playing against golf's greatest player in a playoff for the US Open? The answer was Yes.

Fleck had a one-stroke lead on Hogan through 17 holes. After hitting a good drive up the 18th fairway, Fleck watched as his hero hit his ball into the deep rough to the left of the fairway. Accounts said Hogan hooked his tee shot after his foot slipped on the tee. Fleck reflected years later that Hogan in fact "neck-pulled the shot" into the rough. With Fleck looking on, Hogan took two slashes at the ball to get it out of the rough. He finally got on the green in five and holed a 40-footer for double bogey six. Fleck, meanwhile, hit the green in regulation, made par and won the title by three shots.

The golfing world was stunned, and the press had a field day. They named Fleck "Jack the Giant Killer" and "The Winner Nobody Knew." "Who is Jack Fleck?" was the headline in *Sports Illustrated* after the upset, with Herbert Warren Wind, the professor emeritus of American golf, asking the question that was on everyone's lips. He was the man responsible for one of the biggest upsets in the history of golf.

RIGHT: SURPRISE WINNER JACK FLECK (LEFT) HAD MUCH TO SMILE ABOUT AFTER DEFEATING BEN HOGAN (RIGHT) IN A PLAYOFF FOR THE 1955 US OPEN.

# Ralph Guldahl

RALPH GULDAHL CAME CLOSE TO QUITTING PROFESSIONAL GOLF BUT WAS PERSUADED TO PERSEVERE BY FRIENDS AND FAMILY. JUST AS WELL, FOR HE WENT ON TO WIN THREE MAJOR CHAMPIONSHIPS.

## Fact File

**BORN** 1911, Dallas, Texas, USA

**CAREER HIGHLIGHTS**
1936 Western Open
1937 Western Open
1937 US Open
1938 Western Open
1938 US Open
1939 Masters

**INTERNATIONAL HONORS**
Ryder Cup: 1937

Trivia enthusiasts will delight in the fact that Ralph Guldahl was the last player to win a major championship wearing a tie. However, there was nothing trivial about his golf.

Guldahl won three major championships in his career, and three Western Opens, which in his day were accorded major status. However, there was a time when he nearly quit golf altogether.

After finishing second in the 1933 US Open by a stroke to amateur Johnny Goodman, the Texan's game fell apart. His confidence dropped to the point that in 1935 he considered leaving the tournament circuit for good. Friends and family persuaded him to persevere, and Guldahl put in many hours on the practice ground working on his game. It paid off.

A tall, powerful man, Guldahl developed a swing that involved very little lower body action. His feet remained rooted to the ground while he made a full shoulder turn. As he completed the backswing, he let his right hand slide down the grip and then delivered a solid smack to the back of the ball. He was also known as a very good putter, who would often spend a lot of time staring at the hole before striking the ball.

Four years after his disappointment in America's national championship, Guldahl triumphed in the first of two successive championships when he won the title at the tough Oakland Hills course near Detroit, Michigan. It was a magnificent performance from a player at the top of his game. He was one of only five players to finish the tournament under par, and the only one to shoot par or better in all four rounds, the first player to do so in US Open history. A 69 in the final round gave him the title by two strokes over Sam Snead. His performance at Cherry Hills Country Club in Denver, Colorado, a year later was even more impressive. Guldahl ran away with the championship when he won the title by six strokes from Dick Metz.

The years just before 1940 were Guldahl's best. In 1937 and 1938 he finished runner-up in the Masters, missing out by two strokes each year, first to Byron Nelson, then to Henry Picard. He laid that particular ghost to rest in 1939, when he edged Snead by one stroke to win the coveted title. Thirty-three strokes over the final nine holes on the last day allowed him to overtake Snead and win the tournament.

All in all, Guldahl won 16 tournaments on the American professional circuit. But he disappeared from the winner's circle just as quickly as he had arrived: he won one tournament in 1940 and never won again.

# JAY HAAS

JAY HAAS HAS ONE OF THE BEST RECORDS IN THE MASTERS WITHOUT ACTUALLY WINNING THE TOURNAMENT. NOT SURPRISING REALLY—HE IS THE NEPHEW OF 1968 CHAMPION BOB GOALBY.

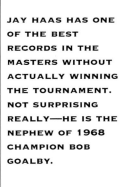

Jay Haas got the best start possible in golf—he was coached by a former Masters winner.

Haas is the nephew of 1968 Masters winner Bob Goalby. It's no surprise then that of the four majors the Masters is the one in which Haas has performed best. For three consecutive years, from 1985 to 1987, Haas finished fifth, sixth, and seventh at Augusta. In 1994 and 1995, he placed fifth and third respectively.

Haas has had top-ten finishes in other majors, but Augusta seems to bring out the best in him. For example it's where he shot a second round 64 there in 1995 for a one-shot lead going into the weekend. He trailed by just one after three rounds, but a final round 70 was just three shots shy of tying the lead.

While the St Louis-born professional has one of the best records in the Masters without actually winning the Georgia classic, he has won the mini-Masters. He's twice won the par-3 contest at Augusta, the tournament around Augusta's short nine-hole course that precedes the main event. Haas won it in 1976 as a 22-year-old amateur, and then 20 years later in 1996.

The 5-foot, 10-inch professional had an outstanding amateur career. He played in the 1975 Walker Cup at St Andrews and won all three matches he played in to help the United States to a 15½ to eight- and-a-half point victory.

He attended Wake Forest University along with two-time US Open champion Curtis Strange, and the two have remained good friends into the professional ranks.

At Wake Forest, Haas won the 1975 NCAA Championship. He was voted All-American in 1975 and 1976, and was awarded the Fred Haskins Trophy in 1975 as the outstanding collegiate golfer.

The likable professional with the slow, deliberate golf swing has a three and zero record in playoffs on the US Tour. In 1982 he defeated John Adams to win the Hall of Fame Classic, he bettered Buddy Gardner in 1987 to win the Big I Houston Open, and in 1993 he defeated Bob Lohr in extra holes to win the H-E-B Texas Open.

Haas has twice played on American Ryder Cup teams. His debut came in the victorious 1983 match at Walton Heath, when he appeared on what many believe was the best US team ever assembled. He also played in the 1995 match at Oak Hill, Country Club, New York, when his side, although clear favorites, lost to an underdog European team.

## FACT FILE

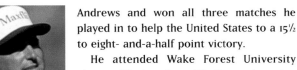

**BORN** 1953, St Louis, Missouri, USA

**CAREER HIGHLIGHTS**
1978 Andy Williams-San Diego Open
1981 Greater Milwaukee Open
1982 Hall of Fame Classic
1982 Texas Open
1993 H-E-B Texas Open

**INTERNATIONAL HONORS**
Ryder Cup: 1983, 1995
Presidents Cup: 1994
Walker Cup: 1975

# WALTER HAGEN

ABOVE: WALTER HAGEN WAS ONE OF THE MOST FLAMBOYANT GOLFERS TO GRACE THE PROFESSIONAL GAME, A PLAYER WHO STOOD OUT FROM THE PACK.

RIGHT: THE HAGEN SWING WASN'T A THING OF GREAT BEAUTY, HE TENDED TO LURCH AT THE BALL. BUT IT WAS A SWING HE HAD PERFECTED, PROBABLY FROM PLAYING BASEBALL—AND ONE THAT MADE HIM A LOT OF MONEY.

Walter "The Haig" Hagen is not only one of the immortals of golf, he's responsible for one of the best quotes made in the game's history. "So many people today never have time to stop off and smell the flowers as they go through life," Hagen once said. Wouldn't it be nice if some of today's "superstars," in all sports, were to heed that advice?

Hagen was one of the greatest characters the game of golf has ever seen. Everything about him marked him apart from the rest of the pack. He dressed in hand-made suits, walked in two-tone shoes, and wore monogrammed shirts with gold cuff-links. He traveled first class everywhere, even turning up at British golf clubs in Rolls Royces he had rented.

Hagen had risen from the caddie yard to become one of the greatest players in the game. Yet when he was in his prime, professionals were still looked down upon by golf club members. That did not sit too well with Hagen, and he went out of his way to highlight the situation whenever possible. For example, when he finished runner-up in the 1923 British Open at Troon, Scotland he refused to enter the clubhouse for the presentation. As defending champion and runner-up, Hagen's presence would have been required. The American declined the invitation on the grounds that the professionals had not been allowed in the clubhouse during the tournament. Instead, he invited spectators to the pub where he had been living for the week.

To look at him, you wouldn't have thought he would be good at golf. He played from a wide stance, and made a definite lurch at the ball. The action may have come from his early days when he played baseball. But it was a move that was simply grooved into his swing, and he knew exactly what he was doing.

The Haig's favorite form of golf was match play, which explains why he won the USPGA Championship five times in that format. Hagen's four consecutive victories between 1924 and 1927 remains a USPGA record.

His penchant for match play was instrumental in setting up the Ryder Cup. Hagen had been involved in an unofficial match between USA and Great Britain at Gleneagles, Scotland, in 1921. The Americans were soundly beaten nine to three on that occasion. Then in 1926 Hagen got an American team to travel to Wentworth in what has become known as the forerunner to the current Ryder Cup. The Americans were comprehensively beaten then as well, losing by 13½ to one-and-a-half. In the gallery at Wentworth was the St Albans seed merchant Samuel Ryder. He was so taken with the match that he donated a trophy, and the greatest team event in golf was born.

Hagen was involved in the official Ryder Cup between 1927 and 1937. He played captain for the first five matches and non-playing captain for the 1937 match. The first four matches went with home course advantage, and Hagen's record was a predictable seven wins, one loss and one half from the nine games he played. In 1937, he led his team to victory at Southport & Ainsdale, Lancashire, England the first time the USA won the Cup on British soil—though it was certainly not to be the last.

The flamboyant New York professional wasn't just a great match-play golfer, he was just a great golfer. He won the US Open twice and the British Open four times, including back-to-back victories in 1928 and 1929.

The only blemish on his record is that he never won the Masters. However, by the time it got started, Hagen was already in his 40s. No doubt he would have won it a few times had it been around when The Haig was in his prime.

In later years, Hagen traveled the world giving exhibitions and clinics, often with the trick shot artist Joe Kirkwood. Golf not being what it is today, a large part of Hagen's income came from exhibitions, even when he was competing for major championships. The money was important—it was needed to finance his lavish lifestyle.

It has often been said that Hagen was the first golfer to make a million dollars, and the first one to spend a million, too! His like will never be seen again.

## FACT FILE

**BORN** 1892, Rochester, New York, USA

**DIED** 1969

**CAREER HIGHLIGHTS**
1914 US Open
1919 US Open
1921 USPGA Championship
1922 The Open Championship
1924 USPGA Championship
1924 The Open Championship
1925 USPGA Championship
1926 USPGA Championship
1927 USPGA Championship
1928 The Open Championship
1929 The Open Championship

**INTERNATIONAL HONORS**
Ryder Cup: 1927 (captain), 1929 (captain), 1931 (captain), 1933 (captain), 1935 (captain), 1937 (captain)

# Chandler Harper

CHANDLER HARPER'S CAREER SPANNED NEARLY 40 YEARS, DURING WHICH TIME HE WON MANY TOURNAMENTS, INCLUDING THE 1950 USPGA CHAMPIONSHIP.

## Fact File

**BORN** 1914, Portsmouth, Virginia, USA

**CAREER HIGHLIGHTS**
1950 Tucson Open
1950 USPGA Championship
1953 El Paso Open
1954 Texas Open
1955 Colonoial National Invitation

**INTERNATIONAL HONORS**
Ryder Cup: 1955

Chandler Harper won three Virginia State Amateur Championships before he decided to turn professional. His first victory in the event came just after his 16th birthday in 1930. Harper was still winning golf tournaments 38 years later.

Harper turned professional in the mid 1930s and went a long time before he gained celebrity in the world of professional golf. Of course World War II intervened, but Harper went another five seasons after the war ended before he gained fame and fortune. After years of hard work, Harper finally found success in the USPGA Championship.

The Virginia professional won the 1950 USPGA Championship at the Scioto Country Club in Columbus, Ohio, defeating a couple of big names to get to the final. Harper had to overcome two tough Texans in the quarter and semi-finals. In his quarter-final match he faced Lloyd Mangrum and watched as a four-hole lead disappeared at the 30th hole. Four halves followed and then Harper won the match with birdies on the last two holes.

He had an even tougher opponent in the semi-finals when he came up against Jimmy Demaret, who had lost in two previous semi-finals, going down to Ben Hogan in 1946 and 1948. No one expected him to get beaten by Harper, but the underdog prevailed to win the match two and one. Harper was pleased to reach the finals where he came up against Henry Williams. It wasn't a pretty match to watch. Despite shooting 75 in the morning round, Harper was three up heading into the final 18 holes. In the first 11 holes Williams found five bunkers and only hit one green in regulation. Harper won the match at the 33rd hole, winning by a score of four and three.

Harper also won the Tucson Open in 1950, and started a run of years where he found much success on the US Tour. When he won the 1954 Texas Open, Harper tied the US Tour record for the lowest 72-hole total with 259, set by Byron Nelson in 1945. That total is still the third lowest in US Tour history. Harper's 25 under par score gave him the title by two shots over Johnny Potts. After an opening one under par 70, Harper then shot three consecutive 63s to win the tournament.

The Virginian was a good enough player to make the 1955 Ryder Cup team. Although he lost in his only match, a foursomes defeat with Jerry Barber to John Fallon and John Jacobs, the US side won the contest.

In 1968, Harper won the World Senior Championship when he defeated England's Max Faulkner for the title.

# Dutch Harrison

ARKANSAS NATIVE DUTCH HARRISON LEARNED HIS CRAFT BY HUSTLING GAMES, WHICH IS HOW HE FIRST MET SAM SNEAD. HARRISON EVENTUALLY PLAYED AGAINST SNEAD, BEN HOGAN, AND BYRON NELSON DURING HIS US TOUR CAREER.

Before Ernest Joe Harrison, or "Dutch," became a regular winner on the US Tour, he went years without making a single dollar in official prize money. Harrison made his living from hustling in money games just to cover expenses. That's how he met one of the greatest golfers who ever lived.

Harrison and his friend Bob Hamilton were hustled by a complete stranger in 1937. They didn't know who the player was, just that he was a country boy who was able to match them shot for shot. Whenever Harrison or Hamilton hit a good shot, their opponent hit one better. Later when they were paying the country boy the wager, he asked if they wanted to play tomorrow. "Son, you work your side of the road, and we'll work ours," replied Harrison. The opponent's name? Sam Snead.

Harrison spent a lot of time in the company of Snead, and Byron Nelson, and Jimmy Demaret, and even roomed with Ben Hogan on the US Tour. Hogan kept Harrison awake by beating his fists against the posts of his bed one night. When Harrison asked him what he was doing, Hogan said he was strengthening his wrists.

The Arkansas professional's big breakthrough came in the 1939 season, when he won twice, winning the Bing Crosby tournament and the Texas Open. After that Harrison was a regular winner on the US Tour in a career that spanned nearly 40 years. In total he had won 18 tournaments by the time he retired from competitive golf. One of those wins came in the 1953 Western Open, a big tournament in Harrison's day. He won the title at the tough Bellerive Country Club in Chicago by four strokes over Lloyd Mangrum, Ed Furgol, and Fred Haas.

Despite his success, Harrison was never able to win the major championship that would have put the icing on a great career. He did make it to the semi-finals of the 1939 USPGA Championship but was routed by the lopsided score of nine and eight at the hands of Nelson.

Harrison served in the US Army for three years in World War II, but resumed his winning ways when his tour was over. He had a couple good showings in the US Open after the war, finishing fourth in 1950 at Merion, when he shot a closing 76 to miss a playoff by just one shot. He was also third in the 1960 US Open at Cherry Hills, even though he was in the twilight of his career.

One of the best Harrison anecdotes concerns the time he slapped the Duke of Windsor on the back after a round of golf and said, "Attaboy, Dukie."

## Fact File

**BORN** 1910, Conway, Arkansas, USA

**DIED** 1982

**CAREER HIGHLIGHTS**
1939 Bing Crosby Pro-Am
1939 Texas Open
1953 Western Open
1954 Bing Crosby Pro-Am
1956 All-American Open

**INTERNATIONAL HONORS**
Ryder Cup: 1947, 1949, 1951

# Sandra Haynie

CHRONIC ARTHRITIS FORCED SANDRA HAYNIE TO RETIRE FROM COMPETITIVE GOLF, BUT NOT BEFORE SHE HAD WON FOUR MAJOR CHAMPIONSHIPS.

## Fact File

**BORN** 1943, Fort Worth, Texas, USA

**CAREER HIGHLIGHTS**
1962 Austin Civitan Open
1965 LPGA Championship
1974 US Women's Open
1974 LPGA Championship
1982 Du Maurier Classic

Sandra Haynie is a remarkable woman. Not only was she a champion golfer in her prime, but she was able to win while coping with an illness which isn't exactly compatible with good golf.

Haynie discovered she had arthritis in 1976, when she was only 33. By that time she had won just about everything in women's golf. Her record included 39 victories in just 13 seasons, including three major championships. The illness and other related injuries set her back for a few years between 1977 and 1980, when she played only in a limited number of tournaments. However, it did not stop her.

Haynie rejoined the LPGA tour in 1981 to compete in 25 tournaments. That year she marked her comeback with a victory in the Henredon Classic, in which she tied her career low score of 64. The following season she went one better by winning twice, including a major championship when she triumphed in the Du Maurier Classic. Indeed, 1982 was her best financial year ever as a professional: Haynie won just short of $250,000.

Injuries forced the tough Texan to sit on the sidelines in 1985, when she had electrode treatment to lessen the sensitivity in her lower back. She also had knee surgery that year. However, quitting has never been part of Haynie's vocabulary, and in 1988 she returned to the Tour to play in 12 tournaments and surpass the $1 million mark in career earnings. The following season she played in 23 events before retiring for good.

The 5-foot, 6-inch Texan turned professional after a good amateur career that saw her win the 1957 and 1958 Texas State Public Links and the Texas Amateur Championship in 1958 and 1959. She was also a winner of the 1960 Trans-Mississippi.

Before being plagued with injuries, Haynie had become one of the best players on the LPGA Tour. She joined the Tour in 1961, won her first tournament in 1962 and until 1975 she won at least one tournament a season. Her best year came in 1974 when she won six times, including the US Women's Open and the LPGA Championship. She is one of only four women to have won those two majors in the same season; Pat Bradley, Meg Mallon, and Se Ri Pak are the others.

Haynie has done much to help the cause of arthritis sufferers. She still heads an annual tournament called Swing Against Arthritis, from which all proceeds go to the NEC Texas Chapter of the National Arthritis Foundation.

# JAY HEBERT

JAY HEBERT WAS FASCINATED WITH BEN HOGAN, AND WENT TO GREAT LENGTHS TO TRY TO DISCOVER HOGAN'S SECRET. HEBERT ETCHED HIS NAME IN THE RECORD BOOKS WHEN HE WON THE 1960 USPGA CHAMPIONSHIP.

Jay Hebert was one of the most consistent US Tour players in the 1950s, winning his fair share of tournaments. However, he came close to not making it after he was injured in World War II.

Hebert enlisted in the US Marines in World War II and made it as far as the rank of lieutenant. He was wounded at Iwo Jima but made it home to attend Louisiana State University, from which he graduated in 1948. Hebert joined the US Tour the same year.

The likable Louisiana professional won a number of tournaments in the 1950s, even though by his own admission he had a poor short game. However, it wasn't bad enough to stop him from winning the 1960 USPGA Championship.

Along with brother Lionel, the Heberts are the only two American brothers to win the same major championship, and the only brothers to win the USPGA. Lionel won the championship in 1957, the last time it was contested at Match Play. Jay won his title at the tough Firestone Country Club in Akron, Ohio, venue for the World Series of Golf for many years. A fine 67 in the second round helped Hebert to victory. Despite a double bogey at the tenth hole, Hebert managed a level par 70 in the final round for a one-stroke victory over Jim Ferrier.

The victory was sandwiched between two seasons when Hebert made the American Ryder Cup team, following brother Lionel's appearance in the 1957 match. The Heberts are one of two sets of brothers to play for the American side, the others are Joe and Jim Turnesa. Hebert lost only one of the four matches he played, a singles match to Dai Rees in 1961. Of the other three, he won two and halved the other.

Like many golfers in the 1950s, Hebert was fascinated with Ben Hogan. Prior to a 1953 exhibition match at Moon Brook Golf Club in Jamestown, New York, in which Hebert and club professional Toby Lyons played against Hogan and 1950 US Amateur champion Sam Urzetta, Hebert took pictures of Hogan's swing. Hebert lay on his stomach 10 yards away and shot the pictures with his own single shot Roloflex camera, trying to catch Hogan's swing at impact.

Hebert and Lyons won the match, after which Hebert drove Hogan to the train station. They talked for only about five minutes of the 45-minute drive, and it was only later that Hebert found out Hogan was on his way to contest the British Open. Hogan hadn't bothered to mention it.

Once, during a rain delay, Hebert found Hogan hitting balls from inside a tent. Hogan had rolled up one side of the tent and was hitting balls to his caddie in the rain. When Hebert asked him what he was doing, Hogan explained, "Jay, if you miss one day, you've got to work twice as hard the next."

## FACT FILE

**BORN** 1923, St Martinville, Louisiana, USA

**CAREER HIGHLIGHTS**
1957 Bing Crosby National
1957 Texas Open
1958 Lafayette Open
1960 USPGA Championship
1961 American Golf Classic

**INTERNATIONAL HONORS**
Ryder Cup: 1959, 1961

# Lionel Hebert

LIONEL HEBERT HOLDS THE UNIQUE DISTINCTION OF BEING THE LAST PLAYER TO WIN THE USPGA CHAMPIONSHIP AT MATCH PLAY. HEBERT WON THE 1957 FINAL BY DEFEATING DOW FINSTERWALD.

## Fact File

**BORN** 1928, Lafayette, Louisiana, USA

**CAREER HIGHLIGHTS**
1957 USPGA Championship
1958 Tucson Open
1960 Cajun Classic
1962 Memphis Open
1966 Florida Citrus Open

**INTERNATIONAL HONORS**
Ryder Cup: 1957

Lionel Hebert followed his older brother Jay onto the US Tour. Despite being some six years younger, he was the first of the two brothers to win the USPGA Championship.

Like his brother, Lionel attended Louisiana State University where he took a degree in music. Lionel finished runner-up in the Louisiana Amateur Championship before he turned professional in 1950.

Hebert holds a unique distinction—he is the last player to have won the USPGA Championship at match play. Between its inception in 1916 and 1957, the USPGA was held annually as a match play championship. After the 1957 final, the championship was changed to a 72-hole stroke play championship, like the other three majors.

The influence of television had much to do with the change, although discussions had been taking place since 1952 about changing the format. Ironically, Dow Finsterwald, Hebert's victim in the 1957 final, was the first player to win the USPGA at stroke play when he triumphed in the 1958 championship.

Hebert had beaten 1948 Masters champion Claude Harmon by the score of two and one in the quarter-finals, and 1953 USPGA champion Walter Burkemo three and one in the semi-finals to get to the deciding match. For much of the final Hebert and Finsterwald were neck and neck. His break came at the 32nd hole when he went one up with a 15-foot birdie putt. Finsterwald made bogey at the 34th hole even though he was allowed a free drop from a footbridge that was ruled an artificial obstruction. Two up with two to play, Hebert closed out the match with par at the 35th hole, winning two and one.

Hebert earned $8,000 for his first US Tour victory, but more importantly he made history as the last golfer to win the USPGA at match play. It is this claim to fame that has resulted in Hebert being featured in golf trivia quizzes ever since.

Hebert's victory put him on the American Ryder Cup side that traveled to the Lindrick Golf Club in Yorkshire, England, in 1957. However, unlike his brother Jay who played in the next two matches and won both times, Hebert's experience wasn't that great. Great Britain & Ireland won the match that year, their first win in 24 years. Hebert played only one of the two sessions, losing a singles match to Ken Bousfield by the score of four and three. To make matters worse, Bousfield's point sealed the victory for the home side.

Hebert was a good enough player to go on and win more tournaments in America, and in 1962 and 1963 he was chairman of the PGA Tournament Committee.

# SANDY HERD

ST ANDREWS GOLFER SANDY HERD WON ONE ONLY MAJOR CHAMPIONSHIP, THE 1902 BRITISH OPEN. NO DOUBT HE WOULD HAVE WON MORE HAD HIS CAREER NOT COINCIDED WITH THOSE OF THE GREAT TRIUMVERITE.

Sandy Herd was one of the best golfers of his generation. However, as with many golfers throughout the game's history, his best years just happened to coincide with those of players marginally better than him.

Herd triumphed in only one British Open Championship, but he probably should have won a few more. A certain trio by the name of the Great Triumvirate did its best to keep Herd's name off the British Open trophy. James Braid, Harry Vardon and J. H. Taylor were the champion golfers of the day, players who dominated the British Open for 20 years. Between them, they won the grand old trophy 16 times. That Herd was able to win it once was a credit to his talent.

Herd first announced his intentions in the British Open in 1892, when he finished as joint runner-up behind Harold Hilton at Muirfield. Three years later, he again placed second, this time on his own, finishing four strokes behind J. H. Taylor at St Andrews.

The fine St Andrews golfer was able to break the Triumvirate's hold on the championship when he won the 1902 tournament at Hoylake, in England. Fittingly, Vardon and Braid finished tied for second. Despite Herd's obvious prowess, many attributed the win to his adoption of the new Haskell ball. The Haskell was a rubber-cored ball that had just been introduced to Great Britain. Herd initially disliked the ball but was persuaded to use it after watching John Ball play one in a practice round. The fact that Herd used the Haskell while Vardon used the old gutty ball was not lost on the public, and the ball became an instant success, eventually replacing the gutty.

Herd finished second twice after the turn of the century, too. In 1910 Braid got the better of him at St Andrews, shooting 299 to Herd's 303. Then in 1920, he placed second to George Duncan at Royal Cinque Ports in Deal.

Many were of the opinion that Herd's temperament kept him from winning more tournaments. He was prone to prepare his victory speech before he had actually won, and often found himself losing tournaments down the stretch to players better able to focus on the task at hand.

Despite that, Herd played excellent golf for many years. In 1926, he won the British Professional Match Play championship at the age of 58, a full 20 years after his first victory in the tournament.

## FACT FILE

**BORN** 1868, St Andrews, Fife, Scotland

**DIED** 1944

**CAREER HIGHLIGHTS**
1902 The Open Championship
1906 British Professional Match Play
1926 British Professional Match Play

# Dave Hill

DAVE HILL WASN'T AFRAID TO SPEAK HIS MIND, AND COURTED CONTROVERSY THROUGHOUT HIS CAREER. HIS 1977 BOOK IS ONE OF THE BEST WRITTEN ABOUT PROFESSIONAL GOLF.

## Fact File

**BORN** 1937, Jackson, Michigan, USA

**CAREER HIGHLIGHTS**
1961 Denver Open
1967 Memphis Open
1974 Houston Open
1976 Greater Milwaukee Open
1988 MONY Senior Tournament of Champions

**INTERNATIONAL HONORS**
Ryder Cup: 1969, 1973, 1977

Dave Hill never won a major championship; the closest he came was in the 1970 US Open, when he finished runner-up to England's Tony Jacklin. However, he won 13 US Tour events during his prime, and was one of the best ball strikers of his day. More importantly, Hill was not afraid to speak his mind.

Golf's not a game for generating controversy. The professionals are usually happy enough to play for the large purses, and are loath to bite the hands that feed them, so to speak. Not Hill.

The Michigan native made headlines at the 1970 US Open at Hazeltine in Chaska, Minnesota, when he openly criticized the course. When asked what he thought the course lacked to make it a true championship layout, Hill's reply was to the point. "Eighty acres of corn and a few cows," he replied.

The remark earned him a fine, but Hill wasn't too far off the mark. Set in the middle of farming country near Minneapolis, Hazeltine was staging its first major championship. Most of the professionals agreed privately that the course wasn't up to the usual standard expected for the US Open. Only Hill was brave enough to speak out.

In 1977 Hill wrote a book called *Teed Off*, a candid look inside the US Tour, which became very well-known. The opening two sentences tell the reader that this won't be the usual obsequious "golf is great and so is the professional" golfer book. "The average touring pro today is living off the fat of the land and thinks the world owes him $200,000 a year. Most golf pros couldn't do anything else for a living, but they always have their hands out looking for a freebie," wrote Hill. And so it continues in the same vein. It's a compulsory book for anyone wanting to know what the US Tour was really like in the 1970s.

At least Hill could back up his controversial claims. He wasn't just some journeyman professional mad at the world because he couldn't break into the winner's circle. Hill made many champion's speeches during his career. He won 13 times as a regular US Tour professional, and has added another six victories on the US Senior Tour.

Hill turned professional in 1959 and joined the US Tour the same year. He won tournaments in 1961, 1963, and 1969. However, his best season was 1969, when he won three times. Despite his previous three victories, Hill said that year was the end of a five-year slump which came about after his wife stopped him from playing golf for two months when she locked his clubs in the garage!

Hill played in the Ryder Cup three times, compiling a record of six wins and three losses from the nine games in which he played.

# Harold Hilton

DURING HIS LONG CAREER, AMATEUR HAROLD HILTON WON TWO BRITISH OPENS, THE BRITISH AMATEUR CHAMPIONSHIP FIVE TIMES, AND ONE US AMATEUR CHAMPIONSHIP.

Harold Hilton was the first golfer to win the British Open over 72 holes when he won the championship in 1892. Until 1891 the championship had been contested over 36 holes. Hilton's win gave him much satisfaction, for it came over one of his greatest opponents.

John Ball finished tied for second in the 1892 British Open, three strokes behind Hilton's winning total of 305. It is the only time in the tournament's history that two amateurs have finished in the top two spots.

Ball was Hilton's great rival at the turn of the century. He, too, won the British Open, taking the championship in 1890 at Prestwick. He also won the British Amateur title seven times, three more than Hilton. However, Hilton also won the US Amateur, and one more British Open.

Hilton won the 1892 British Open at Muirfield with two superb closing rounds to lift the old claret jug. After opening with 78, 81, Hilton then scored 72, 74 to win his first British Open. His second was just as spectacular.

The Cheshire golfer seemed to have thrown the 1897 title away. Just one stroke behind the powerful professional James Braid after two rounds at Hoylake, Hilton had apparently shot himself in the foot with an 84. However, Braid shot 82 to give Hilton a chance. The amateur shot a closing 75 and then had to wait to see if Braid could beat that score. Hilton spent the time playing billiards and then went out to the 18th to see Braid play the last hole. Braid couldn't get the three he needed to force a playoff, and Hilton had won his second British Open.

Hilton remains one of only three amateurs to win the British Open. Ball and Bobby Jones are the others. Jones went one better than Hilton by winning three British titles in his career.

Although his forte was said to be stroke play, Hilton was a decent match player. If he had been then he would not have won four British Amateurs and the US Amateur title. His first victory in the former event came in 1900 at Royal St George's. He defended his title the following year at St Andrews, won his third at Prestwick in 1911, and his fourth at Hoylake in 1913.

It was no surprise that Hilton won two of his championships at Hoylake, for it was there that he learned to play golf. He was born in the same year the club was formed, and was a member of the club for many years.

Hilton became the first editor of *Golf Monthly* magazine when it was formed in 1911. He is also the editor of several books on the game.

## Fact File

**BORN** 1869, West Kirby, Cheshire, England

**DIED** 1942

**CAREER HIGHLIGHTS**
1892 The Open Championship
1897 The Open Championship
1900 British Amateur
1901 British Amateur
1911 British Amateur
1911 US Amateur
1913 British Amateur

# Scott Hoch

Scott Hoch came close to winning the 1989 Masters in a playoff with Nick Faldo. Hoch missed a short putt at the first extra hole and was later vilified by the press.

## Fact File

**BORN** 1955, Raleigh, North Carolina, USA

**CAREER HIGHLIGHTS**
1980 Quad Cities Open
1989 Las Vegas Invitational
1994 Bob Hope Chrysler Classic
1996 Michelob Championship at Kingsmill
1997 Greater Milwaukee Open

**INTERNATIONAL HONORS**
Ryder Cup: 1997
Presidents Cup: 1994, 1996
Walker Cup: 1979

In 1989 Scott Hoch lost a playoff to Nick Faldo in the Masters and was vilified in the press for doing so. The criticism he received wasn't fair.

Hoch tied with Faldo for the 72-hole lead at Augusta National in 1989. The two players teed off on the tenth hole for a sudden death playoff. After hitting their drives, the two marched down the steep hill to the middle of the tenth fairway. Faldo had hit the poorer of the two drives, leaving him a long iron second. He put his approach shot into the right-hand greenside bunker. Hoch had a beautiful drive down the hill, leaving him a short iron to the green. He followed up the drive with a marvelous shot to just two-and-a-half feet.

The Englishman played a fine bunker shot and was able to hole out for his par. The stage was set for Hoch to win his first major, but he missed the short putt, throwing the putter up in the air as the ball slid past the hole. Faldo eventually won the title after holing a long birdie putt on the 11th green.

Hoch took a beating in the press. They called him a choker for missing the short putt. What the papers didn't say was that there's no such thing as an easy short putt at Augusta National. Faldo was fully aware that Hoch's putt was by no means easy. That's why he made sure he holed out for his par.

Three weeks later, Hoch put the disappointment behind him when he won the Las Vegas Invitational in a playoff over Robert Wrenn. The North Carolina native immediately donated $100,000 to the Arnold Palmer Children's Hospital in Orlando, Florida, an affiliate of the Orlando Regional Medical Center where Hoch's son Cameron underwent successful treatment for a rare bone infection in his leg.

Hoch then went winless on the US Tour for the next four seasons. That period wasn't helped by shoulder surgery in 1992. However, by 1994 Hoch was back in the winner's circle, with a victory in the Bob Hope Chrysler Classic.

Hoch has also won further afield. He won back-to-back Korean Opens in 1990 and 1991, and in 1995 he triumphed on the European Tour when he won the Heineken Dutch Open. Hoch didn't endear himself to the media when he skipped the previous week's British Open at St Andrews, making some ill-founded criticisms of the Old Course.

In 1997, Hoch became the second oldest American Ryder Cup rookie when he made his debut in the match at Valderrama, Spain, at the age of 42. (Lee Elder was 45 when he played in his first Ryder Cup in 1979.)

# Tommy Horton

EUROPEAN GOLF OWES TOMMY HORTON A LOT. THE NEW JERSEY PROFESSIONAL HAS TAKEN A KEEN INTEREST IN THE DEVELOPMENT OF YOUNG PROFESSIONALS DURING HIS CAREER.

They say life begins at 40—not so for Tommy Horton. His life, in professional golf anyway, changed dramatically upon turning 50.

Horton has been a phenomenon since reaching the five-decade mark. Between reaching that milestone and the end of the 1998 season, the Jersey Island professional had won 20 tournaments and showed no signs of slowing down.

Great things were always expected of Horton. He was reared to be a true champion at an early age. Along with Brian Barnes he was one of the Butten Boys, a group of British players given expert advice in the hope of producing a home-grown British Open champion. The experiment didn't work, for not one of the players won the oldest golf tournament in the world.

Horton wasn't exactly a prolific winner in his regular Tour career. In 20 full seasons on the European Tour he won only seven times. While he also had five other professional victories outside Europe, including the 1970 South African Open, nothing really pointed toward Horton dominating the European Seniors Tour in the way he has.

Between 1992 and 1998, Horton topped the Seniors money list four times, and also placed second, third, and fourth. In 1997 alone he won six times to finish the season with nearly £170,000. In his entire career on the European Tour, Horton won just over £240,000. It took him only five full seasons on the over-50 circuit to surpass that figure.

Horton is one of the most respected figures in the game, a true gentleman, who is always approachable. He sits on the European Tour's Board of Directors and is a chairman of the Seniors Tour committee. Besides that, he still holds a job as a club professional at Royal Jersey.

The former Ryder Cup player has never forgotten the head start he was given in professional golf from being a Butten Boy. He drew on that experience to set up an annual school for young professionals setting out on the European Tour. It's now called MacGregor Week and is highly organized, with a select group of young professionals receiving advice on their swings, diets, their mental approach to golf, finance, scheduling, fitness—in short everything they need to excel at the top level of European golf. However, in the early days Horton organized the week himself, even going so far as to cajole sponsors into giving money to finance the week.

European golf owes a lot to Tommy Horton.

## Fact File

**BORN** 1941, St Helens, England

**CAREER HIGHLIGHTS**
1970 PGA Match Play Championship
1978 Dunlop Masters
1992 Forte PGA Seniors
1997 Player Championship
1998 The Belfry PGA Seniors Championship

**INTERNATIONAL HONORS**
Ryder Cup: 1975, 1977
World Cup: 1976

# Ben Hogan

Go to any professional tournament today and you will see a long line of professionals on the practice ground beating balls into the distance. On any tour anywhere, the busiest place is the practice ground. Ben Hogan is the man responsible for that.

No one worked harder on the golf swing than Hogan. Before the Texan came along, professional golfers just played. They may have hit a few shots prior to playing, just to loosen up, but they wouldn't have finished a round and spent hours on the practice ground afterwards. Ben Hogan did.

Hogan claimed his lack of natural talent meant he had to work hard. When asked the key to his success, he usually answered the same way. "The secret's in the dirt," would be his terse reply. What he meant was that the only way to learn was to hit golf balls, and Hogan did, shot after shot until his hands were literally bleeding.

The pain paid off, for Hogan is still widely recognized as one of the best swingers of a golf club in the history of the game. His book *Five Lessons: The Modern Fundamentals of Golf* is considered a seminal work on the golf swing.

Hogan had a mastery over the golf ball that no one had before and no one has arguably had since. All his hard work paid off; Hogan is one of only four men to have won golf's Grand Slam—the Masters, US Open, British Open, and USPGA Championship. (The others are Jack Nicklaus, Gary Player, and Gene Sarazen.) Yet a near fatal car accident almost stopped him from attaining that honor.

Hogan and his wife Vicky were returning from a tournament to their home in Fort Worth in 1950 when their car collided with a bus on a foggy highway. Hogan saw the bus's headlights at the last moment and instinctively dived across the passenger seat to protect his wife.

Hogan suffered horrible injuries. It was thought he would never play golf again. However, giving in was not part of Hogan's nature. While lying in his hospital bed, Hogan used the time to think about his golf swing. Plagued by the occasional destructive right to left hook, Hogan devised a way to change his swing to eradicate the problem.

Soon after he got out of the hospital, Hogan started working on the new swing. His new method meant a shorter, more controlled backswing, and he faded the ball from left to right rather than his old right to left shot.

The new ball flight gave him more control. So much so that in 1953 he won three of the game's four majors, the Masters, the US Open, and the British Open, a record that no one else has ever achieved. His Open victory at Carnoustie came in the only time he played in the championship. He couldn't compete in the USPGA that year because it conflicted with the British Open.

Hogan's final major championship tally rests at nine, but who knows how many he would have won had the accident, and World War II, not deprived of him of some of his best years?

## Fact File

**BORN** 1914, Fort Worth, Texas, USA

**DIED** 1997

**CAREER HIGHLIGHTS**
1946 USPGA Championship
1948 US Open
1948 USPGA Championship
1950 US Open
1951 Masters
1951 US Open
1953 Masters
1953 US Open
1953 The Open Championship

**INTERNATIONAL HONORS**
Ryder Cup: 1947 (captain) 1949 (captain), 1951, 1967 (captain)
World Cup: 1956

ABOVE: EVEN IN HIS 70S BEN HOGAN STILL HAD A MASTER SWING, ACQUIRED THROUGH LONG HOURS OF PRACTICE.

ABOVE RIGHT: HOGAN MADE ONE APPEARANCE IN THE BRITISH OPEN, WINNING THE TITLE IN 1953 AT CARNOUSTIE.

RIGHT: POETRY IN MOTION. CLASSIC ACTION BY HOGAN AT THE TOP OF HIS BACKSWING. NO PLAYER CAME AS CLOSE TO PERFECTION AS THE FORT WORTH, TEXAS, PROFESSIONAL.

# Brian Huggett

BRIAN HUGGETT IS FONDLY REFERRED TO AS THE "WELSH BULLDOG," A TERM THAT APTLY DESCRIBES HIS FIGHTING SPIRIT. HE WAS A PERENNIAL RYDER CUP PLAYER DURING THE 1960S AND '70S.

## Fact File

**BORN** 1936, Porthcawl, Wales

**CAREER HIGHLIGHTS**
1962 Dutch Open
1968 British Match Play Championship
1970 Dunlop Masters
1974 Portuguese Open
1998 Senior British Open

**INTERNATIONAL HONORS**
Ryder Cup: 1963, 1967, 1969, 1971, 1973, 1975, 1977 (captain)
World Cup: 1963, 1964, 1965, 1968, 1969, 1970, 1971, 1976, 1979

Brian Huggett achieved his biggest victory in golf in 1998 when he won the Senior British Open at Royal Portrush in Northern Ireland. It may have come as a surprise to many people when they discovered that Huggett was 62 when he lifted the title, but not to those who knew him.

Huggett wasn't given the nickname the "Welsh Bulldog" for nothing. He got the affectionate title because of his fighting spirit, his never-say-die attitude. That was certainly true at Royal Portrush. Huggett battled over the tough Antrim, Northern Ireland course to record a 72-hole total of 283, five under par, then won the title in a playoff with Eddie Polland.

Huggett had come close on a couple of occasions to winning the real thing. The Porthcawl-born professional finished tied for third in the 1962 British Open at Troon, Scotland, behind Arnold Palmer and Kel Nagle. In 1965, at Royal Birkdale he finished equal second with Christy O'Connor, two strokes behind Peter Thomson.

Huggett, all 5-foot, 6-inches of him, was a giant killer in his days on the European Tour. He won 16 titles during a 19-year career on the regular circuit. His best two years came in 1968 and 1970 when he had three tournament wins in each season, including important tournaments like the British Match Play Championship, the Carrolls International and the Dunlop Masters. In 1968 he topped the European Order of Merit with just over £8,000 in total prize money.

The son of a professional golfer, Huggett turned pro in 1951 and didn't start as a regular tournament professional until 1962. He made his first Ryder Cup appearance a year later in the 1963 match at East Lake Country Club in Atlanta, Georgia. The Welshman gave a good account of himself in a losing cause, winning two matches, losing two and halving one.

Huggett was involved in the famous halved match at Royal Birkdale on England's west coast in 1969. He made a valuable contribution on the final day when he faced Billy Casper in the afternoon singles. Huggett had to hole a four-foot putt on the final green to halve his match with Casper. The Welsh Bulldog drained the putt. It meant the Cup now hinged on the final match on the course between Jack Nicklaus and Tony Jacklin. However, Huggett thought his putt had been to share the Cup and he left the final green in tears.

Of course, the Cup was shared when Nicklaus graciously conceded Jacklin a two-and-a-half foot putt on the final green, but had Huggett missed at 18, the USA would have won the match.

# BERNARD HUNT

BERNARD HUNT PLAYED THE EUROPEAN TOUR ALONG WITH HIS BROTHER GEOFFREY DURING THE 1960S. THE TWO ALSO APPEARED ON THE SAME 1963 RYDER CUP SIDE.

Bernard Hunt was one of the early pioneers of the European Tour. He worked hard to create a Tour where professionals could make a decent living. No wonder: Hunt topped the European Order of Merit three times and the most money he ever won for doing so was just over £7,200 in 1963.

The 1963 season was his best ever as a professional. He won four times and became the first player to collect four £1,000 winner's cheques in the same year. His wins inspired the most frequently used newspaper headline of the season: "Big Ben Strikes Again." At 6-foot, 2-inches tall, the headline was appropriate.

Hunt was born into golf. His father was a professional and his younger brother Geoffrey also played the European circuit for a short spell. The two played together on the 1963 Ryder Cup side, only the second set of British brothers to play in the match since Charles and Ernest Whitcombe in 1935. The Hunts weren't played together in foursomes or fourball play, as the Whitcombe pair had been in 1935.

The Ryder Cup saw Bernard Hunt achieve one of his greatest ambitions in professional golf. The English professional was a member of the 1957 side that won the cup at Lindrick, Yorkshire, England. Hunt teamed up with Peter Alliss in the opening foursomes on day one but the pair lost their match to Doug Ford and Dow Finsterwald by a score of two and one. After day one, it looked likely to be another American whitewash, as the visitors led by three points to one going into the singles. However, the home side mounted a tremendous comeback on the final day to win the cup for the first time since 1933.

Hunt contributed a valuable point that memorable day when he defeated Doug Ford by an impressive score of six and five. He was a regular Ryder Cup player until his final match in 1969 at Royal Birkdale. He was later honored with the captaincy, leading both the 1973 and 1975 sides.

The eight-time Ryder Cup player won 21 tournaments in a career that spanned nearly 27 years. Hunt had some good years in the British Open, most notably in 1960, 1964, and 1965, when he was third, fourth, and fifth respectively. His services to golf saw him achieve the MBE (Member of the British Empire), and in 1966 he was honored with the captaincy of the Professional Golfers Association.

## FACT FILE

**BORN** 1930, Atherstone, England

**CAREER HIGHLIGHTS**
1953 Gor-Ray Cup
1957 Belgian Open
1963 Dunlop Masters
1965 Dunlop Masters
1967 French Open

**INTERNATIONAL HONORS**
Ryder Cup:1953, 1957, 1959, 1961, 1963, 1965, 1967, 1969, 1973 (captain), 1975 (captain)
World Cup: 1958, 1959, 1960, 1962, 1963, 1964, 1968

# Horace Hutchison

HORACE HUTCHISON ACHIEVED THE DISTINCTION OF BECOMING THE CAPTAIN OF THE ROYAL NORTH DEVON GOLF CLUB AT THE AGE OF 16. HE WENT ON TO WIN TWO BRITISH AMATEUR TITLES.

## Fact File

**BORN** 1859, London, England

**DIED** 1932

**CAREER HIGHLIGHTS**
1886 British Amateur
1887 British Amateur

Horace Hutchison was thrown into a position of power at the tender age of 16, although it came as a shock to him and the club he was a member of.

The Westward Ho! Golf Club, or Royal North Devon to give it its official name, in Devon had a rule in 1875 which said the player that won the scratch medal at the club's autumn meeting automatically became the club president. Hutchison won the medal and found himself chairing meetings for the following 12 months.

Needless to say, Hutchison was a very good player. So good that he played golf for Oxford University. It was said that Hutchison could extricate himself from just about anywhere on the golf course. No matter how impossible the shot looked, Hutchison seemed able to pull it off. That ability and his obvious talent helped him make a big impact in the first three British Amateur Championships. The Londoner lost in the first ever final in 1885, going down to seven and six to A. F. MacFie at Royal Liverpool. It did not take long for Hutchison to atone for the defeat. A year later he captured the first of two consecutive British Amateur titles when he defeated Henry Lamb by the score of seven and six over the Old Course at St Andrews.

While the victory was a great accomplishment, his win the following year was an even greater achievement. Hutchison came up against John Ball in the 1887 final at Hoylake. Not only was Hoylake Ball's home course, but Ball had featured in the championship in the previous two years, losing in the semi-finals. Moreover, Ball was recognized as one of the top amateurs in the game, a reputation he lived up to by winning the championship eight times between 1888 and 1912, and finishing runner-up twice. Ball gave Hutchison a tough match in the 1887 final, but the defending champion outlasted the local favorite, winning the title by one hole.

In later years, Hutchison often employed a young caddie by the name of John Henry Taylor when he played at Westward Ho! Taylor would go on to make a name for himself in golf history by winning the British Open five times.

In 1908, Hutchison had the distinction of becoming the first Englishman to captain the Royal and Ancient Golf Club of St Andrews. After retiring from competitive action, Hutchison wrote a number of books on the game that are still sought after by enthusiasts even today.

# Jock Hutchison

ST ANDREWS NATIVE JOCK HUTCHISON LEARNED TO PLAY GOLF OVER THE OLD COURSE. HE EMIGRATED TO AMERICA AND FOUND MUCH SUCCESS THERE, BEFORE RETURNING TO SCOTLAND TO WIN THE 1921 BRITISH OPEN.

Jock Hutchison grew up in St Andrews, Scotland and learned the game on the famous old links before moving to North America, where he settled in Pittsburgh. He won several Western Pennsylvania Opens before coming to national prominence in the 1916 US Open, at the Minikahda Club in Minnesota, when he finished second by two strokes to amateur star Chick Evans. He also lost in the final of the USPGA Championship the same year, losing to Jim Barnes on the final green. Hutchison had defeated Walter Hagen in the semi-finals, but a missed five-footer on the 35th green of the final cost him his first major championship.

The war years interrupted Hutchison's progress, but he more than made up for it when play resumed after the hostilities. In 1920 he won the first of two Western Opens, and also recorded his first major victory when he triumphed in the USPGA Championship at Flossmoor Country Club in Chicago, a tournament he shouldn't have played in.

In those days, competitors had to qualify for the USPGA over 36 holes. Hutchison failed to qualify, but got into the event when George Fotheringham and Arthur Clarkson were unable to play. Hutchison gladly took a place in the field and won the tournament. The transplanted Scot defeated Douglas Edgar by a score of one up in his toughest match of the tournament. In his previous four matches before the final he hadn't been taken beyond the 33rd hole.

A short missed putt on the 69th hole of the 1920 US Open saw him miss out on a playoff for the title with Ted Ray. Hutchison finished in a four-way tie for second. He seemed to perform well in the United States' national championship, also placing third in 1919 and 1923, but sadly he never won the prestigious event.

In 1921, Hutchison returned to Scotland to play in the British Open. The championship that year was held at St Andrews, Hutchison's home course, so to speak. The expatriate golfer traveled back home early to visit relatives, while playing the course many times in preparation for the championship.

It was a glorious homecoming because Hutchison won the tournament. After scoring an ace at the short eighth hole in round one, the St Andrews man went on to shoot 70 in the final round to tie Roger Wethered. Hutchison won the ensuing playoff by nine strokes.

A short golfer, lightweight at just 140 pounds, Hutchison was highly strung. He was renowned for talking incessantly between shots in an effort to relieve his frequent nervous tension.

## Fact File

**BORN** 1884, St Andrews, Fife, Scotland

**DIED** 1977

**CAREER HIGHLIGHTS**
1920 USPGA Championship
1920 Western Open
1921 The Open Championship
1921 North and South Open
1923 Western Open

# Watson Chips In at Pebble Beach

Tom Watson and Jack Nicklaus have had some tremendous battles in the heat of major championships. Their head-to-head at Turnberry in the 1977 British Open is perhaps their best, but the one they had at Pebble Beach will long be remembered because of the dramatic way the tournament was decided.

Watson had already proved he was a major specialist. With three British Opens and two Masters titles already in his trophy cabinet, the Kansas native was in the prime of his golfing life. So when he came to Pebble Beach in 1982 for the US Open, he was one of the heavy favorites. So, too, was Nicklaus, who was chasing a record fifth title to take him out of a deadlock with Willie Anderson, Bobby Jones and Ben Hogan as the only men to win the U.S. national championship four times.

The final round of 1982 came down to a straightforward battle between the two giants of golf. Nicklaus started the ball rolling with five straight birdies from the third hole. That put him into a tie for the lead with Bill Rogers, with Watson just one behind, tied with Bruce Devlin. Both Rogers and Devlin fell out of contention with bogeys, leaving the stage set for an epic finale.

By the time Watson birdied the 11th hole, he had built a two-stroke lead over Nicklaus, who was playing ahead. A bogey at 12 cut Watson's lead to just one, and when Nicklaus birdied the 15th, the two were tied. Watson holed a 40-foot birdie putt on 14 to take the lead, but a bogey at 16 after a poor drive put him level again. Then came the real drama of the afternoon.

The 17th hole at Pebble Beach is one of the hardest par-3s in golf. At 209 yards into a strong breeze, it calls for a long iron to a tough, two-level green with the Pacific Ocean providing a dramatic backdrop. In 1982 Watson hit a 2-iron to the 17th that swung too much to the left in the air. The ball landed in deep rough to the left of the pin. Watson was faced with a hellish shot from a downhill lie to a green that sloped away from him. At best, Watson could hope to hole a long putt for a par, at worst he would make bogey and walk to the next tee tied with Nicklaus, who had already finished. When Watson got to his ball, though, he found he had a good lie and his confidence soared. His caddie told him just to get it close. Watson said,. "I'm not going to get the ball close–I'm going to sink it." Watson slid the face of his sand wedge under the ball and it popped up out of the grass nice and high and landed on the green, took two short bounces and started rolling towards the hole. When the ball was about five feet away Watson started moving, when it rolled into the hole he nearly danced into the Pacific. He turned and pointed to his caddie and yelled, "I told you." Watson's chip won him his only US Open. His birdie at the last was just the icing on the cake.

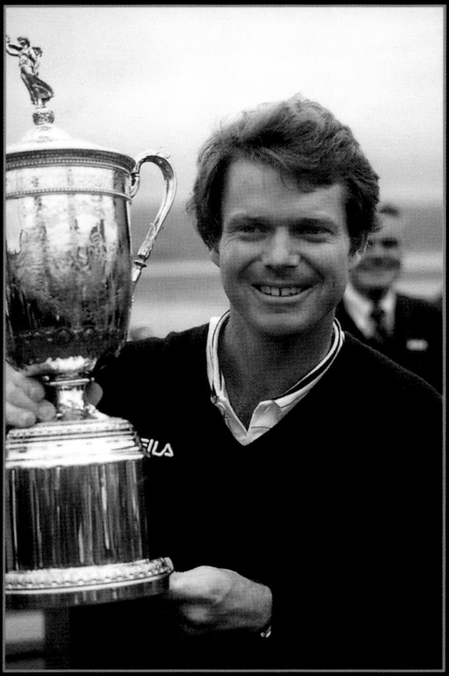

RIGHT: WATSON FINALLY GOT HIS HANDS ON THE US OPEN AT PEBBLE BEACH IN 1982.

ABOVE AND RIGHT: WATSON HAD TOLD HIS CADDIE BRUCE EDWARDS THAT HE WAS GOING TO HOLE HIS DIFFICULT CHIP AT THE 71ST HOLE. HE DID AND THEN DANCED WITH JOY AROUND THE GREEN.

17
U.S.
OPEN

# Juli Inkster

INKSTER IS ONE OF ONLY TWO WOMEN TO WIN THE WOMEN'S GRAND SLAM. IN 1999, SHE WON THE US WOMEN'S OPEN AND LPGA CHAMPIONSHIP, TO ADD TO HER DU MAURIER CHAMPIONSHIP AND NABISCO DINAH SHORE.

## Fact File

**BORN** 1960, Santa Cruz, California, USA

**CAREER HIGHLIGHTS**
1980 US Women's Amateur
1981 US Women's Amateur
1982 US Women's Amateur
1984 Nabisco Dinah Shore
1984 Du Maurier Classic
1989 Nabisco Dinah Shore
1999 US Women's Open
1999 McDonald's LPGA Championship

**INTERNATIONAL HONORS**
Solheim Cup: 1992
Curtis Cup: 1982

Long before Tiger Woods became the first male golfer to capture three consecutive US Amateur Championships in the 1990s, Juli Inkster had already accomplished the feat in women's golf some ten years earlier.

Inkster won three consecutive US Women's Amateur Championships between 1980 and 1982, and was one of the game's best amateur golfers before turning professional. She was a member of the 1982 American Curtis Cup team that won the trophy in Denver, Colorado, contributing a perfect four points from the four matches she played in. She won the California Amateur Championship in 1981, and in that season and the following year she was voted the number one amateur golfer by *Golf Digest* magazine. The Californian attended San Jose State University, where she was a four-time All-American.

Big things were expected of Inkster when she joined the professional ranks. She did not disappoint. The 5-foot, 7-inch golfer became the first rookie in LPGA history to win two majors in the same year. Inkster won the Nabisco Dinah Shore and the Du Maurier Classic in 1984, and finished the season by earning the Rookie of the Year Award. She won the Dinah Shore after beating Pat Bradley in a playoff.

The US Amateur champion had triumphed the previous year on the LPGA Tour when she won the SAFECO Classic. It was only Inkster's fifth event as a professional. In 1986 Inkster won four times and twice recorded scores of 64. The 1988 season saw her win three times and record 12 top-ten finishes during the year. She lifted her third major championship when she won her second Nabisco Dinah Shore tournament.

In 1992 Inkster lost playoffs in two major championships. Dottie Pepper got the better of her in the Dinah Shore, while she lost to Petty Sheehan in the US Women's Open. Inkster played in one Solheim Cup match, appearing in a losing cause at Dalmahoy. She faced a tough opponent in Alison Nicholas in the singles and won the match by a score of three and two. She was one of only three Americans to win on the final day, as Europe took the trophy for the first time.

But Inkster made history in 1999 when she became only the second player after Pat Bradley to win the women's grand slam. In the space of a month Inkster won the US Women's Open and then added the McDonald's LPGA Championship to take her place among players like Bradley, Gene Sarazen, Ben Hogan, Gary Player, and Jack Nicklaus.

# HALE IRWIN

HALE IRWIN'S THREE US OPEN WINS ARE PROOF THAT HE IS ONE OF THE GRITTIEST COMPETITORS IN THE PROFESSIONAL GAME.

Hale Irwin doesn't look like a golfer. His glasses make him look like an accountant or a bank manager. Don't let appearances fool you though, Irwin is one of the best golfers ever to play the game. More importantly, bank managers, or accountants would love to handle Irwin's accounts. The Missouri resident has made millions from playing the game.

Irwin was already a successful US Tour player when he turned his attention to the US Senior Tour. He had won three major championships in the shape of the US Open, and had added another 17 tournament wins, including big events like the Western Open (1975) and the Memorial Tournament, which he won twice (1983 and 1985). He had made a fortune from those wins, but that was nothing compared to the money he made when he turned 50.

The University of Colorado graduate is the pre-eminent player on the US Senior Tour. It took him just three seasons to equal the number of wins he recorded on the regular circuit. In 1997 alone Irwin won nine times to top the US Senior Tour money list with a phenomenal $2,343,364 in earnings, a record amount not only for the Senior Tour, but any Tour anywhere. Not even Tiger Woods's amazing 1997 season matched Irwin's in dollars earned.

The 1998 season was even better. The six-footer made even more money, topping the Order of Merit with $2,861,945, even though he had two fewer victories than the previous year. The most money Irwin ever made on the regular US Tour was just over $838,000 in 1990. Among Irwin's 20 Senior Tour wins through the end of the 1998 season were four senior majors, one more than he won on the regular circuit.

Irwin is noted for being one of the best long iron players the game has ever seen. Mentally he is also very tough, and has been called a grinder in the past because of his ability to grind out good scores over tough courses. That's evident from his three US Open wins.

His first victory in the US Open came at Winged Foot, Mamaroneck, New York, in 1974. Five years later he won the title again when he triumphed at Inverness, Toledo, Ohio. However, his most dramatic victory was his last.

In 1990 at Medinah Country Club, near Chicago, he holed a dramatic 60-foot birdie putt on the final green to force a playoff for the championship with Mike Donald. Irwin danced jubilantly around the green after the putt went in. He won in the playoff the next day, beating Donald at the 19th hole after the two had tied over the 18 holes of regulation.

## FACT FILE

**BORN** 1945, Joplin, Missouri, USA

**CAREER HIGHLIGHTS**
1974 US Open
1975 Western Open
1979 US Open
1990 US Open
1998 US Senior Open

**INTERNATIONAL HONORS**
Ryder Cup: 1975, 1977, 1979, 1981, 1991
World Cup: 1974, 1979

# TONY JACKLIN

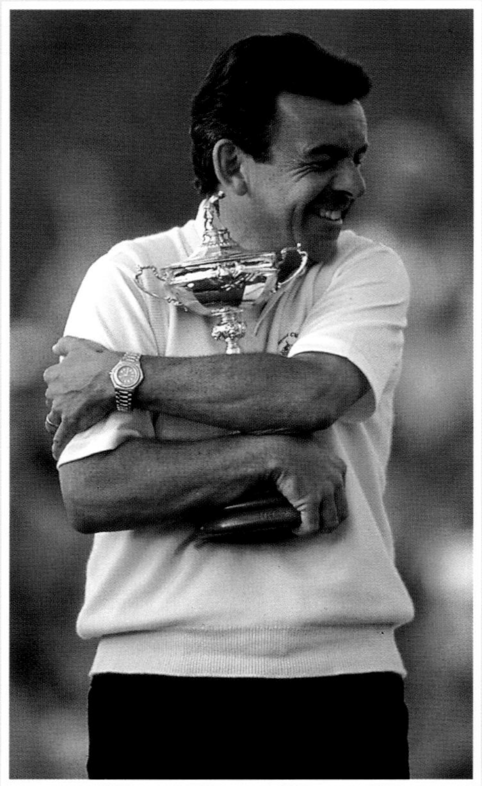

Tony Jacklin peaked at just the right time. Until he won the British Open in 1969, it looked as if a British player would never again win the oldest championship in golf.

Jacklin won the British Open at Royal Lytham & St Annes, to become the first British player in 18 years to win the prestigious tournament. Although it would be another 14 years before another British player won the British Open—Sandy Lyle in 1985 at Royal St George's—it was Jacklin who proved that the Americans weren't invincible on the world's fairways.

From a working-class family in Scunthorpe, England, Jacklin went on to become one of the best golfers Britain has ever produced. On the European Tour, he won 16 times, including the PGA Championship and the Dunlop Masters, which he won twice.

His belief that he could beat the best drove him to try his luck on the US Tour. He was successful there, too, winning the Jacksonville Open twice along with one of the biggest tournaments in golf. In 1970, Jacklin won the US Open, the first Briton to do so since Ted Ray 50 years earlier. He not only won it, he ran away with it. He won the title by seven shots, a margin of victory that was second only to Jim Barnes in 1921.

It was Jacklin's belief that European golfers could challenge the Americans and win that drove him to take on the Ryder Cup captaincy. Until Jacklin came along, the USA had lost the Cup only once in 20 matches, in 1957 at Lindrick. In his own Ryder Cup career, Jacklin had played on six losing sides and had been involved in the first tied match in Cup history.

The shrewd Scunthorpe native knew, though, that in players like Seve Ballesteros, Nick Faldo, Bernhard Langer, Sandy Lyle, and Ian Woosnam he had the backbone of a team that could beat the Americans. In his first match as captain in 1983, Europe lost narrowly by one point at Palm Beach Gardens, Florida, and only because of a heroic shot by Lanny Wadkins at the 18th to tie his match with Jose Maria Canizares. The European performance proved to Jacklin that he was right to believe a European side could win the Ryder Cup.

From the outset of his captaincy, Jacklin insisted on his players getting first-class treatment. He believed that if you treated people as winners, they would be winners. So his team traveled first class and were treated like champions. It worked.
Jacklin's dream came true at The Belfry in 1985, when Europe won the Cup for the first time in 28 years. He went one better in 1987 when Europe won the Cup for the first time on American soil when they triumphed at Muirfield Village, Ohio. In 1989 his side tied at The Belfry to retain the Cup.

Thanks to Jacklin, no more would Europe be underdogs in the biennial competition.

## FACT FILE

**BORN** 1944, Scunthorpe, Lincolnshire, England

**CAREER HIGHLIGHTS**
1967 Dunlop Masters
1969 The Open Championship
1970 US Open
1970 Lancôme Trophy
1982 Sun Alliance PGA Championship

**INTERNATIONAL HONORS**
Ryder Cup: 1967, 1969, 1971, 1973, 1975, 1977, 1979, 1983 (captain), 1985 (captain), 1987 (captain), 1989 (captain)

ABOVE: JACKLIN EMBRACES THE RYDER CUP IN 1989 AFTER EUROPE RETAINED THE CUP IN THE TIED MATCH AT THE BELFRY.

ABOVE: JACKLIN JOYOUSLY ACCEPTS THE 1970 US OPEN TROPHY, HELD AT HAZELTINE NATIONAL, MINNESOTA

RIGHT: DURING HIS PRIME JACKLIN WAS A MATCH FOR ANYONE, AS HE PROVED BY WINNING THE 1969 BRITISH OPEN AND THE 1970 US OPEN.

# Peter Jacobsen

OREGON PROFESSIONAL PETER JACOBSEN ISN'T A PROLIFIC WINNER ON THE US TOUR, BUT HE DRAWS HUGE GALLERIES WHEREVER HE PLAYS BECAUSE OF HIS ENGAGING PERSONALITY.

## Fact File

**BORN** 1954, Portland, Oregon, USA

**CAREER HIGHLIGHTS**
1980 Buick-Goodwrench Open
1984 Colonial National Invitation
1984 Sammy Davis, Jr-Greater Hartford Open
1990 Bob Hope Chrysler Classic
1995 AT&T Pebble Beach National Pro-Am

**INTERNATIONAL HONORS**
Ryder Cup: 1985, 1995
Alfred Dunhill Cup: 1995

Peter Jacobsen is widely known throughout the world of golf for his upbeat personality and his quick-witted ability to make galleries laugh. As a result he is a big draw wherever he plays.

The Portland, Oregon, native has one of the best clinics in the game. Jacobsen's exhibition normally features a session where he imitates other professionals, including Craig Stadler, Arnold Palmer, Jack Nicklaus. The shows are so successful that even those pros he makes fun of show up to watch.

Along with fellow professionals Payne Stewart, Larry Rinker, and Mark Lye, Jacobsen was one of the founders of Jake Trout and the Flounders, a musical group that often performed at US Tour events. He has also written a popular book that takes a look at the funnier side of professional golf. Entitled *Buried Lies: True Tales and Tall Stories from the PGA Tour*, the book lives up to its billing.

Yet Jacobsen is more than just an engaging personality. A three-time All-American at the University of Oregon before turning pro in 1976, Jacobsen has had good years on the US Tour. It took the 6-foot, 3-inch professional only a few seasons to establish himself among America's best players. That happened in 1980 when he came from six strokes back heading into the final round to win his first tournament, the Buick-Goodwrench Open.

A few seasons later, in 1984, Jacobsen won twice. His first win that season came when he defeated Payne Stewart in a playoff for the Colonial National Invitation, a victory he dedicated to his father who had just undergone surgery. He also captured the Sammy Davis, Jr-Greater Hartford Open that season. The wins helped him to his best finish on the US Tour money list when he placed tenth.

The 1995 season also saw Jacobsen triumph twice, winning the AT&T Pebble Beach National Pro-Am and the Buick Invitational of California. The former victory was important because the Pebble Beach event is a tournament well suited to Jacobsen's personality. It involves professionals playing with showbiz celebrities, and for years Jacobsen has teamed up with Jack Lemmon. It's become a long running saga to see if Lemmon can actually make the cut. He never has, and it's probably a safe bet that it hurts Jacobsen more than it does the movie star.

Jacobsen has played twice in the Ryder Cup. Proof that he is one of the classiest acts in golf came when singles opponent Howard Clark made a hole in one at Oak Hill in the 1995 match. Jacobsen applauded his European counterpart all the way to the green.

Needless to say, Jacobsen is one of the game's true ambassadors.

# Mark James

ONCE THE BAD BOY OF THE EUROPEAN TOUR, MARK JAMES IS NOW ONE OF THE MOST RESPECTED FIGURES IN EUROPEAN GOLF. HE CAPTAINED THE EUROPEAN RYDER CUP SIDE IN THE 1999 MATCH.

Mark James got one of the biggest rewards in his long career when he was made European Ryder Cup captain for the 1999 match at Brookline, Massachusetts. It was a fitting honor for a man who has served the European game so well. Yet there was a time when James would have been considered the worst possible candidate for the job.

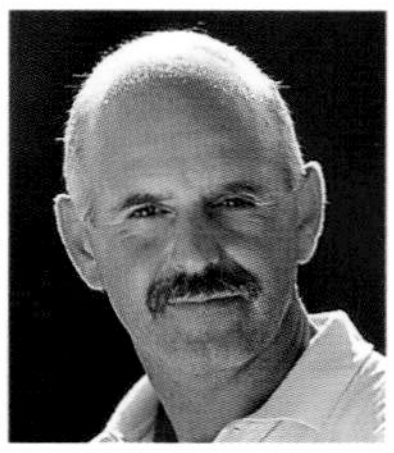

James made headlines in the 1979 Ryder Cup when, along with team-mate Ken Brown, he did his best to undermine captain John Jacobs's authority. James's antics were not in keeping with the tradition of the match, and he was fined accordingly. It is a mark of the man that he has changed over the years to become one of Europe's leading golf statesmen.

The man known affectionately as "Jesse" by his European colleagues has grown so much in stature that he is now chairman of the European Tour Tournament Committee. He is one of the biggest supporters of European golf. For example, when Nick Faldo lambasted the European Tour in the early 1990s for playing on allegedly inferior golf courses, James took it upon himself to walk into the press tent and defend the integrity of the European Tour. When James talks, people listen.

The Yorkshire-based professional has been one of Europe's top golfers since he joined the tour in his rebellious youth. Winner of the Rookie of the Year Award in 1976, through to the 1998 season James had won 18 titles and amassed just under £3 million in earnings. Included in those victories were wins in events like the Carrolls Irish Open (1979, 1980), the Italian Open (1982), the Benson & Hedges International Open (1986), the English Open (1989, 1990), the British Masters, and the Spanish Open. The last win came in 1997, when Jesse outgunned Greg Norman in a playoff to take the title.

In the Ryder Cup, James has been one of the stalwarts of the European side. Between 1977 and 1995, he played in the match seven times. Unfortunately he missed out on the winning sides of 1985 and 1987. However, he was a member of the team that retained the Cup in the drawn match at The Belfry in 1989, and he played on the side that won the Cup in a comeback at Oak Hill, New York, in 1995. James contributed to that victory by beating Jeff Maggert four and three on the final day.

The Manchester-born professional has one of the driest senses of humor in European golf. He is also known for not taking either himself or the game too seriously, a much admired trait in these days of often over-inflated egos.

## Fact File

**BORN** 1953, Manchester, England

**CAREER HIGHLIGHTS**
1978 Sun Alliance Match Play Championship
1986 Benson & Hedges International Open
1989 Karl Litten Desert Classic
1990 Dunhill British Masters
1997 Peugeot Open de Espana

**INTERNATIONAL HONORS**
Ryder Cup: 1977, 1979, 1981, 1989, 1991, 1993, 1995, 1999 (captain)
World Cup: 1978, 1979, 1982, 1984, 1987, 1988, 1990, 1993, 1997
Alfred Dunhill Cup: 1988, 1989, 1990, 1993, 1995, 1997

# Betty Jameson

BETTY JAMESON'S GOLF SWING WAS MUCH ADMIRED, BY MALE AND FEMALE PROFESSIONALS ALIKE. LAWSON LITTLE CALLED IT ONE OF THE BEST HE HAD SEEN IN THE HISTORY OF THE GAME.

## Fact File

**BORN** 1919, Norman, Oklahoma, USA

**CAREER HIGHLIGHTS**
1939 US Women's Amateur
1940 US Women's Amateur
1947 US Women's Open
1952 World Championship
1954 Women's Western Open

Betty Jameson was a child prodigy from the age of 13 when she won the Texas State Public Links Championship and the Texas State Championship. Two years later, Jameson became the youngest woman to win the Southern Championship, a tournament she went on to win in four consecutive seasons.

From Norman, Oklahoma, Jameson learned to play golf at age 11 after taking her father's left-handed clubs, turning them around and upside down, and trying to hit them right handed. Her father bought her a set of cut-down hickory-shafted clubs for Christmas and during the summer Jameson would often play 50 holes a day. Later, Jameson was taken under the wing of Francis Sheider of the Brook Hollow Golf Club in Dallas, one of the best clubs in the city.

Jameson was a tall, strong, athletic woman with good hand-eye coordination. Under Sheider's guidance she developed an outstanding golf swing.

Jameson had a brilliant amateur career. After back-to-back wins in the US Women's Amateur tournaments through 1939 and 1940, she became the first player to win the Western Open and Western Amateur in the same year, 1942.

Jameson turned professional in 1945 at the end of World War II. The Spalding golf company persuaded her to join the paid ranks by offering her the then fortune of $5,000 a year plus expenses to play Spalding clubs. Two years later she won the US Women's Open. Her 295 total for the four rounds was the first time a woman had broken the 300 barrier for 72 holes.

The Oklahoma pro was a founding member of the WPGA in 1945, and later the LPGA in 1950. She donated a trophy to the women's game in 1952. Called the Vare Trophy after Jameson's idol, Glenna Collett Vare, the award goes to the player with the lowest scoring average for the year on the LPGA Tour.

Jameson had one of the best swings in women's golf. Lawson Little once said about her: "Betty Jameson has the soundest swing, the best pivot and the greatest follow through of the hips, of any woman player except Joyce Wethered."

In 1951, she was inducted into the Hall of Fame at the age of 32. At the time she was one of the big four of women's golf, along with Louise Suggs, Babe Zaharias, and Patty Berg.

During her professional career, Jameson won ten times, including five tournaments in 1955.

# Don January

DON JANUARY'S BIGGEST CAREER WIN CAME WHEN HE WON THE 1967 USPGA CHAMPIONSHIP. HOWEVER, HE HAD MORE SUCCESS AFTER TURNING 50, WINNING 22 TIMES IN SEVEN YEARS.

Don January's biggest moment in golf came on July 25, 1967. That's when he joined the most elite club in golf and put to rest an old ghost.

January won the USPGA Championship that day. The victory saw him finally join the major club, that group of golfers who have won one of the game's four major championships. Yet for a time it seemed the tall Texan was never fated to join this illustrious group.

January had been close in the majors before. He'd had good finishes in the Masters, the US Open and the USPGA, including a runner-up spot to Jerry Barber in the 1961 USPGA at Olympia Fields Country Club, Los Angeles. January should have won that tournament. He was four shots clear with three holes remaining, but he made two bogeys and Barber made two birdies to force an 18-hole playoff. January twice held leads of two strokes the following day but his 68 wasn't good enough to take the title.

That 1961 playoff was the first time the USPGA needed extra holes to decide a winner since it switched from Match Play to stroke play in 1958. Ironically, the second time extra holes were required, January was also involved.

In 1967, January tied for the 72-hole lead with fellow Texan Don Massengale. January entered the final round four shots behind leader Dan Sikes, but played brilliantly on the final day, shooting a four under par 68. However, Massengale played the course two strokes better and the two men had to come back the following day to decide the title.

This time January was not to be denied. He shot 69 to his opponent's 71 to take the $25,000 first prize cheque.

January was a good player in the late 1950s, 1960s, and early 1970s. The graduate of North Texas State University, where he received a BA, won ten US Tour events, starting with the 1956 Dallas Centennial Open and finishing with the 1976 MONY Tournament of Champions. In fact, he won the Tournament of Champions twice, taking the title in 1968 as well. His best year on Tour financially was in 1976, when he earned just over $163,000. He was 46 years old that year and also won the Vardon Trophy for having the lowest stroke average on Tour.

His success on the regular Tour, however, was nothing compared to what January has achieved as a senior golfer. For a while in the early 1980s, January all but owned the US Senior Tour. Between 1980, when he turned 50, and 1987, January won 22 tournaments, at the time a senior record. His earnings on the Senior Tour far outstripped the money he made as a regular Tour player. He became the first senior player to surpass the $1 million mark when he passed that milestone in 1985.

## Fact File

**BORN** 1929, Plainview, Texas, USA

**CAREER HIGHLIGHTS**
1956 Dallas Centennial Open
1967 USPGA Championship
1968 Tournament of Champions
1976 MONY Tournament of Champions
1987 MONY Senior Tournament of Champions

**INTERNATIONAL HONORS**
Ryder Cup: 1965, 1967

# LEE JANZEN

LEE JANZEN'S TWO US OPEN WINS MAKE HIM ONE OF THE BEST GOLFERS OF THE 1990S. ON BOTH OCCASIONS JANZEN DENIED PAYNE STEWART THE TITLE.

## FACT FILE

**BORN** 1964, Austin, Maryland, USA

**CAREER HIGHLIGHTS**
1992 Northern Telecom Open
1993 US Open
1995 Players Championship
1995 Kemper Open
1998 US Open

**INTERNATIONAL HONORS**
Ryder Cup: 1993, 1997
Alfred Dunhill Cup: 1995
Presidents Cup: 1998

Lee Janzen seemed to come out of nowhere to win the 1993 US Open. Although he had twice won on the US Tour, few, except probably friends and family, seriously expected him to mount a strong challenge in America's national championship. Yet Janzen didn't just win it, he did so in style.

The Orlando, Florida, resident won the title by beating Payne Stewart by two strokes after shooting four consecutive rounds in the 60s at Baltusrol Golf Club in Springfield, New Jersey. His 72-hole total of 272 tied Jack Nicklaus's record for the lowest score in US Open history.

Known as one of the best pressure putters in the game, Janzen received a little bit of help from the man whose record he equaled at Baltusrol. A few weeks before the US Open, Janzen had the privilege to sit down with Nicklaus. The game's greatest player told his young charge that when faced with difficult holes, he would set out a game plan to make those holes easier. Janzen took that advice to the US Open and planned his strategy for each hole. It worked.

Janzen first took up golf after his family moved to Florida from Maryland when he was 14. Until that time he had been content to play Little League Baseball, and is still a huge fan of America's national pastime. After he turned 15, Janzen won his first golf tournament while he was a member of the Greater Tampa Junior Golf Association.

The future double US Open champion attended Florida Southern College and took a degree in marketing as well as playing on the golf team. He was a first-team All-American in the years 1985-86, and he won the 1986 Division II National Championship during his college career.

Payne Stewart also featured in Janzen's second US Open win at the Olympic Club in San Francisco in 1998. Stewart led the tournament on the final day but faltered over the closing holes. He got a bad break in the final round when a good drive found the fairway but landed in a sand-filled divot. It cost Stewart a bogey and, ultimately, a playoff for the title. He shot a final round 74 and missed a playoff by one stroke.

There was nothing faltering about Janzen's play on the final day, though. The six-footer was five shots behind Stewart heading into the final round but shot a closing 68 to win the title. He was the only player to shoot under par on the final day, and the only player to match par for the four days.

# Per-Ulrik Johansson

SWEDEN'S PER-ULRIK JOHANSSON IS ONE OF THE HARDEST WORKERS ON THE EUROPEAN TOUR. TWICE JOHANNSON HAS WON THE EUROPEAN OPEN, IN 1996 AND 1997.

Per-Ulrik Johansson set a European Tour record when he won just under £360,000 in the 1991 season, the most ever won by a rookie in a single season.

The talented Swede represented his country at junior and senior level before getting a golf scholarship to attend Arizona State University. He took top honors in his college career when he was the 1990 NCAA champion. Phil Mickelson was also a member of the same team, and he and Johansson have remained friendly in the professional ranks.

The 5-foot, 8-inch professional is one of a large number of Swedes on the European Tour. Like his compatriots, Johansson is a tireless worker. He spends many hours on the practice ground working on every facet of his game. It's time that has paid off, for Johansson has won many top honors in his short career on the European Tour. He has twice won the prestigious European Open, winning the title in consecutive years, 1996 and 1997.

His inaugural victory came in 1991 in the Renault Belgian Open. Johansson took the title after defeating England's Paul Broadhurst in a playoff. The Swede had five other top-10 finishes that year, and it helped him gain the European Tour's Sir Henry Cotton Award as Rookie of the Year.

Johansson made his debut appearance in the Ryder Cup in 1995 at Oak Hill Country Club in Rochester, New York; only the second Swedish player to play in the match. (Joakim Haeggman was the first in 1993.) As fate would have it, he was drawn against old college team-mate Phil Mickelson in the singles. Mickelson won the battle but Johansson won the war, so to speak, as Europe lifted the trophy. Johansson helped contribute a point that year when he teamed with Germany's Bernhard Langer in the opening foursomes to defeat Curtis Strange and Ben Crenshaw by a score of one up.

Johansson made history in the following match at Valderrama, Spain, in 1997. When he was paired with countryman Jesper Parnevik in the opening fourballs, the duo became the first Swedish pair to play together in a Ryder Cup. This time Johansson did not face Mickelson in singles play. Instead he was drawn against a tough opponent in the shape of Davis Love III. Johansson prevailed to win his match three and two to contribute a valuable point on the final day. The Swede was one of only three Europeans to win a singles match on the last day as Europe scraped home to a one-point victory.

The Swede is one of the most likable players on the European Tour and is always easily approached, whether it be by fans seeking an autograph or media people looking for an interview.

## Fact File

**BORN** 1966, Uppsala, Sweden

**CAREER HIGHLIGHTS**
1991 Renault Belgian Open
1994 Chemapol Trophy Czech Open
1996 Smurfit European Open
1997 Alamo English Open
1997 Smurfit European Open

**INTERNATIONAL HONORS**
Ryder Cup: 1995, 1997
World Cup: 1991, 1992, 1997
Alfred Dunhill Cup: 1991, 1992, 1995, 1997, 1998

# The Maestro Sets 60-Year Record

Henry Cotton's first British Open win was the most remarkable of the three championships he would eventually win. His performance at Royal St George's in 1934 set a record that would stand for 56 years.

Difficult though it is to believe and considering what happened in the first two rounds, Cotton arrived at Royal St George's a week before the championship not feeling confident about his game. He took four different sets of clubs with him, trying to find something to rejuvenate his poor form. He was making changes to his swing at the time and had no real idea where he was going wrong. Things were so bad that he even considered withdrawing from the tournament, and did not practice the Sunday before qualifying.

In those days, everyone had to qualify for the British Open, even past champions and rising stars. The day's rest helped, for the next day he was just about invincible. Cotton duly took his place among the hopefuls and promptly shot 66 on what he later called, "18 of the most perfect holes I have ever played ... without a long putt going in." The score broke the course record by two shots, but it was only a taste of things to come. A second round of 75 at Royal Cinque Ports meant he qualified for the tournament with ease.

French champion Marcel Dallemagne was Cotton's playing companion for the opening round. After a birdie at the first hole, Dallemagne played well and shot 71. Perhaps it was the Frenchman's sterling play that influenced Cotton, because he made only one bogey all day to finish the round in 67 for a three-stroke lead over the field.

His confidence now at its peak, Cotton played even better in the second round. Out in 33 strokes, the Englishman knew he needed to treat St George's finishing holes with the utmost respect if he was to reap the rewards of his fine outward nine. The last five holes are particularly treacherous at St George's, yet Cotton played them in three under par to come home in 32. The Maestro birdied the last two holes to break his own two-day-old course record by a stroke.

Cotton's 132 for the opening two rounds set a record that stood until 1990—36 years—when Greg Norman and Nick Faldo equaled it at St Andrews. Faldo later broke the record by two strokes at Muirfield in 1992. Cotton held a seven-stroke lead over Alf Padgham going into the final two rounds, and only had to play par golf to win the championship. After a third round of 72 in difficult conditions, Cotton took a ten-stroke lead into the final round. He couldn't lose, or so everyone thought.

Stomach cramps caused Cotton to play poorly in the final round. After scoring 40 on the front nine, it looked as though Cotton was going to throw away all the work of the previous three rounds and lose the title he so coveted. There was very little he could do though. His condition wouldn't allow him to make a full swing. Yet he rallied over the closing holes and eventually shot 79 to win by five shots.

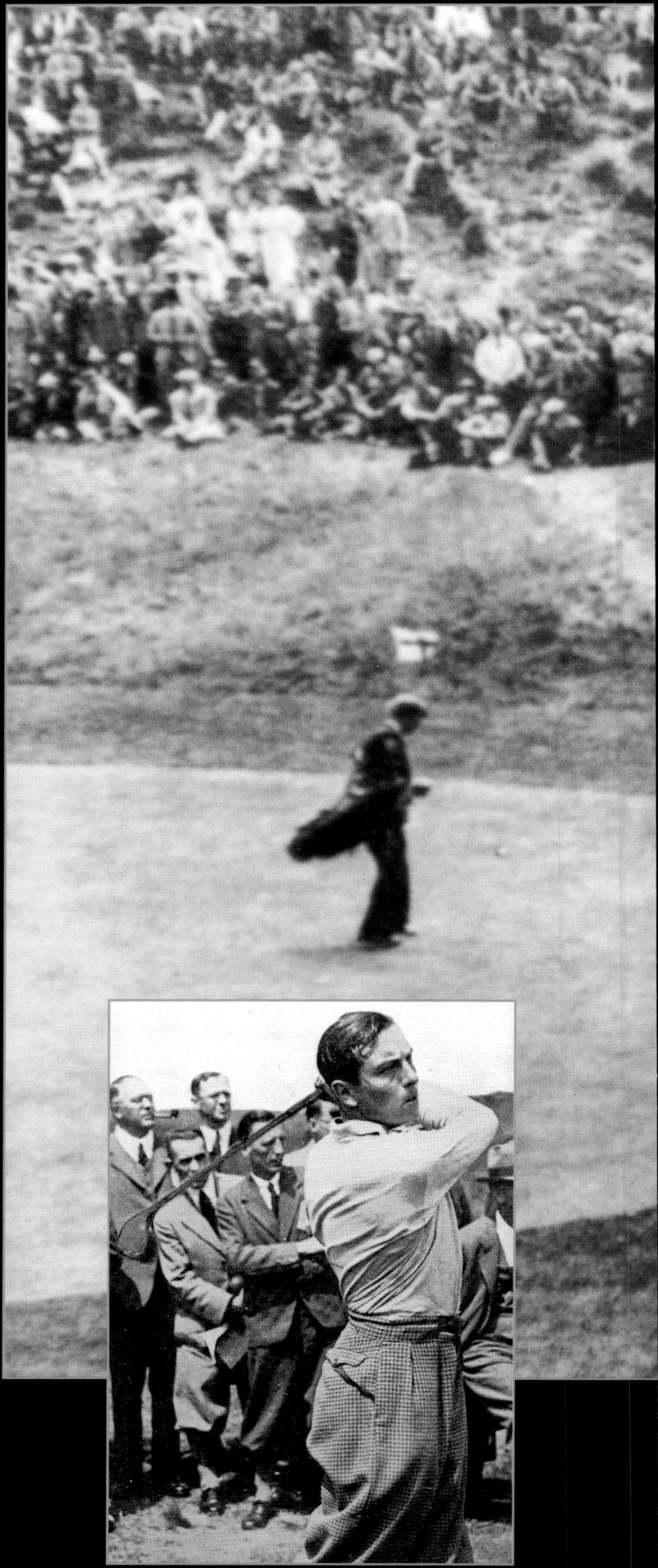

RIGHT INSET: A PICTURE OF CONCENTRATION, COTTON WAS TOTALLY FOCUSED ON WINNING THE 1934 BRITISH OPEN.

ABOVE: COTTON DIDN'T FIND TOO MUCH TROUBLE ON HIS WAY TO VICTORY IN 1934, BUT HERE HE HAS TO PLAY A CHIP SHOT OUT OF THE ROUGH AS HUGE GALLERIES LOOK ON.

RIGHT INSET: COTTON HAS THE BRITISH OPEN TROPHY IN HIS GRASP AT LAST, AFTER SETTING A RECORD THAT STOOD FOR SIX DECADES.

# Chris Johnson

JOHNSON FINALLY ACHIEVED HER DREAM OF WINNING A MAJOR CHAMPIONSHIP WHEN SHE WON THE 1997 LPGA CHAMPIONSHIP AFTER 18 YEARS ON THE LPGA TOUR.

## Fact File

**BORN** 1958, Arcata, California, USA

**CAREER HIGHLIGHTS**
1984 Samaritan Turquoise Classic
1984 Tucson Conquistadores Open
1991 Ping Welch's Championship
1997 McDonald's LPGA Championship
1997 Safeway Golf Championship

**INTERNATIONAL HONORS**
Solheim Cup: 1998

They say good things come to those who wait. Chris Johnson knows that's true. It seemed Johnson would go her entire career and never win the major championships that would elevate her status in women's golf. Then came the 1997 season.

Johnson was an outstanding amateur golfer. She won the Northern California Junior Girls' Championship in 1975 and went on to become an All-American at the University of Arizona in 1979 and 1980. In 1985, she was honored with induction into the University of Arizona Sports Hall of Fame.

It took Johnson only three years on the LPGA Tour to win her first tournament. That came in 1984 when she won the Samaritan Turquoise Classic. A week later she made it two in a row when she won the Tucson Conquistadores Open. She then won tournaments in the 1986, 1987, 1990, 1991, and 1995 seasons, but never a major. She did finish fifth in the 1991 US Women's Open, but she looked destined to miss out on one of the big tournaments.

The 1997 season was Johnson's 18th on the LPGA Tour, and it was to be her best ever. The LPGA Championship was held at the Du Pont Country Club in Wilmington, Delaware, that season. Despite her

experience, Johnson wasn't really seen as one of the favorites, not with the likes of Laura Davies, Annika Sorenstam and Karrie Webb in the field.

Davies shot an opening 67 to lead the tournament, but Johnson scored 68 to give herself a chance. Poor second and third rounds by Davies saw her drop back while Johnson stayed in contention with rounds of 73, 69. After a level par 71 on the last day, she found herself in a playoff with Leta Lindley. Johnson prevailed in the playoff when she got up and down from behind the 10th green to make par while Lindley made a bogey. At the age of 39, Johnson had finally won her first major championship. "There was a time when I realized I could wait for my week to come along, and when everything goes your way, God comes down and says it's your week," said Johnson afterwards.

Johnson capped the season by winning the Safeway Golf Championship. Her two victories helped her to fourth on the LPGA Order of Merit with just over $720,000, more than triple her previous best season. After her Safeway triumph, Johnson summed up the year when she said: "I knew I was capable of doing something like this, but I'm exceeding everything I thought."

# TRISH JOHNSON

RISH JOHNSON URNED ROFESSIONAL FTER AN UTSTANDING MATEUR CAREER. HE QUICKLY STABLISHED ERSELF AS A PRO, INNING THREE OURNAMENTS IN ER ROOKIE YEAR.

It's too bad Trish Johnson was born a female, because there is nothing she likes better than soccer, especially rsenal of the English Premier League. It's safe bet that had Johnson been born a ale, she would have played for the amous team at one stage in her life.

Johnson is mad about Arsenal, to the point here she has even played in tournaments earing the team's shirt. That stunt earned her a fine, ut it didn't dampen Johnson's love for the team.

From the time she realized she couldn't become a rofessional soccer player, Johnson was always estined for a career in golf. She was an outstanding mateur, winning the English Ladies' Match Play and nglish Ladies' Stroke Play Championships in 1985. A ear later, she played in the Curtis Cup, playing a big art in Great Britain & Ireland's 13 to five victory at rairie Dunes, Kansas. She was the top points earner f both teams, winning all four matches she played. hat same season she entered the US Women's mateur and reached the quarter-finals.

Johnson turned professional in 1987 and quickly roved she could play for money as well as pride. ohnson won three tournaments in Europe and ran away with the Rookie of the Year Award, placing fifth on the European Order of Merit. Three seasons later she won the Order of Merit when she had four tournament victories in 1990.

With women's professional golf finding hard times in Europe in the 1990s, Johnson has turned more of her attention to the LPGA Tour. She has found much success there, too. Through the 1998 season, Johnson recorded her second and third victories on the LPGA Tour. Her first was in 1996, at the Fieldcrest Canon Classic. That win was especially sweet for Johnson because it gave her a modicum of revenge over Dottie Pepper. A few weeks earlier, Johnson lost a singles match to Pepper in the Solheim Cup, despite being ahead after nine holes. The loss was particularly hard as the US won the Cup only by virtue of dominating the singles on the final day. In the Fieldcrest tournament Johnson was three strokes behind Pepper going into the last round but shot a career best 64 to defeat Pepper by four shots.

Johnson still plays in Europe, but most of her golf is played in North America. The only problem with that is it means she has to spend time away from her beloved Arsenal.

## FACT FILE

**BORN** 1966, Bristol, Avon, England

**CAREER HIGHLIGHTS**
1987 McEwan's Wirral Classic
1990 European Open
1996 French Open
1993 Las Vegas LPGA at Canyon Gate
1996 Fieldcrest Canon Classic

**INTERNATIONAL HONORS**
Solheim Cup: 1990, 1992, 1994, 1996, 1998
Curtis Cup: 1986

# Tony Johnstone

ZIMBABWE'S TONY JOHNSTONE IS RECOGNIZED AS ONE OF THE BEST BUNKER PLAYERS IN THE WORLD. IT'S A TALENT THAT HAS EARNED HIM MANY TOURNAMENT WINS DURING HIS CAREER.

## Fact File

**BORN** 1956, Bulawayo, Zimbabwe

**CAREER HIGHLIGHTS**
1984 Quinta do Lago Portuguese Open
1990 Murphy's Cup
1991 Murphy's Cup
1992 Volvo PGA Championship
1992 Philips South African Open
1998 Alfred Dunhill South African PGA Championship

**INTERNATIONAL HONORS**
World Cup: 1994, 1995, 1996, 1997, 1998
Alfred Dunhill Cup: 1993, 1994, 1995, 1996, 1997, 1998

Tony Johnstone had the best start in golf—he grew up in Rhodesia, now Zimbabwe, playing against two of the future greats of the game. Not that he needed much encouragement, for Johnstone is a very determined individual.

Johnstone grew up playing with future stars Mark McNulty and Nick Price. Through their careers the three players competed against one another and were often team-mates playing for their country. They propelled each other along in much the same way Ben Crenshaw and Tom Kite did when they were growing up in Austin, Texas, or Ben Hogan and Byron Nelson in Fort Worth in the 1920s. The rivalry worked, for the three have gone on to win many championships around the world, and still remain close friends. Indeed, for many years they have played together at St Andrews in the Alfred Dunhill Cup.

Johnstone was always the smallest of the three, but he made up for what he lacked in physique with hard work and determination. The latter quality was evident in the way Johnstone earned his nickname. The 5-foot, 8-inch professional is called "Ovie" by McNulty and Price, and it stems back to when they were playing in their junior days.

Johnstone hit a tee shot that headed down the right-hand side of one fairway, struck a tractor and bounced out of bounds. Johnstone thought the tractor shouldn't have been there and asked to retake the shot. When he was refused, Johnstone kept demanding that he be allowed to take it "over," which in his accent sounded like "Ovie." The name has stuck ever since.

Johnstone is one of the hardest workers in golf. He has spent more time hitting balls than just about any other player. The work has paid off because Johnstone has won many tournaments on his home continent, and through the 1998 season he had won five times on the European Tour.

The 1992 Volvo PGA Championship was Johnstone's first big victory on the European Tour. Although he had won three tournaments prior to that, the PGA is one of the flagship European events, and always gets a good field. Johnstone had to play with Nick Faldo in the final round, but it didn't faze him in the slightest. The Zimbabwean shot a final round 65 to win the prestigious title by two strokes.

Johnstone is known as one of the best bunker players in the world. He used that skill to good effect in winning the South African PGA Championship in 1998. Johnstone bunkered his approach shot to the final green then hit his sand shot to within inches of the hole to make par and win by two shots over Ernie Els.

# Steve Jones

JONES ACHIEVED FAME WHEN HE WON THE 1996 US OPEN AT OAKLAND HILLS, FIVE YEARS AFTER A DIRT BIKE ACCIDENT NEARLY COST HIM HIS CAREER.

A dirt bike accident at the end of 1991 nearly cost Steve Jones his career. The four-time winner on the US Tour, including three victories in 1989, suffered ligament and joint damage in his left ring finger, making it nearly impossible for him to hold a golf club, let alone swing one.

It took the 6-foot, 4-inch professional nearly four seasons to recover from the injury, and included a drastic grip change in order for him to do so. He now overlaps the index finger of his left hand over the little finger of his right hand in a reverse overlapping grip. It's proved successful, because when Jones did come back, he did so with a bang.

When the New Mexico native showed up for the 1996 US Open at Oakland Hills, he came with a copy of a biography of Ben Hogan. Hogan had conquered Oakland Hills when he won the 1951 US Open, and afterwards called the tough Michigan course a "monster." Jones finished the book just before he played at Oakland Hills, and was inspired by Hogan's life story. So inspired that he went out and won his first major championship. "I honestly don't think I could have won this tournament without reading that book," Jones said afterwards.

Inspiration also came from another source in Jones's march to victory. Normally golfers don't expect someone they are trying to beat to offer them words of encouragement, but that's what Jones got on the final day from playing companion Tom Lehman. Both deeply religious men, Lehman quoted words from the Bible to Jones as they set out on the final 18 holes. "You know the Lord wants us to be courageous and strong, for that is the will of God," said Lehman on the first tee.

Both men were strong, but as it turned out Jones was the stronger of the two. After 17 holes they were tied for the lead with Davis Love III who was playing ahead of them. Jones hit a beautiful drive up the 18th fairway. Lehman did, too, but it turned just enough to catch the left-hand fairway bunker. From there Lehman made bogey, to follow the five Love had made minutes earlier when he three putted the 18th. A solid par from Jones handed him his first major championship.

The victory spurred Jones on to another successful season in 1997 when he won twice, taking the Phoenix and Canadian Opens.

## Fact File

**BORN** 1958, Artesia, New Mexico, USA

**CAREER HIGHLIGHTS**
1988 AT&T Pebble Beach National Pro-Am
1989 MONY Tournament of Champions
1989 Canadian Open
1996 US Open
1997 Canadian Open

# BOBBY JONES

Debate has raged over the years about who was best: Jack Nicklaus, Ben Hogan, or Bobby Jones. All three have their supporters, but those in the Bobby Jones camp perhaps have the most persuasive argument.

While Nicklaus and Hogan compiled their records as professionals, Jones conquered the golfing world as an unpaid amateur. Hogan and Nicklaus won titles in their 30s and 40s, whereas Jones's trophy cabinet was full by the time he was 28 years old.

The "immortal" Bobby as he was often referred to, packed seven major championships, 13 if you throw in amateur majors, into a span of just seven years. Then he shocked the world of golf by quitting the game he loved so dearly.

Quite simply, Jones was a phenomenon. The boy from Atlanta grew up to become the greatest golfer of his age, and many a player still epitomize him as the model professional. He learned his golf at East Lake Country Club, where he developed a swing he copied from Stewart Maiden, the Carnoustie-born professional who taught Jones as a youngster. Maiden must have had some golf swing, for Jones possessed one of the most classic swings ever seen in the history of the game.

By the time Jones was just nine he had won the East Lake Junior Championship, and by 14 he had taken his first Georgia State Amateur Championship. At 15 he finished runner-up in both the Canadian Open and the US Amateur, and won the Southern Amateur Championship. In 1923, at the age of 21, Jones won his first of four US Open Championships, becoming the first amateur to win America's national championship. Indeed, he is one of only two amateurs to win the coveted trophy, the other being Johnny Goodman, who won the title in 1933.

Jones won the first of his five US Amateur titles in 1924, then successfully defended his title in 1925. He also won back-to-back championships in 1927 and 1928.

While it didn't take Jones long to conquer America, he didn't take to British golf so readily. His first experience with links golf came when he competed in the 1921 British Amateur Championship at St Andrews. Jones lost in the fourth round and was so frustrated with the nuances of the Old Course and links golf that he ripped up his scorecard. Jones did not enjoy his first experience of golf at the seaside, yet in later years it would become his favorite form of golf. In 1958, he said that if he had to play on only one course in the world, he would choose the Old Course.

By 1926, Jones had learned the subtleties of links golf, and he won his first of three British Opens, taking the trophy at Royal Lytham & St Annes. A year later he defended the title when he won at his beloved St Andrews.

By the beginning of the 1930 season, Jones had won just about everything there was to win in golf, in the professional and amateur games. Everything except the British Amateur, which he would win that year during a display of golf not likely to be seen again.

The year 1930 saw Jones achieve the ultimate in golf at the time. He finally won his first and only British Amateur at St Andrews, when he overcame Roger Wethered in the final by a score of seven and six. He went on to win the British Open at Hoylake, to finish the first half of what was then the grand slam of golf. Jones returned to the United States to win the US Open at Interlachan Country Club in Minnesota, taking the title in temperatures that soared above 100°F (38°C). He then traveled to Merion, Pennsylvania in September for the US Amateur, and the last leg of his incredible journey. Jones took the title by defeating E.V. Homans eight and seven in the final.

Jones achieved what many at the time had considered the impossible, the grand slam of golf, or the "Impregnable Quadrilateral" as it was termed in those days. With no more mountains to conquer, Jones retired, aged just 28.

The decision shocked many in the world of golf, but those close to him knew why he had chosen to walk away from the game. Jones suffered from the heavy strain of competitive golf, often losing as much as ten pounds in weight while winning championships.

Jones retired to create his dream course at Augusta National, a place where he could get away from the constant attention he had been under for nearly 15 years in his playing days. The Masters stands forever as Jones's legacy to golf—it's a fitting tribute to a great man.

## FACT FILE

**BORN** 1902, Atlanta, Georgia, USA

**DIED** 1971

**CAREER HIGHLIGHTS**
1923 US Open
1924 US Amateur
1925 US Amateur
1926 US Open
1926 The Open Championship
1927 The Open Championship
1927 US Amateur
1928 US Amateur
1929 US Open
1930 US Open
1930 US Amateur
1930 British Amateur
1930 The Open Championship

**INTERNATIONAL HONORS**
Walker Cup: 1922, 1924, 1926, 1928 (captain), 1930 (captain)

ABOVE: BOBBY JONES CONQUERED THE WORLD OF GOLF BY THE TIME HE WAS 28, THEN SHOCKED EVERYONE WHEN HE RETIRED TO BUILD HIS DREAM COURSE AT AUGUSTA NATIONAL.

RIGHT: JONES IN ACTION DURING THE BRITISH OPEN. JONES DID NOT INITIALLY LIKE LINKS GOLF, BUT HE WENT ON TO WIN THE BRITISH OPEN THREE TIMES.

# Herman Keiser

HERMAN KEISER WAS A SURPRISE WINNER OF THE 1946 MASTERS. BUT HE BELIEVED THAT AUGUSTA OFFICIALS TRIED TO STOP HIM FROM WINNING THE TOURNAMENT.

## Fact File

**BORN** 1914, Springfield, Missouri, USA

**CAREER HIGHLIGHTS**
1939 Iowa Open
1946 Masters
1946 Knoxville Invitation
1946 Richmond Invitation
1947 Esmeralda Open

**INTERNATIONAL HONORS**
Ryder Cup: 1947

They say revenge can bring out the best in a person. It certainly helped Herman Keiser win the 1946 Masters.

Nicknamed the "Missouri Mortician" for his somber appearance, Keiser was the darkest of dark horses to win the Masters. Yet he has always maintained that Augusta National officials did their best to keep his name off the trophy. Why? Because of large gambling stakes by two Augusta members.

Following World War II, the 1946 tournament was the first for four years, and the bookmakers were very busy. The top players had returned from service in the war—Keiser was in the navy and spent 30 months at sea—and everyone was excited at the prospect of watching the best players in the world fight it out for the title.

Two Augusta members had bet $50,000 on Hogan at odds of four to one, huge money in those days, roughly the equivalent of $250,000 today. Years afterwards, Keiser remained convinced that everything was done to stop him from winning so that the members could collect on their bet. First, he wasn't allowed to replace his caddie on Saturday, and then his tee-time was changed without any official informing him. Keiser was eating lunch when a fellow competitor, Bob Hamilton, told him he was on the tee in 15 minutes. Then on the 14th hole, Keiser was warned for slow play.

Of course Keiser had the lead going into Saturday's round, which makes the conspiracy theory all the more intriguing. After rounds of 69 and 68 he led the field by five shots, with Hogan seven behind. Even with the shenanigans and distractions, Keiser shot 71 on Saturday to lead by five shots.

When Keiser was put out in the fifth-last twosome with Byron Nelson, instead of in the last group, his suspicions that Augusta officials were trying to prevent him from winning were confirmed. It should be noted, though, that Keiser's earlier tee-time wasn't that unusual—things have always been done differently at the Masters.

Determined more than ever to win the tournament, Keiser hung on to his lead on the final day. A three putt at the last after his 4-iron hit the flag didn't help his cause. But when Hogan three putted from the back of the green, Keiser was champion. Keiser won $2,500 for his victory. However, he added to that when he picked up $1,400 from the bookmakers. Keiser had spent $70 backing himself at odds of 20-1.

Keiser retired from the US Tour in the 1950s. Despite his dislike for Augusta officials, for years afterwards Keiser attended the Masters every year to attend the champions' dinner and pick up the $1,500 honorarium that went to former winners.

# BETSY KING



IT TOOK BETSY KING SEVEN SEASONS TO WIN ON THE LPGA TOUR, BUT ONCE SHE WON HER FIRST TOURNAMENT THERE WAS NO STOPPING HER.

Betsy King gave herself an ultimatum when she joined the LPGA Tour. "If I don't win in my first year, I don't belong here," she told herself. That was in 1977. By 1983 she still hadn't won, yet she was still playing the Tour.

It took King a long time to win as a professional. By 1983 her motto had changed. Then, she was saying: "I'm going to be the best non-winner I can." Thankfully, the Pennsylvania native was able to discard that philosophy the following year.

King made up for a lot of lost time during the 1984 season. She won three times to finish first on the money list, despite never placing inside the top ten in her previous seven seasons as a professional. From that season on, King became one of the top women golfers in the world.

The confidence she gained from her first win in the 1984 Women's Kemper made the difference between a good golfer and a great one. Suddenly King had the self-belief to go all the way to the top. And she did just that—between 1984 and 1992 she won at least two tournaments per year.

Her first big win, a major championship victory, came in the 1987 Nabisco Dinah Shore. She won four more times that year to place second on the money list. The following season she won three times and placed eighth. Then came her biggest season ever. King totally dominated women's golf in 1989. She won six times to earn just over $650,000 and place first on the money list for the second time. More importantly, she added another major that season, lifting her first US Women's Open. In 1990 she not only successfully defended her US Women's Open title, but added another Nabisco Dinah Shore.

King got her name on a third major trophy when she captured the LPGA Championship in 1992. She won the tournament in great style. She didn't score higher than 68 for the four rounds, returning a record 72-hole total of 267, 17 under par, to win by 11 shots. She now only needs the Du Maurier Classic to win the women's grand slam.

A devout Christian, King won her 30th LPGA tournament when she birdied the final two holes in the 1995 Shop Rite Classic. It was a historic victory. The win enabled her to become only the 14th woman to enter golf's Hall of Fame.

## FACT FILE

**BORN** 1955, Reading, Pennsylvania, USA

**CAREER HIGHLIGHTS**
1987 Nabisco Dinah Shore
1989 US Women's Open
1990 Nabisco Dinah Shore
1990 US Women's Open
1992 Mazda LPGA Championship

**INTERNATIONAL HONORS**
Solheim Cup: 1990, 1992, 1994, 1996, 1998

# Tom Kite

TOM KITE WAS COACHED THROUGHOUT HIS CAREER BY THE LEGENDARY GOLF GURU HARVEY PENICK. KITE'S VICTORY IN THE 1992 US OPEN WAS JUSTIFICATION FOR HIS HARD WORK OVER THE YEARS.

## Fact File

**BORN** 1949, Austin, Texas, USA

**CAREER HIGHLIGHTS**
1984 Doral Eastern Open
1985 MONY Tournament of Champions
1986 Western Open
1989 Players Championship
1992 US Open

**INTERNATIONAL HONORS**
Ryder Cup: 1979, 1981, 1983, 1985, 1987, 1989, 1993, 1997 (captain)
World Cup: 1984, 1985
Alfred Dunhill Cup: 1989, 1990, 1992, 1994
Walker Cup: 1971

Until 1992, Tom Kite had the dubious honor of being the best player never to have won a major championship. The Texan had had a steady rate of success and set all sorts of records for money earned, but it didn't matter a jot because he still didn't have a major trophy on his mantelpiece. He changed that over four days in June 1992.

Pebble Beach was the venue for the US Open in 1992. The California course is one of the most scenic in the world; it's also one of the toughest. It was especially so for the US Open. Narrow fairways, deep rough, and rock-hard greens were the order of the day that year, making it a nightmare for the world's top professionals.

The course became almost unplayable in the final round, as the wind blew in hard from the Pacific Ocean. Scores in the high 70s and low 80s were commonplace. Kite had an advantage over the rest of the field, though. As a boy growing up in Texas, Kite learned early to play in the wind. He handled the conditions brilliantly in the final round, shooting a level par 72 to finish two strokes ahead of Jeff Sluman.

Kite had come close in America's national championship before. He had a three-stroke lead going into the final round at Oak Hill in 1989, but stumbled in with a 78 to finish ninth, allowing Curtis Strange to win his second consecutive US Open. He also had a number of top-10 finishes in other majors, but it looked like he would always be a bridesmaid and never actually make it to the altar. His win at Pebble Beach was long overdue.

Kite began playing golf when he was just six years old. He was fortunate to grow up in Austin, Texas, for it was there that the revered coach Harvey Penick resided. Penick took Kite under his wing at an early age, helping to build a swing that would earn him a fortune and many victories around the world.

It took more than Penick, however, to get Kite to the top. The 5-foot, 8-inch professional is one of the hardest workers the game has ever seen. Tireless, he spends hours on the practice ground hitting balls, refining his swing. He does the same around the practice green, working on his pitching and chipping, honing his putting stroke. He has one of the best short games in the world as a result.

Kite also had a fierce competitor to urge him on through the years, against whom he has been measured throughout his career. Ben Crenshaw also grew up in Austin, Texas, and also took lessons from Penick. Naturally, the two competed against each other as youngsters, then as professionals. It's a rivalry that has been very healthy for the two men's careers. Though, given Kite's dedication to the game, he probably would have made it to the top anyway.

# Emilee Klein

EMILEE KLEIN WAS A STAR IN THE AMATEUR RANKS BEFORE SHE TURNED PROFESSIONAL. IT DIDN'T TAKE HER LONG TO FIND SUCCESS AS A PROFESSIONAL, WINNING TWICE IN HER SECOND FULL SEASON ON THE LPGA TOUR.

Emilee Klein's performance in 1996 was overshadowed by that of Karrie Webb, but Klein proved over the course of the season that she is one to watch in the 21st century.

Klein is another LPGA professional to enter the Tour with an exemplary amateur record. She was the 1988 California Women's champion, the 1991 US Junior Girls' champion, then she won two big championships in 1993, including the North and South Championship, and was named 1993 amateur Player of the Year. At Arizona State University she was a first team All-American between 1989 and 1991. In other words, she couldn't miss. Nor did she.

As a rookie on the 1995 LPGA Tour, Klein finished second in the Safeco Classic and the State Farm Rail Classic, losing a playoff to Mary Beth Zimmerman in the latter event. That set the stage for 1996 and her first two wins.

In every tournament she plays, Klein always calls her parents after she leaves the scoring tent. No matter what score she has shot, they want to know. She did that after the final round of the 1996 Ping Welch's Championship at the Blue Hill Country Club in Canton, Massachusetts. When mom and dad asked how she did, Klein replied, "Oh, I did okay." When her dad asked for more specifics, Klein replied, "I shot 65—I won." She had to call them back later. Both parents couldn't talk because they were crying.

Klein won her first tournament in style. She shot rounds of 71, 69, 68, and then closed like a champion with a 65 and a two-shot victory over Karrie Webb. "I've been waiting for this, dreaming of it," she said afterwards. "I wanted it badly, and now I have it. To win it against a field like this makes it more special."

A week later it wasn't tears that were flowing, but champagne. Klein had flown over to Britain with her parents to contest the Women's British Open over the Dukes Course at Woburn, north of London. Klein didn't defeat Webb for this title, but she followed her as champion. Webb had won the title a year earlier over the same course.

It was obvious that Klein had enjoyed the experience of winning the week before and had no intention of letting it go. For most of the week, the talk was about who would finish second. Opening rounds of 68, 66 gave her a commanding lead and she was never overtaken. Klein won the championship by seven shots over Amy Alcott and Penny Hammel. She was doused with champagne on the 18th green to celebrate the victory.

## Fact File

**BORN** 1974, Santa Monica, California, USA

**CAREER HIGHLIGHTS**
1988 California Women's Championship
1991 US Junior Girls' Championship
1994 NCAA Champion
1996 Ping Welch's Championship
1996 Weetabix Women's British Open

**INTERNATIONAL HONORS**
Curtis Cup: 1994

# CATHERINE LACOSTE

LACOSTE TURNED DOWN HER COUNTRY TO PLAY IN THE 1967 US WOMEN'S OPEN. IT WAS A GOOD DECISION FOR SHE WON THE TOURNAMENT, BECOMING THE FIRST FOREIGNER TO WIN THE PRESTIGIOUS TITLE.

## FACT FILE

**BORN** 1945, Paris, France

**CAREER HIGHLIGHTS**
1967 US Women's Open
1968 French Ladies' Close Championship
1969 British Ladies' Amateur
1969 US Women's Amateur
1969 French Ladies' Close Championship

In 1967 Catherine Lacoste did what no woman had ever done before—she became the first foreigner to win the US Women's Open.

Lacoste came from good stock. Her father was the famous tennis player René Lacoste, while her mother was Thion de la Chaume, winner of the 1927 British Ladies' Amateur. Lacoste learned her golf on the fairways of Chantaco, the course her family owned in southern France. There she took lessons from Jean Garaialde, the fine French player who won several European professional events in the 1960s.

Garaialde's pupil didn't need too much guidance. A competitive sportswoman, Lacoste had a natural swing that let her hit the ball a long way. She was a fine long iron player and a good driver of the ball.

Lacoste won everything as a young amateur in France. She lifted her first Ladies' French Open trophy in 1967. That year she made the biggest decision of her career when she chose to play in the US Women's Open at Hot Springs, Virginia, rather than contest the European team championship for her country. Lacoste shot a second round 70 that gave her a five-shot lead over a field that included the top women professionals in the game. She went on to win the tournament by two strokes.

Not only was she the first foreigner to win the prestigious tournament, but Lacoste was the first amateur to do so, and the youngest ever to lift the trophy.

One of Lacoste's biggest ambitions was to follow her mother as winner of the British Ladies' Amateur Championship. Her mother had lifted the title after winning at Royal County Down in Northern Ireland. So when the 1969 British Ladies' was held at Portrush in Northern Ireland, Lacoste took her mother to help her win the championship.

Lacoste arrived a week early to practice. It worked, because she won her way through to the final, where she met a formidable opponent in Ann Irvin. Lacoste was four down at one stage in the final, but such was her determination to win the tournament that she fought back to lift the trophy.

The talented Frenchwoman traveled to the United States that year to try for a unique double of winning the US Women's Amateur to add to her British title. Las Colinas, Texas, was the venue for that year's championship, and in temperatures exceeding 100°F (38°C) Lacoste lifted the trophy. Only 24 years old, she had won just about everything in golf, including the French Ladies' Open four times.

After marrying in 1970, Lacoste retired from full-time competitive golf. She remains one of the best amateurs ever to grace the world's fairways.

# BERNHARD LANGER

GERMANY'S BERNHARD LANGER HAS OVERCOME PUTTING PROBLEMS TO WIN THE MASTERS TWICE, AS WELL AS COUNTLESS TOURNAMENTS AROUND THE WORLD.

Bernhard Langer is probably the most determined player ever to play the European Tour. He has suffered from an affliction that would have driven most players into another line of work, but three times he has battled the problem and won.

Langer is famous for suffering from the "yips," a nervousness in the hands that makes it just about impossible to putt, especially from short distances.

The German has suffered from the condition at various stages of his career, yet each time he has found a way to combat it. He even invented a highly unorthodox grip to help him keep the putter blade steady through the stroke. This involved extending the shaft of the putter up the left forearm and clamping it there with the right hand. In recent years, Langer has adopted the long putter to help him overcome the affliction.

Mere putting problems were never going to deter the hard-working German, though. No one is more dedicated to getting the most out of their talent than Langer. Not only is he one of the hardest working players on the European Tour, but he is also one of the fittest.

Proof of his victory over his putting woes is evident from his record. Through the 1998 season, Langer had won some 37 tournaments in Europe. Indeed, from 1980 to 1995 he won at least one tournament annually on the European Tour. The streak ended in 1996, but the German made up for it the next year with four victories.

A deeply religious man, Langer's biggest achievements in golf have come on a course that no player with a case of the yips could hope to do well on: Augusta National, home of the Masters, is famous for having the quickest putting surfaces in the world. Only the best putters win there. Langer has won the coveted green jacket twice. His first victory came in 1985. That was the year of Curtis Strange's famous collapse. Strange found water at the 13th and 15th holes to throw the title away. Langer sneaked in and won the tournament by two strokes from Strange, Seve Ballesteros, and Ray Floyd.

He didn't need any help in winning his second title in 1993, winning the tournament with a dazzling display of golf over the four days. An eagle at the par-5, 13th hole on the last day helped him to a final round 70 and a four-stroke victory over Chip Beck.

## FACT FILE

**BORN** 1957, Anhausen, Germany

**CAREER HIGHLIGHTS**
1980 Dunlop Masters
1985 Masters
1993 Masters
1993 Volvo PGA Championship
1995 Volvo PGA Championship

**INTERNATIONAL HONORS**
Ryder Cup: 1981, 1983, 1985, 1987, 1989, 1991, 1993, 1995, 1997
World Cup: 1976, 1977, 1978, 1979, 1980, 1990, 1991, 1992, 1993, 1994, 1996
Alfred Dunhill Cup: 1992

# Palmer Saves the British Open

LEFT: PALMER WAS ALREADY ONE OF THE MOST RECOGNIZED FACES IN SPORT BY THE TIME HE SHOWED UP FOR THE 1960 BRITISH OPEN.

BELOW: PALMER WITH CADDIE TIP O'NEIL, WHO CARRIED THE BAG IN 1960 AND IN NEARLY EVERY SUBSEQUENT BRITISH OPEN THEREAFTER.

When Arnold Palmer came down the final fairway after competing in his last British Open at St Andrews in 1995, he was given a standing ovation. Many players joined the gallery to pay tribute to the great man. Among them was Nick Faldo.

Faldo is not one to display emotion. He is the last person you would expect to see engaged in a nostalgic tribute to a professional long past his best. Yet Faldo was beside the Old Course's 18th fairway for Palmer's final march. When asked afterward why he was there, Faldo acknowledged what Palmer had done for the oldest championship in all of golf. "If it hadn't been for Arnold, we'd probably be huddled in a shed on the beach," Faldo told reporters. Faldo realized, as everyone in the game realizes, that it was Palmer's decision to play in the 1960 British Open that revitalized the tournament. Until Palmer made the trip to St Andrews in 1960, many of the top American names had skipped the tournament year after year. Ben Hogan won the tournament in 1953, yet didn't defend his title the year after, or play in the tournament ever again. Most of North America's big names followed Hogan's lead. Travel not being what it is today, American stars chose to ignore the British Open. It was expensive to get there, it meant losing nearly three weeks of the American circuit and in those days everyone had to play 36 holes to qualify. It wasn't an attractive proposition—until Palmer came along.

Palmer started the 1960 season by winning the Masters and the US Open, so playing in the British Open gave him a chance to become the first player since Ben Hogan to win the three tournaments in the same season. Plus, if he could win the British Open, then he would have a chance of becoming the first player to win all four majors in the same year, a challenge he couldn't resist. Another reason Palmer wanted to play in the 1960 tournament was to mark the event's 100-year anniversary. Palmer recognized the tournament's importance in the game, and wanted to take part in the celebrations.

Sadly, Palmer did not win the 1960 Open, but he came close. After rounds of 70, 71, and 70, he entered the final round with a good chance. Then four strokes behind with six holes to play, he mounted one of his famous charges to shoot 68. It was one stroke short of Australian Kel Nagle's winning total of 278. Successive bogeys on the two closing holes in the third round had cost Palmer his dream. Palmer won the following two years, when he triumphed at Royal Birkdale in 1961, then successfully defended his title at Troon the next year. It was his last victory in the tournament, yet Palmer would play in every Open Championship thereafter until 1995. His presence inspired every other top international to take part. The British Open owes a lot to Arnold Palmer.

RIGHT: PALMER'S REPUTATION HAD PRECEDED HIM AT ST ANDREWS IN 1960, AND HE WAS VERY POPULAR WITH THE HUGE NUMBER OF FANS WHO CAME TO WATCH HIM PLAY.

FAR RIGHT: PALMER'S POWER HELPED HIM ON THE OLD COURSE AT ST ANDREWS, BUT HE FELL SHORT OF KEL NAGLE'S WINNING SCORE BY JUST ONE SHOT.

# Marie Laure de Lorenzi

THERE WAS NO STOPPING MARIE LAURE DE LORENZI DURING 1988 WHEN SHE WON SEVEN TIMES AND RAN AWAY WITH THE EUROPEAN ORDER OF MERIT.

## Fact File

**BORN** 1961, Biarritz, France

**CAREER HIGHLIGHTS**
1978 British Girls' Championship
1987 BMW Ladies' German Open
1988 French Open
1994 Spanish Open
1997 Swiss Open

**INTERNATIONAL HONORS**
Solheim Cup: 1990, 1992, 1994, 1996, 1998

Marie Laure de Lorenzi is the greatest French woman golfer since the great Catherine Lacoste graced the world's fairways in the late 1960s. While she hasn't achieved a major championship victory like her compatriot, the stylish swinger from Biarritz in southwest France has been one of the mainstays of women's European golf since she turned professional in 1986.

De Lorenzi had an outstanding amateur career before turning professional. As an unpaid player she won the French Close Championship in 1983, the Spanish Ladies' Championship three times between 1978 and 1983, and the South African Ladies' Championship and the South African Ladies' Stroke Play in 1981. She also took top honors as a girl, winning the French Girls' Championship in 1976 and the British Girls' Championship two years later.

Needless to say, big things were expected of the French sensation when she turned professional at the age of 25. It didn't take her long to take the professional game by storm either. Indeed, despite her obvious pedigree, many were surprised that de Lorenzi was able to become such a force in women's European golf so soon after turning pro.

Her first professional victories came in the 1987 season, when de Lorenzi won the BMW Ladies' German Open and the Belgian Ladies Godiva Open. Those two victories were but a mere appetizer of what was to come the following year. In 1988 de Lorenzi won seven times on the Women's European Tour to place first on the Order of Merit by a long shot. She also capped that season off by winning the Benson & Hedges Trophy with Mark McNulty.

The 1989 season saw de Lorenzi go into something of a slump when she only won three times. Still it was good enough to give her a second consecutive European Order of Merit title.

Through the 1998 season, de Lorenzi had won 19 tournaments on the Women's European Tour. She has also been a perennial Solheim Cup player since its inception in 1990. Despite her talent, her record in that contest isn't great, with just three wins and eight losses from her 11 matches. However, she was a member of the 1992 team that won the cup at Dalmahoy.

Given her success in Europe, de Lorenzi has surprisingly not been tempted by the lucrative purses to be found across the Atlantic Ocean on the LPGA Tour, as many of her contemporaries have been. She remains loyal to the Women's European Tour and has served as one of its best selling points through its difficult history.

# Tom Lehman

LEHMAN HAS EARNED HIS SUCCESS THE HARD WAY—HONING HIS GAME AROUND THE WORLD BEFORE HE FINALLY MADE THE US TOUR.

For years Tom Lehman was the epitome of the journeyman golfer. The powerful Arizona native did not find much success when he first played the US Tour in the early 1980s, forcing him to find other places to ply his trade. It was an invaluable learning experience.

Lehman finished 182nd, 184th, and 158th on the US Tour money list between 1983 and 1985. Not good enough to retain his card by a long shot, or for that matter make a decent living. So Lehman left America to play in South Africa and Asia. He also played the mini tours in Florida, the Dakotas, the Carolinas, and anywhere else where he could play golf. Things got so bad that at one point he considered taking a coaching position at the University of Minnesota. He turned the job down only because it would have meant selling ski equipment in the winter.

Lehman chanced his luck one more time, and put 180,000 miles on his car traveling across the States in search of his golfing grail. He eventually found success on the Hogan Tour, the US Tour's second division. He won three times on that circuit in 1991 and was named Hogan Player of the Year. It earned him a ticket onto the US Tour and Lehman hasn't looked back since.

Lehman has become one of the United States' best players since joining the US Tour in 1992. Top-35 finishes on the money list in 1992 and 1993 saw him establish himself as a Tour regular. A victory in the prestigious Memorial Tournament in 1994 signaled that Lehman was there to stay. He added his second US Tour win in 1995 when he triumphed in the Colonial National Invitation.

His most memorable moment in golf to date, however, came in the 1996 British Open at Royal Lytham & St Annes.

Rounds of 67, 67, 64 helped Lehman establish a new 54-hole British Open record of 198. More importantly, it gave him a six-stroke lead over the field. However, Lehman had one very important obstacle to overcome in the final round—Nick Faldo. Winning a major is never an easy task, but it isn't helped when you have to go head to head with one of the pre-eminent players in the world.

The American had to play with Faldo on the final day. The three-time Open champion had overcome a six-stroke deficit earlier in the year to steal the Masters from Greg Norman. There was to be no similar collapse from Lehman, though. He shot 73 on the final day to win the tournament by two strokes. Lehman's years of struggling had all been worthwhile.

## Fact File

**BORN** 1959, Scottsdale, Arizona, USA

**CAREER HIGHLIGHTS**
1994 Memorial Tournament
1995 Colonial National Invitation
1996 The Open Championship
1996 Tour Championship
1997 Gulfstream Loch Lomond Invitational

**INTERNATIONAL HONORS**
Ryder Cup: 1995, 1997
World Cup: 1996
Presidents Cup: 1994, 1996

# Cecilia Leitch

CECILIA LEITCH WON FOUR BRITISH LADIES' AMATEUR TITLES DURING HER CAREER, AND WAS INVOLVED IN SOME EPIC BATTLES WITH JOYCE WETHERED.

## Fact File

**BORN** 1891, Silloth, Cumberland, England

**DIED** 1977

**CAREER HIGHLIGHTS**
1914 British Ladies' Amateur
1914 English Ladies' Amateur
1919 English Ladies' Amateur
1920 British Ladies' Amateur
1921 British Ladies' Amateur
1926 British Ladies' Amateur

Charlotte Cecilia Pitcairn Leitch, or Cecilia, won 12 national titles during her long career as one of Britain's finest women golfers. In her day she was just about unbeatable.

Leitch learned her golf at Silloth on Solway, a championship course about 25 miles west of Carlisle, England. The course is a links layout *par excellence*, and is considered one of the true hidden gems of British golf. One look at it and it becomes obvious why Leitch was one of the best players of her generation. "If you can play Silloth, you can play anywhere," Leitch once said about her home course. She was living proof of that. Silloth's best female golfer went on to win four British Ladies' Amateur Championships, winning one in each of Scotland, England, Wales, and Ireland.

Of the five Leitch girls who played on the Silloth links, Cecilia was the one who would become the most famous. She initially came to prominence in the 1908 British Ladies' at St Andrews when she reached the semi-final. It was her first attempt at the title. However, she had to wait six years before gaining the first of her four victories in the pre-eminent women's amateur championship. That win came at Hunstanton, Norfolk, England in 1914.

The key to Leitch's game lay in her woods and long irons. She had tremendous power and used it to her full advantage. World War I put a halt to Leitch's trophy collection, but she resumed where she left off when the war ended.

She won her second English Ladies' in 1919, and the following year became the British Ladies' champion for the second time when she won the title at Royal County Down. She defended her title the following year at Turnberry, when she bettered her great rival Joyce Wethered by a score of four and three.

Wethered and Leitch had some fine battles during the 1920s. They first met in the final of the English Ladies' at Sheringham, Norfolk, in 1920, when Wethered upset the form book by beating the Silloth golfer. Leitch's win in the 1921 British Ladies' was sweet revenge.

They met in the finals of the British at Prince's in 1922 and at Troon in 1925, with Wethered winning both encounters. The 1925 final was a close-fought affair, with Wethered eventually winning the title on the 37th hole. The battles between the two did much to promote women's golf in the British Isles.

Leitch had much success abroad, too. She won the French Ladies' Open five times and triumphed in the 1921 Canadian Ladies' Open, winning the title by the huge margin of 17 and 15.

# Tony Lema

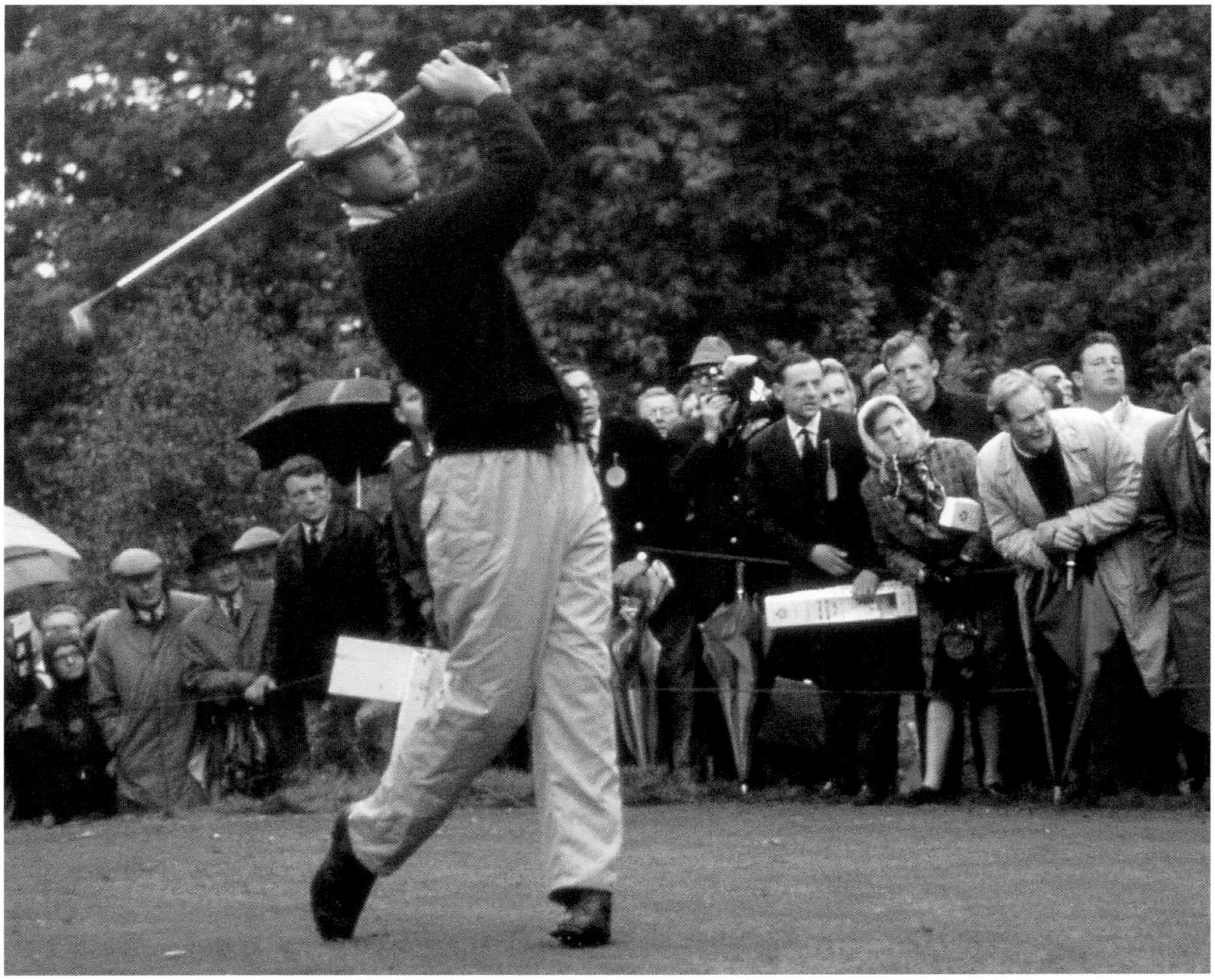

TONY LEMA'S CAREER WAS CUT SHORT WHEN HE DIED IN AN AIR CRASH. ALREADY A WINNER OF THE 1964 BRITISH OPEN, THERE'S NO TELLING HOW MANY MAJORS HE WOULD HAVE WON HAD HE NOT DIED AT THE PEAK OF HIS CAREER.

Perhaps it was his tough upbringing that made Tony Lema crave the finer things the world had to offer. They called him "Champagne Tony Lema" because of his love of the high life, and because he would treat the press to champagne when he won.

Not since the days of Walter Hagen had a golfer lived life to the full. Lema often gave the impression that he was simply enjoying himself when he was on the golf course. Yet underneath that devil may care attitude was a golfer able to beat the toughest players on any given day.

Lema grew up in a working-class environment on the San Francisco waterfront. At 12 he started caddying and later became an assistant at the San Francisco Golf Club. He served in Korea for a spell then came home and joined the US Tour in 1958. The first few years were tough, and Lema struggled. He eventually found his feet in the early 1960s, and became one of the best Americans in the game.

Lema's best year was 1964. He captured three US Tour events—the Bing Crosby Pro-Am, the Buick Open and the World Series—then traveled to Great Britain to play in his first British Open at St Andrews. It normally takes years to learn to play links golf well, and can take a lifetime to master the intricacies of the Old Course. It took Lema just a couple of days.

The American seemed at home on the most famous links in golf. Even on the first day when the course was buffeted by gale force winds, Lema appeared unaffected. He went around the Old Course in 73, a wonderful score considering the conditions. Two successive rounds of 68 gave him the lead. However, fellow countryman Jack Nicklaus positioned himself in contention with a third round 66 to put the pressure on Lema. If Lema felt any pressure at all then, it didn't show. He closed with a final round 70 to take the title by five strokes.

The closest Lema came in the American majors was a second place finish in the Masters in 1963 when he finished a stroke behind Nicklaus. However, he was a big threat in every tournament he contested in the early 1960s, and found the winner's circle many times.

Lema's time at the top was short, though. He and his wife died in a plane crash in 1966 when the aircraft in which they were flying was attempting to land. Lema was at the peak of his game at the time and would no doubt have gone on to win more tournaments and more majors.

## Fact File

**BORN** 1934, Oakland, California, USA

**DIED** 1966

**CAREER HIGHLIGHTS**
1964 World Series
1964 The Open Championship
1965 Carling World Tournament

**INTERNATIONAL HONORS**
Ryder Cup: 1963, 1965
World Cup: 1965

# Justin Leonard

LEONARD IS FAMOUS FOR HIS METICULOUS ATTENTION TO DETAIL. HE HAD EVERYTHING IN PERFECT ORDER WHEN HE WON THE 1997 BRITISH OPEN AT ROYAL TROON.

## Fact File

**BORN** 1972, Dallas, Texas, USA

**CAREER HIGHLIGHTS**
1996 Buick Open
1997 The Open Championship
1997 Kemper Open
1998 Players Championship

**INTERNATIONAL HONORS**
Ryder Cup: 1997
World Cup: 1997
Alfred Dunhill Cup: 1997
Presidents Cup: 1996, 1998
Walker Cup: 1993

Texas has produced many fine champions over the years in the shape of Ben Hogan, Byron Nelson, Jack Burke, Tom Kite, Ben Crenshaw, and a host of others too numerous to mention but certainly, add Justin Leonard's name to that roll of honor.

Born in Dallas, Texas, Leonard attended the University of Texas on a golf scholarship and graduated with a business degree. It was a good choice of study, for he needs a numerate brain to keep track of all the money he has won and will continue to win in the future.

Leonard is famous for his meticulous attention to detail. Jokes abound among his peers about the way Leonard's life is so ordered. Contemporary Brad Faxon once said that Leonard was the only player he knew who actually unpacked his suitcase and folded his clothes away the minute he checked into his hotel. And that he is the only player who color-coordinates his sock drawer. This tidiness is also applied to his golf game.

Leonard was a good enough player to earn his way onto the US Tour courtesy of invites he received after graduating from college. It meant he avoided the dreaded US Tour Qualifying School. A third place finish in the 1994 Anheuser-Busch Golf Classic earned him a cheque of just under $75,000 and he finished the season with over $140,000 to earn his card for the following year. No one doubted his ability to make the grade. After all, as an amateur he had played eight US Tour events and had made the cut in five of them.

The 1995 season consolidated Leonard's place on the US Tour. He finished 22nd on the money list that year to set himself up for his first victory. That came in 1996 when he captured the Buick Open with a five-stroke win over Chip Beck.

Given his upbringing in Texas, it was no surprise when Leonard won the 1997 British Open at Royal Troon. Texas is known for strong winds, and any golfer growing up there learns at an early age to shape the ball in the breeze. However, it wasn't so much Leonard's ability to cope with the conditions that won him the title, but his brilliant display of putting on the final day.

After rounds of 69, 66, 72, the young Texan entered the final round three strokes behind leader Jesper Parnevik. Over the last 18 holes, however, Leonard holed just about every putt he looked at. He shot 65 on the final day to win his first major by the comfortable margin of three strokes. No doubt the first of many.

# BRUCE LIETZKE

BRUCE LIETZKE IS ESSENTIALLY A PART TIME GOLFER. EVEN WITH A SHORTENED SCHEDULE, LIETZKE HAS MANAGED TO WIN MANY US TOUR EVENTS.

Bruce Lietzke is an enigma among the world's top golfers. He plays less competitive golf than any other player, yet has remained one of the best players on the US Tour.

Lietzke basically takes the summer off. While others are trying to win the US Open or the British Open, Lietzke is back home in Dallas, Texas, doing everything else but playing golf. Lietzke plays early in the season and then at the end of the year. Since the mid 1980s he has played less than 20 tournaments a season, yet he still manages to break into the top ranks of the US money list.

By his own admission, Lietzke would rather spend the summer with his family than chase a little white ball over a large green field. He admitted as much when he was in contention for the 1992 USPGA Championship at Crooked Stick in Carmel, Indiana. John Daly won the tournament that year, but Lietzke was in contention after three rounds. In the press room he was asked if winning would make him change his ways. "No," said Lietzke.

A natural player who plays every shot with a left to right fade, Lietzke never practices. He warms up before a round, but you won't find him spending hours on the range as some of his contemporaries do. One of his peers decided to test the Kansas native to see if he was being honest about not practicing when he was away from the Tour. Just before one of his extended breaks, a banana peel was placed inside the headcover of his driver and slipped over the club. Three months later when Lietzke came back on Tour the banana peel was still there. He was true to his word.

His limited schedule has meant that Lietzke hasn't contested a US Open since 1985, and hasn't played in the British Open since 1983. It also means he has only ever made one Ryder Cup team. He appeared in the 1981 match at Walton Heath, when America fielded its best ever side in the biennial competition. Lietzke lost both matches in which he partnered Bill Rogers, but halved his singles match with Bernhard Langer.

Despite his schedule, the University of Houston graduate had managed to win 13 times through the 1998 season. Two of those victories came in the Canadian Open at Glen Abbey Golf Course near Toronto. He also has two second place finishes in the event, one a playoff loss to Greg Norman in 1992.

## FACT FILE

**BORN** 1951, Kansas City, Kansas, USA

**CAREER HIGHLIGHTS**
1978 Canadian Open
1980 Colonial National Invitation
1981 Bob Hope Desert Classic
1982 Canadian Open
1994 Las Vegas Invitational

**INTERNATIONAL HONORS**
Ryder Cup: 1981

# LAWSON LITTLE

LAWSON LITTLE'S PERFORMANCE IN THE 1934 BRITISH AMATEUR WAS SIMPLY OUTSTANDING. HIS MARGIN OF VICTORY IS STILL THE BIGGEST IN THE CHAMPIONSHIP'S HISTORY.

## FACT FILE

**BORN** 1910, Newport, Rhode Island, USA

**DIED** 1968

**CAREER HIGHLIGHTS**
1934 British Amateur
1934 US Amateur
1935 British Amateur
1935 US Amateur
1940 US Open

**INTERNATIONAL HONORS**
Walker Cup: 1934

Lawson Little holds a unique distinction. In 1934 he won the British and US Amateur championships, then in 1935 he repeated the achievement. Not even the great Bobby Jones was able to do that. Little's double double involved winning 31 straight matches against the best amateur players in the world.

The Rhode Island golfer was one of the most powerful men ever to play the game. Often there was simply no one to match his tremendous length. That was the case when Little won his first British Amateur Championship in 1934. He put on a display of golf that hadn't been seen before and probably hasn't been seen since.

Prestwick was the venue for the British Amateur in 1935, and a local Scottish golfer by the name of J. Wallace had the misfortune of facing Little in the final. It was a complete mismatch. Little went round the Prestwick course with a 66 in the morning round, and the match finished on the 23rd hole, with Little winning the title by a score of 14 and 13, the biggest margin of victory in British Amateur Championship history. Little scored a three on 12 of the 23 holes he played in the final. Bernard Darwin, the doyen of British golf writing, called the performance "one of the most terrific exhibitions in all golfing history."

An exhibition of Little's power came on the final hole of the morning round. Little drove the last green, hitting his ball 270 yards off the tee. That's not long by today's standards, but it was in 1935.

It was no surprise when Little turned professional in 1936. He immediately found success as a paid player, too, winning the Canadian Open that year at St Andrews Golf Club in Toronto. Little didn't show any mercy to his professional opponents either. He won the title by eight shots from Jimmy Thompson, another long-hitting player whom Little often played against in exhibition matches.

Little's biggest moment as a professional came in the 1940 US Open at Canterbury Golf Club in Cleveland, Ohio. The powerful golfer had come close the year before in Philadelphia, when an opening 69 had given him a chance. However, he slipped up with a final round of 81. He was in no mood for failure the following year, even after tying for the 72-hole lead with Gene Sarazen. Little defeated the grand slam winner by three strokes in the playoff.

# SALLY LITTLE

HEALTH PROBLEMS HAVE PLAGUED SALLY LITTLE THROUGHOUT HER CAREER, BUT SHE STILL MANAGED TO CAPTURE THREE MAJOR CHAMPIONSHIPS.

Sally Little was the first South African woman to turn professional, which she did in 1971 after winning most of South Africa's top amateur tournaments.

The only teacher Little had was her father, who started her in golf when she was just 12. He persuaded her to go to the golf course with him by paying her to pull his cart, then she started playing with her father. By 15, she had a handicap of seven but was involved in a motorbike accident that year. With her leg in a brace, she passed the time chipping and putting, and it was then she decided she wanted a career in golf.

As an amateur, Little won the Western Province Championship twice, the Transvaal Strokeplay tournament, and the 1971 South African Amateur Championship. The best amateur woman golfer in her homeland, Little turned professional with high expectations. She was quickly sent crashing down to earth.

The Cape Town girl joined the LPGA Tour when she was just 19 years old, playing seven events in the 1971 season. Although she won the Rookie of the Year Award with $1,670, it was not what Little had envisaged when she left South Africa. She quickly realized that she would need to work hard to earn her stripes in North America. She suffered a few setbacks early on before she finally found the winner's circle.

In a tournament in Orlando in the early 1970s, Little once led after three rounds. However, she went to pieces when she was paired with Kathy Whitworth, the LPGA's dominant player at the time, and actually shanked shots into the gallery because she was so nervous. Rather than let the experience upset her, Little drew on it to become a better player.

Little's breakthrough came in 1976 when she won the Women's International by holing an 80-foot bunker shot on the last hole to finish ahead of Jan Stephenson.

Although she had two operations in 1977 for a hysterectomy and ovarian cysts, and was plagued by health problems throughout her career, it is a credit to her perseverance that Little was able to win tournaments despite her physical problems. In 1980, she took her highest honor when she won the LPGA Championship.

Little's best season came in 1982 when she won three times and finished third on the LPGA Order of Merit with just under $230,000. She triumphed in the Nabisco Dinah Shore that season, a year before it was designated a major championship. Little ended the season by undergoing abdominal surgery and knee surgery.

She battled back valiantly and in 1988 capped off her career when she won the Du Maurier Classic, one of the four major championships in the women's game. That victory earned her the Ben Hogan Award, given to golfers who overcome serious illness. She was a deserving winner.

## FACT FILE

**BORN** 1951, Cape Town, South Africa

**CAREER HIGHLIGHTS**

1976 Women's International
1980 LPGA Championship
1981 Olympia Gold Classic
1982 Nabisco Dinah Shore
1988 Du Maurier Classic

# Gene Littler

FEW GOLFERS CAN SWING A CLUB BETTER THAN GENE LITTLER, FOR WHICH HE WAS KNICKNAMED "GENE THE MACHINE". BECAUSE OF HIS EFFORTLESS SWING, LITTLER WON THE 1961 US OPEN.

## Fact File

**BORN** 1930, San Diego, California, USA

**CAREER HIGHLIGHTS**
1953 US Amateur
1954 San Diego Open
1961 US Open
1965 Canadian Open
1966 World Series

**INTERNATIONAL HONORS**
Ryder Cup: 1961, 1963, 1965, 1967, 1969, 1971

Few golfers have ever hit golf shots as pure as Gene Littler did in his prime. He was called "Gene the Machine" because his swing was so effortlessly smooth and repetitive. Henry Cotton called him "one of the game's supreme stylists."

When Littler won the 1953 US Amateur Championship, he seemed destined for an outstanding future as a professional. It didn't take him long to live up to expectations. Born and raised in San Diego, it was fitting that Littler's first victory should come in the 1954 San Diego Open. He then won four times the following year, including a victory in the lucrative Los Angeles Open, and a 13-shot winning margin in the Tournament of Champions.

The 1959 season saw Littler win five times on the US Tour. In 1960 he won twice but picked up only one tournament victory in 1961. However, it was the biggest of his career.

Littler's 1961 US Open win was the only time the smooth swinger ever lifted one of the game's major trophies. The win came over the tough Oakland Hills layout near Detroit, Michigan. His four-round total of 281 was a stroke better than Bob Goalby and Doug Sanders, and tied Ralph Guldahl's 72-hole record at Oakland Hills, in Missouri.

Littler's US Open win should have been the first of many major championships for him, but he never won another. He lost an 18-hole playoff to boyhood rival Billy Casper for the 1970 Masters, and in 1977 lost a playoff to Lanny Wadkins for the USPGA Championship.

Many experts believe that Littler's poor showing in the majors stemmed from his personality. He seemed to lack the fire needed to win the big tournaments. In fact, it was said he spent only as much time on the tournament circuit as was needed to make a decent living. A lover of classic cars, particularly Rolls Royces, Littler liked nothing better than to be at home working on his collection of vintage automobiles.

Gene the Machine won 29 times on the US Tour during his career. Although he had to undergo surgery for a cancerous growth under his left arm in 1972, it did not stop him winning tournaments. Proof that his swing was one of the best lies in the fact that Littler's victory in the 1977 Houston Open came a full 23 years after his maiden win.

Upon turning 50 in 1981, Littler joined the US Senior Tour and used his classic golf swing to rack up victories on that circuit as well.

# Bobby Locke

SOUTH AFRICAN BOBBY LOCKE PLAYED EVERY SHOT THE SAME WAY, HITTING THE BALL WITH A PRONOUNCED DRAW. LOCKE USED THE TECHNIQUE TO WIN FOUR BRITISH OPENS.

Bobby Locke was one of the most unflappable characters the game of golf has ever seen. Locke never rushed anything he did, even off the golf course. His approach to life and to golf was unhurried and deliberate. He played every shot the same way, hitting everything with a big swinging hook. It was a swing he developed as a youngster growing up in South Africa, and one from which he never deviated when he turned professional.

The son of Irish immigrants, Locke won every major amateur honor in his native South Africa, including the South African Amateur twice and the 1935 South African Open before turning professional at the age of 20. In fact, Locke went on to win a further eight South African Opens as a pro.

World War II delayed Locke's assault on the British Open, but he won his first of four championships in 1949 at Royal St George's, defeating Ireland's Harry Bradshaw by 12 strokes in a 36-hole playoff for the title. He defended the championship in 1950 at Troon when he bettered Roberto de Vicenzo by two strokes and won his third in four years at Royal Lytham in 1952, edging out Peter Thomson by a shot.

Thomson took over Locke's mantle as British Open specialist, winning the title three straight times between 1954 and 1956. However, Locke won the old trophy one last time when he captured the title at St Andrews in 1957.

Besides his unflappable approach to the game, Locke's other strength lay in his short game. He ranks as one of the best putters ever to play the game, and his wedge play was second to none.

Locke's game was so good that Sam Snead persuaded him to try his hand on the US circuit. Snead had witnessed Locke's prowess during a tour of South Africa when he lost 12 of a series of 16 matches to him. Locke obliged and played in the States for a few years.

He more than held his own in the United States. Locke won six events in 1947, and in 1948 he won the Chicago Victory National Championship by the huge margin of 16 strokes. His presence in America was not appreciated by the rank and file tournament professionals, who did not like the fact that Locke was able to win large portions of their tournament purses. Locke had no great love of the United States or its professionals, and so returned to Great Britain to play most of his golf.

The South African was not a great practicer, but he played at least nine holes every day and had a passion for the game which lasted throughout his life until his death in 1987.

## Fact File

**BORN** 1917, Germiston, Transvaal, South Africa

**DIED** 1987

**CAREER HIGHLIGHTS**
1947 Canadian Open
1949 The Open Championship
1950 The Open Championship
1952 The Open Championship
1957 The Open Championship

# Nancy Lopez

NO GOLFER HAS HELPED POPULARIZE THE WOMEN'S GAME AS HAS NANCY LOPEZ. SHE IS ADORED BY GALLERIES WHEREVER SHE PLAYS.

## Fact File

**BORN** 1957, Torrance, California, USA

**CAREER HIGHLIGHTS**
1978 Colgate European Open
1978 LPGA Championship
1985 LPGA Championship
1989 LPGA Championship
1993 Youngstown-Warren LPGA Classic

**INTERNATIONAL HONORS**
Solheim Cup: 1990
Curtis Cup: 1976

If smiles could be bottled and marketed to the general public, then Nancy Lopez's would have made her millions over the years.

Lopez did for the LPGA Tour what Seve Ballesteros did for the men's European Tour. Both brought charisma to the game, helping make their respective tours more popular by drawing fans through the admission gates.

Lopez first joined the LPGA Tour in 1978 and made an immediate impression. In her rookie year, she won nine times and topped the end of season money list with nearly $190,000. She was the first player to win five consecutive tournaments on the LPGA Tour, and became the first player in the history of the game, man or woman, to win Rookie of the Year and Player of the Year awards in the same season. More importantly, her dazzling good looks and affable personality made her instantly popular. She became the LPGA's most valuable asset, helping promote the women's game for more than 20 years.

Lopez came from a poor working-class family in New Mexico and has never forgotten her humble beginnings. Her mother died in 1977, and the death had a profound effect on Lopez. It made her even more determined to do well. When she won her first LPGA Tour event, the Bent Tree Classic in Sarasota, Florida, she dedicated the victory to the memory of her mother.

Not surprisingly, Lopez's bond with her father, Domingo, is a strong one. He started her in golf by introducing her to the game when she was just seven years old. Despite his lack of disposable income, Lopez senior supported his daughter's desire to become a top-class golfer.

It was evident from an early age that Lopez would make it to the top. She won her first tournament at the age of nine, and went on to compile an outstanding amateur career that saw her win two USGA Junior Girls' Championships and play on the 1976 Curtis Cup team.

Through the 1998 season, Lopez had recorded 48 victories on the LPGA Tour to make her one of the top women golfers ever to play the game. Sadly, Lopez has not won the US Women's Open, the tournament she most covets. In 1977, she finished second as an amateur, and in 1997 fell just short of a playoff with Great Britain's Alison Nicholas. Not surprisingly, the Hall of Fame golfer isn't that concerned if it never happens. "I don't really worry about winning the US Open," she once said. "If it's going to happen, it will." All of golf wants to see her win the title—there would be no more popular winner than Lopez.

# DAVIS LOVE III

LOVE CAST OFF THE UNWANTED LABEL OF "BEST PLAYER NEVER TO HAVE WON A MAJOR" WHEN HE CAPTURED THE 1997 USPGA CHAMPIONSHIP, WINNING THE TITLE BY FIVE STROKES FROM JUSTIN LEONARD.

For years it seemed Davis Love III was destined to be a great US Tour player who would never win one of the game's four major championships. There were a few who argued that Love was a talented golfer, but that he didn't have what it takes to win a major. That changed in 1997.

Love's win in the USPGA Championship at Winged Foot, New York, rid him of the unwanted title of best player in the world not to have won a major. In previous years, he had finished second in the Masters (1995) and in the US Open (1996). Love would have been involved in a playoff for the latter championship had he not three putted the 72nd green at Oakland Hills from just 20 feet. That seemed to be ample proof that he didn't have the nerve to win the biggest titles in golf. But that changed when he won the USPGA by a convincing five strokes over Justin Leonard.

Of all the major titles in golf, it was fitting that Love's first would come in the USPGA. Love's father had been a golf professional, and one of the game's outstanding teachers. He had a huge influence on his son's life until he died in a plane crash in 1988. However, he lived long enough to watch his son achieve success on the US Tour, which came in Love's win in the 1987 MCI Heritage Classic.

Love Jr has often admitted that his father's teachings are never too far from his mind. Indeed, there were many who felt Davis Love II had a supernatural presence at Winged Foot in 1997. Upon holing out for a birdie on the final green, a huge rainbow appeared in the sky, as if his father was honoring the victory from another world.

One of the longest hitters in the modern game, Love's power is allied to a superb temperament for golf. He never lets himself get too excited on the golf course, keeping himself on an even keel no matter whether he is leading a tournament down the stretch or a few shots behind.

Through the 1998 season, Love had won 13 times on the US Tour, most of the victories coming with his brother Mark caddying for him. Since 1993 he has been a perennial member of the US Ryder Cup side. Indeed, it was his ability to come back from one down with two to play to defeat Italy's Costantino Rocca that won the USA the Cup that year.

## FACT FILE

**BORN** 1964, Charlotte, North Carolina, USA

**CAREER HIGHLIGHTS**
1987 MCI Heritage Classic
1992 Players Championship
1993 Infiniti Tournament of Champions
1997 USPGA Championship
1998 MCI Classic

**INTERNATIONAL HONORS**
Ryder Cup: 1993, 1995, 1997
World Cup: 1992, 1993, 1994, 1995, 1997
Presidents Cup: 1994, 1996, 1998
Walker Cup: 1985

# The Most Famous Miss in Golf

Doug Sanders should have won the 1970 British Open at St Andrews. One of the most colorful men in all of golf, the Georgia native came to the home hole needing a par to win the championship. After hitting his second shot too far past the hole, Sanders stroked his first putt to within 30 inches and was barely three feet from winning the British Open.

The American lined up the putt as usual, then stood over the ball with a Blue Goose putter he had bought for $3 earlier in the week. Instead of hitting the ball, though, Sanders backed away. Then he bent down to brush away some sand that was on the line of his putt. He stood over the ball again, and weakly hit it past the hole. The ball never looked like dropping in. Twenty-five years later, Sanders talked about the putt in a 1995 interview with a British golf magazine. "Do I ever think about it? Hell, I've been known to go as long as five minutes without thinking about it," was Sanders's reply.

What still bothered him even after all the years that had passed, was the way he had behaved. He said someone in the gallery sniggered when he backed away from the putt, and that put him off. "I looked round and it disturbed me, but I'm a professional. I should be able to get over that," said Sanders. "But it was all going through my mind instead of making the putt. I thought I'll get back at them when I hole it. What an amateurish thought process that is, isn't it? I'd prepared the victory speech before the battle was over. That's not the way a champion thinks. He doesn't let these things confuse him. It was indescribable the feelings I had and I didn't take hold of them. I didn't get the job done. I knew the putt was going to miss straight away. I moved on it. The most expensive missed putt in the history of the game."

The miss forced a playoff the next day with Jack Nicklaus, which Sanders lost by one stroke, scoring a 73 to Nicklaus's 72. Ironically, Sanders birdied the last hole.

What many people forget about that British Open is that Sanders made one of the best pars on the 17th hole. After placing his approach shot in the Road Bunker, Sanders got the ball up and down in two shots to preserve his one-shot lead, hitting the ball out of the sand to within inches of the hole. "It would have been one of the great bunker shots in history if it hadn't been wasted by the three putt on the next hole," admitted Sanders in 1995.

No one remembers the 17th, but the world of golf remembers the 18th—the biggest miss in golf history.

TOP: SANDERS'S SWING WASN'T EXACTLY TEXTBOOK, BUT IT NEARLY WON HIM THE 1970 BRITISH OPEN.

RIGHT: SANDERS (LEFT) AND NICKLAUS POSE WITH THE BRITISH OPEN TROPHY BEFORE THEIR 18 HOLE PLAYOFF, WHICH NICKLAUS WON.

FAR RIGHT: THE MOMENT SANDERS THINKS ABOUT EVERY DAY OF HIS LIFE, AS HIS WEAK PUTT FOR VICTORY SLIDES PAST THE HOLE.

# Sandy Lyle

SCOTLAND'S SANDY LYLE TOOK THE GREEN JACKET AT THE 1988 MASTERS WITH ONE OF THE BEST SHOTS SEEN IN THE HISTORY OF THE TOURNAMENT.

## Fact File

**BORN** 1958, Shrewsbury, Shropshire, England

**CAREER HIGHLIGHTS**
1985 The Open Championship
1987 Players Championship
1988 Masters
1988 Suntory World Match Play Championship
1992 Volvo Masters

**INTERNATIONAL HONORS**
Ryder Cup: 1979, 1981, 1983, 1985, 1987
World Cup: 1979, 1980, 1987
Alfred Dunhill Cup: 1985, 1986, 1987, 1988, 1989, 1990
Walker Cup: 1977

Sandy Lyle is responsible for one of the greatest shots in Masters history and one of the best ever hit in a major championship. In the 1988 Masters, Lyle put his 1-iron tee shot into the bunker on the 72nd hole, then hit a glorious 7-iron onto the green to about ten feet past the pin and holed the putt for a birdie. The shot won him the Masters. Lyle took the title by one stroke from Mark Calcavecchia.

Lyle's victory at Augusta made him the first British player to win the coveted green jacket. However, it came as no surprise. Lyle had been an outstanding talent from an early age.

As an amateur Lyle was taught by his late father Alex, who for many years was the professional at Hawkstone Park in Shropshire, England. Lyle junior won the English Boys' Amateur Stroke Play Championship, and the English Amateur Stroke Play Championship twice prior to turning professional. He represented England many times and was a member of the 1977 Great Britain & Ireland Walker Cup side. Later he would adopt the nationality of his father and play professionally for Scotland.

Upon turning professional after his Walker Cup appearance, Lyle immediately made an impression in the paid ranks. He won the 1977 European Tour Qualifying School and in 1978 was named Rookie of the Year. His first European victory came in 1979 when he won the Jersey Open, adding the Scandinavian Enterprise Open and the European Open to finish the year as leading money winner.

Through the 1985 season, Lyle had earned ten victories in Europe, but that year, in Sandwich on the south coast of England, would see him win the biggest tournament of his career.

The British Open was held at Royal St George's in 1985, and Lyle won the tournament with fine play over the final few holes. On the long, 508-yard, par-5, 14th hole, Lyle hit a poor shot into the rough, played a wedge shot onto the fairway and then covered the flag with a brilliant 2-iron from 220 yards. He holed the subsequent 40-foot putt for a birdie, and he birdied the next when he hit a 6-iron to less than ten feet. Around him others were dropping strokes, and Lyle came to the 18th thinking he needed a four to win. After getting his ball to the side of the 18th in two strokes, Lyle chipped poorly and watched the ball roll back to his feet. The Scotsman sank to his knees in despair, thinking he had blown his chance. However, he managed to get down in two and eventually won the championship by a shot from Payne Stewart.

Despite losing his way somewhat in the 1990s, Lyle remains one of the greatest players Great Britain has ever produced.

# Jeff Maggert

MAGGERT BECAME A MILLION DOLLAR MAN WHEN HE WON THE INAUGURAL ANDERSEN CONSULTING MATCH PLAY CHAMPIONSHIP. MAGGERT HAD TO GO EXTRA HOLES WITH ANDREW MAGEE BEFORE HITTING THE JACKPOT.

When Jeff Maggert holed a 20-foot chip on the 38th hole in the final of the 1999 Andersen Consulting Match Play Championship, he not only won himself $1 million, but he finally cast off the impression that he was little more than a professional runner-up.

Until the Andersen event, Maggert was a player who normally got himself into contention only to finish either second or third. His only previous US Tour win had come six years earlier, when he triumphed by three strokes over Greg Kraft in the Walt Disney/Oldsmobile Classic. He had plenty of top-ten finishes in the intervening years, including 13 seconds and seven thirds. But he just couldn't close the deal and earn his second victory.

"I needed to win for me, myself, and I," said Maggert after defeating Andrew Magee to win the richest prize in golf. In other words, the win was needed to prove that he could beat the best in the game when it mattered. He did exactly that.

Maggert's route to the final included wins against Bernhard Langer and the tournament favorite Tiger Woods, whom he beat in the quarter-finals by the score of two and one to upset the form book.

Maggert's game is characterized by an efficient, compact swing that has made him an accurate driver of the ball and lets him hit a lot of greens in regulation. He also has the perfect temperament for professional golf. He is one of the quieter players on Tour and never gets too excited or agitated on the course.

The resident of Texas has had several close calls in major championships. Twice he has finished fourth in the US Open, in 1995 and 1997, with the latter championship being particularly disappointing. Maggert entered the final round at the Congressional Club two strokes behind Tom Lehman, but had taken the lead by the fourth hole on four under par. However, he made a series of errors during the rest of the round to shoot 74 and finish five strokes behind eventual winner Ernie Els.

Twice Maggert has finished third in the USPGA Championship, in 1995 at Riviera, and in 1997 at Winged Foot when he shot a final round 65 to fall short of Davis Love's 269 winning total by seven strokes.

Maggert's victory in the Andersen tournament was obviously the biggest check of his career. It gave him a three-year exemption on the US Tour but, more importantly, provided him with the belief that he can win one of the game's major championships.

## Fact File

**BORN** 1964, Columbia, Missouri, USA

**CAREER HIGHLIGHTS**
1989 Malaysian Open
1990 Vines Classic
1993 Walt Disney/Oldsmobile Classic
1999 Andersen Consulting Match Play Championship

**INTERNATIONAL HONORS**
Ryder Cup: 1995, 1997
Presidents Cup: 1994

# John Mahaffey

JOHN MAHAFFEY MADE UP FOR LOSING A PLAYOFF IN THE 1975 US OPEN BY WINNING THE 1978 USPGA CHAMPIONSHIP, HIS ONE MAJOR VICTORY.

## Fact File

**BORN** 1948, Kerrville, Texas, USA

**CAREER HIGHLIGHTS**
1973 Sahara Invitational
1978 USPGA Championship
1980 Kemper Open
1986 Tournament Players Championship
1989 Federal Express St Jude Classic

**INTERNATIONAL HONORS**
Ryder Cup: 1979
World Cup: 1978, 1979

John Mahaffey's biggest victory in a US Tour career that spanned 27 years came in the 1978 USPGA Championship at Oakmont Country Club, Pennsylvania. Despite the fact he had won only once as a professional—the 1973 Sahara Invitational—and had gone four years without a victory, Mahaffey won the tournament in style.

The Texan began the tournament with a four over par 75, but an excellent 67 on the second day put him up among the leaders. A third round 68 kept him in contention. However, he entered the final round seven shots behind Tom Watson. Mahaffey made up the difference with a 66, equaling Jerry Pate and Gil Morgan for the lowest score of the week. Meanwhile, Watson shot 73 while Pate scored 68 to put the three men in a tie for the lead. The playoff ended on the second extra hole, when Mahaffey rolled in a 12-foot birdie putt to win his only major championship.

The win made up for the disappointment Mahaffey suffered in 1975. That year he tied Lou Graham for the US Open at Medinah, only to lose the ensuing 18-hole playoff, shooting 73 to Graham's 71.

Mahaffey was the 1970 NCAA champion while he was at the University of Houston, where he graduated with a degree in psychology.

Early in his professional career, Mahaffey specialized in doing impressions of other leading players. His imitation of Puerto Rico's Chi Chi Rodriguez was so good that many thought it was better than the real thing.

The 5-foot, 9-inch professional's other big win on the US Tour came in the Tournament Players Championship, now called the Players Championship, on the tough Tournament Players Course at Sawgrass in Florida. A third round 65 put Mahaffey into contention, and he won the tournament by one stroke over Larry Mize. The victory earned him a ten-year exemption on the US Tour.

Mahaffey's only appearance in the Ryder Cup came in the 1979 match at The Greenbrier, West Virginia. The USA won the Cup that year by the score of 17 to 11 points, and Mahaffey contributed a point on the final day when he defeated Brian Barnes by a score of one up. Mahaffey also helped the United States win the World Cup twice, in 1978 and 1979.

The resident of Houston turned 50 on May 9, 1998, and immediately joined the US Senior Tour. Despite playing a shortened season, Mahaffey was still able to finish the season among the top 50 on the money list, with earnings of over $365,000.

# Meg Mallon

MALLON'S WINS IN THE US WOMEN'S OPEN AND LPGA CHAMPIONSHIP IN 1991 EARNED HER MEMBERSHIP OF AN ELITE GROUP ON THE LPGA TOUR. SHE BECAME ONE OF ONLY FIVE WOMEN TO WIN THE TWO MAJORS IN THE SAME SEASON.

The words "never compromise" grace the back of Meg Mallon's putter. The words are apropos because there is nothing compromising about the way Mallon plays golf.

Since 1991, when she won four times on the LPGA Tour, Mallon has been one of the top players in women's golf. Of her four wins that season, two of them came in major championships. Mallon won the LPGA Championship and the US Women's Open to become only the fifth woman to win those two majors in the same season (Sandra Haynie, Pat Bradley, Se Ri Pak, and Juli Inkster are the others).

It took Mallon a while to find her feet on the LPGA Tour. After winning the 1983 Michigan Amateur Championship and attending Ohio State University where she earned all-conference honors, Mallon turned professional in 1987.

She started to show signs of promise in 1990 when she had four top-ten finishes. Then came her tremendous season in 1991. Her four victories and eight other top-ten finishes that year helped her to her best financial season on the LPGA Tour, with over $630,000 in earnings. Her performance that year also earned the prestigious Golf Digest Most Improved Player award.

Through the 1998 season Mallon had won nine times on the LPGA Tour, and had also won the J.C. Penney Classic with Steve Pate in 1998. She broke through the $1 million mark in 1992, the $2 million barrier in 1995, and $3 million in 1997.

The 5-foot, 6-inch professional has been a regular Solheim Cup player since 1992 when she appeared in a losing cause at Dalmahoy, Scotland. Every other appearance since then has been on a winning side, and through the 1998 match she had amassed an excellent record of seven wins, three losses, and four halves in the 14 times she had played.

Mallon nearly added her third major championship at the beginning of the 1999 season when she finished runner-up to Dottie Pepper in the Nabisco Dinah Shore tournament. Mallon's 13 under par total would have won the tournament in most other years, but Pepper was just too good that week. Tremendous golf by Pepper saw her run out a six-stroke champion on 19 under par, the best score ever in a women's major.

The strength of Mallon's game lies in her accurate iron play. Most years she is one of the leading players when it comes to hitting greens in regulation. Although she isn't the longest driver on the LPGA Tour, she is by no means short. However, she is normally very straight off the tee and hits a lot of fairways.

## Fact File

**BORN** 1963, Natick, Massachusetts, USA

**CAREER HIGHLIGHTS**
1991 Mazda LPGA Championship
1991 US Women's Open
1993 Ping Welch's Championship
1996 Cup Noodles Hawaiian Ladies' Open
1998 Star Bank LPGA Classic

**INTERNATIONAL HONORS**
Solheim Cup: 1992, 1994, 1996, 1998

# LLOYD MANGRUM

MANGRUM WAS ONE OF THE TOUGHEST COMPETITORS EVER TO PLAY THE US TOUR. THE TEXAS PROFESSIONAL WAS KNOWN FOR HIS OUTSTANDING ABILITY AROUND THE GREENS.

## FACT FILE

**BORN** 1914, Trenton, Texas, USA

**DIED** 1973

**CAREER HIGHLIGHTS**
1938 Pennsylvania Open
1946 Argentine Open
1946 US Open
1948 All-American Open
1948 World Tournament

**INTERNATIONAL HONORS**
Ryder Cup: 1947, 1949, 1951, 1953 (captain)

Lloyd Mangrum was perhaps the biggest gambler ever to play the US professional circuit. The bigger the stake, the better Mangrum liked it. And that wasn't just golf. Mangrum was also a serious poker player during his career.

Another great player to come out of Texas, Mangrum went on the professional circuit with just $250 given to him by a singer called John Boles. It was enough to get him on the road and into card games. Poker, gin rummy, or whatever else was being played, it didn't matter to Mangrum. He'd ante up and sometimes win the pot. Stories about his gambling winnings were legendary. Most of them were blown out of proportion in the retelling, but it only served to enhance Mangrum's image.

The Texan was as tough on the golf course as he was at the card table. He was not the best player when it came to hitting woods and long irons, but he more than made up for his deficiencies in those areas with his short game. Mangrum was outstanding within 30 yards of the hole. More often than not he would get the ball up and down in two strokes to salvage par. And when he did hit greens in regulation, he was a safe bet to walk away without three putting.

Mangrum twice finished runner-up in the Masters. In 1940 he placed second, four shots behind fellow Texan Jimmy Demaret. Then in 1949 he tied for second with Johnny Bulla, three strokes behind Sam Snead.

His only major triumph came in the 1946 US Open at the Canterbury Golf Club in Cleveland, Ohio. After four rounds, Mangrum found himself tied for the lead with Vic Ghezzi and Byron Nelson. The three men tied with scores of 72 in the ensuing 18-hole playoff and had to play another 18 holes to determine the winner. Mangrum won the second playoff by shooting 72 to 73s by Ghezzi and Nelson. With six holes to play in the second extra round, Mangrum was three strokes behind Ghezzi and two behind Nelson. However, he birdied the last three holes in driving rain to win the title.

Mangrum was involved in another playoff for the US Open in 1950, when he tied Ben Hogan for the 72-hole lead. Mangrum lost the playoff by four shots, two of which came on a penalty on the 16th hole when he picked up his ball to remove a fly.

Mangrum may have been a tough competitor, but he was an honest one too. He once called a penalty shot on himself in the Masters when his ball moved in the rough after he had addressed it.

# Carol Mann

MANN'S BEST TWO SEASONS ON THE LPGA TOUR CAME IN 1968 AND 1969, WHEN SHE WON AN INCREDIBLE 18 TOURNAMENTS. THE FORMER LPGA PRESIDENT WON 38 TIMES DURING HER CAREER.

Carol Mann had a huge impact on the LPGA Tour in the 1960s and 1970s. Mann was not only one of its star players, but she served as LPGA president from 1973 until 1976, a period during which the LPGA underwent a drastic modernization process.

Mann began playing golf at the age of nine when she was given a set of right-handed clubs. Mann is left-handed, but in those days it was hard to find a set of left-handed clubs so Mann persevered. In the summers she would play against her four younger brothers, and by the time she was 17 she was good enough to win the Junior Women's Western Open.

Patty Berg helped Mann get sponsorship from Wilson Sporting Goods when she turned professional in October 1960. Her first tournament turned out to be a nightmare, featuring an 89 that included a five putt on one green because she didn't know how to take relief from casual water. In her second event, though, Mann won $300 and that helped boost her confidence.

Her game was transformed in 1962 when she met Manuel de la Torre, the professional at Milwaukee Country Club. He altered her swing, and the two worked together for the next 16 years.

Torre's influence helped Mann win her first tournament, the 1964 Western Open. In those days there were no scoreboards or hi-tech communications that proliferate at modern golf tournaments. So when Mann finished the last hole she asked who was leading. She was. Mann had won the tournament by two strokes. Her first place check was for $1,200, and she spent $120 of it on champagne for the press.

In 1965 Mann won twice, including her only major championship when she won the US Women's Open. In 1966 she won four times, three times in 1967 and then went on a romp for the next two seasons.

Mann hit double figures in 1968 when she won ten tournaments to finish second on the money list. In 1969 she won eight times and topped the Order of Merit with just under $50,000. Those were her best two seasons as a professional.

Her last victory came in the 1975 Lawson's Open, her 38th win on the LPGA Tour, ninth best in LPGA history. That same season saw her establish an LPGA record of seven consecutive birdies during the Borden Classic, which she went on to win.

Mann was inducted into the LPGA Hall of Fame in 1977, and the Women's Sports Hall of Fame in 1982.

## Fact File

**BORN** 1941, Buffalo, New York, USA

**CAREER HIGHLIGHTS**
1964 Western Open
1965 US Women's Open
1969 Tournament of Champions
1972 Orange Blossom Classic
1975 Dallas Civitan Classic

# Dave Marr

THE GOLF WORLD MOURNED THE LOSS OF DAVE MARR WHEN HE DIED OF CANCER IN 1997. THE 1965 USPGA CHAMPION WAS ONE OF THE MOST POPULAR FIGURES IN THE GAME.

## Fact File

**BORN** 1933, Houston, Texas, USA

**DIED** 1997

**CAREER HIGHLIGHTS**
1961 Greater Seattle Open
1962 Azalea Open
1965 USPGA Championship

**INTERNATIONAL HONORS**
Ryder Cup: 1965, 1981 (captain)

There probably hasn't been a finer gentleman to play the game of golf than Dave Marr. Nor has there been a player who squeezed more out of his talent than the man from Houston, Texas.

Marr was never a world beater. There was nothing spectacular about his driving or his iron play or his short game; in fact, he was by his own admission a poor putter. Yet he worked hard and maximized his talent to the point where he won a major championship.

Marr was fortunate enough when he was a young hopeful to meet Claude Harmon, the 1948 Masters champion. Harmon took Marr under his wing and taught him the facts of golf and life. Marr went to work for Harmon when Harmon was based at Winged Foot in the summer, and at Seminole in the winter. But Harmon taught Marr more than just how to conduct himself as a professional: he made him the man he turned out to be. "Claude Harmon not only taught me most of what I know about the golf swing, he did something almost as important," Marr once revealed. "Man, he took me out of Argyll socks."

When Marr passed away in 1997 after a long battle with cancer, the golf world mourned the passing of one of the game's true characters. Marr was one of the most personable players ever to play the game. He was just as comfortable in the company of other sports stars and show business celebrities as he was with top-class golfers. Then there was his wit, examples of which come from the Masters. Marr played the final round of the 1964 Masters with Arnold Palmer. Standing on the 18th tee, Palmer was six strokes ahead with Marr in second place along with Jack Nicklaus. Palmer looked over at his good friend and asked if there was anything he could do for him. "Yeah," replied Marr. "Make a 12."

Earlier in the round Palmer hit a huge shot to the 15th hole which he lost in the sun. Worried that it might have landed in the pond fronting the green, Palmer asked Marr if the ball got over the water. "Hell, Arnold, your divot got over," replied Marr.

A year later Marr won his only major championship when he triumphed in the USPGA Championship at Laurel Valley, a long course. Marr made up for his lack of length off the tee by grinding his way around the course. He eventually won by two shots from Jack Nicklaus and Billy Casper.

After his playing days ended, Marr became an excellent TV commentator, a role he held until his untimely death.

# Graham Marsh

MARSH NEVER WON A MAJOR CHAMPIONSHIP DURING HIS REGULAR PLAYING DAYS. HE MADE UP FOR THAT BY WINNING THE 1997 US SENIOR OPEN.

Graham Marsh started playing golf as an eight-year-old in Western Australia. By the time he was 18 he had got his handicap down to scratch, and would represent Western Australia for six straight seasons as an amateur. Despite that, Marsh had to be persuaded to turn professional.

Marsh was a schoolmaster when he won the 1967 Western Australian Amateur Championship and placed second in the Australian Amateur Championship. On the advice of Peter Thomson, five-time winner of the British Open, he packed away his books and his pointer and turned professional.

A year later Marsh recorded his first victory when he won the Watties Tournament in New Zealand. He also finished runner-up to Bob Charles in the New Zealand Open and won the Swiss Open. His golfing career was off and running.

Although Marsh now plays almost all his golf on the US Senior Tour, as a young man he was quite content to play everywhere around the world. His passport has been well stamped. Besides winning in New Zealand and Australia, the man they call "Swampy," for obvious reasons, has won all over the world. He holds the title of Open champion of the following countries: Switzerland, India, Germany, Thailand, Malaysia, Holland, and Scotland. Before his senior career started he had won over 50 tournaments around the world. Included in that number was the 1977 Heritage Classic, the only tournament he won on the US Tour. Marsh defeated Tom Watson by one stroke to earn the title.

The Australian spent much of his prime golfing years on the lucrative Japanese Tour, banking a lot of yen in the process. He won 24 tournaments in total on the tough Japanese circuit.

Marsh's best season came in 1977 when he won six times on three different tours. Besides his victory over Watson, Marsh also won the prestigious Lancôme Trophy and the World Match Play Championship at Wentworth, defeating strong American player Ray Floyd by a score of five and three in the final.

The Australian joined the US Senior Tour in 1994 and a year later won his first tournament when he triumphed in the Bruno's Memorial Classic. His finest moment as a senior occurred in 1997 when he won the US Senior Open at Olympia Fields Country Club. He won the title by one stroke from good friend John Bland, and by two from Gil Morgan and Tom Wargo to win his first senior major.

## Fact File

**BORN** 1944, Kalgoorlie, Western Australia

**CAREER HIGHLIGHTS**
1970 Swiss Open
1977 Colgate World Match Play Championship
1979 Dunlop Masters
1982 Australian Masters
1997 US Senior Open

**INTERNATIONAL HONORS**
Alfred Dunhill Cup: 1985

# Casey Martin

MARTIN MADE LEGAL HISTORY IN 1998 WHEN HE TOOK THE US TOUR TO COURT OVER THE RIGHT TO RIDE IN A GOLF CART. MARTIN WON HIS CASE AND WENT ON TO COMPETE IN THE US OPEN.

## Fact File

**BORN** 1972, Eugene, Oregon, USA

**CAREER HIGHLIGHTS**
1998 NIKE Lakeland Classic

Don't look for Casey Martin's name in any list of major champions. Don't even look for his name in any list of US, European, Australian, or Japanese Tour winners. It isn't there. Martin's only tournament victory so far came in the 1998 Lakeland Classic on the NIKE Tour. He is in this book for a bigger victory than emerging as the winner of a four-round golf tournament.

Martin suffers from a disease known as Klippel-Trenauney-Webber Syndrome. The affliction impedes the flow of blood in Martin's right leg, making it almost impossible to walk, let alone play golf. Yet the Eugene, Oregon, native has overcome the disease to make it all the way to the US Open.

The 6-foot, 3-inch golfer attended Stanford University at the same time as Tiger Woods. Martin was a second team All-American in 1994 while at Stanford, and was a member of the team that won the NCAA Championship. He graduated in 1995 with a degree in economics and turned professional before joining the NIKE Tour.

Martin hit the headlines in 1998 when he took the US Tour to court over the right to ride in a golf cart.

US Tour rules forbid golfers from riding during a round. Martin went to court and won his case in what became an important precedent for handicapped golfers. The debate polarized the US Tour. Big names like Arnold Palmer and Jack Nicklaus backed the Tour's position, while players like Tom Lehman, John Daly, and Payne Stewart voiced their support for Casey's right to ride. Stewart put it best when he said, "This gentleman is handicapped, but he has the ability to play golf. Let him play. So what if he has to be transported around in a cart."

That same year Martin qualified to play in the US Open at the Olympic Club, where he was allowed to ride during the four rounds. It was obvious from the support he received from the San Francisco galleries that public opinion was firmly on his side on the cart issue. Martin did himself proud by making all four rounds. Scores of 74, 71, 74, and 72 saw him tie for 23rd place, just nine shots behind winner Lee Janzen.

Martin may never realize his dream of playing on the US Tour. His performance in the US Open, however, and his brave decision to take on the might of the US Tour makes him one of the true champions of golf.

# Shigeki Maruyama

MARAYUMA WAS THE STAR OF THE 1998 PRESIDENTS CUP. THE POPULAR JAPANESE GOLFER WAS THE ONLY PLAYER TO COMPILE A PERFECT RECORD.

Shigeki Maruyama was the star of the 1998 Presidents Cup, when the international team shocked their American rivals at Royal Melbourne Golf Club in Australia by winning the cup for the first time by the landslide score of $20\frac{1}{2}$ to $11\frac{1}{2}$ points. Maruyama was the only player on either team with a perfect record of five matches and five wins.

Maruyama came to the attention of the golfing public with his Presidents Cup performance. Until that time no one had really heard of him. He did enjoy a brief spell in the limelight in the 1997 British Open at Royal Troon when he finished tenth, but it was seen as something of a flash in the pan, just one good week. Japanese golf fans knew differently.

Just a few months after the Presidents Cup, Maruyama was back in the limelight again with his showing in the Andersen Consulting Match Play Championship at the La Costa Resort and Spa in Carlsbad, California. The field was one of the best ever assembled for a tournament other than a major championship. Of the top 64 players in the world, only Maruyama's countryman Jumbo Ozaki failed to turn up for the world's richest golf tournament, where the total purse was $5 million and where the winner, Jeff Maggert, picked up $1 million.

As in Australia, however, Maruyama confounded the form book by upsetting three of America's strongest players. In the first round, he knocked out Steve Stricker three and two. In the second, he took care of 1997 British Open champion Justin Leonard by the surprising score of four and three. Then Maruyama defeated Loren Roberts, runner-up in the 1994 US Open, by two holes to one. The Japanese player finally ran out of steam in his fourth match when he lost at the last hole to Andrew Magee.

Maruyama's play was exemplary over the four matches, but then Japanese golf fans could have predicted that. Through the 1998 season, Maruyama had won eight times on his home circuit.

His first victory came in 1993, when he won the Pepshi-Ubekousan. Another win followed in 1996 when he triumphed in the Bridgestone Open. Then he came close to dethroning the king of Japanese golf the following season.

With four victories on the 1997 Japanese Tour, Maruyama did his best to unseat Jumbo Ozaki as the Japanese number one golfer. He didn't quite make it, but with the equivalent of just over $1.38 million, he only fell short of Ozaki's winning total by just under $40,000. Ozaki took the Order of Merit because he won one more tournament than Maruyama.

The small but powerful golfer says his ambition is to win a tournament on the US Tour. There are not many people who doubt he will do it.

## Fact File

**BORN** 1969, Chiba, Japan

**CAREER HIGHLIGHTS**
1993 Pepshi-Ubekousan
1996 Bridgestone Open
1997 Japan PGA Championship
1997 Japan Match Play Championship
1998 PGA Philanthropy

**INTERNATIONAL HONORS**
Presidents Cup: 1998

# Arnaud Massy

FRENCHMAN ARNAUD MASSY ACTUALLY STARTED PLAYING THE GAME LEFT HANDED, BUT SWITCHED SIDES AND WENT ON TO WIN THE 1907 BRITISH OPEN.

## Fact File

**BORN** 1877, Biarritz, France

**DIED** 1958

**CAREER HIGHLIGHTS**
1906 French Open
1907 The Open Championship
1907 French Open
1911 French Open
1925 French Open

Nowadays there are many fine French golfers—Jean Van de Velde, Marc Farry, Fabrice Tarnaud, to name a few—but at the turn of the century it was exceptional to see a Frenchman in a golf tournament, especially any one of the major championship. Arnaud Massy was the exception to the rule.

Massy won the British Open in 1907 at Hoylake to become the first foreigner to triumph in the tournament. Winning the championship was no easy feat, however, because Massy triumphed at a time when the Great Triumvirate of Harry Vardon, James Braid, and J.H. Taylor were at their peak and winning the British Open on a regular basis. Massy got the better of them at Hoylake, particularly Taylor who finished second, two strokes behind the Frenchman. Massy nearly won the championship again in 1911 when he tied Vardon for the 72-hole lead at Royal St George's. However, Vardon won the ensuing playoff.

Massy actually started playing golf left-handed when he was in France, because that was the only set of clubs available to him. However, when Massy went to North Berwick, Scotland, in 1902, he was given a set of right-handed clubs and so had to start all over again. Massy practiced hard and was able to master the clubs to the extent that he played in the British Open at St Andrews in 1905 and finished fifth. A year later he placed sixth at Muirfield before recording his famous victory at Hoylake.

The Frenchman was one of the best wind players in the game, and was at his most commanding when the wind blew hard. In the year he tied Vardon he said he wanted the wind to blow so strong that it would knock down all the trees in Sandwich. Obviously the wind didn't blow hard enough or he may have won his second British Open.

As was perhaps to be expected, Massy played the game with much *élan*. He walked tall and proud and had that certain air that all great champions have.

Massy triumphed not only in the British Open, but won several French and Spanish national opens. He won the French title four times, and lifted three Spanish Opens during his playing days.

Upon retiring from full-time competitive golf he became the professional at Chantaco at the base of the Pyrenees, the course owned by the Lacoste family.

# BILLY MAYFAIR

MAYFAIR HIT THE JACKPOT IN 1995 WHEN HE IMPROVED HIS EARNINGS BY NEARLY $1.4 MILLION. MAYFAIR WON THREE TIMES, INCLUDING THE END OF SEASON TOUR CHAMPIONSHIP.

Billy Mayfair looks like the sort of guy who would deliver your milk, or fix your car, or sell you hardware materials. If you were to pass him in a shopping mall you wouldn't think of him as a professional golfer. Looks can be deceiving.

After a glittering amateur career that saw him win the 1987 US Amateur Championship and the 1986 US Amateur Public Links Championship, Mayfair turned professional in 1988. It took the Arizona native a while to find his true form on the US Tour, but once he did he made up for lost time.

In his first full season on the US Tour Mayfair finished 116th on the money list. He followed that up the next season by finishing 12th, courtesy of seven top-ten finishes, including two seconds. He faded into the background slightly over the next four seasons, and even came close to losing his card in 1994 when he finished 113th on the money list. Then came a banner year in 1995.

Mayfair's earnings in 1994 totaled just $158,159. Not much when you consider the costs of full-time travel and accommodation on the US Tour. The following season he gave himself a record pay raise when he won $1,543,192, a jump of $1,385,033 from the previous year and a US Tour record year to year increase. Mayfair won twice that season, picking up the Western Open and then capping the season with a first-place check of $540,000 in the end of year Tour Championship. That win catapulted him to second on the final money list.

After two winless seasons in 1996 and 1997, Mayfair won twice in 1998 for another $1 million-plus year. The former Arizona State player twice shot final rounds of 67 to win the Nissan and Buick Opens.

The strength of Mayfair's game lies in his driving accuracy. Not long off the tee, Mayfair normally finishes in the top-30 ranking for fairways hit. The same cannot be said for his putting.

The former amateur champion has one of the oddest putting strokes in the game. He tends to take the club away from the ball outside the ball-to-target line, and then cuts across it at impact, pushing the ball toward the hole. It's not a stroke that inspires confidence. Indeed, for six of his seven years on the US Tour through the 1998 season, Mayfair had finished well down in the putting statistics. However, with over $4 million in career earnings he's obviously in no hurry to try a different stroke.

## FACT FILE

**BORN** 1966, Scotsdale, Arizona, USA

**CAREER HIGHLIGHTS**
1987 US Amateur
1993 Greater Milwaukee Open
1995 Motorola Western Open
1995 Tour Championship
1998 Nissan Open

**INTERNATIONAL HONORS**
Walker Cup: 1987

# MARK McCUMBER

MCCUMBER HAS BEEN CLOSE TO A MAJOR CHAMPIONSHIP ON A NUMBER OF OCCASIONS BUT HAS NARROWLY MISSED THE FIRST PLACE PRIZE EACH TIME. HE HAS, HOWEVER, WON MANY TIMES ON THE US TOUR.

## FACT FILE

**BORN** 1951, Jacksonville, Florida, USA

**CAREER HIGHLIGHTS**
1979 Doral-Eastern Open
1983 Western Open
1989 Beatrice Western Open
1988 Players Championship
1994 Tour Championship

**INTERNATIONAL HONORS**
Ryder Cup: 1989
World Cup: 1988, 1989
Alfred Dunhill Cup: 1988

Mark McCumber has finished second in major championships on two separate occasions, once in the US Open and once in the British Open. That's not too surprising given the Floridian's good all-round game. What is surprising is that he has never been able to win one of the game's four coveted trophies.

McCumber has won the so-called fifth major, the name given to the Players Championship. McCumber won this title in 1988 over the demanding TPC course at Sawgrass. McCumber's four-shot victory over Mike Reid was one of the most popular in the tournament's history, given that he was the local favorite. In fact, McCumber has made it a habit to win quite often in his home state.

Besides the Players Championship, he has won the Pensacola Open, and the Doral-Eastern Open on two occasions, in 1979 and 1985. Winning Doral is no easy task, for it means having to conquer the famous Blue Monster course. That he has won the title twice is a measure of the quality of McCumber's game.

Not surprisingly, McCumber's first near miss in a major championship came in his home state. PGA National Golf Club in Palm Beach Gardens was the venue for the 1987 USPGA Championship, and the local boy entered the final round with a real chance to win the title. After rounds of 74, 69, 69, McCumber started the last day tied for the lead with D.A. Weibring. However, a disastrous 77 knocked him back to fifth place, just two shots behind eventual winner Larry Nelson.

Two years later, McCumber had a chance to win the US Open at Oak Hill in Rochester, New York. Rounds of 70, 68, 72, 69 gave the Floridian a four-round total of 279, a score good enough to win in some years. However, Curtis Strange went one stroke better to deny McCumber the title; he tied for second with Chip Beck.

Nine years later, McCumber entered the final round of the 1996 British Open at Royal Lytham & St Annes nine strokes behind fellow countryman Tom Lehman. An excellent final round 66 saw McCumber cut the deficit to two shots. He finished tied for second with Ernie Els.

Injury hampered McCumber's presence on the Tour in the late 1990s. He underwent surgery in August 1996 for a rotator cuff injury, and played just 15 tournaments that year as a result.

One of the few players on the US Tour not to come through the US college route, McCumber has moved into golf course design with his brothers. One of their creations is the Heron Bay course in Coral Springs Florida, venue for the Honda Classic.

# JOHN J. MCDERMOTT

MCDERMOTT'S TIME AT THE TOP WAS BRIEF. HE SUFFERED A NERVOUS BREAKDOWN AT THE AGE OF 23 AND NEVER PLAYED GOLF AGAIN.

John J. McDermott made history in 1911 when he became the first home-grown player to win the US Open. Until then, the tournament had been dominated by Scottish immigrants who had moved to America to capitalize on the riches the game had to offer there.

McDermott was a small man who used clubs that were extra long, a factor that no doubt contributed to his very flat swing. He actually tied for the 72-hole lead at the Philadelphia Cricket Club in 1910 with two Scotsmen from Carnoustie, the Smith brothers, Alex and MacDonald. McDermott lost the subsequent playoff when he shot 75 to Alex's 71 and a 77 from MacDonald. A year later at the Chicago Golf Club he also tied for the lead after four rounds. His 307 score put him into a playoff for the title with Mike Brady and George Simpson. This time McDermott prevailed, even though he shot 80 in the extra round. It won him the title by two shots from Brady, and by five from Simpson. At just 19 years old, he was the youngest player to win the prestigious championship, a record that remains to this day.

When McDermott defended the title a year later at the Country Club of Buffalo, he became the second man since Willie Anderson to win consecutive US Opens. Tom McNamara, another American-born player, was McDermott's main rival that year. He finished runner-up by two shots despite two rounds under 70, a rare feat in those days.

After his two US Open victories, McDermott won the Western Open, one of the biggest tournaments in golf in his day. The professional again got the better of Mike Brady, taking the title from him by seven shots. McDermott also won the 1913 Shawnee Open and the North and South Open in 1914. In 1913, he tied fifth in the British Open at Hoylake when J. H. Taylor won the last of his five championships.

McDermott's story after his few brief moments in the spotlight is one of the saddest in golf history. He lost money on the stock market, and was once shipwrecked in the English Channel while sailing to the British Open. Then in 1915 he suffered a nervous breakdown at the age of 23.

Just a few years after his greatest moments in golf, McDermott's career was over. He was plagued by mental illness for the rest of his life. He had worked so hard to get to the top that many felt he had burned himself out in the process. Even though he lived to the age of 80, McDermott never played another golf tournament in his life.

## FACT FILE

**BORN** 1891, Philadelphia, Pennsylvania, USA

**DIED** 1971

**CAREER HIGHLIGHTS**
1911 US Open
1912 US Open
1912 Philadelphia Open
1912 Western Open
1914 North and South Open

# The Birth of a Legend

Severiano Ballesteros was just 19 years old when he competed in the 1976 British Open. Strong, handsome, and with a smile that could light up a room, Seve Ballesteros would not win the British Open that year, but he gave warning to the golfing world that it wouldn't be long before he would.

It was Ballesteros who set the pace after an opening round of 69. Another 69 in the second round gave him the halfway lead. Seve was two strokes ahead of Johnny Miller, who, three years earlier, had won the US Open Championship at Oakmont with a brilliant closing round of 63. Miller could play. So could Seve. The galleries were thrilled by the way Seve played the game. Not since Palmer had a golfer attacked a course with such reckless abandon. Seve hit the ball all over the place, but a marvelous short game saw him save par from the unlikeliest of places.

After Ballesteros and Miller scored matching 73s in the third round, Ballesteros entered the final round needing a good score to win his first British Open. It was the more experienced player, however, who kept his nerves over the final 18 holes. Early in the final round Ballesteros actually increased his lead to three strokes, but a bogey six at the sixth and Miller's 33 over the opening nine saw him slip. Ballesteros made a triple bogey seven at the par-4 11th hole. When Miller made eagle at the par-5 13th, it was clear the American was going to win the championship. Yet it was the way the Spaniard finished that established his reputation as a player willing to take on the hardest of shots and execute them to perfection in the heat of competition.

Ballesteros eagled the 17th and then needed to birdie the last to tie Jack Nicklaus for second place. A hooked second shot to the home hole looked like he would have to settle for third place. His ball had come to rest about 30 yards from the flag, but between Seve's ball and the hole were a pair of bunkers with a narrow path running between them. Most players would have played a pitch over the bunkers. However, such a shot had little chance of getting the ball close to the hole. Ballesteros had other ideas. The Spaniard chose to play a chip and run shot between the two bunkers. In the circumstances it was an extremely brave shot to play, because he could have been playing his next shot from sand. Instead he ran the ball up between the two bunkers to within a few feet of the hole. When he holed the subsequent putt he had finished second in the British Open. The shot was the mark of a genius, a master stroke by a player who would go on to become one of the masters of the game.

RIGHT: SEVE IN DETERMINED MOOD. A 19-YEAR-OLD BALLESTEROS HAS THE EYES OF A TIGER AS HE CONTENDS FOR THE 1976 BRITISH OPEN AT ROYAL BIRKDALE.

FAR RIGHT: SEVE IN FAMILIAR TERRITORY, PLAYING FROM THE ROYAL BIRKDALE ROUGH. IT WAS HIS ABILITY TO GET OUT OF JAIL FROM ALMOST ANY SITUATION THAT ENDEARED HIM TO THE FANS.

# Mark McNulty

MCNULTY IS ONE OF THE BEST PUTTERS IN THE MODERN GAME, A TALENT ACQUIRED PUTTING ON BROWN GREENS IN HIS NATIVE ZIMBABWE.

## Fact File

**BORN** 1953, Bindwa, Zimbabwe

**CAREER HIGHLIGHTS**
1980 German Open
1987 Dunhill British Masters
1987 Million Dollar Challenge
1994 BMW International Open
1996 Volvo Masters

**INTERNATIONAL HONORS**
World Cup: 1993, 1994, 1995, 1996, 1997, 1998
Alfred Dunhill Cup: 1993, 1994, 1995, 1996, 1997, 1998
Presidents Cup: 1994, 1996

Mark McNulty's nickname is "McMagic," a title given to him by his peers for his wonderful putting stroke. Few players in the history of the game have stroked the ball better than McNulty.

The Zimbabwean's silky smooth stroke was developed on sand greens when he was growing up in Zimbabwe. These are hard-packed greens formed from oil-treated sand that are called browns. To have any success on them, players have to make sure they accelerate the putter head through the ball toward the hole. Acceleration through the ball is an important asset on grass as well. Nobody in professional golf does that better than Mark McNulty.

The other reason for the McMagic moniker comes from his wedge play. McNulty is one of the best chippers and pitchers of a ball in the game. He has to be. The 5-foot, 10-inch professional isn't one of the longest hitters in the game; in fact, he's one of the shortest. However, he hits the ball on the fairway with amazing regularity, hits a lot of greens in regulation, and when he does come up short or miss the green then he has his magic short game to rely on.

McNulty grew up playing alongside good players like Tony Johnstone and Nick Price, the latter a winner of three major championships. Although the three are the greatest of friends and have represented Zimbabwe in many Alfred Dunhill Cups together, it is because of their intense but healthy rivalry in their younger days that they have made it to the top. Throughout their careers they have spurred one another along to greater and greater heights.

Through the 1998 season, McNulty had won 15 times on the European Tour, including four German Opens. He is also a past winner of big events like the Dunhill British Masters and the Volvo Masters.

The resident of Sunningdale, England, has won 30 other titles around the world, most of them in South Africa and his native Zimbabwe. In 1987 he picked up the biggest check of his career when he won the Million Dollar Challenge in Sun City, South Africa.

McNulty came closest to winning a major championship when he finished second to Nick Faldo at the Old Course, St Andrews in the 1990 British Open. McNulty tied with Payne Stewart for second place honors that year after both men finished with a four-round total of 275, 13 under par. In previous years that score would have meant a playoff for the title, but they were second by five strokes to an outstanding display of golf by Nick Faldo.

# Bill Mehlhorn

WILD BILL MEHLHORN'S SWING DREW PRAISE FROM BEN HOGAN, BUT NOT HIS PUTTING STROKE. MEHLHORN WOULD NO DOUBT HAVE WON MORE TOURNAMENTS HAD HE BEEN A BETTER PUTTER.

Few golfers have hit a golf ball as sweetly as Wild Bill Mehlhorn. From tee to green he was one of the greatest players ever to swing a golf club. His problems started when he got onto the putting green.

"Wild Bill" was the nickname given to Mehlhorn by his friend and competitor Leo Diegel. The title was entirely fitting for Mehlhorn looked nothing like a golfer. Celebrated British golf writer Bernard Darwin once said that Mehlhorn looked like a bricklayer's carrier. Looks can and do deceive, especially in Mehlhorn's case.

The Mehlhorn swing was so good that even Ben Hogan loved to watch Wild Bill hit balls, and Hogan was particularly choosy about who he watched play golf. Hogan had probably the best golf swing in the history of the game, but he said Mehlhorn was one of the best ball strikers he ever saw. You can bet though that Hogan often looked away when Mehlhorn putted.

More tournaments would have gone Mehlhorn's way had his putting stroke matched his golf swing. Twice he finished third in the US Open, in 1924 and 1926. He made it to the final of the 1925 USPGA Championship only to lose to USPGA specialist Walter Hagen by a score of six and five. Mehlhorn reached the semi-finals of the USPGA in 1936 but poor putting cost him a place in the final. Two up with four to play, Mehlhorn's putting woes got the better of him. He missed two four-foot putts on the 33rd and 34th holes and eventually lost the match with a bogey at the last.

Stories of Mehlhorn's putting are legendary. He had the "yips" long before the term came into vogue. Playing in a pairs tournament once with Earl Holland in Miami, Mehlhorn's second shot was 10 feet from the hole when he told Holland to pick up his ball. Mehlhorn then took six putts to get the ball in the hole. Once, in Dallas, Mehlhorn had a four-footer to tie for the lead. Standing in the fringe at the back of the green Craig Wood had to jump as the ball raced past him. Then there was the time he played with Hogan and hit his approach shot two feet from the hole. Hogan watched as Mehlhorn played his fourth from a bunker.

Despite his putting problems, Mehlhorn still managed to win 20 tournaments during his career. He went on to become an excellent teacher.

## Fact File

**BORN** 1898, Elgin, Illinois, USA

**DIED** Date unknown

**CAREER HIGHLIGHTS**
1924 Western Open
1926 South Florida Open
1928 Hawaiian Open
1928 Texas Open
1929 El Paso Open

**INTERNATIONAL HONORS**
Ryder Cup: 1927

# PHIL MICKELSON

MICKELSON IS THE MOST TALENTED LEFT-HANDED GOLFER SINCE NEW ZEALAND'S BOB CHARLES. THE POPULAR AMERICAN GOLFER HAS ONE OF THE BEST SHORT GAMES IN GOLF.

## FACT FILE

**BORN** 1970, San Diego, California, USA

**CAREER HIGHLIGHTS**
1991 Northern Telecom Open
1993 Buick Invitational
1996 Phoenix Open
1996 NEC World Series of Golf
1997 Bay Hill Invitational

**INTERNATIONAL HONORS**
Ryder Cup: 1995, 1997
Alfred Dunhill Cup: 1996, 1997
Presidents Cup: 1994, 1996, 1998
Walker Cup: 1989, 1991

Phil Mickelson was always destined to be a superstar. As an amateur, he won three NCAA Championships while at Arizona State, the 1990 US Amateur Championship, and also a professional tournament, the 1991 Northern Telecom Open in Tucson.

Mickelson didn't hurry his decision to turn professional. He didn't have to. His one-stroke victory over Bob Tway and Tom Purtzer in Tucson gave him a free pass onto the Tour, meaning he didn't have to go through the US Tour Qualifying School.

The Arizona State graduate is actually right-handed. He plays left-handed because when he was younger he would stand in front of his father and watch as he demonstrated the golf swing. Mickelson just mirrored what his dad was doing. When he won the 1990 US Amateur at Cherry Hills in Colorado, he became the only left-hander to win the title, a distinction he still holds. He also shares a unique record with Ben Crenshaw, Curtis Strange, and Billy Ray Brown—all four won the NCAA Championship as freshmen.

Mickelson's first win as a professional came in the 1993 Buick Invitational, when he won the title by four strokes over Dave Rummels. The victory was particularly sweet because he won it in his home town of San Diego, at the Torrey Pines course.

Mickelson set another unique record in 1995, when he became the first player to win the same event as an amateur and as a professional, when he logged his second victory in the Northern Telecom Open. He successfully defended his title in 1996.

Renowned for having one of the best short games in golf, Mickelson's putting stroke has often been compared to that of Ben Crenshaw, one of the best putters in the game. The two do look like mirror images of each other, even down to the fact that they use the same type of blade putter. Besides his putting, Mickelson's wedge play is perhaps the best of the modern-day players. His trademark is a towering flop shot. Mickelson lays the face of his wedge wide open and cuts the club under the ball, causing the ball to float high in the air and land softly, usually next to the pin.

Not many left-handed players have reached the pinnacle of golfing success. One of the few to do so is New Zealander Bob Charles, who won the 1963 British Open. Many think Mickelson is probably the best lefty ever, a fact that will be confirmed when he finally wins one of golf's four major championships.

# CARY MIDDLECOFF

MIDDLECOFF TRAINED AS A DENTIST BUT NEVER SET UP A PRACTICE, CHOOSING A MORE LUCRATIVE CAREER IN GOLF INSTEAD. THE DOCTOR WON TWO US OPENS DURING HIS CAREER.

"Dr" Cary Middlecoff got his title because as an amateur player he was training to follow his father and two uncles into the dental profession. However, before going into the army in 1943, Middlecoff won the North and South Open, the only amateur to win the event, and his life changed course. Middlecoff never really practiced dentistry, but the title stuck throughout his career.

The doctor made the right decision by choosing a life in golf. Middlecoff triumphed in the third tournament in which he competed after turning professional, winning the Charlotte Open in 1947. It was the start of an excellent career.

In 1949 Middlecoff took his first big honor when he won the US Open at the Medinah Country Club, Chicago. These were the halcyon days of players like Ben Hogan, Sam Snead, and Jimmy Demaret. Indeed, Snead finished second, a stroke behind Middlecoff. The doctor also denied Hogan a record fifth US Open title when he won the 1956 championship at Oak Hill. Hogan tied for second, one stroke behind with Julius Boros. The Tennessee professional almost made a successful defense of his title a year later but lost a playoff to Dick Mayer. The loss was a pity because Middlecoff had shot two 68s on the final day, equaling Gene Sarazen's 1931 record for the lowest score over the final two rounds.

Besides two US Opens, Middlecoff also found success in the Masters. In 1948, he finished runner-up to Claude Harmon, finishing five shots adrift of Harmon's 279 total. He made up for that disappointment by winning the title in 1956. His seven-shot triumph over Ben Hogan was the biggest margin of victory in the tournament's history, a record that stood until Jack Nicklaus won by nine shots over Arnold Palmer in 1965.

The 6-foot-plus professional was noted for his proficiency with the driver. He was one of the longest hitters in the game. However, he had a reputation for slow play, especially on the greens, where he would spend a lot of time studying the line of the putt. The doctor was something of a perfectionist, which probably accounted for his slow play.

Middlecoff's career was highly successful until he experienced problems in the 1960s. He won 40 US Tour events in total, including six in 1955, the most by any player that season.

## FACT FILE

**BORN** 1921, Halls, Tennessee, USA

**CAREER HIGHLIGHTS**
1947 Charlotte Open
1949 US Open
1950 St Louis Open
1955 Masters
1956 US Open

**INTERNATIONAL HONORS**
Ryder Cup: 1953, 1955, 1959
World Cup: 1959

# Johnny Miller

NO ONE COULD CATCH MILLER WHEN HE WAS ON FORM. HE STILL HOLDS THE RECORD FOR THE LOWEST FINAL ROUND IN US OPEN HISTORY, A 63 IN 1973.

## Fact File

**BORN** 1947, San Francisco, California, USA

**CAREER HIGHLIGHTS**
1971 Southern Open
1973 US Open
1976 Open Championship
1981 Glen Campbell Los Angeles Open
1994 AT&T Pebble Beach National Pro-Am

**INTERNATIONAL HONORS**
Ryder Cup: 1975, 1981
World Cup: 1973, 1975, 1980

There was no one who could touch Johnny Miller when he was at the top of his game. No one. Not even Jack Nicklaus, Tom Watson, Gary Player or any of the other great players. At his best Miller was simply phenomenal.

That's the only adjective that can describe Miller's golf between 1973 and 1976, especially 1974. Miller won 17 tournaments in that spell, including two major championships. In the 1974 season alone, the California golfer won seven times to top the money list with over $350,000 in earnings, smashing Jack Nicklaus's record by over $30,000 for most money won in a single season.

Miller was always destined for greatness. As an amateur he had won the 1964 US Junior Amateur Championship. Then as a 16-year-old he qualified for the 1966 US Open at the Olympic Club in San Francisco and finished eighth. Seven years later, he made the championship his own.

Miller's final round 63 at Oakmont in 1973 still ranks as the lowest final round in US Open history. In fact, until Jack Nicklaus and Johnny Miller shot identical 63s in the 1980 Open, Miller's score was the lowest in US Open history. Miller's still ranks better than those by Nicklaus and Tom Weiskopf as his score was eight under the par of 71, while Nicklaus and Weiskopf were seven under.

The 63 at Oakmont came out of nowhere. A graduate of Brigham Young University, Miller had scored 76 in the third round and was six strokes behind the leaders. No one expected Miller to win the title. Although he had a habit of shooting low rounds in the 60s when he was on form, he had never done it in a big event. Two years earlier he had blown the Masters title when he bogeyed two of the last three holes after taking the lead. Those two lost strokes were Charles Coody's margin of victory.

While overnight rain had softened the greens, Miller's 63 over a course as tough as Oakmont was almost unbelievable. He romped away with a championship no one thought he had any right to win, taking the title by one shot from John Schlee, one of four players who shared the overnight lead.

That victory set Miller's game alight. He was almost unbeatable the next two seasons and capped the period with his only win in the British Open, when he won the title at Royal Birkdale in 1976.

Miller won tournaments in the 1980s and his last US Tour win came in the 1994 AT&T Pebble Beach Pro-Am when he outlasted old rival Tom Watson for the title.

Miller is now a full-time TV commentator for NBC Sports. His penchant for speaking his mind on air has made him one of the most highly regarded analysts in the business.

# ABE MITCHELL

MITCHELL NEVER ATTAINED THE MAJOR CHAMPIONSHIP THAT WOULD HAVE CAPPED HIS CAREER. A WEAKNESS ON THE GREENS DENIED HIM MANY TITLES, ESPECIALLY THE BRITISH OPEN.

Although Abe Mitchell died in 1947, every two years his image is paraded before the world of golf in the most exciting event on the golfing calendar. Mitchell is the figure that adorns the top of the Ryder Cup.

By the 1920s, Mitchell was one of the greatest players in the British game. A huge hitter who hit the ball close to 300 yards with a hickory-shafted driver, Mitchell is one of the best players never to have won the British Open. He came close a few times, finishing in the top six five times.

The Sussex native also came close in the British Amateur. He was a semi-finalist at Hoylake in 1910 when he lost to eventual winner John Ball. He had a chance to make amends for that defeat in the 1912 final at Westward Ho! Mitchell had a four-foot putt to win the match but missed and eventually lost to Ball at the 38th hole.

Putting was Mitchell's great weakness. He was highly strung, and nerves and anxiety would get the better of him. Had he been better on the greens, then Mitchell could have been one of the best golfers Britain ever produced.

Mitchell's Ryder Cup connection came about because he happened to be the professional at Verulam Golf Club in St Albans at the time Samuel Ryder took up golf. Ryder was advised to take up the game on doctor's orders. The St Albans seed merchant had been ill and was told he needed fresh air and exercise. Golf was prescribed.

Ryder was soon hooked on the game and employed Mitchell as his exclusive instructor, paying the professional an annual fee of £1,000. When Ryder decided to donate a trophy to a biennial match between the professionals of America and the British Isles, he insisted that Mitchell's likeness sit atop the trophy.

Mitchell appeared in the forerunner of the Ryder Cup, playing in the 1926 match at Wentworth, when he and George Duncan defeated Walter Hagen and Jim Barnes. Mitchell should have captained the Great Britain & Ireland team in the first official match in 1927, but had to withdraw due to appendicitis. He then played in the next three matches.

The powerful professional never lost any of the three foursomes matches he contested. He wasn't so lucky in singles play, however. He lost to Leo Diegel by the score of nine and eight in the 1929 match, then by three and one to Wilfred Cox in the 1931 contest. He finally found singles success in 1933. Mitchell trounced Olin Dutra by a score of nine and eight. Fittingly, it came in the last match Samuel Ryder ever attended.

## FACT FILE

**BORN** 1887, East Grinstead, Sussex, England

**DIED** 1947

**CAREER HIGHLIGHTS**
1919 British Professional Match Play
1920 British Professional Match Play
1929 British Professional Match Play

**INTERNATIONAL HONORS**
Ryder Cup: 1929, 1931, 1933

# Larry Mize

MIZE PRODUCED ONE OF THE GREATEST SHOTS IN MASTERS HISTORY, HOLING A PITCH SHOT FROM 140 FEET TO DEFEAT GREG NORMAN IN A PLAYOFF FOR THE 1987 MASTERS.

## Fact File

**BORN** 1958, Augusta, Georgia, USA

**CAREER HIGHLIGHTS**
- 1983 Danny Thomas-Memphis Classic
- 1987 Masters
- 1993 Northern Telecom Open
- 1993 Buick Open
- 1993 Johnnie Walker World Championship

**INTERNATIONAL HONORS**
Ryder Cup: 1987

Larry Mize grew up in Augusta, Georgia, home of the Masters. As a young boy he worked at the course during the tournament, operating the scoreboard at the third hole. Mize's dream was one day to play in the Masters, and obviously winning formed a big part of that dream. Little did he know that he would make Masters history.

By the time spring 1987 rolled around, Mize had won only once on the US Tour, the 1983 Danny Thomas-Memphis Classic. A 25-foot birdie putt on the final hole had given him a one-shot lead over Fuzzy Zoeller, Sammy Rachels, and Chip Beck. Mize was seen as a good, solid professional who played steadily but who would never be a world beater. Needless to say, no one expected him to win one of the majors. No one except Larry Hogan Mize.

Mize played well over the first three rounds of the 1987 Masters, staying in contention throughout the three days. On the final day, he needed to sink a five-foot putt on the 72nd hole to get into a playoff with Greg Norman and Seve Ballesteros. Mize's putt was straight and true.

Mize was the distinct underdog in the three-man playoff. Ballesteros had won the title twice before, while Norman was the heir apparent to Jack Nicklaus. Seve went out at the first extra hole when he three putted the 10th. On the 11th it looked like Mize had thrown away his chances when he missed the green to the right by 140 feet. Norman's ball was safely on the right-hand side of the green and the Australian looked odds-on to make his par. Then came one of the greatest shots in Masters history.

The flag on the last day was cut very close to the pond that guards the left side of the green. Mize knew he had to land the ball short of the green and then let it trickle down to the hole. If he hit the shot too strongly the ball would go in the water, too soft and he would leave himself a long par putt. Mize landed his ball about three feet short of the green and watched it roll onto the green. About 10 feet away it looked like it was going to get close to the hole, five feet away and it looked like it had a chance of going in the hole. It did. The ball went down and Mize went up. He leapt about three feet in the air and ran around the 11th green in celebration. When Norman missed his putt, Mize had lived his boyhood dream.

# Colin Montgomerie

**MONTGOMERIE'S RECORD OF SIX CONSECUTIVE EUROPEAN NUMBER ONE TITLES BETWEEN 1993 AND 1998 IS A RECORD THAT MIGHT NEVER BE BROKEN.**

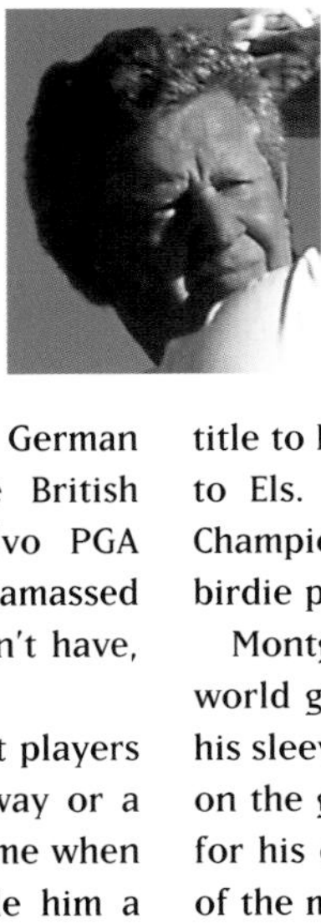

No player has dominated European golf the way Colin Montgomerie has done in the 1990s. Between 1993 and 1998, Montgomerie set a record that may never be broken, winning six straight European Order of Merit titles.

Through the 1998 season, the Scotsman had won 17 tournaments on the European Tour, including prestigious titles like the German Open (twice), the Irish Open (twice), the British Masters, the Volvo Masters, and the Volvo PGA Championship. In only 12 seasons he had amassed close to £8 million in earnings. What he didn't have, though, was a major championship.

The Scotsman is one of the most consistent players in the game today. He rarely misses a fairway or a green and is one of the best putters in the game when he is on form. His straight hitting has made him a favorite in every US Open and USPGA Championship since 1993, since those two tournaments put such a premium on accuracy. He's come close to winning both titles, too.

The Scotsman nearly snatched the 1992 US Open at Pebble Beach. Out a couple of hours before the leaders, Montgomerie managed to shoot a final round 70 before the wind picked up and made it tough for those still on the golf course. As he sat in the clubhouse watching events unfold, Montgomerie gradually climbed up the leaderboard as those above him shot high scores in the wind. However, Tom Kite and Jeff Sluman managed to persevere to finish number one and two respectively. Montgomerie placed third.

The Scotsman lost a playoff for the 1994 title to Ernie Els and then placed second in 1997, again to Els. He also lost a playoff for the 1995 USPGA Championship, when Steve Elkington rolled in a long birdie putt on the first extra hole.

Montgomerie is one of the toughest competitors in world golf. He's a player who wears his emotions on his sleeve and who often looks like he's in a bad mood on the golf course. While he's taken a lot of criticism for his on-course demeanor, off the course he is one of the most engaging and delightful people you would ever want to meet.

Besides the fire in his belly, one of the reasons for Montgomerie's success lies in his refusal to change his golf swing. The Scotsman's swing does not look textbook, but it works. Montgomerie is smart enough to know that and has never really tried to change it. Many experts think it isn't a matter of if he will win a major championship, but when. He certainly has the game for it.

## Fact File

**BORN** 1963, Glasgow, Scotland

**CAREER HIGHLIGHTS**
1989 Portuguese Open
1993 Volvo Masters
1996 Dubai Desert Classic
1997 Andersen Consulting World Championship of Golf
1998 Volvo PGA Championship

**INTERNATIONAL HONORS**
Ryder Cup: 1991, 1993, 1995, 1997
World Cup: 1988, 1991, 1992, 1993, 1997
Alfred Dunhill Cup: 1988, 1991, 1992, 1993, 1994, 1995, 1996, 1997, 1998
Walker Cup: 1985, 1987

# Orville Moody

MOODY WAS A SURPRISE WINNER OF THE 1969 US OPEN, THE ONLY REGULAR US TOUR EVENT THE FORMER ARMY SARGEANT EVER WON. HOWEVER, MOODY WON ELSEWHERE AROUND THE WORLD AND ON THE US SENIOR TOUR.

## Fact File

**BORN** 1933, Chickacha, Oklahoma, USA

**CAREER HIGHLIGHTS**
1969 US Open
1969 World Series of Golf
1971 Hong Kong Open
1984 Senior Tournament of Champions
1989 US Senior Open

**INTERNATIONAL HONORS**
World Cup: 1969

Orville Moody triumphed in only one US Tour event, but it was a big one—the 1969 US Open Championship.

Moody was a career army man before he ever became a somebody in golf. The Oklahoma native served in the US Army for 14 years before turning professional. During that time, he won three Korean Opens and was the 1962 All-Service Champion.

The son of a golf course superintendent, Moody won the Oklahoma State Scholastic Golf Championship and was offered a golf scholarship to the University of Oklahoma. He took it, but left college in 1953 to enlist in the service.

Upon leaving the army in 1967, Moody decided to try his hand on the professional golf circuit. He joined the US Tour and gave himself two years to make it. He was right on schedule.

Moody surprised everyone when he won the US Open at the Champions Club in Houston, Texas. After a week's holiday, Moody turned up at the tournament and played the best golf of his life. He opened with rounds of 71, 70 before an excellent third round 68 put him in second place. With others finding trouble in the last round, a final 72 was good enough to give him the championship by one stroke over the trio of Bob Rosburg, Deane Beman, and Al Geiberger.

There had been nothing previously to suggest Moody would become America's national champion. He made just short of $13,000 in 1968 and had previously never won on Tour. Indeed, his only other time in the limelight came in the 1969 Greater Greensboro Open, when he lost in a playoff. Moody then won the World Series of Golf that year, an unofficial contest that pitted the winners of the four majors against each other. Moody triumphed over Tony Jacklin, George Archer, and Ray Floyd.

Moody picked up the Player of the Year award for his performance in 1969, a season that saw him earn just under $80,000.

The ex-army man never won another tournament on the US Tour. He won abroad, taking titles like the Hong Kong Open, and the Morocco Grand Prix, which he won in 1971. He also won the 1977 International Caribbean Open, but he never achieved the same level of success as a regular Tour player that he had found in the 1969 season.

Moody's best golfing years came once he turned 50. He joined the Senior Tour and won 11 times on that circuit, including the 1989 US Senior Open. He also won the Mazda Senior Tournament Players Championship that year, and ended the season with more than $600,000 in prize money, his richest season as a pro.

# GIL MORGAN

MORGAN HAD A CHANCE TO WIN THE 1992 US OPEN BUT LOST THE CHAMPIONSHIP OVER THE FINAL TWO ROUNDS, DESPITE BECOMING THE FIRST PLAYER TO REACH 10 UNDER PAR IN THE TOURNAMENT.

After starting golf at the age of 15, Gil Morgan went to East Central State College to pursue a medical career. During his junior year, Morgan decided he wanted to play golf professionally. However, he waited until he got his degree as a Doctor of Optometry from the Southern College of Optometry, just in case he didn't make it as a pro. Although he still holds a doctor's license, he has never practiced. He's made so much money as a professional golfer he hasn't had to.

Morgan is another player whose best years have come after turning 50. He was successful on the main Tour, winning seven events, including the 1978 World Series of Golf after defeating Hubert Green in a playoff for the title. That win enabled him to finish the season as number two on the money list behind Tom Watson. But there was nothing from Morgan's 22 years on the regular Tour to suggest he would blossom as an over-50 golfer.

The 5-foot, 9-inch professional should have won the 1992 US Open at Pebble Beach on California's Monterey Peninsula. He led after 36 holes and early in the third round he made history when he became the first player to reach 10 under par in the tournament. He was 12 under after 43 holes before a spectacular collapse. In the next seven holes he dropped nine shots. Morgan told the press afterwards that his parachute developed a hole. He shot 77 that round, and then followed it with an 81 in horrible conditions on the final day. Morgan eventually finished 13th. He had thrown away the biggest tournament of his life. The championship that had been his to win had also been his to lose. It was one of the most dramatic freefalls in US Open history.

No sooner had Morgan joined the US Senior Tour than he was racking up wins and challenging Hale Irwin as best player on the over-50 circuit. He was also making heaps of money.

Just 11 days after turning 50 in 1996, Morgan celebrated by winning the Ralphs Senior Classic to become the youngest winner on the Senior Tour. Through the 1998 season, Morgan had won 13 times as a senior, including six victories in each of the 1997 and 1998 seasons. He topped the $2 million mark both years. In 22 years on the regular Tour, Morgan made over $5.2 million. He appeared to be easily surpassing that mark heading into the 1999 season, after just three years as a senior.

## FACT FILE

**BORN** 1946, Wewoka, Oklahoma, USA

**CAREER HIGHLIGHTS**
1977 BC Open
1978 World Series of Golf
1990 Kemper Open
1997 Energizer Senior Tour Championship
1998 Ford Senior Players Championship

**INTERNATIONAL HONORS**
Ryder Cup: 1979, 1983

# Old Tom Morris

OLD TOM MORRIS WAS THE FIRST GOLFING SUPERSTAR, A PLAYER WHO DOMINATED THE BRITISH OPEN BY WINNING THE TITLE FOUR TIMES BETWEEN 1861 AND 1867.

## Fact File

**BORN** 1821, St Andrews, Fife, Scotland

**DIED** 1908

**CAREER HIGHLIGHTS**
1861 The Open Championship
1862 The Open Championship
1864 The Open Championship
1867 The Open Championship

Old Tom Morris was one of the very first professionals in the history of the game, and the first to dominate the British Open. In fact, Old Tom was probably the first acknowledged golfing superstar.

Morris was born on North Street in St Andrews. The son of a letter carrier who later became a caddie, Morris started golf at the age of 10. He began by playing with his left hand below his right but soon changed to a conventional method as he became more proficient at the game.

He was supposed to become a carpenter when he reached his teenage years, but went to work for Allan Robertson on the advice of Sandy Herd. Morris served his apprenticeship under Robertson as a ball and club maker. There could have been no better man to serve under than Robertson. He was the best player of his age, and generally regarded as the first true professional golfer. It is golf's misfortune that Robertson never had the chance to win the British Open, but the championship did not start until 1860, a year after Robertson's death.

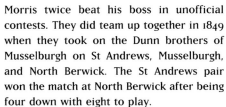

Under Robertson's tutelage, Morris soon perfected his game to the point where the two men had to play each other on level strokes. The pair never played each other in an official match, but it was said that Morris twice beat his boss in unofficial contests. They did team up together in 1849 when they took on the Dunn brothers of Musselburgh on St Andrews, Musselburgh, and North Berwick. The St Andrews pair won the match at North Berwick after being four down with eight to play.

Old Tom later parted company with Robertson and went into business by himself. Then in 1851 he accepted a job at Prestwick, as custodian of the new links course there.

When the British Open began in 1860, it was staged at Prestwick, on Scotland's Ayrshire coast, where it would be held for the first 12 years. The inaugural tournament was won by Willie Park with Old Tom finishing runner-up. It came as no surprise when Old Tom won the next two championships. He was runner-up to Park again in 1863, and then Old Tom won the 1864 championship. Three years later, he won his fourth and last championship. A year later, his mantle as Britain's dominant golfer was taken over by his son, Young Tom Morris. Young Tom won four times between 1868 and 1872, with his father finishing second in his first two wins.

The British Open began when Old Tom was 39 years old. There is no doubt he would have won more had it been in existence during his prime.

# YOUNG TOM MORRIS

YOUNG TOM TOOK OVER HIS FATHER'S MANTLE AS BRITAIN'S BEST GOLFER BY WINNING THE BRITISH OPEN FOUR TIMES IN SUCCESSION. YOUNG TOM DIED AT THE AGE OF JUST 24.

If Old Tom Morris was the first golfing superstar, then Young Tom Morris was the first golfing phenomenon.

Young Tom took over from his father as Britain's dominant player, winning the British Open Championship four times in succession between 1868 and 1872 (no championship was held in 1871), the first and only player to do so in the history of the game.

Young Tom was born in St Andrews and grew up under the influence of his famous father. He was an accomplished golfer by the time he was 13, when he won the then princely sum of £5 in an exhibition match at Perth. He won his first professional tournament at the age of 16 when he defeated Bob Andrew and four-time British Open champion Willie Park in a playoff at Carnoustie.

Young Tom's first two British Open victories came at the expense of his father. Old Tom finished runner-up to his son in 1868 and 1869. When Young Tom won the title for a third time in 1870, he was given custody of the championship belt as three-time winner. That tournament saw Young Tom establish himself as the pre-eminent player in the game. His margin of victory was 12 shots over David Strath and Bob Kirk, and he established a record that was never broken. In those days the championship was played over 36 holes, and Young Tom had set the scoring record with 157 in 1868, the first player to shoot under 160. He bettered that score by three strokes the following year and then smashed it in 1870 with a score of 149. Until 1891, when the championship was extended to 72 holes, no player would break 150. In fact, no player would come even close to that score. Willie Park Jr and Andrew Kirkaldy shot 155 in 1889, but that was as close as any player got.

After another British Open win in 1872, Young Tom finished runner-up in 1874. Then in 1875, after a foursomes match with his father against the Parks of Musselburgh, Young Tom was given a telegram that said his wife was seriously ill. He managed to secure a yacht to take him from North Berwick to St Andrews, but then received another message telling him his wife and new-born child were dead.

Young Tom never really recovered from the tragedy. On Christmas Day, 1875, Young Tom died at the age of just 24. Cause of death was said to be pneumonia, but many believed he died of a broken heart.

There is no telling how many British Opens Young Tom would have won had he not experienced such tragedy in his life.

## FACT FILE

**BORN** 1851, St Andrews, Fife, Scotland

**DIED** 1875

**CAREER HIGHLIGHTS**
1868 The Open Championship
1869 The Open Championship
1870 The Open Championship
1872 The Open Championship

# Kel Nagle

KEN NAGLE'S BIGGEST CAREER WIN CAME WHEN HE WON THE 1960 CENTENARY BRITISH OPEN, DEFEATING ARNOLD PALMER TO TAKE THE TITLE.

## Fact File

**BORN** 1920, Sydney, New South Wales, Australia

**CAREER HIGHLIGHTS**
1959 Australian Open
1960 Open Championship
1961 French Open
1964 Canadian Open
1971 World Seniors

**INTERNATIONAL HONORS**
World Cup: 1954, 1955, 1958, 1959, 1960, 1961, 1962, 1965, 1966

It took Kel Nagle a while to get started in golf, but he made up for lost time once he did.

Nagle became an assistant professional at the age of 15, when he went to work at the Pymble Club near Sydney. He started out picking up balls on the practice ground and then couldn't join the Australian PGA because they said there were too many assistants at that time. World War II broke out and he had to serve time in New Guinea before finally getting onto the professional circuit when the war ended.

In 1949, Nagle won the Australian Professional Championship. He won it again in 1954, 1958, 1959, 1965, and 1968. He also won the New Zealand Open seven times during his career. By the 1950s, he was a well-established player in the southern hemisphere, but he wasn't that well-known on the world stage. That soon changed.

Nagle was one of a strong contingent that showed up to compete for the 1960 British Open at St Andrews, the Centenary Open. In the field was Arnold Palmer, winner of the Masters and the US Open that year and contesting his first British Open. He was the hot favorite, while at 40 years old Nagle wasn't heavily backed.

Palmer badly wanted the tournament. A win and he would emulate Ben Hogan in 1953, when the Texan won the Masters, the US Open, and then the British Open on his first and only attempt. Victory at St Andrews would also give Palmer a chance to win golf's grand slam if he could add the USPGA Championship later that summer.

It was testament to Nagle's nerve that he was able to survive Palmer's assault on the tournament. When Palmer birdied the 72nd hole to post a score of 279, it meant Nagle had to par the last two holes to win the title. Palmer had whittled Nagle's four-stroke lead down to just one solitary shot.

The Australian used good common sense when he played the treacherous 17th hole. Rather than attack the flag and risk the wrath of the Road Bunker, he played short of the green, and put his faith into chipping and putting for par. He chipped up to 10 feet and then needed to hole the putt to maintain his lead. His nerve did not fail him, and when he made another four at the last, Nagle had won the championship and defeated the greatest player of that era.

Nagle had a chance to win the 1965 US Open at Bellerive but eventually tied with Gary Player. Player won the ensuing playoff by a score of 71 to Nagle's 74.

# TOMMY NAKAJIMA

TOMMY NAKAJIMA ONCE TOOK FOUR STROKES TO ESCAPE THE ROAD BUNKER AT ST ANDREWS, LEADING THE LOCALS TO DUB THE BUNKER "THE SANDS OF NAKAJIMA."

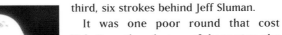

No Japanese player has ever won a major championship, but for many years it was thought Tsuneyuki "Tommy" Nakajima would be the first.

Nakajima is one of the best players ever to come out of Japan. At one point he was ranked fourth best player in the world. After winning the Japan Amateur in 1973, Nakajima turned professional two years later and went on to win many tournaments on his own Japanese circuit. Besides his four Japan Opens, Nakajima has also recorded four victories in the Japan PGA Championship, taking the title in 1983, 1984, 1986, and 1992. Indeed, between 1984 and 1995, Nakajima won no less than 23 tournaments on the lucrative Japanese circuit.

Like Jumbo Ozaki, Nakajima's heroics are mainly confined to his home Tour. Nakajima has never won a big tournament outside his homeland, yet over the years he has featured in a few major championships. In the 1988 USPGA Championship, Nakajima was just four shots behind Paul Azinger heading into the final two rounds. A poor 74 in the third round left him with too much work to do and Nakajima eventually finished third, six strokes behind Jeff Sluman.

It was one poor round that cost Nakajima the chance of becoming the first Japanese player to win the British Open. After three rounds at Turnberry in 1986, Nakajima entered the final round just one shot behind Greg Norman, with whom he was paired on the last day. Nakajima's chance of winning went early. He bunkered his approach shot to the first hole, splashed out and took three putts for a double bogey six. His second putt was from 12 inches.

The Japanese player will always be remembered for a couple of incidents he would rather forget. In the 1978 Masters Nakajima took 13 at the par-5 13th hole in the second round that included two two-stroke penalties. Then in the same year he was in contention in the third round of the British Open when he put his approach shot into the infamous Road Bunker at the par-4 17th hole. Four times Nakajima tried to splash the ball out of the little pot bunker, and four times he failed. He eventually got the ball out on his fifth attempt, took two putts and made a nine. The bunker has often been referred to as "The Sands of Nakajima" ever since.

## FACT FILE

**BORN** 1954, Kiryu City, Gumma, Japan

**CAREER HIGHLIGHTS**
1973 Japan Amateur
1985 Japan Open
1986 Japan Open
1990 Japan Open
1991 Japan Open

**INTERNATIONAL HONORS**
World Cup: 1996
Alfred Dunhill Cup: 1986

# THE DUEL IN THE SUN

Turnberry was new to the British Open Championship rota when the oldest tournament in the world was held over the Ayrshire links in 1977. What a baptism of fire it turned out to be.

The 1977 British Open goes down as the best seen in the grand old tournament—perhaps the best major championship in the history of the game. It pitted the top two golfers in the world over four days, two golfers so far ahead of the field that they may as well have played the tournament alone. Tom Watson and Jack Nicklaus arrived at Turnberry as tournament favorites. Watson had won the British Open two years earlier and his first Masters that year. Nicklaus was well established as the best in the game, a winner of two British Opens, five Masters, three US Opens and four USPGA Championships. His status as the game's number one player was undisputed. He and Watson would take Turnberry apart.

Watson had already got the better of Nicklaus that year. At the Masters, he birdied the 71st hole to defeat his great rival by a stroke. Nicklaus was looking for revenge at Turnberry. Normally scores of 68, 70, and 66 for the first three rounds would have set him on his way, but Watson matched him score for score.

Nicklaus nosed ahead early in the final round. Birdies at the first and fourth holes along with a Watson bogey at the second saw him take a three-shot lead. Watson then birdied the fifth, seventh and eighth holes. Heading to the par-3 13th, Nicklaus was still one shot ahead when Watson pulled his tee shot to the left of the green some 65 feet from the hole. He then rattled the long putt into the hole to tie Nicklaus. Watson didn't take the lead that final day until the 17th. He hit two shots onto the par-5 hole to about 15 feet from the hole. Nicklaus, meanwhile, had missed the green with his second, chipped to five feet and missed the putt. Watson had a one-stroke lead going down the last.

Watson's tee shot found the last fairway, but Nicklaus's didn't. He pushed his drive wildly and the ball came to rest at the base of a small bush. Watson played first and hit his 7-iron to within three feet of the hole. It looked like a lost cause for Nicklaus. Most players couldn't have advanced the ball let alone considered reaching the green, but Nicklaus was one of the strongest players in the game. He knocked the ball onto the front edge of the putting surface a long way from the hole. Watson's caddie congratulated his man on winning, but Watson told him to wait, that Nicklaus could hole the putt. Nicklaus duly knocked the 30-footer into the hole for a miraculous birdie. It made Watson's putt feel longer than it actually was. But Watson's nerves were made of steel and he holed the putt to win by a stroke.

After battling each other over the four rounds, it seemed unfair that one had to lose. Nicklaus had done his best and lost to a better player. He acknowledged as much when he put his arm around Watson and escorted him from the final green. Hubert Green finished third, 11 shots behind Watson.

TOP: NICKLAUS (STANDING) AND WATSON STOOD APART FROM THE REST OF THE FIELD. SO FAR APART THAT HUBERT GREEN FINISHED THIRD, 11 SHOTS BEHIND WATSON.

BELOW LEFT: THE CONTENDERS TAKE A BREAK ON THE ROCKY SHORES OF THE AYRSHIRE COASTLINE DUE TO THE THREAT OF LIGHTENING.

RIGHT: NICKLAUS (RIGHT) CONGRATULATES WATSON ON WINNING THEIR EPIC BATTLE. THEIR RESPECT FOR EACH OTHER WAS OBVIOUS WHEN THEY LEFT THE FINAL GREEN.

FAR RIGHT: WATSON POSES WITH THE OLD CLARET JUG, FOR A SECOND TIME, AFTER WINNING THE 1977 BRITISH OPEN.

WATSON

# Byron Nelson

BYRON NELSON SET A RECORD IN 1945 WHEN HE WON 18 TOURNAMENTS ON THE US TOUR, INCLUDING AN INCREDIBLE 11 IN A ROW.

## Fact File

**BORN** 1912, Forth Worth, Texas, USA

**CAREER HIGHLIGHTS**
1937 Masters
1939 US Open
1940 USPGA Championship
1942 Masters
1945 USPGA Championship

**INTERNATIONAL HONORS**
Ryder Cup: 1937, 1947, 1965 (captain)

Byron Nelson established a record in 1945 that will never be broken. The Texan won 11 tournaments in succession and 18 in total.

From March 11 until August 19, 1945 there was no one in the game that could match Nelson. That year he went five months without losing a golf tournament. That year he won everything in his sights, taking 18 of the 31 tournaments he played. In fact, between 1944 and 1946, Nelson won 32 of the 72 professional tournaments in which he competed.

Of course, this was during World War II, when many of the top American players were in the armed forces. Nelson's health precluded him from active service, and it's always been hinted that he would never have played the way he did had he faced tougher opposition. Despite the lack of some good players, though, Nelson still played phenomenal golf. For example, his stroke average for 1945 was 68.33, and during one spell he shot 19 straight rounds under 70.

Nelson grew up in Fort Worth, Texas playing golf against Ben Hogan. As youngsters the two caddied at the same golf club, Glen Garden, and first faced each other in the annual caddie championship. Nelson got the better of Hogan after a playoff. Things started out the same way once they turned professional, with Nelson establishing himself as a great player long before Hogan.

By the time Hogan really started to dominate the world of golf, Nelson had virtually retired from the game. By 1946 he had won the Masters twice, the USPGA twice, and the US Open once. Then he quit. Meanwhile, Hogan did not win his first major, the USPGA, until Nelson retired at the end of the 1946 season.

One of the true gentlemen of the game, and a man who seemed to have time for everybody, tournament golf took its toll on Nelson. He retired to spend time on the ranch he had bought with his winnings from professional golf, and to concentrate on a career as a broadcaster. He did make a few forays back into tournament golf, showing up to compete in the 1955 British Open at St Andrews. He did not play well, but then traveled to Paris to compete in the French Open, winning the title with a dazzling display of golf.

Nelson was a supreme stylist in his prime. A tremendous driver of the ball and a great iron player, the Texan could take a course apart. Ironically, he wasn't known as a great putter.

Long after his playing days were over, he became a mentor to Tom Watson, often accompanying the Kansas City professional to the British Open.

# Larry Nelson

LARRY NELSON DIDN'T TAKE UP GOLF UNTIL HIS 20S, BUT HE MADE UP FOR LOST TIME BY WINNING THREE MAJORS, INCLUDING THE 1983 US OPEN.

Larry Nelson is one of golf's most natural practitioners. He did not start playing the game until his 20s, and went on to win three major championships.

Nelson had never played the game as a youngster. His first experience of golf came after he had served in Vietnam. He broke 100 the first time he played and was soon breaking par. While others spend a lifetime trying to master the game's intricacies, Nelson took to it as if it were the easiest sport in the world.

The Alabama native turned professional in 1971 and attended the US Tour Qualifying School in 1973, where he got his US Tour card. While it took him five seasons before he won his first tournament, the 1979 Jackie Gleason-Inverary Classic, Nelson never really struggled on the US Tour. Solid performances earned him a good living until he finally entered the winner's circle.

Nelson also won the Western Open in 1979, and recorded nine top-10 finishes in total. His play was good enough to earn him second place on the end of season money list behind Tom Watson. By the time the 1981 USPGA Championship took place, Nelson was already a four-time winner on the US Tour. A fourth place finish in the 1979 US Open, and sixth place in the 1980 Masters marked him as a player who could win a major. His low-key approach to the game did not make him one of the most charismatic figures in golf, but it was probably the reason he won the 1981 USPGA and went on to win two more majors.

Nelson won the 1981 USPGA at the Atlanta Athletic Club near his home in Marietta, Georgia. An opening round of 70 was followed by two successive 66s and Nelson's challenge was never really threatened. He wound up winning the tournament by four strokes over Fuzzy Zoeller.

His second major didn't come so easily. Nelson trailed Seve Ballesteros and Tom Watson by a shot heading into the final round of the 1983 US Open at Oakmont, but managed a closing 67 to take the title by a stroke over Watson.

Nelson completed his trio of major wins when he lifted the 1987 USPGA Championship at PGA National Golf Club in Florida. On one of the toughest courses to have staged the USPGA, Nelson's one under par total of 287 tied him with Lanny Wadkins. Nelson won the title at the first playoff hole.

Nelson was one of the most respected figures in the game and many people were upset when Ben Crenshaw was made captain of the 1999 US Ryder Cup side. There was a groundswell of opinion that said Nelson should have got the job.

## Fact File

**BORN** 1947, Fort Payne, Alabama, USA

**CAREER HIGHLIGHTS**
1979 Western Open
1981 USPGA Championship
1983 US Open
1987 USPGA Championship
1988 Georgia-Pacific Atlanta Classic

**INTERNATIONAL HONORS**
Ryder Cup: 1979, 1981, 1987

# Liselotte Neumann

LOTTA NEUMANN IS ONE OF THE BEST GOLFERS PRODUCED BY THE SWEDISH GOLF FEDERATION. HER FIRST LPGA VICTORY CAME IN THE 1988 US WOMEN'S OPEN.

## Fact File

**BORN** 1966, Finspang, Sweden

**CAREER HIGHLIGHTS**
1988 US Women's Open
1991 Mazda Japan Classic
1994 Weetabix Women's Open
1996 Ping Welch's Championship
1998 Standard Register Ping

**INTERNATIONAL HONORS**
Solheim Cup: 1990, 1992, 1994, 1996, 1998

Liselotte Neumann, or Lotta as she is called, is another of the many magnificent Swedish players to grace the fairways of the top professional tours.

Like many fellow Swedes, Neumann received excellent coaching from the Swedish Golf Federation when she was an amateur. Prior to turning professional she won the Swedish Amateur Championship in 1982 and 1983, the Swedish Match Play Championship in 1983, and represented Sweden in the 1984 European Team Championship and the World Team Championships of 1982 and 1984.

Now an established player on the LPGA Tour, Neumann's apprenticeship was served in Europe, where she learned how to win. In 1985 she won the European Open, the French Open in 1987, and three consecutive German Opens between 1986 and 1988. Neumann's rookie year on the LPGA Tour also coincided with the biggest win of her career. In the 1988 US Women's Open in Baltimore, Neumann put together four brilliant rounds to take the title. Her 277 total for the four days was at the time the lowest aggregate score in the tournament's history, and wasn't bettered until compatriot Annika Sorenstam posted a 272 in 1996.

Neumann's win followed on the heels of Laura Davies's victory in 1987, making her the first Swede to take the coveted title. Neumann was just 22 at the time of her victory, yet she played with the poise of a player with great experience. It was her first victory on the LPGA Tour, and at the time made her one of only 12 players to make the US Women's Open their first LPGA win. Neumann's victory earned her the LPGA Rookie of the Year Award for the 1988 season.

The Swedish star makes golf look like the easiest game in the world. Her golf swing is a model of simplicity. Her backswing is quite short for a top player but it is a controlled action. More importantly, it allows Neumann to hit a lot of fairways and greens. Allied to a silky putting touch and a good short game, she is a factor in most tournaments she enters.

Although most of her time is spent in America, Neumann still plays as many European events as she can fit into her schedule.

Along with fellow Swede Helen Alfredsson, whom she has partnered on many occasions, Neumann has played in every Solheim Cup since the inaugural match in 1990. She went unbeaten in the European victory in 1992 at Dalmahoy in Scotland, defeating the strong American player Betsy King by a score of two and one in the singles.

Neumann is one of the best players in women's golf, one who is sure to add more major championships before her career is over.

# Alison Nicholas

LISON NICHOLAS'S MOTIONAL CTORY OVER ANCY LOPEZ IN HE 1997 US OMEN'S OPEN AS ONE OF THE OST GRIPPING ONTESTS EVER ITNESSED IN OLF.

Alison Nicholas is affectionately known as "Big Al" by her friends. At just 5 feet in her stockinged feet, Nicholas may not live up to the title physically. If heart size is anything to by, however, then the Englishwoman fully deserves the nickname.

Nicholas started playing golf as a 17-year-old in Yorkshire, England where her family moved after Alison was born in Gibralter. In no time at all, she was playing golf to an excellent standard, winning the 1982 and 1983 Northern Girls Amateur Open. The 1983 season also saw her win the Ladies' British Open Amateur Stroke Play Championship at Moortown. Nicholas's 292 total was at the time a record low score for the tournament. Needless to say, big things were expected of little Alison Nicholas when she turned professional.

Nicholas soon established herself on the Women's Professional Golf European Tour, lifting such prestigious titles as the 1987 Women's British Open at St Mellion and the German and Swedish Opens of 1989. When the Solheim Cup was created in 1990, Nicholas played a big part in the European team. The Yorkshire golfer made quite a pairing with fellow Englishwoman Laura Davies.

The "little and large" team certainly stood out on the golf course, and the duo managed to defeat the strong pairing of Pat Bradley and Nancy Lopez in the opening foursomes match. They later lost to Betsy King and Beth Daniel in the four-balls, but the chemistry between them was established and they became a feature of the early matches, winning a lot of valuable points along the way.

With the women's game suffering in Europe from lack of sponsorship, Nicholas turned her attention to the United States and the LPGA Tour. Her first success there came in 1995 when she won twice. Two years later, however, she would win the biggest tournament in the women's game.

Nicholas had initially been persuaded by Nancy Lopez to play more in the United States. As a youngster growing up, Nicholas had watched Lopez play and idolised the popular American player. The two had become firm friends from their meetings at tournaments, and so when Lopez spoke Nicholas listened. Little did the Englishwoman know that her biggest win in golf would come over her hero.

In the 1997 US Women's Open at Pumpkin Ridge Golf Club in Cornelius, Oregon, Lopez became the first player to shoot four rounds in the 60s, scoring 275 for the four rounds. Nicholas went one shot better to steal the title from Lopez, the sentimental favourite, in one of the most exciting head to head final round contests ever seen in golf.

## Fact File

**BORN** 1962, Gibraltar

**CAREER HIGHLIGHTS**
1987 Weetabix Women's British Open
1989 German Open
1989 Swedish Open
1995 LPGA Corning Classic
1997 US Women's Open

**INTERNATIONAL HONOURS**
Solheim Cup: 1990, 1992, 1994, 1996, 1998

# Jack Nicklaus

Jack William Nicklaus is without doubt the greatest player the game of golf has ever seen. There may have been better swingers of a golf club, better putters, more charismatic figures, but there hasn't been a better player. It is even questionable whether anyone in the future will be able to break the phenomenal record Nicklaus set during his long career.

Neither Vardon, nor Jones, nor Hogan, nor Palmer dominated golf the way Nicklaus did. Between 1962 and 1986, Nicklaus won 18 major championships, 11 more than Vardon, Jones, and Palmer, and nine more than Hogan. In addition he won two US Amateur championships before turning professional.

Nicklaus grew up in Ohio where he had the benefit of coaching from Jack Grout, who first saw Nicklaus in a junior clinic and immediately recognized his potential. Until his death, Grout was the only teacher Nicklaus ever had. There was nothing technical in what Grout told Nicklaus, just basic fundamentals. In fact, every year Nicklaus would go to Grout for a tune-up, in which the two men would ensure Nicklaus's grip, stance, set-up and alignment were correct.

Even as an amateur, Nicklaus was a phenomenon. He very nearly won the 1960 US Open as an unpaid player, finishing second to Arnold Palmer by two shots at Cherry Hills in Colorado. It was no surprise then that the US Open would be Nicklaus's first professional win. Nicklaus lifted his first of four US Opens in 1962 at Oakmont, in Pennsylvania. This time he reversed the tables on Palmer, beating him by three shots in a playoff for the title.

Nicklaus won the US Open three more times to equal the record held by Willie Anderson, Bobby Jones, and Ben Hogan. He also finished runner-up four times, but could not add a fifth title.

The man they call the Golden Bear also put his mark on the Masters, winning the title six times. In 1966, he became the first player to successfully defend the title when he defeated Tommy Jacobs and Gay Brewer in a playoff. Such was Nicklaus's driving length that it forced the Augusta authorities to make alterations to the golf course. The bunkers that now sit on the left-hand side of the 18th fairway were placed there to catch Nicklaus's booming tee shots.

It was after one of Nicklaus's performances in the Masters that led to Bobby Jones's often quoted line about the golfing phenomenon. "He plays a game with which I'm not familiar," said Jones.

Nicklaus's last Masters win came in 1986, when at the age of 46 he turned back the years to produce one of the most emotional tournaments in the history of golf. Nicklaus wasn't even on the leaderboard going into the last round, but shot an amazing 65, including a back nine of 30, to win his sixth green jacket.

Nicklaus's run in the USPGA Championship has also been nothing short of amazing. Five times he has picked up the Wanamaker Trophy that goes to the winner. Nicklaus's wire to wire victory at the PGA National Golf Club in 1971 made him the only player to win the grand slam of golf for a second time. His victory at Oak Hill in 1980 gave him his fifth and last title, tying him with Walter Hagen as the two players with the most wins in the tournament.

Of all the majors, the British Open is the one Jack has won the least—only won three times! Twice he won the game's oldest championship at St Andrews, in 1970 and 1978, to go with his first victory at Muirfield in 1966. Nicklaus also finished second in the tournament seven times, and third three times.

Including the majors, Nicklaus racked up 70 official US Tour titles, and another 27 victories around the world. Between 1962 and 1982, he was probably the favorite against the rest of the field in most tournaments he played. In short he is a phenomenon the world of golf is unlikely to see again.

The final word on Nicklaus goes to Gene Sarazen, who over his 97 years saw just about every great player that ever lived. In 1975 Sarazen had this to say about the Golden Bear: "Nicklaus is the greatest tournament player we have ever had. He's the longest hitter under pressure and a fighter to the last putt."

## Fact File

**BORN** 1940, Columbus, Ohio, USA

**CAREER HIGHLIGHTS**
1962 US Open
1963 Masters
1963 USPGA Championship
1965 Masters
1966 Masters
1966 The Open Championship
1967 US Open
1970 The Open Championship
1971 USPGA Championship
1972 Masters
1972 US Open
1973 USPGA Championship
1975 Masters
1975 USPGA Championship
1978 The Open Championship
1980 US Open
1980 USPGA Championship
1986 Masters

**INTERNATIONAL HONORS**
Ryder Cup: 1969, 1971, 1973, 1975, 1977, 1979, 1983 (captain), 1987 (captain)
World Cup: 1963, 1964, 1965, 1966, 1967, 1971, 1973
Walker Cup: 1959, 1961

ABOVE: NO ONE HIT THE BALL FURTHER THAN JACK NICKLAUS DID WHEN THE GOLDEN BEAR WAS IN HIS PRIME.

RIGHT: NICKLAUS WASN'T RENOWNED FOR HIS SHORT GAME, BUT HE WAS THE BEST CLUTCH PUTTER IN THE GAME.

# Bobby Nichols

A TERRIBLE CAR ACCIDENT NEARLY COST NICHOLS (RIGHT) HIS LIFE, BUT HE BATTLED THROUGH SERIOUS INJURIES TO PLAY GOLF AT THE TOP LEVEL.

## Fact File

**BORN** 1936, Louisville, Kentucky, USA

**CAREER HIGHLIGHTS**
1962 St Petersburg Open Invitational
1964 USPGA Championship
1973 Westchester Classic
1974 Canadian Open
1989 Southwestern Bell Classic

**INTERNATIONAL HONORS**
Ryder Cup: 1967

Bobby Nichols is living proof that hard work, determination, and sheer willpower can overcome just about any obstacle in life. The Kentuckian survived a life threatening accident to become one of the best players on the US Tour in the 1960s and '70s.

Nichols was involved in a horrific car accident in high school just as he was about to enter his junior year. A good sports player who excelled at football as well as golf, Nichols suffered a broken pelvis, concussion, plus back and internal injuries. For 13 days he was paralyzed from the waist down and lay in a coma. When he regained consciousness, he was told he would never walk again. He was released from hospital after 96 days and then, miraculously, later regained the use of his legs and found he could still play golf.

The youngster won two high school golf championships and was awarded a football scholarship at Texas A&M, as there were no golf scholarships available at the time. In 1960, he turned professional and joined the US Tour. Two years later he won twice, when he triumphed in the 1962 St Petersburg Open Invitational and the Houston Classic. Those two victories earned him the Ben Hogan Award that goes annually to the golfer who has overcome injuries to play well on the US Tour. Hogan himself came back from a near fatal car injury to win major championships, and the great man sent two inspirational letters to Nichols after his accident.

Nichols did not stop after his two wins. In 1964 he lifted the USPGA Championship by defeating two of the biggest names in golf. The tournament was held that year at Columbus Country Club in Ohio, and Nichols established an early three shot lead with an opening 64, the low round of the week. Successive rounds of 71, 69, and 67 saw him win the title by three shots over Jack Nicklaus and Arnold Palmer. His 271 total set the record for the lowest winning score in USPGA history, one that stood for 30 years until Nick Price's win at Southern Hills in 1994.

Nichols was runner-up to Gay Brewer in the 1967 Masters, finishing one stroke short of a playoff for the title. However, seven more US Tour victories followed his USPGA win. By the time his regular playing days were over, Nichols had won 11 times.

He also won once on the Senior Tour, triumphing in the 1989 Southwestern Bell Classic. Not bad for a guy who was told he would be disabled for the rest of his life.

# Frank Nobilo

FRANK NOBILO IS ONE OF NEW ZEALAND'S BEST GOLFERS. THE STYLISH SWINGER HAS REPRESENTED HIS COUNTRY MANY TIMES AND WON TOURNAMENTS AROUND THE WORLD.

Frank Nobilo has a unique background. His ancestors were Italian pirates who settled in New Zealand in the early 1900s after running out of things to pillage on the Adriatic. At least that's Nobilo's version of events. Maybe that explains why the New Zealander has been able to plunder the riches of the European and US Tours.

Nobilo represented New Zealand as an amateur, appearing in the 1978 Eisenhower Trophy. That same season saw him triumph in the New Zealand Amateur Championship. He turned professional in 1979 and found success in New Zealand and Australia before graduating to the European and US Tours. The 5-foot, 11-inch professional won the 1982 New South Wales PGA Championship, and twice won the New Zealand PGA Championship, in 1985 and 1987.

Nobilo's next stop was the European Tour, which he joined in 1985. He was one of a large group of Australasian golfers who based themselves in Surrey, England, a group that included the likes of Craig Parry, Mike Harwood, Wayne Riley, Brett Ogle, and other antipodean stars. Like Parry *et al*, Nobilo soon found success in Europe. He won his first European Tour event in 1988 when he picked up the PLM Trophy. Over the next eight seasons, Nobilo won four more tournaments, including the 1991 Lancôme Trophy.

In 1997, the New Zealander moved permanently to the United States and soon found the winner's circle there, too. In April, he won the Greater Greensboro Chrysler Classic after a playoff with Brad Faxon. The irony is that Nobilo was thinking of skipping the tournament until his friend Ernie Els told him to play. Nobilo had missed three cuts in the previous five tournaments and wanted a week off, but he played on Ernie's advice.

The way Nobilo won his first US Tour event was a measure of his ability. Despite three successive rounds of 69, Nobilo never led the tournament. However, he birdied six of the last 11 holes in the final round to tie Faxon, and won at the first extra hole with a par to Faxon's bogey.

One of the most unassuming of players on the professional golf scene, Nobilo is a popular figure among his peers. The New Zealander is respected for the quality of his golf swing, one he has worked hard on over the years with top teacher Denis Pugh. The swing has stood up to the tests of championship golf, and Nobilo has had some good top ten finishes in the majors.

## Fact File

**BORN** 1960, Auckland, New Zealand

**CAREER HIGHLIGHTS**
1988 PLM Open
1991 Lancôme Trophy
1995 BMW International Open
1996 Deutsche Bank TPC of Europe
1997 Greater Greensboro Chrysler Classic

**INTERNATIONAL HONORS**
World Cup: 1982, 1987, 1988, 1990, 1993, 1994, 1995, 1998
Alfred Dunhill Cup: 1985, 1986, 1987, 1990, 1992, 1994, 1995, 1996, 1997, 1998
Presidents Cup: 1994, 1996, 1998

# Greg Norman

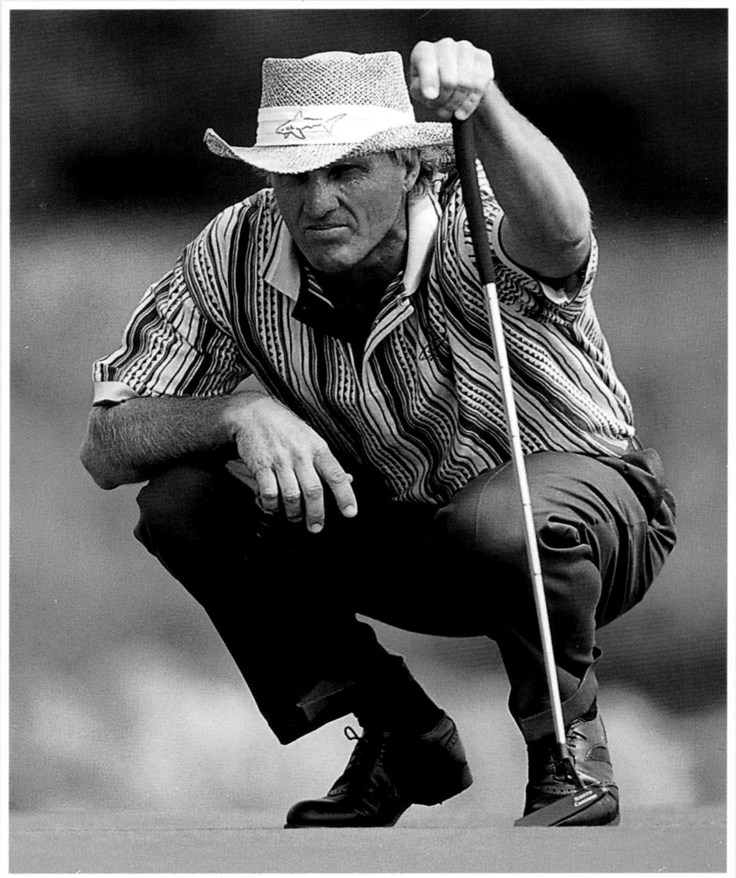

Gregory John Norman is either the victim of cruel fate or the biggest underachiever the game of golf has ever seen, depending on your point of view.

Norman is one of the most charismatic figures ever to pick up a golf club. His natural blond hair, his dazzling smile, his movie star good looks, his athletic physique all combine to make him a marketing man's dream. Indeed, off the golf course the tall Australian has made a fortune in endorsements.

Norman has won two major championships, both of them British Opens, and has won over 70 tournaments around the world. However, most experts agree it should be more.

Norman is one of only two men to have lost playoffs for all four of golf's major championships. (Craig Wood is the other.) By common consent, Norman should have won at least six majors by now. However, either he has contrived to throw them away or they have been stolen from his grasp by miracle shots.

Norman first came to prominence during the 1981 Masters when he tied for fourth. Beside his appearance, his all-out attacking style of play marked the 26-year-old as a player to watch. He also finished fourth in the USPGA Championship that year, his first full season on the US Tour. It was a sign of things to come—big things.

The Australian stamped his identity on the US Tour for good in 1984 when he won the Kemper and Canadian Opens. It was also the season he came closest to winning his first major, the US Open. Norman finished in a tie for first place with Fuzzy Zoeller at Winged Foot in the 1984 US Open before losing the 18-hole playoff. However, it was clear from that performance that it wouldn't be long before he won a major.

Norman won his first British Open in 1986 at Turnberry. The Australian played brilliantly over the four days in sometimes foul weather and over a course with very deep rough. Of particular note was his 63 in the second round to give him a lead that he never squandered.

Norman could easily have won all four majors in 1986. He led each one after the third round. A poor shot to the 72nd hole at the Masters resulted in a bogey that saw him miss a playoff with Jack Nicklaus. A bad final round at Shinnecock Hills in the US Open saw him slip to a tie for 12th. He won at Turnberry and should have won the USPGA at the Inverness Club in Ohio. However, miracle shot number one denied him the title.

Norman held a four-shot lead after three rounds of the 1986 USPGA, and played the final round with Bob Tway. As it turned out, Norman only had to shoot even par to win. However, by the 11th hole his lead had vanished and he found himself in a dogfight with Tway. Going down the last, the two were all square. When Tway's second shot found the bunker fronting the green, it looked like Norman would win his first USPGA. Norman's own ball spun back off the green but left him with an easy chip and putt for par. A playoff looked certain until Tway holed out from the bunker. It was a phenomenal shot under the circumstances, but it wasn't the last to deny Greg Norman a major championship.

Eight months later, Norman found himself in a playoff for the Masters with Larry Mize and Seve Ballesteros. Ballesteros parted company with the trio after a bogey at the first playoff hole, Augusta's tenth. With Norman on the green at the 11th, and Mize about 30 yards to the right with an impossible pitch, Norman looked certain to be slipping on his first green jacket. Then came miracle shot number two. Mize holed out from off the green to win the title.

Lesser mortals would not have recovered from such setbacks, but Greg Norman is made of strong stuff. The Australian continued to win tournaments, and in style. For example, he won the 1993 British Open Championship at Royal St George's by coming from one stroke behind Nick Faldo and Cory Pavin to win by two shots. Norman shot a near flawless final round 64 to take the title.

Norman's biggest heartbreak came in the 1996 Masters. He entered the final round with a six-stroke lead over Nick Faldo and seemed a certainty to finally win the green jacket. However, Faldo shot 67 while Norman struggled to a 78 to lose the title by five shots.

In total, Norman has finished second in the majors eight times. He completed the playoff grand slam when he lost in extra holes to Paul Azinger for the 1993 USPGA title.

## Fact File

**BORN** 1955, Mount Isa, Queensland, Australia

**CAREER HIGHLIGHTS**
1986 The Open Championship
1990 Memorial Tournament
1993 The Open Championship
1994 Players Championship
1995 Memorial Tournament

**INTERNATIONAL HONORS**
Presidents Cup: 1994 (withdrew due to illness), 1996, 1998

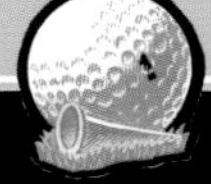

ABOVE: A PENSIVE-LOOKING NORMAN STUDIES A PUTT. MANY HEARTBREAKS OVER THE YEARS HAVE GIVEN THE AUSTRALIAN MUCH TO THINK ABOUT, ON AND OFF THE GOLF COURSE.

RIGHT: NORMAN'S ALL-OUT ATTACKING STYLE OF PLAY HAS MADE HIM ONE OF THE WORLD'S MOST EXCITING PLAYERS TO WATCH IN ANY GOLF TOURNAMENT, ESPECIALLY THE MAJORS.

# Moe Norman

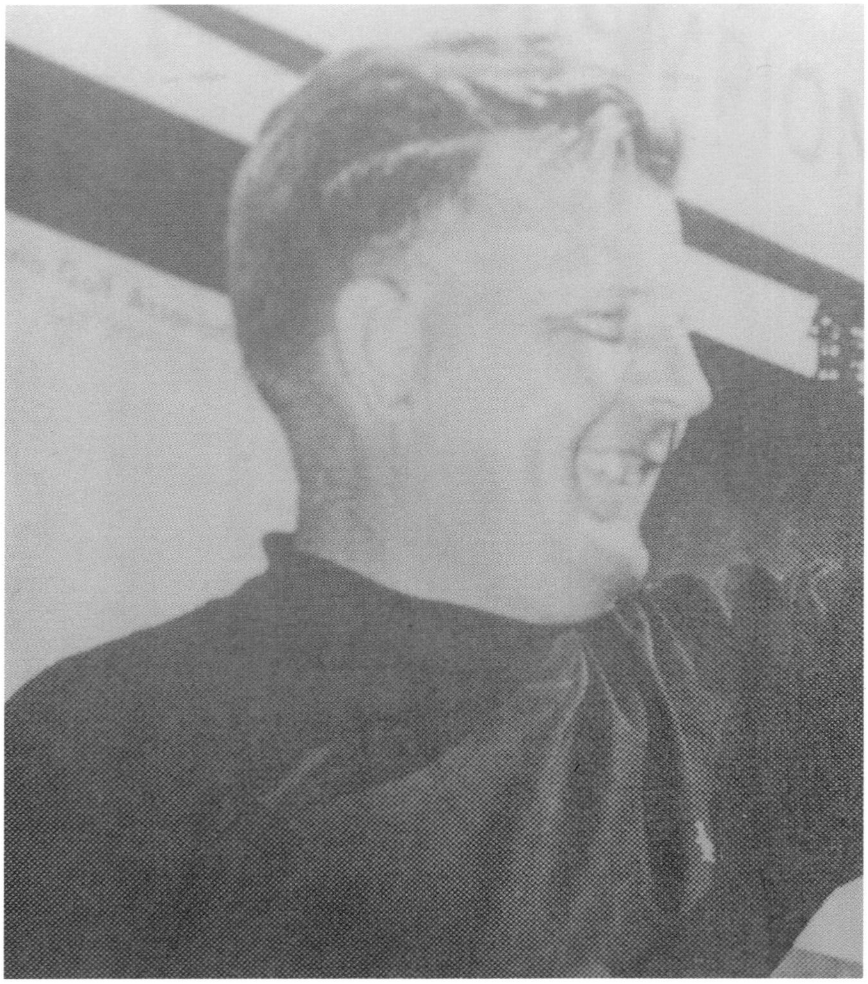

MOST GOLF FANS HAVE NEVER HEARD OF MOE NORMAN, BUT THE ECCENTRIC CANADIAN IS ONE OF THE BEST BALL STRIKERS THE GAME HAS EVER SEEN.

## Fact File

**BORN** 1929, Kitchener, Ontario, Canada

**CAREER HIGHLIGHTS**
1955 Canadian Amateur
1956 Canadian Amateur
1966 Canadian PGA Championship

Moe Norman is relatively unknown outside the world of golf. Even inside it there are people who will say "Moe who?" But players like Tom Watson, Paul Azinger, Ben Crenshaw, and Lee Trevino know him to be one of the purest swingers of a golf club ever to play the game.

The players mentioned above all have Moe Norman stories. For example, whenever anyone asks Watson who is the straightest hitter in golf, Norman's name is usually one of the players mentioned in Watson's reply. Paul Azinger first saw him in Florida when the future USPGA champion was a freshman at Brevard Junior College. One day Azinger was practicing with his team-mates when his coach John Redman, announced, "Boys, here comes the best ball-striker that ever lived."

Azinger took one look at Norman and thought his coach was crazy. "I couldn't believe what I was seeing," said Azinger later. "I've hit balls for a couple of hours, it's 100 degrees, and here comes this guy in a long sleeve turtleneck. I watched him hit drivers at the 250 yard sign, and he never hit one more than ten yards left or right of the marker."

Moe is one of the most eccentric players ever to grace a golf course. As in Azinger's experience, he usually wore a long-sleeved shirt, no matter what the weather, and trousers that were about three inches too short for him. Then there's his swing. Norman addresses the ball with the clubhead about a foot behind the ball, takes a short swing and hits it arrow-straight down the fairway every time. He is called "Pipeline Moe" because he hits it so straight, and very fast too. Norman's pre-shot routine is one look at the target and hit. Anyone who looks away will miss it.

Norman grew up in Kitchener, Ontario, Canada, where he played golf at the Rockway Golf Club, the municipal course. As a five-year-old he was hit by a car while sledding, and dragged 100 yards. He went home apparently unhurt, but the accident may have caused his fast speech and movement.

While he was at ease with himself on the golf course, Norman wasn't comfortable with people he didn't know. According to Canadian golf writer Lorne Rubenstein, Norman's personality kept him back from becoming one of the greatest players that ever lived. "He suffers from an inferiority complex so pervasive that it's kept him out of the mainstream of golf," Rubenstein once wrote. That was true in 1958 when he joined the US Tour only to quit because he felt the players were superior to him.

Norman finally got the respect his game deserved when the Titleist organization, whose equipment Norman uses, decided to pay him an annual $5,000 for the rest of his life.

# Andy North

**ANDY NORTH WON ONLY THREE TIMES ON THE US TOUR, BUT TWO OF HIS VICTORIES CAME IN THE US OPEN CHAMPIONSHIP.**

Andy North is probably the most maligned major winner in the history of golf. North won only three tournaments in his professional career, but two of them were US Opens. Even that did not impress many people. Of North's US Open wins, *Golf Monthly* magazine wrote the following: "How such an uninspiring player managed to even win one US Open is a mystery, but to win two seems almost criminal." That's unfair, very unfair.

As a youngster, North had been a good all-around sports player, especially in basketball and football, but an unusual ailment in his knee forced him to give up those two sports. A bone had stopped growing and was starting to disintegrate. Doctors felt that North could do serious damage to the leg if he persisted in playing sports that involved too much leg action. He was told he could play golf, but only so long as he used a cart.

The decision turned North to a career in golf. Before turning professional, he won the 1969 Wisconsin State Amateur and later the Western Amateur, and attended the University of Florida where he was a three-time All-American.

North joined the US Tour in 1973 and for four seasons finished no worse than 64th on the money list. His breakthrough win came in 1977 when he triumphed by two strokes over George Archer in the Westchester Classic. A year later he added his first US Open when his 285 at Cherry Hills in Denver, Colorado, was one stroke better than Dave Stockton and J. C. Snead.

North's second US Open victory was even sweeter than the first because it came on arguably the toughest layout to host the US Open. Oakland Hills Country Club is the course Ben Hogan once dubbed a "monster" after his victory there in 1951. Hogan's total that year was a seven over par 287. When North won it on the same layout in 1985, he did so with a one under par 279, the lowest US Open score posted there until Steve Jones bettered it by one stroke in 1996.

North's victory at Oakland Hills in Missouri is one of the main reasons the criticism of him is unfair. Poor players don't win the US Open at Oakland Hills. True, North shot a final round 74 to win, including a bogey on the last hole, but anyone who knows the layout will tell you that 74 is no embarrassment on Oakland Hills, especially in the last round of the US Open. Besides, four rounds in one under par is the work of a true champion.

Injuries forced North to quit the Tour in the mid-1990s to concentrate on a broadcasting career with ESPN.

## Fact File

**BORN** 1950, Thorpe, Wisconson, USA

**CAREER HIGHLIGHTS**
1971 Western Amateur
1977 American Express-Westchester Classic
1978 US Open
1985 US Open

**INTERNATIONAL HONORS**
Ryder Cup: 1985
World Cup: 1978

# CHRISTY O'CONNOR

NOT MANY PLAYERS HAVE HAD THE FLAIR OF CHRISTY O'CONNOR. THE IRISHMAN WAS ONE OF THE BEST SHOTMAKERS.

## FACT FILE

**BORN** 1924, Galway, Ireland

**CAREER HIGHLIGHTS**
1956 Dunlop Masters
1957 News of the World PGA Match Play
1964 Martini International Club
1970 John Player Classic
1972 Carrolls International

**INTERNATIONAL HONORS**
Ryder Cup: 1955, 1957, 1959, 1961, 1963, 1965, 1967, 1969, 1971, 1973
World Cup: 1956, 1957, 1958, 1959, 1960, 1961, 1962, 1963, 1964, 1966, 1967, 1968, 1969, 1971, 1975

Christy O'Connor is a legend in his native Ireland, a man they give the simple but revered title of "Himself."

O'Connor grew up on the west coast of Ireland in the town of Galway. Like many Irish youngsters he started out as a caddie and would practice his golf on the beach at Galway, where he would hit balls off the smooth sands. Seve Ballesteros was another who developed his golf by playing on beach sand as a youngster, and it is probably no coincidence that he and O'Connor are two of the greatest shot makers the game has ever seen.

O'Connor's swing was free, loose and rhythmic. Like many Irish players, he grew up playing in windy conditions, and was always comfortable playing in any type of breeze.

For years, O'Connor never ventured outside his homeland. He was 30 years old by the time he finally played golf outside the Emerald Isle, traveling to Llandudno in 1954 to compete in the Penfold tournament, which at the time was played at match play. O'Connor lost in the semi-finals to eventual winner Henry Cotton.

Himself made his Ryder Cup debut in 1955, the first of ten consecutive appearances in the biennial competition. O'Connor lost his singles match by the score of four and two to Tommy Bolt. However, in 1957 he helped contribute to Great Britain & Ireland's first victory in 24 years when he easily defeated Dow Finsterwald seven and six in the singles.

The Irishman's first attempt at the British Open came in 1951, when the tournament was held at Royal Portrush, Northern Ireland. He came close to winning the tournament on a couple of occasions. He missed a playoff for the title in 1958 when the tournament was held at Royal Lytham & St. Annes in England. He fell short of Peter Thomson and Dave Thomas's four-round total of 278. Then in 1965 he finished runner-up with Brian Huggett at Royal Birkdale, when Thomson won the last of his five titles.

The ten-time Ryder Cup player won 24 times on the European Tour during his prime, and twice won the Harry Vardon Trophy as leading money winner on the European Order of Merit, which he topped in 1961 and 1962. In 1958, he and Harry Bradshaw recorded a historic first for Ireland when they won the World Cup in Mexico City.

Now a senior golfer with six victories in the PGA Seniors Championship between 1976 and 1983, O'Connor's services are still very much in demand. It is said there is no greater pleasure than to play 18 holes with "Himself."

# CHRISTY O'CONNOR JR

CHRISTY O'CONNOR JR HAS WON MANY TOURNAMENTS IN HIS CAREER, BUT HIS GREATEST MOMENT CAME IN THE 1989 RYDER CUP.

When Christy O'Connor Jr retires to his home in Galway on the west coast of Ireland, he will do so with a lot of memories. One will stand out above all others. It involves a glorious 2-iron shot at The Belfry in the 1989 Ryder Cup, a shot O'Connor Jr and those who saw it will never forget.

The Irishman made his second appearance in the Ryder Cup in the 1989 match. His first in 1975 hadn't been that memorable. He played only twice that year, losing in the first day's fourballs with fellow countryman Eamonn Darcy, and then in the foursomes on the second day with another compatriot, John O'Leary. O'Connor wasn't selected for either session of singles on the final day when his side was thrashed 21 points to 11 at Laurel Valley in Pennsylvania.

It looked like 1989 wouldn't be much different. O'Connor had played only once prior to the singles, losing with Ronan Rafferty in a fourball match to Mark Calcavecchia and Ken Green. The draw for the final day didn't work in the Irishman's favor either. He was pitted against Fred Couples, one of the United States' top players.

However, like his famous uncle, O'Connor is a fighter who can produce top quality golf when he's playing well. He certainly did that in his match against Couples.

The American was sometimes 50 yards longer off the tee than his opponent, and at one point was two up. But O'Connor showed great nerve to battle back and square the match with a good putt on the 16th. The pair came to the last hole all square, but Couples hit a monster tee shot down the last fairway leaving himself only a 9-iron to the green. O'Connor, meanwhile, had 230 yards to go. He selected a 2-iron, told himself to "make a good turn," and hit the ball to within six feet of the cup. The shot may have unnerved his opponent, for Couples pushed his second shot and took three more strokes to hand the point to O'Connor. It was an important one, too, because it gave Europe 13 points. When Jose Maria Canizares won his match immediately after O'Connor, it meant that Europe had retained the cup. The match was eventually drawn when America won the last four matches.

O'Connor is one of the most congenial of players, and it was no surprise when he and Couples later became friends, drawn together by their memorable encounter.

Now a player on the European Seniors Tour, O'Connor won four times during his years on the regular European Tour, plus another nine victories around the world. In 1985 he came close to winning the British Open at Royal St George's when he finished third behind Sandy Lyle.

## FACT FILE

**BORN** 1948, Galway, Ireland

**CAREER HIGHLIGHTS**
1975 Carrolls Irish Open
1975 Martini International
1989 Jersey European Airways Open
1990 555 Kenya Open
1992 Dunhill British Masters

**INTERNATIONAL HONORS**
Ryder Cup: 1975, 1989
World Cup: 1974, 1975, 1978, 1985, 1989, 1992
Alfred Dunhill Cup: 1985, 1989, 1992

# Ayako Okamoto

AYAKO OKAMOTO WAS A LATECOMER TO GOLF. THE JAPANESE STAR WAS A STANDOUT IN SOFTBALL BEFORE SHE TOOK UP GOLF.

## Fact File

**BORN** 1951, Hiroshima, Japan

**CAREER HIGHLIGHTS**

1984 Weetabix Women's British Open
1987 Nestlé World Championship
1988 Greater Washington Open
1989 LPGA Corning Classic
1992 McDonald's Championship

Ayako Okamoto is a superstar in her native Japan, a golfer much revered by the golf-mad population. Yet the irony is that she only took up the game as an afterthought.

Okamoto was a star softball player until she took up golf. In fact, she was the number one player in Japan. It wasn't until just before her 23rd birthday that Okamoto started playing golf. She practiced for a few months at a private club in Osaka, and shot 47 for her first nine holes.

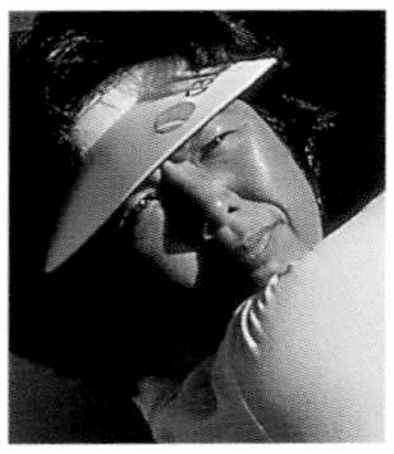

The Japanese professional is known as a player who works hard and gives 100 percent to her game. That was the case when she started golf. Okamoto practiced from morning until night and soon mastered the game.

It didn't take long for Okamoto to become the number one player in Japan, but at the age of 30 she had a premonition that she would become one of the top three players in the world, so she decided to leave the Japanese Tour and concentrate on the American circuit.

In 1981 Okamoto played seven events on the LPGA Tour and finished 76th on the Order of Merit. She moved up to 14th the following season with her first LPGA victory in the Arizona Classic. She was tenth the following year with another victory, and third in 1984 when she won twice and also captured the Women's British Open over the tough Dukes course at Woburn. In appalling conditions, the Japanese star ran away with the tournament, winning the title by 11 shots.

Okamoto's presence on the LPGA Tour was the subject of much attention by the Japanese media. There were times when the number of Japanese press people covering Okamoto was more than that covering the rest of the field—a sure indication of Okamoto's popularity in Japan.

It wasn't long before the Hiroshima native gave the Japanese press corps something big to write about. After suffering from a herniated spinal disc in 1985 which halted her progress, Okamoto returned to fine form the following season when she placed ninth on the end of season money list. Then came her finest year as a professional.

In 1987 Okamoto won four times and topped the money list with over $465,000 to become the first foreign player in LPGA history to achieve that honor. That season also saw her become the first visitor to take the Player of the Year Award.

# Jose Maria Olazabal

JOSE MARIA OLAZABAL ALMOST GAVE UP GOLF BECAUSE OF A FOOT AILMENT. HOWEVER, THE SPANIARD BATTLED BACK TO WIN THE MASTERS FOR A SECOND TIME.

There was a time when it looked as if Jose Maria Olazabal would never play golf again. Then a chance meeting with an old amateur competitor led him to a German doctor who gave the Spaniard a new lease of life.

Olazabal was diagnosed with rheumatoid arthritis in his feet at the end of the 1995 season. His condition was so bad that he voluntarily withdrew from the 1995 Ryder Cup. Olazabal suffered much until he chanced upon a former amateur competitor who put him in touch with Doctor Hans-Wilhelm Muller-Wohlfahrt who cured his ailment.

Olazabal was out of the game for 18 months, during which time he was often so incapacitated as to be unable to get out of bed. He returned in 1997 and was soon back to his winning ways with an emotional victory in the Turespana Masters.

The son of a Real Sebastian greenkeeper, Olazabal grew up on a golf course and was a child prodigy by the time he was in his teens. He remains the only player to make a clean sweep of the British Boys', Youth, and Amateur Championships. He triumphed in the latter over Scotland's Colin Montgomerie, winning the 1984 title at Formby Golf Club by the score of five and four.

It wasn't long before Olazabal was competing on a

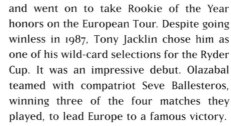

and went on to take Rookie of the Year honors on the European Tour. Despite going winless in 1987, Tony Jacklin chose him as one of his wild-card selections for the Ryder Cup. It was an impressive debut. Olazabal teamed with compatriot Seve Ballesteros, winning three of the four matches they played, to lead Europe to a famous victory.

By the 1994 season Olazabal had won 13 times on the European Tour. He had been victorious twice in the United States, including a runaway win in the 1990 NEC World Series of Golf when he headed the field by 12 shots.

Prior to 1994, the nearest Olazabal had come to a major championship was a second place finish to Ian Woosnam in the 1991 Masters. A bogey at the final hole that year cost him a playoff for the title. He made amends in 1994.

The Spaniard is one of the best short game players in the world. As a youngster he would spend hours around the practice green chipping and putting. All those hours paid off when he won the 1994 Masters at Augusta National, a course where a brilliant short game is a must. Glorious golf over the four days saw the young Spaniard win the title from Tom Lehman by two shots.

Olazabal won his second Masters title in 1999 by

## Fact File

**BORN** 1966, Fuenterrabia, Spain

**CAREER HIGHLIGHTS**
1984 British Amateur
1990 NEC World Series of Golf
1994 Masters
1994 Volvo PGA Championship
1999 Masters

**INTERNATIONAL HONORS**
Ryder Cup: 1987, 1989, 1991, 19
1997
World Cup: 1989
Alfred Dunhill Cup: 1986, 1987, 1
1989, 1992, 1993, 1998

# BALLESTEROS DENIES WATSON

There are many great photographs of Seviano Ballesteros, but the sequence that stands out is the one shot at St Andrews in 1984 when Ballesteros won the British Open at the "home of golf." The images capture Ballesteros punching the air with unbridled joy. The Spaniard had sunk a birdie putt on the final hole to win his second British Open Championship.

Every golfer dreams of winning a major championship. As children they play games on the practice putting green: "This putt is for the Open," they will say to themselves. And if it is for the British Open, then you can bet the course in their heads is St Andrews.

Watson arrived at St Andrews in 1984 seeking his third consecutive British Open. More importantly, he was looking for his sixth title to tie the legendary Harry Vardon as winner of most British Opens. The fact that it was at St Andrews made the occasion all the more special. Ballesteros was looking for his second British title to add to the championship he won five years earlier at Royal Lytham & St Annes. He, too, was desperate to win the title at St Andrews, the birthplace of the game.

The galleries were divided that year. Both men were extremely popular. On the one hand, Watson was respected not only for the way he played the game, but for his adherence to its traditions and its history, and for his love of links golf and the British Open. Ballesteros was admired for his style of play, for his go-for-broke attitude, yet he would win the championship by playing one of the toughest holes in golf in a conservative manner. Dressed in his traditional final round navy blue outfit, Ballesteros declined to go for the flag on the 17th in the final round. Instead he hit his approach shot to the right and played a chip and a putt to get his par. A drive at the last left him with just a wedge to the home hole. The putt broke from right to left and Seve hit the ball with just enough pace. For a brief moment it looked like the ball would hang on the lip, but it dropped in and the champion thrilled the galleries on the 18th green by repeatedly punching the air, turning to sections of the crowd as he did so.

Meanwhile, Watson was having his problems in the group behind, by overhitting his approach shot to the 17th, leaving him with an almost impossible angle against the wall behind the green. A short stab at the ball sent it scooting across the road and a long way from the hole. Two putts cost him a bogey. Watson had witnessed Seve's delight at the last, and knew he now needed to eagle the last to force a playoff. After a good drive, he walked from his ball to the green to survey the situation. Watson had to hole his shot to take the tournament to extra holes. He didn't and Ballesteros had earned the most famous victory in his career.

RIGHT: BALLESTEROS'S PUTTER HELPED HIM TO HIS SECOND BRITISH OPEN VICTORY, INCLUDING A BIRDIE AT THE LAST TO SEAL VICTORY OVER TOM WATSON.

**ABOVE: CLASSIC SEVE. BALLESTEROS WAS MAGNIFICENT IN WINNING THE 1984 BRITISH OPEN.**

**ABOVE RIGHT: SEVE'S WIN AT ST ANDREWS, THE HOME OF GOLF, RANKS AS ONE OF HIS GREATEST ACHIEVEMENTS.**

**RIGHT: A WINNING TEAM. CADDIE NICK DEPAUL GUIDED SEVE TO VICTORY AT ST ANDREWS IN 1984.**

# Ed Oliver

ED "PORKY" OLIVER DID NOT WIN A MAJOR , BUT HE CAME CLOSE ON A NUMBER OF OCCASIONS. A RULES INFRINGEMENT DENIED HIM THE 1940 US OPEN.

## Fact File

**BORN** 1916, Wilmington, Delaware, USA

**DIED** 1961

**CAREER HIGHLIGHTS**
1940 Bing Crosby National Pro-Am
1940 Phoenix Open
1941 Western Open
1947 Texas Open
1958 Houston Open

**INTERNATIONAL HONORS**
Ryder Cup: 1947, 1951, 1953

Ed "Porky" Oliver is probably the unluckiest golfer ever to play the game. A popular figure on the US Tour for over 20 years, Oliver won a number of tournaments but never won one of the majors, despite coming close on several occasions.

Oliver was runner-up in around 20 tournaments during his career, but it was for his second place finishes in the majors that people will remember him. The Delaware native was the victim of a rules infringement in 1940 that denied him the US Open. Oliver, Johnny Bulla, and Dutch Harrison teed off before their scheduled start in the fourth round. Their excuse was that they wanted to avoid a storm threatening the round. It never materialized but the three players were disqualified nevertheless. That was a pity, because Oliver's final round 71 tied him for the 72-hole lead with Lawson Little and Gene Sarazen.

In 1946, Oliver fought his way through to the final of the USPGA Championship, beating Byron Nelson by a score of one up in the quarter finals. Oliver then came up against Ben Hogan in the final. After the first 18 holes Oliver was three up and looked to be on his way to his first major victory. However, Hogan shot 30 on the front nine in the afternoon and ran out a six and four winner.

Hogan got the better of Oliver again in 1953 when he finished five shots ahead of the heavyweight professional in the Masters. Oliver was particularly unlucky that year. His 279 total would have won the championship in every previous year except two, when it would have got him into a playoff for the title. Oliver was the unfortunate victim of a phenomenal four rounds by Hogan.

Oliver also finished second, officially, in the US Open, when he was runner-up to Julius Boros in 1952 at Northwood Country Club in Dallas.

The popular player competed in three Ryder Cups during his career. In his debut match in 1947, Oliver combined with Lew Worsham to inflict a ten and nine foursomes drubbing of Henry Cotton and Arthur Lees. The win equaled the highest winning margin in Ryder Cup history, tying the mark set by Walter Hagen and Denny Shute in 1931, when they defeated George Duncan and Arthur Havers.

Oliver recorded the win of his career in 1941, when he triumphed in the Western Open, one of the biggest tournaments in world golf at the time. His 275 total was three shots better than the formidable duo of Hogan and Nelson.

The world of golf mourned Oliver's death deeply when he died of cancer in 1961.

# MARK O'MEARA

FOR MOST OF HIS CAREER IT LOOKED AS THOUGH MARK O'MEARA WOULD NOT WIN A MAJOR CHAMPIONSHIP, BUT IN 1998 THE AMERICAN HAD THE SEASON OF HIS LIFE, WINNING TWO.

Mark O'Meara will never forget the 1998 season for as long as he lives. That was the year the popular American finally put his mark on the game.

Through nearly 16 seasons as a professional, the 1979 US Amateur champion had won 25 tournaments around the world, including 18 on the US Tour alone. Yet he had never won a major championship. He'd been fourth in the Masters, third in the US Open and third in the British Open, but had never managed to land the one victory that would ensure his status in the game. If ever there was a golfer worthy of the title "the best player never to have won a major," then O'Meara was the man.

O'Meara had turned 41 as the 1998 season got into full swing; an age when many golfers are well past their prime and readying themselves for the Senior Tour. However, O'Meara was ready for his most successful campaign ever.

A friend of the young phenomenon Tiger Woods, O'Meara showed up at Augusta, Georgia, for the Masters as a player who was expected to do well but who wasn't really seen as a serious contender to Woods's title. However, O'Meara followed his young friend as champion by shooting a final round 65 that included two birdies on the 71st and 72nd holes. He became only the third winning player to record that particular feat, following Art Wall in 1959, and Arnold Palmer in 1960.

O'Meara then showed his first major victory was no fluke by winning the British Open at Royal Birkdale that summer. Already a winner over the Birkdale layout having won the 1987 Lawrence Batley Invitational, O'Meara looked comfortable all week and eventually fought his way into a playoff for the title with fellow American Brian Watts. O'Meara won over the four extra holes to become the first player since Nick Price in 1994 to win two majors in the same season.

O'Meara then topped the year off by defeating Woods in the final of the World Match Play Championship at Wentworth in England. His phenomenal season earned him Player of the Year honors on the US Tour. More importantly, it finally put him among the game's elite.

One of the most likable players in the game, O'Meara has marked himself as different from his American contemporaries by his willingness to travel to different countries. During his career he has competed in many tournaments around the world. For example, among his victories are the 1986 Australian Masters, the 1994 Argentine Open and two tournament wins in Japan.

## FACT FILE

**BORN** 1957, Goldsboro, North Carolina, USA

**CAREER HIGHLIGHTS**
1984 Greater Milwaukee Open
1995 Canadian Open
1996 Mercedes Championship
1998 Masters
1998 The Open Championship

**INTERNATIONAL HONORS**
Ryder Cup: 1985, 1989, 1991, 1997
Alfred Dunhill Cup: 1985, 1986, 1987, 1996, 1997, 1998
Presidents Cup: 1996, 1998

# PETER OOSTERHUIS

PETER OOSTERHUIS WAS AN OUTSTANDING EUROPEAN TOUR PLAYER IN THE 1970S. FOR FOUR STRAIGHT SEASONS BETWEEN 1971 AND 1974 HE WAS EUROPE'S NUMBER ONE PLAYER.

## FACT FILE

**BORN** 1948, London, England

**CAREER HIGHLIGHTS**
1971 Piccadilly Medal
1973 Viyella PGA Championship
1973 French Open
1974 French Open
1981 Canadian Open

**INTERNATIONAL HONORS**
Ryder Cup: 1971, 1973, 1975, 1977, 1979, 1981
World Cup: 1971, 1973
Walker Cup: 1967

Until Colin Montgomerie came along, Peter Oosterhuis held the record for the most consecutive years as Europe's number one player. "Oosty" achieved that honor between 1971 and 74, when he was the best player on the European Tour.

Oosterhuis turned professional in 1968 after a glittering amateur career that saw him captain the England Boys' team, win the British Youth Championship at Dalmahoy in 1966, and play in the 1967 Walker Cup at Royal St George's. The latter achievement came when he was still a schoolboy at Dulwich College.

Oosterhuis' transformation to the professional game was nothing short of amazing. He won the Rookie of the Year Award for his performance on the 1969 European Tour, when he ranked 16th on the European money list. He triumphed in his first professional event in 1970 when he won the South African General Motors Open, and then the next year took the first of his four consecutive money titles.

The 1971 season saw Oosterhuis make the first of six consecutive appearances in the Ryder Cup. He made an impressive debut in the biennial match, defeating Gene Littler by a score of four and three in the morning singles and then bettering Arnold Palmer by three and two in the afternoon.

Oosterhuis was the player everyone expected to succeed Tony Jacklin as Britain's next great golfer. Jacklin had won two majors, the 1969 British Open and 1970 US Open, by the time Oosterhuis got into his stride. London-born Oosterhuis certainly gave it his best shot. He was runner-up in the 1974 British Open at Royal Lytham & St Annes, finishing four shots behind Gary Player. However, that was as close as he got to a major championship.

A wonderful iron player and an excellent putter, Oosterhuis tried his luck on the US Tour for a number of seasons. He lost a playoff to Lee Elder for the 1974 Monsanto Open, and finally found success seven years later when he captured the Canadian Open. The 6-foot, 5-inch golfer won the 1984 tournament at the Glen Abbey Golf Club near Toronto by one shot from Andy North, Bruce Lietzke, and Jack Nicklaus.

After his playing days were over, Oosterhuis became the director of golf at the famous Riviera Club in Los Angeles. He is now a full-time golf commentator and is considered one of the best in the business.

# FRANCIS OUIMET

FRANCIS OUIMET SHOCKED THE WORLD OF GOLF WHEN HE DEFEATED HARRY VARDON AND TED RAY IN A PLAYOFF FOR THE 1913 US OPEN.

Francis Ouimet is generally credited with starting the boom in American golf because of his shock victory in the 1913 US Open.

Ouimet was a complete unknown outside his native Massachusetts when he entered the championship at Brookline that year. He only played in the tournament to get a closer look at the immortal Harry Vardon, and because the course was across the street from his house. No one gave the amateur and part-time caddie a chance in the tournament, especially since Vardon and fellow Englishman Ted Ray were the tournament favorites. Yet Ouimet found himself in contention coming down the stretch. He needed a birdie over the last four holes to tie the two professionals and promptly got it at the 17th.

Everyone expected the 20-year-old to crack in the ensuing 18-hole playoff, but Ouimet held his nerve to shoot 72 against the 77 by Vardon and Ray's 78 to win his national title.

A year later Ouimet won the French Amateur and the US Amateur. He repeated as US Amateur champion in 1931, 17 years after his first victory.

Ouimet's victory in the US Open did not initially end the British challenge in the tournament. After all, Ted Ray won the title in 1920 while Vardon came second. However, Ouimet's win proved to Americans that they could compete on a world level. Moreover, the victory captured the imagination of the American public. He was an ordinary blue-collar American who wasn't privileged to belong to the country club set as so many golfers did. If he could do it, then anyone could.

Despite his historic win, Ouimet remained an amateur golfer for the rest of his life. Neither did the victory inflate his ego, for Ouimet was known as the most unassuming and modest of golfers.

No American golfer in the early part of the century had such an allegiance with the Walker Cup as Ouimet. He played in every match between 1922 and 1934, captaining the side in 1932 and 1934. In that time he played 16 matches and won nine, lost five, and halved two. He was also non-playing captain four times between 1936 and 1949.

After his playing days were over, Ouimet served on many USGA committees and was responsible for administration of the game in America. In 1951 he was honored with the captaincy of the Royal & Ancient Golf Club of St Andrews, the first foreigner to hold that post.

## FACT FILE

**BORN** 1893, Newton, Massachusetts, USA

**DIED** 1967

**CAREER HIGHLIGHTS**
1913 US Open
1914 US Amateur
1914 French Amateur
1931 US Amateur

**INTERNATIONAL HONORS**
Walker Cup: 1922, 1923, 1924, 1926, 1930, 1932 (captain), 1934 (captain), 1936 (captain), 1938 (captain), 1947 (captain), 1949 (captain)

# Jumbo Ozaki

JUMBO OZAKI HAS WON OVER 100 TOURNAMENTS ON THE JAPANESE TOUR, MAKING HIM JAPAN'S GOLFING SUPERSTAR.

## Fact File

**BORN** 1947, Kaiman Town, Tokushima, Japan

**CAREER HIGHLIGHTS**
1974 Japan Open
1988 Japan Open
1989 Japan Open
1994 Japan Open

**INTERNATIONAL HONORS**
World Cup: 1974, 1988
Presidents Cup: 1996

No player has won more times on the Japanese Tour than Masashi "Jumbo" Ozaki. Since turning professional in 1970, Ozaki has made the Japanese circuit his own.

A large golfer who hits the ball a long way, Ozaki has won over 100 times on the Japanese circuit. When he won the Dunlop Phoenix tournament in November 1996, it marked the 100th win of his career. Two weeks later he won his 101st when he triumphed in the Japan Series Hitachi Cup, and was still going strong the last time anyone checked his record. In fact, Ozaki had won 109 tournaments through the 1998 season, 110 if you throw in the 1972 New Zealand PGA Championship, his only win outside Japan.

In 1997 Ozaki won five tournaments and topped the Japanese Order of Merit with just over $1.4 million in earnings. It was the 11th year Ozaki had won the Japanese money list, and the fourth year in succession. Ozaki first won the Order of Merit in 1973, then in 1974, 1977, 1988, 1989, 1990, 1992 and from 1994 to 1997.

Besides his five Japan Opens, Ozaki has won the Japan PGA Championship six times, six Japan Series Championships, six Fuji-Sankei Opens, six Ana Opens and five Jun Classics, and many, many more tournaments besides. Ozaki is a superstar in his homeland, a player who enjoys almost cult status. Whenever he plays abroad, especially in a major championship, a huge Japanese press contingent follows his every move.

Noted for his colorful attire and his baggy trousers and roomy shirts, Ozaki has never really traveled well outside Japan. He has appeared in many majors over the years but has not threatened to win one during his career. The closest he has come is an eighth place finish in the 1973 British Open at Troon, and sixth place at the US Open at Oak Hill Country Club, New York in 1989.

His dominance of the Japanese circuit has made him one of the leading players in the world according to the Official Golf Ranking. Between 1989 and 1998 he was no worse than 30th on the ranking, reaching fifth twice, in 1996 and 1997. As of the 1998 season he was, at 51, the oldest player in the top 15.

Despite his success at home, and unlike his brother Joe who has successfully combined playing both Tours, Ozaki has never been tempted to play the US Tour. Indeed, Ozaki's best finish in a regular US Tour event was a tie for fourth place in the 1993 Memorial Tournament. But then with the millions of yen in prize money Ozaki has won over the years, there has been no need to play anywhere else but at home.

# ALF PADGHAM

WHEN ALF PADGHAM WON THE 1936 BRITISH OPEN, HE CAPPED A BRILLIANT CAREER THAT SAW HIM WIN MANY TOURNAMENTS THROUGHOUT EUROPE.

Alf Padgham won many titles in his career. His greatest season ever came in 1936, when he won three tournaments before laying his hands on the biggest trophy in golf.

Padgham's family had connections with Royal Ashdown Forest, and the Surrey professional served his apprenticeship at the course before joining the tournament circuit.

A player with huge hands, Padgham had one of the most elegant swings ever to grace the game. Although it was short, his swing looked effortless, yet he hit the ball a long way. He was also a very accurate iron player. His putting was another story.

The Englishman looked anything but elegant on the greens. Indeed, one look at his putting stroke was enough to make people think he wasn't a professional but a high handicapper. He held his hands well out from his body and hit the ball as if he were playing a short chip. However, the stroke was good enough to win the British Open.

Padgham had announced his intentions of winning the world's oldest golf tournament when he finished runner-up to Alf Perry at Muirfield in 1935. Padgham finished four strokes short of Perry's winning margin, but his performance obviously told him he could win the tournament, because he came back and won it the next year. Padgham's victory came on the links of Hoylake. Ironically it was his putting that was to win him the championship. Padgham holed a 12-foot birdie putt on the last green to win the championship by one stroke over Scotland's James Adams.

The Surrey professional's fine play during the 1930s earned him three appearances in the Ryder Cup between 1933 and 1937. Despite his obvious talent, Padgham never recorded a win in the biennial match. He played six matches and lost every one, including singles losses to Gene Sarazen (1933), Olin Dutra (1935), and Ralph Guldahl (1937), the latter by the lopsided score of eight and seven.

A quiet man who often appeared on the course as a player without a care in the world, Padgham was nevertheless a tough competitor. Despite his disappointing Ryder Cup performances, Padgham had a fairly good record in match play. For example, he twice won the British Professional Match Play, with both victories coming at Royal Mid-Surrey.

It was said of Padgham that he lost his putting touch after a trip to South Africa in the winter following his British Open win. There he had to putt on grainy greens and was never the same player again.

## FACT FILE

**BORN** 1906, Surrey, England

**DIED** 1966

**CAREER HIGHLIGHTS**
1931 British Professional Match Play Championship
1934 German Open
1935 British Professional Match Play Championship
1936 The Open Championship
1938 Dutch Open

**INTERNATIONAL HONORS**
Ryder Cup: 1933, 1935, 1937

# Arnold Palmer

There can be no doubting Arnold Palmer's influence on the game of golf. It was simply huge. He took it from being a sport often ignored by most of the American population, and popularized it as no player before had ever done.

Not even Bobby Jones or Ben Hogan came close to gaining the sort of stardom that befell Arnold Palmer. They came close, but Arnold had a distinct advantage. His prime happened to coincide with the biggest influence on American sensibilities—the television.

Palmer was the first genuine superstar of the TV age. Americans had to follow Jones's progress on radio, and, in effect, that of Hogan as well. Television was around when Hogan was winning major championships, but not to the same extent as when Palmer was in his prime.

Palmer's career includes a lot of firsts. He was the first player to win the Masters four times, the first player to win $1 million in prize money, and the first to travel the world in his own private jet.

Palmer's success came from two things: the way he played the game and his background. Palmer didn't just shoot low scores, he battered golf courses into submission. He became famous for mounting last round charges to win golf's biggest titles. In 1960 he birdied the final two holes at Augusta to steal the title from Ken Venturi. That same season he came from seven shots behind going into the final round to win his only US Open Championship.

People all over America watched his exploits on television and flocked to see him play golf. Palmer's inclusion in the field of any tournament was guaranteed to increase the gate receipts substantially. Americans also loved the fact that he hailed from a predominantly working-class background. Palmer's father had been a club professional in Latrobe, Pennsylvania, and so Arnold became a blue-collar hero in the minds of most Americans. His chasing was so strong that the galleries chasing him became known as "Arnie's Army."

Even when the Pennsylvania phenomenon was well past his prime, people still flocked to see him play. Palmer won his last major championship, the Masters, in 1964, yet for years afterwards the army turned up in huge numbers to cheer him on.

It was Palmer's decision to play in the 1960 British Open at St Andrews that helped repopularize the event for American players. Until Palmer made the trip, and every other after that, American professionals had largely ignored the tournament.

Palmer pioneered the way for future professionals to make huge amounts of money off the golf course. Managed by Mark McCormack, who would later found the hugely successful and influential International Management Group, Palmer made more money off the course than he ever did on it. Even well into the 1990s Palmer was making millions in endorsement deals.

Despite his success, and despite his immense wealth, Palmer has never forgotten his roots. He continues to be one of the most approachable professionals in the game, always courteous to fans, officials, and media alike.

Golf has been very good to Arnold Palmer, but today's professionals owe a lot to him for paving their way. Without Palmer, golf might still be a second-rate sport with professionals playing for low stakes instead of the huge pots of money for which they compete today.

## Fact File

**BORN** 1929, Latrobe, Pennsylvania, USA

**CAREER HIGHLIGHTS**
1954 US Amateur
1958 Masters
1960 Masters
1960 US Open
1961 The Open Championship
1962 Masters
1962 The Open Championship
1964 Masters

**INTERNATIONAL HONORS**
Ryder Cup: 1961, 1963, 1965, 1967, 1971, 1973, 1975 (captain)
World Cup: 1960, 1962, 1963, 1964, 1966, 1967
Presidents Cup: 1996 (captain)

ABOVE: PALMER WAS ONE OF THE BEST PUTTERS DURING HIS PRIME. THE POPULAR AMERICAN HOLED MANY VITAL PUTTS WHILE WINNING MAJOR CHAMPIONSHIPS.

RIGHT: A CLASSIC PALMER FOLLOW THROUGH. ARNIE GAVE EVERY SHOT 150 PERCENT

# Se Ri Pak

SE RI PAK IS THE BEST GOLFER EVER TO EMERGE FROM KOREA. PAK WAS A COMPLETE UNKNOWN PRIOR TO THE 1998 SEASON, BUT MADE HEADLINES BY WINNING TWO MAJOR CHAMPIONSHIPS.

## Fact File

**BORN** 1977, Daejeon, Korea

**CAREER HIGHLIGHTS**
1998 McDonald's LPGA Championship
1998 US Women's Open
1998 Jamie Farr Kroger Classic
1998 Giant Eagle LPGA Classic

Se Ri Pak came out of nowhere to take the LPGA Tour by storm in 1998, setting a string of records that make her one of the players to watch in the 21st century.

Pak simply ran away with the LPGA's Rookie of the Year Award, and nearly ran away with the Order of Merit title, too. She ended the season second on the LPGA money list with just over $870,000. In the competition for Rookie of the Year, Pak was so far ahead of nearest rival Janice Moodie that she actually won the award with nine events left to play in the season.

Prior to turning professional, Pak won 30 amateur tournaments in her native Korea. When she turned professional in 1996, Pak played 14 tournaments on the Korean LPGA Tour, winning six and finishing runner-up in another seven. That was impressive in itself, but the American LPGA Tour is the strongest in women's golf. No one expected Pak to do what she did in 1998.

In her first major championship as a professional, Pak went to the wire to win the LPGA Championship. Her victory made her the first rookie since Sweden's Liselotte Neumann in 1988 to make a major championship her first LPGA win. Her maiden victory took the golf world by complete surprise. So, too, did her second.

Pak then won the US Open to make her first two wins on the LPGA Tour major championships. Pak had to playoff against amateur Jenny Chuasiriporn and the pair went to extra holes before Pak won at the 20th. The 92-hole tournament was the longest in women's professional golf history. In winning the championship, Pak became the youngest winner of the US Women's Open. She also joined Juli Inkster as the only two players to win two majors in their rookie seasons. Moreover, she became one of only three women to win the US Open and the LPGA Championship in the same season. (The others are Meg Mallon and Mickey Wright.) However, Pak is the only one of the three to record the feat in her rookie year.

Six days after winning the US Open, Pak triumphed in the Jamie Farr Kroger Classic to join Jane Geddes and Louise Suggs as the only three LPGA players to win a tournament the week after winning the US Open. Pak's second round 61 set a record for the lowest total in LPGA history, and her total score of 261 set the LPGA record for lowest 72-hole score.

Then, just for good measure, Pak won the Giant Eagle LPGA Classic. Four victories in her rookie year and the youngest winner of all four: it leaves pundits wondering what she does for an encore during the rest of her career.

# WILLIE PARK

MUSSELBURGH-BORN WILLIE PARK WON THE FIRST BRITISH OPEN EVER CONTESTED, TAKING THE 1860 CHAMPIONSHIP AT PRESTWICK.

Willie Park has the distinction of being the first player to win the British Open, taking the inaugural title at Prestwick in 1860. Although there were only eight competitors in the tournament, Park still won the title by beating the predominant player of the time, Old Tom Morris.

Until Young Tom Morris took the first of four straight titles in 1868, the first seven British Opens were normally a straightforward fight between Park and Old Tom. Park finished second to Old Tom in the British Opens of 1861 and 1862. He then got the better of Old Tom by winning his second title in 1863. He finished second to Andrew Strath in 1865, won the title in 1866 and finished second again to Old Tom the following year. Park also won a fourth time in 1875, a year after his brother Mungo had picked up the title.

The Parks were the dominant golfing family of Musselburgh, Scotland. Besides Mungo, Willie's brother David was also a good player, good enough to finish second when Willie won the championship in 1866.

Willie was recognized as a great shot maker and a player willing to accept any challenge. He was known as one of the best putters in the game, an art he perfected on the Musselburgh links. It was said that Park's putting was honed over the links' four "baker's holes," where a local baker sold pies to the golfers and engaged in putting matches at the same time. Park spent much time there as a youngster.

Besides the British Open, Park had many famous matches against Old Tom Morris, most involving huge stakes. In one match at Musselburgh, the partisan crowd had become so unruly that Old Tom and the referee walked in with only a few holes left to play. They left Park on the golf course and retired to Foreman's Public House. Park sent a message saying that if Morris did not come out and finish the round then he would complete the remaining holes and claim the prize. When Old Tom declined the offer, Willie played the last few holes and claimed the stakes.

Challenge matches were the way professionals made their money in Park's day. For 20 years the four-time British Open champion had a standing challenge in *Bell's Life*, London, to play "any man in the world for £100 a side," a huge sum in those days.

Willie passed on much of his golfing talent to his son Willie Jr, who went on to win two British Opens.

## FACT FILE

**BORN** 1833, Musselburgh, Midlothian, Scotland

**DIED** 1903

**CAREER HIGHLIGHTS**
1860 The Open Championship
1863 The Open Championship
1866 The Open Championship
1875 The Open Championship

# Willie Park Jr

WILLIE PARK JR (FRONT ROW FAR LEFT, PICTURED WITH THE SCOTTISH 1903 TEAM AT PRESTWICK) FOLLOWED IN HIS FATHER'S FOOTSTEPS BY WINNING THE BRITISH OPEN, TAKING THE TITLE TWICE. PARK WAS SAID TO BE ONE OF THE BEST PUTTERS IN THE GAME.

## Fact File

**BORN** 1864, Musselburgh, Midlothian, Scotland

**DIED** 1925

**CAREER HIGHLIGHTS**
1887 The Open Championship
1889 The Open Championship

Like his father, Willie Park Jr was one of the greatest putters in the game. It seems the greatest putters have names for their putters—Ben Crenshaw has "Little Ben" and Bobby Jones had "Calamity Jane," for example—and Park Jr was no exception. His was called "Old Pawky" and with it he was deadly. The famous golf expression, "a man who can putt is a match for anyone" belongs to Park Jr.

There was never going to be any line of work other than a career in golf for Park Jr, given his background was immersed in golfing traditions. Surrounded as he was by famous golfing uncles and a father who was a four-time British Open champion, it was no surprise when at the age of 16 Park Jr went to Ryton Golf Club in Tyne and Wear, England, to serve as the professional/greenkeeper. It was while he was there that he won his first professional tournament, taking a title at Alnmouth at the age of just 17.

Park returned to Musselburgh after his time at Ryton and set himself up as a club and ball maker. He soon made his mark in the British Open, finishing fourth in 1884 at Prestwick. Three years later he won the title outright with a score of 161, one better than runner-up Bob Martin.

His performance in winning the 1887 British Open had been outstanding, but his play in the 1889 championship was even better. Andrew Kirkaldy of St Andrews had finished the tournament on 155, a total everyone thought was good enough to give him the title. However, the championship was held at Musselburgh that year, Park Jr's home course. The local boy needed to make up two strokes over the last three holes to tie Kirkaldy and he used his knowledge of the layout to do just that, despite the fact that he finished in almost total darkness.

The championship playoff was held three days later, and Park Jr took his second and last British Open title by five strokes from the St Andrews man.

Like his father, Park Jr made the most of his playing income from challenge matches. After his second British Open victory, he laid down the gauntlet to anyone who would challenge him for £100 a side. Kirkaldy assumed a modicum of revenge for his British Open loss by beating Park Jr by a score of eight and seven over 144 holes in one such match.

In the 1890s, Park Jr started designing golf courses, finding as much success in that field as he had done on the golf course. He created, among others, such gems as Sunningdale Old, West Hill, and Worplesdon, three courses in Surrey, England.

# Jesper Parnevik

SWEDEN'S JESPER PARNEVIK IS KNOWN FOR HIS ECCENTRICITY. ONE OF HIS UNUSUAL HABITS IS EATING VOLCANIC DUST TO CLEANSE HIS SYSTEM.

Jesper Parnevik is one of the true characters of the game of golf. For example, he lists shark fishing as one of his hobbies, wears outlandish clothes, and eats volcanic dust to cleanse his system.

Parnevik gets his eccentricity from his father, Bo who is famous in Sweden as a comedian and impressionist. Now a regular on the US Tour, where he has won the Phoenix Open, Parnevik is easily recognizable on the golf course. He plays in drainpipe trousers and with the peak of his cap turned up, his trademark.

Another of the talented young Swedes to make their mark on the European Tour, Parnevik first gained notoriety when he won the 1993 Scottish Open on the King's Course at Gleneagles. Parnevik's win was all the more impressive because he was up against the formidable American Payne Stewart. Despite a seven-shot lead heading into the final day, many weren't sure if the Swede's nerve would hold up against Stewart. It did. Parnevik won his first European title by five strokes from the American.

The talented Stockholm native nearly became the first Swede to win the British Open when the championship was played at Turnberry in 1994. On the last hole of the final round, Parnevik thought he needed a birdie to win the title and went for the flag. He had refused to look at the leaderboard during the last round and it cost him. Parnevik went for the pin and missed the green. Three more shots handed him a bogey and he lost the title by just one shot. Had he gone for the center of the green and made his par, he would have played off for the title with Nick Price.

Parnevik came close three years later at Royal Troon. The Swede entered the last round two strokes ahead of Darren Clarke. He was still two shots clear when he birdied the 11th, with American Justin Leonard now his closest pursuer. However, while Leonard holed putt after putt down the stretch, Parnevik struggled. He came home in 38 shots, five worse than the 33 he had taken over the back nine in each of the previous three days. For the second time in three years, Parnevik finished runner-up in the world's oldest tournament.

Not surprisingly, his performances in the British Open make him the hot favorite to become the first Swede to win not only that major, but one of the other three as well.

## Fact File

**BORN** 1965, Danderyd, Stockholm, Sweden

**CAREER HIGHLIGHTS**
1993 Bell's Scottish Open
1995 Volvo Scandinavian Masters
1996 Lancôme Trophy
1998 Volvo Scandinavian Masters
1998 Phoenix Open

**INTERNATIONAL HONORS**
Ryder Cup: 1997
World Cup: 1994, 1995
Alfred Dunhill Cup: 1993, 1994, 1995, 1997

# Craig Parry

CRAIG PARRY IS CALLED "POPEYE" BY HIS PEERS, A REFERENCE TO HIS STRONG ARMS. THE AUSTRALIAN HAS USED HIS STRENGTH TO POWER HIS WAY TO MANY VICTORIES.

## Fact File

**BORN** 1966, Sunshine, Victoria, Australia

**CAREER HIGHLIGHTS**
1987 New South Wales Open
1989 German Open
1991 Scottish Open
1992 Australian PGA Championship
1996 Australian Masters

**INTERNATIONAL HONORS**
Alfred Dunhill Cup: 1993, 1995, 1996, 1998
Presidents Cup: 1994, 1996, 1998

Like many fine Australian golfers, Craig Parry has followed a familiar route to the US Tour. After starting out in his homeland, Parry graduated to the European Tour before establishing himself in America. It's worked for Parry—almost.

Parry joined the US Tour in 1992, and through the 1998 season he had yet to win in America. Strange, for the diminutive professional has won everywhere else in the world.

Standing just 5-foot, 6-inches in his stockinged feet, Parry would seem to be too small to play golf. However, he is sturdily built and has huge forearms for a little man, earning him the nickname "Popeye" among his peers. The Australian has no problem keeping up with most players off the tee as a result.

The Sunshine, Victoria, native was helped into a career in golf through the Graham Marsh program, which was in operation in Western Australia when Parry was growing up. It turned him into a fine player. Prior to turning professional, Parry was low amateur in the 1985 Australian Masters, the Tasmanian Open, and the South African Open. He turned professional the same year and took only two years to win as a pro, lifting the 1987 New South Wales Open. He also added the Canadian TPC the same year before gaining his playing card at the 1987 European Tour Qualifying School.

Parry was a popular figure during his days on the European Tour, with both Australian and non-Australian players. He was one of a large contingent who based themselves in the town of Bagshot, in Surrey, England, during the late 1980s and early 1990s.

After finishing 24th on the European Order of Merit in his rookie 1988 season, Parry won his first European Tour event when he captured the 1989 German Open. He also won the Wang Four Stars Pro-Celebrity that year, victories that helped him to third place in Europe with nearly £300,000.

Parry won further European Tour events when he triumphed in the Italian and Scottish Opens in 1991. Armed with those experiences he took his clubs to America, where he has been a regular ever since.

The little professional has made several successful forays to his homeland. He is a three-time winner of the Australian Masters, picking up the title in 1992, 1994 and 1996. He has also won in Japan and played in the first three Presidents Cup matches, helping the international side to a famous victory in the 1998 match in Australia.

# Jerry Pate

A SEVERE SHOULDER INJURY FORCED JERRY PATE OUT OF THE GAME, BUT NOT BEFORE HE HAD WON THE US AMATEUR AND US OPEN CHAMPIONSHIPS.

Jerry Pate has a funny way of celebrating victory—he gets very wet. The only problem is, those around him usually get wet as well.

When Pate won the Danny Thomas Memphis Classic in 1981, he dove into the lake beside the 18th green. When he triumphed in the Players Championship a year later at the tough Sawgrass course in Florida, he pushed US Tour Commissioner Deane Beman into the lake beside the final green. He then threw in Pete Dye, the course architect, before joining them himself. Pate had reason to celebrate. He had just birdied four of the last seven holes, including the notorious 17th and 18th holes, to win the title by two shots from Scott Simpson and Brad Bryant.

The University of Alabama graduate burst onto the professional golf scene in fine style. Already a winner of the 1974 US Amateur Championship and a member of the 1975 US Walker Cup side, Pate won the 1976 US Open in his first year as professional. The six-footer hit a 5-iron to within two feet of the final hole at the Atlantic Athletic Club for a two-shot victory over Tom Weiskopf and Al Geiberger.

That victory was the start of a tremendous run for the Georgia native. He won the Canadian Open the same year to help him to tenth place on the US money list, setting a then rookie earnings record with over $153,000, a mark that stood until Hal Sutton bettered it in 1982. Six more victories followed in the next six years, including two Southern Opens. He came close again in the US Open when he finished two strokes behind Hale Irwin at the Inverness Club in Toledo, Ohio, in 1979.

Pate was a serious contender in any tournament he entered during those years. He was supremely confident in his abilities and seemed to relish being in the heat of contention coming down the stretch, as he proved over the closing holes in the Players Championship.

Pate's excellent play made him a Ryder Cup player for the 1981 match at Walton Heath in Surrey, England. Pate played four matches, winning two and losing two. His two wins came in partnership with Lee Trevino in the fourballs and foursomes of the second day.

The former US Amateur champion's career was dealt a severe blow when he suffered a shoulder injury in 1982. Pate tried many times to come back from the injury but was never the same player again. He now serves as a TV commentator for ABC television in the United States.

## Fact File

**BORN** 1953, Macon, Georgia, USA

**CAREER HIGHLIGHTS**
1974 US Amateur
1976 US Open
1976 Canadian Open
1977 Phoenix Open
1982 Players Championship

**INTERNATIONAL HONORS**
Ryder Cup: 1981
Walker Cup: 1975
World Cup: 1976

# TWAY BLASTS NORMAN

Greg Norman could have won the 1986 USPGA Championship at Inverness in Ohio, but a once-in-a-lifetime shot denied the Australian his second major championship.

The 1986 season was a mixture of agony and ecstasy for Norman. A bogey five at the 72nd hole in the Masters had cost him a playoff for the title with Jack Nicklaus. A poor final round in the US Open at Shinnecock Hills on Long Island had lost him that major. He had made up for it by winning the British Open over the links of Turnberry, Scotland. So when he came to the USPGA he was looking to make it two majors out of four.

After three rounds, it appeared Norman would end the season with two major championships. He led the field by four strokes after scores of 65, 68, and 69. Victory looked certain, but that had been the case in the previous three majors. Norman had led after three rounds of every major that season, but he had only closed the deal on the British Open. Now he led at Inverness, winner of the Saturday Slam, as some were describing his feat, of leading all four majors heading into the final round.

Mother Nature played her hand in Norman's quest for glory. Heavy rain had flooded the course soon after play began on Sunday, and action had to be halted and resumed the following day. Who knows what went through Norman's mind that Sunday? Certainly that extra time to dwell on the possibilities did not play into his hand, and he wasn't the same player on Monday. For ten holes he maintained his lead over Bob Tway, the tall professional from Oklahoma partnering Norman in the final round. At the 11th hole Norman's nerves began to fray. A double bogey six halved his lead to two shots. A birdie by Tway at the 13th cut the lead to one, and Norman's advantage disappeared when he bogeyed the 14th hole.

The two men were tied as they stepped onto the 18th tee, but after the tee shots it appeared Norman was destined to win the trophy. Tway hit his ball into heavy rough while the Australian's tee shot split the fairway. All Tway could do was hack at the ball, and into the bunker fronting the green. It was the best possible place to be in the circumstances.

Meanwhile, Norman's approach shot had landed near the pin but the ball had so much spin on it that it backed up into the fringe of the green. At worst, Norman was thinking about a playoff for the title. He had a relatively easy up and down from the fringe. Tway had the harder of the two shots. He needed to hit his bunker shot with precision to get it to stop near the hole. He did better. He holed it. All of a sudden, Tway became a jumping jack, leaping up and down in the sand with his arms spread in pure unbridled joy. Norman had to hole his chip shot to force a playoff but he missed. Tway had won his first major championship. The trophy should have been Norman's, but a poor final round of 76 didn't help his cause. Neither did Tway's miracle shot.

**RIGHT: GREG NORMAN LAMENTS HIS DOUBLE BOGEY AT THE 11TH GREEN, AT THE INVERNESS CLUB, DURING THE 1986 USPGA CHAMPIONSHIP.**

**TOP AND FAR RIGHT: MASTER BLASTER. TWAY PLAYS FROM THE GREENSIDE BUNKER ON THE 72ND HOLE, THEN CELEBRATES WITH HIS CADDIE AFTER THE BALL WENT INTO THE HOLE TO WIN HIM THE CHAMPIONSHIP.**

# Billy Joe Patton

BILLY JOE PATTON CAME CLOSE IN 1954 TO BECOMING THE FIRST AMATEUR TO WIN THE MASTERS. HOWEVER, CRUCIAL MISTAKES AT THE 13TH AND 15TH HOLES COST HIM THE TITLE.

## Fact File

**BORN** 1922, Morganton, North Carolina, USA

**CAREER HIGHLIGHTS**
1954 North and South Amateur
1961 Southern Amateur
1962 North and South Amateur
1963 North and South Amateur
1965 Southern Amateur

**INTERNATIONAL HONORS**
Walker Cup: 1955, 1957, 1959, 1963, 1965, 1969 (captain)

Billy Joe Patton would have become the first amateur to win the Masters if he had only gone against his natural tendencies one Sunday in 1954.

Patton possessed one of the fastest swings in golf, an action that helped him hit the ball a long way. By nature Patton wasn't a player to hold anything back. He seemed to hit every ball as hard as he could and took on the most daring of shots. That was his undoing in the final round of the 1954 Masters.

After leading the field at the halfway stage, Patton slipped back slightly in the third round only to take the lead when he aced the sixth hole in the final round. Playing with the immortal Ben Hogan, after 12 holes Patton was still in the lead when he came to the par-5, 13th hole. This shortish par-5 allows players the ideal opportunity for a birdie if they can carry Rae's creek that fronts the green with their second shot. That was the choice facing Patton after his drive. Not surprisingly, Patton went for the green. However, his ball landed in the creek and he ran up a triple bogey seven.

Patton then made the same mistake at the par-5, 15th. He went for the green in two, only to see his ball come to rest in the pond that guards the green.

Despite that, Patton still finished only a stroke behind Sam Snead and Ben Hogan. Snead defeated Hogan in an 18-hole playoff for the title.

Patton's story has become part of Augusta lore. For years golfers have played the 13th hole in the final round and wondered whether or not to go for the 13th and 15th greens with their second shots. Many have had Patton's experience in the forefront of their minds. Ben Crenshaw chose to lay up short of the water on both holes when he won the title in 1984. He said the decision was made for him when he saw Patton, now an Augusta member, on duty at the 13th hole during the final round. However, Patton says he was nowhere near when Crenshaw was playing the 13th hole. Crenshaw's experience has become just one of the many mysteries that surrounds the Masters.

Unfortunately, Curtis Strange didn't learn from Patton's example. Strange took the Patton route in 1985 and found the water at both holes to hand the title to Germany's Bernhard Langer.

The Masters aside, Patton was one of America's outstanding amateurs in the 1950s and 1960s. Twice he was low amateur in the US Open, in 1954 and 1957. The North Carolina native also played in no less than five Walker Cups, compiling a fine record of 11 wins and just three losses from the 14 matches he played.

# COREY PAVIN

COREY PAVIN'S WIN IN THE 1995 US OPEN CAME AFTER HE HIT ONE OF THE BEST SHOTS EVER SEEN IN A MAJOR CHAMPIONSHIP, A 230-YARD 4-WOOD TO THE FINAL GREEN.

Corey Pavin hit one of the best shots ever seen on the 72nd hole of any US Open, a shot that ultimately gave him his first major championship.

Shinnecock Hills was the venue for the 1995 championship, and Pavin entered the final round three strokes behind Greg Norman. The 5-foot, 9-inch golfer may be small in stature, but he has the heart of a lion. He is known for being one of the grittiest competitors in world golf, and that's just what he was over the final 18 holes at Shinnecock.

Pavin fashioned a two under par 68 on the final day, the highlight of which was his approach shot to the final green. After holing a crucial five-foot putt for par at the 17th, Pavin came to the final hole with a one-shot lead. His drive on the 18th landed in the fairway but still left him with nearly 230 yards to the flag. Pavin selected a 4-wood and watched as his ball landed in the rough and bounced up to within five feet of the hole. Two putts later and Pavin had won the title by two shots from Norman, who could only manage a final round 73.

The diminutive golfer isn't the longest hitter in the world; in fact, he's one of the shortest. However, he makes up for what he lacks in length with pure talent. As he proved on the last hole of the US Open, Pavin is one of the best shot makers in the game. He can work the ball from left to right, right to left, hit it high or hit it low depending on the situation.

The US Open victory did not come as a surprise. Pavin had come close in previous majors, including a third place finish in the 1992 Masters, fourth place in the 1993 British Open, and second in the 1994 USPGA Championship. What was surprising was that the 1995 US Open was only his first major victory.

Prior to Shinnecock, Pavin had won 12 tournaments on the US Tour, as well as another seven tournaments internationally. He had topped the US Tour money list in 1991 with just under $1 million in earnings. When he won the 1988 Texas Open, he did so with a score of 259, 21 under par, to become only the fifth player in US Tour history to break 260 for four rounds. In other words, it wasn't a matter of if Pavin would win his first major, but when.

## FACT FILE

**BORN** 1959, Oxnard, California, USA

**CAREER HIGHLIGHTS**
1984 Houston Coca-Cola Open
1988 Texas Open
1994 Nissan Los Angeles Open
1995 US Open
1996 Mastercard Colonial

**INTERNATIONAL HONORS**
Ryder Cup: 1991, 1993, 1995
Presidents Cup: 1994, 1996
Walker Cup: 1981

# Calvin Peete

CALVIN PEETE IS LIVING PROOF THAT GOLF DOESN'T HAVE TO BE PLAYED WITH A STRAIGHT LEFT ARM. PEETE REACHED THE TOP WITH A SWING IN WHICH THE LEFT ARM WAS NEVER FULLY EXTENDED.

## Fact File

**BORN** 1943, Detroit, Michigan, USA

**CAREER HIGHLIGHTS**
1979 Greater Milwaukee Open
1982 Pensacola Open
1984 Texas Open
1985 Players Championship
1986 Mony Tournament of Champions

**INTERNATIONAL HONORS**
Ryder Cup: 1983, 1985

Like Ed Furgol, who won the 1954 US Open, Calvin Peete is a player who cannot straighten out his left arm. He broke his elbow in an accident in childhood and was never able to extend it fully for the rest of his life. And like Furgol, he was one of the few golfers to disprove the myth of the importance of the straight left arm in golf.

Unlike Furgol, though, Peete had another handicap: his color. Peete is one of the few black golfers to make it in the predominantly white world of professional golf. While that's a huge feat in itself, it is all the more remarkable as he didn't take up the game until he was 23 years old.

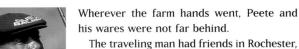

Although he was born in Detroit, Peete spent much of his youth on a Florida farm with his 18 brothers and sisters from his father's two marriages. Times were hard on the family and Peete was forced to drop out of school at a young age. He was an enterprising youngster who as a teenager started selling goods to migrant farm workers. Peete knew they had little chance of getting into town to shop, so he packed his car full of clothes, jewelry, and anything else he could squeeze into his station wagon and followed the migrants around. His territory extended from Florida to New York State. Wherever the farm hands went, Peete and his wares were not far behind.

The traveling man had friends in Rochester, New York, who invited him to play golf whenever he was in town. At first he resisted, but when he was 23 he finally relented and tried the game. It was a wise decision.

Peete turned professional just five years after taking up the game. He joined the US Tour in 1975 and within four years had won his first tournament, the 1979 Greater Milwaukee Open. Despite his left arm, Peete had one of the best swings on the US Tour during his prime. For nearly ten years he hit more fairways than any other player, taking the driver accuracy statistic for an unprecedented ten straight years.

His best year on Tour came in 1982 when he won four times, including a second Greater Milwaukee Open title. Those victories helped him to place fourth on the money list with over $318,000. Two more victories in 1983 saw him again finish fourth on the money list, while two wins in 1985, including the prestigious Players Championship, saw him finish the season as the third best player in America.

Lower back problems in 1987 and 1989 halted Peete's progress on the regular Tour. He now plays on the US Senior Tour.

# Dottie Pepper

NO WOMAN PLAYER IN THE MODERN GAME HAS PLAYED GOLF WITH THE SAME COMPETITIVE FIRE AS DOTTIE PEPPER, MAKING HER POPULAR WITH HEADLINE WRITERS EVERYWHERE.

Newspaper and magazine headline writers have had to stop themselves from using the line "Red Hot Pepper" on many occasions, so often has that particular header been used in reference to Dottie Pepper.

You can't blame the editors for wanting to splash the headline across their newspapers and magazines—it fits the New York native like a glove.

Pepper is the fieriest competitor in women's golf. No player wears her emotions on her sleeve more than Pepper. One look at her will tell you whether or not she is in contention. When she is, look out.

Pepper's actions haven't always endeared her to her fellow competitors or her opponents, especially in match play. Pepper has played on every US Solheim Cup side since the competition began. More often than not she has been the biggest thorn in the sides of her European counterparts. She had a much publicized bust-up with Laura Davies in the 1998 Solheim Cup. The European player accused Pepper of bad sportsmanship when she cheered a missed European putt. Pepper was unrepentant.

It is not only in the Solheim Cup that Pepper shows her emotions. No player tries to exert influence over the ball while it is airborne more than Pepper. Sometimes it seems to listen. That was obvious when she won her second major championship at the start of the 1999 season.

A graduate of Furman University, where she was twice named female athlete of the year, won her first major when she triumphed in the 1992 Nabisco Dinah Shore Championship after a playoff with Juli Inkster. At that time she was called Dottie Mochrie, her married name. Her second victory came seven years later under her maiden name, even though she had since divorced and remarried. This time there was to be no playoff.

Pepper made history with her second Nabisco Dinah Shore victory in March 1999. Her 19 under par total broke the previous record by four strokes, and also set a record for the lowest 72-hole total in a women's major. The previous record was 18 under par.

Pepper was simply invincible in winning her second major. She started the final round with a three-stroke lead and didn't try to play safe. It's not in her nature anyway. Pepper fired a final round 66 to take the title by six strokes over Meg Mallon. Pepper then celebrated the same way she had celebrated seven years previously—with a dive into the pond beside the 18th hole.

The victory broke a lean two-year winless period, and signaled that there are many more major victories in Dottie Pepper.

## Fact File

**BORN** 1965, Saratoga Springs, New York, USA

**CAREER HIGHLIGHTS**
1989 Oldsmobile LPGA Classic
1992 Nabisco Dinah Shore
1993 World Championship of Women's Golf
1996 Safeway LPGA Golf Championship
1999 Nabisco Dinah Shore

**INTERNATIONAL HONORS**
Solheim Cup: 1990, 1992, 1994, 1996, 1998

# ALFRED PERRY

ALFRED PERRY HAD TO OVERCOME HENRY COTTON TO WIN HIS ONLY MAJOR CHAMPIONSHIP, THE 1935 BRITISH OPEN AT MUIRFIELD.

## FACT FILE

**BORN** 1904, Coulsdon, Surrey, England

**DIED** 1974

**CAREER HIGHLIGHTS**
1935 The Open Championship
1938 Dunlop Metropolitan

**INTERNATIONAL HONORS**
Ryder Cup: 1933, 1935, 1937

Trivia buffs will rejoice in the fact that when Alfred Perry won the 1935 British Open, he used the same ball, a Dunlop 65, for the last 36 holes. Nowadays, professionals change balls as regularly as every three holes. Things were a lot different in Perry's day.

Perry's victory in the British Open at Muirfield came as something of a surprise. It followed hard on Henry Cotton's first British Open victory the previous year, at Sandwich, and the two men were complete opposites. Like Alf Padgham who succeeded him in 1936, and who finished second to him at Muirfield, Perry was a quiet, unassuming man. However, there was nothing unassuming about his game.

The Surrey native possessed a sound swing despite an unorthodox right-hand grip and a stance that put him a long way from the ball. Allied to his reliable swing was an excellent short game that often got him out of trouble.

Cotton was the obvious favorite at Muirfield in 1935, given his complete dominance of the field the previous year at Sandwich. Indeed, the defending champion opened the tournament with the first round lead, but

Perry was just one stroke behind after an opening 69. A second round 75 seemed to have denied him his chances but Perry came roaring back with a 67 in the third round to put him a stroke ahead of Charles Whitcombe heading into the final 18 holes. Despite a double bogey six at the opening hole of the final round, Perry was not to be denied the title. A birdie at the second steadied him and thereafter Perry attacked the course. For example, he had the nerve to try a 3-wood shot out of a bunker at the 14th hole. Hitting woods out of bunkers is normally a surefire way of throwing a tournament away, but Perry was able to reach the green with the outrageous shot. A closing round 72 gave him the title by four strokes over Padgham.

Perry never really got the credit his game deserved, no doubt because of his demeanor. However, he was a good enough golfer to play on three consecutive Ryder Cup sides between 1933 and 1937. Although he won only one half point from his three matches played, which came in his 1935 singles encounter with Sam Parks, he was a member of the 1933 side that defeated the Americans at Southport, England, the last American defeat for 24 years.

# Henry Picard

GOLF OWES HENRY PICARD QUITE A LOT, FOR THE STYLISH SWINGER HAD A BIG INFLUENCE ON THE CAREERS OF SAM SNEAD AND BEN HOGAN.

There were few better players in the 1930s than Henry Picard, the stylish swinger from Plymouth, Massachusetts.

Picard based himself at the Hershey Country Club, a factor that earned him the nickname the "Chocolate Soldier." A quiet man who dressed elegantly, Picard chose to let his clubs do his talking. They more than made up for his relative silence. Picard won 26 tournaments during his career on the US Tour. His greatest triumphs came in the 1938 Masters and the 1939 USPGA Championship.

Prior to 1938, Picard had played in the previous four Masters tournaments, since its inception in 1934. The stylish swinger had been a favorite every year, and it came as no surprise when his 285 total gave him the title by two strokes from Ralph Guldahl and Harry Cooper.

The Chocolate Soldier's second major came the next season when he defeated Byron Nelson in the final of the USPGA Championship. Despite leading for most of the 36-hole final, Picard fell behind when Nelson birdied the 32nd hole. Picard saved himself from going two down when he holed from 25 feet at the 34th to halve the hole with Nelson. He then birdied the 36th to take the final to an extra hole, and added another birdie at the 37th to win the championship.

Despite his many victories and his two appearances in the Ryder Cup in 1935 and 1937, where he had a record of three wins and one loss, Picard's gift to the game was in helping the careers of two young professionals who would go on to eclipse his own record.

In 1937 Picard gave Sam Snead a driver which Snead said turned him from a hooker of the ball into one of the longest straight drivers in the game. The Hershey-based pro also had much to do with the start of Ben Hogan's career. Hogan had financial problems early in his career that nearly saw him give up tournament golf. Hogan was virtually down to his last few dollars when Picard gave him much needed backing. After hearing Hogan and his wife Valerie arguing in a hotel lobby, Picard approached and asked what the problem was. When Hogan told him that he was thinking about quitting because he couldn't finance his life on Tour, Picard said: "I'm not the richest man in the world, but go ahead and play. If you run out of money, I'll take care of it."

Hogan accepted the offer, although he never had to go to Picard for the money. Years later, in his book *Power Golf,* Hogan wrote about Picard's generous offer. "Knowing that help was there if I needed it helped me forget about my troubles."

## Fact File

**BORN** 1907, Plymouth, Massachusetts, USA

**DIED** 1997

**CAREER HIGHLIGHTS**
1936 North and South Open
1937 Argentine Open
1938 Masters
1939 USPGA Championship
1939 Metropolitan Open

**INTERNATIONAL HONORS**
Ryder Cup: 1935, 1937

# GARY PLAYER

No player in the history of the game worked harder at becoming a champion than Gary Player. Certainly no one worked on fitness more than Player.

Even in the late 1990s, while in his 60s, Player was still one of the fittest players in the game of golf. No golfer ever did more sit-ups, more pushups, or lifted more weights than Player. In his book *Fit For Golf*, Player talks about the part physical fitness played in making him a great golfer. "Without my life-long commitment to fitness, I would not have achieved half as much as I did as a golfer. I knew that if I were ever to become a champion professional golfer I would have to work at it, harder than the average man, for my size, a mere five foot seven inches, and weight, 145 pounds, were both against me."

That's just what Player did. As a youngster he ran up and down the gold-mine hills of his native South Africa to strengthen his legs. He lifted weights to build up his muscles. To strengthen his hands he did 70 fingertip pushups a day. He did hundreds of sit-ups to strengthen his torso. Player was driven to become a champion.

This drive extended to the practice ground, too. Player would spend hours hitting balls on the range, he would spend a similar amount on the practice putting green, developing that short jabby stroke that won him so many titles around the world.

Player first traveled to Great Britain as a raw 20-year-old in 1955. He seemed to have too many technical flaws to become a great champion, but he soon showed his caliber by winning the Dunlop tournament at Sunningdale the following year. Three years later all his hard work was justified when he won the British Open at Muirfield. It was the first of nine major championships.

Only four men have managed to win the grand slam of golf in their careers. Gary Player is one of them, along with Gene Sarazen, Ben Hogan, and Jack Nicklaus. Two more British Opens followed his 1959 victory. His first of three Masters championships came in 1961, making him the first non-American golfer to wear the green jacket. Victory in the 1962 USPGA Championship and the 1965 US Open made him the first South African winner of those titles. Player's last major championship came in the 1978 Masters, when he won his third green jacket by a stroke over Hubert Green, Tom Watson, and Rod Funseth.

Now a successful senior golfer with many victories on the over-50 circuit, Player at last count had over 100 victories worldwide. He is truly one of the legends of the game.

## FACT FILE

**BORN** 1935, Johannesburg, South Africa

**CAREER HIGHLIGHTS**
1959 The Open Championship
1961 Masters
1962 USPGA Championship
1965 US Open
1968 The Open Championship
1972 USPGA Championship
1974 Masters
1974 The Open Championship
1978 Masters

**INTERNATIONAL HONORS**
World Cup: 1956, 1957, 1958, 1959, 1960, 1962, 1963, 1964, 1965, 1966, 1967, 1968, 1971, 1972, 1973, 1977
Alfred Dunhill Cup: 1991

ABOVE: PLAYER'S PHYSICAL FITNESS REGIME MADE HIM ONE OF THE STRONGEST PLAYERS IN THE GAME; HE SELDOM HAD PROBLEMS ESCAPING FROM DEEP ROUGH.

RIGHT: PLAYER USED TO SPEND HOURS PRACTICING HIS BUNKER PLAY, AND HE WAS ONE OF THE BEST BUNKER PLAYERS IN THE WORLD AS A RESULT.

# Manuel Pinero

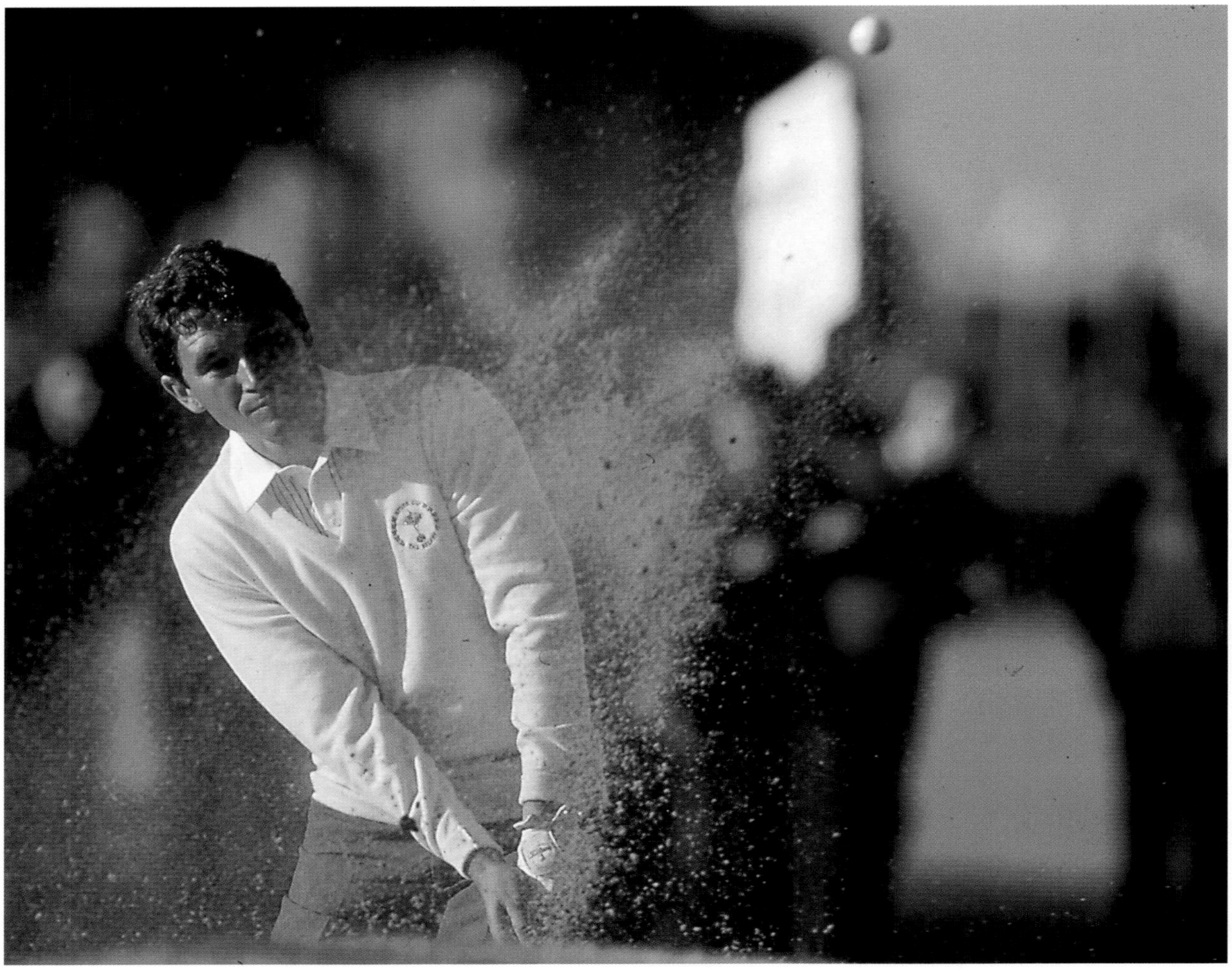

LIKE MANY SPANISH PLAYERS, PINERO HAS A GREAT IMAGINATION AROUND THE GREENS. HIS SHORT GAME HAS EARNED HIM PLAUDITS OVER THE YEARS.

## Fact File

**BORN** 1952, Badajoz, Spain

**CAREER HIGHLIGHTS**
1974 Madrid Open
1976 Swiss Open
1977 Penfold PGA Championship
1982 European Open
1985 Italian Open

**INTERNATIONAL HONORS**
Ryder Cup: 1981, 1985
World Cup: 1974, 1976, 1978, 1979, 1980, 1982, 1983, 1985, 1988
Alfred Dunhill Cup: 1985

Along with Jose Maria Canizares and Antonio Garrido, Manuel Pinero was one of the first Spaniards to make a big impact on the European Tour, and one of the first to play in the Ryder Cup.

Like his more famous compatriot Seve Ballesteros, the professional from Marbella on the Mediterranean coast is one of the best wedge players to have walked the fairways of Europe. On many occasions, his ability to turn what looked like three shots into two has saved him strokes.

Fittingly, Pinero's first tournament win came in his home country, in the 1974 Madrid Open. It allowed the Spaniard to finish 22nd on the European money list that year, and started a run which never saw Pinero finish lower than 37th on that list over the next 14 seasons.

It was a pity continental Europeans were not allowed into the Ryder Cup until 1979, for Pinero would have made several appearances before then. For example, he finished fourth on the Order of Merit in both 1976 and 1977, and would have been a valuable addition to the 1977 European side which lost to the Americans at Royal Lytham & St Annes.

Pinero made his debut in the 1981 match, where he teamed up with Germany's Bernhard Langer three times. The pair triumphed in the second day fourballs with a victory against the powerful duo of Ray Floyd and Hale Irwin. Pinero then defeated Jerry Pate in the final day's singles. It was one of only three European wins on the last day, as the powerful American side crushed the Europeans by the score of 18½ to nine-and-a-half points at Walton Heath in Surrey, England.

Although Pinero recorded significant wins during his regular European Tour career, including victories in the 1977 PGA Championship and the 1982 European Open, probably his best three days of golf came in the 1985 Ryder Cup at The Belfry.

Pinero forged a successful partnership with compatriot Seve Ballesteros in the historic 1985 match. The duo won three of the four matches in which they were paired, leading the European charge. Then Pinero led the victory parade on the final day. Out first in the singles, Pinero recorded the first European point with a three and one victory over Lanny Wadkins, and Europe went on to win the title for the first time since 1957.

A wrist injury hampered Pinero's progress in the 1990s, and he turned his attention to golf course design. One of his creations is the La Quinta course on the Costa del Sol, Spain.

# Nick Price

NICK PRICE WAS THE DOMINANT GOLFER OF THE EARLY 1990S, WINNING MANY TOURNAMENTS, INCLUDING THREE MAJOR CHAMPIONSHIPS IN TWO YEARS.

No player in the early 1990s was as successful as Nick Price, the popular Zimbabwe professional.

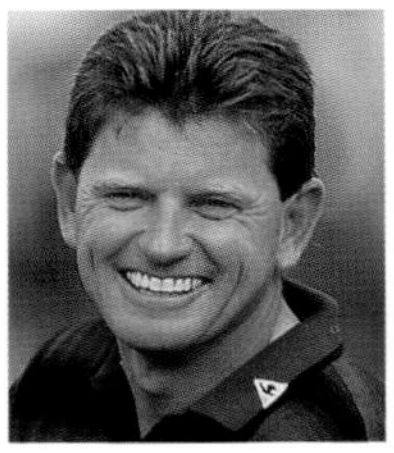

For a stretch between 1992 and 1994 Price was the dominant force in the game, a favorite in every tournament he entered. During that two-year reign Price won 16 tournaments around the world, and 11 on the US Tour alone. He was the US Tour's leading money winner in both the 1993 and 1994 seasons, earning just under $1.5 million in each year.

Price was born in South Africa but grew up in Rhodesia, now Zimbabwe, where he was a contemporary of Mark McNulty, Tony Johnstone, and David Leadbetter, who would later coach Price.

Price first came to the attention of the golf world when he finished second in the British Open at Royal Troon in 1982. He led the championship in the final round but stumbled to let Tom Watson win his fourth title. A year later Price established himself in America when he won the 1983 World Series of Golf by four shots over Jack Nicklaus.

Price's love affair with the British Open continued in 1988 at Royal Lytham when he led the tournament going into the final day. Normally, Price's final round 69 would have been good enough to give him the title, but Seve Ballesteros's 65 denied him the championship.

Ironically, Price's first major championship victory didn't come in the British Open but in the 1992 USPGA Championship. Although he was two strokes behind Gene Sauers going into the final round, Price's closing 70 to Sauers's 75 gave him the title by three shots over Sauers, Nick Faldo, John Cook, and Jim Gallagher Jr.

The next season Price took the US Tour by storm, winning four times, including the prestigious Players Championship. However, that was but a taste of what was to come in 1994.

The affable six-footer won six tournaments in 1994, adding two more majors to his collection. A second USPGA Championship came courtesy of a six-shot victory at Southern Hills in Tulsa, Oklahoma. His 11 under par total of 269 broke the old USPGA record set by Bobby Nichols in 1964 by two shots. More importantly, Price finally won the British Open. Price's eagle at Turnberry's par-5, 17th hole in the final round ultimately gave him his one-stroke victory over Sweden's Jesper Parnevik. After two heartbreaks, Price had at last got his hands on the trophy he coveted most.

Now a resident of Hobe Sound, Florida, where his good friend Greg Norman resides, Price is one of the dominant players in world golf.

## Fact File

**BORN** 1957, Durban, South Africa

**CAREER HIGHLIGHTS**
1983 World Series of Golf
1992 USPGA Championship
1993 Players Championship
1994 The Open Championship
1994 USPGA Championship

**INTERNATIONAL HONORS**
World Cup: 1993
Alfred Dunhill Cup: 1993, 1994, 1995, 1996, 1997, 1998
Presidents Cup: 1994, 1996, 1998

# Ronan Rafferty

RONAN RAFFERTY FOUND SUCCESS EARLY IN THE GAME AS AN AMATEUR. THE LOVER OF FINE WINE FOUND MUCH SUCCESS AS A PROFESSIONAL TOO.

## Fact File

**BORN** 1964, Newry, Northern Ireland

**CAREER HIGHLIGHTS**
1979 British Boys' Championship
1989 Volvo Masters
1990 PLM Open
1992 Portuguese Open
1993 Hohe Brucke Austrian Open

**INTERNATIONAL HONORS**
Ryder Cup: 1989
World Cup: 1983, 1984, 1987, 1988, 1990, 1991, 1992, 1993
Alfred Dunhill Cup: 1986, 1987, 1988, 1989, 1990, 1991, 1992, 1993, 1995
Walker Cup: 1981

Ronan Rafferty was a teenage prodigy who first came to prominence when he won the British Boys' Championship as a 15-year-old. He then played in the Walker Cup at the age of just 17 years and seven months.

A connoisseur and collector of fine wines, Rafferty's vintage year came in the 1989 season when he won three times and ended the season as European number one. He had to beat out one of Europe's best players to take the title, but the Northern Ireland native was equal to the task.

There are many who would bow to the prowess of Jose Maria Olazabal in many contests. Rafferty isn't one of them. He went head to head with the Spaniard in the race to top the 1989 European Order of Merit. Many thought Olazabal would win the race hands down, with one leading European golf magazine even prematurely handing the award to Olazabal as it went to print before the last counting event, the Volvo Masters. However, Rafferty won the tournament by holing a five-foot putt on the last to become European number one.

That victory capped a fine season for Rafferty as he won two other events and made his debut in the Ryder Cup at The Belfry. He did not let his side down either.

Despite going winless in his opening two matches, Rafferty earned a valuable point in the final day's singles with a victory over Mark Calcavecchia. The point was important, for Europe retained the cup when the two sides tied the match at 14 points apiece.

Although Rafferty turned professional in 1981 with a handicap of plus two and a wealth of top amateur experience behind him, he did not gain his European Tour card on his first attempt. Rafferty missed his card at the 1981 Qualifying School and so took his clubs to South Africa over the winter of 1981 and 1982. There he finished in the top 50 in the South African Order of Merit and got onto the European Tour that way. After that he was off and running and has been one of Europe's leading professionals ever since.

Like many Irish players, Rafferty has a swing that is anything but textbook. He uses a ten-finger baseball grip, and his swing has a lot of hand action as a result. However, it gets the job done quite effectively, and through the 1998 season he had won seven events on the European Tour and many more around the world.

A thumb injury in 1998 saw him play very few events in Europe.

# JUDY RANKIN

NOW A TELEVISION COMMENTATOR, JUDY RANKIN HAD A BRILLIANT PROFESSIONAL CAREER. SHE WAS THE FIRST FEMALE PLAYER TO WIN OVER $100,000 IN A SINGLE SESSION.

Judy Rankin never played golf for the glory. She played because it was the one way she could guarantee to make a good living.

When Rankin was just six years old her mother developed a malignant brain tumor. She never walked again, and died when Judy was 11 years old. The years of illness meant thousands of dollars of medical bills and the family suffered as a result. It was that experience which made Rankin want to earn as much from the game as possible.

Not surprisingly, Rankin was very close to her father. He introduced her to golf when she was six and soon recognized her aptitude for the game. Although she was slightly built, Rankin was able to hit the ball well because she could generate a lot of clubhead speed. The game came easy to her and she started winning tournaments at the age of seven. When she was 14 Rankin won the 1959 Missouri Amateur. Her victory still stands as a record for the youngest winner of that event. Then, after she turned 15 that year, she became the youngest player to finish as low amateur in the US Women's Open.

Rankin joined the LPGA Tour in 1962 at the tender age of 17. She was homesick for the first couple of years, and didn't win her first tournament until 1968, the Corpus Christi Open. Until that point she had been trying too hard to win. After a number of seconds she quit trying to win and decided to try to make as much money as possible. She won in Corpus Christi the following week.

Her maiden victory opened the floodgates. Over the next 11 years she won 26 tournaments on the LPGA Tour. Between 1970 and 1979 she won at least one tournament per season. Her best years came in 1976 and 1977 when she topped the Order of Merit both seasons. In 1976 she racked up six victories and then recorded five the year after. She became the first player to earn over $100,000 in a single season when she made $150,734 in prize money in 1976. She also set a record in 1977, which still stands, for the most top-ten finishes, with 25 to her credit.

Chronic back problems in the early 1980s forced Rankin off the Tour. Her last full season was 1983, and in 1985 she underwent surgery. Since then she has worked as TV commentator for ABC network.

Rankin was honored with the captaincy of the 1996 and 1998 American Solheim Cup sides, leading her teams to victory on both occasions.

## FACT FILE

**BORN** 1945, St Louis, Missouri, USA

**CAREER HIGHLIGHTS**
1968 Corpus Christi Open
1974 Baltimore Open
1976 Colgate Dinah Shore
1977 Orange Blossom Classic
1979 WUI Classic

**INTERNATIONAL HONORS**
Solheim Cup: 1996 (captain), 1998 (captain)

# Betsy Rawls

BETSY RAWLS WAS SET ON A CAREER AS A PHYSICIST, BUT SHE MADE A WISE CHOICE BY TURNING PROFESSIONAL AFTER WILSON SPORTING GOODS OFFERED HER A CONTRACT.

## Fact File

**BORN** 1928, Spartanburg, South Carolina, USA

**CAREER HIGHLIGHTS**
1951 US Women's Open
1953 US Women's Open
1957 US Women's Open
1960 US Women's Open
1959 LPGA Championship
1969 LPGA Championship

Betsy Rawls is another champion golfer to have had lessons from the late great Harvey Penick. At the age of 17, Rawls went to Penick for instruction at Austin Country Club. Penick charged her $1.50 for the lesson but never charged her for another lesson in her life, he recognized her talent. She was a natural for whom the game came very easily. Winning came easy, too. Rawls was a player who believed she would win tournaments, and she did. She never let emotion affect her performance, even under the most intense pressure. Yet despite winning some amateur tournaments soon after taking up the game, Rawls rarely gave professional golf a thought. She was dead set on a career as a physicist, having majored in physics at the University of Texas.

Rawls graduated from university in 1950, fully intent on being a physicist. She never even knew a professional women's golf circuit existed until she was approached by Wilson Sporting Goods. The company offered her a contract to play its equipment and to do exhibitions. Rawls decided it was probably more fun than physics and signed on the dotted line.

It was a wise career move because Rawls's temperament was ideally suited to tournament golf. "I always played well under pressure because it didn't bother me, which is why I won so many tournaments," Rawls once admitted to the English golf journalist Liz Kahn. "I could perform under tense situations. It was in my physical makeup to allow that to happen."

Rawls proved that particular talent by winning the US Women's Open in her first year as a professional. It was the first of four wins in the tournament, the others coming in 1953, 1957, and 1960. Of the four, the 1957 win is the one that Rawls is least proud of. She was declared the winner when Jackie Pung was disqualified for an error on her scorecard.

The South Carolina native also won the LPGA Championship twice, and her second victory in the event was the biggest thrill of her career. It came in 1969, at a point in Rawls's life when, by her own admission, she wasn't sure if she would ever win again. Yet she won the event on the toughest course the women played that year, the Concord Country Club in New York. Rawls didn't have a bogey in the final round and as a result she collected her second LPGA title.

Rawls played a big part in the history of the LPGA. Not only did she win over 50 tournaments, but she was also LPGA president for the years 1960 to 1961.

# TED RAY

JERSEY GOLFER TED RAY WAS ONE OF THE MOST POWERFUL GOLFERS TO PLAY AT THE TURN OF THE CENTURY. POWERFUL ENOUGH TO WIN THE US AND BRITISH OPEN.

Ted Ray has a special place in the history of golf—he is one of only three British men to capture the British and US Open championships.

Until Tony Jacklin triumphed in the US Open at Hazeltine in 1970, Ray was the last British player to have won America's national championship, a feat he accomplished in 1920 at the Inverness Club in Toledo, Ohio. It gave Ray considerable pleasure to win the title. The victory made up for disappointment in 1913 when he lost a playoff for the championship to Francis Ouimet at Brookline. Moreover, winning both the US and British Opens equaled the feat of his great friend and rival Harry Vardon. The two men were the only Britons to have won both championships at that time. The fact that Vardon finished equal second to Ray at Inverness made the victory even sweeter.

Ray grew up within a mile of Vardon on the island of Jersey, and throughout his career he was measured against the six-time British Open winner. Indeed, it is probably safe to say that had it not been for Vardon and the other two members of the Great Triumvirate, James Braid and J.H. Taylor, Ray would probably have won more championships. On more than one occasion the great British trio denied Ray a big tournament victory. For example, Ray lost three British Match Play finals to members of the Great Triumvirate. In 1903 and 1911 he lost to James Braid, while Vardon got the better of him in 1912.

A huge man, who usually played with a pipe clenched between his teeth, Ray used his size to hit the ball a long way. He had a pronounced sway in his swing which led to the occasional wild shot, but when his timing was on he was a match for anyone.

One of the best stories concerning Ray underscores his simple approach to golf. When once asked how to hit the ball further, he passed on this advice: "Hit it a bloody sight harder, mate."

The Jersey man was honored with the captaincy of the first Ryder Cup in 1927 when the Great Britain & Ireland side traveled to the Worcester Country Club in Massachusetts. Unfortunately his side lost by the wide margin of nine-and-a-half to two-and-a-half points, with Ray losing both matches in which he appeared, including a seven and five singles defeat at the hands of Leo Diegel.

## FACT FILE

**BORN** 1877, Grouville, Jersey, Channel Islands

**DIED** 1943

**CAREER HIGHLIGHTS**
1912 The Open Championship
1920 US Open

**INTERNATIONAL HONORS**
Ryder Cup: 1927 (captain)

# VICTORY AT LAST

The Ryder Cup hasn't always produced the type of epic confrontations that have typified the event throughout the 1980s and '90s. For years it might as well have been called the Rollover Cup, because that is exactly what the Americans did to their British and Irish opponents every two years. There was one exception, one time when Great Britain & Ireland produced a miracle.

There was nothing to suggest that the 1957 Ryder Cup at Lindrick Golf Club in Yorkshire, England, would be any different from the previous seven matches. The Americans had won those contests, usually with ease. Ten years earlier, for example, they had crushed their opponents by the score of 11 points to one.

The 1957 match appeared to be heading toward a similar conclusion after the opening day's foursomes. The U.S.A. led by three points to one. Only a three and two victory by Ken Bousfield and Dai Rees over Art Wall and Fred Hawkins had given the home side some respect. With a three to one lead heading into the singles, though, all the U.S.A. needed to do was win three matches of the eight being played, and the cup was theirs. That didn't seem a tall order, given the team consisted of players like Tommy Bolt, Jack Burke, Doug Ford, and Dow Finsterwald. The home side however, wasn't about to roll over and die. A partisan crowd played its part on the final day, causing some of the American players to lose their composure. "This isn't golf—it's war," was Tommy Bolt's predictable remark. Either the galleries got to him or he was beaten by a better player on the day.

Out first, Bolt lost his match to Scotland's Eric Brown by a score of four and three. All over the course, the home side was rallying to captain Dai Rees. He handed Ed Furgol a seven and six thrashing. Christy O'Connor downed Dow Finsterwald by the same score. The only American to win a match was Fred Hawkins. He defeated Peter Alliss two and one. Dick Mayer managed to halve his match with Harry Bradshaw, but elsewhere the visitors were no longer invincible. Burke, the American captain, was beaten five and three by Peter Mills, while Doug Ford was hammered six and five by Bernard Hunt.

The moment of glory fell to Ken Bousfield. The diminutive professional suffered a setback in his match against Lionel Hebert when he lost three straight holes on Lindrick's back nine. Rees appeared with Max Faulkner to give Bousfield support, and he rallied to win four and three and give Great Britain & Ireland its first win in 34 years. It was a historic occasion. It was the last time Great Britain & Ireland won the Ryder Cup. The next time the Americans lost—in 1985—they did so to a European side.

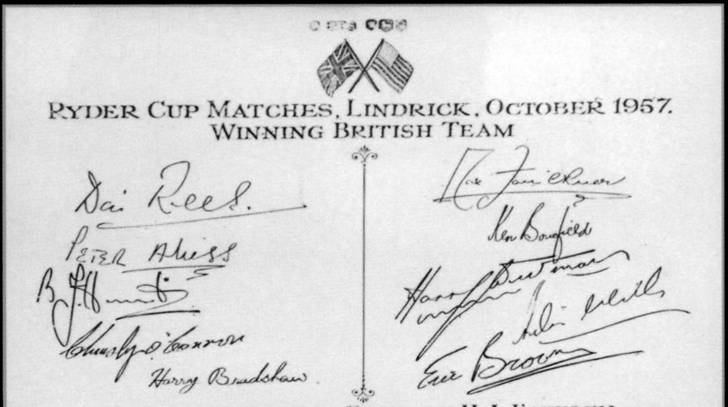
RYDER CUP MATCHES, LINDRICK, OCTOBER 1957.
WINNING BRITISH TEAM
PRESENTED TO DAI REES, BY H. I. EARDLEY,
PRESIDENT, LINDRICK GOLF CLUB.

TOP: CHRISTY O'CONNOR'S SEVEN AND SIX SINGLES WIN OVER DOW FINSTERWALD HELPED HIS SIDE TO VICTORY.

ABOVE: DICK MAYER WAS UNBEATEN IN BOTH HIS MATCHES IN 1957, BUT HIS SIDE STILL LOST THE MATCH.

LEFT: THE GREAT BRITAIN & IRELAND SIDE WROTE THEIR NAMES INTO THE HISTORY BOOKS AT LINDRICK IN 1957.

RIGHT: DAI REES FINALLY GOT HIS HANDS ON THE RYDER CUP IN HIS SIXTH MATCH, CAPTAINING THE SIDE TO A HISTORIC WIN.

# Dai Rees

Welshman Dai Rees never won a major championship, but had a stellar career in Europe. He won many tournaments and appeared in nine Ryder Cups.

## Fact File

**BORN** 1913, Barry, Glamorgan, Wales

**DIED** 1983

**CAREER HIGHLIGHTS**
1936 British Professional Match Play
1938 British Professional Match Play
1949 British Professional Match Play
1950 British Professional Match Play
1954 Belgian Open

**INTERNATIONAL HONORS**
Ryder Cup: 1937, 1947, 1949, 1951, 1953, 1955 (captain), 1957 (captain), 1959 (captain), 1961 (captain)

Dai Rees had one of the longest careers of any British professional ever to play the game, stretching for nearly 40 years from the 1930s to the 1960s. During that time Rees achieved many honors.

After starting out as an assistant professional in Wales, Rees found fame when he won the 1936 British Professional Match Play Championship. Despite being five down with 14 to play against Ernest Whitcombe, Rees won the final. That was a measure of the man. He was a very positive person who believed he could overcome any obstacle.

Part of the reason for Rees's success was his dedication to fitness. He was the Gary Player of his day, and it allowed him a long and happy career.

The victory earned him a place in the 1937 Ryder Cup. Rees acquitted himself handsomely even though he was ultimately involved in a losing cause. He went unbeaten in both matches in which he appeared, and even inflicted a three and one defeat on the legendary Byron Nelson in the singles.

That was the beginning of a long run in the Ryder Cup for the Welshman, the highlight of which was captaining his side to victory at Lindrick in 1957. Rees led the Great Britain & Ireland side four times, but 1957 was his finest hour. Despite losing the opening foursomes by three points to one, with Rees and Ken Bousfield gaining the single point, Rees rallied his troops on the last day. He inflicted a seven and six defeat on 1954 US Open champion Ed Furgol, then watched as his side hammered the Americans by six-and-a-half to one-and-a-half points on the final day, to take the cup for the first time in 24 years.

In all, Rees played in nine Ryder Cup matches, making 17 appearances, a commendable record given that he played at a time of almost total American dominance. His record stands at seven wins, nine losses, and one half, including a five and four won/lost record in singles play.

Indeed, the Welsh native was something of a match-play specialist. He won the British Professional Match Play Championship four times between 1936 and 1950, and was runner-up on three occasions, his last final appearance coming in 1969 when he was in his mid 50s.

Despite his talent, Rees never captured the one tournament that would have capped his career. Three times he finished runner-up in the British Open, in 1953, 1954, and 1961. One of his best chances to win came in 1946 when he finished five strokes behind Sam Snead after a heartbreaking final round of 80.

# Johnny Revolta

JOHNNY REVOLTA IS ONE OF THE MANY PLAYERS FROM THE EARLY PART OF THE 20TH CENTURY WHO STARTED OUT IN THE GAME AS A CADDIE.

Like many players of his era, Johnny Revolta learned to play golf as a caddie. Many fine players have developed this way, but Revolta was one of the best to take that route to professional golf.

Revolta won the Wisconsin Caddie Championship at the age of 14 to get his first taste of winning a golf tournament. Four years later, Revolta turned professional and found success in smaller tournaments and challenge matches in the American Midwest. He realized he had the potential to go all the way to the top when he beat the better ball of Gene Sarazen and Tommy Armour in the early 1930s. Little did he know then that he would go on to beat Armour in one of the biggest championships in golf.

Revolta's first big professional win came in 1933 when he won the Miami Open. A year later he won four times and had the best season of his life.

The Western Open was considered a major championship in Revolta's day, second in importance only to the US Open. The St Louis professional took the title in 1935 when he won by four shots over Willie Goggin at South Bend Country Club in Indiana.

The 1935 season was a great year for Revolta. He led the money list with just over $9,500, a lot of money in the years immediately following the Great Depression. More importantly, he won a major championship.

Revolta was known for having a great short game, and he used it to good effect in the 1935 USPGA Championship at Twin Hills Country Club in Oklahoma City. Despite his talent, he probably didn't appreciate his first round draw. Revolta was pitted against USPGA specialist Walter Hagen. A five-time winner of the championship in the 1920s, including four in a row, Hagen was the best match player in the world at the time. However, he found himself three down to Revolta after seven holes. Hagen fought back to just one down playing the 18th and had a chance to extend the match when Revolta bogeyed the hole. However, Hagen missed his par putt.

Revolta had easier matches over the next few rounds but then came up against Tommy Armour in the final. Armour was 16 years older and had won three major championships, including the 1930 USPGA, and just about every other professional tournament. Revolta started the match off positively by birdying the first hole. In cold conditions, Revolta ran out a five and four winner over Armour. The secret to his victory lay in his short game. In the 31 holes they played, Revolta one-putted 13 greens and never three-putted.

The war years interrupted Revolta's career, and he was never the same player once the circuit resumed, after the war ended. However, he still managed to win 18 times on the US Tour during his career.

## Fact File

**BORN** 1911, St Louis, Missouri, USA

**CAREER HIGHLIGHTS**
1933 Miami Open
1935 Western Open
1935 USPGA Championship
1938 St Petersburg Open
1944 Texas Open

**INTERNATIONAL HONORS**
Ryder Cup: 1935, 1937

# Jose Rivero

SPANIARD JOSE RIVERO NEEDED TO BORROW MONEY EARLY IN HIS CAREER TO MAKE ENDS MEET. HE WAS SOON ABLE TO REPAY THE LOAN WITH INTEREST.

## Fact File

**BORN** 1955, Madrid, Spain

**CAREER HIGHLIGHTS**
1984 Lawrence Batley International
1987 Peugeot French Open
1988 Monte Carlo Open
1992 Open Catalonia

**INTERNATIONAL HONORS**
Ryder Cup: 1985, 1987
World Cup: 1984, 1987, 1988, 1990, 1991, 1992, 1993, 1994
Alfred Dunhill Cup: 1986, 1987, 1988, 1989, 1990, 1991, 1992, 1993, 1994, 1995

Another of the many fine golfers to emerge from Spain along with Seve Ballesteros and Jose Maria Olazabel, Jose Rivero has been one of the mainstays of the European Tour since his rookie year of 1983.

Like a lot of golfers of his age, Rivero worked as a caddie before he finally became a professional in Madrid. Although he turned professional in 1973, Rivero did not start his European Tour career until he was 28, after two trips to the European Tour Qualifying School. He finished first at the Tour School in 1982 to earn his playing rights, and has not looked back since.

In 1984 the man from Madrid was given a £2,500 loan by the Spanish Golf Federation to help him play the European Tour. Rivero made good use of the money. He was able to repay the debt when he won the 1984 Lawrence Batley International at The Belfry with a score of 280.

Rivero found himself at The Belfry in 1985 when European Ryder Cup captain Tony Jacklin selected him as one of his wild cards to play against the Americans in the biennial match. Rivero responded by partnering compatriot Jose Maria Canizares to a seven and five drubbing of Tom Kite and Calvin Peete in the second day's foursomes, as Europe went on to win the cup.

Rivero was also a member of the European Ryder Cup side that made history two years later at Muirfield Village, Ohio, when the Americans lost the cup for the first time on US soil. Rivero contributed to the 15 to 13 point European victory when he teamed up with Gordon Brand Jr in the second day's fourballs to defeat Ben Crenshaw and Scott Simpson by the score of three and two.

Besides his Ryder Cup appearances, Rivero has turned out many times for his country in both the World and Alfred Dunhill Cups. In 1984 he helped Jose Maria Canizares to victory when the World Cup was held in Rome.

With four wins up to the 1998 season, Rivero's best campaign on the European Tour came in 1988 when he finished tenth on the money list with a victory in the Monte Carlo Open and six other top-ten finishes. His most lucrative season occurred in 1992 when he won the Open Catalonia and finished the year with over £300,000 in prize money, £50,000 of which came in the Catalan event.

# Kelly Robbins

IT DIDN'T TAKE KELLY ROBBINS LONG TO MAKE HER MARK IN PROFESSIONAL GOLF. THE PLAYER FROM MICHIGAN NOTCHED UP HER FIRST MAJOR CHAMPIONSHIP WHEN SHE WON THE 1995 LPGA CHAMPIONSHIP.

Kelly Robbins is one of the best women golfers to emerge in the 1990s, a player who within six years of turning professional had won eight tournaments, including a major championship.

The 5-foot, 9-inch Michigan professional was an outstanding amateur while she was at the University of Tulsa. During her time there, Robbins was a quarter-finalist in the 1988 and 1990 US Women's Amateur, and in 1991 she won the North and South Championship. The 1991 season saw her play all four rounds of the US Women's Open. Robbins won a total of seven tournaments during her collegiate career, and was twice named an All-American.

Robbins turned professional in 1992 and quickly made a name for herself. She won her first LPGA tournament when she triumphed in the 1993 LPGA Corning Classic. Since then she had won at least one tournament a year through the 1998 season.

A natural sportswoman, who lists fishing, swimming, basketball, and tennis as her other main hobbies, Robbins started playing golf at the age of eight with her parents. Little did she know then that it would lead her to the top of the women's game.

Robbins' finest hour in her short professional career came in 1995 at the McDonald's LPGA Championship, one of the LPGA's four majors. Robbins had to overcome Laura Davies to win her first major title, and she did it in style.

Davies is one of the longest and most intimidating players in the women's game. She is the John Daly of women's golf, a player who simply grips it and rips it at the flag, hitting every shot with tremendous power and aggression. Most players would have succumbed to Davies's power. Not Robbins.

The Michigan professional led the tournament by two shots after fine opening rounds of 66, 68. However, Davies shot a third round 69 to a 72 by Robbins to take the lead into the final day. Davies had built up a three-shot cushion over Robbins after 11 holes, and was cruising to victory. Robbins made birdies at the 12th and 14th holes to cut the deficit to one. She gained the lead when Davies double-bogeyed the 16th while Robbins got up and down from a bunker to save her par. That was the chance Robbins wanted and she took full advantage of it. She hung on for a one-stroke victory.

Despite lagging behind Davies off the tee, Robbins proved that sometimes precision can overcome length. Robbins was five under for the par-5s that week, while Davies was only one under par.

Most experts agree Robbins will win many more majors in her career.

## Fact File

**BORN** 1969, Mount Pleasant, Michigan, USA

**CAREER HIGHLIGHTS**
1993 LPGA Corning Classic
1994 Jamie Farr Toledo Classic
1995 McDonald's LPGA Championship
1996 Twelve Bridges LPGA Classic
1998 HealthSouth Inaugural

**INTERNATIONAL HONORS**
Solheim Cup: 1994, 1996, 1998

# Loren Roberts

THE "BOSS OF THE MOSS" IS THE NICKNAME GIVEN TO LOREN ROBERTS BY HIS PEERS, A TITLE HE EARNED BECAUSE OF HIS GREAT PUTTING STROKE.

## Fact File

**BORN** 1955, San Luis Obispo, California, USA

**CAREER HIGHLIGHTS**
1994 Nestlé Invitational
1995 Nestlé Invitational
1996 MCI Classic
1996 Greater Milwaukee Open
1997 CVS Charity Classic

**INTERNATIONAL HONORS**
Ryder Cup: 1995
Presidents Cup: 1994

Loren Roberts is arguably the best putter on the US Tour. In fact, he's so good he is known by his peers as the "Boss of the Moss," a nickname given to him in 1985 by fellow professional David Ogrin.

The Californian usually ranks in the top ten in the putting statistics maintained by the US Tour. For example, in 1982 he finished eighth in that category, first in 1994, third in 1997, and tenth in 1998, the latter resembling something of a bad year for Roberts on the greens. It's just as well Roberts can putt, for he normally finishes well down in the driving distance category, averaging in the 250-yard range year after year, not long by modern standards. However, Roberts is very accurate off the tee, hits his fair share of greens in regulation, and then puts his magic wand to work on the greens.

Through 1998 the Boss of the Moss won five tournaments on the US Tour, and used his tremendous touch on the greens to fashion two 62s and three 63s.

Although Roberts won twice in 1996, his best season to date remains 1994, when he won once, finished second three times, and in total recorded nine top-ten finishes to finish the season ninth on the US money list with just over $1 million. It was also the year that saw him nearly win his first major championship.

Roberts was involved in a playoff with Ernie Els and Colin Montgomerie for the 1994 US Open at Oakmont Country Club in Pennsylvania. Roberts's total of 279, one under par, tied Els and Montgomerie for the 72-hole lead. In the three-man playoff the following day, Roberts matched Els's 74 while Montgomerie could only manage a 78. Els and Roberts played a sudden death to decide the title and Els won when Roberts took five to the South African's four at the second extra hole. Ironically, it was his putting that let Roberts down in the playoff. Afterward he admitted, "I was kind of hanging on with the putter today. It let me down a little bit."

That same year also saw Roberts finish fifth in the Masters and ninth in the USPGA Championship. A steady player who keeps the ball in play and works to his strengths, Roberts is the type of player who normally wins the US Open. But then with his slow, deliberate and highly effective putting stroke he is a good bet in many tournaments.

# Allan Robertson

ALLAN ROBERTSON IS GENERALLY REGARDED AS THE FIRST TRUE PROFESSIONAL GOLFER. IT IS SAID HIS DEATH IN 1859 WAS THE IMPETUS BEHIND THE CREATION OF THE BRITISH OPEN.

Allan Robertson's name doesn't adorn the British Open trophy. Robertson died in 1859, the year before the championship began. However, his death was probably one of the reasons why the tournament was inaugurated in the first place.

Robertson was the greatest golfer of his age. He was the first man to go round the Old Course at St Andrews in under 80 strokes, shooting a 79 in September 1858, the year before his death. The mark stood for 30 years until Young Tom Morris recorded a 77. Legend has it that the first British Open was only held to see who would assume Robertson's mantle as the champion golfer of the time.

Robertson's family had been club and ball makers in St Andrews for years when Allan finally took over the shop that looked out over the 18th green and first tee of the Old Course. For a while he employed Old Tom Morris as his assistant, and the business turned out high-quality featheries, leather-covered balls stuffed with feathers.

Robertson not only employed Morris as his assistant, but partnered him in many challenge matches. Even when the two men had a falling out over Morris's use of the gutta percha ball, they remained partners on the golf course. They were a formidable force, but then Robertson was seemingly unbeatable no matter whom he partnered. According to ancient golfing lore, the master of St Andrews never lost a single foursome challenge match in his life.

One such match involved Robertson and Morris against the Dunn brothers, Willie and Jamie, twins from Musselburgh. In 1849 the Dunns challenged the St Andrews pair to a match for £400 a side, a phenomenal sum in those days. The match was played over three courses, St Andrews, Musselburgh, and North Berwick, with 36 holes played at each to decide the 108-hole thriller. The Dunns easily won the first match on their own course, winning by the huge margin of 13 and 12. The St Andrews pair won narrowly on the Old Course, which meant that North Berwick would be the decider. The match came down to the last holes amid a wild scene at North Berwick, where huge crowds had gathered to watch the final of the epic contest. Four down with eight to play, the St Andrews pair halved three and won five of the last eight holes to take the match.

Wooden clubs were the fashion in those days, but Robertson is said to have been the first to pioneer the use of iron clubs to help make approach shots, and shots played around the green, easier.

A memorial to Robertson today stands in St Andrews cemetery.

## Fact File

**BORN** 1815, St Andrews, Fife, Scotland

**DIED** 1859

# Costantino Rocca

COSTANTINO ROCCA'S ROUTE TO PROFESSIONAL GOLF WAS ANYTHING BUT CONVENTIONAL. THE ITALIAN IS NOW ONE OF EUROPE'S MOST CONSISTENT PERFORMERS.

## Fact File

**BORN** 1956, Bergamo, Italy

**CAREER HIGHLIGHTS**
1993 Open V33 Du Grand Lyon
1993 Peugeot Open de France
1996 Volvo PGA Championship
1997 Canon European Masters

**INTERNATIONAL HONORS**
Ryder Cup: 1993, 1995, 1997
Alfred Dunhill Cup: 1986, 1987, 1989, 1991, 1992, 1996
World Cup: 1988, 1990, 1991, 1992, 1993, 1994, 1995, 1996, 1997, 1998

There aren't many golfers who have gone straight from the factory floor to the most famous fairways of the world. Constantino Rocca is one of them.

While many players are helped to the top by their privileged backgrounds, Rocca paid his own way into professional golf. He worked long hours making polystyrene boxes in a factory in his hometown of Bergamo, Italy, to help finance his career in golf.

Rocca is a throwback to the early days when the best players were entirely self-taught and learned their craft through watching the players they caddied for. Rocca carried golf bags as a boy at the Bergamo Golf Club. In 1978 he won the Caddie Championship and then became the caddie master. He turned professional in 1981 at the age of 24.

The first seven years of Rocca's life as a professional were a series of trials and errors. He would get his card only to lose it with ease, traveling to the European Tour Qualifying School four times. He was a good enough player to win minor events in his native Italy, but he just couldn't crack the European Tour. In 1989 he changed tack. He spent a year on the European Challenge Tour trying to gain playing privileges for the main European circuit. It paid off. Rocca won three times on the Challenge Tour that season to finish third on its Order of Merit and gain his playing rights for the 1990 European Tour. Rocca has not looked back since.

The Italian has never finished worse than 48th on the money list since finally taking his place among Europe's elite. Throughout the '90s he established himself as one of the best players in European golf. That was evident from his 1996 victory in the prestigious Volvo PGA Championship. It is also evident in his Ryder Cup record, where he has six wins and five losses from the three matches he has played, including a four and two defeat of Tiger Woods in their singles encounter at Valderrama in 1997.

Rocca nearly became the first Italian to win the British Open when he lost to John Daly in a playoff for the 1995 title at St Andrews. The Bergamo man needed a birdie at the 72nd hole to win, but flubbed his chip. He then holed a 60-foot putt to force the playoff. Known as one of the more expressive players in the game, Rocca celebrated his miracle putt by throwing himself down onto the St Andrews turf and beating it with his fists.

# Phil Rodgers

Phil Rodgers was one of the most consistent American professionals during the 1960s, winning many tournaments on the US Tour.

Phil Rodgers spent only one year on the University of Houston golf team, but he made it worthwhile. Rodgers won the only three tournaments he entered in 1958, including the NCAA Championship.

After spending time in the US Marines, Rodgers turned professional in 1961 and soon made a name for himself on the US Tour. He won twice in the 1962 season, triumphing in the Los Angeles and the Tucson Open. Rodgers won the Los Angeles event by nine strokes over Bob Goalby and Fred Hawkins, with a four-round total of 268, 16 under par, and the largest margin of victory in the tournament's history.

The 1962 season was the same year that Jack Nicklaus made his professional debut, and Nicklaus somewhat overshadowed Rodgers's fine performance by winning the US Open at Oakmont that year. Nicklaus defeated Arnold Palmer in a playoff for the title. Rodgers did his best to upstage Nicklaus. An opening 74 cost Rodgers because he finished tied for third, two strokes out of the playoff.

Paul Runyan once said that Rodgers knew more about the golf swing as a 16-year-old than any other youngster he had ever known. And Runyan, a two-time USPGA champion, had seen quite a few in his time. Runyan was also aware of Rodgers's temper, which could be colossal at times. However, Runyan maintained that Rodgers was one of the few players who could make their anger work for them.

Rodgers traveled to his first British Open in 1962 where he finished third behind Arnold Palmer in the year that Palmer set the 72-hole British Open record with 276. Rodgers finished 13 shots behind Palmer.

Rodgers returned to Britain for the 1963 championship and had his best chance at winning the title, shooting three rounds under 70 that year to tie Bob Charles after 72 holes. Scores of 67, 68, 73, and 69 gave him a four-round total of 277, one shot off Palmer's record. Rodgers lost the last 36-hole playoff in the British Open by eight shots.

Rodgers also had a chance to win the 1966 British Open at Muirfield, but again Nicklaus got the better of him. The former marine had lost 30 pounds, trimming his weight from 200 to 170 pounds. A fine 66 in the second round helped Rodgers's cause. So too did his 70 in the third which featured an inward nine of 30 that put him in the lead. However, a poor 76 in the final round cost him dearly. Rodgers fell short of Nicklaus's winning total by four shots—his last great chance to win a major championship.

## Fact File

**BORN** 1938, San Diego, California, USA

**CAREER HIGHLIGHTS**

1962 Los Angeles Open
1962 Tucson Open
1963 Texas Open
1966 Buick Open
1966 Doral Open

# Chi Chi Rodriguez

YOU MAY NOT FIND CHI CHI RODRIGUEZ'S NAME AMONG GOLF'S ELITE, BUT AS AN AMBASSADOR FOR THE GAME HE HAS DONE MORE THAN MOST.

## Fact File

**BORN** 1935, Rio Piedras, Puerto Rico

**CAREER HIGHLIGHTS**
1963 Denver Open
1964 Western Open
1967 Texas Open
1972 Byron Nelson Classic
1973 Greater Greensboro Open

Don't look for Chi Chi Rodriguez's name in any list of major champions. You won't find it. Rodriguez doesn't have a major championship to his name, but in the hearts of many he is one of golf's true champions.

Rodriguez was elected to the World Golf Hall of Fame in 1992. He's in pretty classy company: Nicklaus, Watson, Player, Palmer, Vardon, Hogan, Cotton—name the great major winners and you'll find them there. Then there's Rodriguez.

The Puerto Rican never really set the US Tour alight during his prime. He won eight times in a career that spanned 25 years. In that time he broke into the top 20 on the money list only twice. Yet his humor, his trick shots, and his clinics for charity made him star billing on the US Tour.

Rodriguez has done more to promote the game than many multiple major winners. He is a showman. He can turn a routine birdie into an impromptu theatrical act. In his trade-mark routine, Rodriguez will draw his putter as if it were an imaginary sword. After administering the *coupe de grâce*, he wipes the putter as if removing blood from a blade, before sheathing it back into its scabbard by his waist. Or he will remove his Panama hat and toss it over the hole to stop the ball from jumping back out. The crowds love it, and they still turn up in their hundreds to watch him play.

Rodriguez is also in the World Golf Hall of Fame for the amount of work he has done for charity. His Chi Chi Rodriguez Foundation for underprivileged children has raised more than $4 million over the years. He has a special rapport with children, and has coached thousands of them, encouraging a legion of youngsters to take up the game.

Despite Chi Chi's modest return for his 25 years on the US Tour, his time on the US Senior Tour has brought handsome dividends. Rodriguez joined the Senior Tour upon turning 50 at the end of 1985. The following season he won three events on the over-50 circuit. In 1987 he more than doubled that figure, winning seven times and earning more than $500,000. Not that he became selfish upon turning 50, though. During that phenomenal season he took part in numerous exhibitions and clinics to raise money for charity.

By the end of the 1993 season, Rodriguez had won 22 tournaments on the Senior Tour. Included in that run were back-to-back years in 1990 and 1991 when he triumphed four times in each season. He still holds the Senior Tour record of eight consecutive birdies, made during the 1987 Silver Pages Classic.

# Bill Rogers

BILL ROGERS'S FINEST MOMENT IN THE SUN CAME WHEN HE WON THE 1981 BRITISH OPEN. HOWEVER, WITHIN A FEW SHORT YEARS OF THAT WIN HE STOPPED PLAYING COMPETITIVE GOLF.

Bill Rogers had the year of his life in 1981, when he won six tournaments and was named the US Tour's Player of the Year. Then within just a few short years he had left the tournament circuit, with no enthusiasm left for the game that had given him such glory.

Rogers's father, Bill, was a lieutenant colonel in the US Air Force and the family moved around quite a bit when Rogers was a small boy. For example, he lived in Germany and then Morocco before he was eight. By the time he was nine the family had moved to Montgomery, Alabama, and Rogers took up golf. Shortly afterward the Rogers were on the road again, this time to Texarkana, Texas. Rogers continued to develop his game. The move to Texas helped Rogers, for he came under the tutelage of Jerry Robinson, professional at the Northridge Country Club. It was Robinson who developed Rogers into a good golfer.

As an amateur, Rogers won the 1972 Southern Amateur and attended the University of Houston, where he was an All-American in 1973. Bruce Lietzke was Rogers's roommate at university and was responsible for giving Rogers the nickname "Panther," because he was jumpy by nature and never seemed able to settle down.

After solid seasons between 1975 and 1977, Rogers earned his first US Tour victory when he won the Bob Hope Desert Classic. The 1979 season saw him travel to England and triumph in the World Match Play Championship. Although he went winless that season in the States, he managed to finish fifth on the money list with over $315,000. Two years later, he had the type of season most players can only dream about.

In 1981 Rogers won three U.S. tournaments—the Heritage Classic, the Texas Open, and the World Series of Golf—the last victory giving him a ten-year exemption to play the US Tour. However, it was his victory in the British Open that year that catapulted him onto the world stage. It was probably his undoing as well.

Rogers won the British title by four strokes from Germany's Bernhard Langer at Royal St George's. His victory came at a time when another American, Tom Watson, was dominating the world's oldest championship.

The victory opened all kinds of doors for Rogers, and he took advantage of his new-found status. He played all over the world for the next couple of years, winning tournaments in Japan and Australia. While he did win the 1983 USF&G Classic, by then Rogers had lost his enthusiasm for the game, burned out at just 32. After 1983 he rarely played tournament golf again.

## Fact File

**BORN** 1951, Waco, Texas, USA

**CAREER HIGHLIGHTS**
1978 Bob Hope Desert Classic
1981 The Open Championship
1981 World Series of Golf
1981 Texas Open
1983 USF&G Classic

**INTERNATIONAL HONORS**
Ryder Cup: 1981
Walker Cup: 1973

# THE GREATEST AMERICAN TEAM EVER

It wasn't a case of if the U.S.A. would win the 1981 Ryder Cup at Walton Heath in Surrey, England, but by *how much.* Quite simply, it was the greatest Ryder Cup team the United States has ever produced. Dave Marr was the American captain in 1981. Not to belittle Marr's acumen as a team leader, but his wasn't really a difficult job that year. The Texan could probably have thrown all the names in a hat, closed his eyes and selected pairings at random. The United States would still have won the Cup by a wide margin.

Between them, the American team members had won 36 major championships, 17 of which belonged to Jack Nicklaus. Eventually they would go on to win 49 majors in total. Only one player on the 1981 team would not win a major in his career; Bruce Lietzke has that dubious honor, but then he's a player who by choice doesn't play in most major championships. Lietzke stopped playing in the US Open in 1986, and hasn't played in the British Open since 1982. America's major tally went like this (the figures in brackets indicate the number players would eventually win in their careers): Nicklaus 17 (18), Tom Watson 5 (8), Lee Trevino 5 (6), Ray Floyd 2 (4), Hale Irwin 2 (3), Johnny Miller 2, Jerry Pate 1, Larry Nelson 1 (3), Bill Rogers 1, Tom Kite 0 (1), Ben Crenshaw 0 (2), Bruce Lietzke 0.

On the European side, the team had won a grand zero majors. Players like Nick Faldo, Sandy Lyle and Bernhard Langer would eventually make their mark on the game, but at that time they were completely majorless. Langer was making his debut in the side, as were the Spaniards Jose Maria Canizares and Manuel Pinero. Their compatriot Seve Ballesteros didn't play that year.

Against the form book, it was the European side that drew first blood. The home side won two of the opening foursomes matches to tie after the morning session of the first day, then won two and halved one of the four afternoon fourballs matches to finish the day a point ahead of the Americans. That seemed to wake the American side up, because thereafter it became a whitewash.

The visitors won seven of the following day's eight matches. Only rookies Langer and Pinero managed to win a point on day two, defeating Ray Floyd and Hale Irwin by a score of two and one in the morning fourballs. Everywhere else it was complete disaster for the home side.

Three of the points from the first two days came from the outstanding pairing of Nicklaus and Watson. There were other attractive pairings on the visiting side, too. How about Trevino and Nelson, Kite and Miller, Floyd and Irwin? Not surprisingly, the Americans entered the last day with a five-point lead, then steamrollered to victory. Of the 12 singles matches, U.S.A. won seven, halved two and lost just three. They completed a resounding nine-point victory to take the Cup. It wasn't just a case of the better team winning, but the best Ryder Cup team ever.

RIGHT: JACK NICKLAUS (STANDING) AND TOM WATSON WERE A FORMIDABLE FORCE IN THE 1981 RYDER CUP, GOING UNBEATEN IN THE THREE MATCHES THEY PLAYED.

RIGHT: DAVE MARR (CENTER) WAS GIVEN THE ENVIABLE TASK OF CAPTAINING THE GREATEST AMERICAN RYDER CUP TEAM EVER ASSEMBLED.

BELOW RIGHT: RAY FLOYD CONTRIBUTED THREE POINTS TO THE AMERICAN VICTORY IN 1981.

BELOW: NICK FALDO (LEFT) AND PETER OOSTERHUIS WERE NO MATCH FOR THE POWERFUL AMERICANS.

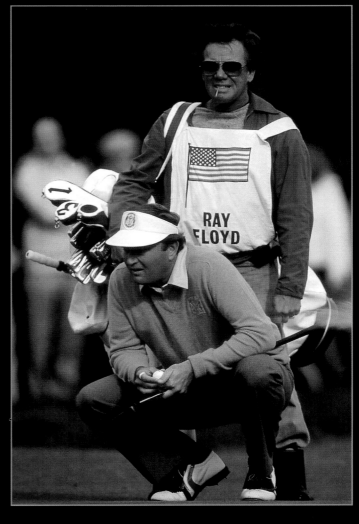

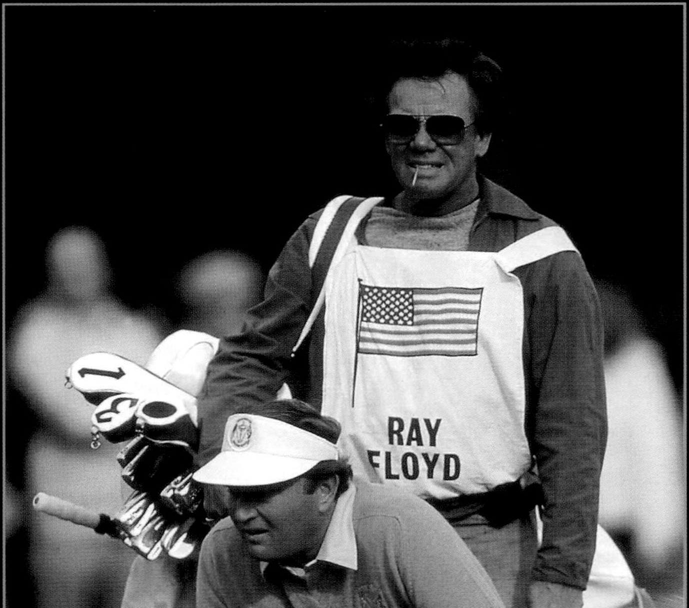

# Eduardo Romero

EDUARDO ROMERO'S FIRST EUROPEAN TOUR VICTORY CAME IN THE 1989 LANCÔME TROPHY, WHEN THE POWERFUL ARGENTINIAN OVERCAME A STRONG FIELD THAT INCLUDED MANY OF EUROPE'S BEST PLAYERS.

## Fact File

**BORN** 1954, Cordoba, Argentina

**CAREER HIGHLIGHTS**
1989 Lancôme Trophy
1990 Volvo Open de Firenze
1991 Peugeot Spanish Open
1991 Peugeot French Open
1994 Canon European Masters

**INTERNATIONAL HONORS**
World Cup: 1983, 1984, 1987, 1988, 1991, 1993, 1994, 1995
Alfred Dunhill Cup: 1988, 1989, 1990, 1993, 1995, 1997, 1998

Eduardo Romero goes by the nickname "El Gato," the cat, a title given to him because of the way he stalks his opponents around the golf course.

The son of a club professional who grew up in Cordoba, Argentina, where he still lives, Romero was always destined for a career in golf. He was already one of Argentina's best players when he established himself on the European Tour. The powerful 6-foot, 2-inch golfer had won 25 times in South America by the time he won his first tournament in Europe.

Romero's maiden win in Europe came in the 1989 Lancôme Trophy, one of the most prestigious events on the European circuit. Romero had to overcome two of Europe's big guns to take the tournament. Spain's Jose Maria Olazabal and Germany's Bernhard Langer were gunning for the title and made things hard for the Argentinean in the final round. Both players shot closing 65s to put pressure on Romero. However, after holing a 40-yard pitch shot for an eagle on the 16th hole, Romero closed with a 66 to add to the 66 he scored in the third round. Romero took the title by one shot from Langer and Olazabal.

"It was so important for me to win for the first time here in such company," said Romero afterwards. "Only the [British] Open Championship has a stronger field." He was right. Besides the runners-up, the field included players like Greg Norman, Curtis Strange, Seve Ballesteros, Nick Faldo, and Sandy Lyle. That Romero was able to win over such prestigious names signaled to the golfing world that he was a player to be reckoned with.

There is no more popular player on the European Tour than Romero. He always seems to be laughing and smiling as he plays, and there is no more approachable player in world golf.

Besides his father, Romero was fortunate enough to take lessons from Roberto de Vicenzo, the greatest Argentinean player of all time, and the winner of the 1967 British Open. Romero has done his best to equal de Vicenzo's British Open win. However, the closest he's come has been an eighth place finish at Royal Troon in 1989, and seventh over the same course in 1997.

Through the 1998 season, Romero had won six times in Europe, as well as three Argentine PGA Championships, an Argentine Open, and two victories in the Chile Open, in 1984 and 1986.

# Bob Rosburg



BOB ROSBURG IS MORE FAMOUS FOR HIS ON-COURSE TELEVISION COMMENTARY, BUT "ROSSIE" WAS A GOOD ENOUGH PLAYER TO WIN THE 1959 USPGA CHAMPIONSHIP.

Bob Rosburg became synonymous with the phrase "How's it lying, Rossie?" In the late 1970s and through most of the 1980s, Rosburg worked as an on-course commentator for American television, telling viewers what sort of shot players were facing. Rosburg knew better than most what the professionals were up against. He had been in every sort of lie during his sterling career.

Rosburg had been a fine player as an amateur. After graduating from Stamford University in 1948, Rosburg turned professional and soon made a name for himself on the US Tour.

The San Francisco native was not noted for having a brilliant swing, but when he was hot he was one of the deadliest putters in the game. His putting helped him win the San Diego and Motor City Opens in 1956, defeating Ed Furgol in a playoff for the latter title. Three years later, he won his biggest tournament when he won the 1959 USPGA Championship at the Minneapolis Golf Club.

After the third round of the USPGA, Rosburg was actually sitting in sixth place, six shots behind leader Jerry Barber. However, he used that silky smooth putting stroke to fashion a four under par 66 on the last day. Barber by contrast shot 73 and Rosburg had won the biggest championship of his life. His 66 was the lowest final round shot by a winner until John Mahaffey equaled the score in 1978. David Graham then shot 65 the following year to break that record.

Rosburg earned a spot on the Ryder Cup team that year as a result of his USPGA victory. He did himself proud, too, winning both matches in which he played. He and Mike Souchak defeated Bernard Hunt and Eric Brown five and four in the opening foursomes. Then Rosburg defeated Harry Weetman six and five in the singles, America winning the match by five strokes.

Rosburg won the Bing Crosby National tournament in 1961, and for a long time it seemed that would be his last Tour victory. Rosburg won the tournament by one shot over Roberto de Vicenzo and Dave Ragan.

It is a credit to his game and his perseverance that 11 years later Rosburg was able to win another US Tour event. His victory in the Bob Hope Desert Classic came when Rosburg was well into his mid 40s. Given that the tournament was played on four different courses and over five rounds, it showed that Rosburg was still fit enough to play with the young guns. His 344 total gave him the title by one stroke over Lanny Wadkins.

## Fact File

**BORN** 1926, San Francisco, California, USA

**CAREER HIGHLIGHTS**
1956 Convair-San Diego Open
1956 Motor City Open
1959 USPGA Championship
1961 Bing Crosby National
1972 Bob Hope Desert Classic

**INTERNATIONAL HONORS**
Ryder Cup: 1959

# Paul Runyan

EVEN IN HIS 80S PAUL RUNYAN WAS A GREAT WEDGE PLAYER, A TALENT THAT WON HIM TWO USPGA CHAMPIONSHIPS IN FIVE YEARS.

## Fact File

**BORN** 1908, Hot Springs, Arkansas, USA

**CAREER HIGHLIGHTS**
1934 USPGA Championship
1938 USPGA Championship
1938 Argentine Open
1961 World Senior Professional Championship
1962 World Senior Professional Championship

**INTERNATIONAL HONORS**
Ryder Cup: 1933, 1935

Paul Runyan was one of the shortest hitters ever to play the game at the top level, but what he lacked in length he more than compensated for around the greens.

Runyan was one of the finest wedge players the game has ever seen, a skill he possessed well into his 80s. For example, even in the 1980s and 1990s, Runyan would still show up at the USPGA Championship and give demonstrations along with professionals much younger than himself. The gallery would be full of Tour professionals who would show up to learn something from the legendary wizard of the wedge.

The Arkansas native earned his fame in the USPGA Championship, winning the event twice in the 1930s. In 1934 he was involved in the closest final in many years. Runyan came up against his former instructor Craig Wood in the deciding match. Despite giving the powerful Wood many yards in length off the tee, Runyan was able to give his mentor a tough time. One down after the morning round, Runyan squared the match soon after lunch. The match seesawed back and forth over the closing holes, but it ended all square and extra holes had to be played. The match was decided at the 38th hole when Runyan played a delicate chip over a bunker and holed an eight-foot par putt to win the title.

Four years later, Runyan beat another long hitter to win his second USPGA title. This time he thrashed the legendary Sam Snead by a score of eight and seven, then the tournament's biggest margin of victory.

His wonderful short game saw him go around the Shawnee Country Club in Pennsylvania in 67 for a five-hole lead on Snead in the final's morning round. The match ended at the 29th hole with "Slammin' Sam" well beaten.

The short-game master made two Ryder Cup appearances in the 1930s, playing in the 1933 and 1935 matches. Although he obviously enjoyed the cut and thrust of match play, his debut wasn't exactly sparkling. He lost both matches in which he played in the 1933 contest when America was defeated in Southport, England, by a single point. However, he made up for that disappointment with two wins in his two 1935 matches.

It was a credit to Runyan's longevity that in the early 1960s he was winning events as a senior golfer, taking the US Senior Professional Championship in 1961 and 1962, and also winning the World Senior Professional Championship in both those years.

# DOUG SANDERS

DOUG SANDERS'S FAMOUS MISS ON THE LAST GREEN OF THE 1970 BRITISH OPEN CHAMPIONSHIP AT ST ANDREWS MADE HIM A HOUSEHOLD NAME THROUGHOUT THE WORLD.

Doug Sanders will always be remembered for one of the saddest misses in golf history, a two-and-a-half-foot putt that cost him the British Open Championship.

Sanders arrived at the 72nd hole, of the 1970 British Open at St Andrews needing a par to win his first major championship. After a magnificent four at the 17th hole, when he got up and down in two shots from the Road Bunker to save par, Sanders only needed a four on the Old Course's 18th, one of the most straightforward holes in all of golf.

Sanders's approach shot was too strong, leaving him a long putt down the green. He knocked his first putt short and then had that famous two-and-a-half-footer to win the oldest championship in golf. He settled over the ball, then bent over to remove something from his line to the hole. When he finally hit the ball it was with a weak stroke, and the ball missed on the right-hand side. Playing companion Lee Trevino could only look away in despair.

The following day Sanders lost the playoff by one shot to Jack Nicklaus, shooting 73 to Nicklaus's 72. Despite his misfortune, Sanders accepted the defeat with the grace and dignity of a true champion. The Georgian's performance at St Andrews came as something of a surprise. Sanders had been one of the stalwarts of the US Tour in the late 1950s and early 1960s.

After winning the 1956 Canadian Open as an amateur—the last player to record that particular feat—Sanders turned professional and won a number of tournaments on the US Tour. In total, he won 20 during his career, including five in 1961. However, he went into something of a slump after the 1967 season. A win at St Andrews would have capped his career.

One of the game's true characters, Sanders was the most colorful player of his generation—literally. His wardrobe had every color imaginable, and he possessed one of the largest collections of shoes of any sportsman. Even in the late 1990s, long past his prime, Sanders remained one of the most colorful players in the game.

It was said of Sanders that he had the shortest backswing of any top player, with a follow-through to match. It was a swing he developed as a youngster playing over the narrow fairways of his home club in Cedartown, Georgia. His action was highly effective and earned him much in prize money throughout his career. One of the best natured of players with a happy-go-lucky attitude to life, Sanders was also in high demand away from the tournament scene, earning a lot of money from exhibitions and clinics.

## FACT FILE

**BORN** 1933, Cedartown, Georgia, USA

**CAREER HIGHLIGHTS**
1956 Canadian Open
1958 Western Open
1961 Colonial National Invitational
1963 Greater Greensboro Open
1966 Bob Hope Desert Classic

**INTERNATIONAL HONORS**
Ryder Cup: 1967

# Gene Sarazen

Gene Sarazen was one of only four men to win the grand slam of golf—the Masters, US Open, British Open, and USPGA Championship. The others are Ben Hogan, Gary Player, and Jack Nicklaus. However, Sarazen has pre-eminence over those other three great champions as he was the first to accomplish the feat.

Sarazen was born in New York of Italian parents and was originally called Eugene Saraceni. He changed the name because he thought it made him sound more like a musician than a golfer. He first competed in the US Open in 1920 and within two years had won the tournament. He traveled to Britain for his first British Open in 1923 at Royal Troon, but failed to qualify for the championship proper. Fifty years later, in his 70s, he would play his last British Open on those links and cap his performance with a hole in one at the 8th hole, the famous Postage Stamp. Twenty years later, by then in his 90s, Sarazen was at Royal St George's to honor Greg Norman's victory in the 1993 championship.

Gene Sarazen is one of the true ambassadors of the game of golf. Besides his sparkling performances on the golf course, he was the man responsible for the sand wedge. Sarazen created the club because he had so much difficulty getting out of the sand. When he first used the club in tournament play, he had to hide it in case the authorities banned him from using it.

Sarazen was also responsible for persuading Ben Hogan to play in the British Open. The New Yorker told Hogan that he would not be a great champion until he had won the British title. After winning the Masters and US Open of 1953, Hogan took Sarazen's advice and won the British Open at Carnoustie in his only appearance in the world's oldest golf championship.

Of his many victories, Sarazen's most famous came in the 1935 Masters. He had skipped the inaugural tournament the year before because of other commitments, but made up for it the following year by hitting the most famous shot in golf. In the final round Sarazen holed his 4-wood approach shot to the par-5, 15th hole for a two, an albatross, to get himself into a playoff with Craig Wood, which he won by five shots the following day.

Even shortly before his death in 1999, at the age of 97, Sarazen was still turning up at the Masters to serve as an honorary starter with Sam Snead and Byron Nelson. The "Squire," as he was known, was still hitting the ball straight and true.

## Fact File

**BORN** 1902, Harrison, New York, USA

**DIED** 1999

**CAREER HIGHLIGHTS**
1922 US Open
1922 USPGA Championship
1923 USPGA Championship
1932 US Open
1932 The Open Championship
1933 USPGA Championship
1935 Masters

**INTERNATIONAL HONORS**
Ryder Cup: 1927, 1929, 1931, 1933, 1935, 1937

ABOVE AND RIGHT: GENE SARAZEN HAD ONE OF THE LONGEST CAREERS IN GOLF, ONE THAT SPANNED OVER 70 YEARS, FROM HIS 1922 US OPEN VICTORY TO THE 1999 MASTERS.

RIGHT: SARAZEN SERVED AS AN HONORARY STARTER UNTIL HIS DEATH IN 1999. THE SQUIRE WOULD PLAY NINE HOLES IN THE COMPANY OF BYRON NELSON AND SAM SNEAD. HERE HE PLAYS OUT OF A BUNKER AT AUGUSTA.

# Peter Senior

PETER SENIOR IS THE FIRST TO ADMIT THAT HIS SWING IS NO THING OF GREAT BEAUTY, BUT THE AUSTRALIAN HAS USED IT TO EARN A LOT OF MONEY IN PROFESSIONAL GOLF.

## Fact File

**BORN** 1959, Singapore

**CAREER HIGHLIGHTS**
1986 PLM Open
1987 Australian Open
1987 Australian PGA Championship
1990 Panasonic European Open
1992 Benson & Hedges International Open

**INTERNATIONAL HONOURS**
World Cup: 1988, 1990
Alfred Dunhill Cup: 1987
Presidents Cup: 1994, 1996

Peter Senior's career nearly came to a complete halt because he couldn't find a way to get the ball into the hole. Then Sam Torrance came to his rescue.

Torrance was one of the first players to adopt the long putter, the broomhandle. It saved his career because before he used it he was having big problems on the greens. Peter Senior was having his own difficulties on the putting surfaces when Torrance gave him one of his own long putters. Senior has openly admitted that the Scotsman put his career back on track. "Before Sam gave me one of his putters I was having a terrible time on the greens. He, and it, saved my career."

The stocky Australian has used his broomstick to good effect. Despite winning a host of tournaments around the world before switching putters, since his conversion Senior has recorded many more victories.

The Singapore-born professional was one of many Aussies who plied their trade on the European Tour in the 1980s and 90s. Basing himself in Bagshot, in Surrey, England, with other compatriots such as Brett Ogle, Mike Harwood, Craig Parry, and many others, Senior found much success in Europe. Between 1984 and 1992 when he was focusing mainly on the European circuit, Senior won four tournaments.

Since 1992, Senior has concentrated more of his play in the Far East and on his home circuit. Through the 1998 season the Queensland resident had won three times on the lucrative Japanese circuit.

Although he does not possess one of the most graceful swings in golf, Senior uses it to great effect. His action looks like that of a middle handicapper, and even the Australian is honest enough to admit his swing isn't a thing of great beauty: "My swing isn't pretty at the best of times but my rhythm usually keeps me afloat."

The 5-foot, 6-inch golfer turned professional in 1978 and earned his stripes the following year when he won the 1979 Dunhill South Australian Open. Two victories on the Australian circuit in 1984 allowed him to play on the European Tour as one of the top 50 players on the Australasian Order of Merit. Through the 1998 season, Senior had won a total of 18 times in his homeland, including the Aussie grand slam of the Australian Masters, Australian Open, and Australian PGA Championship.

# PATTY SHEEHAN



NOT MANY FEMALE GOLFERS HAVE SHOWN AS MUCH GRIT AND DETERMINATION AS PATTY SHEEHAN. SHEEHAN REALIZED A DREAM WHEN SHE WON THE 1992 US WOMEN'S OPEN.

Patty Sheehan recorded the most significant win of her career when she won the 1992 US Women's Open at Oakmont Country Club, Pennsylvania, after a playoff with Juli Inkster.

The petite Vermont professional had won over 20 tournaments before then, including two LPGA Championships, but her win at Oakmont is the victory that has satisfied her most. Two years earlier Sheehan had America's national championship in her hands only to throw the tournament away. At Atlanta Athletic Club in 1990, Sheehan led the US Women's Open by 11 shots at one stage only to lose by a stroke to Betsy King.

The experience was devastating for Sheehan. Nevertheless, like the true sportswoman she is, the 5-foot, 3-inch Sheehan, with tears streaming down her face, had the courtesy to talk to television about her experience. Sheehan's interview with ABC-TV's Judy Rankin earned her many fans. Indeed, she probably gained more friends from losing that tournament than she would had she taken the title.

The golf world rejoiced when Sheehan came back two years later to win the title she coveted most. As she said later, "That 1992 Open victory made me a different person—much happier and more content. If I never win another tournament, I'm still complete because that was the one I wanted." Of course, Sheehan was too good a player not to win another tournament. In fact, she has won many tournaments since then, including another US Women's Open, which she picked up in 1994. Her four-round total of 277 tied the record for the lowest 72-hole score at the time.

Born to a middle-class family in Vermont, Sheehan was involved in sports almost from birth. Her father was an Olympic skiing coach and her three brothers were natural athletes. Patty was on skis as soon as she could walk, and as a 13-year-old was considered the best downhill racer in the country in that age bracket.

Sheehan started golfing because everyone in the family played. She was a scratch player by the time she was 18 and later was the number one player on the San Jose State University golf team.

In 1980 Sheehan played in the Curtis Cup and won all her matches. A year later she joined the LPGA Tour and won her first tournament, the Mazda Japan Classic. That victory and a lot of other good finishes helped her to 11th place on the LPGA money list. In 1981, she won the Rookie of the Year Award.

Sheehan was honored in 1995 with induction into the LPGA Hall of Fame.

## FACT FILE

**BORN** 1956, Middlebury, Vermont, USA

**CAREER HIGHLIGHTS**
1983 LPGA Championship
1984 LPGA Championship
1992 US Women's Open
1993 LPGA Championship
1994 US Women's Open
1996 Nabisco Dinah Shore

**INTERNATIONAL HONORS**
Solheim Cup: 1990, 1992, 1994, 1996, 1998
Curtis Cup: 1980

# Denny Shute

IN 1933 DENNY SHUTE WENT FROM VILLAIN TO HERO IN THE SPACE OF JUST TWO WEEKS, CULMINATING IN HIM WINNING THE BRITISH OPEN CHAMPIONSHIP.

## Fact File

**BORN** 1904, Cleveland, Ohio, USA

**DIED** 1973

**CAREER HIGHLIGHTS**
1930 Los Angeles Open
1930 Texas Open
1933 The Open Championship
1936 USPGA Championship
1937 USPGA Championship

**INTERNATIONAL HONORS**
Ryder Cup: 1931, 1933, 1937

The 1933 season was a strange one for Denny Shute. In June that year he was seen as the player responsible for causing the USA to lose the Ryder Cup; two weeks later he was king of the world.

Shute faced the little-known British player Syd Easterbrook in the singles of the Ryder Cup at Southport and Ainsdale in 1933. Both men were all square on the final green but facing par putts of about 30 feet each. Easterbrook putted first and left his ball within tap-in range. Shute followed and ran his ball four feet past the hole. When he missed the return, he lost his match and with it the Ryder Cup. The half point would have tied the scores overall, and the USA would have retained the Cup because they were the holders.

Shute made amends two weeks later at St Andrews when he won the British Open Championship. The Cleveland native shot four rounds of 73 to find himself in a playoff with fellow Ryder Cup team-mate Craig Wood. In those days the playoff was decided over 36 holes, and Shute won the championship by five strokes from Wood.

A winner of 15 tournaments on the US Tour during his career, Shute's two finest seasons in the US came in 1936 and 1937. He won the USPGA Championship

both seasons to establish himself as one of the US's best players during the 1930s. The slightly built professional had already been involved in one USPGA final, when he lost the 1931 championship to Tom Creavy. Despite the fact that Creavy was a young unknown, Shute lost by a score of two and one when he bogeyed the 35th hole.

Five years later Shute atoned for his loss to Creavy when he beat the long-hitting Jimmy Thomson three and two in the final. Shute was as much as 60 yards behind Thomson off the tee, but accurate approach shots and excellent putting allowed him to stay ahead of his opponent. When he hit a spectacular second shot to three feet of the 34th hole, a par-5, and knocked in the eagle putt. Shute had won his first USPGA title.

A year later, Shute successfully defended the championship when he defeated the 1936 US Open champion Tony Manero one up in a semi-final that was billed the battle of the champions, then took care of Harold McSpaden by the same score in the deciding match.

Shute came close to winning the US Open in 1939. He tied for the 72-hole lead with Byron Nelson and Craig Wood but shot 76 in the playoff as Nelson went on to win the title.

# Jay Sigel

JAY SIGEL SPENT MOST OF HIS GOLFING CAREER AS AN AMATEUR, WINNING MANY BIG TITLES. HE TURNED PROFESSIONAL UPON TURNING 50 AND WENT ON TO WIN A LOT OF MONEY ON THE SENIOR TOUR.

Jay Sigel was a career amateur player until the riches of senior golf lured him into professional golf. It was a wise career move—in his first four years as a professional he earned $3.5 million.

Sigel wasn't just any amateur player, he was America's pre-eminent amateur player. In fact, during his time he was the best amateur in the world. The Pennsylvania native captured every top amateur championship worth winning, including the British Amateur Championship, back-to-back US Amateur Championships and three US Mid-Amateur Championships. Between 1977 and 1993, Sigel played in every Walker Cup, setting a record for the most matches played in the event by any player on either side.

His total of 33 matches easily eclipses the 25 played by Sir Michael Bonallack. In an age when good amateur players readily jump to the lucrative professional tours in Europe and America, it's probably a safe bet to say that Sigel's appearance record will stand for a long time. So, too, will his record for the most wins in the biennial competition. Of his 33 matches Sigel won 18, lost ten, and halved just five. Indeed, of the nine contests in which he played, Sigel only ever appeared on one losing side. That occurred in 1989 at Peachtree Golf Club in Atlanta, when the Great Britain & Ireland side shocked the Americans with a one-point victory. Ironically, it was a slip-up by Sigel that cost America the cup.

In the final day's singles, Sigel was up against Jim Milligan, a 26-year-old Scottish joiner. With just three holes to play, Sigel was two holes to the good, and cruising. His point would give America the victory. However, he lost the 16th to a birdie, the 17th to a par, and when he double bogeyed the 18th, Milligan had won the point that gave Great Britain & Ireland the cup.

Sigel made up for the gaffe by winning four of the next six matches he played in his last two competitions, helping America win both times.

Sigel turned 50 after his last Walker Cup in 1993, and a year later joined the US Senior Tour. He won the GTE West Classic in his senior rookie year when he rallied from ten strokes behind to catch Jim Colbert. He then won the tournament at the fourth playoff hole for his first professional victory. He finished the season as the Senior Tour's Rookie of the Year.

A mighty long hitter of the ball, Sigel was always going to do well in senior golf. So it has proved. Through the 1998 season he had won six tournaments.

## Fact File

**BORN** 1943, Narberth, Pennsylvania, USA

**CAREER HIGHLIGHTS**
1979 British Amateur
1982 US Amateur
1983 US Amateur
1997 Bruno's Memorial Classic
1998 Bell Atlantic Classic

**INTERNATIONAL HONORS**
Walker Cup: 1977, 1979, 1981, 1983 (captain), 1985, 1987, 1989, 1991, 1993

# Scott Simpson

SCOTT SIMPSON'S BIGGEST CAREER WIN CAME IN THE 1987 US OPEN CHAMPIONSHIP AT THE OLYMPIC CLUB IN SAN FRANCISCO, A VICTORY THAT BROKE MANY HEARTS.

## Fact File

**BORN** 1955, San Diego, California, USA

**CAREER HIGHLIGHTS**
1980 Western Open
1987 US Open
1989 BellSouth Atlanta Classic
1993 Byron Nelson Classic

**INTERNATIONAL HONORS**
Ryder Cup: 1987
Walker Cup: 1977

Scott Simpson is one of a trio of golfers who have broken hearts in San Francisco. It was there that the tall professional earned his most famous victory.

The Olympic Club in San Francisco has been the scene of a few upsets in the US Open Championship over the years. Unknown Jack Fleck defeated the immortal Ben Hogan there in 1955, Billy Casper denied Arnold Palmer the championship on that course in 1966, and Simpson became part of that trio in 1987.

Tom Watson was the sentimental favorite at the Olympic Club in the 1987 US Open. Watson had spent several majorless years and almost the entire golfing world was willing him on to victory. Everyone except Scott Simpson and his small band of supporters. The San Diego native trailed Watson by one stroke heading into the final round but fashioned a final round 68, including three birdies on the back nine, to take the title deservedly by one stroke from Watson.

Simpson came close to another US Open title in 1991, leading the championship with three holes to play, he bogeyed two of the holes and found himself in a playoff with Payne Stewart. Simpson also led the playoff but again found trouble over the last three holes, bogeying each one to hand the title to Stewart.

That Simpson has done so well in America's national championship comes as no surprise. The 6-foot, 2-inch professional is a player who hits the ball straight, keeps it in play, and can grind out a score—exactly the type of player who wins the US Open.

There is nothing flamboyant about Simpson. In fact, he is one of the quietest players in the game. A deeply religious man who lists Bible study as one of his hobbies, Simpson lets his clubs do the talking for him. He was a brilliant amateur player at the University of Southern California where he gained a degree in business administration. There he was an All-American and twice won back-to-back NCAA Championships in 1976 and 1977.

Simpson turned professional in 1977, and by 1980 he had triumphed in the Western Open, winning the prestigious title by five strokes from Andy Bean. Through the 1998 season he recorded six victories on the US Tour as well as three wins in Japan, including two Chunichi Crowns.

A good friend of the actor/comedian Bill Murray, whom he partners in the annual AT&T Pebble Beach National Pro-Am, Simpson has for many years hosted a pro-am in Los Angeles established to help a local home for brain-injured children

# Vijay Singh

VIJAY SINGH'S WIN AT THE 1998 USPGA CHAMPIONSHIP AT THE SAHALEE COUNTRY CLUB IN SEATTLE WAS JUST REWARD FOR ALL THE HARD WORK HE HAD PUT IN DURING HIS CAREER.

Vijay Singh is well named. His first name means "victory" in Hindu, and he's more than lived up to the title.

Singh is the only Fijian golfer to win a major championship; in fact, he is the only golfer from the Pacific island to find success in professional golf. It's an island not noted for golf. Rugby is the main sport, so Singh was something of an oddity growing up.

The tall, powerful swinger had to find places to play when he was learning his craft, and his travels took him to many out of the way destinations far removed from the golfing hot spots of the world. For two years, Singh worked as a club professional in Borneo, where he would often hit balls in temperatures exceeding 100°F (38°C). Not that he minded much; Singh is noted for his love of practice.

Stories abound about Singh's work ethic. He is one of the hardest workers in world golf. At any golf tournament he plays, you will usually find him on the practice ground beating ball after ball after ball. European Tour pros used to joke that the Tour was going to install lights on every European practice ground so Vijay could hit more balls, for he would always be the last one to leave.

The hard work has paid off. After serving his time by winning tournaments like the Malaysian PGA Championship, the Nigerian Open, and the Ivory Coast Open, among others, in the 1980s, Singh finally qualified for the European Tour in 1988 on his second attempt. He made his European breakthrough in his rookie year, winning the Volvo Open. After four European victories through the 1992 season, Singh joined the US Tour where he found even greater success.

Singh also won in his first year on the US Tour, taking the 1993 Buick Classic in a playoff with Mark Wiebe. The win helped him earn the Rookie of the Year Award. Two victories followed in 1995, and another two in 1997, including the prestigious Memorial Tournament. Then came his best season to date.

Singh's victory in the 1998 USPGA Championship at Sahalee Country Club in Seattle, Washington, was both justification and reward for all the hard work he has put in throughout his career. Singh led from the second round and never looked like faltering. He eventually won by two shots from Steve Stricker after holing a number of clutch putts throughout the four days.

Experts agree that Singh's first major championship victory won't be his last.

## Fact File

**BORN** 1963, Lautoka, Fiji

**CAREER HIGHLIGHTS**
1989 Volvo Open
1993 Buick Classic
1994 Lancôme Trophy
1997 Memorial Tournament
1998 USPGA Championship

**INTERNATIONAL HONORS**
Presidents Cup: 1994, 1996, 1998

# Jeff Sluman

A BRILLIANT FINAL ROUND 65 IN THE 1988 USPGA CHAMPIONSHIP EARNED JEFF SLUMAN HIS FIRST MAJOR CHAMPIONSHIP. HE THEN WAITED NINE YEARS UNTIL HIS NEXT WIN.

## Fact File

**BORN** 1957, Rochester, New York, USA

**CAREER HIGHLIGHTS**
1985 Tallahassee Open
1988 USPGA Championship
1997 Tucson Chrysler Classic
1998 Greater Milwaukee Open

Jeff Sluman should have won the 1987 Players Championship. In a playoff with Sandy Lyle, Sluman had a short birdie putt at the 17th hole for victory. While he was settled over the ball, a drunken fan jumped into the water that surrounds the green. His concentration disturbed, Sluman backed off the shot. When he finally hit the putt he missed and eventually lost the title to Lyle.

Sluman was gracious enough to say later that he didn't think the fan had a bearing on the putt, but given that it was for his first US Tour victory, the interruption was the last thing he needed. A year later, Sluman put the incident behind him when he won his first US Tour event, and it was one of the biggest in golf, too.

The 1988 USPGA Championship was held at Oak Tree Golf Club in Edmond, Oklahoma, a difficult course that is rated one of the hardest in the United States. Sluman made it look like one of the easiest. Despite trailing Paul Azinger by three shots going into the final round, Sluman won the title with a brilliant closing 65 that included an eagle on the par-5, 9th hole when he holed a 100-yard wedge shot. Sluman ran out a three-stroke winner over Azinger to win his first major championship.

Slightly built and one of the shortest players on the US Tour at just 5 feet 7 inches, Sluman has proved that it doesn't take enormous power to compete at the highest level. The strength of Sluman's game lies in his ability to put together good scores. Annually he ranks high in the scoring average statistics kept by the US Tour.

But Sluman's USPGA win didn't exactly open the floodgates. He went another nine seasons before he won his second official US Tour event. In that period he had many second place finishes, including runner-up in the 1992 US Open at Pebble Beach when he was one of only four players to return sub-par rounds in difficult conditions on the final day. In 1992, he recorded the first ever hole in one at the par-3 4th hole in the Masters, and eventually finished fourth.

A one-time player director on the PGA Tour policy board, the popular player finally cracked the winner's circle again when he triumphed in Tucson in 1997. He added another victory in 1998 when he won the Greater Milwaukee Open to earn $340,000, the largest check of his career.

# ALEX SMITH

ALEX SMITH WAS ONE OF THREE GOLFING BROTHERS TO EMIGRATE TO THE UNITED STATES FROM CARNOUSTIE AT THE TURN OF THE 20TH CENTURY, FINDING MUCH SUCCESS. SMITH WON TWO US OPENS DURING HIS CAREER.

Alex Smith was one of a band of Scottish professionals who emigrated to America at the turn of the century and completely dominated the early days of American golf.

Brought up in Carnoustie on the east coast of Scotland, Smith learned his golf over the town's championship links. There can be no better place to learn to play golf than Carnoustie, and his education there was to make him one of the most successful Scotsmen to play on American soil.

Smith gained fame for his performances in both the Western and US Opens. In Smith's day the Western Open was considered one of the biggest championships in golf, a major at the time. Smith won the title twice, in 1903 and 1906. Indeed, when Smith won the 1906 title and the US Open the same year, he emulated his brother Willie, who had captured the two titles in 1899. Moreover, his 1906 victory was at the expense of his brother. Willie finished runner-up in 1906, seven strokes behind Alex.

His performance in 1906 was notable for another reason—it was the first time any player had broken 300 for four rounds of the US Open. The previous best score had been 303 by Willie Anderson in 1904, but Smith smashed that score by eight shots, recording a 72-hole score of 295 at the Onwentsia Club in Lake Forest, Illinois. The Scotsman was never over 75 in any round, shooting scores of 73, 74, 73, and 75.

Alex's second US Open win also came at the expense of another Smith sibling, younger brother MacDonald. He was arguably the best golfer of the Smith brothers, but he never managed to win a major championship like his two older brothers. In 1910, Alex denied MacDonald the title when he defeated him and John McDermott in a playoff at the Philadelphia Cricket Club after the three had tied on 298. Alex shot 71 in the extra round, to Macdonald's 77 and McDermott's 75 to lift his second and last US Open title.

Alex could have won more than just the two championships. On three other occasions he finished runner-up. In 1898 he placed a distant seven shots behind Fred Herd. He lost a playoff by one stroke to Willie Anderson at the Myopia Hunt Club in 1901, scoring 86 to Anderson's 85. He also lost to Anderson in 1905, finishing two strokes behind Anderson's winning total of 314.

## FACT FILE

**BORN** 1872, Carnoustie, Angus, Scotland

**DIED** 1930

**CAREER HIGHLIGHTS**
1903 Western Open
1906 US Open
1906 Western Open
1910 US Open

# Horton Smith

HORTON SMITH HOLDS THE DISTINCTION OF BEING THE FIRST PLAYER TO WIN THE MASTERS, TAKING THE INAUGURAL TITLE IN 1934. SMITH ALSO WON THE TOURNAMENT IN 1936.

## Fact File

**BORN** 1908, Springfield, Missouri, USA

**DIED** 1963

**CAREER HIGHLIGHTS**
1929 Fort Myers Open
1934 Masters
1936 Masters
1941 Florida West Coast Open

**INTERNATIONAL HONORS**
Ryder Cup: 1929, 1931, 1933, 1935, 1937

Horton Smith will be forever remembered in trivia quizzes as the first player to win the Masters, a tournament he eventually won twice.

Augusta National, home of the Masters, is noted for fast, sloping greens and only the best putters in the world win there. It's no surprise then that Horton won the tournament twice, because in his day he was reputedly the best putter in the world. Bernard Darwin once said as much when he wrote, "The United States have sent us a number of great putters from whom to choose models, but I am disposed to doubt if they have sent a better than Horton Smith."

Smith once defined the importance of putting in golf when he said, "Too much is done with too little thought—it must always be mind over putter!"

It wasn't just his putter that helped him win tournaments, though. He was recognized as one of the finest swingers of a golf club of his generation. Not surprisingly, Darwin had something to say about that, too. The revered journalist called Smith "a joy to watch, easy, elegant and of a horrid certainty."

Smith had used his graceful swing and sure putting touch to good effect prior to the Masters. In 1929 he won no less than eight tournaments on the American professional circuit to finish the season as leading money winner. Throughout his career he would record 32 tournament victories in America. As of the 1998 season that tally placed him 12th on the all-time list of tournament winners in America. Moreover, in 1936 Smith led the money list with just under $8,000, a lot of money in the 1930s.

His brilliant 1929 season earned him his first Ryder Cup appearance, and the elegant swinger was well worthy of his place in the squad. Smith played once in a losing cause at Moortown Golf Club in Leeds, England. He was one of only two Americans on the final day to record singles victories—the other was Leo Diegel—when he won his match with Fred Robson by a score of four and two. Smith never lost a match in the competition. Of his four matches he won three and halved one.

Smith was a contemporary of the indomitable Walter Hagen, and the two were great friends. Smith once accompanied Hagen on a round-the-world golf exhibition.

Tragically, Smith's career was cut short when he broke his wrist in a car accident while being driven by a friend. He was never the same player after that.

# MACDONALD SMITH



MACDONALD SMITH WAS THE BEST OF THE THREE SMITH BROTHERS FROM CARNOUSTIE, SCOTLAND, YET THE TALENTED SCOTSMAN NEVER MANAGED TO WIN A MAJOR TITLE.

MacDonald Smith was probably the best of the Smith brothers who emigrated from Carnoustie to America at the turn of the century.

The younger brother of Alex and Willie, who between them captured three US Opens, Macdonald never won a major championship. He was close on a number of occasions, but he never managed to win a tournament that would have capped his career. His failure to do so makes him another of those players eligible for the unwanted title of best player to have never won a major.

Like his older brothers, Macdonald learned golf on the windswept links of Carnoustie. And like his siblings he found success in America. Before he was 20 years old Smith had tied for the US Open, only to lose a playoff to his brother Alex, when Alex won his second title in 1910. Twenty years later, Smith finished runner-up to Bobby Jones at Interlachan in the year of Jones's grand slam. Smith finished two strokes behind Jones's 287 total.

Smith also came close to winning the British Open on a number of occasions. As fate would have it, he also finished second to Jones in the 1930 championship at Hoylake, again by the margin of two strokes. Two years later he finished second to Gene Sarazen at Prince's in Kent, England, five shots adrift of Sarazen's winning total of 283.

Another chance in the British championship came at Prestwick in 1925. On that occasion, the Scottish crowds were rooting for Smith so much that his concentration was upset just when he needed it most. All he required in the final round was a 78, but he scored 82 to hand the title to Jim Barnes.

A quiet man with a most elegant swing, Smith actually quit the professional scene for a few years and went to work in a shipyard. He returned, however, in 1923 and went on to win many tournaments. He would eventually go on to win 24 times on the American circuit, far in excess of his brothers. He won five times in the 1926 season alone. He was always a threat in the Western and Los Angeles Opens, two huge tournaments at the time. He won the Western title three times and triumphed four times in the Los Angeles tournament, including back-to-back victories in 1928 and 1929.

## FACT FILE

**BORN** 1890, Carnoustie, Angus, Scotland

**DIED** 1949

**CAREER HIGHLIGHTS**
1912 Western Open
1925 Western Open
1926 Canadian Open
1933 Western Open
1933 Los Angeles Open

# Europe Wins after 28-Year Wait

One photograph captures the jubilant scenes that surrounded Europe's historic Ryder Cup victory at The Belfry in 1985. It depicts Sam Torrance standing on the final green with his arms spread wide in victory, tears streaming down his face, after defeating Andy North to clinch Europe's first Ryder Cup in 28 years. After that, it was bedlam. The European team climbed atop the roof of the Belfry Hotel and sprayed champagne, the aircraft, Concorde did a victory flight over the course, and the party lasted well into the night.

Despite the years of total domination by the Americans, the win at The Belfry was not surprising. Two years earlier, Europe had come close to victory. They lost to the American side by just one point. Only a brilliant wedge shot by Lanny Wadkins on the last hole saved the match from being tied. The shot allowed Wadkins to halve his match with Jose Maria Canizares. There would be no such American magic in 1985.

In Nick Faldo, Bernhard Langer, Seve Ballesteros, and Sandy Lyle, European captain Tony Jacklin had a solid team with which to build a winning squad. Throw in experienced players like Ken Brown, Jose Maria Canizares, Manuel Pinero, Ian Woosnam, Howard Clark and Sam Torrance, plus Ryder Cup rookies Jose Rivero and Paul Way, and this was a team without fear of the Americans. Then there was Jacklin.

Jacklin was an inspirational leader. The former British and US Open winner had never been overawed by the Americans, and he certainly didn't fear them as a Ryder Cup player or captain. Upon taking the job, he had insisted his side be treated as champions by demanding they fly first class, stay in five-star hotels and dress like a championship side. He also drummed into his players the fact that they were good enough to beat the Americans. So it proved.

The U.S.A. took the lead after the first day, squeezing out a one-point lead after dominating the morning foursomes by three matches to one. On the second day, Craig Stadler, playing with Curtis Strange, missed a short putt on the final green to give Langer and Lyle a half point in their fourballs match. That seemed to turn the tide in Europe's favor. The home side won the afternoon foursomes three matches to one to take a two-point lead into the singles. Europe only needed five-and-a-half points from the 12 on offer to win.

Five of the six Europeans out before Torrance on Sunday helped put the Scotsman into a position to win Europe the cup. Pinero beat Wadkins three and one, Way defeated Ray Floyd two up, Ballesteros halved with Tom Kite, Lyle defeated Peter Jacobsen three and two, and Langer easily downed Hal Sutton five and four. Only Ian Woosnam lost his singles match, going down two and one to Stadler. The scene was set for Torrance's finest hour. The Scotsman was three down in his match to North, but by the time they came to the 18th tee they were all square. Torrance hit a huge drive down the 18th fairway while North hooked his into the lake. It took the American four strokes to reach the green, Torrance two. When the home player knocked in his 18 foot birdie putt, the home crowd produced a thunderous ovation. After 28 years, Europe had finally won the Ryder Cup.

ABOVE: SAM TORRANCE'S GREATEST MOMENT. THE SCOTSMAN'S SINGLES VICTORY OVER ANDY NORTH SEALED EUROPEAN VICTORY IN 1985.

RIGHT: BERNHARD LANGER CELEBRATES AFTER HOLING A PUTT AGAINST THE UNITED STATES AT THE BELFRY.

TOP RIGHT: THE SPANISH CONNECTION. FROM LEFT TO RIGHT: MANUEL PINERO, SEVE BALLESTEROS, JOSE MARIA CANIZARES AND JOSE RIVERO PLAYED A BIG PART IN EUROPE'S HISTORIC WIN.

FAR RIGHT: A BELOW PAR NICK FALDO ONLY PLAYED TWICE IN THE MATCH, LOSING BOTH TIMES.

# SAM SNEAD

"SLAMMIN SAM" SNEAD WAS ONE OF THE GREATEST SWINGERS OF A GOLF CLUB EVER TO GRACE THE FAIRWAYS OF THE WORLD. SNEAD WON A RECORD 81 TIMES ON THE US TOUR.

## FACT FILE

**BORN** 1912, Hot Springs, Virginia, USA

**CAREER HIGHLIGHTS**
1942 USPGA Championship
1946 The Open Championship
1949 Masters
1949 USPGA Championship
1951 USPGA Championship
1952 Masters
1954 Masters

**INTERNATIONAL HONORS**
Ryder Cup: 1937, 1947, 1949, 1951, 1953, 1955, 1959

No male professional golfer has won more American tournaments than Sam Snead. His total of 81 far exceeds that of Jack Nicklaus (70), Ben Hogan (63), Arnold Palmer (60), or Byron Nelson (52). Indeed, it's mark that may stand forever.

Slammin' Sam, as he is referred to, is one of the immortals of the game, a player who was born in the same year as his two great contemporaries and rivals, Hogan and Nelson. Unlike those two, though, who caught the eye of experts as youngsters growing up in Texas, Snead came out of nowhere.

Snead's background as a barefoot hillbilly from the backwoods of Virginia has become part of golfing lore. It is often difficult to separate fact from fiction, for stories about Snead abound: how he started playing barefoot because he was too poor to afford shoes; how he once took the branch of a swamp maple tree, made a club out of it and shot 72; how he once said that a photo of him in the *New York Times* had to be a fake because he had never been to the city.

Whether or not the stories are true, the indisputable fact is that Sam Snead was one of the best swingers the game has ever seen.

A natural athlete with superb coordination and agility, Snead's swing was graceful and elegant. No less than the late Sir Henry Cotton marveled at Snead's golf swing, calling it "perhaps the greatest ever."

As his tournament tally indicates, Snead's swing earned him a lot of money during his career. Besides his tournament victories, Snead was one of the biggest hustlers in the game, making a lot of dollars in money games against pros and amateurs alike.

By 1942 Snead had won his first major championship, taking the first of three USPGA Championships. He recorded his only British Open victory at St Andrews in 1946, when he triumphed by four strokes over Bobby Locke and Johnny Bulla. His first of three Masters wins came in 1949. Then he shared the title with Ben Hogan over the next four years as both men won the tournament twice. Indeed, Snead's last victory came in a playoff with Hogan for the 1954 title.

The only blot on Snead's career is his failure to win the US Open. He finished runner-up in his national championship four times, including a playoff to Lew Worsham for the 1947 title. His biggest heartbreak, though, came in 1939. He needed only a five at the par-5, final hole to win, or a bogey to tie but took eight to finish fifth behind Nelson.

Snead still thrills fans every year at the Masters, where he is one of the honorary starters.

# Annika Sorenstam

**THERE HAVE BEEN MANY GREAT GOLFERS TO COME OUT OF SWEDEN, BUT ANNIKA SORENSTAM IS PROBABLY THE BEST. DURING THE LATE 1990S SHE WAS ARGUABLY THE BEST GOLFER IN THE WORLD.**

When Annika Sorenstam won the 1996 US Women's Open at Pine Needles Golf Club in Southern Pines, Georgia, she became the first foreign player to win the championship in consecutive years, and only the sixth woman to defend the title successfully.

There was no one to touch Sorenstam in the 1996 championship. She romped away with the title, winning by six strokes over Kris Tschetter, the largest margin of victory in the tournament since Amy Alcott won by nine shots in 1980. The Swede's golf was simply phenomenal. She started with a 70, then fired rounds of 67, 69, and a closing 66 to seal the victory. Sorenstam missed only five fairways all week and made 16 birdies and an eagle in her 72 holes, leading Tschetter to remark, "What golf course is she playing anyway?"

Sorenstam's first victory in the US Women's Open wasn't quite as clear cut, but it was just as impressive. In 1995 at The Broadmoor in Colorado Springs, she had come from five shots behind the experienced Meg Mallon to win the title. It was Sorenstam's debut in the tournament, and her first LPGA win. While many players couldn't have coped with the pressure of contending their first US Women's Open, Sorenstam didn't see what the fuss was all about. "Other players have won for the first time in the US Open, so why not me?" said the Swede.

That Sorenstam would win majors was always obvious. She was a stand out at the University of Arizona, winning seven collegiate titles and earning the 1991 College Player of the Year award in a season that saw her win the NCAA championship. Moreover, as an amateur Sorenstam had been a member of the Swedish national team from 1987 to 1992, and in 1992 she won the World Amateur Championship.

After her successful college career, Sorenstam joined the European Tour and was the 1993 Rookie of the Year. She also picked up that award on the LPGA Tour when she moved across the Atlantic for the 1994 season. Since then she has been the best player in women's golf.

By the end of the 1998 season, Sorenstam had won 16 times in America. She had won the Player of the Year award three times in four years, in 1995, 1996, and 1998. She also won the Vare Trophy in those years, an award that goes to the player with the lowest scoring average on the LPGA Tour. Her 69.99 in 1998 set an all-time LPGA record for the lowest stroke average ever, the first time any player had broken the 70 barrier.

Quite simply, Sorenstam is a phenomenon.

## Fact File

**BORN** 1970, Stockholm, Sweden

**CAREER HIGHLIGHTS**
1995 US Women's Open
1995 World Championship of Women's Golf
1996 US Women's Open
1996 World Championship of Women's Golf
1997 Tournament of Champions

**INTERNATIONAL HONORS**
Solheim Cup: 1994, 1996, 1998

# Mike Souchak

MIKE SOUCHAK IS A HUGE MAN WHO HIT THE BALL GREAT DISTANCES IN HIS PRIME. HE ONCE SET A US TOUR RECORD BY SHOOTING 27 FOR NINE HOLES.

## Fact File

**BORN** 1927, Berwick, Pennsylvania, USA

**CAREER HIGHLIGHTS**
1955 Texas Open
1959 Tournament of Champions
1959 Western Open
1960 San Diego Open Invitational
1961 Greater Greensboro Open

**INTERNATIONAL HONORS**
Ryder Cup: 1959, 1961

When John Huston won the 1998 Hawaiian Open, he broke a record Mike Souchak had shared with Ben Hogan for 43 years. Huston's 28 under par score was one better than the 27 under that Souchak recorded in winning the 1955 Texas Open and the score by which Hogan won the 1945 Portland Open.

A huge man who in his prime, hit the ball for miles, Souchak still holds the record for the lowest 72-hole total. His 257 in Texas still stands. Souchak's margin of victory at Brackenridge Park Golf Club in San Antonio was by seven strokes over Fred Haas. Souchak shot rounds of 60, 68, 64, and 65 in compiling his 257. Over the final nine holes of his first round, Souchak shot 27 with scores of 2, 4, 4, 3, 3, 3, 3, and 2. Souchak still shares that nine-hole record with Andy North.

Souchak turned professional in 1952 after serving time in the US Navy. During his career he won 15 tournaments, although he was never able to win a major championship. He had a chance to win the 1959 USPGA Championship at Minneapolis Golf Club in Minnesota. He was two behind the lead going into the final round, but a closing 74 saw him slip back to fifth place.

The big-hitting professional was a good enough player to earn his way onto two American Ryder Cup teams in 1959 and 1961, where he had a sterling record. From the six matches he played, Souchak won five and lost just the one, a foursomes match at Royal Lytham & St Annes in the 1961 match, when he and Bill Collins lost four and two to Dai Rees and Ken Bousfield.

Souchak was undefeated in Ryder Cup singles play, recording victories over Bousfield in 1959, and defeating Ralph Moffitt and Bernard Hunt in 1961. Souchak was one of the top American points earners in 1961, taking three from the four matches he played.

Besides his phenomenal scoring in the Texas Open, the highlight of Souchak's career came in 1959 when he won the Western Open, an event that was considered a major in Souchak's day. The Pennsylvania professional had finished runner-up in the tournament in 1955 when he finished two strokes behind Cary Middlecoff. In 1959, at the Pittsburgh Field Club, he got the better of Arnold Palmer by one stroke to take the prestigious title.

Souchak's name will be in the US Tour record books until someone shoots 256, which may take some time.

# HOLLIS STACY

HOLLIS STACY'S NICKNAME IS "SPACY STACY" BECAUSE HER CONCENTRATION TENDS TO WANDER. SHE KEPT HER FOCUS IN THE 1977 AND 1978 US WOMEN'S OPEN, WINNING THE TITLE BOTH YEARS.

Hollis Stacy grew up in a family of ten children in Savannah, Georgia, and went on to become one of the best players on the LPGA Tour.

Hollis was taken to the Masters when she was a girl. It was there that she found the golf swing she would copy for the rest of her life. "When I was young I went to the Masters at Augusta, where I got autographs and watched Julius Boros. He was my idol. I would imitate his swing and copy his tempo, and he remained one of my favorites," Stacy once revealed. The Savannah native picked an excellent role model—Boros's swing earned him three major championships.

Stacy possesses one of the most elegant swings in the game, a natural action that is fluid and rhythmical. She has used it to good effect over the years.

As an amateur she won three consecutive USGA Junior Girls' Championships between 1969 and 1971, one of only two players to win three in a row. Her 1969 victory came when she was just 15 years and four months, making her the youngest player ever to take the title. Stacy also won the 1970 North and South Open and played on the 1972 Curtis Cup team.

It came as no surprise when Stacy won the 1977 Lady Tara Classic, just three years after turning professional. She was helped to victory by the intervention of her father, who approached her on the 12th hole of the final round and told her to "quit choking." Stacy promptly reeled off four birdies in the next six holes to win the tournament by one shot from JoAnne Carner.

Her first win out of the way, Stacy immediately set her sights on winning a major that year. It came when she triumphed in the US Women's Open at Hazeltine Golf Club in Chaska, Minnesota. In 100°F and high humidity, Stacy won the title by two strokes from Nancy Lopez. A year later Stacy defended her title when she won the championship in Indianapolis. A third victory came in 1984, making her one of only four women to win the prestigious title three times.

Needless to say, the US Open is the tournament Stacy puts above every other in golf. She admits to the fact that she often can't get motivated in regular LPGA events and often loses interest. In fact, she is noted for her wandering mind, which has earned her the nickname "Spacy Stacy." The US Open, however, always gets her full attention.

## FACT FILE

**BORN** 1954, Savannah, Georgia, USA

**CAREER HIGHLIGHTS**
1977 US Women's Open
1978 US Women's Open
1979 Mayflower Classic
1984 US Women's Open
1991 Crestar-Farm Fresh Classic

**INTERNATIONAL HONORS**
Curtis Cup: 1972

# CRAIG STADLER

CRAIG STADLER NEVER HIDES HIS EMOTIONS ON THE GOLF COURSE. ONE LOOK AT HIS FACE WILL TELL YOU JUST HOW WELL OR HOW POORLY STADLER IS PLAYING.

## FACT FILE

**BORN** 1953, San Diego, California, USA

**CAREER HIGHLIGHTS**
1973 US Amateur
1982 Masters
1982 World Series of Golf
1991 Tour Championship
1996 Nissan Open

**INTERNATIONAL HONORS**
Ryder Cup: 1983, 1985
Walker Cup: 1975

Craig Stadler is the most expressive player to play golf in the modern age. One look at Stadler and it is immediately obvious what his mood is like. He, more than any other golfer, wears his emotions well and truly on his sleeve.

Known as "the Walrus" for his uncanny resemblance to the animal, Stadler first found fame when he won the 1973 US Amateur Championship at the Inverness Club in Toledo, Ohio. He also won All-American honors twice while he was at the University of Southern California.

Stadler turned professional in 1975 and joined the US Tour in 1976. Within four years he had won his first tournament, the Bob Hope Desert Classic, and within two he had won the US Tour's Order of Merit.

The 1982 season remains Stadler's best ever as a professional. He won four tournaments that year, including his first major championship, the Masters. Despite starting the tournament with a 75 in the first round, the Walrus bounced back to get into a playoff for the title with Dan Pohl. A par at the first extra hole, the tenth, to Pohl's bogey earned Stadler the green jacket.

Stadler closed out his season by winning the World Series of Golf. A closing 65 made up five shots on the lead and put Stadler into a playoff with Ray Floyd, which Stadler won. His four victories that year earned him just short of $450,000, good enough for number one spot and the Arnold Palmer Award that goes to the leading money winner.

By the end of 1998 season, Stadler had recorded 12 victories on the US Tour. Most had come in the 1980s, but victory in the 1996 Nissan Open, formerly the Los Angeles Open, proved that even in his mid 40s the Walrus can still beat the new kids on Tour.

The San Diego native was involved in one of the most bizarre rules of golf incidents ever seen in the game's history. Playing in the 1987 Shearson Lehman Brothers Andy Williams Open, Stadler's ball came to rest under a tree. To save getting his trousers dirty, Stadler knelt on a towel to play his shot. He was disqualified for "building a stance." He eventually got revenge on the tree, however. He was given the honor of felling the tree when tournament officials gave him a chain saw to cut down the then diseased tree. Stadler accepted the task with much relish.

# JAN STEPHENSON

AUSTRALIAN JAN STEPHENSON WAS THE UNOFFICIAL GLAMOR GIRL OF THE LPGA TOUR. THE GOOD-LOOKING AUSTRALIAN MADE MORE OFF THE COURSE THAN SHE DID ON IT. BUT STEPHENSON COULD PLAY.

Jan Stephenson is probably better known for her stunning good looks than her golf. However, Stephenson is more than just a beautiful woman, she is one of the best women golfers ever.

In the 1970s Stephenson appeared on the covers of countless magazines, often in very skimpy clothing. She had the greatest sex appeal of any player in women's golf, and the LPGA capitalized on that to full effect. Indeed, she is probably the only professional golfer to grace the pages of *Playboy* magazine. Stephenson didn't appear nude—she was offered the chance but turned it down—but in a Twenty Questions article.

Stephenson was the dominant player in her homeland in the early 1970s. She won the Australian Open in 1973, and four other tournaments, and gained a lot of publicity. Stephenson joined the LPGA Tour for the 1974 season and earned the Rookie of the Year Award in her first year. She recorded her first victory in the 1976 Sarah Coventry Naples Classic, confirmation that she had ability to match her looks. If there were any doubts of her talent, then she put them to rest when she won her first major in 1981, taking the Du Maurier Classic and winning two other tournaments to finish the season as the fifth highest money winner on the LPGA Tour.

Stephenson won her second major in 1982 when she triumphed in the LPGA Championship. A year later she recorded the biggest victory of her career. The 1983 US Women's Open was held in Tulsa, Oklahoma, in temperatures often reaching 105°F (40°C). The Australian won the championship by one stroke over JoAnne Carner and Patty Sheehan. Stephenson wanted the title so badly that she even went to the length of flying to Chicago during the tournament to take a putting lesson from her coach Ed Oldfield.

Obviously Stephenson's image has put her into conflict with some of her peers, who feel the LPGA should be promoted on the strength of its golf rather than its sex appeal. In 1981 Stephenson posed on a bed in a photograph that appeared in the LPGA's *Fairway* magazine. The image upset a lot of players, and Jane Blalock even went so far as to accuse the LPGA of "quasi-pornography." Needless to say, the ensuing arguments earned the LPGA much publicity.

Stephenson's private life has often been under the public gaze. She has gone through three divorces and lost a lot of money in the process. However, she remains one of the best to play the game, and probably the greatest Australian woman to play at the top level.

## FACT FILE

**BORN** 1951, Sydney, New South Wales, Australia

**CAREER HIGHLIGHTS**
1973 Australian Open
1978 Australian Open
1981 Du Maurier Classic
1982 LPGA Championship
1983 US Women's Open

# Payne Stewart

PAYNE STEWART'S TWO US OPEN WINS IN THE 1990S MAKE HIM ONE OF THE BEST GOLFERS OF THE LAST DECADE OF THE 20TH CENTURY. HIS SECOND US OPEN WIN CAME IN DRAMATIC FASHION.

## Fact File

**BORN** 1957, Springfield, Missouri, USA

**CAREER HIGHLIGHTS**
1982 Quad Cities Classic
1987 Bay Hill Classic
1989 USPGA Championship
1991 US Open
1995 Shell Houston Open
1999 US Open

**INTERNATIONAL HONORS**
Ryder Cup: 1987, 1989, 1991, 1993
World Cup: 1987, 1990
Alfred Dunhill Cup: 1993

There is no mistaking Payne Stewart on a golf course who is easily the most recognizable player in all of golf.

Stewart is one of the most colorful dressers in the game who always wears plus-fours, or knickers, when he competes. At one time he had a contract with the NFL and would adopt the colors of each of the NFL teams on different days. Now he has his own range of clothes.

If you're going to dress loud, as Stewart does, then you'd better be able to back it up. Stewart has no problem doing that. Throughout the 1980s and 90s, he has been one of the most consistent American players. However, it wasn't always that way.

Stewart developed a reputation as something of a choker in the mid 1980s. Even though he had won the 1982 Quad Cities Open and the 1983 Walt Disney World Classic, a string of second place finishes and near misses had people questioning whether he had the nerve to win the big tournaments. Stewart soon proved the doubters wrong.

The Missouri native recorded his first major championship victory when he triumphed in the 1989 USPGA Championship at Kemper Lakes Golf Club in Hawthorn Woods, Illinois. Despite an opening round of 74, two over par, Stewart fought his way into contention with rounds of 66 and 69. Heading into the last round he was tied for 11th spot and needed a good final round to put pressure on Mike Reid. He did just that. Stewart shot 67 on the final day, including a 31 on the inward nine that featured four birdies over the last five holes. Stewart won the title by a shot over Reid and Andy Bean.

Two years later, Stewart added his second major championship when he won the US Open in an 18-hole playoff with Scott Simpson at Hazeltine Golf Club in Chaska, Minnesota. He should have added a second US Open in 1998, when he led the field by four shots heading into the final day at the Olympic Club in San Francisco. A closing 74 saw him lose the title by one stroke to Lee Janzen, who shot 68.

Stewart made up for the disappointment in 1998 by winning the last US Open of the 20th century at Pinehurst in North Carolina. Stewart had to hole three crucial putts over the last three holes, including an 18-foot par putt on the 72nd hole to clinch victory.

# DAVE STOCKTON

DAVE STOCKTON WON TWO USPGA CHAMPIONSHIPS DURING HIS CAREER, AND WAS REWARDED WITH THE CAPTAINCY OF THE US RYDER CUP TEAM IN 1991, WHEN HE LED HIS SIDE TO VICTORY.

Dave Stockton is one of the few professional golfers to have a son follow in his footsteps. Dave Stockton Jr now plays on the US Tour. However, he has a long way to go to match the record of his famous father.

The senior Stockton made a name for himself during the 1960s and 70s when he won 11 times on the US Tour. His two most famous victories came in the USPGA Championships of 1970 and 1976.

In 1970, at the age of 28, Stockton came out of the pack in the third round to take the lead with a fine 66 on the tough Southern Hills Country Club in Tulsa, Oklahoma. Then in the final round, with Arnold Palmer breathing down his neck, Stockton fired a nervy three over par 73 to win the title by two shots from Palmer and Bob Murphy. Stockton nearly threw the tournament away when he put his second shot at the 13th hole into a pond. But made a brilliant recovery when he hit a wedge shot to within inches and salvaged a bogey.

Stockton managed to hold his nerve when he won his second title in 1976 at the Congressional Country Club in Bethesda, Maryland. Stockton shot a level par 70 on the final day to take the title. However, he had to hole a ten-foot par putt on the 72nd hole to avoid a playoff with Ray Floyd and Don January.

The Californian twice played in the Ryder Cup, in 1971 and 1977. His record for the match stands at a very respectable three wins, one loss, and a half from the five matches he played. However, his greatest moment in the biennial competition came in 1991.

The two-time USPGA champion was given the captaincy of the American side for the match at Kiawah Island. It was no easy task, for the Americans had failed to win the competition in their previous three attempts. In one of the closest matches ever, the USA won the Cup by just one point when Bernhard Langer missed a six-foot putt on the last hole. The American players celebrated by throwing Stockton into the nearby Atlantic Ocean.

Stockton now competes on the US Senior Tour, where he has won many times and earned a lot of money. His crowning moment on that circuit came when he won the 1996 US Senior Open by two strokes over Hale Irwin at the Canterbury Country Club in Cleveland, Ohio. Noted throughout his career for his excellent wedge play, his victory in the US Senior Open gave him much satisfaction for the way he played from tee to green, which he said was "as flawless as I have ever played in a major."

## FACT FILE

**BORN** 1941, San Bernardino, California, USA

**CAREER HIGHLIGHTS**
1967 Colonial National Invitation
1970 USPGA Championship
1974 Glen Campbell Los Angeles Open
1976 USPGA Championship
1996 US Senior Open

**INTERNATIONAL HONORS**
Ryder Cup: 1971, 1977, 1991 (captain)
World Cup: 1970, 1976

# FRANK STRANAHAN

FRANK STRANAHAN (RIGHT) WAS ONE OF THE GREATEST AMATEURS EVER TO PLAY THE GAME, WINNING MANY BIG TITLES. HE NEARLY WON THE 1947 BRITISH OPEN AS AN UNPAID PLAYER.

## FACT FILE

**BORN** 1922, Toledo, Ohio, USA

**CAREER HIGHLIGHTS**
1947 Canadian Amateur
1948 Canadian Amateur
1948 British Amateur
1950 British Amateur
1958 Los Angeles Open

**INTERNATIONAL HONORS**
Walker Cup: 1947, 1949, 1951

Frank Stranahan never found much success as a professional golfer, which was strange because he was one of the greatest players ever to grace the unpaid ranks.

Stranahan was almost unbeatable as an amateur. With his list of achievements as an unpaid player, it is almost inconceivable that he didn't win many tournaments as a pro. Stranahan won every major amateur trophy with the exception of the US Amateur. The closest he came in that tournament was a runner-up finish to Sam Urzetta in 1950. Stranahan put up a brave fight and took Urzetta to extra holes, only to lose the match on the 39th hole. That is the only blot on Stranahan's amateur record.

Aside from his failure to win the American championship, Stranahan won five consecutive Tam O'Shanter World Amateur Championships between 1950 and 1954, and six straight Tam O'Shanter All-American Amateur titles between 1949 and 1953. He won the British Amateur Championship twice, taking the title at Royal St George's in 1948 and at St Andrews in 1950. He won the Canadian Amateur twice, the North and South Amateur three times and the Western Amateur four times.

Not surprisingly, he was a stalwart in the American Walker Cup team in his time. He appeared in the biennial competition three times, posting a record of three wins, two losses, and one half from his six matches.

On two occasions Stranahan was close to winning the British Open. In 1947, he came within inches of holing his second shot on the 72nd hole at Hoylake, which would have tied him with Fred Daly. Stranahan placed second. Then he finished runner-up to Ben Hogan at Carnoustie in 1953, four strokes adrift of Hogan's winning margin of 282.

The son of a spark plug millionaire, Stranahan was almost obsessive about his attention to detail. He worked extremely hard on his game and was devoted to a strict physical fitness regime. He would even take weights with him when he traveled abroad.

With very few mountains left to conquer in the amateur game, Stranahan turned professional in 1952. However, he never found the same success as a money player as he did while playing for pride. His biggest moment as a professional came when he triumphed in the 1958 Los Angeles Open, one of the biggest tournaments on the US circuit at the time. Stranahan won the title by three shots from E.J. Harrison at the Rancho Municipal Golf Club in Los Angeles.

# CURTIS STRANGE

CURTIS STRANGE BECAME THE FIRST PLAYER SINCE BEN HOGAN TO WIN BACK TO BACK US OPENS, TAKING THE TITLE IN 1988 AND 1989, AND ONE OF ONLY FIVE MEN TO WIN THE TITLE TWO YEARS IN A ROW.

For a short period during the 1980s Curtis Strange was almost unbeatable. When he was at his best there was nobody who could touch him, especially in the US Open.

Strange made history in 1989 when he successfully defended his US Open title at Oak Hill Country Club in Rochester, New York. Strange's one-shot victory over Chip Beck, Mark McCumber, and Ian Woosnam made him the first player to defend the title successfully since Ben Hogan in 1950 and 1951, and one of only five men to win back-to-back championships.

A year earlier Strange had won his first US Open when he defeated England's Nick Faldo in a playoff for the title at The Country Club in Brookline, Massachusetts. Beat Faldo by four shots in the extra round, Strange shot 71 to the Englishman's 75.

Strange had recorded 17 US Tour victories through the 1998 season. He set a US Tour record in 1988 when he became the first player to break the $1 million barrier in earnings for a single season. Strange ended the year atop the US money list, a feat he also accomplished in 1985 and 1987.

A star on the Wake Forest University golf team, where he was a teammate of Jay Haas, Strange started golf at the age of seven. His father owned the White Sands Country Club in Virginia Beach, Virginia, and Strange spent many hours there as a boy dreaming about holing putts to win the US Open. So, too, did his identical twin brother Alan. Like Curtis, he too played the US Tour, although he never found the same success as his brother.

Strange enjoyed many victories as an amateur. He triumphed in the 1973 Southeastern Amateur, the 1974 NCAA Championship, the 1974 Western Amateur, and in the North and South Amateur Championships of 1975 and 1976. He turned professional in 1976 and joined the US Tour in 1977. It wasn't long before Strange was racking up the wins. His breakthrough came in 1979 when he won the Pensacola Open.

The Virginia native is one of the most intense competitors on the US Tour. He has been known to let his temper get the better of him on the golf course, and on more than one occasion he has "let off steam" to the detriment of his game. Off the golf course, he is one of the nicest people anyone could ever want to meet.

Although he still competes, he also works part-time as a TV commentator for ABC Television.

## FACT FILE

**BORN** 1955, Norfolk, Virginia, USA

**CAREER HIGHLIGHTS**
1985 Canadian Open
1987 Canadian Open
1988 Memorial Tournament
1988 US Open
1989 US Open

**INTERNATIONAL HONORS**
Ryder Cup: 1983, 1985, 1987, 1989, 1995
Alfred Dunhill Cup: 1985, 1987, 1988, 1989, 1990, 1991, 1994
Walker Cup: 1975

# Louise Suggs

LOUISE SUGGS HAD ONE OF THE BEST SWINGS IN THE GAME, MALE OR FEMALE. EVEN THE IMMORTAL BEN HOGAN WAS A GREAT ADMIRER OF THE SUGGS SWING.

## Fact File

**BORN** 1923, Atlanta, Georgia, USA

**CAREER HIGHLIGHTS**
1947 US Women's Amateur
1948 British Ladies' Championship
1949 US Women's Open
1952 US Women's Open
1957 LPGA Championship

**INTERNATIONAL HONORS**
Curtis Cup: 1948

Louise Suggs has had many admirers in the world of golf, not least of whom was Ben Hogan.

Hogan partnered Suggs once in the 1945 Chicago Victory Open at Medinah when Suggs was still an amateur. They won the tournament. When Suggs published a book in 1953 called *Par Golf For Women*, Hogan wrote the foreword. In it he had this to say about his one-time playing partner. "If I were to single out one woman in the world today as a model for any other woman aspiring to ideal golf form it would be Miss Suggs. Her swing combines all the desirable elements of efficiency, timing and coordination. It appears to be completely effortless." High praise indeed from a player many considered to have the greatest golf swing ever.

Suggs virtually grew up on a golf course. Her father, a one-time member of the New York Yankees baseball team, owned a golf course in Lithia Springs, Georgia. There Louise started playing golf when she was ten.

At the age of 14 she had won the Georgia State Championship and went on to do the double of the US Women's Amateur and British Ladies' championships of 1947 and 1948 respectively. By the time she turned professional after her British victory, Suggs was already being called the "Georgia Peach."

The Georgia Peach was just as dominant in the professional ranks as she had been against amateur competition. With her flawless swing and her cool temperament, Suggs could beat anybody on her day, and usually did. In her first full year as a professional, Suggs won three tournaments, including the US Women's Open.

In 1952 Suggs won her second US Open and another five LPGA events from the 11 she contested. A year later she won ten tournaments and $19,568 in prize money to top the money list, a record and a phenomenal sum for women's golf at the time.

One of the founding members of the LPGA Tour, Suggs was rewarded for her commitment to the Tour when she was made LPGA president between 1955 and 1957. She capped off her last year as president by winning her only LPGA Championship.

A proud woman who took offense easily, Suggs quit the LPGA in 1962 when she was fined for not turning up to play a tournament in Milwaukee. Suggs actually started out to play the tournament but decided to return home when she felt her emotional state was not right. She appealed the fine but the LPGA stuck to its guns. Suggs quit the Tour in protest and never played full-time again.

# Hal Sutton

HAL SUTTON MADE A GREAT COMEBACK WHEN HE WON THE 1995 BC OPEN, AFTER SPENDING YEARS IN THE DOLDRUMS. THE VICTORY SPURRED THE 1983 USPGA CHAMPION ON TO MORE WINS IN 1998.

Hal Sutton is one of a number of golfers to be hailed the next Jack Nicklaus—Ben Crenshaw and Greg Norman are just two others to fall into that category. Filling Nicklaus's shoes is no easy task, as Norman and Crenshaw have found out. Nevertheless, Sutton has made himself one of America's top players over a long period of time.

From the time he won the US Amateur Championship in 1980 and was voted College Player of the Year by one of America's leading magazines, Sutton was earmarked for greatness. Within one year of turning professional, Sutton had lived up to expectations, recording his first victory when he won the 1982 Walt Disney World Golf Classic. That win and three second place finishes saw him finish the season in 11th place on the US Tour Order of Merit, good enough for him to take the Rookie of the Year Award. A year later he improved his Order of Merit position by ten places.

Sutton's win in the 1983 USPGA Championship confirmed the Louisiana native as a player for the big occasion. The link with Nicklaus was only strengthened when he beat Nicklaus to win the title.

Sutton opened the 1983 USPGA with a 65 on the tough Riviera Country Club in Los Angeles and a one-shot lead over the field. He then led the tournament from wire to wire with further rounds of 66, 72, and 71. Even a last day charge by Nicklaus, who closed with a 66, could not stop Sutton from earning his first major.

Coupled with his win in the Tournament Players Championship earlier in the year, and a host of other good finishes, Sutton's USPGA victory propelled him to the top of the US money list with just over $426,000. Over the next two years he won four more tournaments, including the 1986 Memorial, Nicklaus's tournament. Then, just as quickly as he had found the winning touch, he lost it.

Between 1986 and 1995, Sutton spent eight years in the golfing wilderness without a victory. His low point came in the 1992 season when he made only eight cuts from the 29 tournaments he entered, finishing the season 185th on the money list.

Sutton found his old form again in 1995 when he won the BC Open, then proved in 1998 that he was still able to win big tournaments. Sutton triumphed twice in the 1998 season, taking the Texas Open and the end of season US Tour Championship.

## Fact File

**BORN** 1958, Shreveport, Louisiana, USA

**CAREER HIGHLIGHTS**
1980 US Amateur
1983 USPGA Championship
1983 Tournament Players Championship
1986 Memorial Tournament
1998 Tour Championship

**INTERNATIONAL HONORS**
Ryder Cup: 1985, 1987
Walker Cup: 1979, 1981

# Freddie Tait

FREDDY TAIT'S CAREER WAS CUT SHORT WHEN HE WAS KILLED IN ACTION IN THE BOER WAR. ALREADY A WINNER OF TWO BRITISH AMATEURS, THERE'S NO TELLING HOW MANY CHAMPIONSHIPS HE WOULD HAVE WON.

## Fact File

**BORN** 1870, Dalkeith, Midlothian, Scotland

**DIED** 1900

**CAREER HIGHLIGHTS**
1896 British Amateur
1898 British Amateur

There is no telling how many British Opens or British Amateur Championships Freddie Tait would have won had he not died at such a young age.

Tait was only 30 when he was killed in the Boer War. Serving in the Black Watch regiment, Tait was leading his men into battle at Koodoosberg Drift in South Africa when he was killed. The Scotsman had already made a name for himself in the world of golf by winning two British Amateurs and coming close in two British Opens.

The son of a professor at Edinburgh University, Tait spent much of his boyhood at St Andrews, where he played golf on the town's famous links. He was an excellent rugby player and cricketer in his youth, but it was at golf that he excelled. One of the strongest amateurs in the game at the time, Tait could hit the ball for miles. A member of the Royal & Ancient Golf Club of St Andrews, Tait once hit a tee shot 340 yards on the 13th hole of the Old Course. True, the shot was hit over frozen ground, but it was a mammoth hit for that era nevertheless. He had a fine touch too, and used it to establish a course record on the Old Course when he scored 77 in 1890. He went round the same layout in 1894 in 72, although it wasn't considered a

record because Tait wasn't playing in a competition.

When Tait won his first British Amateur title at Sandwich in 1896, he did so by defeating Harold Hilton eight and seven in the final. In getting to that stage, however, he had beaten Horace Hutchison, John Ball, John Laidlay, Charles Hutchings, and, G.C. Broadwood, the top amateurs of the period. Two years later Tait added a second title at Hoylake when he defeated Mure Ferguson by the score of seven and five.

Tait came close to winning the British Open in his short career. Twice he finished third in the world's oldest championship. He was just three shots away from a playoff with Harry Vardon and J.H. Taylor at Muirfield in 1896. Two scores of 83 and 84 in the first and third rounds respectively did not help his cause. A year later he missed out on the title at Hoylake when his rounds of 79, 79, 80, and 79 gave him a 317 total, three strokes short of Harold Hilton's winning score.

Tait was well liked in his day. He was known for his forthright views and magnetic personality. He was honored posthumously in 1925 with the creation of the Freddie Tait Cup, presented annually to the top amateur golfer in the South African Open.

# J. H. TAYLOR



J. H. TAYLOR WAS THE LAST SURVIVING MEMBER OF THE GREAT TRIUMVIRATE, THE THREE GOLFERS AT THE TURN OF THE 20TH CENTURY WHO WON 16 BRITISH OPENS BETWEEN THEM. TAYLOR WON FIVE.

When John Henry Taylor died in 1963 just a month short of his 92nd birthday, it marked the passing of the last of the great golfers of the 19th century.

Taylor was one of a trio of British golfers who dominated golf at the turn of the century. Along with Harry Vardon and James Braid, Taylor was part of the Great Triumvirate, who between them would win 16 British Opens.

Born in Northam, Devon, Taylor learned his golf on the famous links of Westward Ho!, and the Royal North Devon Golf Club. It was there that he also spent his retirement, in a house overlooking the course. On the Devon links Taylor developed a swing that was perfect for winning the British Open. It was a short swing with a lot of punch through the ball, perfect for boring shots through the wind.

Taylor was the first of the Great Triumvirate to make his mark on the game. He won his first British Open in 1894 at Sandwich, when his 326 total was good enough for a five-shot victory over Douglas Rolland. A year later he successfully defended his title at St Andrews, when he won by four shots over Sandy Herd. He nearly added a third title the following year when his 316 total tied Harry Vardon. However, Taylor lost the ensuing 36-hole playoff by four shots as Vardon recorded his first of six victories in the British Open.

The Devonshire golfer came close to winning the US Open in 1900 when he finished second on two strokes behind Vardon at the Chicago Golf Club. An 82 in the second round cost Taylor the championship, but he got his own back on Vardon in the British Open that year at St Andrews, when he won his third championship by eight shots over Vardon.

James Braid kept Taylor out of the limelight for a few years and he had to wait until 1909 to add his fourth open title. His fifth and last came at Hoylake in 1913 when he won the championship by eight shots from Ted Ray.

Besides the British Open, Taylor also won the British Professional Match Play twice, the French Open twice and the German Open once. He was responsible for setting up the British Professional Golfers Association, bringing much-needed organization to Britain's club professionals.

In 1949 he was made an honorary member of the Royal & Ancient Golf Club of St Andrews, and in 1957 he was honored with the presidency of the Royal North Devon Golf Club.

## FACT FILE

**BORN** 1871, Northam, Devon, England

**DIED** 1963

**CAREER HIGHLIGHTS**
1894 The Open Championship
1895 The Open Championship
1900 The Open Championship
1909 The Open Championship
1913 The Open Championship

**INTERNATIONAL HONORS**
Ryder Cup: 1933 (captain)

# EUROPE WINS FOR THE FIRST TIME ON US SOIL

Two factors contributed to make the 1987 Ryder Cup at Muirfield Village in Dublin, Ohio, one of the greatest moments in golf. One saw the birth of the greatest partnership ever seen in match play. Two, a first was achieved by the European team.

Muirfield Village saw Jose Maria Olazabal make his debut in the biennial competition. Eyebrows were raised when Tony Jacklin chose the 21-year-old as one of his wild-card selections. Although he had already won two tournaments on the European Tour and finished second on the 1986 European Order of Merit, some felt the Spaniard was just a little green to take part in the intense pressure of a Ryder Cup. Not Jacklin. The European captain saw in Olazabal a tremendous talent. He also saw him as the perfect partner for Seve Ballesteros. The veteran Spaniard had forged a strong alliance with countryman Manuel Pinero in 1985, winning three out of the four matches they contested. The safe bet would have been to select Pinero to partner Ballesteros. However, Ballesteros was used to breaking rookies into the match. In 1983, he teamed with Paul Way, and the pair won three of the four matches they played. Jacklin knew Olazabal was in safe hands. So it proved. The two lost only once in the four matches they competed, going down two and one to the underdog pair of Hal Sutton and Larry Mize in the second day fourballs.

The dynamic duo were the inspiration behind the European team. It was a role they would assume in future Ryder Cups. Through to the 1999 match the two Spaniards had played together 15 times and won 11, halved twice and lost just two matches.

It wasn't just Jacklin's acumen in pairing the two Spaniards that won Europe the cup, but his pairings in general. The unlikely twosome of Nick Faldo and Ian Woosnam was unbeatable, winning three matches and halving the other. So, too, was the pairing of Bernhard Langer and Sandy Lyle. They won all three matches they played together. Europe won the match in the foursomes and fourballs. Of the 16 matches played, the visitors won ten and halved one to take a five-point lead heading into the final day.

In the previous 13 matches played on American soil, the visiting team had yet to win a match. But with Europe dominating the previous two days, it looked an odds-on certainty they would win for the first time in the United States. The home side had other ideas.

The U.S.A. won the singles on the final day easily, but with Europe needing only four points to win the Cup, it was always going to be a difficult proposition for Nicklaus's side to actually win. Howard Clark scored the first European point when he defeated Dan Pohl on the final green. Sam Torrance added a half point when he tied with Larry Mize. Then the unlikely figure of Irishman Eamonn Darcy holed a five-foot putt on the final green to halve his match with Ben Crenshaw. When Langer halved with Larry Nelson, and Ballesteros defeated Curtis Strange two and one, Europe had the Ryder Cup. Gordon Brand Jr's half point against Hal Sutton in the last match gave Europe victory. The Americans had lost the match on home soil for the first time.

ABOVE: IRISHMAN EAMONN DARCY (LEFT) IS ESCORTED OFF THE 18TH BY NICKLAUS AFTER DARCY'S VITAL WIN OVER BEN CRENSHAW.

TOP RIGHT: SEVE BALLESTEROS (RIGHT) RAISES EUROPEAN CAPTAIN TONY JACKLIN'S HAND IN VICTORY.

RIGHT: THE EUROPEAN CELEBRATIONS LASTED WELL INTO THE NIGHT. HERE NICK FALDO CELEBRATES THE HISTORIC EUROPEAN VICTORY.

COME O

# Dave Thomas

DAVE THOMAS WAS ONE OF BRITAIN'S BEST PLAYERS DURING THE 1950S AND '60S, ONLY A POOR SHORT GAME PREVENTED HIM WINNING A MAJOR CHAMPIONSHIP.

## Fact File

**BORN** 1934, Newcastle upon Tyne, England

**CAREER HIGHLIGHTS**
1955 Belgian Open
1958 Dutch Open
1959 French Open
1963 British Professional Match Play
1966 Penfold

**INTERNATIONAL HONORS**
Ryder Cup: 1959, 1963, 1965, 1967
World Cup: 1957, 1958, 1959, 1960, 1961, 1962, 1963, 1966, 1967, 1969, 1970

Dave Thomas is another of those great players who falls into the category, the best player never to have won a major championship, although he came close, very close. Had it not been for one obvious weakness in his game, Thomas might have won the British Open and many other big tournaments in his day.

Thomas had trouble with pitch shots during his career. Although he worked hard to master that vital part of his game, he never did. In his book *Thanks for the Game*, the late Sir Henry Cotton described Thomas's problems with one of the shortest shots in golf. "He simply could not pitch the ball," wrote Cotton. "If you gave him a good lie and a shot from 40 yards or less to the green, he would make an awful mess of it. I tried to help, every other player, friend and coach tried, but we never achieved any lasting success in making Dave play this length of pitch shot well."

It was this problem that probably cost Thomas the 1958 British Open at Royal Lytham & St Annes. His approach shot to the 72nd hole rolled through the back of the green. Down in two shots and Thomas would have won the tournament, but he took three for a bogey and lost the ensuing playoff with Peter Thomson by four shots.

Despite his problems with the pitching wedge, Thomas was one of his generation's best drivers of the ball. A massive player, he hit the ball tremendous distance off the tee, and usually straight. That asset saw him nearly win another British Open, at Muirfield in 1966. That year the course called for accurate driving off the tee, and Thomas did just that. Jack Nicklaus started the championship with rounds of 70, and 67, and was the man to beat. Thomas made up six strokes on Nicklaus by shooting a 69 in the third round. But another 69 in the final round saw him miss a playoff with Nicklaus by just one stroke.

Thomas was a good enough player to play in four Ryder Cup matches, and to represent Wales 11 times in the World Cup. He also won many big tournaments during his career, but because of his weak short game he never quite lived up to expectations.

After his playing days were over, Thomas became a respected golf course architect. One of his creations is The Belfry, scene of so many Ryder Cups which he designed in partnership with Peter Alliss.

# PETER THOMSON

AUSTRALIAN PETER THOMSON WAS THE FIRST PLAYER IN THE MODERN AGE TO WIN THE BRITISH OPEN FIVE TIMES. THOMSON WON THE TOURNAMENT FOUR TIMES IN FIVE YEARS DURING THE 1950S.

Peter Thomson was the first player of the modern era to win the British Open five times, a feat he accomplished in the 1950s and 1960s. Indeed, Thomson is one of only five men to win the coveted title five times, and one of only four to win it three years in succession.

Thomson was the epitome of a player with an old head on young shoulders. He originally took up the game because he lived near a golf course in Melbourne. Thomson taught himself to play the game, developing a swing that was built on sound fundamentals. In 1949, at the age of 19, he had become quite proficient and turned professional.

The lack of tournaments to play in Australia brought Thomson to Great Britain, where he quickly made a name for himself. He finished equal sixth in his first British Open in 1951, when Max Faulkner won the championship at Royal Portrush. He was second to Bobby Locke in 1952 at Royal Lytham, second again the following year at Carnoustie when Ben Hogan won his only British Open. Then came the onslaught.

The 1954 championship saw Thomson take hold of the world's oldest golf tournament with a grip so tight that it seemed he would never let go. Thomson won the title at Royal Birkdale that year, defended his title at St Andrews in 1955, then won his third straight in at Hoylake in 1956. Bobby Locke denied Thomson the chance of winning the title for an unprecedented five straight years when he beat him to the title by three strokes at St Andrews in 1957. However, Thomson returned the following year at Royal Lytham to win his fourth title.

Gary Player won the British title in 1959 and then came the American invasion in 1960, led by Arnold Palmer. Prior to Palmer's involvement in the British Open, only a handful of Americans made the effort to travel to Britain. It was a credit to Thomson's talent that he was able to win his fifth championship at Royal Birkdale in 1965 at a time when the best players in the world were in the field, including Palmer, Player, and Jack Nicklaus.

Besides the British Open, Thomson won a string of tournaments in Britain in the 1950s and 1960s. He won the British PGA Match Play Championship four times, the British Masters twice, and a host of other big tournaments. Although he didn't have the same success across the Atlantic, Thomson also won tournaments in America, including the 1956 Texas Open. His main success in the United States came as a senior golfer. In 1985 he won nine tournaments on the US Senior Tour.

Thomson is one of the most respected players in world golf. An educated man, he has written widely on the game of golf in newspapers and magazines, and has regularly appeared as a TV commentator.

## FACT FILE

**BORN** 1929, Melbourne, Australia

**CAREER HIGHLIGHTS**
1954 The Open Championship
1955 The Open Championship
1956 The Open Championship
1958 The Open Championship
1965 The Open Championship

**INTERNATIONAL HONORS**
World Cup: 1953, 1954, 1955, 1956, 1957, 1959, 1960, 1961, 1962, 1965, 1969
Presidents Cup: 1996

# Cyril Tolley

CYRIL TOLLEY REMAINS THE ONLY PLAYER TO WIN THE FRENCH OPEN AS AN AMATEUR. TOLLEY WON THE TITLE TWICE IN THE 1920S, AS WELL AS TWO BRITISH AMATEUR TITLES.

## Fact File

**BORN** 1895, London, England

**DIED** 1978

**CAREER HIGHLIGHTS**
1920 British Amateur
1924 French Open
1928 French Open
1929 British Amateur

**INTERNATIONAL HONORS**
Walker Cup: 1922, 1923, 1924 (captain), 1926, 1930, 1934

Cyril Tolley was one of the best amateur golfers ever produced in the British Isles, a player with such talent that he was twice able to win a big professional tournament.

Tolley won his first British Amateur Championship in 1920 while he was still an undergraduate at Oxford University. Tolley defeated American Bob Gardener at Muirfield, winning the title at the 37th hole. However, it was by good fortune that he was in the championship at all.

A member of Rye Golf Club on the south coast of England, Tolley served in World War I in a tank regiment. After fighting in the Battle of Ypres in 1917, Tolley was captured later in the year and spent 13 months as a prisoner of war. He was released in December 1918 and a year later entered Oxford, where he started playing golf again.

Tolley's 1920 British Amateur victory came about only because Roger Wethered cajoled him into making the trip to Muirfield from London. Wethered didn't want to go all the way to Scotland by himself and persuaded Tolley to join him. Wethered was knocked out in the second round but Tolley won the championship.

One of the longest drivers of his day, Tolley used his skills to win two French Open titles. In 1924 he defeated a strong field that included Walter Hagen. Tolley finished three shots ahead of Hagen to take the title. He won the championship again four years later, and remains the only amateur player to have won the prestigious tournament.

Tolley added a second British Amateur Championship to his record in 1929 at Royal St George's. He was favorite to win the title again in 1930 at St Andrews but ran into Bobby Jones in the fourth round. It was the year of Jones's grand slam, when he won the US Amateur, US Open, British Open, and British Amateur. However, Tolley came close to stopping Jones's great march to glory.

Jones defeated Tolley at St Andrews by the narrowest of margins. The two men swapped the lead for much of their match and were all square when they came to the 17th. Jones hit an approach shot that seemed headed for disaster but it hit a spectator and Jones was able to halve the hole. The American eventually won the match at the first extra hole.

Tolley was a member of six Walker Cup sides, captaining the team in 1924. In 1938 the Englishman was made chairman of the selectors of the British team, and in 1948 he was given one of the game's ultimate honors by being made captain of the Royal & Ancient Golf Club of St Andrews.

# Sam Torrance

**SAM TORRANCE'S GREATEST MOMENT IN GOLF CAME IN THE 1985 RYDER CUP AT THE BELFRY, WHEN THE SCOTSMAN HOLED THE PUTT THAT GAINED EUROPE THE CUP FOR THE FIRST TIME SINCE 1957.**

The most famous photograph of Sam Torrance is one that takes pride of place in his home in Surrey, England. It depicts Torrance in a red sweater with his arms spread wide on the 18th green at The Belfry in 1985, the scene of one of the most famous European victories in the Ryder Cup.

Prior to 1985, America had lost only one Ryder Cup contest in 42 years, at Lindrick in 1957. Torrance had already played on two losing teams, in 1981 and 1983. The 1985 match made up for the two previous disappointments.

Torrance won his singles match against Andy North in 1985. By doing so he secured the point that gave Europe its famous victory. Tears streamed down Torrance's cheeks as he acknowledged the ovations on the final hole. It was a moment the Scotsman had been dreaming about his entire life.

Not surprisingly, Torrance seems to play his best golf in odd-numbered years, when the Ryder Cup is held. Between 1981 and 1995 Torrance was a perennial member of the European squad, playing in three winning sides and in the tied match of 1989.

Torrance was always going to be a golf professional, even from a small boy. He was given his start by his father Bob, a golf professional and one of the most respected teachers in the game. Torrance senior taught his son well, for Sam has one of the best swings in the game.

It is a credit to the Scotsman's talent that through the 1998 season he was one of the longest serving members of the European Tour. The 1998 campaign marked his 28th as a professional, and he set a European Tour record at the Lancôme Trophy when it became his 600th tournament. It was estimated that by that time Torrance had walked over 14,000 miles, taken almost 150,000 shots, and earned around $1,000 per round, or $15 per stroke.

During his 28 years on Tour, Torrance has won 21 tournaments. Twice he has finished second on the European Order of Merit, in 1984 and 1995. He took part in an epic battle with fellow Scotsman Colin Montgomerie for the 1995 title. Torrance just missed the accolade when he finished behind Montgomerie in the last tournament of the season.

Torrance was awarded the royal honor of Member of the British Empire (an MBE) in 1995 for his services to golf. Three years later he proved that he was still a match for the young kids on the European Tour when he won the 1998 French Open.

## Fact File

**BORN** 1953, Largs, Scotland

**CAREER HIGHLIGHTS**
1976 Piccadilly Medal
1981 Carrolls Irish Open
1984 Benson and Hedges International
1990 Mercedes German Masters
1998 Peugeot French Open

**INTERNATIONAL HONORS**
Ryder Cup: 1981, 1983, 1985, 1987, 1989, 1991, 1993, 1995
World Cup: 1976, 1978, 1982, 1984, 1985, 1987, 1989, 1990, 1991, 1993, 1995
Alfred Dunhill Cup: 1985, 1986, 1987, 1989, 1990, 1991, 1993, 1995

# JERRY TRAVERS

JERRY TRAVERS PLAYED GOLF ONLY WHEN HE REALLY FELT LIKE IT. ON THE OCCASIONS WHEN HE DID SHOW UP TO PLAY HE PUT HIS MIND TO THE TASK. TRAVERS WON THE 1915 US OPEN.

## FACT FILE

**BORN** 1887, New York, New York, USA

**DIED** 1951

**CAREER HIGHLIGHTS**
1907 US Amateur
1908 US Amateur
1912 US Amateur
1913 US Amateur
1915 US Open

Jerome Dunstan Travers, or Jerry, never really took golf seriously. He was an enigma who only played when he felt like it, often missing important tournaments—even when he was the defending champion.

Travers won four US Amateur Championships and one US Open during his career. You would think someone with that record would take the game very seriously indeed. Not Travers. His philosophy was best summed up from something he wrote in 1924. "I believe that many of us here are prone to take the game too seriously, which doesn't help in the slightest to mold the proper mental attitude toward it," wrote Travers.

He believed golfers should treat the game as casually as possible. In the same passage he said: "We have a tendency to be too deliberate. That is a real handicap. Step out on any golf course and watch the average American golfer as he fiddles around before swinging the club. I am convinced that the average player would get more enjoyment and better scores if he abandoned the national habit of overemphasizing the care necessary in every shot."

Travers came from a wealthy family in New York and learned the game at his father's estate on Long Island. Later he was taught at the Nassau Country Club by Alex Smith of Carnoustie, winner of the 1910 US Open. Travers had a long backswing with very fast hands that would whip the clubhead into the back of the ball. His strength lay in his temperament. He was icy cool on the course and never let his opponents or the galleries disturb his concentration. Even when he hit poor shots he seemed to be able to put them behind him and somehow scramble a good score.

Travers was one of America's best amateurs during his time. His controlled temperament made him a supreme match player, a factor that helped him win four US Amateur titles. In his four victories, Travers was never taken beyond the 32nd hole.

The New Yorker was one of the best putters in the game after the turn of the century, and it was no surprise when he won America's most important championship. He became the second amateur to win the US Open when he triumphed at Baltusrol in 1915. Travers played the last six holes in one under par to win the title. True to his nature, Travers didn't bother to defend the title the following year.

# WALTER TRAVIS

WALTER TRAVIS WAS A LATECOMER TO GOLF, BUT IT DIDN'T TAKE HIM LONG TO MASTER THE GAME. ONCE HE DID, HE WON SOME OF GOLF'S BIGGEST AMATEUR TOURNAMENTS, INCLUDING THE BRITISH AND US AMATEUR TITLES.

Walter Travis didn't start golf until he was 35, and yet went on to become one of the supreme champions of the sport.

On a trip to London, England, in 1896, Travis bought a set of golf clubs. Some friends were thinking of starting a club and Travis thought he should join. Never someone who did things by halves, Travis poured all of his energy into learning to play the game.

He read everything he could about the game over the winter of 1896 and 1897. He hardly played in the summer of 1897. Instead he hit ball after ball, trying to groove his swing. He also made an important discovery. He soon realized that putting represented almost half the game, and set out to make himself as good a putter as possible. He did so by putting balls into a hole that was just a little wider than the ball itself.

He soon became so proficient at his new sport that he made the semi-finals of the 1898 US Amateur, losing eight and six to Findlay S. Douglas, the eventual winner. He made the semi-finals again the following year, losing to Douglas again, this time by the narrower margin of two and one.

He finally found success in 1900 when he won the prestigious tournament at the age of 38. This time Travis got the better of Douglas, defeating him by two holes. Travis beat Douglas again the following year in the semi-finals, and went on to repeat as champion. Travis won his third championship in four years at Nassau, New York, in 1903 when he defeated Eben Byers five and four in the final.

The Australian-American tried to win the British Amateur Championship only once, and succeeded. However, it wasn't a happy experience. Travis became the first foreigner to win the British event when he won the title at Sandwich. Travis felt the British were trying to prevent him from winning. He was refused a locker and had to change in a corridor. Then he was given a caddie whom he described as "one of the worst caddies it had ever been my misfortune to be saddled with." Despite his efforts, Travis couldn't get another caddie. However, he gained his revenge by winning the championship, defeating Ted Blackwell four and three in the final.

Travis's putter was the subject of some controversy in the British Amateur Championship. It was a center-shafted Schenectady putter with the shaft inserted into the middle of the putter head. No such design existed in Britain at the time.

Travis chose not to defend his British title. And then, a few years later, as if to add insult to his injury, the Schenectady putter was banned in Great Britain.

## FACT FILE

**BORN** 1862, Maldon, Victoria, Australia

**DIED** 1927

**CAREER HIGHLIGHTS**
1900 US Amateur
1901 US Amateur
1903 US Amateur
1904 British Amateur

# Lee Trevino

NOT MANY GOLFERS HAVE COME FROM BACKGROUNDS LIKE LEE TRAVINO, ONE OF THE GAME'S TRUE RAGS TO RICHES SUCCESS STORIES. TREVINO WORKED HARD TO REACH THE TOP, AND WON MANY MAJOR TITLES.

## Fact File

**BORN** 1939, Dallas, Texas, USA

**CAREER HIGHLIGHTS**
1968 US Open
1971 US Open
1971 The Open Championship
1972 The Open Championship
1974 USPGA Championship
1984 USPGA Championship

**INTERNATIONAL HONORS**
Ryder Cup: 1969, 1971, 1973, 1975, 1979, 1981, 1985 (captain)
World Cup: 1968, 1969, 1970, 1971, 1974

Lee Trevino was the first player ever to record four rounds under 70 in the US Open, a feat that surprised many people who thought Trevino would never amount to a great champion.

Trevino had finished fifth in the 1967 US Open at Baltusrol, eight shots behind Nicklaus. Despite that performance, he was not seen as a player capable of winning America's national championship. Trevino's victory the following year at Oak Hill Country Club in Rochester, New York, was a clear sign that he would be one of the dominant players over the next decade.

The Dallas-born professional is one of the greatest success stories in the history of the game. He was brought up in a poor family in Texas, where his family lived in an old shack. He taught himself to play golf at a municipal par-3 course and eventually became one of the legends of the game.

Known for his constant chatter on the golf course and for having a readily quotable quip about anything, Trevino was a journalist's dream. He received much press coverage in newspapers and magazines, not least for the quality of his golf.

After his shock win in the 1968 US Open, Trevino won the championship again three years later at Merion, Pennsylvania, in 1971, when he defeated Jack Nicklaus in a playoff. That turned out to be his greatest season ever. Shortly afterwards he went on to win the Canadian and British Opens. Indeed, in the space of just 23 days, Trevino held three national championships.

His 1971 British Open victory came at Royal Birkdale in a famous battle with Taiwan's Mr Lu. A year later he won the title again with his immaculate short game. Trevino seemed to hole everything from off the green that year to deny crowd favorite Tony Jacklin his second British Open trophy. Trevino had practically given Jacklin the title but then chipped in for a par at the 17th hole. Jacklin was so rattled that he took three putts at the hole.

Trevino added the first of two USPGA Championships in 1974, again denying Nicklaus a major title. Jack finished a stroke behind Trevino that year. Trevino's second and last USPGA title came in 1984 at Shoal Creek in Birmingham, Alabama. Then 44 years old, Trevino rolled back the years to win the championship by four strokes over Gary Player and Lanny Wadkins.

Part of the reason for initial doubts over Trevino rested in the fact that the man they call the "Merry Mex" doesn't have a swing that is even close to textbook. It is a classic slicer's swing. Trevino has hit the ball from left to right throughout his career, but it is a controlled action. Besides, Trevino's swing through impact is nothing short of classic.

# Bob Tway

ALTHOUGH BOB TWAY WON THE 1985 USPGA CHAMPIONSHIP IN DRAMATIC STYLE, THE MOST IMPORTANT VICTORY OF HIS CAREER CAME IN 1995 IN THE MCI CLASSIC.

Bob Tway tried to pass off the 1986 USPGA Championship as just another tournament. It became obvious that was anything but the case when in the final round Tway hit one of the greatest shots ever seen in the history of golf.

The 1986 USPGA was held at Inverness and Tway seemed to be heading for a second place finish to Greg Norman. He hung in, however, and eventually tied Norman for the lead when the Australian faltered down the stretch. All square on the 18th, Tway seemed destined to be but a bridesmaid when he put his second shot into a bunker. However, he holed the shot to win his first major championship. Tway couldn't stop jumping up and down with delight afterward, proof of just how much the tournament really meant to him.

The 1986 season was a banner year for Tway; besides the USPGA, he won three other titles and ended the season second on the US Tour money list with over $650,000. He was named Player of the Year that season, and appeared headed for greatness. He did win titles in 1989 and 1990, but then went into a spiral of bad play that culminated in a 179th place on the US money list in 1992. Tway made only 12 cuts of the 21 tournaments he entered that season. Things did not get much better over the next two years and it looked like Tway was fading away into obscurity.

Then in 1995 Tway put his three miserable years behind him by winning the MCI Classic at Hilton Head after a playoff with Nolan Henke and David Frost. There were tears in his eyes afterwards as he told the press that the win was even more important than his victory over Norman nine years previously. "This means more than any of the other tournaments," said Tway. "Those other tournaments I won, they all seemed easy. This wasn't easy. This was very, very special. When you have been down so long, you think you'll never get up. You wonder, 'Why bother?' I guess the key is never give up."

The signs from the 1998 season were that Tway would not be giving up the game in a hurry. Although he failed to win that year, he won over $1 million with a lot of good finishes. He placed third in the US Open at the Olympic Club behind Lee Janzen and Payne Stewart, proof that he still has the game to win golf's biggest championships.

However, even if he wins another major, he will be forever remembered for that miracle shot in 1986.

## Fact File

**BORN** 1959, Oklahoma City, Oklahoma, USA

**CAREER HIGHLIGHTS**
1986 Westchester Classic
1986 USPGA Championship
1989 Memorial Tournament
1990 Las Vegas Invitational
1995 MCI Classic

# HARRY VARDON

NO PLAYER HAS EVER EQUALLED HARRY VARDON'S RECORD OF SIX BRITISH OPEN VICTORIES. THE JERSEY GOLFER ALSO ADDED A US OPEN VICTORY TO HIS LIST OF ACCOMPLISHMENTS.

## FACT FILE

**BORN** 1870, Grouville, Jersey, Channel Islands

**DIED** 1937

**CAREER HIGHLIGHTS**
1896 The Open Championship
1898 The Open Championship
1899 The Open Championship
1900 US Open
1903 The Open Championship
1911 The Open Championship
1914 The Open Championship

No player has won more British Opens than Harry Vardon, his record of six has stood since 1914, a number that may never be beaten given the high level of competition in the modern game.

Of the three members of the Great Triumvirate, Vardon was the best. While James Braid and J. H. Taylor helped Vardon dominate the British Open around the turn of the century, the Jersey golfer was the acknowledged master of the three. Besides, neither Braid nor Taylor was able to match Vardon's victory in the US Open.

Vardon learned the game as a caddie growing up at Grouville in the Channel Islands. Unlike his contemporaries, Vardon's swing was markedly different because it was more upright than the normal flat sweeping arc of the great players of the time. He was also the man to make popular the overlapping grip, although Vardon didn't invent it.

The Jersey golfer first announced his intentions of winning the British Open in 1894 when he finished equal fifth at Sandwich behind J. H. Taylor. Two years later he denied Taylor a third consecutive championship by defeating him in a playoff for the title at Muirfield. He won consecutive championships in 1898 and 1899 and placed runner-up in the next three tournaments, before winning his fourth title in 1903 at Prestwick. His fifth followed at Sandwich in 1909 and he eventually won his last in 1914 at Prestwick again. Vardon was 44 years old when he won his record sixth title, taking the championship 18 years after he had won his first. The fact that he finished three shots ahead of Taylor was simply the icing on the cake.

Vardon wasn't only successful in Great Britain. In 1900 he undertook a highly successful tour of the United States where he won many matches. He capped the tour by winning the US Open in Chicago, defeating J. H. Taylor by two shots as the two Englishmen dominated the tournament.

A fine putter in his day, Vardon's touch deserted him as he grew older. However, he was still able to contend for the US Open in 1920 at the ripe old age of 50. Vardon was six strokes ahead with seven holes to play when the weather grew foul. Vardon dropped strokes over the closing holes to shoot 78 for the final round and lost the tournament by one stroke to Ted Ray.

Vardon eventually died in London in 1937. His death marked the passing of the greatest player in the history of the British Open.

# Ken Venturi

KEN VENTURI'S 1964 US OPEN VICTORY WAS ONE OF THE MOST DRAMATIC WINS IN THE HISTORY OF GOLF. VENTURI HAD TO BE ACCOMPANIED BY A DOCTOR FOR THE FINAL 18 HOLES.

The 1964 US Open was Ken Venturi's only major championship win, but it goes down as one of the bravest and most courageous victories in the annals of the game.

The Congressional Country Club was the venue for America's national championship that year. As well as having to contend with a course that measured 7,053 yards, the longest in US Open history, the professionals also had to deal with intense heat and humidity.

Venturi had been a good enough player to twice finish runner-up in the Masters. A final round 80 in 1956 while he was still an amateur saw him lose the title by a shot. Four years later, everyone thought he had won the 1960 tournament. Sitting in the clubhouse after posting a 283, Venturi was being congratulated by all and sundry for winning his first green jacket. The backslapping stopped when Arnold Palmer birdied the last two holes to steal the title from Venturi by one stroke. Perhaps not surprisingly, Venturi went into a slump after that loss.

Early in the 1964 season, Venturi showed that he could still play, when he posted a couple of top-ten finishes. No one gave him much thought in the US Open at Congressional, though.

The 1964 championship was the last time the final two rounds were played over the same day, on "Open Saturday," as it was called. The USGA liked it that way because they were of the belief that stamina played as big a part in winning as skill. They soon changed their minds after Venturi's victory.

The Californian professional entered the last two rounds five shots behind Arnold Palmer, the clear favorite. It soon became obvious that physical endurance was going to play a big part in deciding the tournament. The temperatures were climbing into the 90s as competitors teed off for the final two rounds.

Venturi played brilliantly in the third round, shooting a 66 that included six birdies in the first 12 holes. The heat was beginning to take its toll as the round ended, though, and had much to do with Venturi missing short putts on the 17th and 18th holes. He had been close to collapse over the last five holes. Between rounds he was advised by a doctor to rest.

After taking salt tablets, Venturi headed for the first tee accompanied by the doctor, who stayed with him for the entire last round. How he got through the final 18 holes on his feet remains a mystery to this day because he looked exhausted. Not only did he survive, but he shot 70 and won the tournament by four strokes.

Playing partner Ray Floyd had to fetch Venturi's ball from the 72nd hole. Floyd had tears in his eyes when he handed Venturi his ball.

Venturi is now a highly respected TV commentator.

## Fact File

**BORN** 1931, San Francisco, California, USA

**CAREER HIGHLIGHTS**
1958 Phoenix Open
1959 Los Angeles Open
1960 Bing Crosby National
1964 US Open
1964 Insurance City Open

**INTERNATIONAL HONORS**
Ryder Cup: 1965
Walker Cup: 1953

# The Match Goes to the Wire

The 1991 Ryder Cup at Kiawah Island, South Carolina, will go down in history as one of the most unsavory matches in the history of the competition. Ironically, it will also go down as one of the most exciting. When Sam Ryder created the Ryder Cup, he saw it as a competition that would put sportsmanship, fair play and goodwill between the two sides above all else. His wishes certainly weren't adhered to in the 1991 match played beside the Atlantic Ocean.

Sadly, the match became known as "The War by the Shore," the headline given to the competition by a golf magazine that should have known better. The match was played during the days of the Gulf War, and a few American players wore army combat caps while playing. A local radio DJ tried to unsettle the Europeans by making early morning calls to their hotel rooms. Despite the disagreeable elements, the match turned out to be one of the most exciting ever played.

Seve Ballesteros and Jose Maria Olazabal provided the spark behind the European side. Some other unlikely duos emerged successful, too. Mark James and rookie Steve Richardson won two of the three matches they played, while Bernhard Langer and Colin Montgomerie, and Ian Woosnam and Paul Broadhurst combined to win matches on the second day.

American captain Dave Stockton was no slouch when it came to putting his players together either. He teamed Fred Couples and Ray Floyd and the pair won two of the three matches they played. He also put Payne Stewart and Mark Calcavecchia out twice in the foursomes and watched them win both games.

Through two days the teams were dead level with eight points apiece. A thrilling finale was expected. The players produced it. In a Ryder Cup first, American player Steve Pate had to withdraw from the singles due to injury, meaning his match with David Gilford was halved. Through the next ten singles matches, the U.S.A. held the edge by just one point. With one match left out on the course, they led by 14 points to 13, meaning the entire competition came down to the contest between Germany's Bernhard Langer and Hale Irwin. With four holes to play, Langer was two down to Irwin. He had, however, fought back to all square by the time the pair reached the 18th tee. Irwin missed the final green with his approach shot, while Langer hit the green in regulation. Irwin then chipped poorly and putted up to within a foot of the hole for a conceded bogey five. From 45 feet, Langer ran his first putt six feet past the hole. The Ryder Cup rested on that putt. If the German holed it, Europe would retain the trophy; if not, U.S.A. would win it for the first time since 1983. Langer missed. The anguish on the German's face was evident for all to see. The Americans went wild with delight. They threw Stockton into the Atlantic Ocean during celebrations that lasted well into the Carolina night.

RIGHT TOP: RAYMOND FLOYD (RIGHT) AND FRED COUPLES WERE A TOWER OF STRENGTH FOR THE US SIDE AT KIAWAH, WINNING BOTH THEIR MATCHES ON THE OPENING DAY.

RIGHT: THE PREVIOUSLY SUCCESSFUL PARTNERSHIP OF IAN WOOSNAM (RIGHT) AND NICK FALDO FAILED AT KIAWAH. THE PAIR LOST BOTH MATCHES THEY PLAYED.

**ABOVE: COREY PAVIN (LEFT) AND STEVE PATE LOST A VITAL FOURBALL MATCH ON SATURDAY.**

**ABOVE RIGHT: CAPTAINS AT KIAWAH. BERNARD GALLACHER (LEFT) AND DAVE STOCKTON POSE WITH THE RYDER CUP BEFORE THE HOSTILITIES BEGIN.**

**RIGHT: AFTER EIGHT YEARS WITHOUT A WIN, THE AMERICAN TEAM HAD MUCH TO CELEBRATE AFTER THEIR ONE POINT WIN.**

# Roberto de Vicenzo

ARGENTINIAN GOLFER ROBERTO DE VICENZO MADE THE MOST ELEMENTARY OF MISTAKES TO MISS OUT ON A PLAYOFF WITH BOB GOALBY FOR THE 1968 MASTERS TITLE.

## Fact File

**BORN** 1923, Buenos Aires, Argentina

**CAREER HIGHLIGHTS**
1950 French Open
1960 French Open
1964 German Open
1966 Spanish Open
1967 The Open Championship

**INTERNATIONAL HONORS**
World Cup: 1953, 1954, 1955, 1962, 1963, 1964, 1965, 1966, 1968, 1969, 1970, 1971, 1972, 1973, 1974

Although Roberto de Vicenzo's finest hour came when he won the 1967 British Open at Hoylake, he will be forever remembered for one of the biggest oversights in golf.

De Vicenzo made a birdie three in the final round of the 1968 Masters, and finished the round with a par to tie Bob Goalby. Millions of TV viewers saw the Argentine make his three at the 17th, yet playing partner Tommy Aaron had marked a four on the card. De Vicenzo missed the error and when he signed the card the score had to stand. A playoff that should have taken place never did. Goalby won the tournament by a shot.

The popular Argentine golfer accepted full responsibility for the mistake, but it was a cruel blow to his career. It was the closest de Vicenzo ever came in the prestigious tournament. Although he may have lost the playoff, had he won there could have been no more worthy winner than the man from Argentina. The grace and dignity with which he handled the situation was later rewarded when he was presented with the 1970 Bobby Jones Award for distinguished sportsmanship.

De Vicenzo grew up in Buenos Aires in a working-class family. He and his four brothers used to caddie at a nearby course and all eventually turned professional. De Vicenzo had to travel abroad as golf was not a popular sport in Argentina. He showed early promise in the British Open by finishing third in 1948 and 1949, then runner-up in 1950. He came close throughout the rest of the 1950s and early 1960s, with three more third place finishes. However, he seemed destined not to win the world's oldest championship.

When he arrived at Hoylake in 1967, de Vicenzo was already 44 years old. Moreover, by this time all the top American players were regularly competing in the British Open. De Vicenzo seemed bound for disappointment. However, while others had given up hope of him winning, he certainly hadn't. The stylish swinger fashioned four rounds of 70, 71, 67, and 70 to take the title by two shots from defending champion Jack Nicklaus, winner of that year's US Open.

There was no more popular win in the tournament's history. Although he had won many events around the world, and would go on to eventually win some 140 professional tournaments during his career, the British Open was a fitting tribute to the greatest golfer Argentina has ever produced.

# NORMAN VON NIDA

NORMAN VON NIDA WAS ONE OF THE FIRST AUSTRALIANS TO FIND SUCCESS ON FOREIGN SHORES. THE FORMER CADDIE WAS INSTRUMENTAL IN HELPING PETER THOMSON WHEN HE WAS A YOUNG GOLFER.

Young Australian golfers owe Norman Von Nida quite a lot. He was a pioneer of Australian golf, one of the first to take his skills abroad.

Although he was born in Sydney, Von Nida was raised in Brisbane, where his family had moved. The family was poor, and times were hard. A career in professional golf was a long way from Von Nida's mind when he was a boy. His first job at a young age was in an abattoir, where Von Nida developed strong hands and arms from his work. It was just as well he did, for Von Nida was not endowed with the natural attributes of a sportsman.

Like many golfers who come from humble beginnings, Von Nida learned the game while caddying in his spare time at the Royal Queensland Golf Club. Small of stature, Von Nida used his strong forearms to help him keep up with the longer hitters. However, he worked hard on his short game as a youngster, and became one of the best chippers and pitchers of his generation. At the age of 15 he was good enough to win the Queensland Amateur Championship, and only then did he contemplate a career in professional golf.

Von Nida traveled to Great Britain after World War II and won many tournaments. For example, after two victories in 1946, he was leading money winner the following season when he won four of the first six tournaments he played. He earned a record £3,250 in prize money that season.

Von Nida was a regular contender in the British Open, but he never found the same success in that championship as he did in other tournaments. He finished fourth behind Sam Snead in 1946 at St Andrews; sixth at Royal Liverpool, Hoylake in 1947 when a closing 76 saw him miss Fred Daly's winning score of 293 by three shots; then he placed third at Muirfield in 1948, when the late Sir Henry Cotton won his last championship.

A player known for having nerves of steel, Von Nida spoke his mind. That didn't endear him to a lot of people but it was the way he was. The Australian tried his hand on the American circuit in 1948. However, a well-publicized argument with another professional over the marking of a scorecard, which resulted in a fight in front of a clubhouse, didn't exactly make Von Nida the most popular visiting golfer on that circuit.

Although he didn't personally win the British Open, he was instrumental in ensuring that fellow countryman Peter Thomson did. Von Nida gave Thomson much encouragement when Thomson was a young man. Thomson thanked Von Nida with five British Open victories.

## FACT FILE

**BORN** 1914, Sydney, New South Wales, Australia

**CAREER HIGHLIGHTS**
1947 Penfold
1948 Dunlop Masters
1950 Australian Open
1952 Australian Open
1953 Australian Open

# LANNY WADKINS

LANNY WADKINS IS ONE OF THE TOUGHEST PLAYERS TO PLAY ON THE US TOUR. WADKINS CAME CLOSE IN A LOT OF MAJOR CHAMPIONSHIPS, BUT ONLY MANAGED TO WIN ONE, THE 1977 USPGA CHAMPIONSHIP.

## FACT FILE

**BORN** 1949, Richmond, Virginia, USA

**CAREER HIGHLIGHTS**
1977 USPGA Championship
1977 World Series of Golf
1979 Los Angeles Open
1979 Players Championship
1992 Canon Greater Hartford Open

**INTERNATIONAL HONORS**
Ryder Cup: 1977, 1979, 1983, 1985, 1987, 1989, 1991, 1993, 1995 (captain)
World Cup: 1977, 1984, 1985
Alfred Dunhill Cup: 1986
Walker Cup: 1969, 1971

The Wadkins family had a virtual stranglehold on the Richmond, Virginia, Junior Championship trophy. For six years it sat in the Wadkins's trophy cabinet as Lanny won it four times and brother Bobby won it twice. Both went on to play the US Tour, but it was Lanny who would be the more successful.

Wadkins is known as one of the toughest competitors ever to play the US Tour. In his prime during the 1970s and 80s, he seemed to have nerves of steel, the type of true grit you expect of great champions.

After a glittering amateur career that saw him play in two Walker Cup matches and win the US Amateur, the Western Amateur, and the Southern Amateur Championships of 1970, Wadkins turned pro in 1971. He won the Sahara Invitational in his first full season as a professional and through 1998 had recorded 21 victories on the regular US Tour.

A winner of the Byron Nelson Classic and the USI Classic in 1973, it was only a matter of time before Wadkins won a major. A mini slump followed when he went three seasons without a victory, then came his finest hour. Wadkins found himself in a playoff with Gene Littler for the 1977 USPGA Championship at

Pebble Beach when he shot a final round 70 to Littler's 76. In the first sudden death playoff for a major championship, Wadkins picked up his first major title when he made a six-foot par putt at the third extra hole.

Many more majors were expected of the Virginian but, despite coming close on many occasions, it never happened. Wadkins's record is littered with top-ten finishes in subsequent majors. He has three third-place finishes in the Masters, a second in the US Open of 1986, a fourth in the British Open in 1984, and three further seconds in the USPGA, but sadly he never added to his 1977 victory in the USPGA. While he will no doubt win many tournaments as a senior golfer, including senior majors, his talent deserved more big championships.

Wadkins earned the reputation for being as hard as nails at a young age. He has proved his mettle in the Walker and Ryder Cup matches. In Ryder Cup play between 1977 and 1993, he recorded 20 wins, 11 losses, and three halves from his 34 matches. It is a testament to his talent that he has twice made the side as a captain's wild-card selection, in 1989 and 1993.

Wadkins was honored with the American Ryder Cup captaincy in 1995 at Oak Hill. No one took the team's loss harder than he did that year.

# MICKEY WALKER

MICKEY WALKER WAS AN OUTSTANDING AMATEUR PLAYER WHO NEVER QUITE FOUND THE SAME SUCCESS WHEN A PROFESSIONAL. HOWEVER, SHE IS STILL ONE OF GOLF'S GREAT AMBASSADORS.

Mickey Walker had a phenomenal career as an amateur golfer, and remains one of the best British women amateurs ever to play the game.

Walker was coached by Bill Ferguson at the Ilkley Golf Club in Yorkshire, England. An excellent teacher, Ferguson was responsible for the development of Colin Montgomerie. Like Montgomerie, Walker had the game for the big occasion from an early age. She reached the final of the British Girls' Championship in 1969, and two years later she became the youngest winner of the British Ladies' when she won the title at Alwoodley in her native Yorkshire. Walker was only 18 when she defeated Beverly Huke by a score of three and one in the final.

Walker successfully defended her title the following year at Hunstanton, when she defeated Claudine Cros-Rubin of France by two holes. She reached her third successive final in 1973 only to lose to Ann Irvine by a score of three and two at Carnoustie.

The 1972 season saw Walker travel to America where she won the Trans-Mississippi Championship, a victory that was notable because it came during her first visit to the United States. Walker also won the Portuguese Ladies' Amateur title that year and capped the season off by winning three-and-a-half points from a possible four in the Curtis Cup. Her half point came in an excellent match against Laura Baugh, but her overall performance couldn't stop her team from losing the cup. The 1973 season saw her win the English and Spanish Ladies' titles before she turned professional.

Walker never quite reached the heights in professional golf that she had in the amateur game. She did win a number of tournaments as a professional, and in 1979 finished runner-up in the British Open. Her preference for match play was obvious from the fact that two of her victories as a professional came in that format.

Walker's standing in the women's game has always been of the highest rank, and she is much respected throughout the game, in men's and women's golf, so it came as no surprise when she was selected as captain of the inaugural European Solheim Cup team, a role she held for four matches. Her greatest moment in that competition came at Dalmahoy in 1992 when her European side defeated their American counterparts by five points.

Now a highly respected golf coach, Walker also finds the time to commentate on television and radio.

## FACT FILE

**BORN** 1952, Alwoodley, Yorkshire, England

**CAREER HIGHLIGHTS**
1971 British Ladies' Championship
1972 British Ladies' Championship
1973 English Ladies' Championship
1980 Lambert & Butler Match Play
1984 Lorne Stewart Match Play

**INTERNATIONAL HONORS**
Solheim Cup: 1990 (captain), 1992 (captain), 1994 (captain), 1996 (captain)
Curtis Cup: 1972

# Tom Watson

Tom Watson was virtually unbeatable between 1977 and 1983. Yet there was a time when Watson was considered something of a choker.

Watson earned that label early in his career when he lost three majors in the final rounds, majors he should have won. A 79 in the final round of the 1974 US Open at Winged Foot in New York cost him his first US Open. Watson finished fifth, five strokes behind Hale Irwin. A year later, at Medinah Country Club in Illinois, he led the US Open again in the final round only to slide back to ninth place. It was a similar story in the 1975 Masters. Again he led the field in the final round but somehow managed to finish eighth.

Other players would have let such collapses drive them to despair. Not Watson. These experiences were part of his learning curve, because Watson would soon rid himself of the choker label.

While Watson first stamped his mark on the game when he won the British Open at Carnoustie in a playoff with Australia's Jack Newton, the choker label well and truly vanished with Watson's first Masters victory in 1977. The Kansas City kid had only to take on the might of Jack Nicklaus in the final round. Everyone expected Watson to fold under the pressure, but there was no collapse this time, just pure solid golf. Watson kept his composure to defeat Nicklaus by two shots.

Watson defeated Nicklaus again that year when he went head to head with the world's greatest golfer in the British Open at Turnberry. He matched Nicklaus shot for shot over the four days in the best British Open ever, winning the title by one stroke.

Watson has always insisted that the 1977 season kick-started his career. It's one thing to win two major titles, but to win them from the greatest player the game has ever seen can only help to make you feel like a world beater. That's just what Watson became.

Another Masters title followed in 1981, and Watson's only US Open title came at Pebble Beach in California the following year. Both times Nicklaus finished second to Watson, and in the latter tournament he was beaten only when Watson holed an outrageous chip at the 71st hole. However, it was in the British Open that Watson proved he was one of the game's truly great players.

Other than Peter Thomson in the 1950s and 60s, Watson has come the closest to breaking Harry Vardon's record of six British Open titles. Watson fell in love with links golf, so much so that he would sometimes arrive in the British Isles two weeks before the championship to acclimatize. He would spend time at Ballybunion on the west coast of Ireland, a course he believes to be one of the best in the world.

There was no one to touch Watson in the British Open between 1980 and 1983. Only Bill Rogers was able to stop Watson's grip on the trophy, when Rogers won the title at Royal St George's in 1981. Watson took the title in 1980 at Muirfield, in 1982 at Royal Troon, and at Royal Birkdale in 1983. So when he arrived in St Andrews in 1984, the world of golf expected him to add his sixth title at the home of golf. He would have done, too, if not for a certain Spaniard named Severiano Ballesteros. Watson finished second to Ballesteros by two strokes at St Andrews.

The only blot on Watson's British Open record is that he never won the title over the Old Course, the home of golf. He deserved to win there more than anybody, given his love of traditional golf.

Like Arnold Palmer before him, Watson never won the USPGA Championship. However, that aside he is still one of the greatest ever to play the game.

## Fact File

**BORN** 1949, Kansas City, Missouri, USA

**CAREER HIGHLIGHTS**
1975 The Open Championship
1977 Masters
1977 The Open Championship
1980 The Open Championship
1981 Masters
1982 US Open
1982 The Open Championship
1983 The Open Championship

**INTERNATIONAL HONORS**
Ryder Cup: 1977, 1981, 1983, 1989, 1993 (captain)

ABOVE: TOM WATSON CELEBRATES WINNING THE GREATEST BRITISH OPEN OF ALL TIME, THE 1977 CHAMPIONSHIP AT TURNBERRY.

ABOVE RIGHT: DURING HIS PRIME WATSON WAS THE BEST BALL STRIKER IN THE GAME.

RIGHT: WATSON PLAYING THE TYPE OF GOLF HE LOVES MOST—LINKS GOLF—ON THE SEASIDE COURSES OF THE BRITISH ISLES.

# Art Wall

ART WALL COULD DO NO WRONG IN 1959, WINNING A HOST OF AWARDS. MOST IMPORTANTLY, HE WON HIS ONLY MAJOR CHAMPIONSHIP, THE MASTERS, BY SHOOTING A 66 IN THE FINAL ROUND.

## Fact File

**BORN** 1923, Honesdale, Pennsylvania, USA

**CAREER HIGHLIGHTS**
1954 Tournament of Champions
1959 Bing Crosby National
1959 Masters
1960 Canadian Open
1964 San Diego Invitational

**INTERNATIONAL HONORS**
Ryder Cup: 1957, 1959, 1961

In 1959, Art Wall had the type of year many players can only dream about. Wall was named Player of the Year, he was the US Tour's leading money winner, he won the Vardon Trophy for the lowest stroke average and, more importantly, he won the Masters at Augusta National. A 1949 graduate of Duke University, Wall had found success on the US Tour prior to the 1959 season, but nothing compared to what happened that year.

Even though he had finished sixth the year before, the Pennsylvania native didn't look like he had much of a chance of winning the 1959 Masters. After opening the tournament with rounds of 73, 74, and 71, Wall found himself heading into the final 18 holes six strokes behind Arnold Palmer and Stan Leonard. He played the round of his life, however, and shot a 66, which included five birdies on the last six holes. Palmer could only manage a 74, while Leonard shot 75, and Wall found he'd won the tournament by one stroke from Cary Middlecoff.

Wall never really came close in another major championship after that. He did place fifth in the 1961 USPGA Championship at Olympia Fields in Illinois, when he missed a playoff for the title with Jerry Barber and Don January by five shots, but that was it.

Strange, for he was a very accomplished player in his day. In the 1950s and 60s, Wall won 12 tournaments on the US Tour, including the 1954 Tournament of Champions and the Canadian Open in 1960.

Proof that his game was enduring came in 1971 when he lost a playoff to Lee Trevino for the Canadian Open. Wall was in his late 40s at the time yet he had still managed to shoot 13 under par to tie Trevino.

The Masters winner was a good enough player to play in three Ryder Cup matches. Unfortunately his debut came in the 1957 at Lindrick in Yorkshire, England, when the Americans lost the biennial match for the first time in 24 years. Wall lost in a foursome match with Fred Hawkins on the first day, the pair going down three and two to Ken Bousfield and Dai Rees. He then had to sit on the sidelines and watch his team-mates lose the singles and the cup the following day.

Wall was in the thick of things though when America won the 1959 match at Eldorado Country Club in California. This time he played in the singles, beating Ireland's Christy O'Connor seven and six. Wall's last Ryder Cup appearance came in 1961 when he played three matches and won all three as the Americans triumphed at Royal Lytham & St Annes.

# KARRIE WEBB

AUSTRALIAN KARRIE WEBB HAD TO BORROW $200 FROM HER MOTHER TO GET STARTED IN PROFESSIONAL GOLF. BEFORE LONG SHE HAD TURNED THAT SMALL INVESTMENT INTO A $1 MILLION PROFIT.

Karrie Webb set an LPGA Tour record in 1996 when she became the first rookie to earn $1 million in a single season. She wasted no time in reaching that mark—only ten months and ten days. No rookie on the men's US Tour has ever made $1 million in a season.

Webb won four tournaments in her rookie LPGA year. Only Nancy Lopez has bettered that total, winning nine in her first full season on the LPGA Tour. Se Ri Pak tied Webb's total in 1998.

Not surprisingly, Webb ran away with the Rookie of the Year Award. She had taken that honor the previous year on the European Tour in 1995, courtesy of her victory in the Weetabix Women's British Open. Webb won the British title by six strokes from the formidable Annika Sorenstam over the tough Dukes Course at Woburn. That signaled to the golfing world that she was a player to watch out for.

Webb joined the LPGA Tour for the 1996 season and wasted no time in announcing her arrival. Webb finished second in the first event of the season, the Chrysler-Plymouth Tournament of Champions. Only an outstanding performance by Sweden's Liselotte Neumann denied Webb her first title. Neumann won the title by 11 shots.

A week later Webb secured her first LPGA Tour win when she triumphed in the Healthsouth Inaugural, in a playoff with Martha Nause and Jane Geddes. When Nause bogeyed the first playoff hole, it was left to Webb and Geddes to decide the title. Webb prevailed when Geddes bogeyed the fourth extra hole by three putting. Webb could hardly believe she had won her first LPGA tournament. "In the playoff, I think I was more nervous than in the British Open. I can't believe this is happening so soon," said Webb afterward.

The young Australian nearly made it two wins in succession when she finished second to Meg Mallon a week later. Webb actually had a three-shot lead after nine holes of the final round, but eventually a Mallon birdie on the final denied her another playoff.

The 1996 season only got better and better. She won three more tournaments, the Sprint Titleholders Championship, the SAFECO Classic, and then topped off the season by winning the season-ending Tour Championship by four strokes over Kelly Robbins, Nancy Lopez, and Emilee Klein. The victory made her a millionaire in her first full season on the LPGA Tour. Not bad for a girl who in 1994 had to borrow $200 from her mother to join the Australian Women's Tour.

That $200 was one of the most astute investment Mrs Webb could have made.

## FACT FILE

**BORN** 1974, Ayr, Queensland, Australia

**CAREER HIGHLIGHTS**

1996 HEALTHSOUTH Inaugural
1996 ITT LPGA Tour Championship
1997 Weetabix Women's British Open
1997 Safeco Classic
1998 Australian Ladies' Masters

# Harry Weetman

HARRY WEETMAN WAS ONE OF THE LONGEST HITTERS IN THE GAME DURING HIS PRIME, AN ASSET HE USED TO WIN MANY BIG TOURNAMENTS.

## Fact File

**BORN** 1920, Oswestry, Shropshire, England

**DIED** 1972

**CAREER HIGHLIGHTS**
1951 British Professional Match Play
1952 Dunlop Masters
1957 German Open
1958 British Professional Match Play
1958 Dunlop Masters

**INTERNATIONAL HONORS**
Ryder Cup: 1951, 1953, 1955, 1957, 1959, 1961, 1963, 1965 (captain)
World Cup: 1953, 1954, 1956, 1960

Harry Weetman was one of the first of a string of famous golfers to emerge from the small English county of Shropshire, preceding by nearly 40 years the likes of Ian Woosnam, Sandy Lyle, and Peter Baker.

Weetman was probably the most powerful British player to emerge in the professional ranks after World War II. A huge man with long, muscular arms, Weetman could hit the ball for miles. Fans used to turn up just to watch him drive balls from the tee. He entertained them, too. Weetman never held back on any tee shot, delivering a violent blow to the back of the ball. He reduced most courses to a drive and a pitch and it helped him win many tournaments.

The Shropshire lad developed his arms by chopping trees for extra money as a youth, and it remained one of his favorite exercises throughout his career. Despite his immense power, Weetman also had a deft touch around the greens. He was known as a fine chipper and pitcher of the ball and was an excellent putter during his day.

Weetman twice won the Harry Vardon Trophy on the European circuit for leading the money list. Those honors came in 1952 and 1958, in the same years he won the Dunlop Masters, the forerunner of the current British Masters title, one of the biggest tournaments in European golf.

Not surprisingly, Weetman was a member of every Great Britain & Ireland Ryder Cup side during his prime. He played in every match between 1951 and 1963, later captaining the side in 1965 at Royal Birkdale. Unfortunately, Weetman competed in the event during a time when the US completely dominated the biennial match. Weetman won only two matches of the 15 in which he played, halving two and losing 11. However, his two victories came against excellent players. In 1953 he defeated Sam Snead at Wentworth one up despite being four holes down with six to play. His other singles win came in the 1963 match at East Lake Country Club in Atlanta, Georgia. Weetman defeated Julius Boros in the morning singles by a score of one up.

Weetman was a member of the 1957 side that triumphed at Lindrick. The Shropshire professional actually fell out with captain Dai Rees on that occasion when he was told he wasn't playing in the singles matches on the final day. Weetman was quoted at the time as saying he never wanted to play for Rees again, but he was in the team two years later when Rees was again captain.

In 1972, Weetman was killed in a car accident. He was in the front seat of his Rolls Royce being driven by a friend when the tragedy struck. He was 52.

# TOM WEISKOPF

NO PLAYER SINCE TOMMY BOLT HAD A TEMPERAMENT LIKE THAT OF TOM WEISKOPF. YET WHEN WEISKOPF CONTROLLED HIS EMOTIONS HE WAS CAPABLE OF BEATING THE BEST.

There is no telling how many major championships Tom Weiskopf would have won had he been born either 10 years earlier or 10 years later. Then he wouldn't have been stopped by the game's greatest player.

It was Weiskopf's misfortune to be born just two years after Jack Nicklaus, which meant the two reached their prime at virtually the same time. On more than one occasion Weiskopf was denied a title by Nicklaus. Their paths first crossed at Ohio State University. Nicklaus was a senior when Weiskopf was in his sophomore year. They would meet many times in the professional ranks.

Weiskopf also had another little problem—his temper. Not since the days of Tommy Bolt had a golfer been known to blow a fuse the way Weiskopf could. Often he was his own worst enemy, but when he controlled himself he was one of the best players in the world.

The tall, slim golfer had one of the most beautiful swings ever seen in professional golf, a swing which would serve as a model for golfers everywhere.

The Ohio professional had been one of America's most consistent golfers by the time the 1973 season rolled around. He had won four tournaments and it seemed only a matter of time before he won a major. He had already finished second twice in the Masters, in 1969 when he missed a playoff for the title by a shot, and in 1972 when he placed three strokes behind Nicklaus.

Weiskopf nearly accomplished his dream in the US Open in 1973 when he finished third, just two shots behind Johnny Miller. So when he arrived to play in the British Open at Royal Troon, Weiskopf was one of the favorites. Despite not having a particularly great love of links golf, Weiskopf led the championship from wire to wire. Not since Henry Cotton in 1934 had a golfer led the British Open in all four rounds. Weiskopf did lose the lead to Johnny Miller in the fourth, but he hung on to win by three strokes.

That was to be the only major championship Weiskopf would ever win. He was denied further Masters titles in 1974 and 1975 when he finished second both times. In the latter tournament Weiskopf and Miller lost an epic battle to Nicklaus by just one stroke.

Now a highly respected commentator for CBS Television, Weiskopf delivered one of the all-time great lines when Nicklaus won his sixth green jacket in 1986. Weiskopf was asked what was going through Nicklaus's mind as the world's greatest golfer was charging to victory. "If I knew what was going through Jack Nicklaus's head, I would have won this golf tournament," replied Weiskopf. If not for Jack Nicklaus, Weiskopf would have indeed won the tournament, perhaps more than once.

## FACT FILE

**BORN** 1942, Massillon, Ohio, USA

**CAREER HIGHLIGHTS**
1973 Open Championship
1973 Canadian Open
1975 Canadian Open
1975 Kemper Open
1982 Western Open

**INTERNATIONAL HONORS**
Ryder Cup: 1973, 1975
World Cup: 1972

# LEE WESTWOOD

LEE WESTWOOD ANNOUNCED HIMSELF TO THE WORLD OF GOLF BY WINNING SEVEN TIMES IN 1998, VICTORIES THAT CAME ON THREE DIFFERENT CONTINENTS.

## FACT FILE

**BORN** 1973, Worksop, Nottinghamshire, England

**CAREER HIGHLIGHTS**

1993 British Youths' Championship
1996 Volvo Scandinavian Masters
1997 Volvo Masters
1998 Standard Life Loch Lomond
1998 Freeport McDermott Classic

**INTERNATIONAL HONORS**

Ryder Cup: 1997
Alfred Dunhill Cup: 1996, 1997, 1998

While the United States has Tiger Woods, European golf has Lee Westwood. The Worksop professional has already been compared to the American phenomenon, and the two should win titles well into the twenty-first century.

Westwood took up golf at the age of 13 when his grandparents bought him a half set of clubs. His father John, a math teacher, also took up the game to give his son encouragement. Little did Westwood senior know that his son would go on to become one of Europe's leading professionals.

Westwood was a talented athlete as a schoolboy. He excelled at cricket, rugby, and soccer, but golf was his first love. Westwood was good enough as a boy to win the Peter McEvoy Trophy and the British Youths' Championship. He represented England at Boys', Youths', and Senior levels and turned professional in 1993 with a handicap of plus 4.

Westwood easily got his card at the 1993 European Tour Qualifying School, taking the fifth card. He established himself on the European circuit in 1994 when he finished 43rd on the money list. Within two seasons he had entered the winner's circle.

His maiden victory in the 1996 Volvo Scandinavian Masters confirmed the expectations of many golf pundits, not least Andrew "Chubby" Chandler. A former European Tour golfer turned player-manager, Chandler had recognized Westwood's potential and signed him to his stable of Tour players. It was a wise move.

Another victory followed in 1996 when Westwood won the Sumitomo Visa Taiheiyo Masters in Japan, defeating Jeff Sluman and Constantino Rocca in a playoff. Since that victory, Westwood has successfully defended the title in 1997 and 1998.

Westwood won the 1997 Volvo Masters in Europe, a victory that saw him finish the season third on the European money list. He also won three other tournaments around the world, one in Australia, one in Malaysia, and his Masters title in Japan.

While 1997 was a great year for Westwood, it was nothing compared to what he did in the 1998 season, when he confirmed that he is one of the future greats of golf by winning seven times around the world. Four of those victories came in Europe, and it helped him to a second consecutive third place on the European Order of Merit. Westwood also won the Japanese Masters title for the third year in a row, and added another victory in Japan when he won the Dunlop Phoenix tournament. However, his most significant win of the year came in the United States.

Westwood's three-shot victory in the Freeport McDermott Classic proved that he has the game to win anywhere in the world. And he will. It is only a matter of time before he adds major titles to his record.

# JOYCE WETHERED

AMONG JOYCE WETHERED'S MANY FANS WAS BOBBY JONES, WHO WAS ONCE TOTALLY OUTCLASSED BY HER IN A MATCH AT ST ANDREWS.

Joyce Wethered was a complete unknown when she burst onto the British amateur scene. However, it wasn't long before she became the best player in the women's amateur game.

Wethered only entered the 1920 English Ladies' Championship after a friend had persuaded her to play. To everyone's surprise, her own included, Wethered reached the final. There she came up against the dominant player of the day, Cecilia Leitch, with whom she would have many great encounters.

Wethered downed the favorite to win the first of five consecutive English Ladies' titles, going an amazing 33 matches without defeat. Leitch would get her revenge in other championships, including victory over Wethered in the final of the British Ladies' that year.

Wethered learned much of her golf at Dornoch in the north of Scotland, where the family would spend the summer. It helped that her brother Roger was a natural golfer who would go on to become as dominant in the men's amateur game as Joyce was in women's golf. In her youth Joyce spent many rounds playing against her brother and his friends, all top amateur players.

It wasn't just the English Ladies' title that Wethered dominated. She won her first British Ladies' title in 1922, when she easily defeated Leitch by the score of nine and seven. She won the titles in 1924 and 1925, downing Leitch in a heroic battle at Troon in the latter championship; Wethered won the title at the 37th hole.

After three seasons away from tournament golf, Wethered added her fourth British title in 1929 when she beat the great American player Glenna Collett at St Andrews. Collett seemed to be cruising to victory in the final over the Old Course. She was five up on Wethered after 11 holes. However, her British opponent was made of stern stuff. Wethered fought back to be only two down at lunch and eventually won the championship at the 35th hole.

Wethered was one of the best swingers of a golf club in the game's history. Bobby Jones once said she had the best swing he had ever seen, and he was including male golfers in his appraisal. Jones played many times with Wethered. She scored a 75 at St Andrews once, which Jones was later to comment on. "I had never played golf with anyone, man or woman, amateur or professional, who made me feel so utterly outclassed," wrote Jones about the experience.

Wethered later became Lady Heathcoat Amory and retired to Devon, where she died in 1983.

## FACT FILE

**BORN** 1901, London, England

**DIED** 1983

**CAREER HIGHLIGHTS**
1922 British Ladies' Amateur
1924 British Ladies' Amateur
1925 British Ladies' Amateur
1929 British Ladies' Amateur

# Roger Wethered

ROGER WETHERED WAS SOMEWHAT OVERSHADOWED BY THE EXPLOITS OF HIS SISTER JOYCE. NEVERTHELESS, ROGER WAS A GOOD ENOUGH PLAYER TO WIN THE 1923 BRITISH AMATEUR CHAMPIONSHIP.

## Fact File

**BORN** 1899, Moldon, Surrey, England

**DIED** 1983

**CAREER HIGHLIGHTS**
1923 British Amateur
1927 Golf Illustrated Gold Vase

**INTERNATIONAL HONORS**
Walker Cup: 1922, 1923, 1926, 1930 (captain), 1934

Roger Wethered was one of the best amateur players to play the game between the two World Wars, and the last British amateur golfer to come close to winning the British Open.

Wethered should have won the 1921 British Open at St Andrews, only a penalty shot in the third round and a bogey on the 72nd hole cost him the title. Wethered stepped on his ball in the third round as he was walking backwards. He called the penalty on himself and it cost him a valuable stroke. However, it was the five at the last that really cost him the title. A par-4 there and Wethered would have become the first amateur golfer in the twentieth century to win the title.

The Englishman found himself in a playoff for the title against Jock Hutchison. Wethered didn't want to stay for the playoff as he was keen to return home to play in a cricket match. He stayed, however, and lost the 36-hole playoff by nine shots, scoring 159 to Hutchison's 150. The loss was a pity because Wethered had battled back in the championship after a poor 78 in the opening round.

Apart from the fact that he was an amateur, Wethered's performance was all the more remarkable because at the time he was still an undergraduate at Oxford University.

Two years later Wethered partly avenged the defeat when he won the British Amateur title at Royal Cinque Ports. Wethered came up against the legendary Francis Ouimet in the semi-finals and defeated the talented American two and one. He went on to an emphatic seven and six victory over Scotland's Robert Harris in the final.

Four times Wethered won the President's Putter during his career, an event that drew the top amateur golfers of the day. He was also one of the mainstays of the British Walker Cup side during his prime. Wethered played in the match five times, captaining the side in 1930. His record was exemplary in that competition, too. Wethered won five, lost three, and halved one of the nine matches he played. Two of those losses came at the hands of Bobby Jones in the singles matches of 1922 and 1930, the only player to defeat Wethered in Walker Cup singles play.

Jones and Wethered had not only a great rivalry, but also a mutual respect for each other. Wethered was made captain of the Royal & Ancient Golf Club of St Andrews in 1946, and when Jones died in 1972, Wethered, as the senior of the past 11 captains at the service, delivered the eulogy.

# Kathy Whitworth

NO PLAYER IN THE HISTORY OF THE WOMEN'S GAME HAS WON MORE TIMES THAN KATHY WHITWORTH. HER 88 TOUR VICTORIES IS A RECORD THAT MAY STAND FOREVER.

In the *Little Red Golf Book*, the late Harvey Penick explains why Kathy Whitworth has won more tournaments in America than any other player. "She makes more long putts when she needs them than any other player I ever saw," revealed Penick in his best-selling golfing title.

A lot of great Texas golfers were students of Penick. Whitworth is probably one of the best the revered coach ever taught. That's saying a lot, for Penick coached Ben Crenshaw, Tom Kite, and a host of other great golfers to emerge from that southern state.

During her time Whitworth won just about every LPGA event, with one exception—the US Women's Open. Like Sam Snead in the men's game, Whitworth never won her national championship. She finished runner-up in 1971, but sadly the tournament she wanted most eluded her.

Whitworth began playing golf at the age of 15, using clubs that had belonged to her grandfather. The tall, athletic teenager had no problems using a man's set of clubs. In fact, she quickly became quite adept at her new-found passion. As an amateur she won the New Mexico State Championship and would occasionally play exhibition matches with top women professionals.

The 5-foot, 9-inch Texan turned professional when she was 20 after her father and some local businessmen decided to sponsor her on Tour. She had a hard time adjusting to life in the paid ranks. Whitworth nearly quit after she went six months without making a penny, often shooting scores in the 80s. She was persuaded to continue, however, and it's just as well she did.

She established herself on the LPGA Tour with two wins and eight second place finishes in 1962. In 1963 she won eight times, the first of three seasons when she would win that number of tournaments. However, that isn't her best win tally in one season; in 1967 she won nine times and then won 10 tournaments in the 1968 season alone.

Whitworth was the leading money winner on the LPGA Tour in every year except one, 1969, between 1965 and 1973. When she won the 1982 Lady Michelob tournament, she surpassed Mickey Wright's record of 82 wins on the LPGA Tour. However, her winning habits were not finished, not by a long shot.

In all, Whitworth won 88 tournaments on the LPGA Tour. She was the first woman to surpass the $1 million mark, a feat she accomplished in 1981.

## Fact File

**BORN** 1939, Monahans, Texas, USA

**CAREER HIGHLIGHTS**
1967 LPGA Championship
1971 LPGA Championship
1975 LPGA Championship
Seven-time LPGA Player of the Year
Elected to the LPGA Hall of Fame and World Golf Hall of Fame in 1982

**INTERNATIONAL HONORS**
Solheim Cup: 1990 (captain), 1992 (captain)

# TIGER WOODS

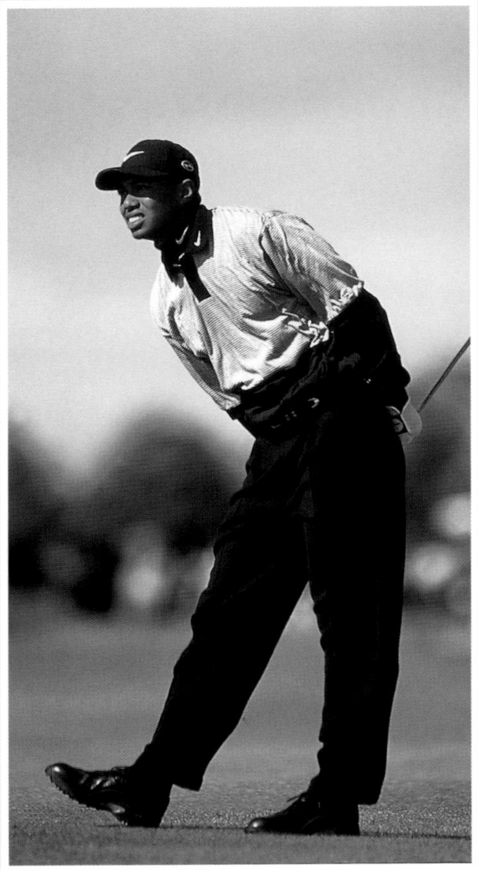

No golfer in recent history has had an impact on the game the way Eldrick Tiger Woods has. Wood's influence on the game in the 1990s has been nothing short of phenomenal.

Tiger Woods was always meant to play golf. Not just amateur golf, or college golf, but golf at the very highest level. He was a child prodigy who appeared on the Mike Douglas Show at the age of two, when he had a putting contest against Bob Hope. He shot 48 for nine holes at the age of three. At five he appeared in *Golf Digest* magazine. In 1991 he won the US Junior Amateur Championship. He defended the title in 1992 and in 1993, becoming the first player to win more than one US Junior Amateur Championship. At 18 he became the youngest golfer to win the US Amateur Championship. He won the title again in 1995 and 1996, becoming the first player to win the event three times. Not even Jack Nicklaus was able to do that. Indeed, Woods holds the US Amateur record for most consecutive match-play victories, with 18.

He turned pro to great fanfare in 1996 and it did not take him long to live up to expectations. Woods won his first professional event that year, taking the Las Vegas Invitational, only his fifth event as a pro. He also won the Walt Disney World/Oldsmobile Classic. In just 11 tournaments in his first year as a professional, Woods earned just under $1 million.

It was no surprise then that Woods arrived at Augusta for the 1997 Masters as the hot favorite. His accuracy and immense length off the tee had everyone looking for him to tear Augusta National apart. He did not disappoint. The phenomenon broke or tied record after record in his march to victory.

Woods's performance at Augusta was just the start of a brilliant year. By June 15 he was the World Number One ranked player, by season's end he was the US Tour's leading money winner, becoming the first player to surpass $2 million in one season.

Like Arnold Palmer before him, Woods has introduced a whole new generation to the game of golf. By becoming the first black man to win the title at Augusta National, which at one time did not allow blacks to become members, Woods proved to many Afro-Americans that there were avenues open to them to play what was once considered an elite, white man's game. All the experts agree that Woods could be the one player to surpass Jack Nicklaus's tally of 18 major championships.

## FACT FILE

**BORN** 1975, Cypress, California

**CAREER HIGHLIGHTS**

1994 US Amateur
1995 US Amateur
1996 US Amateur
1997 Masters
First player to win over $2 million on the US Tour (1997)

ABOVE: NO PLAYER SINCE ARNOLD PALMER HAS MADE AN IMPACT ON THE GAME THE WAY TIGER WOODS HAS. WOODS OPENED UP GOLF TO A WHOLE NEW GENERATION OF FANS.

RIGHT: WOODS CELEBRATES WINNING THE 1997 MASTERS, THE FIRST OF MANY MAJOR TITLES THE LONGEST HITTER IN THE GAME WILL WIN DURING HIS CAREER.

HOLE
PAR
ROCCA
SLUMAN
LANGER
COUPLES
TOLLES

# Craig Wood

CRAIG WOOD (LEFT) LOOKED DESTINED NEVER TO WIN A MAJOR CHAMPIONSHIP. AFTER SEVERAL NEAR MISSES, WOOD THEN WON TWO MAJORS IN THE 1941 SEASON.

## Fact File

**BORN** 1901, Lake Placid, New York, USA

**DIED** 1968

**CAREER HIGHLIGHTS**
1933 Los Angeles Open
1941 Masters
1941 US Open
1942 Canadian Open

**INTERNATIONAL HONORS**
Ryder Cup: 1931, 1933, 1935

Craig Wood shares a unique distinction with Greg Norman—they are the only two players to lose playoffs in all four major championships. Wood was the first, recording this dubious record back in the 1930s.

Like Norman in modern golf, Wood was a player of near misses. For much of his career he seemed destined never to win a major championship, although he would eventually find success when he won two in the 1941 season.

Wood's first experience of playoff defeat occurred in the 1933 British Open at St Andrews. A fine 68 in the third round helped Wood tie Denny Shute for the lead. However, Shute won the 36-hole playoff by five strokes.

A year later, Wood lost in extra holes in the USPGA Championship. Wood beat Shute in the semi-finals and came up against Paul Runyan, a former pupil, in the final. Wood was at times 50 yards longer off the tee than Runyan, but the two remained deadlocked after 36 holes. Runyan won the title when Wood bogeyed the second playoff hole.

Wood nearly won the very first Masters tournament. Only a fine birdie on the 71st hole by Horton Smith denied Wood a playoff for the title. That's what he found himself in the following year, in 1935, when he was the victim of Gene Sarazen's most famous shot in golf. Wood was in the clubhouse being congratulated by all and sundry on winning the Masters when Sarazen holed a 4-wood to tie the lead. Sarazen won the 36-hole playoff the following day by five shots.

Another playoff loss occurred in the 1939 US Open at the Philadelphia Country Club. Wood's 72-hole total of 284 tied with Denny Shute and Byron Nelson. Nelson and Wood had to play a second 18 when they both tied on 68, with Shute taking 76. However, during the course of the round Nelson holed a 1-iron to take a lead that he never relinquished. He won the title by three strokes, shooting 70 to Wood's 73.

Wood finally became a major man when he won the Masters and US Open in 1941. It was fitting that he should take the titles from two men who had earlier denied him major championship victories. Wood defeated Nelson by three strokes to finally win the Masters, and then defeated Shute by a similar score when he won the US's national championship at the Colonial Club in Texas. The victories were well earned, for no one had paid their dues in major championship golf more than Wood.

# Ian Woosnam

AFTER STRUGGLING TO GET HIS CARD EARLY IN HIS CAREER, IAN WOOSNAM HAS BECOME ONE OF EUROPE'S GREATEST PLAYERS. HIS WIN IN THE 1991 MASTERS WAS ONE OF THE MOST POPULAR IN THE TOURNAMENT'S HISTORY.

When Ian Woosnam holed a seven-foot putt on the final green of the 1991 Masters, it justified all the years he had spent trying to make it to the top. Woosnam donned the green jacket with pride. He had earned his title the hard way.

There was a time when Woosnam had to travel around Europe in an old camper van, living off canned beans and potato chips. He, Martin Poxon and D. J. Russell used to drive from tournament to tournament together, trying to make enough money to get to the next Tour stop. Times have changed. Now Woosnam has his own private plane.

Woosnam's parents were Welsh, and the family lived in Oswestry on the Welsh border. Woosnam's golf was played on the local Llanymynech course where 15 holes were played in England and three in Wales. The little golfer soon became quite an accomplished player. What he lacked in natural talent he more than made up for with intense desire to become a professional golfer. As a boy, Woosnam competed against Sandy Lyle, another Shropshire native who would go on to win the Masters.

When he was in his teens, "Woosie," as he is called by his peers, worked on his father's farm where he would spent long summer days lifting bales of hay. That was to help the diminutive golfer add some muscle to his frame, and Woosie became a long hitter as a result.

It took the Welshman three attempts to gain his European Tour card, but when he finally got it in 1978 he made sure he held on to it. His big breakthrough came in 1982 when he won the Swiss Open. That opened the floodgates. For the next 15 seasons, Woosie went only two years without a victory. Over that period he won 28 tournaments on the European Tour alone. He also added two World Match Play Championships, his Masters title, and another US Tour victory when he won the USF&G Classic.

Woosie's two biggest years to date have been 1987 and 1990. Both years he topped the European Order of Merit, and both seasons he won five times in Europe. The Welsh dynamo has also come close in other majors besides winning the Masters. In 1989 he finished second in the US Open, and he finished fourth in the British Open in 1990.

A perennial Ryder Cup player since his debut in 1983, Woosnam has played a big part in four winning matches and the tied match at The Belfry in 1989.

## Fact File

**BORN** 1958, Oswestry, Shropshire, England

**CAREER HIGHLIGHTS**
1987 Bell's Scottish Open
1988 Volvo PGA Championship
1991 Masters
1994 Dunhill British Masters
1997 Volvo PGA Championship

**INTERNATIONAL HONORS**
Ryder Cup: 1983, 1985, 1987, 1989, 1991, 1993, 1995, 1997
World Cup: 1980, 1982, 1983, 1984, 1985, 1987, 1990, 1991, 1992, 1993, 1994, 1996, 1997, 1998
Alfred Dunhill Cup: 1985, 1986, 1988, 1989, 1990, 1991, 1993, 1995

# International Team Shocks America

There have been many unlikely heroes in international team competitions, players who have excelled beyond expectations in the heat of intense competition. Shigeki Maruyama found himself in that role during the 1998 Presidents Cup.

Royal Melbourne Golf Club, Australia, was the scene. One of the toughest courses in the world, it was expected to favor the American team, a side the opposing International captain Peter Thomson said might have been the strongest in the history of the game. With Tiger Woods, Mark O'Meara, Phil Mickelson, Davis Love III, Justin Leonard, Lee Janzen, David Duval, Fred Couples, Scott Hoch, Mark Calcavecchia, John Huston and Jim Furyk playing under captain Jack Nicklaus, Thomson had a point. He just forgot to pass it on to his players. Thomson's team wasn't half bad either. It consisted of Ernie Els, Steve Elkington, Greg Norman, Nick Price, Vijay Singh, Craig Parry, Stuart Appleby, Frank Nobilo, Joe Ozaki, Greg Turner, Carlos Franco and the aforementioned Maruyama. Not quite the same strength as the Americans, but a team with a solid backbone of stars and some good quality players.

The previous two Presidents Cups had gone to the Americans. The first was an easy victory, but the second was won by a narrow one point. That 1998 was going to be different was soon obvious, as the International side raced into an early lead. On the Friday morning, the Americans lost the foursomes by a score of three-and-a-half to one-and-a-half, and lost by a similar score in the afternoon fourballs to enter the second day four points behind. It got worse on Saturday.

The second day saw the International squad win the morning foursomes by a comfortable four-and-a-half points to a half point. Then in the afternoon fourballs they took the series by three points to two to take a commanding 14½ points to five-and-a-half points lead into the singles. It meant they needed to win only two points on Sunday to win the cup. In the event they won four, lost four and halved four to win the cup by a landslide, 20½ to 11½.

Star of the show was the Japanese player Maruyama. He had never even heard of Royal Melbourne until the event started. Yet he was the only player to compile a perfect record of five matches played and five matches won. He had arrived in Australia hoping to win at least one point. When asked why he and Craig Parry had formed such a successful partnership, Maruyama replied, "I hit where Mr Parry told me to hit." The two teamed together in foursomes play to defeat Janzen and Hoch, then Woods and Couples. He also teamed with countryman Joe Ozaki in fourballs to get the better of Calcavecchia and Huston, and Duval and Mickelson. Just for good measure, Maruyama defeated John Huston in singles play—although with the form he was in that week he probably could have taken on Nicklaus in his prime and given him a good thrashing.

ABOVE: NICK PRICE DOWNED DAVID DUVAL IN THE SINGLES AND THEN LET HIS FEELINGS SHOW.

TOP RIGHT: THE INTERNATIONAL TEAM POSES WITH ITS FIRST PRESIDENTS CUP. PROUD CAPTAIN PETER THOMSON (WITH GLASSES) STANDS AT THE FRONT OF HIS WINNING TEAM.

RIGHT: THE STAR OF THE SHOW. JAPAN'S SHIGEKI MARUYAMA WAS THE ONLY PLAYER TO PLAY FIVE MATCHES AND WIN ALL FIVE.

The Presidents Cup

# MICKEY WRIGHT

MICKEY WRIGHT'S SCORE OF 82 CAREER VICTORIES HAS BEEN BEATEN BY ONLY ONE PLAYER, KATHY WHITWORTH. HOWEVER, WRIGHT'S EIGHT MAJOR CHAMPIONSHIP VICTORIES MAKE HER ARGUABLY THE GREATEST WOMAN GOLFER EVER.

## FACT FILE

**BORN** 1935, San Diego, California, USA

**CAREER HIGHLIGHTS**
1958 US Women's Open
1958 LPGA Championship
1959 US Women's Open
1960 LPGA Championship
1961 US Women's Open
1961 LPGA Championship
1963 LPGA Championship
1964 US Women's Open

Mickey Wright is arguably the best woman golfer that ever lived. Certainly her record backs her up, as does the opinion of another living legend of the women's game.

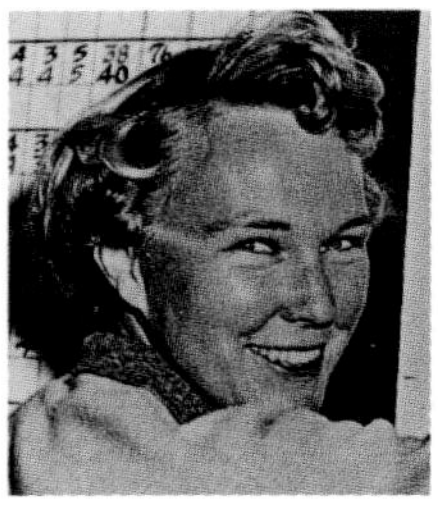

During the course of her career, Wright won 82 professional tournaments. That's one more than the total Sam Snead won on the men's Tour and just six short of Kathy Whitworth's record of 88, the most in LPGA history. However, Wright is considered a better player than Whitworth and would probably have won more had she not taken time away from tournament golf in the mid 1960s.

Wright's record is simply amazing. In 1963 alone she won 13 times, topping the LPGA money list for a fourth consecutive season. Between 1960 and 1964 she won no less than 44 tournaments. She won the US Women's Open four times and the LPGA Championship four times. During her peak there was no one who could touch her.

Betsy Rawls, a legend in her own right, once acknowledged that Wright was the greatest woman golfer ever. "Mickey was the best golfer we've ever had, and that I've ever seen," said Rawls about her one-time great rival. Indeed, it was Rawls who gave Wright invaluable advice early on. Rawls told Wright that she needed to focus more on winning than the mechanics of her golf swing. Wright was prone to be too technical about her swing rather than concentrating on getting the ball into the hole. Once she concentrated on scoring, there was no stopping her.

Wright grew up in San Diego, California, and was introduced to the game by her father at the age of 10. He took her to a professional by the name of Johnny Bellante, who had taught Gene Littler to play. Soon Wright was obsessed by the game. When she was 11 years old a photograph of her appeared in the local newspaper with a caption that said, "The next Babe?" a reference to Babe Zaharias. The caption was right. When Zaharias died in 1956 Wright assumed her mantle as the game's best woman golfer.

Wright's incredible run from 1960 to 1964 can be credited to her work with Earl Stewart, a Dallas professional. Stewart never really touched Wright's swing, which was perfection personified anyway, but he forced her to set goals as high as she could. She did, and had no trouble achieving them.

Wright's proudest victory came when she won the 1964 US Open. She needed to hole a six-foot putt on the last green to force a playoff and did so. She won the title the next day and she did it in front of her mother and her father, who, aged 79, was in poor health.

# Babe Zaharias



Babe Zaharias was the greatest female athlete to walk the fairways of the world. Zaharias won three Olympic medals before she turned her attention to golf.

Babe Zaharias is probably the only professional golfer to claim two Olympic gold medals and one silver medal, which she won in the 1932 Olympic games, long before she ever turned her attention to golf.

Zaharias is arguably the most natural athlete ever to play the women's game. She grew up as Mildred Ella Didrikson in Port Arthur, Texas. When she was a small child her parents moved to Beaumont, Texas, where her father built a gymnasium with weight-lifting equipment and a trapeze. Mildred soon expressed herself in athletics as a result. She was on every sports team at Beaumont High School—baseball, swimming, volleyball, basketball, tennis—you name it, "the Babe" played it. She earned her nickname from hitting home runs in baseball, after the legendary Babe Ruth.

Basketball was her first love, and Babe played the game for a team called the Golden Cyclones in Dallas, Texas. She was introduced to track and field shortly afterward and soon excelled by winning Olympic gold in the low hurdles and javelin, and silver in the high jump.

After her Olympic achievements, Zaharias turned her attention to golf. She went to Los Angeles in 1933 where she worked with a professional called Stan Kertes. For six months the Babe hit hundreds of balls each day in an effort to improve her game. By 1934, she was good enough to win the Texas Women's Amateur Championship.

The Babe's amateur status was called into question because she had played as a professional in other sports. Her status was taken away and she started doing clinics and exhibitions, often with Gene Sarazen.

Zaharias regained her amateur status in 1943 and when World War II ended she started playing amateur tournaments. She had a run from 1946 where she won just about every tournament she entered, including the 1946 US Amateur and the 1947 British Ladies' Championship.

In 1947, Zaharias turned professional and the following year won the first of her three US Opens. Her first championship was won by the margin of eight shots. Further victories followed in 1950 and 1954.

The Babe won 31 professional tournaments during her career, but it could have been a lot more. She was diagnosed with cancer in 1953 and underwent an operation. Despite that she won two tournaments that year. The following year she won five times including her final US Women's Open, which she won by 12 strokes from Betty Hicks. She went on to win twice more in 1955, but following an operation in June that year she never played golf again. She died in September 1956 at just 42 years old, and has always been remembered as one of the greatest female athletes ever.

## Fact File

**BORN** 1914, Port Arthur, Texas, USA

**DIED** 1956

**CAREER HIGHLIGHTS**
1946 US Women's Amateur
1947 British Ladies' Championship
1948 US Women's Open
1950 US Women's Open
1954 US Women's Open

# FUZZY ZOELLER

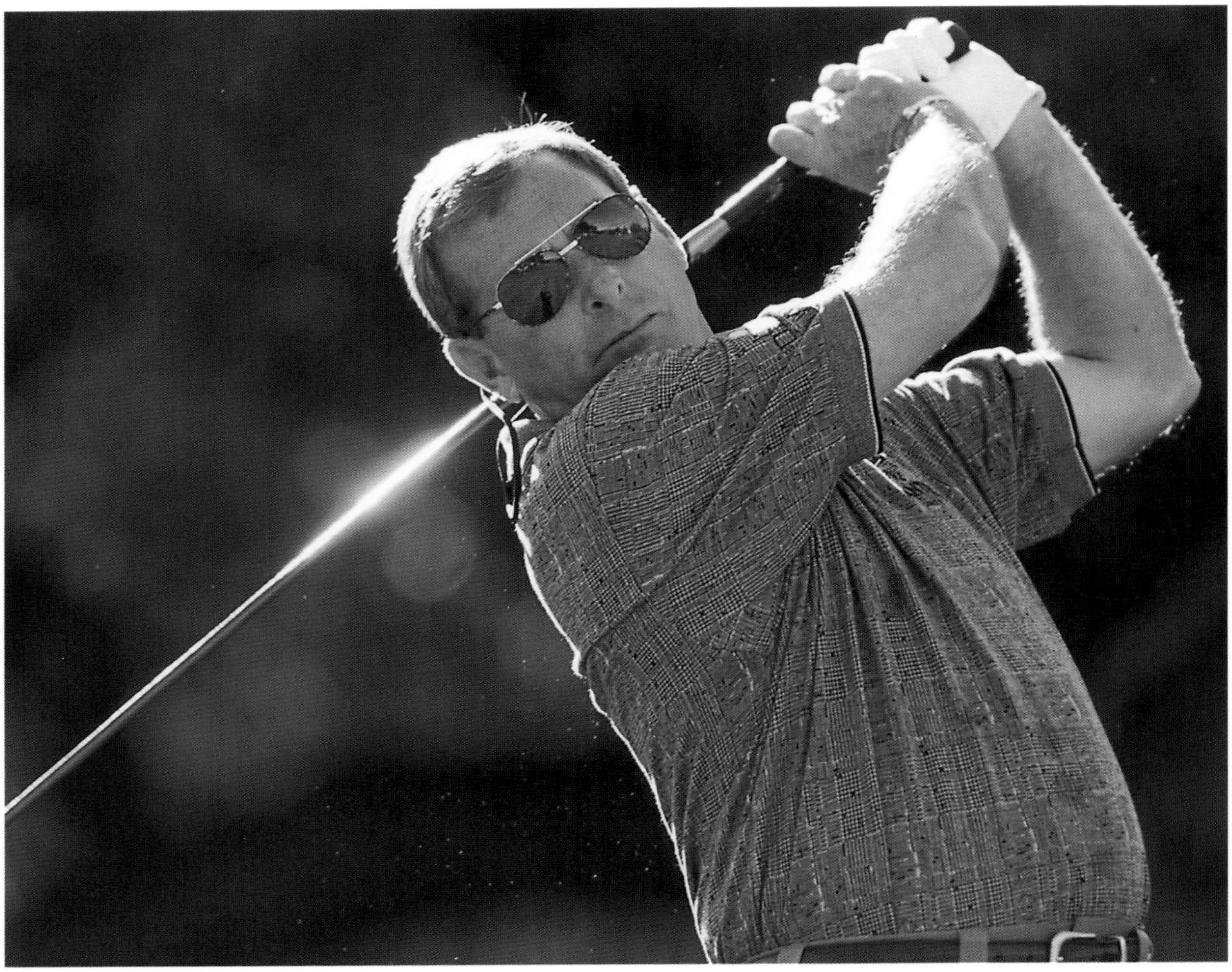

FUZZY ZOELLER IS ONE OF THE MOST POPULAR GOLFERS EVER. THE EASY-GOING PROFESSIONAL IS A GALLERY FAVORITE WHEREVER HE PLAYS.

## FACT FILE

**BORN** 1951, New Albany, Indiana, USA

**CAREER HIGHLIGHTS**
1979 Masters
1981 Colonial National Invitation
1984 US Open
1985 Hertz Bay Hill Classic
1986 AT&T Pebble Beach National Pro-Am

**INTERNATIONAL HONORS**
Ryder Cup: 1979, 1983, 1985

No golfer in recent times has given off such an air of complete nonchalance as Frank Urban Zoeller, or Fuzzy, and that applies even when he's in the heat of a major championship.

Walter Hagen once said that every golfer should take time to stop and smell the flowers as he or she goes through life. That's just what Fuzzy does. He whistles as he walks down the fairways, he chats to the fans, jokes with them, and on the odd occasion has even accepted their offer of a sip from whatever it is they are drinking. That attitude has made Fuzzy a crowd favorite everywhere.

Zoeller has acted like a big brother to John Daly during his career, and has helped the former USPGA and British Open champion through his troubles.

Zoeller is one of only three men to win the Masters at Augusta National on their first attempt. The first was Horton Smith, obviously, as he won the inaugural 1934 tournament. The second was Gene Sarazen in 1935, who had to skip the first Masters because of other commitments. Forty-four years passed and in that time no player ever won the Masters on their first go, until Fuzzy Zoeller.

Zoeller got into the 1979 Masters when he won the Wickes-Andy Williams San Diego Open. He came back from shooting an opening 76 to win the tournament by five strokes. It was his first US Tour victory. His second was accomplished in even greater style.

Zoeller was involved in the first sudden death playoff for the Masters. Until 1979, every other tie had been decided in an 18-hole playoff. In the 1979 tournaments, Ed Sneed had the title virtually in his hand but faltered down the stretch to allow Zoeller and Tom Watson into a playoff. They tied the first extra hole, the 10th, then Fuzzy holed a birdie putt from eight feet on the 11th green to win his first major championship.

Three more victories followed over the next two seasons, and then Zoeller won the US Open at Winged Foot Golf Club in New York. An incident on the final day showed that he is a true sportsman. Playing behind Greg Norman, Fuzzy was standing on the 18th fairway as Norman knocked in a monster putt for par. Zoeller thought it was for a birdie and that Norman had gone one stroke ahead. He immediately reached for the white towel on his bag and started waving it in mock surrender. Fuzzy made par and then found he was in a playoff with Norman the next day. Zoeller easily won the playoff, shooting a 67 to his opponent's 75. Norman returned the compliment by waving a white towel as the two strode down the final fairway.

# MAJOR CHAMPIONSHIP AND RYDER CUP RESULTS

COMPILED BY GEOFFREY S. WILDE

## THE U.S. OPEN CHAMPIONSHIP

| YEAR | WINNER | VENUE | SCORE |
|---|---|---|---|
| 1895 | H. J. Rawlins | Newport, RI | 173 |
| 1896 | J. Foulis | Shinnecock Hills, NY | 152 |
| 1897 | J. Lloyd | Chicago, IL | 162 |
| 1898 | F. Herd | Myopia Hunt Club, MA | 328 |
| 1899 | W. Smith | Baltimore CC, MD | 315 |
| 1900 | H. Vardon | Chicago, IL | 313 |
| 1901 | W. Anderson | Myopia Hunt Club, MA | 331 |
| 1902 | L. Auchterlonie | Garden City, NY | 307 |
| 1903 | W. Anderson | Baltusrol, NJ | 307 |
| 1904 | W. Anderson | Glen View, IL | 303 |
| 1905 | W. Anderson | Myopia Hunt Club, MA | 314 |
| 1906 | A. Smith | Onwentsia, IL | 295 |
| 1907 | A. Ross | Philadelphia Cricket Club, PA | 302 |
| 1908 | F. R. McLeod | Myopia Hunt Club, MA | 322 |
| 1909 | G. Sargent | Englewood, NJ | 290 |
| 1910 | A. Smith | Philadelphia Cricket Club, PA | 298 |
| 1911 | J. J. McDermott | Chicago, IL | 307 |
| 1912 | J. J. McDermott | Buffalo CC, NY | 294 |
| 1913 | F. de S. Ouimet * | Country Club, Brookline, MA | 304 |
| 1914 | W. C. Hagen | Midlothian CC, IL | 290 |
| 1915 | J. D. Travers * | Baltusrol, NJ | 297 |
| 1916 | C. Evans, Jr * | Minikahda, MN | 286 |
| 1917 – 1918 | | No Championship | |
| 1919 | W. C. Hagen | Brae Burn CC, MA | 301 |
| 1920 | E. Ray | Inverness, OH | 295 |
| 1921 | J. M. Barnes | Columbia CC, MD | 289 |
| 1922 | E. Sarazen | Skokie CC, IL | 288 |
| 1923 | R. T. Jones, Jr * | Inwood CC, NY | 296 |
| 1924 | C. Walker | Oakland Hills CC, MI | 297 |
| 1925 | W. MacFarlane | Worcester CC, MA | 291 |
| 1926 | R. T. Jones, Jr * | Scioto CC, OH | 293 |
| 1927 | T. D. Armour | Oakmont CC, PA | 301 |
| 1928 | J. Farrell | Olympia Fields CC, IL | 294 |
| 1929 | R. T. Jones, Jr * | Winged Foot, NY | 294 |
| 1930 | R. T. Jones, Jr * | Interlachen CC, MN | 287 |
| 1931 | B. Burke | Inverness, OH | 292 |
| 1932 | E. Sarazen | Fresh Meadow CC, NY | 286 |
| 1933 | J. G. Goodman * | North Shore, IL | 287 |
| 1934 | O. Dutra | Merion Cricket Club, PA | 293 |
| 1935 | S. Parks, Jr | Oakmont CC, PA | 299 |
| 1936 | T. Manero | Baltusrol, NJ | 282 |
| 1937 | R. Guldahl | Oakland Hills CC, MI | 281 |
| 1938 | R. Guldahl | Cherry Hills, CO | 284 |
| 1939 | J. B. Nelson, Jr | Philadelphia CC, PA | 284 |
| 1940 | W. L. Little, Jr | Canterbury, OH | 287 |
| 1941 | C. R. Wood | Colonial, TX | 284 |
| 1942 – 1945 | | No Championship | |
| 1946 | L. E. Mangrum | Canterbury, OH | 284 |
| 1947 | L. E. Worsham | St Louis CC, MS | 282 |
| 1948 | W. B. Hogan | Riviera CC, CA | 276 |
| 1949 | C. Middlecoff | Medinah CC, IL | 286 |
| 1950 | W. B. Hogan | Merion, PA | 287 |
| 1951 | W. B. Hogan | Oakland Hills CC, MI | 287 |
| 1952 | J. Boros | Northwood, TX | 281 |
| 1953 | W. B. Hogan | Oakmont CC, PA | 283 |
| 1954 | E. J. Furgol | Baltusrol, NJ | 284 |
| 1955 | J. Fleck | Olympic CC, CA | 287 |
| 1956 | C. Middlecoff | Oak Hill CC, NY | 281 |
| 1957 | R. Mayer | Inverness, OH | 282 |
| 1958 | T. Bolt | Southern Hills CC, OK | 283 |
| 1959 | W. E. Casper, Jr | Winged Foot, NY | 282 |
| 1960 | A. D. Palmer | Cherry Hills CC, CO | 280 |
| 1961 | E. A. Littler | Oakland Hills CC, MI | 281 |
| 1962 | J. W. Nicklaus | Oakmont CC, PA | 283 |
| 1963 | J. Boros | Country Club, Brookline, MA | 293 |
| 1964 | K. Venturi | Congressional CC, MD | 278 |
| 1965 | G. J. Player | Bellerive CC, MS | 282 |
| 1966 | W. E. Casper, Jr | Olympic CC, CA | 278 |
| 1967 | J. W. Nicklaus | Baltusrol, NJ | 275 |
| 1968 | L. B. Trevino | Oak Hill CC, NY | 275 |
| 1969 | O. J. Moody | Champions, TX | 281 |
| 1970 | A. Jacklin | Hazeltine National, MN | 281 |
| 1971 | L. B. Trevino | Merion, PA | 280 |
| 1972 | J. W. Nicklaus | Pebble Beach, CA | 290 |
| 1973 | J. L. Miller | Oakmont CC, PA | 279 |
| 1974 | H. S. Irwin | Winged Foot, NY | 287 |
| 1975 | L. Graham | Medinah CC, IL | 287 |
| 1976 | J. Pate | Atlanta Athletic Club, GA | 277 |
| 1977 | H. M. Green | Southern Hills CC, OK | 278 |
| 1978 | A. S. North | Cherry Hills CC, CO | 285 |
| 1979 | H. S. Irwin | Inverness, OH | 284 |
| 1980 | J. W. Nicklaus | Baltusrol, NJ | 272 |
| 1981 | A. D. Graham | Merion, PA | 273 |
| 1982 | T. S. Watson | Pebble Beach, CA | 282 |
| 1983 | L. G. Nelson | Oakmont CC, PA | 280 |
| 1984 | F. U. Zoeller | Winged Foot, NY | 276 |
| 1985 | A. S. North | Oakland Hills CC, MI | 279 |
| 1986 | R. L. Floyd | Shinnecock Hills, NY | 279 |
| 1987 | S. W. Simpson | Olympic Club, CA | 277 |
| 1988 | C. N. Strange | Country Club, Brookline, MA | 278 |
| 1989 | C. N. Strange | Oak Hill CC, NY | 278 |
| 1990 | H. S. Irwin | Medinah CC, IL | 280 |
| 1991 | W. P. Stewart | Hazeltine National, MN | 282 |
| 1992 | T. O. Kite, Jr | Pebble Beach, CA | 285 |
| 1993 | L. M. Janzen | Baltusrol, NJ | 272 |
| 1994 | E. Els | Oakmont CC, PA | 279 |
| 1995 | C. Pavin | Shinnecock Hills, NY | 280 |
| 1996 | S. Jones | Oakland Hills CC, MI | 278 |
| 1997 | E. Els | Congressional CC, MD | 276 |
| 1998 | L. M. Janzen | Olympic Club, CA | 280 |
| 1999 | W. P. Stewart | Pinehurst CC, NC | 279 |

* = Amateur

# The Open Championship

| YEAR | WINNER | VENUE | SCORE |
|---|---|---|---|
| 1860 | W. Park, Sr | Prestwick | 174 |
| 1861 | T. Morris, Sr | Prestwick | 163 |
| 1862 | T. Morris, Sr | Prestwick | 163 |
| 1863 | W. Park, Sr | Prestwick | 168 |
| 1864 | T. Morris, Sr | Prestwick | 167 |
| 1865 | A. Strath | Prestwick | 162 |
| 1866 | W. Park, Sr | Prestwick | 169 |
| 1867 | T. Morris, Sr | Prestwick | 170 |
| 1868 | T. Morris, Jr | Prestwick | 157 |
| 1869 | T. Morris, Jr | Prestwick | 154 |
| 1870 | T. Morris, Jr | Prestwick | 149 |
| 1871 | | No Championship | |
| 1872 | T. Morris, Jr | Prestwick | 166 |
| 1873 | T. Kidd | St Andrews | 179 |
| 1874 | M. Park | Musselburgh | 159 |
| 1875 | W. Park, Sr | Prestwick | 166 |
| 1876 | R. Martin | St Andrews | 176 |
| 1877 | J. Anderson | Musselburgh | 160 |
| 1878 | J. Anderson | Prestwick | 157 |
| 1879 | J. Anderson | St Andrews | 169 |
| 1880 | R. Ferguson | Musselburgh | 162 |
| 1881 | R. Ferguson | Prestwick | 170 |
| 1882 | R. Ferguson | St Andrews | 171 |
| 1883 | W. Fernie | Musselburgh | 159 |
| 1884 | J. Simpson | Prestwick | 160 |
| 1885 | R. Martin | St Andrews | 171 |
| 1886 | D. Brown | Musselburgh | 157 |
| 1887 | W. Park, Jr | Prestwick | 161 |
| 1888 | J. Burns | St Andrews | 171 |
| 1889 | W. Park, Jr | Musselburgh | 155 |
| 1890 | J. Ball * | Prestwick | 164 |
| 1891 | H. Kirkaldy | St Andrews | 166 |
| 1892 | H. H. Hilton * | Muirfield | 305 |
| 1893 | W. Auchterlonie | Prestwick | 322 |
| 1894 | J. H. Taylor | St George's (Sandwich) | 326 |
| 1895 | J. H. Taylor | St Andrews | 322 |
| 1896 | H. Vardon | Muirfield | 316 |
| 1897 | H. H. Hilton * | Royal Liverpool (Hoylake) | 314 |
| 1898 | H. Vardon | Prestwick | 307 |
| 1899 | H. Vardon | St George's (Sandwich) | 310 |
| 1900 | J. H. Taylor | St Andrews | 309 |
| 1901 | J. Braid | Muirfield | 309 |
| 1902 | A. Herd | Royal Liverpool (Hoylake) | 307 |
| 1903 | H. Vardon | Prestwick | 300 |
| 1904 | J. White | Royal St George's (Sandwich) | 296 |
| 1905 | J. Braid | St Andrews | 318 |
| 1906 | J. Braid | Muirfield | 300 |
| 1907 | A. Massy | Royal Liverpool (Hoylake) | 312 |
| 1908 | J. Braid | Prestwick | 291 |
| 1909 | J. H. Taylor | Royal Cinque Ports (Deal) | 295 |
| 1910 | J. Braid | St Andrews | 299 |
| 1911 | H. Vardon | Royal St George's (Sandwich) | 303 |
| 1912 | E. Ray | Muirfield | 295 |
| 1913 | J. H. Taylor | Royal Liverpool (Hoylake) | 304 |
| 1914 | H. Vardon | Prestwick | 306 |
| 1915 – 1919 | | No Championship | |
| 1920 | G. Duncan | Royal Cinque Ports (Deal) | 303 |
| 1921 | J. Hutchison | St Andrews | 296 |
| 1922 | W. C. Hagen | Royal St George's (Sandwich) | 300 |
| 1923 | A. G. Havers | Troon | 295 |
| 1924 | W. C. Hagen | Royal Liverpool (Hoylake) | 301 |
| 1925 | J. M. Barnes | Prestwick | 300 |
| 1926 | R. T. Jones, Jr* | Royal Lytham & St Annes | 291 |
| 1927 | R. T. Jones, Jr* | St Andrews | 285 |
| 1928 | W. C. Hagen | Royal St George's (Sandwich) | 292 |
| 1929 | W. C. Hagen | Muirfield | 292 |
| 1930 | R. T. Jones, Jr* | Royal Liverpool (Hoylake) | 291 |
| 1931 | T. D. Armour | Carnoustie | 296 |
| 1932 | E. Sarazen | Prince's (Sandwich) | 283 |
| 1933 | H. D. Shute | St Andrews | 292 |
| 1934 | T. H. Cotton | Royal St George's (Sandwich) | 283 |
| 1935 | A. Perry | Muirfield | 283 |
| 1936 | A. H. Padgham | Royal Liverpool (Hoylake) | 287 |
| 1937 | T. H. Cotton | Carnoustie | 290 |
| 1938 | R. A. Whitcombe | Royal St George's (Sandwich) | 295 |
| 1939 | R. Burton | St Andrews | 290 |
| 1940 – 1945 | | No Championship | |
| 1946 | S. J. Snead | St Andrews | 290 |
| 1947 | F. Daly | Royal Liverpool (Hoylake) | 293 |
| 1948 | T. H. Cotton | Muirfield | 284 |
| 1949 | A. D. Locke | Royal St George's (Sandwich) | 283 |
| 1950 | A. D. Locke | Troon | 279 |
| 1951 | M. Faulkner | Royal Portrush | 285 |
| 1952 | A. D. Locke | Royal Lytham & St Annes | 287 |
| 1953 | W. B. Hogan | Carnoustie | 282 |
| 1954 | P. W. Thomson | Royal Birkdale | 283 |
| 1955 | P. W. Thomson | St Andrews | 281 |
| 1956 | P. W. Thomson | Royal Liverpool (Hoylake) | 286 |
| 1957 | A. D. Locke | St Andrews | 279 |
| 1958 | P. W. Thomson | Royal Liverpool (Hoylake) | 278 |
| 1959 | G. J. Player | Muirfield | 284 |
| 1960 | K. D. G. Nagle | St Andrews | 278 |
| 1961 | A. D. Palmer | Royal Birkdale | 284 |
| 1962 | A. D. Palmer | Troon | 276 |
| 1963 | R. J. Charles | Royal Lytham & St Annes | 277 |
| 1964 | A. D. Lema | St Andrews | 279 |
| 1965 | P. W. Thomson | Royal Birkdale | 285 |
| 1966 | J. W. Nicklaus | Muirfield | 282 |
| 1967 | R. de Vicenzo | Royal Liverpool (Hoylake) | 278 |
| 1968 | G. J. Player | Carnoustie | 289 |
| 1969 | A. Jacklin | Royal Lytham & St Annes | 280 |
| 1970 | J. W. Nicklaus | St Andrews | 283 |
| 1971 | L. B. Trevino | Royal Birkdale | 278 |
| 1972 | L. B. Trevino | Muirfield | 278 |
| 1973 | T. D. Weiskopf | Troon | 276 |
| 1974 | G. J. Player | Royal Lytham & St Annes | 282 |
| 1975 | T. S. Watson | Carnoustie | 279 |
| 1976 | J. L. Miller | Royal Birkdale | 279 |
| 1977 | T. S. Watson | Turnberry | 268 |
| 1978 | J. W. Nicklaus | St Andrews | 281 |
| 1979 | S. Ballesteros | Royal Lytham & St Annes | 283 |
| 1980 | T. S. Watson | Muirfield | 271 |
| 1981 | W. C. Rogers | Royal St George's (Sandwich) | 276 |
| 1982 | T. S. Watson | Royal Troon | 284 |
| 1983 | T. S. Watson | Royal Birkdale | 275 |
| 1984 | S. Ballesteros | St Andrews | 276 |
| 1985 | A. W. B. Lyle | Royal St George's (Sandwich) | 282 |
| 1986 | G. J. Norman | Turnberry | 280 |
| 1987 | N. A. Faldo | Muirfield | 279 |
| 1988 | S. Ballesteros | Royal Lytham & St Annes | 273 |
| 1989 | M. Calcavecchia | Royal Troon | 275 |
| 1990 | N. A. Faldo | St Andrews | 270 |
| 1991 | I. Baker-Finch | Royal Birkdale | 272 |
| 1992 | N. A. Faldo | Muirfield | 272 |
| 1993 | G. J. Norman | Royal St George's (Sandwich) | 267 |
| 1994 | N. R. L. Price | Turnberry | 268 |
| 1995 | J. P. Daly | St Andrews | 282 |
| 1996 | T. E. Lehman | Royal Lytham & St Annes | 271 |
| 1997 | J. Leonard | Royal Troon | 272 |
| 1998 | M. O'Meara | Royal Birkdale | 280 |
| 1999 | P. Lawrie | Carnoustie | 290 |

* = Amateur

# THE U.S. P.G.A. CHAMPIONSHIP

## MATCHPLAY

| YEAR | WINNER & RUNNER-UP | VENUE | MARGIN |
|---|---|---|---|
| 1916 | J. M. Barnes beat J. Hutchison | Siwanoy CC, NY | 1 Hole |
| 1917 – 1918 | | No Championship | |
| 1919 | J. M. Barnes beat F. R. McLeod | Engineers CC, NY | 6 & 5 |
| 1920 | J. Hutchison beat J. D. Edgar | Flossmoor CC, IL | 1 Hole |
| 1921 | W. C. Hagen beat J. M. Barnes | Inwood CC, NY | 3 & 2 |
| 1922 | E. Sarazen beat E. French | Oakmont CC, PA | 4 & 3 |
| 1923 | E. Sarazen beat W. C. Hagen | Pelham, NY | At 38th |
| 1924 | W. C. Hagen beat J. M. Barnes | French Lick, IN | 2 Holes |
| 1925 | W. C. Hagen beat W. E. Mehlhorn | Olympia Fields CC, IL | 6 & 5 |
| 1926 | W. C. Hagen beat L. Diegel | Salisbury, NY | 5 & 3 |
| 1927 | W. C. Hagen beat Joe Turnesa | Cedar Crest CC, TX | 1 Hole |
| 1928 | L. Diegel beat A. R. Espinosa | Five Farms CC, MD | 6 & 5 |
| 1929 | L. Diegel beat J. Farrell | Hillcrest CC, CA | 6 & 4 |
| 1930 | T. D. Armour beat E. Sarazen | Fresh Meadow CC, NY | 1 Hole |
| 1931 | T. Creavy beat H. D. Shute | Wannamoisett, RI | 2 & 1 |
| 1932 | O. Dutra beat F. Walsh | Keller, MN | 4 & 3 |
| 1933 | E. Sarazen beat W. Goggin | Blue Mound CC, WI | 5 & 4 |
| 1934 | P. S. Runyan beat C. R. Wood | Park Club of Buffalo, NY | At 38th |
| 1935 | J. Revolta beat T. D. Armour | Twin Hills CC, OK | 5 & 4 |
| 1936 | H. D. Shute beat J. Thomson | Pinehurst CC, NC | 3 & 2 |
| 1937 | H. D. Shute beat H. McSpaden | Pittsburgh Field Club, PA | At 37th |
| 1938 | P. S. Runyan beat S. J. Snead | Shawnee CC, PA | 8 & 7 |
| 1939 | H. C. Picard beat J. B. Nelson, Jr | Pomonok CC, NY | At 37th |
| 1940 | J. B. Nelson, Jr beat S. J. Snead | Hershey CC, PA | 1 Hole |
| 1941 | V. Ghezzi beat J. B. Nelson, Jr | Cherry Hills CC, CO | At 38th |
| 1942 | S. J. Snead beat Jim Turnesa | Seaview CC, NJ | 2 & 1 |
| 1943 | | No Championship | |
| 1944 | R. Hamilton beat J. B. Nelson, Jr | Manito CC, WA | 1 Hole |
| 1945 | J. B. Nelson, Jr beat S. Byrd | Morraine CC, OH | 4 & 3 |
| 1946 | W. B. Hogan beat E. Oliver | Portland, OR | 6 & 4 |
| 1947 | J. Ferrier beat M. R. Harbert | Plum Hollow CC, MI | 2 & 1 |
| 1948 | W. B. Hogan beat M. Turnesa | Norwood Hills CC, MS | 7 & 6 |
| 1949 | S. J. Snead beat J. Palmer | Hermitage CC, VA | 3 & 2 |
| 1950 | C. Harper beat H. Williams, Jr | Scioto CC, OH | 4 & 3 |
| 1951 | S. J. Snead beat W. Burkemo | Oakmont CC, PA | 7 & 6 |
| 1952 | Jim Turnesa beat M. R. Harbert | Big Spring CC, KY | 1 Hole |
| 1953 | W. Burkemo beat F. Torza | Birmingham CC, MI | 2 & 1 |
| 1954 | M. R. Harbert beat W. Burkemo | Keller, MN | 4 & 3 |
| 1955 | D. Ford beat C. Middlecoff | Meadowbrook CC, MI | 4 & 3 |
| 1956 | J. Burke, Jr beat T. Kroll | Blue Hill CC, MA | 3 & 2 |
| 1957 | L. Hebert beat D. Finsterwald | Miami Valley, OH | 2 & 1 |

## STROKEPLAY

| YEAR | WINNER | VENUE | SCORE |
|---|---|---|---|
| 1958 | D. Finsterwald | Llanerch CC, PA | 276 |
| 1959 | R. R. Rosburg | Minneapolis, MN | 277 |
| 1960 | J. J. Hebert | Firestone CC, OH | 281 |
| 1961 | J. Barber | Olympia Fields CC, IL | 277 |
| 1962 | G. J. Player | Aronimink, PA | 278 |
| 1963 | J. W. Nicklaus | Dallas Athletic Club, TX | 279 |
| 1964 | B. Nichols | Columbus CC, OH | 271 |
| 1965 | D. Marr | Laurel Valley, PA | 280 |
| 1966 | A. Geiberger | Firestone CC, OH | 280 |
| 1967 | D. January | Columbine CC, CO | 281 |
| 1968 | J. Boros | Pecan Valley CC, TX | 281 |
| 1969 | R. L. Floyd | NCR CC, OH | 276 |
| 1970 | D. Stockton | Southern Hills CC, OK | 279 |
| 1971 | J. W. Nicklaus | PGA National, FL | 281 |
| 1972 | G. J. Player | Oakland Hills CC, MI | 281 |
| 1973 | J. W. Nicklaus | Canterbury, OH | 277 |
| 1974 | L. B. Trevino | Tanglewood, NC | 276 |
| 1975 | J. W. Nicklaus | Firestone CC, OH | 276 |
| 1976 | D. Stockton | Congressional CC, MD | 281 |
| 1977 | J. L. Wadkins | Pebble Beach, CA | 282 |
| 1978 | J. D. Mahaffey | Oakmont CC, PA | 276 |
| 1979 | A. D. Graham | Oakland Hills CC, MI | 272 |
| 1980 | J. W. Nicklaus | Oak Hill CC, NY | 274 |
| 1981 | L. G. Nelson | Atlanta Athletic Club, GA | 273 |
| 1982 | R. L. Floyd | Southern Hills CC, OK | 272 |
| 1983 | H. Sutton | Riviera CC, CA | 274 |
| 1984 | L. B. Trevino | Shoal Creek CC, AL | 273 |
| 1985 | H. M. Green | Cherry Hills CC, CO | 278 |
| 1986 | R. Tway | Inverness, OH | 276 |
| 1987 | L. G. Nelson | PGA National, FL | 287 |
| 1988 | J. Sluman | Oak Tree, OK | 272 |
| 1989 | W. P. Stewart | Kemper Lakes, IL | 276 |
| 1990 | W. Grady | Shoal Creek CC, AL | 282 |
| 1991 | J. P. Daly | Crooked Stick, IN | 276 |
| 1992 | N. R. L. Price | Bellerive CC, MS | 278 |
| 1993 | P. W. Azinger | Inverness, OH | 272 |
| 1994 | N. R. L. Price | Southern Hills CC, OK | 269 |
| 1995 | S. Elkington | Riviera CC, CA | 267 |
| 1996 | M. Brooks | Valhalla, KY | 277 |
| 1997 | D. Love III | Winged Foot, NY | 269 |
| 1998 | V. Singh | Sahalee CC, WA | 271 |
| 1999 | E. Woods | Medinah CC, IL | 277 |

# U.S. Masters Tournament

## Played at Augusta National, Georgia

| YEAR | WINNER | SCORE |
|---|---|---|
| 1934 | H. Smith | 284 |
| 1935 | E. Sarazen | 282 |
| 1936 | H. Smith | 285 |
| 1937 | J. B. Nelson, Jr | 283 |
| 1938 | H. C. Picard | 285 |
| 1939 | R. Guldahl | 279 |
| 1940 | J. N. Demaret | 280 |
| 1941 | C. R. Wood | 280 |
| 1942 | J. B. Nelson, Jr | 280 |
| 1943 – 1945 | No Tournament | |
| 1946 | H. Keiser | 282 |
| 1947 | J. N. Demaret | 281 |
| 1948 | E. C. Harmon | 279 |
| 1949 | S. J. Snead | 282 |
| 1950 | J. N. Demaret | 283 |
| 1951 | W. B. Hogan | 280 |
| 1952 | S. J. Snead | 286 |
| 1953 | W. B. Hogan | 274 |
| 1954 | S. J. Snead | 289 |
| 1955 | C. Middlecoff | 279 |
| 1956 | J. Burke, Jr | 289 |
| 1957 | D. Ford | 283 |
| 1958 | A. D. Palmer | 284 |
| 1959 | A. Wall, Jr | 284 |
| 1960 | A. D. Palmer | 282 |
| 1961 | G. J. Player | 280 |
| 1962 | A. D. Palmer | 280 |
| 1963 | J. W. Nicklaus | 286 |
| 1964 | A. D. Palmer | 276 |
| 1965 | J. W. Nicklaus | 271 |
| 1966 | J. W. Nicklaus | 288 |
| 1967 | G. Brewer, Jr | 280 |
| 1968 | R. Goalby | 277 |
| 1969 | G. Archer | 281 |
| 1970 | W. E. Casper, Jr | 279 |
| 1971 | C. Coody | 279 |
| 1972 | J. W. Nicklaus | 286 |
| 1973 | T. D. Aaron | 283 |
| 1974 | G. J. Player | 278 |
| 1975 | J. W. Nicklaus | 276 |
| 1976 | R. L. Floyd | 271 |
| 1977 | T. S. Watson | 276 |
| 1978 | G. J. Player | 277 |
| 1979 | F. U. Zoeller | 280 |
| 1980 | S. Ballesteros | 275 |
| 1981 | T. S. Watson | 280 |
| 1982 | C. R. Stadler | 284 |
| 1983 | S. Ballesteros | 280 |
| 1984 | B. D. Crenshaw | 277 |
| 1985 | B. Langer | 282 |
| 1986 | J. W. Nicklaus | 279 |
| 1987 | L. H. Mize | 285 |
| 1988 | A. W. B. Lyle | 281 |
| 1989 | N. A. Faldo | 283 |
| 1990 | N. A. Faldo | 278 |
| 1991 | I. H. Woosnam | 277 |
| 1992 | F. S. Couples | 275 |
| 1993 | B. Langer | 277 |
| 1994 | J.-M. Olazabal | 279 |
| 1995 | B. D. Crenshaw | 274 |
| 1996 | N. A. Faldo | 276 |
| 1997 | E. Woods | 270 |
| 1998 | M. O'Meara | 279 |
| 1999 | J.-M. Olazabal | 280 |

# The Ryder Cup

## 1927 WORCESTER, MASSACHUSETTS

CAPTAINS: W. C. HAGEN (USA) and E. RAY (GB)

| FOURSOMES: | |
|---|---|
| W. C. Hagen & J. Golden beat E. Ray & F. Robson | 2 & 1 |
| J. Farrell & Joe Turnesa beat G. Duncan & A. E. W. Compston | 8 & 6 |
| E. Sarazen & A. A. Watrous beat A. G. Havers & H. C. Jolly | 3 & 2 |
| L. Diegel & W. E. Mehlhorn lost to A. B. Boomer & C. A. Whitcombe | 7 & 5 |
| **SINGLES:** | |
| W. E. Mehlhorn beat A. E. W. Compston | 1 Hole |
| J. Farrell beat A. B. Boomer | 5 & 4 |
| J. Golden beat H. C. Jolly | 8 & 7 |
| L. Diegel beat E. Ray | 7 & 5 |
| E. Sarazen halved with C. A. Whitcombe | Halved |
| W. C. Hagen beat A. G. Havers | 2 & 1 |
| A. A. Watrous beat F. Robson | 3 & 2 |
| Joe Turnesa lost to G. Duncan | 1 Hole |

**RESULT: USA 9½, GB 2½**

## 1929 MOORTOWN, ENGLAND

CAPTAINS: G. DUNCAN (GB) and W. C. HAGEN (USA)

| FOURSOMES: | |
|---|---|
| C. A. Whitcombe & A. E. W. Compston halved with J. Farrell & Joe Turnesa | Halved |
| A. B. Boomer & G. Duncan lost to L. Diegel & A R. Espinosa | 7 & 5 |
| A. Mitchell & F. Robson beat E. Sarazen & E. B. Dudley | 2 & 1 |
| E. R. Whitcombe & T. H. Cotton lost to J. Golden & W. C. Hagen | 2 Holes |
| **SINGLES:** | |
| C. A. Whitcombe beat J. Farrell | 8 & 6 |
| G. Duncan beat W. C. Hagen | 10 & 8 |
| A. Mitchell lost to L. Diegel | 9 & 8 |
| A. E. W. Compston beat E. Sarazen | 6 & 4 |
| A. B. Boomer beat Joe Turnesa | 4 & 3 |
| F. Robson lost to H. Smith | 4 & 2 |
| T. H. Cotton beat A. A. Watrous | 4 & 3 |
| E. R. Whitcombe halved with A. R. Espinosa | Halved |

**RESULT: GB 7, USA 5**

## 1931 SCIOTO, OHIO

CAPTAINS: W. C. HAGEN (USA) and C. A. WHITCOMBE (GB)

| FOURSOMES: | |
|---|---|
| E. Sarazen & J. Farrell beat A. E. W. Compston & W. H. Davies | 8 & 7 |
| W. C. Hagen & H. D. Shute beat G. Duncan & A. G. Havers | 10 & 9 |
| L. Diegel & A. R. Espinosa lost to A. Mitchell & F. Robson | 3 & 1 |
| W. Burke & W. H. Cox beat S. Easterbrook & E. R. Whitcombe | 3 & 2 |
| **SINGLES:** | |
| W. Burke beat A. E. W. Compston | 7 & 6 |
| E. Sarazen beat F. Robson | 7 & 6 |
| J. Farrell lost to W. H. Davies | 4 & 3 |
| W. H. Cox beat A. Mitchell | 3 & 1 |
| W. C. Hagen beat C. A. Whitcombe | 4 & 3 |
| H. D. Shute beat B. Hodson | 8 & 6 |
| A. R. Espinosa beat E. R. Whitcombe | 2 & 1 |
| C. R. Wood lost to A. G. Havers | 4 & 3 |

**RESULT: USA 9, GB 3**

# THE RYDER CUP

## 1933 SOUTHPORT & AINSDALE, ENGLAND
CAPTAINS: J. H. TAYLOR (GB) and W. C. HAGEN (USA)

| FOURSOMES: | |
|---|---|
| Percy Alliss & C. A. Whitcombe halved with E. Sarazen & W. C. Hagen | Halved |
| A. Mitchell & A. G. Havers beat O. Dutra & H. D. Shute | 3 & 2 |
| W. H. Davies & S. Easterbrook beat C. R. Wood & P. S. Runyan | 1 Hole |
| A. H. Padgham & A. Perry lost to E. B. Dudley & W. Burke | 1 Hole |
| **SINGLES:** | |
| A. H. Padgham lost to E. Sarazen | 6 & 4 |
| A. Mitchell beat O. Dutra | 9 & 8 |
| A. J. Lacey lost to W. C. Hagen | 2 & 1 |
| W. H. Davies lost to C. R. Wood | 4 & 3 |
| Percy Alliss beat P. S. Runyan | 2 & 1 |
| A. G. Havers beat L. Diegel | 4 & 3 |
| S. Easterbrook beat H. D. Shute | 1 Hole |
| C. A. Whitcombe lost to H. Smith | 2 & 1 |

**RESULT: GB 6½, USA 5½**

## 1935 RIDGEWOOD, NEW JERSEY
CAPTAINS: W. C. HAGEN (USA) and C. A. WHITCOMBE (GB)

| FOURSOMES: | |
|---|---|
| E. Sarazen & W. C. Hagen beat A. Perry & J. J. Busson | 7 & 6 |
| H. C. Picard & J. Revolta beat A. H. Padgham & Percy Alliss | 6 & 5 |
| P. S. Runyan & H. Smith beat W. J. Cox & E. W. Jarman | 9 & 8 |
| O. Dutra & K. Laffoon lost to C. A. Whitcombe & E. R. Whitcombe | 1 Hole |
| **SINGLES:** | |
| E. Sarazen beat J. J. Busson | 3 & 2 |
| P. S. Runyan beat R. Burton | 5 & 3 |
| J. Revolta beat R. A. Whitcombe | 2 & 1 |
| O. Dutra beat A. H. Padgham | 4 & 2 |
| C. R. Wood lost to Percy Alliss | 1 Hole |
| H. Smith halved with W. J. Cox | Halved |
| H. C. Picard beat E. R. Whitcombe | 3 & 2 |
| S. Parks, Jr halved with A. Perry | Halved |

**RESULT: USA 9, GB 3**

## 1937 SOUTHPORT & AINSDALE, ENGLAND
CAPTAINS: W. C. HAGEN (USA) and C. A. WHITCOMBE (GB)

| FOURSOMES: | |
|---|---|
| E. B. Dudley & J. B. Nelson, Jr beat A. H. Padgham & T. H. Cotton | 4 & 2 |
| R. Guldahl & T. Manero beat A. J. Lacey & W. J. Cox | 2 & 1 |
| E. Sarazen & H. D. Shute halved with C. A. Whitcombe & D. J. Rees | Halved |
| H. C. Picard & J. Revolta lost to Percy Alliss & R. Burton | 2 & 1 |
| **SINGLES:** | |
| R. Guldahl beat A. H. Padgham | 8 & 7 |
| H. D. Shute halved with S. L. King | Halved |
| J. B. Nelson, Jr lost to D. J. Rees | 3 & 1 |
| T. Manero lost to T. H. Cotton | 5 & 3 |
| E. Sarazen beat Percy Alliss | 1 Hole |
| S. J. Snead beat R. Burton | 5 & 4 |
| E. B. Dudley beat A. Perry | 2 & 1 |
| H. C. Picard beat A. J. Lacey | 2 & 1 |

**RESULT: USA 8, GB 4**

## 1947 PORTLAND, OREGON
CAPTAINS: B. W. HOGAN (USA) and T. H. COTTON (GB)

| FOURSOMES: | |
|---|---|
| E. Oliver & L. E. Worsham beat T. H. Cotton & A. Lees | 10 & 9 |
| S. J. Snead & L. E. Mangrum beat F. Daly & C. H. Ward | 6 & 5 |
| W. B. Hogan & J. N. Demaret beat J. Adams & M. Faulkner | 2 Holes |
| J. B. Nelson, Jr & H. Barron beat D. J. Rees & S. L. King | 2 & 1 |
| **SINGLES:** | |
| E. J. Harrison beat F. Daly | 5 & 4 |
| L. E. Worsham beat J. Adams | 3 & 2 |
| L. E. Mangrum beat M. Faulkner | 6 & 5 |
| E. Oliver beat C. H. Ward | 4 & 3 |
| J. B. Nelson, Jr beat A. Lees | 2 & 1 |
| S. J. Snead beat T. H. Cotton | 5 & 4 |
| J. N. Demaret beat D. J. Rees | 3 & 2 |
| H. Keiser lost to S. L. King | 4 & 3 |

**RESULT: USA 11, GB 1**

## 1949 GANTON, ENGLAND
CAPTAINS: W. B. HOGAN (USA) and C. A. WHITCOMBE (GB)

| FOURSOMES: | |
|---|---|
| E. J. Harrison & J. Palmer lost to M. Faulkner & J. Adams | 2 & 1 |
| R. Hamilton & S. Alexander lost to F. Daly & K. Bousfield | 4 & 2 |
| J. N. Demaret & C. Heafner beat C. H. Ward & S. L. King | 4 & 3 |
| S. J. Snead & L. E. Mangrum lost to R. Burton & A. Lees | 1 Hole |
| **SINGLES:** | |
| E. J. Harrison beat M. Faulkner | 8 & 7 |
| J. Palmer lost to J. Adams | 2 & 1 |
| S. J. Snead beat C. H. Ward | 6 & 5 |
| R. Hamilton lost to D. J. Rees | 6 & 4 |
| C. Heafner beat R. Burton | 3 & 2 |
| M. R. Harbert beat S. L. King | 4 & 3 |
| J. N. Demaret beat A. Lees | 7 & 6 |
| L. E. Mangrum beat F. Daly | 4 & 3 |

**RESULT: USA 7, GB 5**

## 1951 PINEHURST, NORTH CAROLINA
CAPTAINS: S. J. SNEAD (USA) and A. J. LACEY (GB)

| FOURSOMES: | |
|---|---|
| C. Heafner & J. Burke, Jr beat M. Faulkner & D. J. Rees | 5 & 3 |
| E. Oliver & H. Ransom lost to C. H. Ward & A. Lees | 2 & 1 |
| S. J. Snead & L. E. Mangrum beat J. Adams & J. Panton | 5 & 4 |
| W. B. Hogan & J. N. Demaret beat F. Daly & K. Bousfield | 5 & 4 |
| **SINGLES:** | |
| J. Burke, Jr beat J. Adams | 4 & 3 |
| J. N. Demaret beat D. J. Rees | 2 Holes |
| C. Heafner halved with F. Daly | Halved |
| L. E. Mangrum beat H. Weetman | 6 & 5 |
| E. Oliver lost to A. Lees | 2 & 1 |
| W. B. Hogan beat C. H. Ward | 3 & 2 |
| S. Alexander beat J. Panton | 8 & 7 |
| S. J. Snead beat M. Faulkner | 4 & 3 |

**RESULT: USA 9½, GB 2½**

# The Ryder Cup

## 1953 WENTWORTH, ENGLAND

CAPTAINS: L. E. MANGRUM (USA) and T. H. COTTON (GB)

| | |
|---|---|
| **FOURSOMES:** | |
| D. Douglas & E. Oliver beat H. Weetman & Peter Alliss | 2 & 1 |
| L. E. Mangrum & S. J. Snead beat E. C. Brown & J. Panton | 8 & 7 |
| T. Kroll & J. Burke, Jr beat J. Adams & B. J. Hunt | 7 & 5 |
| W. Burkemo & C. Middlecoff lost to F. Daly & H. Bradshaw | 1 Hole |
| **SINGLES:** | |
| J. Burke, Jr beat D. J. Rees | 2 & 1 |
| T. Kroll lost to F. Daly | 9 & 7 |
| L. E. Mangrum lost to E. C. Brown | 2 Holes |
| S. J. Snead lost to H. Weetman | 1 Hole |
| C. Middlecoff beat M. Faulkner | 3 & 1 |
| Jim Turnesa beat Peter Alliss | 1 Hole |
| D. Douglas halved with B. J. Hunt | Halved |
| F. Haas lost to H. Bradshaw | 3 & 2 |

**RESULT: USA 6½, GB 5½**

## 1955 THUNDERBIRD GOLF & CC, CALIFORNIA

CAPTAINS: M. R. HARBERT (USA) and D. J. REES (GB)

| | |
|---|---|
| **FOURSOMES:** | |
| C. Harper & J. Barber lost to J. Fallon & J. R. M. Jacobs | 1 Hole |
| D. Ford & T. Kroll beat E. C. Brown & S. S. Scott | 5 & 4 |
| J. Burke, Jr & T. Bolt beat A. Lees & H. Weetman | 1 Hole |
| S. J. Snead & C. Middlecoff beat H. Bradshaw & D. J. Rees | 3 & 2 |
| **SINGLES:** | |
| T. Bolt beat C. O'Connor | 4 & 2 |
| M. R. Harbert beat S. S. Scott | 3 & 2 |
| C. Middlecoff lost to J. R. M. Jacobs | 1 Hole |
| S. J. Snead beat D. J. Rees | 3 & 1 |
| E. J. Furgol lost to A. Lees | 3 & 2 |
| J. Barber lost to E. C. Brown | 3 & 2 |
| J. Burke, Jr beat H. Bradshaw | 3 & 2 |
| D. Ford beat H. Weetman | 3 & 2 |

**RESULT: USA 8, GB 4**

## 1957 LINDRICK, ENGLAND

CAPTAINS: D. J. REES (GB) and J. BURKE, JR (USA)

| | |
|---|---|
| **FOURSOMES:** | |
| Peter Alliss & B. J. Hunt lost to D. Ford & D. Finsterwald | 2 & 1 |
| K. Bousfield & D. J. Rees beat A. Wall & F. Hawkins | 3 & 2 |
| M. Faulkner & H. Weetman lost to T. Kroll & J. Burke, Jr | 4 & 3 |
| C. O'Connor & E. C. Brown lost to R. Mayer & T. Bolt | 7 & 5 |
| **SINGLES:** | |
| E. C. Brown beat T. Bolt | 4 & 3 |
| R. P. Mills beat J. Burke, Jr | 5 & 3 |
| Peter Alliss lost to F. Hawkins | 2 & 1 |
| K. Bousfield beat L. Hebert | 4 & 3 |
| D. J. Rees beat E. J. Furgol | 7 & 6 |
| B. J. Hunt beat D. Ford | 6 & 5 |
| C. O'Connor beat D. Finsterwald | 7 & 6 |
| H. Bradshaw halved with R. Mayer | Halved |

**RESULT: GB 7½, USA 4½**

## 1959 ELDORADO CC, CALIFORNIA

CAPTAINS: S. J. SNEAD (USA) and D. J. REES (GB)

| | |
|---|---|
| **FOURSOMES:** | |
| R. R. Rosburg & M. Souchak beat B. J. Hunt & E. C. Brown | 5 & 4 |
| J. Boros & D. Finsterwald beat D. J. Rees & K. Bousfield | 2 Holes |
| A. Wall & D. Ford lost to C. O'Connor & Peter Alliss | 3 & 2 |
| S. J. Snead & C. Middlecoff halved with H. Weetman & D. C. Thomas | Halved |
| **SINGLES:** | |
| D. Ford halved with N. V. Drew | Halved |
| M. Souchak beat K. Bousfield | 3 & 2 |
| R. R. Rosburg beat H. Weetman | 6 & 5 |
| S. J. Snead beat D. C. Thomas | 6 & 5 |
| A. Wall beat C. O'Connor | 7 & 6 |
| D. Finsterwald beat D. J. Rees | 1 Hole |
| J. J. Hebert halved with Peter Alliss | Halved |
| C. Middlecoff lost to E. C. Brown | 4 & 3 |

**RESULT: USA 8½, GB 3½**

## 1961 ROYAL LYTHAM & ST. ANNES, ENGLAND

CAPTAINS: J. BARBER (USA) and D. J. REES (GB)

| | |
|---|---|
| **FOURSOMES (morning):** | |
| D. Ford & E. A. Littler lost to C. O'Connor & Peter Alliss | 4 & 3 |
| A. Wall & J. J. Hebert beat J. Panton & B. J. Hunt | 4 & 3 |
| W. E. Casper, Jr & A. D. Palmer beat D. J. Rees & K. Bousfield | 2 & 1 |
| W. Collins & M. Souchak beat T. B. Haliburton & N. C. Coles | 1 Hole |
| **FOURSOMES (afternoon):** | |
| A. Wall & J. J. Hebert beat C. O'Connor & Peter Alliss | 1 Hole |
| W. E. Casper, Jr & A. D. Palmer beat J. Panton & B. J. Hunt | 5 & 4 |
| W. Collins & M. Souchak lost to D. J. Rees & K. Bousfield | 4 & 2 |
| J. Barber & D. Finsterwald beat T. B. Haliburton & N. C. Coles | 1 Hole |
| **SINGLES (morning):** | |
| D. Ford beat H. Weetman | 1 Hole |
| M. Souchak beat R. L. Moffitt | 5 & 4 |
| A. D. Palmer halved with Peter Alliss | Halved |
| W. E. Casper, Jr beat K. Bousfield | 5 & 3 |
| J. J. Hebert lost to D. J. Rees | 2 & 1 |
| E. A. Littler halved with N. C. Coles | Halved |
| J. Barber lost to B. J. Hunt | 5 & 4 |
| D. Finsterwald beat C. O'Connor | 2 & 1 |
| **SINGLES (afternoon):** | |
| A. Wall beat H. Weetman | 1 Hole |
| W. Collins lost to Peter Alliss | 3 & 2 |
| M. Souchak beat B. J. Hunt | 2 & 1 |
| A. D. Palmer beat T. B. Haliburton | 2 & 1 |
| D. Ford lost to D. J. Rees | 4 & 3 |
| J. Barber lost to K. Bousfield | 1 Hole |
| D. Finsterwald lost to N. C. Coles | 1 Hole |
| E. A. Littler halved with C. O'Connor | Halved |

**RESULT: USA 14½, GB 9½**

## 1963 EAST LAKE, GEORGIA

CAPTAINS: A. D. PALMER (USA) and J. FALLON (GB)

**FOURSOMES (morning):**

| | |
|---|---|
| A. D. Palmer & J. Pott lost to B. G. C. Huggett & G. Will | 3 & 2 |
| W. E. Casper, Jr & D. Ragan, Jr beat Peter Alliss & C. O'Connor | 1 Hole |
| J. Boros & A. D. Lema halved with N. C. Coles & B. J. Hunt | Halved |
| E. A. Littler & D. Finsterwald halved with D. C. Thomas & H. Weetman | Halved |

**FOURSOMES (afternoon):**

| | |
|---|---|
| W. J. Maxwell & R. Goalby beat D. C. Thomas & H. Weetman | 4 & 3 |
| A. D. Palmer & W. E. Casper, Jr beat B. G. C. Huggett & G. Will | 5 & 4 |
| E. A. Littler & D. Finsterwald beat N. C. Coles & G. M. Hunt | 2 & 1 |
| J. Boros & A. D. Lema beat T. B. Haliburton & B. J. Hunt | 1 Hole |

**FOURBALLS (morning):**

| | |
|---|---|
| A. D. Palmer & D. Finsterwald beat B. G. C. Huggett & D. C. Thomas | 5 & 4 |
| E. A. Littler & J. Boros halved with Peter Alliss & B. J. Hunt | Halved |
| W. E. Casper, Jr & W. J. Maxwell beat H. Weetman & G. Will | 3 & 2 |
| R. Goalby & D. Ragan, Jr lost to N. C. Coles & C. O'Connor | 1 Hole |

**FOURBALLS (afternoon):**

| | |
|---|---|
| A. D. Palmer & D. Finsterwald beat N. C. Coles & C. O'Connor | 3 & 2 |
| A. D. Lema & J. Pott beat Peter Alliss & B. J. Hunt | 1 Hole |
| W. E. Casper, Jr & W. J. Maxwell beat T. B. Haliburton & G. M. Hunt | 2 & 1 |
| R. Goalby & D. Ragan, Jr halved with B. G. C. Huggett & D. C. Thomas | Halved |

**SINGLES (morning):**

| | |
|---|---|
| A. D. Lema beat G. M. Hunt | 5 & 3 |
| J. Pott lost to B. G. C. Huggett | 3 & 1 |
| A. D. Palmer lost to Peter Alliss | 1 Hole |
| W. E. Casper, Jr halved with N. C. Coles | Halved |
| R. Goalby beat D. C. Thomas | 3 & 2 |
| E. A. Littler beat C. O'Connor | 1 Hole |
| J. Boros lost to H. Weetman | 1 Hole |
| D. Finsterwald lost to B. J. Hunt | 2 Holes |

**SINGLES (afternoon):**

| | |
|---|---|
| A. D. Palmer beat G. Will | 3 & 2 |
| D. Ragan, Jr beat N. C. Coles | 2 & 1 |
| A. D. Lema halved with Peter Alliss | Halved |
| E. A. Littler beat T. B. Haliburton | 6 & 5 |
| J. Boros beat H. Weetman | 2 & 1 |
| W. J. Maxwell beat C. O'Connor | 2 & 1 |
| D. Finsterwald beat D. C. Thomas | 4 & 3 |
| R. Goalby beat B. J. Hunt | 2 & 1 |

**RESULT: USA 23, GB 9**

## 1965 ROYAL BIRKDALE, ENGLAND

CAPTAINS: J. B. NELSON, JR (USA) and H. WEETMAN (GB)

**FOURSOMES (morning):**

| | |
|---|---|
| A. D. Palmer & D. Marr lost to D. C. Thomas & G. Will | 6 & 5 |
| K. Venturi & D. January lost to Peter Alliss & C. O'Connor | 5 & 4 |
| J. Boros & A. D. Lema beat L. Platts & P. J. Butler | 1 Hole |
| W. E. Casper, Jr & E. A. Littler beat B. J. Hunt & N. C. Coles | 2 & 1 |

**FOURSOMES (afternoon):**

| | |
|---|---|
| A. D. Palmer & D. Marr beat D. C. Thomas & G. Will | 6 & 5 |
| J. Boros & A. D. Lema beat J. Martin & J. Hitchcock | 5 & 4 |
| W. E. Casper, Jr & E. A. Littler lost to Peter Alliss & C. O'Connor | 2 & 1 |
| K. Venturi & D. January lost to B. J. Hunt & N. C. Coles | 3 & 2 |

**FOURBALLS (morning):**

| | |
|---|---|
| D. January & K. T. Jacobs beat D. C. Thomas & G. Will | 1 Hole |
| W. E. Casper, Jr & E. A. Littler halved with L. Platts & P. J. Butler | Halved |
| A. D. Palmer & D. Marr beat Peter Alliss & C. O'Connor | 5 & 4 |
| J. Boros & A. D. Lema lost to B. J. Hunt & N. C. Coles | 1 Hole |

**FOURBALLS (afternoon):**

| | |
|---|---|
| A. D. Palmer & D. Marr lost to Peter Alliss & C. O'Connor | 2 Holes |
| D. January & K. T. Jacobs beat D. C. Thomas & G. Will | 1 Hole |
| W. E. Casper, Jr & E. A. Littler halved with L. Platts & P. J. Butler | Halved |
| K. Venturi & A. D. Lema beat B. J. Hunt & N. C. Coles | 1 Hole |

**SINGLES (morning):**

| | |
|---|---|
| A. D. Palmer beat J. Hitchcock | 3 & 2 |
| J. Boros beat L. Platts | 4 & 2 |
| A. D. Lema beat P. J. Butler | 1 Hole |
| D. Marr beat N. C. Coles | 2 Holes |
| E. A. Littler lost to B. J. Hunt | 2 Holes |
| W. E. Casper, Jr lost to Peter Alliss | 1 Hole |
| K. T. Jacobs beat D. C. Thomas | 2 & 1 |
| D. January halved with G. Will | Halved |

**SINGLES (afternoon):**

| | |
|---|---|
| A. D. Lema beat C. O'Connor | 6 & 4 |
| J. Boros beat J. Hitchcock | 2 & 1 |
| A. D. Palmer beat P. J. Butler | 2 Holes |
| K. Venturi lost to Peter Alliss | 3 & 1 |
| W. E. Casper, Jr lost to N. C. Coles | 3 & 2 |
| E. A. Littler beat G. Will | 2 & 1 |
| D. Marr beat B. J. Hunt | 1 Hole |
| K. T. Jacobs lost to L. Platts | 1 Hole |

**RESULT: USA 19½, GB 12½**

## 1967 HOUSTON, TEXAS

CAPTAINS: W. B. HOGAN (USA) and D. J. REES (GB)

**FOURSOMES (morning):**

| | |
|---|---|
| W. E. Casper, Jr & J. Boros halved with B. G. C. Huggett & G. Will | Halved |
| A. D. Palmer & G. Dickinson beat Peter Alliss & C. O'Connor | 2 & 1 |
| G. D. Sanders & G. Brewer, Jr lost to A. Jacklin & D. C. Thomas | 4 & 3 |
| B. Nichols & J. Pott beat B. J. Hunt & N. C. Coles | 6 & 5 |

**FOURSOMES (afternoon):**

| | |
|---|---|
| W. E. Casper, Jr & J. Boros beat B. G. C. Huggett & G. Will | 1 Hole |
| G. Dickinson & A. D. Palmer beat M. E. Gregson & H. F. Boyle | 5 & 4 |
| E. A. Littler & A. Geiberger lost to A. Jacklin & D. C. Thomas | 3 & 2 |
| B. Nichols & J. Pott beat Peter Alliss & C. O'Connor | 2 & 1 |

**FOURBALLS (morning):**

| | |
|---|---|
| W. E. Casper, Jr & G. Brewer, Jr beat Peter Alliss & C. O'Connor | 3 & 2 |
| B. Nichols & J. Pott beat B. J. Hunt & N. C. Coles | 1 Hole |
| E. A. Littler & A. Geiberger beat A. Jacklin & D. C. Thomas | 1 Hole |
| G. Dickinson & G. D. Sanders beat B. G. C. Huggett & G. Will | 3 & 2 |

**FOURBALLS (afternoon):**

| | |
|---|---|
| W. E. Casper, Jr & G. Brewer, Jr beat B. J. Hunt & N. C. Coles | 5 & 3 |
| G. Dickinson & G. D. Sanders beat Peter Alliss & M. E. Gregson | 3 & 2 |
| A. D. Palmer & J. Boros beat G. Will & H. F. Boyle | 1 Hole |
| E. A. Littler & A. Geiberger halved with A. Jacklin & D. C. Thomas | Halved |

**SINGLES (morning):**

| | |
|---|---|
| G. Brewer, Jr beat H. F. Boyle | 4 & 3 |
| W. E. Casper, Jr beat Peter Alliss | 2 & 1 |
| A. D. Palmer beat A. Jacklin | 3 & 2 |
| J. Boros lost to B. G. C. Huggett | 1 Hole |
| G. D. Sanders lost to N. C. Coles | 2 & 1 |
| A. Geiberger beat M. E. Gregson | 4 & 2 |
| E. A. Littler halved with D. C. Thomas | Halved |
| B. Nichols halved with B. J. Hunt | Halved |

**SINGLES (afternoon):**

| | |
|---|---|
| A. D. Palmer beat B. G. C. Huggett | 5 & 3 |
| G. Brewer, Jr lost to Peter Alliss | 2 & 1 |
| G. Dickinson beat A. Jacklin | 3 & 2 |
| B. Nichols beat C. O'Connor | 3 & 2 |
| J. Pott beat G. Will | 3 & 1 |
| A. Geiberger beat M. E. Gregson | 2 & 1 |
| J. Boros halved with B. J. Hunt | Halved |
| G. D. Sanders lost to N. C. Coles | 2 & 1 |

**RESULT: USA 23½, GB 8½**

## 1969 ROYAL BIRKDALE, ENGLAND

CAPTAINS: E. C. BROWN (GB) and S. J. SNEAD (USA)

**FOURSOMES (morning):**

N. C. Coles & B. G. C. Huggett beat M. Barber & R. L. Floyd 3 & 2
B. J. Gallacher & M. E. Bembridge beat L. B. Trevino & K. A. Still 2 & 1
A. Jacklin & P. M. P. Townsend beat D. Hill & T. D. Aaron 3 & 1
C. O'Connor & Peter Alliss halved with W. E. Casper, Jr & F. Beard Halved

**FOURSOMES (afternoon):**

N. C. Coles & B. G. C. Huggett lost to D. Hill & T. D. Aaron 1 Hole
B. J. Gallacher & M. E. Bembridge lost to L. B. Trevino & E. A. Littler 2 Holes
A. Jacklin & P. M. P. Townsend beat W. E. Casper, Jr & F. Beard 1 Hole
P. J. Butler & B. J. Hunt lost to J. W. Nicklaus & D. D. Sikes 1 Hole

**FOURBALLS (morning):**

C. O'Connor & P. M. P. Townsend beat D. Hill & D. Douglass 1 Hole
B. G. C. Huggett & G. A. Caygill halved with R. L. Floyd & M. Barber Halved
B. W. Barnes & Peter Alliss lost to L. B. Trevino & E. A. Littler 1 Hole
A. Jacklin & N. C. Coles beat J. W. Nicklaus & D. D. Sikes 1 Hole

**FOURBALLS (afternoon):**

P. J. Butler & P. M. P. Townsend lost to W. E. Casper, Jr & F. Beard 2 Holes
B. G. C. Huggett & B. J. Gallacher lost to D. Hill & K. A. Still 2 & 1
M. E. Bembridge & B. J. Hunt halved with T. D. Aaron & R. L. Floyd Halved
A. Jacklin & N. C. Coles halved with L. B. Trevino & M. Barber Halved

**SINGLES (morning):**

Peter Alliss lost to L. B. Trevino 2 & 1
P. M. P. Townsend lost to D. Hill 5 & 4
N. C. Coles beat T. D. Aaron 1 Hole
B. W. Barnes lost to W. E. Casper, Jr 1 Hole
C. O'Connor beat F. Beard 5 & 4
M. E. Bembridge beat K. A. Still 1 Hole
P. J. Butler beat R. L. Floyd 1 Hole
A. Jacklin beat J. W. Nicklaus 4 & 3

**SINGLES (afternoon):**

B. W. Barnes lost to D. Hill 4 & 2
B. J. Gallacher beat L. B. Trevino 4 & 3
M. E. Bembridge lost to M. Barber 7 & 6
P. J. Butler beat D. Douglass 3 & 2
C. O'Connor lost to E. A. Littler 2 & 1
B. G. C. Huggett halved with W. E. Casper, Jr Halved
N. C. Coles lost to D. D. Sikes 4 & 3
A. Jacklin halved with J. W. Nicklaus Halved

**RESULT: GB 16, USA 16**

## 1971 OLD WARSON COUNTRY CLUB, MISSOURI

CAPTAINS: J. J. HEBERT (USA) and D E. C. BROWN (GB)

**FOURSOMES (morning):**

W. E. Casper, Jr & M. Barber lost to N. C. Coles & C. O'Connor 2 & 1
A. D. Palmer & G. Dickinson beat P. M. P. Townsend & P. A. Oosterhuis 2 Holes
J. W. Nicklaus & D. Stockton lost to B. G. C. Huggett & A. Jacklin 3 & 2
C. Coody & F. Beard lost to M. E. Bembridge & P. J. Butler 1 Hole

**FOURSOMES (afternoon):**

W. E. Casper, Jr & M. Barber lost to H. Bannerman & B. J. Gallacher 2 & 1
J. W. Nicklaus & J. C. Snead beat M. E. Bembridge & P. J. Butler 5 & 3
A. D. Palmer & G. Dickinson beat P. M. P. Townsend & P. A. Oosterhuis 1 Hole
L. B. Trevino & E. M. Rudolph halved with B. G. C. Huggett & A. Jacklin Halved

**FOURBALLS (morning):**

A. D. Palmer & G. Dickinson beat P. A. Oosterhuis & B. J. Gallacher 5 & 4
L. B. Trevino & E. M. Rudolph beat C. O'Connor & B. W. Barnes 2 & 1
F. Beard & J. C. Snead beat N. C. Coles & J. R. Garner 2 & 1
J. W. Nicklaus & E. A. Littler beat P. M. P. Townsend & H. Bannerman 2 & 1

**FOURBALLS (afternoon):**

L. B. Trevino & W. E. Casper, Jr lost to B. J. Gallacher & P. A. Oosterhuis 1 Hole
E. A. Littler & J. C. Snead beat A. Jacklin & B. G. C. Huggett 2 & 1
A. D. Palmer & J. W. Nicklaus beat P. M. P. Townsend & H. Bannerman 1 Hole
C. Coody & F. Beard halved with N. C. Coles & C. O'Connor Halved

**SINGLES (morning):**

L. B. Trevino beat A. Jacklin 1 Hole
D. Stockton halved with B. J. Gallacher Halved
E. M. Rudolph lost to B. W. Barnes 1 Hole
E. A. Littler lost to P. A. Oosterhuis 4 & 3
J. W. Nicklaus beat P. M. P. Townsend 3 & 2
G. Dickinson beat C. O'Connor 5 & 4
A. D. Palmer halved with H. Bannerman Halved
F. Beard halved with N. C. Coles Halved

**SINGLES (afternoon):**

L. B. Trevino beat B. G. C. Huggett 7 & 6
J. C. Snead beat A. Jacklin 1 Hole
M. Barber lost to B. W. Barnes 2 & 1
D. Stockton beat P. M. P. Townsend 1 Hole
C. Coody lost to B. J. Gallacher 2 & 1
J. W. Nicklaus beat N. C. Coles 5 & 3
A. D. Palmer lost to P. A. Oosterhuis 3 & 2
G. Dickinson lost to H. Bannerman 2 & 1

**RESULT: USA 18½, GB 13½**

## 1973 MUIRFIELD, SCOTLAND

CAPTAINS: J. BURKE, JR (USA) and B. J. HUNT (GB & I)

**FOURSOMES (1):**

L. B. Trevino & W. E. Casper, Jr lost to B. W. Barnes & B. J. Gallacher 1 Hole
J. W. Nicklaus & A. D. Palmer beat M. E. Bembridge & E. Polland 6 & 5
T. D. Weiskopf & J. C. Snead lost to C. O'Connor & N. C. Coles 3 & 2
L. Graham & J. Rodriguez halved with A. Jacklin & P. A. Oosterhuis Halved

**FOURBALLS (1):**

T. D. Aaron & G. Brewer, Jr lost to B. W. Barnes & B. J. Gallacher 5 & 4
A. D. Palmer & J. W. Nicklaus lost to M. E. Bembridge & B. G. C. Huggett 3 & 1
L. B. Trevino & H. Blancas beat C. O'Connor & N. C. Coles 2 & 1
T. D. Weiskopf & W. E. Casper, Jr lost to A. Jacklin & P. A. Oosterhuis 3 & 1

**FOURSOMES (2):**

J. W. Nicklaus & T. D. Weiskopf beat B. W. Barnes & P. J. Butler 1 Hole
A. D. Palmer & D. Hill lost to P. A. Oosterhuis & A. Jacklin 2 Holes
L. Graham & J. Rodriguez lost to B. G. C. Huggett & M. E. Bembridge 5 & 4
L. B. Trevino & W. E. Casper, Jr beat C. O'Connor & N. C. Coles 2 & 1

**FOURBALLS (2):**

J. C. Snead & A. D. Palmer beat B. W. Barnes & P. J. Butler 2 Holes
G. Brewer, Jr & W. E. Casper, Jr beat A. Jacklin & P. A. Oosterhuis 3 & 2
T. D. Weiskopf & J. W. Nicklaus beat E. Polland & C. A. Clark 3 & 2
L. B. Trevino & H. Blancas halved with M. E. Bembridge & B. G. C. Huggett Halved

**SINGLES (morning):**

W. E. Casper, Jr beat B. W. Barnes 2 & 1
T. D. Weiskopf beat B. J. Gallacher 3 & 1
H. Blancas beat P. J. Butler 5 & 4
T. D. Aaron lost to A. Jacklin 3 & 1
G. Brewer, Jr halved with N. C. Coles Halved
J. C. Snead beat C. O'Connor 1 Hole
J. W. Nicklaus halved with M. E. Bembridge Halved
L. B. Trevino halved with P. A. Oosterhuis Halved

**SINGLES (afternoon):**

| | |
|---|---|
| H. Blancas lost to B. G. C. Huggett | 4 & 2 |
| J. C. Snead beat B. W. Barnes | 3 & 1 |
| G. Brewer, Jr beat B. J. Gallacher | 6 & 5 |
| W. E. Casper, Jr beat A. Jacklin | 2 & 1 |
| L. B. Trevino beat N. C. Coles | 6 & 5 |
| T. D. Weiskopf halved with C. O'Connor | Halved |
| J. W. Nicklaus beat M. E. Bembridge | 2 Holes |
| A. D. Palmer lost to P. A. Oosterhuis | 4 & 2 |

**RESULT: USA 19, GB & I 13**

## 1975 LAUREL VALLEY, PENNSYLVANIA

CAPTAINS: A. D. PALMER (USA) and B. J. HUNT (GB & I)

**FOURSOMES (morning):**

| | |
|---|---|
| J. W. Nicklaus & T. D. Weiskopf beat B. W. Barnes & B. J. Gallacher | 5 & 4 |
| E. A. Littler & H. S. Irwin beat N. D. Wood & M. E. Bembridge | 4 & 3 |
| A. Geiberger & J. L. Miller beat A. Jacklin & P. A. Oosterhuis | 3 & 1 |
| L. B. Trevino & J. C. Snead beat T. A. Horton & J. E. O'Leary | 2 & 1 |

**FOURBALLS (afternoon):**

| | |
|---|---|
| W. E. Casper, Jr & R. L. Floyd lost to P. A. Oosterhuis & A. Jacklin | 2 & 1 |
| T. D. Weiskopf & L. Graham beat E. Darcy & C. O'Connor, Jr | 3 & 2 |
| J. W. Nicklaus & R. J. Murphy halved with B. W. Barnes & B. J. Gallacher | Halved |
| L. B. Trevino & H. S. Irwin beat T. A. Horton & J. E. O'Leary | 2 & 1 |

**FOURBALLS (morning):**

| | |
|---|---|
| W. E. Casper, Jr & J. L. Miller halved with P. A. Oosterhuis & A. Jacklin | Halved |
| J. W. Nicklaus & J. C. Snead beat T. A. Horton & N. D. Wood | 4 & 2 |
| E. A. Littler & L. Graham beat B. W. Barnes & B. J. Gallacher | 5 & 3 |
| A. Geiberger & R. L. Floyd halved with E. Darcy & G. Hunt | Halved |

**FOURSOMES (afternoon):**

| | |
|---|---|
| L. B. Trevino & R. J. Murphy lost to A. Jacklin & B. G. C. Huggett | 3 & 2 |
| T. D. Weiskopf & J. L. Miller beat C. O'Connor, Jr & J. E. O'Leary | 5 & 3 |
| H. S. Irwin & W. E. Casper, Jr beat P. A. Oosterhuis & M. E. Bembridge | 3 & 2 |
| A. Geiberger & L. Graham beat G. Hunt & E. Darcy | 3 & 2 |

**SINGLES (morning):**

| | |
|---|---|
| B. Murphy beat A. Jacklin | 2 & 1 |
| J. L. Miller lost to P. A. Oosterhuis | 2 Holes |
| L. B. Trevino halved with B. J. Gallacher | Halved |
| H. S. Irwin halved with T. A. Horton | Halved |
| E. A. Littler beat B. G. C. Huggett | 4 & 2 |
| W. E. Casper, Jr beat E. Darcy | 3 & 2 |
| T. D. Weiskopf beat G. Hunt | 5 & 3 |
| J. W. Nicklaus lost to B. W. Barnes | 4 & 2 |

**SINGLES (afternoon):**

| | |
|---|---|
| R. L. Floyd beat A. Jacklin | 1 Hole |
| J. C. Snead lost to P. A. Oosterhuis | 3 & 2 |
| A. Geiberger halved with B. J. Gallacher | Halved |
| L. Graham lost to T. A. Horton | 2 & 1 |
| H. S. Irwin beat J. E. O'Leary | 2 & 1 |
| R. J. Murphy beat M. E. Bembridge | 2 & 1 |
| L. B. Trevino lost to N. D. Wood | 2 & 1 |
| J. W. Nicklaus lost to B. W. Barnes | 2 & 1 |

**RESULT: USA 21, GB & I 11**

## 1977 ROYAL LYTHAM & ST. ANNES, ENGLAND

CAPTAINS: D. FINSTERWALD (USA) and B. G. C. HUGGETT (GB & I)

**FOURSOMES:**

| | |
|---|---|
| J. L. Wadkins & H. S. Irwin beat B. J. Gallacher & B. W. Barnes | 3 & 1 |
| D. Stockton & J. McGee beat N. C. Coles & P. Dawson | 1 Hole |
| R. L. Floyd & L. Graham lost to N. A. Faldo & P. A. Oosterhuis | 2 & 1 |
| E. Sneed & D. January halved with E. Darcy & A. Jacklin | Halved |
| J. W. Nicklaus & T. S. Watson beat T. A. Horton & M. H. James | 5 & 4 |

**FOURBALLS:**

| | |
|---|---|
| T. S. Watson & H. M. Green beat B. W. Barnes & T. A. Horton | 5 & 4 |
| E. Sneed & J. L. Wadkins beat N. C. Coles & P. Dawson | 5 & 3 |
| J. W. Nicklaus & R. L. Floyd lost to N. A. Faldo & P. A. Oosterhuis | 2 & 1 |
| D. Hill & D. Stockton beat A. Jacklin & E. Darcy | 5 & 3 |
| H. S. Irwin & L. Graham beat M. H. James & K. J. Brown | 1 Hole |

**SINGLES:**

| | |
|---|---|
| J. L. Wadkins beat H. K. Clark | 4 & 3 |
| L. Graham beat N. C. Coles | 5 & 3 |
| D. January lost to P. Dawson | 5 & 4 |
| H. S. Irwin lost to B. W. Barnes | 1 Hole |
| D. Hill beat T. A. Horton | 5 & 4 |
| J. W. Nicklaus lost to B. J. Gallacher | 1 Hole |
| H. M. Green beat E. Darcy | 1 Hole |
| R. L. Floyd beat M. H. James | 2 & 1 |
| T. S. Watson lost to N. A. Faldo | 1 Hole |
| J. McGee lost to P. A. Oosterhuis | 2 Holes |

**RESULT: USA 12½, GB & I 7½**

## 1979 THE GREENBRIER, WEST VIRGINIA

CAPTAINS: W. E. CASPER, JR (USA) and J. R. M. JACOBS (EUROPE)

**FOURBALLS (morning):**

| | |
|---|---|
| J. L. Wadkins & L. Nelson beat A. Garrido & S. Ballesteros | 2 & 1 |
| L. B. Trevino & F. U. Zoeller beat K. J. Brown & M. H. James | 3 & 2 |
| A. Bean & L. Elder beat P. A. Oosterhuis & N. A. Faldo | 2 & 1 |
| H. S. Irwin & J. D. Mahaffey lost to B. J. Gallacher & B. W. Barnes | 2 & 1 |

**FOURSOMES (afternoon):**

| | |
|---|---|
| L. B. Trevino & G. Morgan halved with A. W. B. Lyle & A. Jacklin | Halved |
| F. U. Zoeller & H. M. Green lost to S. Ballesteros & A. Garrido | 3 & 2 |
| H. S. Irwin & T. O. Kite, Jr beat K. J. Brown & D. J. Smyth | 7 & 6 |
| J. L. Wadkins & L. Nelson beat B. J. Gallacher & B. W. Barnes | 4 & 3 |

**FOURSOMES (morning):**

| | |
|---|---|
| L. Elder & J. D. Mahaffey lost to A. Jacklin & A. W. B. Lyle | 5 & 4 |
| A. Bean & T. O. Kite, Jr lost to N. A. Faldo & P. A. Oosterhuis | 6 & 5 |
| J. L. Wadkins & L. Nelson beat S. Ballesteros & A. Garrido | 3 & 2 |
| F. U. Zoeller & M. Hayes lost to B. W. Barnes & B. J. Gallacher | 2 & 1 |

**FOURBALLS (afternoon):**

| | |
|---|---|
| J. L. Wadkins & L. Nelson beat S. Ballesteros & A. Garrido | 5 & 4 |
| H. S. Irwin & T. O. Kite, Jr beat A. Jacklin & A. W. B. Lyle | 1 Hole |
| L. B. Trevino & F. U. Zoeller lost to B. J. Gallacher & B. W. Barnes | 3 & 2 |
| L. Elder & M. Hayes lost to N. A. Faldo & P. A. Oosterhuis | 1 Hole |

**SINGLES:**

| | |
|---|---|
| J. L. Wadkins lost to B. J. Gallacher | 3 & 2 |
| L. Nelson beat S. Ballesteros | 3 & 2 |
| T. O. Kite, Jr beat A. Jacklin | 1 Hole |
| M. Hayes beat A. Garrido | 1 Hole |
| A. Bean beat M. G. King | 4 & 3 |
| J. D. Mahaffey beat B. W. Barnes | 1 Hole |
| L. Elder lost to N. A. Faldo | 3 & 2 |
| H. S. Irwin beat D. J. Smyth | 5 & 3 |
| H. M. Green beat P. A. Oosterhuis | 2 Holes |
| F. U. Zoeller lost to K. J. Brown | 1 Hole |
| L. B. Trevino beat A. W. B. Lyle | 2 & 1 |
| G. Morgan and M. H. James both withdrew (injured) | Halved |

**RESULT: USA 17, EUROPE 11**

# The Ryder Cup

## 1981 WALTON HEATH, ENGLAND

CAPTAINS: D. MARR (USA) and J. R. M. JACOBS (EUROPE)

| | |
|---|---|
| **FOURSOMES (morning):** | |
| L. B. Trevino & L. Nelson beat B. Langer & M. Pinero | 1 Hole |
| W. L. Rogers & B. Lietzke lost to A. W. B. Lyle & M. H. James | 2 & 1 |
| H. S. Irwin & R. L. Floyd lost to B. J. Gallacher & D. J. Smyth | 3 & 2 |
| T. S. Watson & J. W. Nicklaus beat P. A. Oosterhuis & N. A. Faldo | 4 & 3 |
| **FOURBALLS (afternoon):** | |
| T. O. Kite, Jr & J. L. Miller halved with S. R. Torrance & H. K. Clark | Halved |
| B. Crenshaw & J. Pate lost to A. W. B. Lyle & M. H. James | 3 & 2 |
| W. C. Rogers & B. Lietzke lost to D. J. Smith & J.-M. Cañizares | 6 & 5 |
| H. S. Irwin & R. L. Floyd beat B. J. Gallacher & E. Darcy | 2 & 1 |
| **FOURBALLS (morning):** | |
| L. B. Trevino & J. Pate beat N. A. Faldo & S. R. Torrance | 7 & 5 |
| L. Nelson & T. O. Kite, Jr beat A. W. B. Lyle & M. H. James | 1 Hole |
| R. L. Floyd & H. S. Irwin lost to B. Langer & M. Pinero | 2 & 1 |
| J. W. Nicklaus & T. S. Watson beat J.-M. Cañizares & D. J. Smyth | 3 & 2 |
| **FOURSOMES (afternoon):** | |
| L. B. Trevino & J. Pate beat P. A. Oosterhuis & S. R. Torrance | 2 & 1 |
| J. W. Nicklaus & T. S. Watson beat B. Langer & M. Pinero | 3 & 2 |
| W. C. Rogers & R. L. Floyd beat A. W. B. Lyle & M. H. James | 3 & 2 |
| T. O. Kite, Jr & L. Nelson beat D. J. Smyth & B. J. Gallacher | 3 & 2 |
| **SINGLES:** | |
| L. B. Trevino beat S. R. Torrance | 5 & 3 |
| T. O. Kite, Jr beat A. W. B. Lyle | 3 & 2 |
| W. C. Rogers halved with B. J. Gallacher | Halved |
| L. Nelson beat M. H. James | 2 Holes |
| B. D. Crenshaw beat D. J. Smyth | 6 & 4 |
| B. Lietzke halved with B. Langer | Halved |
| J. Pate lost to M. Pinero | 4 & 2 |
| H. S. Irwin beat J.-M. Cañizares | 1 Hole |
| J. L. Miller lost to N. A. Faldo | 2 & 1 |
| T. S. Watson lost to H. K. Clark | 4 & 3 |
| R. L. Floyd beat P. A. Oosterhuis | 1 Hole |
| J. W. Nicklaus beat E. Darcy | 5 & 3 |

**RESULT: USA 18½, EUROPE 9½**

## 1983 PGA NATIONAL, FLORIDA

CAPTAINS: J. W. NICKLAUS (USA) and A. JACKLIN (EUROPE)

| | |
|---|---|
| **FOURSOMES (morning):** | |
| T. S. Watson & B. D. Crenshaw beat B. J. Gallacher & A. W. B. Lyle | 5 & 4 |
| J. L. Wadkins & C. R. Stadler lost to N. A. Faldo & B. Langer | 4 & 2 |
| R. L. Floyd & R. Gilder lost to J.-M. Cañizares & S. R. Torrance | 4 & 3 |
| T. O. Kite, Jr & C. Peete beat S. Ballesteros & P. G. Way | 2 & 1 |
| **FOURBALLS (afternoon):** | |
| G. Morgan & F. U. Zoeller lost to B. J. Waites & K. J. Brown | 2 & 1 |
| T. S. Watson & J. Haas beat N. A. Faldo & B. Langer | 2 & 1 |
| R. L. Floyd & C. N. Strange lost to S. Ballesteros & P. G. Way | 1 Hole |
| B. D. Crenshaw & C. Peete halved with S. R. Torrance & I. H. Woosnam | Halved |
| **FOURBALLS (morning):** | |
| T. S. Watson & B. Gilder beat S. R. Torrance & I. H. Woosnam | 5 & 4 |
| C. Peete & B. D. Crenshaw lost to N. A. Faldo & B. Langer | 4 & 2 |
| J. L. Wadkins & C. R. Stadler beat B. J. Waites & K. J. Brown | 1 Hole |
| G. Morgan & J. Haas halved with S. Ballesteros & P. G. Way | Halved |
| **FOURSOMES (afternoon):** | |
| T. O. Kite, Jr & R. L. Floyd lost to N. A. Faldo & B. Langer | 3 & 2 |
| T. S. Watson & B. Gilder lost to S. Ballesteros & P. G. Way | 2 & 1 |
| J. Haas & C. N. Strange beat B. J. Waites & K. J. Brown | 3 & 2 |
| J. L. Wadkins & G. Morgan beat S. R. Torrance & J.-M. Cañizares | 7 & 5 |
| **SINGLES:** | |
| F. U. Zoeller halved with S. Ballesteros | Halved |
| J. Haas lost to N. A. Faldo | 2 & 1 |
| G. Morgan lost to B. Langer | 2 Holes |
| R. Gilder beat G. J. Brand | 2 Holes |
| B. D. Crenshaw beat A. W. B. Lyle | 3 & 1 |
| C. Peete beat B. J. Waites | 1 Hole |
| C. N. Strange lost to P. G. Way | 2 & 1 |
| T. O. Kite, Jr halved with S. R. Torrance | Halved |
| C. R. Stadler beat I. H. Woosnam | 3 & 2 |
| J. L. Wadkins halved with J.-M. Cañizares | Halved |
| R. L. Floyd lost to K. J. Brown | 4 & 3 |
| T. S. Watson beat B. J. Gallacher | 2 & 1 |

**RESULT: USA 14½, EUROPE 13½**

## 1985 THE BELFRY, ENGLAND

CAPTAINS: A. JACKLIN (EUROPE) and L. B. TREVINO (USA)

| | |
|---|---|
| **FOURSOMES (morning):** | |
| S. Ballesteros & M. Pinero beat C. N. Strange & M. O'Meara | 2 & 1 |
| B. Langer & N. A. Faldo lost to C. Peete & T. O. Kite, Jr | 3 & 2 |
| A. W. B. Lyle & K. J. Brown lost to J. L. Wadkins & R. L. Floyd | 4 & 3 |
| H. K. Clark & S. R. Torrance lost to C. R. Stadler & H. Sutton | 3 & 2 |
| **FOURBALLS (afternoon):** | |
| P. G. Way & I. H. Woosnam beat F. U. Zoeller & H. M. Green | 1 Hole |
| S. Ballesteros & M. Pinero beat A. S. North & P. Jacobsen | 2 & 1 |
| B. Langer & J.-M. Cañizares halved with C. R. Stadler & H. Sutton | Halved |
| S. R. Torrance & H. K. Clark lost to R. L. Floyd & J. L. Wadkins | 1 Hole |
| **FOURBALLS (morning):** | |
| S. R. Torrance & H. K. Clark beat T. O. Kite, Jr & A. S. North | 2 & 1 |
| P. G. Way & I. H. Woosnam beat H. M. Green & F. U. Zoeller | 4 & 3 |
| S. Ballesteros & M. Pinero lost to M. O'Meara & J. L. Wadkins | 3 & 2 |
| B. Langer & A. W. B. Lyle halved with C. R. Stadler & C. N. Strange | Halved |
| **FOURSOMES (afternoon):** | |
| J.-M. Cañizares & J. Rivero beat T. O. Kite, Jr & C. Peete | 7 & 5 |
| S. Ballesteros & M. Pinero beat C. R. Stadler & H. Sutton | 5 & 4 |
| P. G. Way & I. H. Woosnam lost to C. N. Strange & P. Jacobsen | 4 & 2 |
| B. Langer & K. J. Brown beat R. L. Floyd & J. L. Wadkins | 3 & 2 |
| **SINGLES:** | |
| M. Pinero beat J. L. Wadkins | 3 & 1 |
| I. H. Woosnam lost to C. R. Stadler | 2 & 1 |
| P. G. Way beat R. L. Floyd | 2 Holes |
| S. Ballesteros halved with T. O. Kite, Jr | Halved |
| A. W. B. Lyle beat P. Jacobsen | 3 & 2 |
| B. Langer beat H. Sutton | 5 & 4 |
| S. R. Torrance beat A. S. North | 1 Hole |
| H. K. Clark beat M. O'Meara | 1 Hole |
| N. A. Faldo lost to H. M. Green | 3 & 1 |
| J. Rivero lost to C. Peete | 1 Hole |
| J.-M. Cañizares beat F. U. Zoeller | 2 Holes |
| K. J. Brown lost to C. N. Strange | 4 & 2 |

**RESULT: EUROPE 16½, USA 11½**

## 1987 MUIRFIELD VILLAGE, OHIO

CAPTAINS: A. JACKLIN (EUROPE) and J. W. NICKLAUS (USA)

| | |
|---|---|
| **FOURSOMES (1):** | |
| S. R. Torrance & H. K. Clark lost to C. N. Strange & T. O. Kite, Jr | 4 & 2 |
| K. J. Brown & B. Langer lost to H. Sutton & D. Pohl | 2 & 1 |
| N. A. Faldo & I. H. Woosnam beat J. L. Wadkins & L. H. Mize | 2 Holes |
| S. Ballesteros & J.-M. Olazabal beat L. Nelson & W. P. Stewart | 1 Hole |
| **FOURBALLS (1):** | |
| G. Brand, Jr & J. Rivero beat B. D. Crenshaw & S. Simpson | 3 & 2 |
| A. W. B. Lyle & B. Langer beat A. Bean & M. Calcavecchia | 1 Hole |
| N. A. Faldo & I. H. Woosnam beat H. Sutton & D. Pohl | 2 & 1 |
| S. Ballesteros & J.-M. Olazabal beat C. N. Strange & T. O. Kite, Jr | 2 & 1 |

| | |
|---|---|
| **FOURSOMES (2):** | |
| J. Rivero & G. Brand, Jr lost to C. N. Strange & T. O. Kite, Jr | 3 & 1 |
| N. A. Faldo & I. H. Woosnam halved with H. Sutton & L. H. Mize | Halved |
| A. W. B. Lyle & B. Langer beat J. L. Wadkins & L. Nelson | 2 & 1 |
| S. Ballesteros & J.-M. Olazabal beat B. D. Crenshaw & W. P. Stewart | 1 Hole |
| **FOURBALLS (2):** | |
| I. H. Woosnam & N. A. Faldo beat T. O. Kite, Jr & C. N. Strange | 5 & 4 |
| E. Darcy & G. Brand, Jr lost to A. Bean & W. P. Stewart | 3 & 2 |
| S. Ballesteros & J.-M. Olazabal lost to H. Sutton & L. H. Mize | 2 & 1 |
| A. W. B. Lyle & B. Langer beat J. L. Wadkins & L. Nelson | 1 Hole |
| **SINGLES:** | |
| I. H. Woosnam lost to A. Bean | 1 Hole |
| H. K. Clark beat D. Pohl | 1 Hole |
| S. R. Torrance halved with L. H. Mize | Halved |
| N. A. Faldo lost to M. Calcavecchia | 1 Hole |
| J.-M. Olazabal lost to W. P. Stewart | 2 Holes |
| J. Rivero lost to S. Simpson | 2 & 1 |
| A. W. B. Lyle lost to T. O. Kite, Jr | 3 & 2 |
| E. Darcy beat B. D. Crenshaw | 1 Hole |
| B. Langer halved with L. Nelson | Halved |
| S. Ballesteros beat C. N. Strange | 2 & 1 |
| K. J. Brown lost to J. L. Wadkins | 3 & 2 |
| G. Brand, Jr halved with H. Sutton | Halved |

**RESULT: EUROPE 15, USA 13**

## 1989 THE BELFRY, ENGLAND

CAPTAINS: A. JACKLIN (EUROPE) and, R. L. FLOYD (USA)

| | |
|---|---|
| **FOURSOMES (1):** | |
| N. A. Faldo & I. H. Woosnam halved with T. O. Kite, Jr & C. N. Strange | Halved |
| H. K. Clark & M. H. James lost to J. L. Wadkins & W. P. Stewart | 1 Hole |
| S. Ballesteros & J.-M. Olazabal halved with T. S. Watson & C. Beck | Halved |
| B. Langer & R. P. Rafferty lost to M. Calcavecchia & K. Green | 2 & 1 |
| **FOURBALLS (1):** | |
| S. R. Torrance & G. Brand, Jr beat C. N. Strange & P. W. Azinger | 1 Hole |
| H. K. Clark & M. H. James beat F. S. Couples & J. L. Wadkins | 3 & 2 |
| N. A. Faldo & I. H. Woosnam beat M. Calcavecchia & M. McCumber | 2 Holes |
| S. Ballesteros & J.-M. Olazabal beat T. S. Watson & M. O'Meara | 6 & 5 |
| **FOURSOMES (2):** | |
| I. H. Woosnam & N. A. Faldo beat J. L. Wadkins & W. P. Stewart | 3 & 2 |
| G. Brand, Jr & S. R. Torrance lost to C. Beck & P. W. Azinger | 4 & 3 |
| C. O'Connor, Jr & R. P. Rafferty lost to M. Calcavecchia & K. Green | 3 & 2 |
| S. Ballesteros & J.-M. Olazabal beat T. O. Kite, Jr & C. N. Strange | 1 Hole |
| **FOURBALLS (2):** | |
| N. A. Faldo & I. H. Woosnam lost to C. Beck & P. W. Azinger | 2 & 1 |
| B. Langer & J.-M. Cañizares lost to T. O. Kite, Jr & M. McCumber | 2 & 1 |
| H. K. Clark & M. H. James beat W. P. Stewart & C. N. Strange | 1 Hole |
| S. Ballesteros & J.-M. Olazabal beat M. Calcavecchia & K. Green | 4 & 2 |
| **SINGLES:** | |
| S. Ballesteros lost to P. W. Azinger | 1 Hole |
| B. Langer lost to C. Beck | 3 & 1 |
| J.-M.Olazabal beat W. P. Stewart | 1 Hole |
| R. P. Rafferty beat M. Calcavecchia | 1 Hole |
| H. K. Clark lost to T. O. Kite, Jr | 8 & 7 |
| M. H. James beat M. O'Meara | 3 & 2 |
| C. O'Connor, Jr beat F. S. Couples | 1 Hole |
| J.-M. Cañizares beat K. Green | 1 Hole |
| G. Brand, Jr lost to M. McCumber | 1 Hole |
| S. R. Torrance lost to T. S. Watson | 3 & 1 |
| N. A. Faldo lost to J. L. Wadkins | 1 Hole |
| I. H. Woosnam lost to C. N. Strange | 2 Holes |

**RESULT: EUROPE 14, USA 14**

## 1991 KIAWAH ISLAND, SOUTH CAROLINA

CAPTAINS: D. STOCKTON (USA) and B. J. GALLACHER (EUROPE)

| | |
|---|---|
| **FOURSOMES (1):** | |
| P. W. Azinger & C. Beck lost to S. Ballesteros & J.-M. Olazabal | 2 & 1 |
| R. L. Floyd & F. S. Couples beat B. Langer & M. H. James | 2 & 1 |
| J. L. Wadkins & H. S. Irwin beat D. Gilford & C. S. Montgomerie | 4 & 2 |
| W. P. Stewart & M. Calcavecchia beat N. A. Faldo & I. H. Woosnam | 1 Hole |
| **FOURBALLS (1):** | |
| J. L. Wadkins & M. O'Meara halved with S. R. Torrance & D. Feherty | Halved |
| P. W. Azinger & C. Beck lost to S. Ballesteros & J.-M. Olazabal | 2 & 1 |
| C. Pavin & M. Calcavecchia lost to S. Richardson & M. H. James | 5 & 4 |
| R. L. Floyd & F. S. Couples beat N. A. Faldo & I. H. Woosnam | 5 & 3 |
| **FOURSOMES (2):** | |
| J. L. Wadkins & H. S. Irwin beat D. Feherty & S. R. Torrance | 4 & 2 |
| M. Calcavecchia & W. P. Stewart beat M. H. James & S. Richardson | 1 Hole |
| P. W. Azinger & M. O'Meara beat N. A. Faldo & D. Gilford | 7 & 6 |
| R. L. Floyd & F. S. Couples lost to S. Ballesteros & J.-M. Olazabal | 3 & 2 |
| **FOURBALLS (2):** | |
| P. W. Azinger & H. S. Irwin lost to I. H. Woosnam & P. A. Broadhurst | 2 & 1 |
| C. Pavin & S. Pate lost to B. Langer & C. S. Montgomerie | 2 & 1 |
| J. L. Wadkins & W. Levi lost to M. H. James & S. Richardson | 3 & 1 |
| W. P. Stewart & F. S. Couples halved with S. Ballesteros & J.-M. Olazabal | Halved |
| **SINGLES:** | |
| R. L. Floyd lost to N. A. Faldo | 2 Holes |
| W. P. Stewart lost to D. Feherty | 2 & 1 |
| M. Calcavecchia halved with C. S. Montgomerie | Halved |
| P. W. Azinger beat J.-M. Olazabal | 2 Holes |
| C. Pavin beat S. Richardson | 2 & 1 |
| W. Levi lost to S. Ballesteros | 3 & 2 |
| C. Beck beat I. H. Woosnam | 3 & 1 |
| M. O'Meara lost to P. A. Broadhurst | 3 & 1 |
| F. S. Couples beat S. R. Torrance | 3 & 2 |
| J. L. Wadkins beat M. H. James | 3 & 2 |
| H. S. Irwin halved with B. Langer | Halved |
| S. Pate (injured) and D. Gilford withdrawn at start of day | Halved |

**RESULT: USA 14½, EUROPE 13½**

## 1993 THE BELFRY, ENGLAND

CAPTAINS: T. S. WATSON (USA) and B. J. GALLACHER (EUROPE)

| | |
|---|---|
| **FOURSOMES (1):** | |
| J. L. Wadkins & C. Pavin beat S. R. Torrance & M. H. James | 4 & 3 |
| P. W. Azinger & W. P. Stewart lost to I. H. Woosnam & B. Langer | 7 & 5 |
| T. O. Kite, Jr & D. Love III beat S. Ballesteros & J.-M. Olazabal | 2 & 1 |
| R. L. Floyd & F. S. Couples lost to N. A. Faldo & C. S. Montgomerie | 4 & 3 |
| **FOURBALLS (1):** | |
| J. Gallagher, Jr & L. Janzen lost to I. H. Woosnam & P. Baker | 1 Hole |
| J. L. Wadkins & C. Pavin beat B. Langer & B. Lane | 4 & 2 |
| P. W. Azinger & F. S. Couples halved with N. A. Faldo & C. S. Montgomerie | Halved |
| T. O. Kite, Jr & D. Love III lost to S. Ballesteros & J.-M. Olazabal | 4 & 3 |
| **FOURSOMES (2):** | |
| J. L. Wadkins & C. Pavin lost to N. A. Faldo & C. S. Montgomerie | 3 & 2 |
| F. S. Couples & P. W. Azinger lost to B. Langer & I. H. Woosnam | 2 & 1 |
| R. L. Floyd & W. P. Stewart beat P. Baker & B. Lane | 3 & 2 |
| T. O. Kite, Jr & D. Love III lost to S. Ballesteros & J.-M. Olazabal | 2 & 1 |
| **FOURBALLS (2):** | |
| C. Beck & J. Cook beat N. A. Faldo & C. S. Montgomerie | 1 Hole |
| C. Pavin & J. Gallagher, Jr beat M. H. James & C. Rocca | 5 & 4 |
| F. S. Couples & P. W. Azinger lost to I. H. Woosnam & P. Baker | 6 & 5 |
| R. L. Floyd & W. P. Stewart beat J.-M. Olazabal & J. Haeggman | 2 & 1 |

# The Ryder Cup

| | |
|---|---|
| **SINGLES:** | |
| F. S. Couples halved with I. H. Woosnam | Halved |
| C. Beck beat B. Lane | 1 Hole |
| L.M. Janzen lost to C. S. Montgomerie | 1 Hole |
| C. Pavin lost to P. Baker | 2 Holes |
| J. Cook lost to J. Haeggman | 1 Hole |
| J. L. Wadkins and S. R. Torrance (injured) withdrawn | Halved |
| W. P. Stewart beat M. H. James | 3 & 2 |
| D. Love III beat C. Rocca | 1 Hole |
| J. Gallagher, Jr beat S. Ballesteros | 3 & 2 |
| R. L. Floyd beat J.-M. Olazabal | 2 Holes |
| T. O. Kite, Jr beat B. Langer | 5 & 3 |
| P. W. Azinger halved with N. A. Faldo | Halved |

**RESULT: USA 15, EUROPE 13**

## 1995 OAK HILL, NEW YORK

CAPTAINS: B. J. GALLACHER (EUROPE) and J. L. WADKINS (USA)

| | |
|---|---|
| **FOURSOMES (1):** | |
| N. A. Faldo & C. S. Montgomerie lost to C. Pavin & T. E. Lehman | 1 Hole |
| S. R. Torrance & C. Rocca beat J. Haas & F. S. Couples | 3 & 2 |
| H. K. Clark & M. H. James lost to D. Love III & J. Maggert | 4 & 3 |
| B. Langer & P.-U. Johansson beat B. D. Crenshaw & C. N. Strange | 1 Hole |
| **FOURBALLS (1):** | |
| D. Gilford & S. Ballesteros beat B. Faxon & P. Jacobsen | 4 & 3 |
| S. R. Torrance & C. Rocca lost to J. Maggert & L. Roberts | 6 & 5 |
| N. A. Faldo & C. S. Montgomerie lost to F. S. Couples & D. Love III | 3 & 2 |
| B. Langer & P.-U. Johansson lost to C. Pavin & P. Mickelson | 6 & 4 |
| **FOURSOMES (2):** | |
| N. A. Faldo & C. S. Montgomerie beat J. Haas & C. N. Strange | 4 & 2 |
| S. R. Torrance & C. Rocca beat D. Love III & J. Maggert | 6 & 5 |
| I. H. Woosnam & P. Walton lost to L. Roberts & P. Jacobsen | 1 Hole |
| B. Langer & D. Gilford beat C. Pavin & T. E. Lehman | 4 & 3 |
| **FOURBALLS (2):** | |
| S. R. Torrance & C. S. Montgomerie lost to B. Faxon & F. S. Couples | 4 & 2 |
| I. H. Woosnam & C. Rocca beat D. Love III & B. D. Crenshaw | 3 & 2 |
| S. Ballesteros & D. Gilford lost to J. Haas & P. Mickelson | 3 & 2 |
| N. A. Faldo & B. Langer lost to C. Pavin & L. Roberts | 1 Hole |
| **SINGLES:** | |
| S. Ballesteros lost to T. E. Lehman | 4 & 3 |
| H. K. Clark beat P. Jacobsen | 1 Hole |
| M. H. James beat J. Maggert | 4 & 3 |
| I. H. Woosnam halved with F. S. Couples | Halved |
| C. Rocca lost to D. Love III | 3 & 2 |
| D. Gilford beat B. Faxon | 1 Hole |
| C. S. Montgomerie beat B. D. Crenshaw | 3 & 1 |
| N. A. Faldo beat C. N. Strange | 1 Hole |
| S. R. Torrance beat L. Roberts | 2 & 1 |
| B. Langer lost to C. Pavin | 3 & 2 |
| P. Walton beat J. Haas | 1 Hole |
| P.-U. Johansson lost to P. Mickelson | 2 & 1 |

**RESULT: EUROPE 14½, USA 13½**

## 1997 VALDERRAMA, SPAIN

CAPTAINS: S. BALLESTEROS (EUROPE) and T. O. KITE, JR. (USA)

| | |
|---|---|
| **FOURBALLS (1):** | |
| J.-M. Olazabal & C. Rocca beat D. Love III & P. Mickelson | 1 Hole |
| N. A. Faldo & L. Westwood lost to F. S. Couples & B. Faxon | 1 Hole |
| J. Parnevik & P.–U. Johansson beat T. E. Lehman & J. Furyk | 1 Hole |
| C. S. Montgomerie & B. Langer lost to E. Woods & M. O'Meara | 3 & 2 |
| **FOURSOMES (1):** | |
| C. Rocca & J.-M. Olazabal lost to S. Hoch & L. M. Janzen | 1 Hole |
| B. Langer & C. S. Montgomerie beat M. O'Meara & E. Woods | 5 & 3 |
| N. A. Faldo & L. Westwood beat J. Leonard & J. Maggert | 3 & 2 |
| J. Parnevik & I. Garrido halved with T. E. Lehman & P. Mickelson | Halved |
| **FOURBALLS (2):** | |
| C. S. Montgomerie & D. Clarke beat F. S. Couples & D. Love III | 1 Hole |
| I. H. Woosnam & T. Bjorn beat J. Leonard & B. Faxon | 2 & 1 |
| N. A. Faldo & L. Westwood beat E. Woods & M. O'Meara | 2 & 1 |
| J.-M. Olazabal & I. Garrido halved with P. Mickelson & T. E. Lehman | Halved |
| **FOURSOMES (2):** | |
| C. S. Montgomerie & B. Langer beat L. M. Janzen & J. Furyk | 1 Hole |
| N. A. Faldo & L. Westwood lost to S. Hoch & J. Maggert | 2 & 1 |
| J. Parnevik & I. Garrido halved with J. Leonard & E. Woods | Halved |
| J.-M. Olazabal & C. Rocca beat D. Love III & F. S. Couples | 5 & 4 |
| **SINGLES:** | |
| I. H. Woosnam lost to F. S. Couples | 8 & 7 |
| P.-U. Johansson beat D. Love III | 3 & 2 |
| C. Rocca beat E. Woods | 4 & 2 |
| T. Bjorn halved with J. Leonard | Halved |
| D. Clarke lost to P. Mickelson | 2 & 1 |
| J. Parnevik lost to M. O'Meara | 5 & 4 |
| J.-M. Olazabal lost to L. M. Janzen | 1 Hole |
| B. Langer beat B. Faxon | 2 & 1 |
| L. Westwood lost to J. Maggert | 3 & 2 |
| C. S. Montgomerie halved with S. Hoch | Halved |
| N. A. Faldo lost to J. Furyk | 3 & 2 |
| I. Garrido lost to T. E. Lehman | 7 & 6 |

**RESULT: EUROPE 14½, USA 13½**

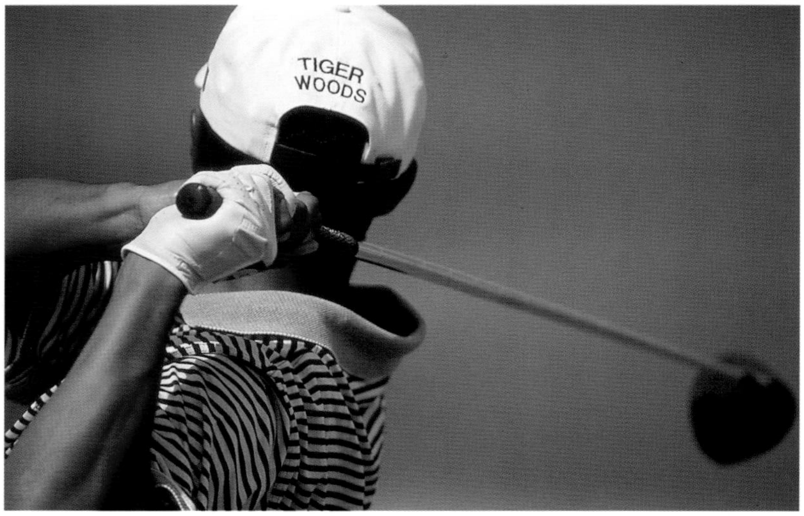

# ACKNOWLEDGMENTS


The images in this book came from the following suppliers:

Allsport - www.allsport.com - part of Getty Images Inc.
3 Greenlea Park, Prince George's Road, London
SW19 2JD, UK
Allsport is the world's leading dedicated sports photographic agency, with offices in New York, Los Angeles, London, Sydney and Melbourne and a network of agents in over 40 countries worldwide. Allsport's team of award-winning photographers are widely recognized as among the world's finest.

Hobbs Golf Collection
5 Winston Way, New Ridley, Stocksfield,
Northumberland NE43 7RF, UK
email: hobbs.golf@btinternet.com

Peter Dazeley Photography
5 Heathman's Road, Parsons Green
London SW6 4TJ, UK
011 44 171 736 3171

Tony Roberts Photography
16615 North 55th Place, Scottsdale,
Arizona 85254, USA
001 602 493 3099

While every effort has been made to ensure this listing is correct, the Publisher apologises for any omissions.

The help of Geoffrey S. Wilde and Ian Penberthy is acknowledged with special thanks.

PAGES ;
**2** David Cannon/Allsport; **6** Stephen Dunn/Allsport; **7** David Cannon/ Allsport (top); Andrew Redington/ Allsport; **8** David Cannon/Allsport (left); Stephen Munday (center); **9** David Cannon/Allsport; **10** Gary Newkirk/Allsport; **11** Andrew Redington/Allsport (top); Stephen Dunn/Allsport; **12** Stephen Munday/ Allsport (top); Stephen Dunn/ Allsport; **13** Andrew Redington/ Allsport (top); David Cannon/Allsport; **14** Allsport Historical Collection (top); David Cannon/Allsport ; **15** Hobbs Golf Collection; **16** Michael Hobbs/ Allsport; **17** Allsport (top); Steve Powell/Allsport; **18/19** Stephen Munday/Allsport (top left); David Cannon/Allsport (top right, bottom left; bottom right); **20** J. D. Cuban/ Allsport; **21** Allsport Historical Collection; **22** David Cannon/Allsport (top); Stephen Munday/Allsport; **23** David Cannon/Allsport; **24** Hobbs Golf Collection; **25** Andrew Redington/Allsport (top); Stephen Munday/Allsport; **26** Stephen Munday/Allsport; **27** David Cannon/ Allsport; **28** Allsport Historical Collection (top); Hobbs Golf Collection; 29 David Cannon/ Allsport; **30** Hobbs Golf Collection; **31** Andrew Redington/Allsport (top); Paul Severn/Allsport; **32** Michael Hobbs/Allsport; **33** David Cannon/ Allsport; **34/5** David Cannon/Allsport (top left, bottom left, right); Hobbs Golf Collection (center left); **36** Michael Hobbs/Allsport; **37** David Cannon/Allsport; **38** Allsport Historical Collection; **39** Hobbs Golf Collection; **40** David Cannon/Allsport (top); John Gichigi/Allsport; **41** Allsport (top); David Cannon/ Allsport; **42** David Cannon/Allsport; **43** David Cannon/Allsport (top); Steve Powell/Allsport; **44** Hobbs Golf Collection; **45** Hobbs Golf Collection; **46** Jamie Squire/Allsport (top); David Cannon/Allsport; **47** David Cannon/ Allsport (top); David Rogers/Allsport; **48** David Cannon/Allsport; **49** Rick Stewart/Allsport (top); Gary Newkirk/ Allsport; **50/1** Hobbs Golf Collection; **52** Tim Matthews/Allsport (top); Andrew Redington/Allsport; **53** J. D. Cuban/Allsport (top); Stephen Munday/Allsport; **54** Allsport; **55** Stephen Munday/ Allsport (top); Bob/Martin/Allsport; **56** David Cannon/Allsport; **57** Allsport (top); Tim Matthews/ Allsport; **58** Hobbs Golf Collection; **59** Hobbs Golf Collection; **60** Peter Dazeley Photography; **61** Craig Jones/Allsport (top); Harry How/ Allsport; **62** Hobbs Golf Collection; **63** Hobbs Golf Collection (top); Allsport Historical Collection; **64** J. D. Cuban/Allsport (top); Hobbs Golf Collection; **65** Michael Hobbs/ Allsport (top); Gary Newkirk/Allsport; **66/7** David Cannon/Allsport; **68** Hobbs Golf Collection; **69** Andrew Redington/Allsport (top); David Cannon/Allsport; **70** Allsport (top); Hobbs Golf Collection; **71** Jamie Squire/Allsport (top); David Cannon/ Allsport; **72** Richard Saker/Allsport (top); David Cannon/Allsport; **73** Simon Bruty/Allsport (top); Andrew Redington/Allsport; **74** Paul Severn/Allsport (top); Stephen Munday/Allsport; **75** Allsport Historical Collection (top); Hobbs Golf Collection; **76** Allsport (top); Allsport Historical Collection; **77** Allsport Historical Collection; **78** Hobbs Golf Collection; **79** Hobbs Golf Collection; **80** Andy Lyons/ Allsport (top); Harry How/Allsport; **81** David Cannon/Allsport; **82/3** David Cannon/Allsport (left and top right); Stephen Munday/Allsport (bottom right); **84** Andrew Redington/ Allsport (top); David Cannon/Allsport; **85** Hobbs Golf Collection; **86** Andrew Redington/Allsport (top); Stephen Munday/Allsport; **87** Allsport Historical Collection (top); Andrew Redington/Allsport; **88** David Cannon/Allsport (top); Harry How/ Allsport; **89** Hobbs Golf Collection; **90** Allspor; **91** Hobbs Golf Collection; **92** David Cannon/Allsport (top); Hobbs Golf Collection; **93** Hobbs Golf Collection; **94** Stephen Munday/ Allsport (top); David Cannon/ Allsport; **95** Hobbs Golf Collection (top); David Cannon/Allsport; **96** Matthew Stockman/Allsport (top); Stephen Munday/Allsport; **97** Michael Hobbs/Allsport (top); Hobbs Golf Collection; **98/99** Allsport Historical Collection; Hobbs Golf Collection; **100** J. D. Cuban/ Allsport (top); Jamie Squire/Allsport; **101** Tony Duffy/Allsport; **102** Andy Lyons/Allsport (top); Andrew Redington/Allsport; **103** Jon Nicholson/Allsport (top); Stephen Dunn/Allsport; **104** Don Morley/ Allsport; **105** David Cannon/Allsport (top); Hobbs Golf Collection; **106** Hobbs Golf Collection; **107** David Cannon/Allsport (top); Hobbs Golf Collection; **108** David Cannon/Allsport (top); Allsport; **109** Allsport; **110** Andy Lyons/ Allsport (top); David Cannon/Allsport; **111** David Cannon/Allsport; **112/3** Hobbs Golf Collection; **114** Hobbs Golf Collection; **115** Gary Newkirk/Allsport (top); David Cannon/Allsport; **116** Allsport Historical Collection; **117** Allsport Historical Collection; **118** Hobbs Golf Collection; **119** Hobbs Golf Collection; **120** Tony Duffy/Allsport; **121** Hobbs Golf Collection; **122** Hobbs Golf Collection; **123** Hobbs Golf Collection (top ); Michael Hobbs/Allsport; **124** Craig Jones/Allsport (top); Don Morley/ Allsport; **125** Hobbs Golf Collection; **126** Allsport (top); Jamie Squire/ Allsport; **127** Stephen Munday/ Allsport (top); Allsport Historical Collection; **128** Allsport (top left); Allsport Historical Collection (top right); **129** Michael Hobbs/Allsport; **130** Phil Cole/Allsport; **131** Don Morley/Allsport (top); Tim Matthews/ Allsport; **132** Hobbs Golf Collection (top); Allsport Historical Collection; **133** Allsport Historical Collection; **134/5** Tony Roberts Photography; **136** David Cannon/Allsport (top); David Cannon/Allsport; **137** David Cannon/Allsport (top); Allsport; **138** Billy Stickland/Allsport (top left); Hobbs Golf Collection (top right); **139** Hobbs Golf Collection; **140** David Cannon/Allsport ; **141** Steve Powell/Allsport (top); Andrew Redington/Allsport; **142** Hobbs Golf Collection; **143** Allsport; **144** Gary Newkirk/ Allsport (top); Andrew Redington/ Allsport; **145** Hobbs Golf Collection; **146/7** Hobbs Golf Collection; **148** David Cannon/Allsport (top); Rick Stewart/Allsport; **149** Hobbs Golf Collection; **150** Hobbs Golf Collection; **151** J. D. Cuban/Allsport (top); J. D. Cuban/Allsport; **152** Michael Hobbs/Allsport; **153** Allsport Historical Collection; **154** Hobbs Golf Collection; **155** Harry How/Allsport (top); Rick Stewart/Allsport; **156** David Cannon/ Allsport (top); David Cannon/Allsport; **157** Andrew Redington/Allsport (top); Stephen Munday/Allsport; **158** Michael Hobbs/Allsport; **159** David Cannon/Allsport (top); David Cannon/Allsport; **160/1** Hobbs Golf Collection (top left, center left, bottom left); Michael Hobbs/Allsport (right); 162 Stephen Munday/ Allsport; **163** Jamie Squire/Allsport (top); David Cannon/Allsport; **164** Allsport Historical Collection; **165** Allsport (top); Hobbs Golf Collection; **166** Rusty Jarrett/Allsport (top); David Cannon/Allsport; **167** Stephen Dunn/Allsport; **168** Allsport Historical Collection; **169** Stephen Dunn/Allsport (top); Hobbs Golf Collection; **170** Hobbs Golf Collection; **171** Allsport Historical Collection; **172** Andrew Redington/Allsport; **173** David Cannon/Allsport (top); David Cannon/Allsport; **174/5** Hobbs Golf Collection (top left, bottom left); Allsport Historical Collection; **176** Steve Powell/Allsport (top); David Cannon/Allsport; **177** Hobbs Golf Collection (top); Craig Jones/ Allsport; 178 Hobbs Golf Collection; **179** Stephen Munday/Allsport (top); Allsport; **180** Allsport Historical Collection; **181** Hobbs Golf Collection; **182** Allsport Historical Collection (top); David Cannon/ Allsport; **183** J. D. Cuban/Allsport; **184** Ezra O. Shaw/Allsport (top); Andy Lyons/Allsport; **185** Craig Jones/Allsport (top); Donald Miralle/ Allsport; **186** Allsport Historical Collection; **187** Harry How/Allsport (top); Matthew Stockman/Allsport; **188** Stephen Munday/Allsport (top); David Cannon/Allsport **189** Hobbs Golf Collection; **190/1** Hobbs Golf Collection/Allsport; **192** David Cannon/Allsport (top); David Cannon/Allsport; **193** Hobbs Golf Collection; **194** Brian Bahr/Allsport (top); Stephen Dunn/Allsport; **195** Hobbs Golf Collection; **196** Allsport Historical Collection; **197** Allsport Historical Collection; **198** David Cannon/Allsport (top); Ezra O. Shaw/Allsport; **199** David Cannon/Allsport (top); Andrew Redington/Allsport ; **200** Allsport (top); Craig Jones/Allsport; **201** Craig Jones/Allsport (top); Andy Lyons/ Allsport; **202** Hobbs Golf Collection; **203** Hobbs Golf Collection; **204** Hobbs Golf Collection; **205** Stephen Munday/Allsport (top); David Cannon/Allsport; **206/7** Allsport (top, bottom center; bottom right); Don Morley/Allsport (bottom left); **208** Stephen Munday/ Allsport (top); Stephen Dunn/ Allsport; **209** Harry How/Allsport (top); Mike Powell/Allsport; **210** David Cannon/Allsport (top); Stephen Dunn/Allsport; **211** Stephen Munday/ Allsport; **212** Hobbs Golf Collection; **213** Steve Powell/Allsport; **214** Hobbs Golf Collection; **215** Stephen Dunn/Allsport; **216** Tim Matthews/ Allsport; **217** Stephen Munday/ Allsport; **218** Hobbs Golf Collection; **219** David Cannon/Allsport (top); Hobbs Golf Collection; **220** Allsport Historical Collection (top); David Cannon/Allsport; **221** David Cannon/ Allsport; **222** David Cannon/Allsport; **223** David Cannon/Allsport; **224/5** David Cannon/Allsport; **226** Hobbs Golf Collection; **227** Andrew Redington/Allsport; **228** Allsport Historical Collection; **229** Allsport Historical Collection; **230** David Cannon/Allsport; **231** Allsport Historical Collection; **232** Gary Newkirk/Allsport (left); Don Morley/Allsport (right); **233** Don Morley/Allsport; **234** Harry How/ Allsport; **235** Hobbs Golf Collection; **236** Hobbs Golf Collection; **237** David Cannon/Allsport; **238** David Cannon/Allsport; **239** David Cannon/Allsport (top); Stephen Munday/Allsport; **240/1** David Cannon/Allsport; **242** Michael Hobbs/Allsport (top); Hobbs Golf Collection; **243** Andrew Redington/Allsport (top); David Cannon/Allsport; **244** David Cannon/ Allsport (top); J. D. Cuban/Allsport; **245** Clive Mason/Allsport; **246** Allsport Historical Collection(top); Hobbs Golf Collection; **247** Hobbs Golf Collection; **248** Allsport (top left); Allsport Historical Collection (top right); **249** Stephen Munday/ Allsport; **250** David Cannon/Allsport (top); Tony Duffy/Allsport; **251** David Cannon/Allsport; **252** Andrew Redington/Allsport (top); David Cannon/Allsport; **253** Tony Duffy/ Allsport; **254** William Vanderson/ Allsport Historical Collection (top); Hobbs Golf;Collection; **255** Allsport Historical Collection; **256/7** Hobbs Golf Collection; **258** Michael Hobbs/Allsport (top); Hobbs Golf Collection; **259** Hobbs Golf Collection; **260** Stephen Munday (top); David Cannon/Allsport; **261** David Cannon/Allsport; **262** Hobbs Golf Collection; **263** Hobbs Golf Collection; **264** David Cannon/Allsport (top); Ross Kinnaird/Allsport; **265** Michael Hobbs/Allsport; **266** Stephen Dunn/ Allsport; **267** Allsport (top); Steve Powell/Allsport; **268/9** Tony Duffy/ Allsport (left); Allsport (top right, bottom left and right); **270** Tim Matthews/Allsport (top); Andrew Redington/Allsport; **271** Allsport Historical Collection (top); Peter Dazeley Photography; **272** Hobbs Golf Collection (top); David Cannon/ Allsport; **273** Allsport; **274** Allsport Historical Collection (left); Matthew Stockman/Allsport (right); **275** David Cannon/Allsport; **276** David Cannon/ Allsport; **277** David Cannon/Allsport (top); Rick Stewart/Allsport; **278** Allsport Historical Collection(top); Hobbs Golf Collection; **279** David Cannon/ Allsport (top); Hobbs Golf Collection; **280** David Cannon/Allsport; **281** David Cannon/Allsport; **282** J. D. Cuban/Allsport; **283** Hobbs Golf Collection; **284** Allsport Historical Collection; **285** Allsport Historical Collection (top); Hobbs Golf Collection; **286/7** David Cannon/Allsport (left, top right, bottom left); Bob Martin/Allsport (bottom right); **288** Allsport Historical Collection (top); J. D. Cuban/Allsport; **289** Ezra Shaw/Allsport (top); Jon Ferrey/Allsport; **290** David Cannon/ Allsport; **291** Peter Dazeley Photography (top); Hobbs Golf Collection; **292** J. D. Cuban/Allsport; **293** Tony Duffy/Allsport (top); David Cannon/Allsport; **294** Craig Jones/ Allsport; **295** Elsa Hasch/Allsport (top); J. D. Cuban/Allsport; **296** Hobbs Golf Collection; **297** David Cannon/Allsport; **298** David Cannon/Allsport; **299** David Cannon/Allsport; **300** Hobbs Golf Collection; **301** Allsport Historical Collecction (top); Michael Hobbs/Allsport; **302/3** David Cannon/Allsport; **304** Allsport; **305** Hobbs Golf Collection; **306** Allsport Historical Collection (top); Hobbs Golf Collection; **307** Hobbs Golf Collection; **308** Hobbs Golf Collection; **309** Hobbs Golf Collection; **310** Allsport Historical Collection (top); Allsport; **311** Jamie Squire/Allsport (top); David Cannon/ Allsport; **312** Hobbs Golf Collection; **313** Allsport; **314** Rusty Jarrett/ Allsport (top left); Stephen Munday/ Allsport **315** Stephen Munday/ Allsport (top left and right); Simon Bruty/Allsport; **316** Allsport (top); Allsport Historical Collection; **317** Michael Hobbs/Allsport; **318** Allsport (top); James Squire/ Allsport; **319** Howard Boylan/Allsport (top); Allsport Historical Collection; **320** Stephen Munday/Allspor; **321** Allsport; **322** David Cannon/ Allsport; **323** Jack Atley/Allsport Australia (top); Anton Want/Allsport; **324** George Douglas/Allsport Historical Collection (top); Hobbs Golf; Collection; **325** Allsport (top); Allsport Historical Collection; **326** Craig Jones/Allsport (top); Andrew Redington/Allsport; **327** Hobbs Golf Collection; **328** Allsport Historical Collection; **329** Allsport (top); Tony Duffy/ Allsport; **330** Andrew Redington/ Allsport (left); J. D. Cuban/Allsport (right); **331** Stephen Munday/ Allsport; **332** Michael Hobbs/Allsport; **333** Stephen Munday/Allsport (top); Andrew Redington/Allsport; **334** Craig Jones/Allsport; **335** Craig Jones/Allsport (top); Mark Dadswell/ Allsport (bottom); **336** Michael Hobbs/Allsport; **337** Allsport Historical Collection; **338** Jon Ferrey/Allsport (top); Harry How/ Allsport; **341** David Cannon/Allsport; **350** Jack Atley/Allsport